Principles of Control Systems Engineering

McGraw-Hill Series in Control Systems Engineering

JOHN R. RAGAZZINI AND WILLIAM E. VANNAH, *Consulting Editors*

Principles of
CONTROL SYSTEMS
ENGINEERING

VINCENT DEL TORO

Professor of Electrical Engineering and Associate Dean
School of Engineering and Architecture
The City College of the City University of New York

SYDNEY R. PARKER

Professor of Electrical Engineering
Cullen College of Engineering
University of Houston

McGRAW-HILL BOOK COMPANY

NEW YORK   TORONTO   LONDON   1960

PRINCIPLES OF CONTROL SYSTEMS ENGINEERING

7 8 9 10 – M P – 9 8 7

16244

Preface

This book presents an integrated treatment of feedback control systems at the senior-graduate level. The need for a book that furnishes an exposition of the various methods of analysis and design and also describes their interrelationships has long been felt by the authors. In fact it was the desire to fulfill this need that led the authors to write a set of notes for classroom use at The City College of New York. These notes have been used for several years and they now represent a major part of this textbook.

In order to emphasize the unified approach referred to, the book is divided into five sections. Each section deals with a fundamental phase of control systems engineering. The order of presentation reflects chronologically the historical development of each phase. It is our opinion that this provides the reader with a maximum motivation for studying each successive phase and for seeking out new tools of analysis and design. Moreover, such an approach offers the merit of furnishing a clearer picture of the role played by each phase, thus making it easier to understand the advantages and limitations of each as well as the manner in which each complements the other. In this way, upon completion of the book, the reader will achieve perspective as well as proficiency in the various methods of analysis and design as they apply to control systems engineering.

Part I of the book furnishes the reader with a careful introduction to the basic concepts of feedback control as well as a treatment of the required mathematical background. At the outset the distinction is made between open-loop and closed-loop control and this distinction is amply illustrated with examples from various fields of engineering. Emphasis is put on the importance of a physical understanding. The mathematics is treated in a fashion which tailors it for direct use to control systems engineering. Thus the classical method of solving differen-

v

tial equations is approached in terms of poles and zeros as well as in terms of transfer functions. The ideas of superposition and related-sources properties are described along with a generalized handling of initial conditions.

Part II of the book presents a comprehensive treatment of the analysis and design of feedback control systems in the time domain. A thorough analysis of the second-order system is made because of the very important role the predominant pair of complex-conjugate roots plays in determining the behavior of higher-order systems. Appropriate charts and curves are included to allow ready identification of the transient response. Moreover, in the interest of enhancing physical understanding as well as the descriptive mathematics, the manner of operation and the characteristics of new components are described as they arise in the study of various systems throughout the book. In addition, an extensive treatment of compensation procedures such as error-rate and output-rate damping is given in terms of the time-domain approach. This section concludes by pointing out the difficulties of the time-domain method of analysis, thus motivating the need for seeking out a simpler approach.

In Part III the analysis and design of feedback control systems are treated by using frequency-domain techniques. Through the use of simple examples there is established at the outset the correlation existing between the steady-state frequency response and the corresponding dynamic behavior in the time domain. Then the transfer characteristics of basic operational functions are treated simultaneously in terms of their pole-zero patterns, polar plots, magnitude vs. frequency plots, and log modulus and phase vs. log frequency plots. This treatment is made independently of the character of the component—electrical, mechanical, hydraulic, or pneumatic. Generalized charts and figures are included for ready use in design. The transfer functions of components from many fields of engineering are considered. Included are electrical networks, amplidynes, hydraulic amplifiers and motors, missiles, accelerometers, gyroscopes, and stabilized platforms for inertial navigation systems.

After development of the block-diagram reduction formulas and other procedures for dealing with the transfer functions of systems, these techniques are applied to those systems described in the introductory chapter. In this way progression as well as integration of the subject matter is served. Moreover, to continue the policy of providing correlation between steady-state sinusoidal frequency response and the dynamic time-domain behavior, there is developed a relationship between damping ratio and phase margin. The study of system stability by using the Nyquist criterion is developed in a manner which offers the reader a basic viewpoint of the technique. The treatment culminates in an easy-to-apply rule called the "shaded area" rule for establishing system stability.

Many examples are included to assure greater understanding of the subject matter.

To emphasize the background furnished by the first eight chapters, system design in the frequency domain is treated by starting with a statement of the problem in terms of meeting proposed specifications and finally coming up with a complete system design including compensation. The design of compensation is accomplished always in terms of providing satisfactory performance in the time domain. In this connection a relationship is developed which enables the designer to relate a frequency-domain quantity, namely phase margin, to a corresponding time-domain quantity, such as the predominant time constant of the compensated system. A careful study is made concerning the design of standard devices (e.g., lag, lead, lag-lead networks) with the expressed intention of revealing the areas in which each shows to advantage over the others.

Part IV of the book deals with the analysis and design of feedback control systems by using complex-frequency-domain techniques (the root-locus method). The transition from the sinusoidal frequency to the complex frequency is described along with the significance involved and the advantages to be gained. The root-locus theory is handled in a general way so that both negative and positive values of the open-loop gain as well as poles and zeros located in the left- and right-half s plane are considered. Moreover, the development of the rules for finding the root-locus plots is done in such a way as to give appreciable emphasis to the role played by the spirule. This viewpoint is taken not only because there often arise pole-zero configurations where there is doubt regarding the specific directions taken by certain branches of the root locus, but also because the important part of the root locus is located in the vicinity of the origin. The spirule allows this part of the root locus to be determined more accurately. Furthermore, as the root-locus method is developed, it is compared with other methods, such as Routh and Nyquist, for obtaining information about critical points of the system behavior.

Analysis by root-locus techniques is amply illustrated with well-chosen examples from industry. The discussions are complete to the extent of describing the influence of introducing zeros in the closed-loop transfer function on the dynamic behavior of systems in the time domain. A critical examination is made to reveal how the root-locus approach furnishes information about the frequency response as well as the time-domain behavior. Constant reference is made to subject matter previously studied in order to emphasize the correlation and to provide the proper perspective.

The inclusion of a chapter on pole-zero design techniques and another on RC network synthesis makes the treatment of the root-locus method one of the most comprehensive to appear in a work of this kind. Thus in Chapter 11 general procedures are developed in terms of poles and zeros

for designing the standard types of compensation devices dealt with previously in the sinusoidal frequency domain.   Comparisons are made, and
the advantages offered are studied critically.   Chapter 12 provides the
reader with insight as to how the placement of poles and zeros in the
complex-frequency plane affects both the form and element values of a
compensation network.   Various techniques for determining the *RC*
network from the zero-pole pattern of the transfer function are developed.
The matter of frequency scaling as well as impedance-level shifting is
presented also.

Part V deals with the analysis and design of feedback control systems
by using the electronic analog and digital computer approach.   A clear
case is made of the important role played by the electronic computer in
the study of the dynamic behavior of control systems in which nonlinearities are significant.   The manner of generating nonlinear functions as
well as multiplying and dividing by variables is treated.   The application
of this approach in solving nonlinear problems is demonstrated.

Chapter 15 is devoted to the special topic of self-adaptive control systems, which represents one of the most significant recent advances in the
field.   The treatment here concerns itself primarily with the basic principles associated with the various viewpoints used in designing such
systems.   Upon becoming familiar with these principles, the reader will
appreciate better why the self-adaptive control system is being looked
upon as the control system of the future, especially where the controlled
system is a complex device such as a chemical process, a guided missile,
or a space ship.

Although this book has no specific section on components, it should not
be concluded that components have received little attention.   On the
contrary, considerable attention is devoted to system components, as is
evident from inspection of Chapters 4, 5, and 6.   The authors have
chosen to treat components as part of the over-all system in order to give
greater emphasis to the unified approach.

A considerable part of the material in this book is presently used to
teach control systems engineering to senior students at The City College
as well as to first-year graduate students with no previous background.
Moreover, the material in the later chapters is used in a subsequent
graduate course.   For students who have had courses in differential
equations and Laplace transform theory, there is no need to include the
subject matter of Chapters 2 and 3, except perhaps as a review.   The
chapter on the Laplace transform theory, however, has been included
because combined with the thorough development of the frequency
response concept along with the use of illustrative examples chosen from
various engineering fields, the book can be readily used by nonelectrical
engineering students.   Perhaps this is especially true for mechanical
engineering students.   Finally, the background provided by the study

of this book should serve well as preparation for advanced study in such topics as synthesis of control systems through pole-zero configurations, analytical design of control systems through use of performance indexes such as the integral-square error and the mean-square error, digital and sampled-data control systems, and nonlinear control systems.

It is with pleasure that we acknowledge gratitude to our colleagues and friends at The City College for the fruitful technical discussions held with them. In particular we wish to note the contributions of Professors A. Abramowitz, G. J. Clemens, L. Echtman, and W. T. Hunt, Jr., who taught from the notes and who made many valuable suggestions.

We are indebted to our students also for the contributions made through their criticism and constructive suggestions concerning the original course notes. They often indicated where the text was in need of clarification. Thanks are also due to all the authors of books and papers dealing with feedback controls which have been published before the date of this book and which have been read by us. Whether in small or large measure, we are certainly indebted to these persons for adding to our own more complete understanding of the subject matter. Finally, we want to express sincere appreciation to Miss Sadie Silverstein, administrative assistant of the Electrical Engineering Department at The City College, for her unstinting dedication and outstanding assistance in the preparation of the manuscript.

Vincent Del Toro
Sydney R. Parker

Contents

xi

PART II—TIME-DOMAIN APPROACH

PART III—FREQUENCY-DOMAIN APPROACH

PART VI—SPECIAL TOPICS

APPENDIXES

I | Introduction and Mathematical Background

1 | Introduction to Feedback Control Systems

The essential feature of many automatic control systems is feedback. Feedback is that property of the system which permits the output quantity to be compared with the input command so that upon the existence of a difference an actuating signal arises which acts to bring the two into correspondence. This principle of feedback is really not new to us; it surrounds every phase of everyday living. It underlies the coordinated motions executed by the human body in walking, reaching for objects, and driving an automobile. It plays an equally important role in the countless applications of control system engineering in the fields of manufacturing, process industries, control of watercraft and aircraft, special-purpose computers for many types of military equipment, and in many other fields including the home and the office.

In this chapter the mechanism through which the feedback action exhibits itself is studied in control systems ranging from elementary ones to those possessing a high degree of complexity. In each the same functional behaviors will be observed, and the general nature of the method of analysis will thus be emphasized. The distinction between an elementary system and one which is complex lies primarily in the difficulty of the task to be performed. The more difficult the task, the more complex the system. In fact with many present-day systems this complexity has reached such proportions that system design has virtually become a science. The functional behavior of each system will be treated in terms of a block-diagram notation and its associated terminology. Following this, attention is focused on the steady-state analysis of the performance of a voltage and a speed control system. Such a study accomplishes two objectives. First, it gives substance to some of the general ideas discussed up to this point, thereby making the operation of the system more vivid. Second, useful results applicable to any feedback control system are developed.

3

1-1. Distinction between Open-loop and Closed-loop (Feedback) Control

It is important in the beginning that the distinction between closed-loop and open-loop operation be clearly understood. Both terms will often be used throughout the book. The following simple definitions point out the difference:[1]

An *open-loop system* is one in which the control action is independent of the output (or desired result).

A *closed-loop system* is one in which the control action is dependent upon the output.

The key term in these definitions is *control action*. Basically, it refers to the actuating signal of the system, which in turn represents the quantity responsible for activating the system to produce a desired output. In the case of the open-loop system the input command is the sole factor responsible for providing the control action, whereas for a closed-loop system the control action is provided by the difference between the input command and the corresponding output.

To illustrate the distinction, consider the control of automobile traffic by means of traffic lights placed at an intersection where traffic flows along north-south and east-west directions. If the traffic-light mechanism is such that the green and red lights are on for predetermined, fixed intervals of time, then operation is open-loop. This conclusion immediately follows from our foregoing definition upon realizing that the desired output, which here is control of the volume of traffic, in no way influences the time interval during which the light shines green or red. The input command originates from a calibrated timing mechanism, and this alone establishes how long the light stays green or red. The control action is thereby provided directly by the input command. Accordingly, the timing mechanism has no way of knowing whether or not the volume of traffic is especially heavy along the north-south direction and therefore in need of longer green-light intervals. A closed-loop system of control would provide precisely this information. Thus, if a scheme is introduced which measures the volume of traffic along both directions, compares the two, and then allows the difference to control the green and red time periods, feedback control results because now the actuating signal is a function of the desired output.

To complete the comparison of closed-loop vs. open-loop operation, it is worthwhile next to list briefly some of the performance characteristics of each. Generally, the open-loop system of control has two outstanding features. First, its ability to perform accurately is determined by its calibration. As the calibration deteriorates, so too does its performance. Second, the open-loop system is usually easier to build since it is not

[1] More precise definitions are given in the next section.

generally troubled with problems of instability. One of the noteworthy features of closed-loop operation is its ability faithfully to reproduce the input owing to feedback. This in a large measure is responsible for the high accuracy obtainable from such systems. Since the actuating signal is a function of the deviation of the output from the input, the control action persists in generating sufficient additional output to bring the two into correspondence. Unfortunately, this very factor (feedback) is also responsible for one of the biggest sources of difficulty in closed-loop systems, namely, the tendency to oscillate. Chapters 8 and 9 are devoted to a thorough study of the conditions which lead to instability and of the methods for avoiding it. A second important feature of closed-loop operation is that it usually performs accurately even in the presence of nonlinearities, which is in direct contrast to what prevails in the open-loop system.

1-2. Block Diagram of Feedback Control Systems. Terminology

Every feedback control system consists of components which perform specific functions. A convenient and useful method of representing this functional characteristic of the system is the block diagram. Basically this is a means of representing the operations performed in the system and the manner in which signal information flows throughout the system. The block diagram is concerned not with the physical characteristics of any specific system but only with the functional relationship among various parts in the system. In general, the output quantity of any linear component of the system is related to the input by a gain factor and combinations of derivatives or integrals with respect to time. Accordingly, it is possible for two entirely different and unrelated physical systems to be represented by the same block diagram, provided that the respective components are described by the same differential equations.

The general form of the block diagram of a feedback control system is shown in Fig. 1-1.[1] Since the differential equation or the gain factor of each block is not specifically identified, lower-case letters are used to represent the input and output variables. When this information is known, capital letters are used. This notation is followed throughout the book. The selection of the symbols in the block diagram was made to avoid those symbols which imply the mechanics of the system such as θ for angle, p for pressure, etc. This helps to preserve the generic nature of the block diagram.

Before proceeding with an explanation of the significance and advantages of the block-diagram notation, it is very important that the mean-

[1] A.I.E.E. Committee Report, Proposed Symbols and Terms for Feedback Control Systems, *Elec. Eng.*, vol. 70, pt. 2, pp. 905–909, 1951.

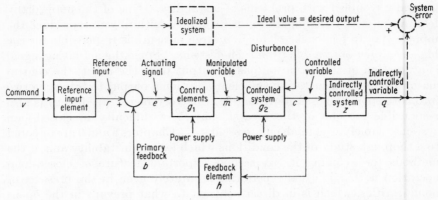

Fig. 1-1. Block diagram of a feedback control system, showing terminology.

ings of the terms used in Fig. 1-1 be clearly understood and remembered. These terms and others are described below:

A *feedback control system* is a control system which tends to maintain a prescribed relationship of one system variable to another by comparing functions of these variables and using the difference as a means of control.

The *controlled variable* is that quantity or condition of the controlled system which is directly measured and controlled.

The *indirectly controlled variable* is that quantity or condition which is controlled by virtue of its relation to the controlled variable and which is not directly measured for control.

The *command* is the input which is established or varied by some means external to and independent of the feedback control system under consideration.

The *ideal value* is the value of the ultimately controlled variable that would result from an idealized system[1] operating from the same command as the actual system.

The *reference input* is a signal established as a standard of comparison for a feedback control system by virtue of its relation to the command.

The *primary feedback* is a signal which is a function of the controlled variable and which is compared with the reference input to obtain the actuating signal. (This designation is intended to avoid ambiguity in multiloop systems.)

The *actuating signal* is the reference input minus the primary feedback.

The *manipulated variable* is that quantity or condition which the controller (g_1) applies to the controlled system.

A *disturbance* is a signal (other than the reference input) which tends to affect the value of the controlled variable.

A *parametric variation* is a change in system properties which may affect the performance or operation of the feedback control system.

---

[1] The idealized system is one which provides the desired output instantaneously.

The *system error* is the ideal value minus the value of the ultimately controlled variable.

The *system deviation* is the negative of the system error.

The *controlled system* is the body, process, or machine a particular quantity or condition of which is to be controlled.

The *indirectly controlled system* is the body, process, or machine which determines the relationship between the indirectly controlled variable and the controlled variable.

The *feedback controller* is a mechanism which measures the value of the controlled variable, accepts the value of the command, and, as a result of comparison, manipulates the controlled system in order to maintain an established relationship between the controlled variable and the command.

The *control elements* comprise the portion of the feedback control system which is required to produce the manipulated variable from the actuating signal.

The *reference-input elements* comprise the portion of the feedback control system which establishes the relationship between the reference input and the command.

The *feedback elements* comprise the portion of the feedback control system which establishes the relationship between the primary feedback and the controlled variable.

The *summing point* is a descriptive symbol used to denote the algebraic summation of two or more signals.

The reference-input element usually consists of a device which converts control signals from one form into another. Such devices are known as *transducers*. Most transducers have an output signal which is in the form of electrical energy. Thus a potentiometer can be used to convert a mechanical position to an electrical voltage. A tachometer generator converts a velocity into a d-c or an a-c voltage. A pressure transducer changes a pressure drop or rise into a corresponding drop or rise in electric potential. There are numerous examples of transducers used in industry. No special attention is directed to a general treatment of these devices at this point. A detailed explanation of each transducer is given as the need for its use in a given system arises. It is felt that introducing transducers in this way provides the reader with a clearer understanding of their function in the over-all system and the manner in which their deviations from the ideal influence the dynamic and static system behavior. For the present, therefore, it is sufficient to understand that the transducer provides the appropriate translation of the command into a form usable by the system.

The feedback element also frequently consists of a transducer of the same kind as the reference-input element. When the two signals of the input and feedback transducers are compared, the result is the actuating

signal.   This portion of the closed-loop system is very important, and it is
usually more descriptively identified as the *error detector* (see Fig. 1-2).
Error detectors may take on a variety of forms depending upon the nature
of the feedback control system.   Some of the more frequently used error
detectors include the following: two bridge-connected potentiometers,
a control-transmitter control-transformer synchro combination, two
linear differential transformers, two tachometer generators, differential
gear, E-type transformers, bellows, gyroscopes.   The application and
operation of most of these error detectors will be described as they are
used in the different systems analyzed throughout the book.

The primary function of the control element g_1 of the block diagram
is to provide amplification of the actuating signal since it is generally
available at very low power levels.[1]   Many types of amplifying devices
are used either singly or in combination.   Some of the more common
types are the following: electronic, solid-state (transistor), electromechanical, hydraulic, pneumatic, magnetic.   Note that the amplifier

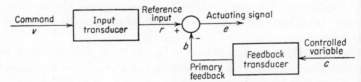

FIG. 1-2. The error-detector portion of a feedback control system.

must have its own source of power.   Indication of this is made in Fig.
1-1 by the use of an external arrow leading to the g_1 block.   It should be
emphasized that the *closed-loop block diagram* refers to the flow of the
control power and not to the main source of energy for the system.   In
essence then the block diagram represents the manner in which the control signal manipulates the main source of power in order to adjust the
controlled variable in accordance with the command.

The block identified as the controlled system g_2 in Fig. 1-1 refers to that
portion of the system which generates the controlled variable in accordance with the dictates of the manipulated variable.   The controlled
system obviously can take on many forms.   It may represent an aircraft frame, the body of a ship, a gun mount, a chemical process, or a
temperature or pressure system.   The milling machine and the lathe are
examples where the controlled system represents a machine as distinguished from a process or body.

The operation of any feedback control system can be described in terms
of the block diagram of Fig. 1-1.   The application of a specific command
causes a corresponding signal at the reference input through the action of

[1] The control element also frequently serves the function of changing the basic time
character of the signal to control the transient system response.   This will be dealt
with at length in Chap. 4.

the input transducer. Since the controlled variable cannot change instantaneously because of the inertia of the system, the output of the feedback element no longer is equal and opposite to the reference input. Accordingly an actuating signal exists, which in turn is received by the control element and amplified, thereby generating a new value of controlled variable. This means that the primary feedback signal changes in such a direction as to reduce the magnitude of the actuating signal. It should be clear that the controlled system will continue to generate a new level of output as long as the actuating signal is different from zero. Therefore only when the controlled variable is brought to a level equal to the value commanded will the actuating signal be zero. The system then will be at the new desired steady-state value.

To have feedback control systems operate in a stable fashion, they must be provided with *negative* feedback; negative feedback simply means that the feedback signal needs to be opposite in sign to the reference input. This helps to assure that, as the controlled variable approaches the commanded value, the actuating signal approaches zero. A moment's reflection reveals that, if the feedback is positive and the controlled variable increases, the actuating signal will also increase. This causes an increased value of controlled variable, which results in a further increase in actuating signal, and so on. The result is an unbounded[1] increase in controlled variable and loss of control by the command source.

Summarizing, we see that the block diagram of a feedback control system is, first of all, a representation of its function characteristics which permits a description of the manner in which the control-signal energy flows through the system. Second, it is a means of emphasizing that the closed-loop system is composed of three principal parts, viz., the error detector, the control element (amplifier and output device), and the controlled system.

1-3. Position Feedback Control System. Servomechanism

A common industrial application of a feedback system is one used to control position. These systems occur so frequently in practice and are so important that they are given a special name—*servomechanism*. A servomechanism is a power-amplifying feedback control system in which the controlled variable is mechanical position. The term also applies to those systems which control time derivatives of position, as, for example, velocity and acceleration. The schematic diagram of a servomechanism is shown in Fig. 1-3.

Consider that the system of Fig. 1-3 is to be used to control the angular position of a table in accordance with a command signal originating from

[1] The nonlinearities inherent in the system would ultimately limit the magnitude of the output.

a remotely located station.   The first step in obtaining the block diagram and understanding the operation of the system is to identify the error-detector portion of the system.   As pointed out in Fig. 1-2, this requires merely finding the input and feedback transducers and the summing point of their output signals.   For the system of Fig. 1-3 the error detector consists of the section blocked off with the broken line.   The second principal part of the system—the control element—consists of the amplifier unit and the output motor.   The latter is more commonly referred

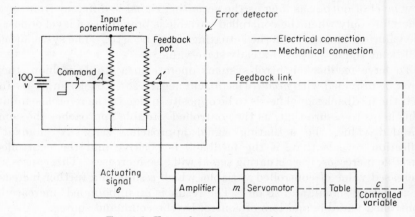

FIG. 1-3. Example of a servomechanism.

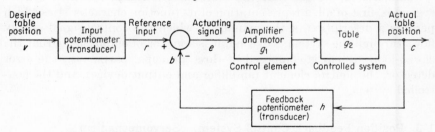

FIG. 1-4. Block diagram of the servomechanism of Fig. 1-3.

to as a servomotor since it requires special design considerations.   The table, the position of which is being controlled, represents the controlled system.   In a specific application it may be a gun mount or the support table for a lathe or milling machine.   The block diagram for the system is shown in Fig. 1-4.

To understand the operation of the system, assume that initially the slider arms of the input and feedback potentiometers are both set at +50 volts.   The voltage of the input potentiometer is the reference input. For this condition the actuating signal is zero, and so the motor has zero output torque.   Next consider that the command calls for a new position of the table, namely, that corresponding to a potentiometer voltage of

+60 volts. When arm A is placed at the +60 volts position, arm A' remains instantaneously at the +50 volts position because of the table inertia. This situation creates a +10 volts actuating signal which is really a measure of the lack of correspondence between the actual table position and the commanded position. A +10 volts input to the amplifier applies an input to the servomotor, which in turn generates an output torque, which repositions the table. With negative feedback present the table moves in a direction which causes the potential of A' to increase beyond +50 volts. As this takes place, the actuating signal gets smaller and finally reaches zero, at which time A' has the same potential as A (this is referred to as the *null* position). The actual table position is therefore equal to the commanded value. Note that, if the table is not exactly at the commanded position, the actuating signal will be different from zero, and hence a motor output torque persists, forcing the table to take the commanded position.[1] On the basis of the foregoing explanation, we can begin to appreciate that a system of this type possesses an integrating property; i.e., the motor output angle is proportional to the integral of the actuating signal and thus stops changing only when the actuating signal itself is zero. This follows from the fact that for any given actuating signal there results a corresponding motor velocity. However, the feedback potentiometer is sensitive not to velocity but rather to motor position, which is the integral of velocity and therefore also of the actuating signal.

One distinguishing feature which the amplifier of this type of control system must have is *sign sensitivity*. It must function properly whether the command places arm A at a higher or a lower voltage than the original value. In terms of position this means that the command should be capable of moving the table in a clockwise or counterclockwise direction. Thus, if arm A had been placed at +40 rather than +60 volts by the command, the actuating signal would have been −10 volts. The amplifier must be capable of interpreting the intelligence implied in the minus sign by applying a reversed signal to the servomotor, thereby reversing the direction of rotation.

The manner in which a feedback control system reacts to an externally applied disturbance may be illustrated by considering further the example of the servomechanism. Assume the disturbance to be in the form of an external torque applied to the table. The effect of this torque will be to offset the feedback potentiometer from its null position. Upon doing this, the actuating signal no longer is zero but takes on such a value that when multiplied by the torque constant (units of torque per volt of actuating signal) the developed torque of the servomotor is equal and

---

[1] This is true provided that the components are all assumed to be perfect. Actually imperfections such as motor dead zone cause the commanded and actual position to be out of correspondence by a small amount.

opposite to the applied disturbance. It should be clear that, as long as the external torque is maintained, the actuating signal cannot be zero. How close it will be to zero depends upon the torque constant of the servo-motor and the magnitude of the external force. Of course, the larger the torque constant, the smaller the actuating signal required. Since the actuating signal can no longer be zero, the potential of arm A' is no longer equal to the commanded value. Hence, for a system of the type described in Fig. 1-3, a steady-state position error exists in the presence of a constantly maintained external disturbance.[1] This characteristic of the system of readjusting itself to counteract the disturbance is referred to as the self-correcting, or automatic control, feature of closed-loop operation.

On the basis of the foregoing description of the servomechanism, a few general characteristics of this type of control system can be stated. A feedback control system is classified as a servomechanism if it satisfies all three of the following conditions: (1) It is error-actuated (i.e., closed-loop operation). (2) It contains power amplification (i.e., operates from low signal levels). (3) It has a mechanical output (position, velocity, or acceleration). Essentially, the servomechanism is a special case of a feedback control system. In regard to performance features we can say at this point that among its salient characteristics are included automatic control, remote operation (of the command station), high accuracy, and fast response. The aspect of remote operation deserves further comment since it is one of the chief factors motivating the development of these systems. It should be apparent from Fig. 1-3 that the input potentiometer (often called the command station) can be far removed from the output device. Thus, if the controlled system is the rudder of a ship, its heading can be easily and accurately manipulated from the ship's bridge. Or if the controlled system is a platform bearing a gun turret, the direction of the gun can be conveniently controlled from a strategically located sighting station.

1-4. Typical Feedback Control Applications

To assure a more thorough understanding of the principles of feedback control, we shall next apply these principles to several widely different situations. For each system the description will revolve about the block-diagram representation, thus again emphasizing the functional nature of the approach. Also, a thorough comprehension of the procedure should develop within us a facility which will make further thinking in terms of block diagrams a routine matter. It is important to establish such a facility before dealing with the general problem of the dynamic behavior of feedback control systems.

[1] This position error may be eliminated by introducing additional control elements.

Pressure Control System for Supersonic Wind Tunnel. Of considerable importance in the aircraft and missile industry nowadays is obtaining information about aircraft stability derivatives and aerodynamic parameters prevailing at Mach[1] numbers ranging from 0.5 to 5 and higher. Several of the leading aircraft companies have built wind tunnels to accomplish this. The wind tunnel is often of the blowdown type, which means that compressors pump air to a specified pressure in a huge storage tank and, when a test is to be performed, the stored air is bled through a valve into a settling chamber, where air flow at high Mach numbers is realized. In such tests, keeping the Mach number constant is of the utmost importance. A problem exists since, as the air is bled from the storage tanks, its pressure drops and so too will the Mach number in the test section unless the valve is opened more. The need for a control system therefore presents itself. The nature of the control system depends upon the means available for monitoring the quantity it is desired to control, which in this case is the Mach number. Since the Mach number can be identified in terms of pressure, it turns out that to keep the Mach number fixed requires keeping the settling-chamber pressure constant. Hence the use of a pressure-activated control system suggests itself. It is interesting to note that the Mach number is now the indirectly controlled variable while the pressure is the directly controlled variable.

A schematic diagram of the wind tunnel[2] without the control system is shown in Fig. 1-5. The block diagram of the complete system including the components required for control is shown in Fig. 1-6. As indicated in Fig. 1-5, the air to operate the tunnel is stored in six tanks at a pressure of 600 psia at 100°F. The tanks discharge into a 30-in.-diameter manifold, which in turn leads to a 24-in.-diameter rotating-plug control rotovalve. The discharge side of this valve is connected to the settling chamber by means of a duct. In Fig. 1-6 the pressure transducer is a device which converts pressure to a corresponding voltage, which then is compared with the reference-input voltage, and the difference constitutes the actuating signal. The controller refers to an amplifying stage plus electrical networks which integrate and differentiate the input signal. (The reason for integration and differentiation will be discussed later in the book.)

The electrohydraulic valve is an electrically operated two-stage hydraulic amplifier. It consists of a coil-magnet motor (which receives the electrical output of the preceding amplifier), a low-pressure pilot valve, and a high-pressure pilot valve. The output motion of the latter

---

[1] *Mach number* refers to the ratio of the speed of the aircraft at a given altitude to the speed of sound at the same altitude.

[2] The wind tunnel discussed here is installed at Convair, a division of General Dynamics Corporation at San Diego, Calif.

drives a positioning cylinder, which in turn positions the rotovalve. For improved performance a position feedback is put round the electrohydraulic valve. The controller, the electrohydraulic valve and its feedback path, and the rotovalve represent that part of the feedback control

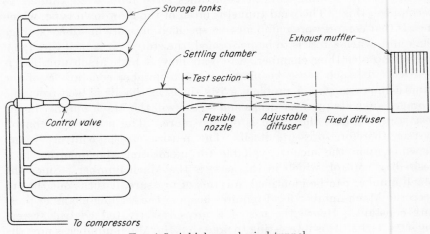

Fig. 1-5. A high-speed wind tunnel.

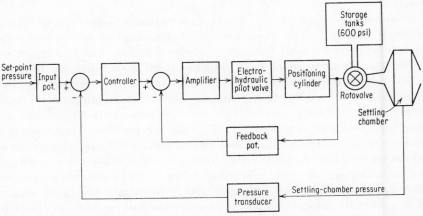

Fig. 1-6. Block diagram of a supersonic wind-tunnel pressure control system.

system identified as the *control elements* g_1. The *error detector* consists of the input potentiometer plus the feedback transducer, while the *controlled system* is the process of pressure build-up in the settling chamber.

Assume that a wind-tunnel test is to be performed at Mach 5, to which the settling-chamber pressure of 250 psia corresponds. Operation is started by putting the input potentiometer at a set-point pressure of 250 psia. An actuating signal immediately appears at the controller, which in turn causes the electrohydraulic pilot valve and its positioning cylinder to open the rotovalve and thereby build up pressure in the chamber. As the rotovalve is opened, the input to the pilot-valve amplifier decreases because of the position feedback voltage. Moreover, as pressure builds up, the actuating signal to the controller decreases. When the settling-chamber pressure has reached the commanded 250 psia, the actuating signal will be zero and no further movement of the rotovalve plug takes place. The time needed to accomplish this is relatively small (about 5 sec), and the attendant decrease in tank pressure is also very small. Consequently, an air flow of Mach 5 is established in the settling chamber. However, as time passes and more and more air is bled from the storage tanks, the storage pressure will decrease and, unless a further opening of the rotovalve is introduced, the settling-chamber pressure will drop also. Of course additional rotovalve opening occurs because of the pressure feedback. Specifically, as the settling-chamber pressure decreases, the corresponding feedback voltage drops and, since the reference input voltage is fixed, an actuating signal appears at the controller, which causes the pilot valve to reposition the rotovalve. This in turn maintains the desired chamber pressure. It should be clear that this corrective action will prevail as long as there is any tendency for the chamber pressure to drop and provided that the rotovalve is not at its limit position, i.e., not fully open.

Automatic Machine-tool Control. Application of the principles of feedback control techniques to machine tools, together with the ability to feed the machine tool programmed instructions, has led to completely automatic operation with increased accuracy as well. Fundamentally, three requirements need to be satisfied to obtain this kind of control. First, the machine tool must receive instructions regarding the size and shape of the workpiece.[1] Second, the workpiece must be positioned in accordance with these instructions. Third, a measurement of the desired result must be made in order to check that the instructions have been carried out. This, of course, is accomplished through feedback.

To understand better the procedure involved, consider the system depicted in Fig. 1-7. It represents the programmed carriage drive for a milling machine. It could just as well represent the vertical and lateral drive of the cutting tool. In practice, for the cutting of a three-dimensional object, three such systems are provided, and so whatever is said about one holds for all three. The information regarding the size and shape of the workpiece usually originates from engineering drawings, equations, or models and is subsequently converted to more usable forms such as punched cards, magnetic tapes, and cams. In Fig. 1-7 this is the box identified as the punched taped input. Frequently this part of the system is referred to as the input memory. The information contained in

[1] *Workpiece* refers here to the desired finished object.

this memory is then applied to a computer, whose function is to make available a command signal indicating a desired position and velocity of the carriage. The computer in the case illustrated is a data-interpreting system and decoding servomechanism. Together with the input memory, this constitutes the total programmed instructions, or command input, to the carriage feedback control system. The transmitter synchro is the transducer, which converts the programmed command to a voltage which is the reference input to the control system. This voltage appears at the amplifier, which generates an output to drive the actuator. The actuator may be of the hydraulic, pneumatic, or electric type or perhaps a clutch. The lead screw is then driven and the carriage positioned in

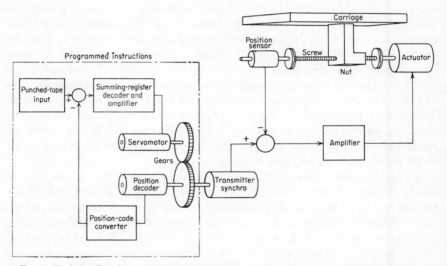

FIG. 1-7. A feedback control system for the carriage drive of a milling machine.

accordance with the instruction. Assurance that the instruction has been followed is provided by the feedback position sensor. Should the instruction fail to be fully carried out, the position sensor will allow an actuating signal to appear at the input terminals of the amplifier, thereby causing additional motion of the carriage. Upon reaching the commanded position the actuating signal is nulled to zero until the next instruction comes along.

The block diagram for the system of Fig. 1-7 is shown in Fig. 1-8. The programmed command refers to the broken-line enclosure and is identified as the programmed instructions in Fig. 1-7. The control elements consist of the amplifier and actuator. The controlled system is the carriage. The error detector is made up of the input and feedback transducers as usual. It is interesting to note, too, that the data-interpreting system is itself a servomechanism.

Automobile Power Steering Servomechanism.   One of the most common servomechanisms is the power steering unit found in the automobile.   A simplified schematic diagram of the system appears in Fig. 1-9.   The corresponding block diagram is given in Fig. 1-10.   The purpose of the

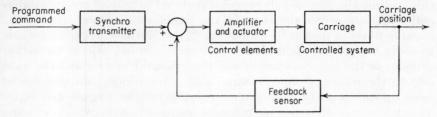

FIG. 1-8. Block diagram of Fig. 1-7.

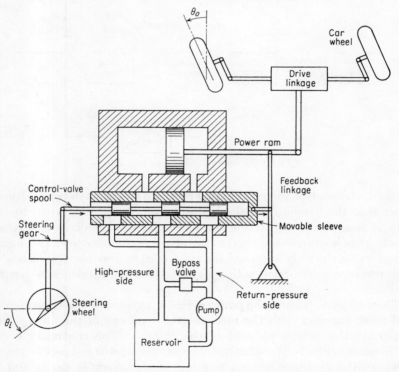

FIG. 1-9. Example illustrating the principle of an automobile power-steering servomechanism.

system is to position the wheels in accordance with commands applied to the steering wheel by the driver.   The inclusion of the hydraulic amplifier means that relatively small torques at the steering wheel will be reflected as much larger torques at the car wheels, thereby providing ease of steering.

The operation is simple and can be explained by applying the same approach that has been applied to the foregoing systems. Initially, with the steering wheel at its zero position (i.e., the crossbar horizontal), the wheels are directed parallel to the longitudinal axis of the car. In this position the control-valve spool is centered so that no pressure differential appears across the faces of the power ram. Upon turning the steering wheel to the left by an amount θ_i, the control-valve spool is made to move toward the right side. This opens the left side of the power cylinder to the high-pressure side of the hydraulic system and the right side to the return, or low-pressure, side. Accordingly, an unbalanced force appears on the power ram, causing motion toward the right. Through proper drive linkage a torque is applied to the wheels, causing the desired displacement θ_0. Of course, as the desired wheel position is

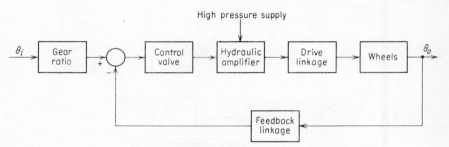

FIG. 1-10. Block diagram of Fig. 1-9.

reached, the control valve should be returned to the centered position in order that the torque from the hydraulic unit will be returned to zero. This is assured through the action of the feedback linkage mechanism. The linkage is so arranged that, as the power ram moves toward the right, the movable sleeve is displaced toward the right also, thereby sealing the high-pressure side. Such action signifies that the system has negative feedback.

The control valve and the power cylinder are part of the same housing, and these together with the mechanical advantage of the linkage ratio constitute the control element of the system. The controlled system in this case refers to the wheels. The error detector consists of the net effect of the feedback output position of the movable sleeve and the displacement introduced by the steering wheel at the control-valve spool. A centered valve position means no lack of correspondence between the command and the output.

Figure 1-10 is a representation of the position feedback loop only. Actually there are several more loops involved, such as the velocity loop and the load loop, which account for such things as car dynamics and tire characteristics. These are omitted for simplicity.

1-5. Steady-state Analysis of an Elementary Voltage Control System

We have studied in the foregoing pages the operation of several feedback control systems from the functional viewpoint. In this section we shall continue this study, but in a more advanced form. Gain factors of the individual elements comprising the system will be introduced and the steady-state performance calculated. (The transient behavior is delayed until Chap. 4.) Our purpose here is not to analyze solely for the sake of arriving at an answer but to analyze in such a way as to emphasize the mechanism underlying the operation of the system. Such an approach will give real substance to the general ideas which have already been described. In addition, it provides an opportunity for discussing such important items as how to establish the initial operating point for the system, the distinction between the direct transmission gain and the

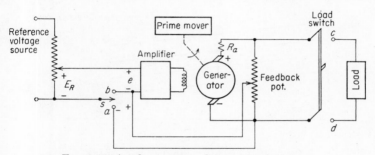

FIG. 1-11. An elementary voltage control system.

closed-loop gain and their significances, and the distinction between open-loop and closed-loop performance in terms of measured quantities. Furthermore, the analysis leads to equations which are used often in later chapters.

The impression should not be created that generally the steady-state analysis needs to proceed as outlined in the following pages. Once familiarity with the mechanics of operation is well understood, a more direct approach is possible. Such a procedure is illustrated at the end of the section.

An elementary voltage regulator is analyzed. The schematic diagram is shown in Fig. 1-11. The d-c generator is the source of voltage for the load. It is driven by a prime mover, which is the source of power for the system. With the generator driven at a constant speed the magnitude of the generated voltage is dependent upon the value of field current, which in turn is determined by the slider-arm setting of the reference voltage potentiometer. The input command to the system takes the form of a specific setting of this slider arm, to which there corresponds a definite field current and in turn a definite generator output voltage.

It is assumed that the amplifier has such a characteristic that increasing input signals result in corresponding increases in field current. Placing the switch S to the (a) position in Fig. 1-11 causes the system to act as a negative feedback control system, whereas putting S to the (b) position gives open-loop operation.

The object of this control system is to provide a preestablished constant voltage at the load terminals in spite of changes in load requirements or changes in prime-mover speed. *Load* in this case refers to the amount of electric current in amperes drawn from terminals cd as shown. If the generator is to be operating alone, with the prime mover running at constant speed, then an increase in load current results in a decreased output voltage because of the internal-resistance drop of the generator. Also if the load current is assumed constant and a drop in prime-mover speed

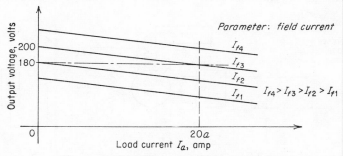

Fig. 1-12. Generator output characteristics.

occurs, the generator output voltage again decreases because the generated voltage is directly dependent upon speed. These generator characteristics are represented in Fig. 1-12. For simplicity the curves are idealized into straight lines. Also, if the prime mover is assumed to be at constant speed, the parameter which distinguishes one drooping straight line from the next is the slider-arm setting of the reference potentiometer. However, a fixed potentiometer setting and a changing prime-mover speed also give a similar set of curves. For our purposes it is convenient to assume the prime-mover speed constant. Let us now proceed with the closed-loop analysis of the system.

Closed-loop Analysis [Switch S at (a)]. The closed-loop steady-state performance is treated first since it leads to results which are readily applicable to open-loop operation. To find the performance requires identifying the equation which determines the output voltage of the generator. As any elementary textbook on electric machinery shows, this equation is

$$E_G = V + I_a R_a \tag{1-1}$$

where E_G = internally induced generator voltage, volts
  V = generator output voltage, volts
  I_a = load current, amp
  R_a = generator internal resistance, ohms

Before proceeding with a study of the automatic regulating action of this system, let us calculate the reference voltage needed to make available a specified no-load output voltage. Assume that the system components have the following gain factors:

Amplifier gain = 2 field amp/volt = K_A
Generator gain = 100 induced volts/field amp = K_G
Feedback gain = 0.5 = h
Generator internal resistance = 1.0 ohm = R_a

The generator gain factor is valid for the given prime-mover speed. The feedback gain factor refers to the slider-arm setting of the feedback potentiometer. Assuming the desired output voltage at no load to be 200 volts,[1] the feedback voltage is $hV = 0.5(200) = 100$ volts, and the required actuating signal is

$$e_0 \text{ (volts) } K_A \left(\frac{\text{field amp}}{\text{volt}} \right) K_G \left(\frac{\text{volts}}{\text{field amp}} \right) = E_G \text{ (volts)}$$

$$e_0(2)(100) = 200$$

$$e_0 = 1 \text{ volt}$$

where subscript 0 refers to no load. However, as a closed-loop system

$$e = E_R - hV \tag{1-2}$$

and from Eq. (1-1) at no load, $I_a = 0$ so that $V = E_G = 200$. Hence,

$$E_R = e_0 + hE_G = 1 + 100 = 101 \text{ volts}$$

This result states that, for the specified system gain factors, the slider arm of the reference potentiometer must be set at a potential of +101 volts.

Next it is appropriate to describe the regulator action which permits the system to adjust itself automatically to try to maintain constant voltage in the presence of increasing load currents. It has already been established that at no load the reference input voltage is 101 volts, while the feedback voltage is −100 volts, thereby giving an actuating signal of 1 volt to generate the desired output voltage. This condition is referred to as the *quiescent operating point*. Since we are concerned now with the operation of the system as a load disturbance is applied, we are essentially concerned with operation about this quiescent point. Accordingly,

[1] Assume that the current drawn by the feedback potentiometer is negligible.

Eq. (1-1) is modified to

$$\Delta E_G = \Delta V + \Delta I_a R_a \qquad (1\text{-}3)$$

where ΔI_a represents the magnitude of the applied disturbance and ΔV the corresponding change in output voltage associated with it at the new steady-state condition.   Thus, if the demand for a new steady-state condition is imposed, Eq. (1-3) indicates that unless a change occurs in the quantity ΔE_G there occurs a change in output voltage equal to $-\Delta I_a R_a$, as long as E_R continues to remain fixed.   However, a study of Fig. 1-11 reveals that a change in ΔE_G does take place to prevent such a drop in output voltage from occurring.   This comes about as follows: An increase in load current causes a decrease in output voltage, which in turn means a decrease in the negative feedback voltage.   Since E_R is kept fixed and the actuating signal is given by Eq. (1-2), it follows that the input to the amplifier (e) increases, thereby producing a larger generator field current, which manifests itself as an increase in induced

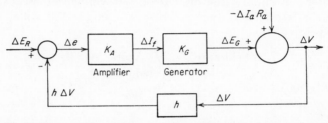

FIG. 1-13. Block diagram of a voltage regulator, showing changes about the initial operating point.

generator voltage, viz., ΔE_G.   It is significant that the increase in actuating signal actually comes about as a result of the decrease in the negative feedback voltage.   A comparison of the actuating signal at no load and at a load different from zero underlines this important fact.   Thus,

At no load: $e_0 = E_R - hV$ where $V = E_G$ = output voltage at no load

At load: $e = E_R - h(V + \Delta V)$ where $V + \Delta V$ = output voltage at load

$e = E_R - hV + h\,\Delta V$ when ΔV is negative   (1-4)

Comparing the two results shows that there is an increase in actuating signal of $h|\Delta V|$ upon application of load.   Equation (1-4) also points out that, for this type of elementary voltage regulator, the corrective action $h\,\Delta V$ depends upon the existence of some drop in voltage.   In other words, this type of control system cannot operate without some deviation from the desired output voltage as load is applied.

The gain factor and the input and output quantity of each component of the system are shown in the block diagram of Fig. 1-13.   To be able to calculate just how much change in output voltage is associated with a given load change and to get a better appreciation of the factors upon which this change depends, it is necessary to obtain a general expression relating ΔV, ΔI_a, ΔE_R, and the system parameters. This is readily accomplished by recognizing that a change in generated induced emf comes about whenever there is a change in actuating signal. From the block diagram it is clear that in going from one operating state to a new one the difference in generated emf is given by

$$\Delta E_G = \Delta e\, K_A K_G \tag{1-5}$$

However, from Eq. (1-2) it follows, too, that the difference in actuating signal between the two states is

$$\Delta e = \Delta E_R - h\, \Delta V \tag{1-6}$$

Accordingly, the change in generated emf is more conveniently written as

$$\Delta E_G = (\Delta E_R - h\, \Delta V)K_A K_G \tag{1-7}$$

Substituting Eq. (1-7) into Eq. (1-3) yields the expression we are seeking,

$$(\Delta E_R - h\, \Delta V)K_A K_G = \Delta V + \Delta I_a\, R_a \tag{1-8}$$

This is a completely general equation for describing the steady-state performance of this type of voltage control system. It is applicable to closed-loop as well as open-loop operation. All that is required to distinguish one mode from the other is the introduction of the appropriate constraints.

With the use of Eq. (1-8) we can now calculate the drop in output voltage corresponding to an increase in load current. Since the system is assumed operating with the loop closed and at a fixed reference voltage, the only constraint needed in Eq. (1-8) is $\Delta E_R = 0$. Hence

$$(-h\, \Delta V)K_A K_G = \Delta V + \Delta I_a\, R_a$$

or

$$\Delta V = \frac{-\Delta I_a\, R_a}{1 + hK_A K_G} \tag{1-9}$$

Equation (1-9) indicates that for an increase in load there is a drop in output voltage which is dependent upon the system parameters. Continuing with the example which has already been introduced, we find that for an increase in load current of $\Delta I_a = 20$ amp there is a change in output voltage of

$$\Delta V = \frac{-20}{1 + 0.5(2)(100)} = \frac{-20}{101} = -0.198 \text{ volt}$$

A glance at Fig. 1-12 shows that when the generator operates in the conventional manner (i.e., without feedback) the associated change in output voltage for the same load increase is -20 volts. Therefore, operation as a closed-loop system automatically corrects for the drop in output voltage to a value which is 101 times smaller. Further thought reveals that it is possible to reduce the magnitude of this voltage drop even more by increasing any one of the gain factors h, K_A, and K_G. However, lest there be a misunderstanding, it must be pointed out that the gain constants cannot be indiscriminately increased in spite of the fact that a decreased steady-state error results. This is because high gain factors can seriously impair the dynamic behavior to such an extent that instability results, which means that the new steady-state condition will never be reached. This subject matter is left to Chap. 4.

For the sake of emphasizing the control action provided by the feedback connection, let us compare the values of the actuating signal for the two load conditions. At no load the actuating signal has already been shown to be equal to 1 volt. For an increase in load of 20 amp an output voltage drop of 0.198 volt occurs so that the new value of output voltage is 199.802 volts. Hence the actuating signal at this load condition is

$$e = E_R - h(V + \Delta V) = 101 - 0.5(199.802) = 1.099$$

Comparison with the original value shows that an increase of 0.099 volt takes place as a result of decreased negative feedback voltage upon application of load. Equation (1-4) shows that in general this increase is $|h \, \Delta V|$. In this illustration, $|h \, \Delta V| = 0.5(0.198) = 0.099$ volt, which checks as expected.

The manner of calculation and the meaning of the closed-loop gain of a feedback control system are the next items for consideration before completing our discussion of the closed-loop analysis. Simply defined, assuming the system to be linear, the closed-loop gain is the ratio of the change in output voltage per unit change in reference voltage at constant I_a. Resorting to Eq. (1-8) with $\Delta I_a = 0$ shows the closed-loop gain to be

$$\frac{\Delta V}{\Delta E_R} = \frac{K_A K_G}{1 + h K_A K_G} \tag{1-10}$$

The form of this equation is a general result which applies to any feedback device. It indicates that the *closed-loop gain* is the ratio of the *direct-transmission gain*[1] divided by 1 plus the loop gain, where the *loop gain* differs from the direct-transmission gain by the feedback gain factor h. In the example being considered the value of this gain is

$$\frac{\Delta V}{\Delta E_R} = \frac{200}{101} = 1.98$$

Since the system is linear, the same result applies to the total quantities at no load so that we can write $V/E_R = 1.98$. Herein lies the significance of the value of the closed-loop gain for the control system. It gives a

[1] The direct-transmission gain is the ratio of output to input with the loop open.

measure of how large a reference voltage is needed to provide a specified level of output voltage.   Thus, to make available an output of 200 volts requires a source of reference voltage in excess of 100 volts.   Similarly, to provide an output of 300 volts requires a reference source in excess of 150 volts, and so on.

Open-loop Analysis [Switch S at (b)].   Placing switch S at position b in Fig. 1-11 removes the feedback connection and so provides open-loop operation for the system.   To find the magnitude of reference voltage needed to give the same value of output voltage as in the closed-loop case, we must first recognize that the difference lies in the removal of the effect of the feedback voltage.   That is, the actuating signal at no load must be the same in both cases, viz., e_0.   Using the figures of the example, this value is $e_0 = 1$ volt.   Now, because of the lack of the feedback voltage, the required reference voltage needed in the open-loop case to generate a no-load voltage of 200 volts is simply 1 volt.   It also follows that the gain as an open-loop system is 200.   The block diagram for this mode of operation is shown in Fig. 1-14.   Note that the actuating signal

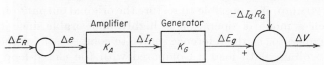

FIG. 1-14. Block diagram of a system operating open-loop.

and the reference voltage are one and the same.   Note, too, that the general form of the gain as an open-loop system is

$$\frac{\Delta V}{\Delta E_R} = K_A K_G \tag{1-11}$$

and is called the direct-transmission gain.   Equation (1-11) may also be obtained from Eq. (1-8) upon introducing the constraints $\Delta I_a = 0$ and $h = 0$.

A glance at Fig. 1-12 makes clear the open-loop performance of the system when subjected to increasing values of load current.   To formalize the procedure, however, let us determine the change in output voltage for a specified load increase by applying the appropriate constraints to Eq. (1-8).   Since the reference voltage is assumed constant and the loop is open, it follows that $\Delta E_R = 0$ and $h = 0$.   Accordingly, Eq. (1-8) becomes

$$0 = \Delta V + \Delta I_a R_a$$

or
$$\Delta V = -\Delta I_a R_a \tag{1-12}$$

which states that the drop in output voltage is equal in magnitude to the internal-resistance drop of the generator.   A comparison of Eq. (1-12) with Eq. (1-9) indicates that operation with the loop closed reduces the change in output voltage compared with open-loop operation by a factor of $1/(1 + hK_AK_G)$. This result is also applicable to feedback devices in general, and for those readers who have studied electronics it is certainly not unfamiliar.

There remains now one final point of interest. If the open-loop system is subjected to a load increase of $\Delta I_a = 20$ amp, then by Eq. (1-12) the corresponding decrease in output voltage for a fixed reference voltage is $\Delta V = -20$ volts. However, a study of Fig. 1-11 reveals that it is possible to restore the original value of output voltage by merely increasing the reference voltage by the proper amount. The required increase is found from Eq. (1-8) upon introducing the constraints $h = 0$ and $\Delta V = 0$. Thus

$$\Delta E_R\, K_A K_G = \Delta I_a\, R_a$$

Therefore, $$\Delta E_R = \frac{\Delta I_a\, R_a}{K_A K_G} = \frac{20}{200} = 0.1 \ \ \text{volt}$$

Accordingly, by increasing the reference voltage by 0.1 volt after a load change of 20 amp, it is possible to restore the original output voltage. Of course such a mode of operation is highly undesirable since it requires placing an operator at the reference source to compensate for the changes in output voltage with load. Compared with the closed-loop mode of operation, it lacks the very important feature of automaticity, i.e., self-correcting action. In fact further thought reveals that placing an operator at the reference source is really equivalent to closed-loop operation where the feedback takes place through the operator. It is interesting to note, too, that, with closed-loop operation the increase in actuating signal for a load change of 20 amp is found to be 0.099 volt, which is just 0.001 volt short of the amount required to give no change in output voltage. As already pointed out, a deviation must always exist for this type of elementary control system. It must be remembered that in a closed-loop system the increase in actuating signal $|h\, \Delta V|$ comes about through a decreased feedback quantity, whereas in the case where an operator is involved it comes about through an increase in the reference voltage.

Now that the mechanics of operation is understood, let us proceed to find the steady-state performance by using a more direct approach. Figure 1-15 is a modified version of the system block diagram shown in Fig. 1-13 and is useful in this connection since it is expressed in terms of the total values of the system variables. Furthermore, it treats the flow of load current as an applied disturbance in the block diagram. A study of this diagram reveals that with the loop closed the expression for the output quantity is simply

$$V = (E_R - hV)K_A K_G - I_a R_a$$

Solving for V yields

$$V = \frac{K_A K_G}{1 + h K_A K_G} E_R - \frac{I_a R_a}{1 + h K_A K_G}$$

It is interesting to note that in situations where the open-loop gain $h K_A K_G$ is very large compared with unity the magnitude of the no-load generator output voltage is E_R/h. This result is significant because it points out that changes in the gain parameters K_A and K_G do not affect the no-load output voltage.

For a fixed reference voltage the change in output voltage due to a change in load current may then be found by applying the operation $\Delta V = (\partial V / \partial I_a) \Delta I_a$ to the preceding equation. Thus

$$\Delta V = \frac{- R_a}{1 + h K_A K_G} \Delta I_a$$

which is the same result as Eq. (1-9).

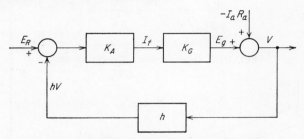

FIG. 1-15. Modified block diagram of Fig. 1-13.

To determine the change in reference voltage needed to offset the decrease in output associated with armature-winding voltage drop, it is merely necessary to formulate

$$\Delta V = \frac{\partial V}{\partial E_R} \Delta E_R + \frac{\partial V}{\partial I_a} \Delta I_a = 0$$

and solve for ΔE_R. Proceeding in this manner yields

$$\Delta V = \left(\frac{K_A K_G}{1 + h K_A K_G} \right) \Delta E_R + \left(\frac{- R_a}{1 + h K_A K_G} \right) \Delta I_a = 0$$

so that

$$\Delta E_R = \frac{\Delta I_a R_a}{K_A K_G}$$

which obviously agrees with the result on page 26.

1-6. Steady-state Analysis of an Elementary Speed Control System

The method of analysis proceeds in a manner similar to that described in the foregoing section. However, instead of the voltage equation, the steady-state performance is derived from the system torque equation. This requires introducing and explaining the concept of the equivalent viscous friction of the motor, which makes available the desired output speeds. The role played by the motor viscous friction is important, not only in determining the steady-state performance, but more so in establishing the nature of the dynamic behavior of the system of which it is a part. Figure 1-16 shows the schematic diagram of a typical elementary speed regulator.

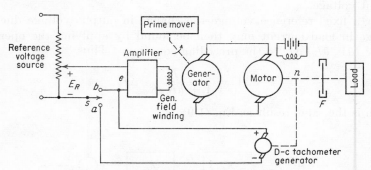

FIG. 1-16. An elementary speed regulator.

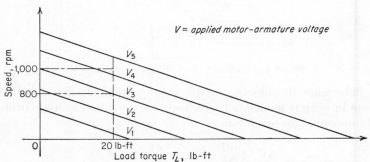

FIG. 1-17. Drooping speed-torque curves of a separately excited d-c motor. $V_5 > V_4 > V_3 > V_2 > V_1$.

Essentially the motor viscous friction is the slope of the speed-torque characteristic. Figure 1-17 shows a typical set of linearized speed-torque curves for a d-c electric motor with a constant field excitation and varying fixed armature voltage. Since the torque equation used in computing the steady-state performance depends upon an understanding of the origin of these curves, we shall now derive them. Assume the actuating signal is of such a value that it applies a voltage V to the motor armature terminals, thereby causing it to run at a speed of n rpm. If a load torque of T_L units is then applied to the load shaft, the equilibrium torque equation is

$$K_T I_a = T_L \qquad\qquad (1\text{-}13)$$

where K_T equals the motor torque constant when expressed in units of lb-ft/armature amp and I_a is the armature current in amperes. Also, for a separately excited d-c machine the armature current may be written as

$$I_a = \frac{V - E}{R_a} = \frac{V - K_n n}{R_a} \tag{1-14}$$

where E = motor counter emf

R_a = motor armature-winding resistance

K_n = motor counter-emf constant, volts/rpm

Substituting Eq. (1-14) into Eq. (1-13) yields

$$K_T \left(\frac{V}{R_a} - \frac{K_n n}{R_a} \right) = T_L$$

or

$$\frac{K_T}{R_a} V = \frac{K_T K_n}{R_a} n + T_L \tag{1-15}$$

An investigation of the units of the coefficient of the n term in the last equation reveals that it has the units of viscous friction. That is,

$$F \equiv \frac{K_T(\text{lb-ft/amp}) K_n(\text{volts/rpm})}{R_a(\text{volts/amp})} = \frac{K_T K_n}{R_a} \left(\frac{\text{lb-ft}}{\text{rpm}} \right) \tag{1-16}$$

Furthermore, the left side of Eq. (1-15) may be looked upon as the maximum (or ideal) developed torque for a specified armature voltage V corresponding to standstill condition (i.e., zero speed). Calling this torque T_{id} and substituting Eq. (1-16) into Eq. (1-15) yields the desired torque equation, namely,

$$T_{id} = Fn + T_L \tag{1-17}$$

A moment's reflection should now make it clear that the speed-torque characteristics of Fig. 1-17 are no more than a plot of Eq. (1-17) in the form

$$T_L = T_{id} - Fn = \frac{K_T V}{R_a} - Fn$$

For a fixed V the T_L curve droops as the speed increases. It is apparent then that the reciprocal of the slope of these curves is the equivalent viscous-friction parameter of the motor.

It is worthwhile at this point to distinguish between the various types of frictional forces or torques that may be encountered, inasmuch as the viscous-friction quantity has already been introduced. The distinction is perhaps best made by referring to Fig. 1-18, which depicts the three types of frictional torques. *Viscous friction* is that torque which opposes motion in a way that is directly proportional to the speed of the output member. *Static friction* refers to the torque required to just barely initiate motion. *Coulomb friction* is that torque which opposes motion but is independent of the output speed.   As is pointed out later in the text, the presence of coulomb friction in any system component adversely affects the steady-state performance and hence must be kept to a minimum if very accurate performance is to result.   Let us now return to the system of Fig. 1-16 and study its performance, assuming that the motor has the characteristics shown in Fig. 1-17.

Closed-loop Analysis.   The system operates closed-loop when switch S is placed at position a.   The purpose of the feedback is to help maintain a predetermined speed in the presence of increased torque demands by the load.   To generate a desired output speed at no load requires a definite value of actuating signal, the magnitude of which depends upon

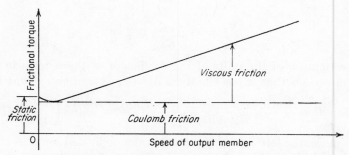

FIG. 1-18. Distinction between various types of frictional torques.

the gain factors of the amplifier, the generator, and the motor.   For purposes of illustration, let us assume the following gain constants:

Amplifier gain $= K_A = 10$ field amp/volt

Generator gain $= K_G = 100$ induced volts/field amp

Motor torque gain $= K_M = \dfrac{K_T}{R_a} = 1$ lb-ft/volt

D-c tachometer gain $= h = 0.01$ volt/rpm

Motor viscous friction $= F = \frac{20}{200} = 0.1$ lb-ft/rpm

Assume that at no load the motor is operating at a speed of 1,000 rpm. To keep the motor turning at this speed requires a developed torque of $Fn = 0.1(1,000) = 100$ lb-ft.   The actuating signal needed is therefore

$$e_0 K_A K_G K_M = 100$$

or

$$e_0 = \frac{100}{1,000} = 0.1 \text{ volt}$$

Since the feedback voltage from the tachometer generator is

$$hn = 0.01(1,000) = 10 \text{ volts}$$

it follows that the reference input voltage needed to generate the output speed of 1,000 rpm is

$$E_R = e_0 + hn = 10.1 \text{ volts}$$

The system block diagram is shown in Fig. 1-19. The input and output quantities of the various components are represented for convenience as changes about the initial operating point. The torque equation as it

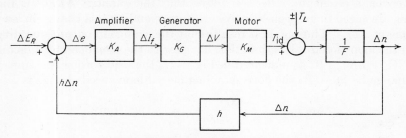

FIG. 1-19. Block diagram of Fig. 1-16.

applies for changes about the quiescent point follows from Eq. (1-17). Thus,

$$\Delta T_{\text{id}} = F \, \Delta n + \Delta T_L \tag{1-18}$$

To put this equation in a general form applicable to both closed-loop and open-loop operaton requires replacing ΔT_{id} by its equivalent, namely,

$$\Delta T_{\text{id}} = (\Delta E_R - h \, \Delta n) K_A K_G K_M \tag{1-19}$$

The last equation merely states that to increase the developed torque of the motor requires increasing the actuating signal. Substituting Eq. (1-19) into Eq. (1-18) yields the desired result.

$$(\Delta E_R - h \, \Delta n) K_A K_G K_M = F \, \Delta n + \Delta T_L \tag{1-20}$$

Since this is still a torque equation and the controlled quantity is speed, it is appropriate to modify the equation so that the terms standing alone represent speed. Dividing both sides of Eq. (1-20) by F accomplishes this. Hence

$$(\Delta E_R - h \, \Delta n) \frac{K_A K_G K_M}{F} = \Delta n + \frac{\Delta T_L}{F} \tag{1-21}$$

For simplicity let $K \equiv K_A K_G K_M / F$ (rpm/volt). The units of K make it clear that it is a speed constant, and more specifically it is the direct-transmission gain of the system. By applying the proper constraints on Eq. (1-21) the particular mode of system performance can be evaluated.

Assume that the system is to function as a regulator, corresponding to the quiescent condition which has already been computed. Accordingly, the constraint to be imposed is $\Delta E_R = 0$. For this mode of operation the relationship between the change in speed and the corresponding change in load is

$$\Delta n = \frac{-\Delta T_L/F}{1 + hK} \tag{1-22}$$

As was the case for the voltage regulator, Eq. (1-22) again points out the dependence of the change in output quantity upon the loop gain hK. Moreover, a moment's reflection shows that the quantity $\Delta T_L/F$ is the change in speed in an open-loop system corresponding to a change in load torque of ΔT_L. Thus again it results that the change in output quantity with the loop closed is less than the change with the loop open by a factor of $1/(1 + hK)$. If, as indicated in Fig. 1-17, the load torque is assumed to change by 20 lb-ft, the corresponding closed-loop speed change is

$$\Delta n = \frac{-200}{1 + 0.01(10,000)} = -1.98 \text{ rpm}$$

Thus, the speed at the new load condition is 998.02 rpm. The corresponding value of actuating signal is

$$
\begin{aligned}
e &= E_R - h(n_0 + \Delta n) \\
&= E_R - hn_0 - h\,\Delta n = e_0 - h\,\Delta n \\
&= 0.1 + 0.01(1.98) = 0.1198 \text{ volt}
\end{aligned}
$$

Again take note of the self-correcting action associated with the feedback connection as it reflects in the increasing portion of the actuating signal $h\,\Delta n$.

The closed-loop gain is conveniently found from Eq. (1-21) by introducing the constraint $\Delta T_L = 0$. The result is

$$\frac{\Delta n}{\Delta E_R} = \frac{K}{1 + hK} \tag{1-23}$$

Open-loop Analysis. As pointed out in the previous section, operation as an open-loop system requires different levels of reference input to duplicate the same no-load operating points. Thus, to generate an output velocity of 1,000 rpm requires a reference input of 0.1 volt, which is the value of the actuating signal at no load.

If this reference input is kept fixed and a load increase is introduced, the introduction of the constraints $\Delta E_R = 0$ and $h = 0$ shows that the attendant drop in speed is

$$\Delta n = -\frac{\Delta T_L}{F}$$

SUGGESTED READING

Brown, G. S., and D. P. Campbell: "Principles of Servomechanisms," chap. 1, John Wiley & Sons, Inc., New York, 1948.

Cage, J. M.: "Theory and Applications of Industrial Electronics," chap. 4, McGraw-Hill Book Company, Inc., New York, 1951.

Fett, G. H.: "Feedback Control Systems," chap. 1, Prentice-Hall, Inc., Englewood Cliffs, N.J., 1954.

Thaler, G. J.: "Elements of Servomechanism Theory," chap. 1, McGraw-Hill Book Company, Inc., New York, 1955.

PROBLEMS

1-1. Prove that the equation for the closed-loop gain of the elementary voltage regulator is the same as that given by Eq. (1-10) under conditions where the load current is fixed at a value other than zero. Assume linear external characteristics as well as uniform spacing for equal increments of the parameter for these curves.

1-2. Verify the result of Eq. (1-22) by analyzing the system, using total quantities in the appropriate block diagram rather than changes about the initial operating point as shown in Fig. 1-19.

1-3. A heavy mass rests on a horizontal slab of steel. The slab is hinge-supported on one side and rests on an adjustable support on the other side. The hinged support is subject to random vertical displacements. The mass is to remain level by changing the height of the adjustable support. Devise a feedback control system to accomplish this task.

1-4. Devise a control system to regulate the thickness of sheet metal as it passes through a continuous rolling mill (see Fig. P1-4). The control system should provide a product which not only keeps the uniformity of thickness within suitable tolerances but permits adjustment of the thickness as well. Show a clearly labeled diagram of the system.

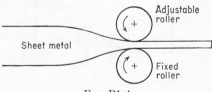

FIG. P1-4

1-5. The control system for remotely positioning the rudder of a ship is shown in Fig P1-5. The resistor coil of the potentiometer is fastened to the ship's frame. The desired heading is determined by the gyroscope setting (which is independent of the actual heading). Explain how the system operates in following a command for a northbound direction.

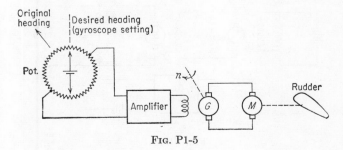

FIG. P1-5

1-6. You are called upon by a medical clinic to design a servo anesthetizer for the purpose of regulating automatically the depth of anesthesia in a patient in accordance with the energy output of the brain-wave activity as measured by an electroencephalograph (EEG). The anesthetic is to be administered by means of a hypodermic syringe which is activated by a stepping relay fed from an appropriate amplifying source.

Show a diagram of the control system, and state clearly what constitutes the error detector, the feedback, and the corrector. Explain the operation of the system.

1-7. Devise an elementary temperature control system for a furnace fed by a valve-controlled fuel line. Use a Wheatstone-bridge error-detector arrangement and a temperature-sensitive resistor. Assume that the disturbance takes the form of changes in ambient temperature. Describe how control is obtained. Also, indicate how the desired reference temperature is established.

1-8. The speed of a gasoline engine is to be controlled in accordance with a command that is in the form of a voltage. Devise a control system which is capable of providing this kind of control. Explain the operation of your system.

1-9. Shown is a simple voltage regulator (Fig. P1-9). The amplifier has a gain of 1 field amp/volt. The generator gain is 50 volts/field amp.

(*a*) The system is operated closed-loop (*s* to *b*). If the generator has a no-load voltage of 250 volts, find the value of the reference voltage.

(*b*) With *s* at *b*, find the change in terminal voltage which occurs when the load current increases by 20 amp.

(*c*) When the system is operated open-loop (*s* to *a*), determine the change needed in the reference voltage to maintain constant terminal voltage for the same current increase.

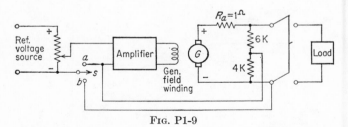

Fig. P1-9

1-10. A voltage regulator equipped with a pilot generator is shown in Fig. P1-10.

(*a*) Explain the operation of this system.

(*b*) Draw the block diagram of the system, identifying specifically the basic elements which make up the closed loop.

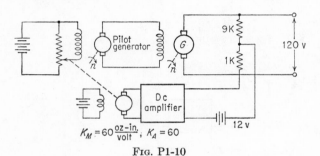

Fig. P1-10

(c) If the coulomb-friction torque of the potentiometer arm is 40 oz-in., what maximum error in generator output voltage will result from a slow change in the speed of the generator?

(d) If this friction could be reduced to zero, would there be a steady-state error in generator output as a result of a change in generator speed or load current? Explain.

1-11. An amplidyne generator is employed to control the charging current to a large storage battery (Fig. P1-11). The amplidyne generates an output current proportional to the difference between reference and control field currents, the current amplification being 200. The charging generator G develops a no-load voltage of 120 volts/amp of field current, and its armature resistance is 0.10 ohm. The internal resistance of battery B is 0.2 ohm.

(a) If the battery generates an emf of 100 volts when charging is begun and the rate of charging is to be 20 amp, determine the current required in the reference winding of the amplidyne.

(b) Assuming that the voltage generated by the battery rises to 115 volts when it is fully charged, what is the total change in current over the charging period?

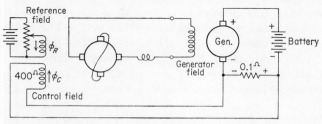

FIG. P1-11

1-12. Using the method of partial derivatives outlined at the end of Sec. 1-5, obtain the results of Eqs. (1-22) and (1-23) for the speed control system.

2 | Classical Solution of Linear Differential Equations

The purpose of this chapter is to provide some of the mathematical background to be used in the remainder of the text. The material is not presented in rigorous mathematical fashion. The reader should be acquainted with many of the ideas. The object is simply to review the available mathematical tools and present them in a unified way, with emphasis on those properties of particular importance to feedback control theory.

Every dynamical physical system can be characterized theoretically by a set of equations. The solution of these equations for various input conditions represents the system's behavior in the real world. If the mathematical solution shows that the system's behavior is incorrect (the system may be unstable or the errors too great), then the original equations can be examined to determine what changes need to be made to obtain the desired operation. These mathematical requirements can then be interpreted in terms of required physical changes. It is certainly more expedient, from both a technical and an economical point of view, to experiment with mathematical coefficients than to build a complex experimental system.

In order to obtain a complete mathematical picture of a system, the engineer must first formulate the governing equations and then proceed to find their solutions. As a practical matter, certain simplifying approximations must be made in the mathematical description, and the reader may correctly point out that these approximations tend to weaken our confidence in the mathematical results. This certainly is true if the system has been oversimplified for the sake of easy mathematics. However, in practice, this should not happen if the engineer employs proper discretion. In fact, it is the very process of evaluating the approximations and simplifications which enables the engineer to reduce a system to its essentials and clear away the clutter of unimportant second-order effects.

In this text we are concerned with both the formulation and the solution of the problem. However, this chapter deals primarily with the latter phase—examining the mathematical equations, finding their solutions, and interpreting the results to instill understanding and insight.

Solving linear differential equations is approached from two points of view: the so-called *classical method*, which is discussed in this chapter, and the *Laplace-transform method*, which is discussed in the next chapter. We shall show that parallel steps are taken with each method and that the difference is primarily one of approach and interpretation. The best physical understanding is obtained by using both. The concept of complex frequency is also introduced to tie the differential-equation approach to the frequency-response and impedance concepts and to serve as an introduction to the problem of system stability. The first few sections discuss some basic system properties and should serve to set the stage and outline the area in which we are working.

2-1. The Linear System

The mathematical equations describing the dynamic behavior of a system can be reduced usually to an integrodifferential equation involving the input and the output. This equation relates the output plus its derivatives and/or integrals to the input plus its derivatives and/or integrals. The input is usually specified as a given function of time (the most common independent variable), and the output as the dependent variable for which a solution is to be determined. The integrodifferential equation formulates the basic relationship between the input and output, i.e., the relationship between the "cause and effect," or the "controlling and controlled variables." The exact nature of the input and output depends upon the specific system; they may take the form of voltage, current, position, velocity, pressure, temperature, etc., and can occur in almost any combination.

We shall restrict our considerations to systems which can be described by the following type of integrodifferential equation, in which a linear combination of the dependent variable (the output c) and its derivatives and integrals is equated to some function of the input $r(t)$ and its derivatives and integrals. Thus

$$\beta_0 c + \beta_1 \frac{dc}{dt} + \cdots + \beta_n \frac{d^n c}{dt^n} + \cdots + \beta_{-1} \int c \, dt + \cdots$$
$$+ \beta_{-m} \int c \, dt^m = f[r(t)] \quad (2\text{-}1)$$

where $r(t)$ is a specified input or driving function. The right-hand side, $f[r(t)]$, is a function of the input and is restricted in this treatment to be a linear combination of the form

$$f[r(t)] = \alpha_0 r(t) + \alpha_1 \frac{dr(t)}{dt} + \cdots + \alpha_p \frac{d^p r(t)}{dt^p}$$
$$+ \alpha_{-1} \int r(t)\, dt + \cdots + \alpha_{-q} \int r(t)\, dt^q$$

The coefficients $\beta_0, \ldots, \beta_n, \ldots, \beta_{-m}$ and $\alpha_0, \ldots, \alpha_p, \ldots, \alpha_{-q}$ may be functions of the variable t or constants. It can be shown that, by successive differentiations or integrations, Eq. (2-1) may be reduced to a pure differential- or integral-equation form. The pure differential-equation form is used most often for pencil-and-paper mathematical analysis.

Equation (2-1) is said to be a linear equation with constant coefficients if the α's and β's are constants. The system it describes is then a linear time-invariant system. The linearity is due to the fact that the dependent variable and its derivatives and integrals are of the first power [terms such as $(dc/dt)^2$ are not permitted] and are combined in a linear equation. It is important to note that linearity *does not* require that the coefficients be constants, but only that their values be independent of the output variable. Thus, in a linear system, $\beta_0, \ldots, \beta_n, \ldots, \beta_{-m}$ cannot be a function of c, but they *may* vary with time. The latter type of system is known as a *linear time-variant system*. This distinction is important because, as is shown in the following sections, linearity implies certain inherent system properties, and the further restriction of constant coefficients adds additional properties.

The restriction of our considerations to linear systems may seem to be a serious limitation upon physical reality. This is true to a certain extent, but nevertheless linear analysis serves the purpose of directing our thinking and provides the basis for understanding how changes in specifically assumed system constants influence system performance. Also, very often nonlinear elements may be considered, as a first approximation, to be linear over a specified dynamic range and the nonlinearities considered to be second-order perturbation effects. Since our mathematical tools and understanding are most fully developed for linear analysis, it is practical to limit our designs to linear elements. Nonlinearities may then be designed into a system, but usually after a linear analysis has laid the groundwork and indicated what is desired.

2-2. Property of Linearity. Superposition

Linear systems have a basic property which sets them apart from all others and which is essential for their study. This property has been given the name of *superposition* and is simple in content.

If a system's response is known for each one of a set of independent driving functions acting alone, then the response, when all act simultaneously, is obtained by adding their independent effects. In other words, each independent source, or drive, produces its own effect, acting as if the other sources were not present. The reader acquainted with electrical-circuit theory will immediately recognize this property as the underlying principle behind the use of Fourier series and Thévenin's theorem in solving electrical-network problems. It should be pointed out that superposition is a property of linearity and does not require constant coefficients. The proof of superposition follows immediately from the linearity of Eq. (2-1).

If $c_1(t)$ is the system's response to input $r_1(t)$ and $c_2(t)$ is the system's response to input $r_2(t)$, then Eq. (2-1) states, for each input acting alone,

$$\beta_0 c_1 + \beta_1 \frac{dc_1}{dt} + \cdots + \beta_n \frac{d^n c_1}{dt^n} + \beta_{-1} \int c_1 \, dt + \cdots$$
$$+ \beta_{-m} \int c_1 \, dt^m = f[r_1(t)]$$

and $$\beta_0 c_2 + \beta_1 \frac{dc_2}{dt} + \cdots + \beta_n \frac{d^n c_2}{dt^n} + \beta_{-1} \int c_2 \, dt + \cdots$$
$$+ \beta_{-m} \int c_2 \, dt^m = f[r_2(t)]$$

Addition of the two preceding equations yields

$$\beta_0 (c_1 + c_2) + \beta_1 \frac{d}{dt}(c_1 + c_2) + \cdots + \beta_n \frac{d^n(c_1 + c_2)}{dt^n}$$
$$+ \beta_{-1} \int (c_1 + c_2) \, dt + \cdots + \beta_{-m} \int (c_1 + c_2) \, dt^m$$
$$= f[r_1(t)] + f[r_2(t)]$$

The foregoing equation can be interpreted as defining a new function, $c_1(t) + c_2(t)$, which is a solution to the equation when the driving function is $f[r_1(t)] + f[r_2(t)]$. This, of course, is exactly what the principle of superposition states. The essential mathematical step in arriving at this conclusion was that we were able to take advantage of linearity and to combine terms, using the property that

$$\frac{d^n c_1}{dt^n} + \frac{d^n c_2}{dt^n} = \frac{d^n(c_1 + c_2)}{dt^n}$$

and $$\int c_1 \, dt^m + \int c_2 \, dt^m = \int (c_1 + c_2) \, dt^m$$

If any of the derivatives or integrals in the original equation had been raised to a power or a product had been involved, the above step could not have been made and we would not have been able to combine the results of the addition to demonstrate superposition, for, as can easily be shown,

$$\left(\frac{d^n c_1}{dt^n}\right)^P + \left(\frac{d^n c_2}{dt^n}\right)^P \neq \left[\frac{d^n(c_1 + c_2)}{dt^n}\right]^P$$

where the letter P represents any arbitrary power other than unity.

Thus we have demonstrated that superposition follows directly from linearity. The importance of superposition in linear automatic control theory will become more obvious in the remainder of the text.

2-3. Property of Constant Coefficient. Related Sources

If the linear differential equation of the previous section also has constant coefficients (time-invariant), then another useful property may be derived. This property has been given the name of *related sources* and may be stated as follows:

If a system's response to a given input function is known, then the response to the derivative, or integral, of this input function may be found by differentiating, or integrating, the original response.

The property of related sources is demonstrated by differentiating Eq. (2-1), assuming that the coefficients are constants. Thus

$$\beta_0 \frac{dc}{dt} + \beta_1 \frac{d^2 c}{dt^2} + \cdots + \beta_n \frac{d^{n+1} c}{dt^{n+1}} + \beta_{-1} c + \cdots$$
$$+ \beta_{-m} \int c \, dt^{m-1} = \frac{d}{dt} \{f[r(t)]\}$$

Rewriting yields

$$\beta_0 \left(\frac{dc}{dt}\right) + \beta_1 \frac{d}{dt}\left(\frac{dc}{dt}\right) + \cdots + \beta_n \frac{d^n}{dt^n}\left(\frac{dc}{dt}\right) + \beta_{-1} c + \cdots$$
$$+ \beta_{-m} \int \left(\frac{dc}{dt}\right) dt^m = \frac{d}{dt} \{f[r(t)]\}$$

It should now be recalled that the right-hand side of Eq. (2-1) is also a linear combination of derivatives and integrals of $r(t)$, similar to the left-hand side. If the coefficients on the right side are also constants, then differentiation of the right side yields the result

$$\frac{d\{f[r(t)]\}}{dt} = f\left[\frac{dr(t)}{dt}\right]$$

Thus the result of differentiating Eq. (2-1) may now be written as

$$\beta_0 \left(\frac{dc}{dt}\right) + \beta_1 \frac{d}{dt}\left(\frac{dc}{dt}\right) + \cdots + \beta_n \frac{d^n}{dt^n}\left(\frac{dc}{dt}\right) + \beta_{-1} \int \left(\frac{dc}{dt}\right) dt + \cdots$$
$$+ \beta_{-m} \int \left(\frac{dc}{dt}\right) dt^m = f\left[\frac{dr(t)}{dt}\right]$$

The foregoing equation is easily recognized as being identical to Eq. (2-1) except that c has been replaced by $\left(\dfrac{dc}{dt}\right)$ and $f[r(t)]$ by $f\left[\dfrac{dr(t)}{dt}\right]$. The interpretation is apparent: the driving function is now $\left[\dfrac{dr(t)}{dt}\right]$, and the solution is given by $\left(\dfrac{dc}{dt}\right)$. Thus the solution for the derivative of an input function is simply the derivative of the response for the original input function. A similar statement can be made for the case of the integral of the driving function, but it should be pointed out that an arbitrary constant must then be added and evaluated separately. This point is demonstrated in an example later on.

The reliance of the related-sources property upon constant coefficients is obvious when one considers the differentiation or integration required for its demonstration. If any of the coefficients had been functions of time, then the corresponding term in Eq. (2-1) would have been differentiated as a product and the related-sources interpretation of the result would not have been possible.

2-4. The Classical Approach

The classical method for the solution of a differential equation is based upon the principle of superposition. Before outlining the procedure it is necessary to differentiate the original integrodifferential equation to obtain a pure differential equation. Thus, if Eq. (2-1) is differentiated enough times to remove all the integral terms, it can be written in the following general form,

$$B_0 c + B_1 \frac{dc}{dt} + B_2 \frac{d^2c}{dt^2} + \cdots + B_n \frac{d^nc}{dt^n} = A_0 r(t) + A_1 \frac{dr(t)}{dt} + \cdots$$
$$+ A_m \frac{d^m r(t)}{dt^m} \quad (2\text{-}2)$$

where the coefficients have now been designated by the letters $A_0, \ldots, A_m, B_0, \ldots, B_n$. [*Note:* n and m in Eq. (2-2) do not have the same meaning as in Eq. (2-1).] For a physically realizable system n is usually greater than m, but the reason for this will not become apparent until later.

The right side of Eq. (2-2) depends upon $r(t)$, the particular driving function being studied. Thus any solution for $c(t)$ which makes the left side equal to the right side is called a *particular* solution and represents the *driven,* or *forced,* behavior of the system in response to a particular driving, or forcing, function.

In a linear system with constant coefficients the driven solution is of the same mathematical form as the driving function. If the input is sinusoidal, the driven response is sinusoidal; if the input is represented by a polynomial, then the driven response is also a polynomial. The reason for this is apparent when it is noted that the left side of Eq. (2-2) involves successive derivatives of the particular solution and that for most functions these derivatives are of the same mathematical form as the original.

The question now arises as to how a system's driven response changes when there is a change in the driving function. The answer lies in the source-free or complementary function, which provides for a continuous transition. The *complementary* function consists of any expression for $c(t)$ which makes the left side of Eq. (2-2) equal to zero. By the principle of superposition, the complementary solution may be added to any particular solution. Also, it represents the system's behavior as it relaxes from a state of stored internal energy in the absence of any input, and it is often called the *source-free*, or *natural*, solution. As is shown, the source-free solution always has some arbitrary constants associated with it which must be evaluated separately. The number of constants is equal to the number of independent energy-storing elements in the system which corresponds to the order of the differential equation.

To obtain a complete picture of a system's behavior, it is necessary to add the source-free solution to every driven solution. The arbitrary constants are then adjusted so that physical conditions at the end of one driven state and the beginning of another are continuous and consistent with the differential equation. When there is a change in driving functions, the source-free solution provides the terms which enable the system's response to change continuously from the conditions required by the first input to those required by the second and still guarantee that the original differential equation is satisfied at all times.

Since the expressions source-free and driven solutions have been introduced, it is worthwhile to clarify their meanings with respect to two other commonly used terms—the *steady-state* and *transient* solutions. In this text the term steady-state refers to that part of the complete solution which *does not* approach zero as time approaches infinity. The term transient refers to that part of the complete solution which approaches zero as time approaches infinity. It should be noted that transient and steady-state are not to be taken as synonymous with source-free and driven. A driven solution may contain transient (or decaying) terms and a source-free solution may contain steady (or sustained) terms.

2-5. The Source-free Solution, or Complementary Function

To reiterate, the source-free or complementary solution to Eq. (2-2) is any function $c(t)$ which, when substituted into the left-hand side, makes it equal to zero. Thus it is any function of time which satisfies the equation

$$B_0 c(t) + B_1 \frac{dc(t)}{dt} + B_2 \frac{d^2c(t)}{dt^2} + \cdots + B_n \frac{d^n c(t)}{dt^n} = 0 \qquad (2\text{-}3)$$

Equation (2-3) is known as the *homogeneous* differential equation. Solution of the homogeneous equation may be found easily when the B coefficients are constants, which is the case with which we are concerned primarily. The source-free solution is determined by assuming that it has the following general exponential form,

$$c(t) = K\epsilon^{st} \qquad (2\text{-}4)$$

where K and s are unknowns whose values are determined by substituting Eq. (2-4) into Eq. (2-3). The assumption of an exponential form is apparent when one considers that all derivatives of the exponential are proportional to the original exponential. That is,

$$\frac{d^n}{dt^n} (K\epsilon^{st}) = K s^n \epsilon^{st}$$

Thus, when the exponential is substituted into Eq. (2-3), $K\epsilon^{st}$ appears as a common factor and the following algebraic equation for s results:

$$B_0 + B_1 s + B_2 s^2 + \cdots + B_n s^n = 0 \qquad (2\text{-}5)$$

The roots of Eq. (2-5) give the specific values of s for which $c(t) = K\epsilon^{st}$ will satisfy Eq. (2-3).[1] The constant K is seen to be arbitrary in that a specific numerical value is not required to satisfy Eq. (2-3).

Equation (2-5) is called the *characteristic* equation for the system. If Eq. (2-5) is compared with Eq. (2-3), it is apparent that the characteristic equation may be obtained directly from this equation by simply replacing d/dt by s and d^n/dt^n by s^n. Several important features may now be described concerning the characteristic equation.

1. All the coefficients $B_0, \ldots, B_n$ are real numbers since each is associated with physical parts of the system. From this fact we can conclude that the roots of the characteristic equation must be real numbers and/or complex conjugate pairs. The latter becomes apparent when one considers that the product of a complex number with its conjugate is always a real number, $(a + jb)(a - jb) = a^2 + b^2$. If the characteristic equation had a complex root without its conjugate counterpart, then the factor corresponding to this root in the original equation would introduce the quantity $j = \sqrt{-1}$ into at least one of the coefficients, which is physically impossible.

[1] Appendix B presents several techniques for determining the roots of any-order characteristic equation.

2. The degree of the characteristic equation is equal to the order of the original differential equation. From the *fundamental law of algebra*[1] this means that the characteristic equation has as many roots as the order of the original differential equation. Each one of these roots represents a solution of the form $c(t) = K\epsilon^{st}$, and the sum of these terms, for all roots, makes up the source-free solution. The constant K is arbitrary, so that each term may have a different value for K associated with it. These are the arbitrary constants mentioned previously. The number of constants is equal to the number of roots, which in turn equals the degree of the characteristic equation or the order of the differential equation.

The foregoing discussion may now be summarized in concise mathematical terms. The characteristic equation is written in factored form as follows,

$$B_0 + B_1 s + \cdots + B_n s^n$$
$$= B_n(s - s_1)(s - s_2)(s - s_2^*) \cdots (s - s_n) = 0 \quad (2\text{-}6)$$

where $s_1, s_2, s_2^*, \ldots, s_n$ are the roots of the characteristic equation and where, for the sake of illustration, s_1 is assumed real and s_2 and s_2^* complex conjugates. Thus

$$s_1 = -\sigma_1$$
$$s_2 = -\sigma_2 + j\omega_2$$
$$s_2^* = -\sigma_2 - j\omega_2$$

Each of these roots gives rise to a term in the solution of the form $K_n \epsilon^{s_n t}$, where the exponent corresponds to a root located at $s = s_n$ and K_n is the arbitary constant associated with that root. Thus the complementary or source-free solution is

$$c(t) = k_1 \epsilon^{s_1 t} + K_2 \epsilon^{s_2 t} + K_2^* \epsilon^{s_2^* t} + \cdots + K_n \epsilon^{s_n t}$$
$$= k_1 \epsilon^{-\sigma_1 t} + K_2 \epsilon^{(-\sigma_2 + j\omega_2)t} + K_2^* \epsilon^{(-\sigma_2 - j\omega_2)t} + \cdots + K_n \epsilon^{s_n t} \quad (2\text{-}7)$$

The coefficients of terms corresponding to real roots are real numbers, such as k_1, and the coefficients of terms corresponding to complex conjugate roots are in general complex conjugate numbers, such as K_2 and K_2^*. The total number of arbitrary constants involved is equal to the number of roots. The reason for complex conjugate powers requiring complex conjugate coefficients is apparent when one considers that Eq. (2-7) must reduce to a real function of time and that the j must disappear or the result will be meaningless physically. This is demonstrated

---

[1] This law states that if a polynomial with a finite number of terms is equated to zero the number of roots is equal to the highest power of the polynomial. See E. A. Guillemin, "The Mathematics of Circuit Analysis," chap. VI, art. 20, John Wiley & Sons, Inc., New York, 1951.

by reducing Eq. (2-7) as follows, where only the first three terms are considered:

$$
\begin{aligned}
c(t) &= k_1 \epsilon^{-\sigma_1 t} + \epsilon^{-\sigma_2 t}(K_2 \epsilon^{+j\omega_2 t} + K_2^* \epsilon^{-j\omega_2 t}) \\
&= k_1 \epsilon^{-\sigma_1 t} + \epsilon^{-\sigma_2 t}[K_2(\cos \omega_2 t + j \sin \omega_2 t) + K_2^*(\cos \omega_2 t - j \sin \omega_2 t)] \\
&= k_1 \epsilon^{-\sigma_1 t} + \epsilon^{-\sigma_2 t}[(K_2 + K_2^*) \cos \omega_2 t + j(K_2 - K_2^*) \sin \omega_2 t] \\
&= k_1 \epsilon^{-\sigma_1 t} + \epsilon^{-\sigma_2 t}(k_2' \cos \omega_2 t + k_2'' \sin \omega_2 t)
\end{aligned}
\tag{2-8}
$$

Since Eq. (2-8) must be a real function of time, it follows that the arbitrary constants $k_2' = K_2 + K_2^*$ and $k_2'' = j(K_2 - K_2^*)$ must be real numbers. This can be true only if K_2 and K_2^* are complex conjugate numbers.

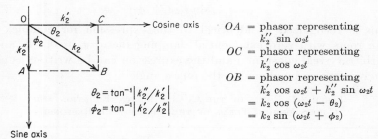

FIG. 2-1. Phasor representation for the sum of a sine and a cosine.

Equation (2-8) may be reduced further by combining the sine and cosine terms. Thus, if sine and cosine are represented as phasors shown in Fig. 2-1, the result is

$$
\begin{aligned}
k_2' \cos \omega_2 t + k_2'' \sin \omega_2 t &= k_2 \cos (\omega_2 t - \theta_2) \\
&= k_2 \sin (\omega_2 t + \phi_2)
\end{aligned}
\tag{2-9a}
$$

where
$$
k_2 = \sqrt{k_2'^2 + k_2''^2} \qquad \theta_2 = \tan^{-1}\left|\frac{k_2''}{k_2'}\right| \qquad \phi_2 = \tan^{-1}\left|\frac{k_2'}{k_2''}\right|
\tag{2-9b}
$$

The source-free response, Eq. (2-7), may now be rewritten in the following alternate forms, where the coefficients and the phase-shift angles are real constants to be evaluated from the initial conditions.

$$
c(t) = k_1 \epsilon^{-\sigma_1 t} + k_2 \epsilon^{-\sigma_2 t} \cos (\omega_2 t - \theta_2)
$$
$$
+ \cdots + \text{terms due to other roots} \tag{2-10a}
$$
$$
c(t) = k_1 \epsilon^{-\sigma_1 t} + k_2 \epsilon^{-\sigma_2 t} \sin (\omega_2 t + \phi_2)
$$
$$
+ \cdots + \text{terms due to other roots} \tag{2-10b}
$$

Examination of Eq. (2-10) indicates that each of the terms involves an exponential damping factor of the form $\epsilon^{-\sigma t}$, the negative exponent coming from the fact that each of the assumed roots has a negative real part. If a root had a positive real part, then its corresponding exponential factor would be $\epsilon^{+\sigma t}$. Such a term would indicate a system whose source-free output increases exponentially with time. This system would tend to "blow up," or be unstable.[1] This topic is discussed in detail in Chap. 8, but for the present we have a basis upon which to formulate the mathematical requirement for system stability. Very simply, it requires that all the roots of the characteristic equation have negative real parts.

The case of pure imaginary roots and multiple roots of the characteristic equation must now be considered. Pure imaginary roots come in pairs of the form $s = \pm j\omega_d$. The corresponding time expression for the source-free response is

$$
\begin{aligned}
c(t) &= K_d \epsilon^{+j\omega_d t} + K_d^* \epsilon^{-j\omega_d t} \\
&= k_d \sin (\omega_d t + \phi_d)
\end{aligned}
\tag{2-11}
$$

This is recognized as identical to the expression for complex conjugate roots with zero exponential damping factor $\sigma_d = 0$. k_d and ϕ_d are arbitrary real constants, and the expression can be written as either a sine or a cosine by changing the phase angle.

TABLE 2-1. ROOTS OF THE CHARACTERISTIC EQUATION AND CORRESPONDING TERMS OF THE SOURCE-FREE RESPONSE

Location of roots of characteristic equation	Source-free response: $c(t)_{\text{source-free}} =$
$s = -\sigma_0$	$k_0 e^{-\sigma_0 t}$
$s = -\sigma_0 \pm j\omega_0$	$k_0 e^{-\sigma_0 t} \sin (\omega_0 t + \phi_0)$
$s = \pm j\omega_0$	$k_0 \sin (\omega_0 t + \phi_0)$
Double root at $s = -\sigma_1$	$(k_0 + k_1 t)e^{-\sigma_1 t}$
Double roots at $s = -\sigma_1 \pm j\omega_1$	$e^{-\sigma_1 t}[k_0 \sin (\omega_1 t + \phi_0) + k_1 t \sin (\omega_1 t + \phi_1)]$
$s = 0$	k_0
Double root at $s = 0$	$k_0 + k_1 t$
Triple root at $s = 0$	$k_0 + k_1 t + k_2 t^2$
"p" multiple root at $s = s_n$	$(k_0 + k_1 t + \cdots + k_{p-1}t^{p-1})e^{s_n t}$

Note: $k_0, k_1, \ldots, k_{p-1}, \phi_0, \phi_1$ are arbitrary constants.

Multiple roots represent the case where the characteristic equation has more than one root at the same point. For example, there may be two roots located at $s = -\sigma_0$. In this case it is possible to show, by substitution into Eq. (2-3), that the source-free response takes the form

$$
c(t) = (k_0 + k_1 t)\epsilon^{-\sigma_0 t}
\tag{2-12}
$$

where k_0 and k_1 are arbitrary constants.

If the double root occurs at a complex conjugate pair (a total of four roots located at $s = -\sigma_2 \pm j\omega_2$), then the source-free response can be

---

[1] Actually most unstable systems do not "blow up" but simply saturate and often go into oscillation.

shown to be of the form

$$c(t) = \epsilon^{-\sigma_2 t}[k_0 \sin (\omega_2 t + \phi_0) + k_1 t \sin (\omega_2 t + \phi_1)] \qquad (2\text{-}13)$$

where k_0, k_1, ϕ_0, and ϕ_1 are arbitrary constants.

In general, if the characteristic equation has a repeated root (let us say of multiplicity p) located at $s = +s_n$, then the corresponding source-free response can be stated as follows,

$$c(t) = (k_0 + k_1 t + k_2 t^2 + \cdots + k_{p-1} t^{p-1})\epsilon^{s_n t} \qquad (2\text{-}14)$$

where k_0, k_1, k_2, . . . , k_{p-1} are arbitrary constants.

Table 2-1 summarizes the location of the roots of the characteristic equation and the corresponding terms of the source-free response.

2-6. System Stability. The Complex Plane

Since the roots of the characteristic equation are, in general, complex numbers, they can be located as points on a complex plane, the abscissa representing the real part of the root and the ordinate the imaginary part. This complex plane is called the *complex-frequency* plane, or *s* plane, and

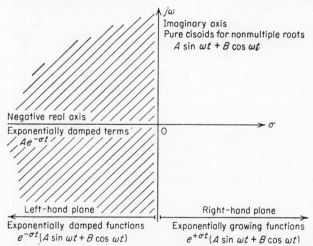

FIG. 2-2. The complex-frequency plane. Location of the roots of the characteristic equation and their corresponding time expressions.

the real axis is usually denoted by the letter σ and the imaginary axis by $j\omega$. Any root $s = -\sigma + j\omega$ is then located at $-\sigma$ units along the abscissa and ω units along the ordinate axis. Figure 2-2 represents the complex-frequency plane and indicates regions of root location and the corresponding source-free response terms.

It is now possible to state a general stability criterion for systems. For a system to be stable, i.e., for the source-free response to involve **only** terms which approach zero as time approaches infinity, the roots of the characteristic equation must lie in the left half side of the complex-frequency plane, excluding the $j\omega$ axis, i.e., the shaded region of Fig. 2-2. Nonmultiple roots on the $j\omega$ axis represent sustained cisoidal (sine or cosine) oscillations, and a root at the origin indicates a constant term. Multiple roots are handled according to Eq. (2-14). It is interesting to note that a multiple root within the left half of the complex plane represents a stable solution, since $\lim_{t \to \infty} t^n \epsilon^{-\sigma t} \to 0$ with n finite, whereas a multiple root on the $j\omega$ axis represents instability since $\lim_{t \to \infty} t^n \cos \beta t \to \infty$ with n finite. The concept of stability presented here forms the basis of all stability criteria and is the starting point for further discussions in Chap. 8. Before leaving the topic it should be noted that stability is solely a function of system parameters (e.g., the characteristic equation) and is independent of the driving function.

2-7. The Particular, or Driven, Solution

The particular solution to Eq. (2-2) consists of expressions for $c(t)$ which make the left side equal to the right side for the particular input being studied. It is immediately obvious that we shall have to confine ourselves to certain specific types of input, or driving, functions. These include two general types: the polynomial and the exponential. By the polynomial is meant a driving function which is represented by a power series with a finite number of terms, i.e., of the form

$$r(t) = r_0 + r_1 t + r_2 t^2 + \cdots + r_n t^n \tag{2-15}$$

where $r_0, r_1, \ldots, r_n$ are constants.

This type of input includes the steady input $r(t) = r_0$, the ramp input $r(t) = r_1 t$, and the parabolic input $r(t) = r_2 t^2$.

The second class of input functions includes those of the form

$$r(t) = \bar{R}_0 \epsilon^{s_g t} \tag{2-16}$$

where s_g is, in general, a complex number of the form $s_g = -\sigma_g + j\omega_g$, and $\bar{R}_0$ is a complex constant. This type of drive includes the pure sine or cosine, the exponentially damped sine or cosine, and the pure exponential.

2-8. Power-series Driving Functions.   The Use of Related Sources and Superposition

As pointed out in Sec. 2-4, the particular solution for a power-series input is also a power series. The method of solution is to assume a power series with undetermined coefficients similar to the input. The assumed power series is substituted into the original differential equation, and coefficients of equal powers of the independent variable on both sides of the equation are equated to solve for the unknown coefficients. This technique is best demonstrated by example.

Example 2-1. Find the particular solution of the system equation given below to a ramp input $r(t) = r_1 t$, where r_1 is a constant. The system is described by the following differential equation, where ζ and ω_n are system constants.

$$\frac{d^2c}{dt^2} + 2\zeta\omega_n \frac{dc}{dt} + \omega_n{}^2 c = \omega_n{}^2 r(t)$$
$$= \omega_n{}^2 r_1 t \qquad (2\text{-}17)$$

The particular solution is assumed to be of the form

$$c(t) = \alpha + \beta t + \gamma t^2$$

where α, β, and γ are coefficients which are to be determined. Actually it is necessary to assume the first two terms only since the driving function involves t as the highest power. The γt^2 term was added to illustrate that any assumed superfluous terms disappear in the solution. Substituting the assumed solution into the differential equation yields

$$(2\gamma + 2\zeta\omega_n\beta + \omega_n{}^2\alpha) + (4\zeta\omega_n\gamma + \omega_n{}^2\beta)t + \omega_n{}^2\gamma t^2 = \omega_n{}^2 r_1 t$$

Equating the coefficients of equal powers of t yields $\gamma = 0$, $\beta = r_1$, and $\alpha = -2\zeta r_1/\omega_n$. The particular solution is then

$$c(t) = r_1 t - \frac{2\zeta r_1}{\omega_n} \qquad (2\text{-}18)$$

The foregoing example may be extended to illustrate the use of related sources.

Example 2-2. Determine the forced system response to an input of the form $r(t) = r_0$. It is recognized that this input is the derivative of the previous input, with r_0 replacing r_1. The forced solution may then be found by differentiating the previous solution with respect to t and substituting $r_0 = r_1$. Thus,

$$c(t) = r_0 \qquad (2\text{-}19)$$

Example 2-3. Determine the forced system response to an input of the form $r(t) = \frac{1}{2} r_2 t^2$. This input is recognized as the integral of the input of Example 2-1, with r_2 replacing r_1. The forced solution is then the integral of the solution of Example 2-1, with an added unknown constant (K_1) which must be evaluated separately. Thus

$$c(t) = \frac{1}{2} r_2 t^2 - \frac{2\zeta r_2 t}{\omega_n} + K_1$$

The constant K_1 is evaluated by substitution into the original differential equation. Thus,

$$(r_2 + K_1\omega_n{}^2 - 4\zeta^2 r_2) + \frac{\omega_n{}^2 r_2}{2} t^2 = \frac{\omega_n{}^2 r_2}{2} t^2$$

Hence

$$K_1 = \frac{r_2(4\zeta^2 - 1)}{\omega_n{}^2}$$

The forced solution is then given by

$$c(t) = \tfrac{1}{2}r_2t^2 - \frac{2\zeta r_2 t}{\omega_n} + \frac{r_2(4\zeta^2 - 1)}{\omega_n{}^2} \tag{2-20}$$

Example 2-4. Determine the forced system response to an input of the form

$$r(t) = r_0 + r_1 t + \tfrac{1}{2}r_2t^2$$

By superposition it is obvious that the forced response in this case is simply the sum of the results of the three previous examples. Thus

$$c(t) = \frac{r_2t^2}{2} + \left(r_1 - \frac{2\zeta r_2}{\omega_n}\right)t + \left(r_0 - \frac{2\zeta r_1}{\omega_n} + \frac{4\zeta^2 - 1}{\omega_n{}^2}r_2\right) \tag{2-21}$$

2-9. Exponential Driving Functions

The first step in determining the forced system response to an exponential driving function is to assume an exponential similar to the driving function with an unknown coefficient. The assumed response is substituted into the original differential equation and the unknown coefficient determined. Although an exponential driving function may seem artificial, it actually includes a variety of practical functions and the generality of the results obtained is important.

Suppose that the input is of the form $r(t) = \bar{R}\epsilon^{s_g t}$, where $\bar{R}$ is a complex constant and s_g is a complex number ($s_g = -\sigma_g + j\omega_g$) known as the complex frequency of the source. The relationship between this generalized exponential driving function and more practical driving functions is discussed in Sec. 2-10. With this type of input Eq. (2-2) reduces to

$$B_0c + B_1\frac{dc}{dt} + \cdots + B_n\frac{d^nc}{dt^n} = \bar{R}(A_0 + A_1s_g + \cdots + A_ms_g{}^m)\epsilon^{s_g t} \tag{2-22}$$

Assume that $c(t)$ is of the form $c(t) = \bar{C}\epsilon^{s_g t}$, where $\bar{C}$ is to be determined. When $c(t)$ is substituted into Eq. (2-22), $\epsilon^{s_g t}$ appears as a common factor on both sides of the equation and therefore $\bar{C}$ is given by

$$\bar{C} = \bar{R}\frac{A_0 + A_1s_g + \cdots + A_ms_g{}^m}{B_0 + B_1s_g + \cdots + B_ns_g{}^n} \tag{2-23}$$

In general $\bar{C}$ is a complex number if s_g is complex, and has a real and imaginary part in rectangular form, or a magnitude and phase angle in polar form. If s_g and $\bar{R}$ are real, then $\bar{C}$ is real.

Substituting Eq. (2-23) into the assumed solution yields the particular solution for a generalized exponential driving function.

$$c(t) = \bar{R}\frac{A_0 + A_1s_g + \cdots + A_ms_g{}^m}{B_0 + B_1s_g + \cdots + B_ns_g{}^n}\epsilon^{s_g t} \tag{2-24}$$

Equation (2-23) may be obtained directly from the differential equation (2-2) as follows:

1. Rewrite Eq. (2-2), letting the letter s replace d/dt and s^n replace d^n/dt^n. Thus

$$(B_0 + B_1 s + \cdots + B_n s^n)c(t) = (A_0 + A_1 s + \cdots + A_m s^m)r(t)$$

or

$$\frac{c(t)}{r(t)} = \frac{A_0 + A_1 s + \cdots + A_m s^m}{B_0 + B_1 s + \cdots + B_n s^n} \tag{2-25}$$

Equation (2-25) is basically a differential equation with s denoting differentiation with respect to time. Such an equation is said to be written in transformed form. The characteristic equation is the denominator polynomial of Eq. (2-25) equated to zero.

2. Equation (2-23) is obtained by replacing s by s_g and substituting $r(t) = \bar{R}\epsilon^{s_g t}$ and $c(t) = \bar{C}\epsilon^{s_g t}$.

The foregoing may be illustrated by an example.

Example 2-5. Consider the system of Example 2-1, and determine the particular solution for the input $r(t) = \bar{R}\epsilon^{s_g t}$.

By rewriting the differential equation of Example 2-1 in transformed form it becomes

$$(s^2 + 2\zeta\omega_n s + \omega_n{}^2)c(t) = \omega_n{}^2 r(t) \tag{2-26}$$

If we let $s = s_g$, $r(t) = \bar{R}\epsilon^{s_g t}$, and $c(t) = \bar{C}\epsilon^{s_g t}$, the result is

$$\bar{C} = \frac{\omega_n{}^2 \bar{R}}{s_g{}^2 + 2\zeta\omega_n s_g + \omega_n{}^2} \tag{2-27}$$

The particular solution is therefore given by

$$c(t) = \frac{\omega_n{}^2 \bar{R}}{s_g{}^2 + 2\zeta\omega_n s_g + \omega_n{}^2} \epsilon^{s_g t} \tag{2-28}$$

An interesting condition occurs when the complex frequency of the exponential source corresponds to one of the roots of the characteristic equation. For this case the assumed solution $c(t) = \bar{C}\epsilon^{s_g t}$ does not yield a result because the left side of Eq. (2-22) becomes zero upon substitution. For this case the assumed solution must be of the form

$$c(t) = \bar{C}t\epsilon^{s_g t} \tag{2-29}$$

The constant $\bar{C}$ is determined by substitution into Eq. (2-22) as before. This condition may be recognized as a generalized type of mathematical "resonance" and is demonstrated in an example in the next section.

2-10. Exponentially Damped and Pure Cisoidal Inputs

To reiterate, the driving function of the previous section was of the form $r(t) = \bar{R}\epsilon^{s_g t}$ where s_g, the complex frequency, is of the form

$$s_g = -\sigma_g + j\omega_g$$

and R is a complex constant. This type of input includes many important possibilities.

1. If s_g is a real number ($s_g = -\sigma_g$) and $\bar{R} = R$ a real constant, then pure exponential drives are obtained. That is, $r(t) = R\epsilon^{-\sigma_g t}$. It would be meaningless physically for the coefficient to be complex if the exponent were real.

2. If σ_g is also zero (that is, $s_g = 0$), we have the case of a constant input $r(t) = R$.

3. If $s_g = j\omega_g$, a pure imaginary, then pure cisoidal (sine or cosine) drives are included; and if s_g is a complex number ($s_g = -\sigma_g + j\omega_g$), then exponentially damped (or growing) cisoidal drives are included. This may be shown by considering the exponential expansions for trigonometric functions.[1]

$R \sin (\omega_g t + \theta)$

$$= \frac{R}{2j} (\epsilon^{j(\omega_g t+\theta)} - \epsilon^{-j(\omega_g t+\theta)})$$

$$= \mathrm{Im}\ (R\epsilon^{j\omega_g t}\epsilon^{j\theta})$$

$$= \mathrm{Im}\ (\bar{R}\epsilon^{s_g t}) \qquad \text{where } \bar{R} = R\epsilon^{j\theta} \text{ and } s_g = j\omega_g \qquad (2\text{-}30a)$$

$R \cos (\omega_g t + \theta)$

$$= \frac{R}{2} (\epsilon^{j(\omega_g t+\theta)} + \epsilon^{-j(\omega_g t+\theta)})$$

$$= \mathrm{Re}\ (R\epsilon^{j\omega_g t}\epsilon^{j\theta})$$

$$= \mathrm{Re}\ (\bar{R}\epsilon^{s_g t}) \qquad \text{where } \bar{R} = R\epsilon^{j\theta} \text{ and } s_g = j\omega_g \qquad (2\text{-}30b)$$

$R\epsilon^{-\sigma_g t} \sin (\omega_g t + \theta)$

$$= \frac{R\epsilon^{-\sigma_g t}}{2j} (\epsilon^{j(\omega_g t+\theta)} - \epsilon^{-j(\omega_g t+\theta)})$$

$$= \mathrm{Im}\ (R\epsilon^{(-\sigma_g+j\omega_g)t}\epsilon^{j\theta})$$

$$= \mathrm{Im}\ (\bar{R}\epsilon^{s_g t}) \qquad \text{where } \bar{R} = R\epsilon^{j\theta} \text{ and } s_g = -\sigma_g + j\omega_g \qquad (2\text{-}30c)$$

$R\epsilon^{-\sigma_g t} \cos (\omega_g t + \theta)$

$$= \frac{\epsilon^{-\sigma_g t}}{2} R(\epsilon^{j(\omega_g t+\theta)} + \epsilon^{-j(\omega_g t+\theta)})$$

$$= \mathrm{Re}\ (R\epsilon^{(-\sigma_g+j\omega_g)t}\epsilon^{j\theta})$$

$$= \mathrm{Re}\ (\bar{R}\epsilon^{s_g t}) \qquad \text{where } \bar{R} = R\epsilon^{j\theta} \text{ and } s_g = -\sigma_g + j\omega_g \qquad (2\text{-}30d)$$

It should be noted that Eq. (2-30a) and Eq. (2-30b) are really special cases of Eq. (2-30c) and Eq. (2-30d) with $\sigma_g = 0$.

Each sinusoidal function may thus be written as an exponential in terms of a complex frequency. There are two possible representations. The first involves two exponentials raised to complex conjugate powers. These terms may each be treated as independent exponential sources and the results combined by superposition. The second representation involves either the real or the imaginary part of a single exponential.

[1] Re ( ) means "the real part of ( )," and Im ( ) means "the imaginary part of ( )."

The latter representation is easier to use in solving differential equations. The particular solution for the exponential is determined first and then either the real or the imaginary part of the result taken as required. This procedure is permissible because of the following identities:

$$\frac{d^n[\text{Re } (\epsilon^{s_g t})]}{dt^n} \equiv \text{Re} \left[\frac{d^n(\epsilon^{s_g t})}{dt^n} \right]$$

$$\frac{d^n[\text{Im } (\epsilon^{s_g t})]}{dt^n} \equiv \text{Im} \left[\frac{d^n(\epsilon^{s_g t})}{dt^n} \right]$$

The point is that the differentiations required by the differential equation may be performed on the exponential first and then the real or imaginary part of the result taken for the final answer.

Example 2-6. Determine the forced response satisfying the following equation for a driving function of the form $r(t) = R\epsilon^{-\sigma_g t} \cos \omega_g t$, where R, σ_g, and ω_g are real numbers. The system equation is

$$\frac{dc}{dt} + \alpha c = \alpha r(t) \tag{2-31}$$

where α is a system constant.

The input function may be written as an exponential in terms of a complex frequency. Thus

$$r(t) = \text{Re } (R\epsilon^{(-\sigma_g + j\omega_g)t})$$
$$= \text{Re } (R\epsilon^{s_g t})$$

where $s_g = -\sigma_g + j\omega_g$.

Rewriting the differential equation in transformed form gives

$$(\alpha + s)c(t) = \alpha r(t)$$

Substituting $s = s_g$, $r(t) = R\epsilon^{s_g t}$, and $c(t) = \bar{C}\epsilon^{s_g t}$ yields the result

$$\bar{C} = R \frac{\alpha}{\alpha + s_g}$$

Letting $s_g = -\sigma_g + j\omega_g$,

$$\bar{C} = \frac{R\alpha}{\alpha - \sigma_g + j\omega_g} = \frac{R\alpha}{\sqrt{(\alpha - \sigma_g)^2 + \omega_g^2}} \epsilon^{-j \tan^{-1} [\omega_g/(\alpha-\sigma_g)]}$$

The particular solution to the exponential source is

$$c(t) = \frac{R\alpha}{\alpha - \sigma_g + j\omega_g} \epsilon^{(-\sigma_g + j\omega_g)t}$$

$$= \frac{R\alpha}{\sqrt{(\alpha - \sigma_g)^2 + \omega_g^2}} \epsilon^{-j \tan^{-1} [\omega_g/(\alpha-\sigma_g)]} \epsilon^{(-\sigma_g + j\omega_g)t} \tag{2-32}$$

Since the driving function is $r(t) = \text{Re } (R\epsilon^{s_g t})$, we must take the real part of $c(t)$ to find the particular solution we want. Thus

$$\text{Re } [c(t)] = \frac{R\alpha}{\sqrt{(\alpha - \sigma_g)^2 + \omega_g^2}} \epsilon^{-\sigma_g t} \cos \left(\omega_g t - \tan^{-1} \frac{\omega_g}{\alpha - \sigma_g} \right) \tag{2-33}$$

Example 2-7. Determine the forced response of the previous example to the driving function $r(t) = R\epsilon^{-\sigma_g t}$.

The solution required is the exponential response with $s_g = -\sigma_g$. Thus

$$c(t) = \frac{R\alpha}{\alpha - \sigma_g} \epsilon^{-\sigma_g t} \tag{2-34}$$

When $\sigma_g = \alpha$, that is, $r(t) = R\epsilon^{-\alpha t}$, a condition of "mathematical resonance" occurs in that the complex frequency of the driving function corresponds to a root of the characteristic equation (which is $s + \alpha = 0$). The particular solution may now be found by assuming that it has the form

$$c(t) = \overline{C} t \epsilon^{-\alpha t}$$

Substituting into the original differential equation yields the result $\overline{C} = R\alpha$, and the particular solution for this special case is

$$c(t) = R\alpha t \epsilon^{-\alpha t} \tag{2-35}$$

Example 2-8. Determine the forced response of the system of Example 2-1 to a driving function of the form $r(t) = R \sin \omega_g t$, where R and ω_g are real constants.

The input function may be written as an exponential function in terms of complex frequency as follows:

$$r(t) = \mathrm{Im}\ (R\epsilon^{j\omega_g t})$$
$$= \mathrm{Im}\ (R\epsilon^{s_g t})$$

where $s_g = j\omega_g$.

In Example 2-5 it was seen that the solution to an exponential input is

$$c(t) = \frac{\omega_n{}^2 R}{s_g{}^2 + 2\zeta\omega_n s_g + \omega_n{}^2} \epsilon^{s_g t}$$

Substituting $s_g = j\omega_g$ and taking the imaginary part of the result yields the particular solution we want.

$$\mathrm{Im}\ [c(t)] = \frac{\omega_n{}^2 R}{\sqrt{(\omega_n{}^2 - \omega_g{}^2)^2 + 4\zeta^2 \omega_n{}^2 \omega_g{}^2}} \sin\left(\omega_g t - \tan^{-1} \frac{2\zeta\omega_n\omega_g}{\omega_n{}^2 - \omega_g{}^2}\right) \tag{2-36}$$

Example 2-9. Determine the forced response of the system of Example 2-1 to a driving function of the form $r(t) = R\epsilon^{-\sigma_g t}$.

Here we have the case where $s_g = -\sigma_g$, and we may write the result directly from the results of Example 2-5, letting $s_g = -\sigma_g$.

$$c(t) = \frac{\omega_n{}^2 R}{\omega_n{}^2 + \sigma_g{}^2 - 2\zeta\omega_n\sigma_g} \epsilon^{-\sigma_g t} \tag{2-37}$$

When $\sigma_g = 0$, $r(t) = R$ and $c(t) = R$, which is the same result as obtained in Example 2-2.

2-11. Complex Frequency and the Transfer-function Concept

Equations (2-23) and (2-24) express, in a general form, the relationship between the forced response and the drive for exponential sources. For such inputs one can define a *transfer function* $\overline{T}(s)$ between input and output. Rather than specify a particular complex frequency s_g, Eq. (2-23) may be left in terms of s. Thus it becomes

$$\overline{T}(s) = \frac{\overline{C}}{\overline{R}} = \frac{A_0 + A_1 s + \cdots + A_m s^m}{B_0 + B_1 s + \cdots + B_n s^n} \tag{2-38}$$

so that, when $s = s_g$, the time expression, Eq. (2-24), becomes

$$c(t) = \bar{R}\bar{T}(s_g)\epsilon^{s_g t} \tag{2-39}$$

Equation (2-38) may be written in factored form. Thus

$$\bar{T}(s) = \frac{A_m(s - s_a)(s - s_b)(s - s_b^*) \cdots (s - s_m)}{B_n(s - s_1)(s - s_2)(s - s_2^*) \cdots (s - s_n)} \tag{2-40}$$

The denominator of (2-40) is recognized as the factored form of the characteristic equation whose roots are located at $s = s_1, s_2, s_2^*, \ldots, s_n$ as discussed in Sec. 2-5. The numerator of Eq. (2-40) is a factored

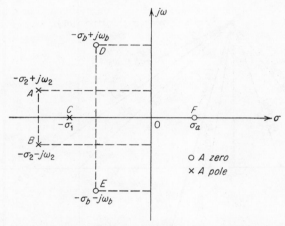

FIG. 2-3. A typical pole-zero configuration for a transfer function.

$$T(s) = \frac{(s - \sigma_a)(s + \sigma_b + j\omega_b)(s + \sigma_b - j\omega_b)}{(s + \sigma_1)(s + \sigma_2 + j\omega_2)(s + \sigma_2 - j\omega_2)}$$
$$= \frac{(s - \sigma_a)[(s + \sigma_b)^2 + \omega_b^2]}{(s + \sigma_1)[(s + \sigma_2)^2 + \omega_2^2]}$$

polynomial with roots at $s = s_a, s_b, s_b^*, \ldots, s_m$. It is apparent that these roots must also be real numbers or complex conjugate pairs. The roots of the numerator polynomial are called *zeros* of $\bar{T}(s)$, and the roots of the denominator (the characteristic equation) polynomial are called the *poles* of $\bar{T}(s)$, poles denoting points in the s plane were $\bar{T}(s)$ becomes infinite. It is possible to locate the zeros and poles of the transfer function in the s plane. Figure 2-3 illustrates a zero-pole configuration for the case where

$$\bar{T}(s) = \frac{(s - \sigma_a)(s + \sigma_b + j\omega_b)(s + \sigma_b - j\omega_b)}{(s + \sigma_1)(s + \sigma_2 + j\omega_2)(s + \sigma_2 - j\omega_2)}$$
$$= \frac{(s - \sigma_a)[(s + \sigma_b)^2 + \omega_b^2]}{(s + \sigma_1)[(s + \sigma_2)^2 + \omega_2^2]} \tag{2-41}$$

If the system is stable, then the poles of $\overline{T}(s)$ are restricted to the left half of the s plane. In general, there is no such restriction for the zeros of $\overline{T}(s)$, and the numerator influences only the magnitude of the terms of the complementary function. When $s = s_g$, Eq. (2-40) becomes

$$\overline{T}(s_g) = \frac{A_m(s_g - s_a)(s_g - s_b)(s_g - s_b^*) \cdots (s_g - s_m)}{B_n(s_g - s_1)(s_g - s_2)(s_g - s_2^*) \cdots (s_g - s_n)} \quad (2\text{-}42)$$

Equation (2-42) may be interpreted graphically since s_g can be located as a point in the complex plane. Thus each factor in the numerator and denominator can be represented as a line in the complex plane. This is

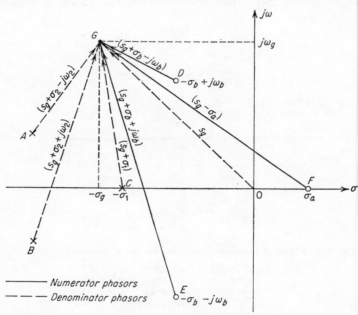

FIG. 2-4. Phasor representation of the transfer function of Fig. 2-3 when $s = s_g = -\sigma_g + j\omega_g$.

illustrated in Fig. 2-4 for the case of the transfer function of Fig. 2-3, where s is arbitrarily located at $s_g = -\sigma_g + j\omega_g$. The solid lines represent factors in the numerator of $\overline{T}(s_g)$ and the dashed lines factors in the denominator. $\overline{T}(s_g)$ is thus the product of the numerator factors divided by the denominator factors, each being treated as a complex number or phasor.

$$\overline{T}(s_g) = \frac{(DG)(EG)(FG)}{(AG)(BG)(CG)} = |\overline{T}(s_g)|\epsilon^{j\phi(s_g)} \quad (2\text{-}43a)$$

$$|\overline{T}(s_g)| = \frac{|DG|\,|EG|\,|FG|}{|AG|\,|BG|\,|CG|} \quad (2\text{-}43b)$$

$$\phi(s_g) = (\angle DG + \angle EG + \angle FG) - (\angle AG + \angle BG + \angle CG) \quad (2\text{-}43c)$$

Thus $\bar{T}(s_g) = |\bar{T}(s_g)|\epsilon^{j\phi(s_g)}$. All angles are measured counterclockwise with respect to a line parallel to the $+\sigma$ axis.

The significance of the graphical interpretation lies in the insight it gives concerning system behavior. Consider, for example, the particular solution of Example 2-5. Here

$$T(s) = \frac{\bar{C}}{\bar{R}} = \frac{\omega_n{}^2}{s^2 + 2\zeta\omega_n s + \omega_n{}^2} \tag{2-44}$$

The characteristic equation is given by $s^2 + 2\zeta\omega_n s + \omega_n{}^2 = 0$, and if $\zeta < 1$, the roots are located at $s = -\zeta\omega_n \pm j\omega_n \sqrt{1 - \zeta^2}$. $\bar{T}(s_g)$ is given below and is illustrated graphically in Fig. 2-5.

$$
\begin{aligned}
\bar{T}(s_g) = \frac{\bar{C}}{\bar{R}} &= \frac{\omega_n{}^2}{s_g{}^2 + 2\zeta\omega_n s_g + \omega_n{}^2} \\
&= \frac{\omega_n{}^2}{(s_g + \zeta\omega_n + j\omega_n \sqrt{1 - \zeta^2})(s_g + \zeta\omega_n - j\omega_n \sqrt{1 - \zeta^2})} \\
&= \frac{\omega_n{}^2}{(AG)(BG)} \\
&= \frac{\omega_n{}^2}{|AG| \, |BG|} \epsilon^{-j(\alpha+\beta)}
\end{aligned}
\tag{2-45}
$$

The graphical representation of the particular solution to an exponential input is therefore

$$c(t) = \frac{\omega_n{}^2 \bar{R}}{(AG)(BG)} \epsilon^{s_g t} \tag{2-46}$$

When $s_g = -\sigma_g$, that is, for driving functions of the form $r(t) = R\epsilon^{-\sigma_g t}$, point G lies on the negative real axis and the complex product $(AG)(BG)$ becomes a real number. This product is a minimum when point G lies at the intersection of line AB and the negative real axis, i.e., when $s_g = -\zeta\omega_n$. For this case $(AG)(BG) = \omega_n{}^2(1 - \zeta^2)$, and $c(t)$ is given by

$$c(t) = \frac{R}{1 - \zeta^2} \epsilon^{-\zeta\omega_n t} \tag{2-47a}$$

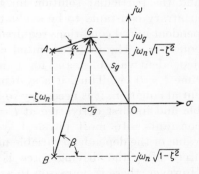

FIG. 2-5. Phasor representation of Example 2-5.

It is interesting to note that when $\zeta = 1$ the poles of $\bar{T}(s)$ occur at $s = -\omega_n$ and the foregoing solution does not apply because there is a condition of mathematical resonance since the complex frequency of the source occurs at the same point as the double pole of $\bar{T}(s)$. For this condition the assumed solution for $c(t)$ must be of the form $c(t) = \bar{C}t^2\epsilon^{s_g t}$, which, upon substitution into the original differential equation, gives the result

$$c(t) = \frac{\omega_n^2 R}{2} t^2 \epsilon^{-\omega_n t} \qquad (2\text{-}47b)$$

If $s_g = j\omega_g$, point G lies on the $j\omega$ axis. For sine or cosine inputs either the imaginary or the real part of the complex product must be taken. If either the damping factor σ_g or the angular frequency ω_g varies, then the behavior of the particular solution can be predicted from the locus of point G in the complex plane. In a similar way the effect of changes in the location of the roots of the characteristic equation can be visualized on the diagram. Thus the complex-frequency plane becomes a very useful tool for understanding system behavior. In fact it forms the basis of the *root-locus method*, which is discussed later in the text.

2-12. Initial Conditions and Continuity

The question of initial conditions comes up in all methods for the solution of differential equations. In the classical method, the initial conditions are used to evaluate the arbitrary constant associated with the source-free solution. In the Laplace-transform approach, they come into the solution automatically but must be evaluated independently. Unfortunately initial conditions are often a major source of difficulty, particularly in higher-order differential equations, and the discussion presented here is intended as a general approach to the problem.

Suppose that a system is in a given condition (not necessarily at rest) and that, at time $t = 0$, a driving function is suddenly applied. The system's behavior is now described by the sum of the source-free solution and the particular solution for the driving function. The number of arbitrary constants to be evaluated, and therefore the number of independent initial conditions required, is equal to the order of the differential equation. The required initial conditions are numerical values for the dependent variables, and for as many of its derivatives as necessary, at time $t = 0^+$.† Thus, if a system is described by a second-order differential equation, it is necessary to know the value of the dependent variable and its first derivative at $t = 0^+$ in order to evaluate the arbitrary constants. In most physical systems, because of inertial effects, the value of the dependent variable may be assumed to be the same immediately after the driving force is applied $(t = 0^+)$ as before $(t = 0^-)$. However, there is no reason to assume that successive derivatives of the dependent variable have the same value at $t = 0^+$ as at $t = 0^-$. The values of these derivatives must be calculated from the differential equation and the physical conditions prevailing at $t = 0^-$. In other words,

---

† $t = 0^+$ is used to denote time immediately after the driving function has been applied and $t = 0^-$ time immediately before the driving function is applied.

the differential equation contains continuity relationships between deriva-tives immediately before and immediately after the application of a driving function.

Consider a system described by Eq. (2-2), which is reproduced below with the right side written as $f[r(t)]$ for convenience:

$$B_0c + B_1\frac{dc}{dt} + B_2\frac{d^2c}{dt^2} + \cdots + B_n\frac{d^nc}{dt^n} = f[r(t)] \tag{2-48}$$

$r(t)$ is to be considered a driving function which is applied suddenly at $t = 0$. At $t = 0^-$ the value of the dependent variable and the first $n - 1$ derivatives are assumed to be known from a previous state.

The values of the required initial conditions at $t = 0^+$ may be derived by successive integrations of Eq. (2-48) over the interval $t = 0^-$ to $t = 0^+$. If Eq. (2-48) is integrated n times with respect to dt over this interval, then the result is[1]

$$B_n[c(0^+) - c(0^-)] = \int_{0^-}^{0^+}\!\!\!\int \cdots \int f[r(t)]\,dt^n \tag{2-49}$$

If Eq. (2-48) is integrated $n - 1$ times over this interval, the result is[2]

$$B_{n-1}[c(0^+) - c(0^-)] + B_n\left(\frac{dc}{dt}\bigg|_{t=0^+} - \frac{dc}{dt}\bigg|_{t=0^-}\right) = \int_{0^-}^{0^+}\!\!\!\int \cdots \int f[r(t)]\,dt^{n-1} \tag{2-50}$$

---

[1] The mathematics involved may not be immediately obvious to the reader. Integrate Eq. (2-48) n times with respect to t over the interval stated. Thus,

$$\int_{0^-}^{0^+}\!\!\!\int \cdots \int B_0c\,dt^n + \int_{0^-}^{0^+}\!\!\!\int \cdots \int B_1c\,dt^{n-1} + \cdots$$
$$+ \int_{0^-}^{0^+} B_{n-1}c\,dt + \left[B_nc\right]_{0^-}^{0^+} = \int_{0^-}^{0^+}\!\!\!\int \cdots \int f[r(t)]\,dt^n$$

The integral terms on the left side are zero because of the infinitesimal limits of the integration, so that Eq. (2-49) results. The integral on the right side depends upon the exact nature of $f[r(t)]$.

[2] Integrate Eq. (2-48) $n - 1$ times with respect to t over the interval stated. Thus,

$$\int_{0^-}^{0^+}\!\!\!\int \cdots \int B_0c\,dt^{n-1} + \int_{0^-}^{0^+}\!\!\!\int \cdots \int B_1c\,dt^{n-2} + \cdots + \left[B_{n-1}c\right]_{0^-}^{0^+}$$
$$+ B_n\left[\frac{dc}{dt}\right]_{0^-}^{0^+} = \int_{0^-}^{0^+}\!\!\!\int \cdots \int f[r(t)]\,dt^{n-1}$$

This reduces to Eq. (2-50).

If Eq. (2-48) is integrated $n - 2$ times over this interval, the result is

$$B_{n-2}[c(0^+) - c(0^-)] + B_{n-1}\left(\frac{dc}{dt}\Big|_{t=0^+} - \frac{dc}{dt}\Big|_{t=0^-}\right)$$

$$+ B_n\left(\frac{d^2c}{dt^2}\Big|_{t=0^+} - \frac{d^2c}{dt^2}\Big|_{t=0^-}\right) = \int_{0^-}^{0^+}\int \cdots \int f[r(t)]\, dt^{n-2} \quad (2\text{-}51)$$

Equation (2-49) is used to solve for $c(0^+)$ in terms of $c(0^-)$ and $r(t)$. Equation (2-50) is used to solve for $dc/dt\Big|_{t=0^+}$ in terms of $dc/dt\Big|_{t=0^-}$, $c(0^+)$, $c(0^-)$, and $r(t)$. Similarly Eq. (2-51) gives $d^2c/dt^2\Big|_{t=0^+}$ in terms of $d^2c/dt^2\Big|_{t=0^-}$ and the previous values. Each integration thus gives a continuity relationship for another derivative at $t = 0^+$.

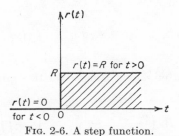

FIG. 2-6. A step function.

The usefulness and generality of the foregoing results may be demonstrated best by several examples.

Example 2-10.   Consider a system described by the following differential equation:

$$J\frac{d^2c}{dt^2} + (F + K_2)\frac{dc}{dt} + K_1 c = K_1 r(t) + K_2 \frac{dr(t)}{dt} \quad (2\text{-}52a)$$

where J, F, K_2, and K_1 are system constants. As a matter of practicality, this equation corresponds to a servomechanism where the developed torque is proportional to both the magnitude and the rate of change of the actuating signal. Determine the required initial values $c(0^+)$ and $dc/dt\Big|_{t=0^+}$ for the conditions where the system is initially at rest [that is $c(0^-) = dc/dt\Big|_{t=0^-} = 0$] and a constant input $r(t) = R$ is suddenly applied at $t = 0$. This is the well-known step input function which is sketched in Fig. 2-6.

Integrating the system equation with respect to t over the interval $t = 0^-$ to $t = 0^+$ gives

$$J\left(\frac{dc}{dt}\Big|_{t=0^+} - \frac{dc}{dt}\Big|_{t=0^-}\right) + (F + K_2)[c(0^+) - c(0^-)] + K_1\int_{0^-}^{0^+} c\, dt$$

$$= K_1\int_{0^-}^{0^+} r(t)\, dt + K_2[r(0^+) - r(0^-)] \quad (2\text{-}52b)$$

Integrating the system equation a second time with respect to t over the interval $t = 0^-$ to $t = 0^+$ gives

$$J[c(0^+) - c(0^-)] + (F + K_2) \int_{0^-}^{0^+} c \, dt + K_1 \iint_{0^-}^{0^+} c \, dt^2$$

$$= K_1 \iint_{0^-}^{0^+} r(t) \, dt^2 + K_2 \int_{0^-}^{0^+} r(t) \, dt \quad (2\text{-}52c)$$

The terms in the foregoing expressions in integral form are zero because of the infinitesimal limit. Also, $r(0^+) = R$, $r(0^-) = 0$, and $c(0^-) = dc/dt \big|_{t=0^-} = 0$, as given. Thus the foregoing expressions yield

$$c(0^+) = c(0^-) = 0 \quad (2\text{-}53)$$

and

$$\frac{dc}{dt}\bigg|_{t=0^+} = \frac{K_2 R}{J} \quad (2\text{-}54)$$

It is interesting to note that the first initial condition is predictable from inertial effects.

Example 2-11. If the system of the previous example is extended to a servomechanism in which the developed torque is proportional to the magnitude, derivative, and integral of the actuating signal, the system equation becomes

$$J \frac{d^3c}{dt^3} + (F + K_2) \frac{d^2c}{dt^2} + K_1 \frac{dc}{dt} + K_3 c = K_3 r(t) + K_1 \frac{dr(t)}{dt} + K_2 \frac{d^2r(t)}{dt^2} \quad (2\text{-}55)$$

Determine the required initial conditions $c(0^+)$, $dc/dt \big|_{t=0^+}$, $d^2c/dt^2 \big|_{t=0^+}$ when $r(t) = R$ is suddenly applied at $t = 0$, all conditions at $t = 0^-$ being zero.

If the system equation is integrated three, two, and one times with respect to dt over the interval $t = 0^-$ to $t = 0^+$, the following results are obtained, respectively:

(1)
$$J[c(0^+) - c(0^-)] = 0$$

Hence
$$c(0^+) = c(0^-) = 0 \quad (2\text{-}56)$$

(2) $\quad J\left(\dfrac{dc}{dt}\bigg|_{t=0^+} - \dfrac{dc}{dt}\bigg|_{t=0^-}\right) + (F + K_2)[c(0^+) - c(0^-)] = K_2[r(0^+) - r(0^-)]$

$$(2\text{-}57)$$

Substituting the values $c(0^+) = c(0^-) = dc/dt \big|_{t=0^-} = r(0^-) = 0$ and $r(0^+) = R$ yields the result

$$\frac{dc}{dt}\bigg|_{t=0^+} = \frac{K_2 R}{J} \quad (2\text{-}58)$$

(3) $\quad J\left(\dfrac{d^2c}{dt^2}\bigg|_{t=0^+} - \dfrac{d^2c}{dt^2}\bigg|_{t=0^-}\right) + (F + K_2)\left(\dfrac{dc}{dt}\bigg|_{t=0^+} - \dfrac{dc}{dt}\bigg|_{t=0^-}\right) + K_1[c(0^+) - c(0^-)]$

$$= +K_1[r(0^+) - r(0^-)] + K_2\left(\frac{dr}{dt}\bigg|_{t=0^+} - \frac{dr}{dt}\bigg|_{t=0^-}\right) \quad (2\text{-}59)$$

Substituting the appropriate values, the result is

$$\frac{d^2c}{dt^2}\bigg|_{t=0^+} = \frac{1}{J}\left[K_1 R - (F + K_2)\frac{K_2 R}{J}\right] = \frac{R}{J^2}\left[K_1 J - (F + K_2)K_2\right] \quad (2\text{-}60)$$

Example 2-12. Consider the differential equation of Example 2-1 where the input is a unit impulse $r(t) = \delta(t)$, the system being previously at rest, $c(0^-) = dc/dt \big|_{t=0^-} = 0$. Determine the complete response for all $t > 0$.

The unit impulse may be derived mathematically from the pulse drawn in Fig. 2-7, where

$$\begin{array}{ll} r(t) = 0 & \text{for } t < 0 \\ r(t) = h & \text{for } 0 < t < 1/h \\ r(t) = 0 & \text{for } t > 1/h \end{array} \tag{2-61a}$$

The unit impulse $\delta(t)$ is the limit of this pulse as $h \to \infty$. Note that as $h \to \infty$ the pulse area remains unity so that $\int_{0^-}^{0^+} \delta(t)\,dt = 1$. Although the unit impulse is a mathematical fiction, it is useful for determining the system's response to a very narrow pulse input. In a sense the impulse may be considered a way of getting initial energy into a system in infinitesimal time.

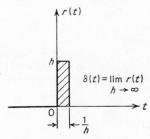

$$\delta(t) = \lim_{h \to \infty} r(t)$$

FIG. 2-7. An impulse function $\delta(t)$.

The particular solution for an impulse is zero since it does not exist for $t > 0$. The complete response is therefore given by the complementary solution alone with the proper initial conditions for $c(0^+)$ and $dc/dt \big|_{t=0^+}$. Hence the complete solution is given by the following equation, where it is assumed that $\zeta < 1$ so that the roots of the characteristic equation are located at $s = -\zeta\omega_n \pm j\omega_n \sqrt{1 - \zeta^2}$,

$$c(t) = k_1 \epsilon^{-\zeta\omega_n t} \sin\left(\omega_n \sqrt{1 - \zeta^2}\, t + k_2\right) \tag{2-61b}$$

where k_1 and k_2 are constants to be evaluated from the initial conditions.

Integration of the differential equation of Example 2-1 twice yields the following results:

$$c(0^+) - c(0^-) = \omega_n^2 \int_{0^-}^{0^+}\!\!\int \delta(t)\,dt^2 = \omega_n^2 \int_{0^-}^{0^+} dt = 0 \tag{2-62}$$

Hence

$$c(0^+) = c(0^-) = 0 \qquad \text{if } c(0^-) = 0 \tag{2-63}$$

Integrating the differential equation once yields the result

$$\frac{dc}{dt}\bigg|_{t=0^+} - \frac{dc}{dt}\bigg|_{t=0^-} + 2\zeta\omega_n[c(0^+) - c(0^-)] = \omega_n^2 \int_{0^-}^{0^+} \delta(t)\,dt = \omega_n^2 \tag{2-64}$$

Hence

$$\frac{dc}{dt}\bigg|_{t=0^+} = \omega_n^2 \tag{2-65}$$

Substituting the initial conditions of Eqs. (2-63) and (2-65) into Eq. (2-61b) yields the final result

$$c(t) = \frac{\omega_n}{\sqrt{1 - \zeta^2}} \epsilon^{-\zeta\omega_n t} \sin\left(\omega_n \sqrt{1 - \zeta^2} t\right) \qquad (2\text{-}66)$$

SUGGESTED READING

Brenner, E., and M. Javid: "Analysis of Electric Circuits," chaps. 11 and 13, McGraw-Hill Book Company, Inc., New York, 1959.

Kaplan, W.: "Advanced Calculus," chap. 8, Addison-Wesley Publishing Company, Reading, Mass., 1957.

Kells, L. M.: "Elementary Differential Equations," 2d ed., chap. 6, McGraw-Hill Book Company, Inc., New York, 1960.

Pipes, L. A.: "Applied Mathematics for Engineers and Physicists," 2d ed., chap. 6, McGraw-Hill Book Company, Inc., New York, 1958.

PROBLEMS

2-1. Write the source-free response for the following characteristic equations:

(a) $s^2 + 2s + 2 = 0$ (b) $(s + 1)^2(s^2 + 2s + 2) = 0$

(c) $(s + 1)(s^2 + 2s + 2)^2 = 0$

2-2. Given

$$\frac{d^3c}{dt^3} + 3\frac{d^2c}{dt^2} + 4\frac{dc}{dt} + 2c = r(t) + \frac{dr(t)}{dt} + \frac{d^2r(t)}{dt^2}$$

determine the driven response (the particular solution) when $r(t)$ is given by the following inputs:

(a) $r(t) = 1$ (b) $r(t) = t$ (c) $r(t) = t^3$ (d) $r(t) = 1 + t^3$

(e) $r(t) = \epsilon^{-2t}$ (f) $r(t) = \epsilon^{-t}$ (g) $r(t) = \cos t$ (h) $r(t) = \epsilon^{-2t} \cos t$

2-3. The transfer function for a system is given by

$$\bar{T}(s) = \frac{\bar{C}}{\bar{R}} = \frac{s + 1}{s^2 + 4s + 5}$$

Locate the poles and zeros of $\bar{T}(s)$ on the complex s plane. Using graphical techniques, determine the driven response of this system to the following input functions:

(a) $r(t) = 1$ (b) $r(t) = \sin t$ (c) $r(t) = \epsilon^{-t} \cos t$

2-4. Given a system whose behavior is described by the differential equation of Prob. 2-2. The system is initially at rest, $c(0^-) = \frac{dc}{dt}(0^-) = \frac{d^2c}{dt^2}(0^-) = 0$. Determine the initial conditions $c(0^+)$, $\frac{dc}{dt}(0^+)$, $\frac{d^2c}{dt^2}(0^+)$ when the input is

(a) A unit step   (b) A unit ramp

2-5. Determine the complete solution of the equation of Prob. 2-2 for a unit-step input. The system is initially at rest.

2-6. The behavior of an inertial guidance system is described by the following differential equation, where a, β, and g are constants of the system:

$$\beta \frac{d^2c}{dt^2} + gc = a \frac{d^2r(t)}{dt^2} + gr(t)$$

Determine the complete response of the system, assuming that the system is initially at rest, to the following inputs:

(a) $r(t) = u(t)$, a unit step   (b) $r(t) = tu(t)$, a unit ramp
(c) $r(t) = t^2u(t)$, a unit parabola

2-7. A simple second-order system has the following response to a unit-ramp input:

$$c(t) = t - 1 + (1 + t)\epsilon^{-t}$$

where the first two terms represent the driven response. It is known that the system has some stored energy at $t = 0^-$.

(a) What is the characteristic equation for this system?
(b) Determine the differential equation which describes the behavior of this system.
(c) Determine the complete response of this system to a unit-step input, assuming that the energy stored in the system at $t = 0^-$ is the same as when the unit-ramp input was applied.

2-8. Given $k' = K + K^*$ and $k'' = j(K - K^*)$, show that if k' and k'' are real numbers then K and K^* must be complex conjugates. Express K and K^* in terms of k' and k''.

2-9. Prove the identities of Eqs. (2-30a) to (2-30d).

2-10. If $c_1(t)$ and $c_2(t)$ are two arbitrary polynomials in the variable t show that, in general,

$$\left(\frac{dc_1}{dt}\right)^P + \left(\frac{dc_2}{dt}\right)^P \neq \left[\frac{d(c_1 + c_2)}{dt}\right]^P$$

where P is a real number greater than unity.

2-11. Show that

$$\frac{d^n[\text{Re } (\epsilon^{s_g t})]}{dt^n} = \text{Re} \left[\frac{d^n(\epsilon^{s_g t})}{dt^n}\right]$$

$$\frac{d^n[\text{Im } (\epsilon^{s_g t})]}{dt^n} = \text{Im} \left[\frac{d^n(\epsilon^{s_g t})}{dt^n}\right]$$

where $s_g = -\sigma_g + j\omega_g$.

3 | Laplace-transform Solution of Linear Differential Equations

The Laplace transform is a tool which can be used to find the complete solution of linear differential equations. In the preceding chapter the method of finding such a solution by using the classical approach was carefully outlined. Although either method may be used to determine the solution in any given situation, application of the Laplace-transform method has come to be preferred by control systems engineers, as is reflected by the prevalence of its use in much of the literature. As greater familiarity with both methods is gained, the reasons for the preference becomes more apparent. Unlike the classical approach, the Laplace-transform method starts with the integrodifferential equation and proceeds directly to the solution. It does not require that the source-free and the forced solutions be found individually and then summed to yield a general solution which is then adapted to fit the particular problem of interest through evaluation of the constants of integration from the initial conditions. This three-part procedure of the classical approach is replaced by a single-step formulation with the Laplace-transform method. Thus the latter method offers the advantage of providing a systematic, simplified, and convenient way of determining the total solution. Furthermore, as is pointed out in the development of the subject matter in this chapter, the Laplace-transform method of solution provides a way of organizing and tabulating, for future reference, all previous experience gained in working with this approach. Moreover, it shows to advantage as against the classical method, with regard to the labor required, when the number of integration constants is large. For these reasons, then, and for others which are pointed out subsequently, attention is deservedly focused on the Laplace-transform method. It should be understood, however, that the following presentation is not intended to be mathematically rigorous with the inclusion of proofs. Such a treatment is found in several textbooks solely devoted to the topic.[1]   Our purpose here is to describe the mechanics of applying the Laplace transform and to convey as much insight concerning the method as is possible with the limited treatment.

3-1. Nature of a Mathematical Transform

A transform has the characteristic of simplifying the analytical procedure which leads to the solution of a problem, irrespective of whether the problem is concerned with numbers, functions, or the calculus of differential equations.   Specifically, the Laplace transform is a tool for transforming functions.   In the analysis of linear systems it serves the purpose of converting functions and operations in time into simpler *algebraic* functions of an intermediate variable.   Before discussing this feature at any length, let us briefly discuss the basic ideas involved by considering a situation where finding the solution to a problem is simplified through use of a transform with which we are all familiar, i.e., the logarithm.   The logarithm is essentially a number transform which allows multiplication to be performed by means of the simpler operation of addition.   Consider, for example, the problem of finding the product of 4.15(928)(2,460) by using the method of number transforms.   First, the transform (or logarithm) of each number is obtained.   For convenience these are listed in the table below.   Logarithms to the base 10 are used.

Original number	Number transform
4.15	0.6180
928.00	2.9675
2,460.00	3.3909
9,472,000.00	6.9764

Next the solution is actually performed in the transformed domain, which, in this case, involves an addition yielding 6.9764.   Finally, the solution in the original system is obtained by use of the logarithm table by reading the number corresponding to the transformed solution.   This last step is known as *performing the inverse transformation*.   Although, for the example cited, little effort is needed to get the result by longhand multiplication, nonetheless it should be apparent that less effort and time are involved when the transform method is used.   Certainly, evaluating a quantity such as $(614)^{0.312}$ would better emphasize the saving to be gained.   The important thing, however, is to understand the procedure

[1] See, for instance, M. F. Gardner and J. L. Barnes, "Transients in Linear Systems," John Wiley & Sons, Inc., New York, 1942; or R. V. Churchhill, "Modern Operational Methods in Engineering," McGraw-Hill Book Company, Inc., New York, 1944.

involved, because it is this very same procedure which underlies the solution of integrodifferential equations by using the Laplace transform. In order to solve an integrodifferential equation, three basic steps are required. (1) The Laplace transform is used to convert the integrodifferential equation into an algebraic equation. (2) The simpler operation of solving the algebraic equation is performed in the transformed domain. (3) The solution in the original time domain is found by consulting appropriate tables and thereby performing the inverse operation.

3-2. Definition of the Laplace Transform and Its Usefulness

The differential equation describing the behavior of a particular feedback control system may be of the form

$$\beta_2 \frac{d^2c(t)}{dt^2} + \beta_1 \frac{dc(t)}{dt} + \beta_0 c(t) + \beta_{-1} \int c(t) \, dt = r(t) \tag{3-1}$$

where $r(t)$ is the driving force and $c(t)$ is the response. To solve this equation by a transformation method implies that application of the transform will introduce simplicity in the procedure. The use of the Laplace transform in Eq. (3-1) exhibits precisely such a property. To Laplace-transform the differential equation requires that we identify first the Laplace transforms of $r(t)$ and $c(t)$ in a manner analogous to obtaining the logarithms of two numbers to be multiplied. This is accomplished by direct application of the Laplace integral to the time function of interest. The nature of this integral is our next concern.

The direct Laplace transform of a time function $f(t)$ is

$$F(s) \equiv \mathcal{L}f(t) \equiv \int_{0^+}^{\infty} f(t)\epsilon^{-st} \, dt \tag{3-2}$$

where s is a complex variable. The lower limit is taken as $t = 0^+$ in order to avoid any uncertainties at $t = 0$. Equation (3-2) states that, to find the Laplace transform of a function $f(t)$, it must be multiplied by ϵ^{-st} and then integrated from $t = 0^+$ to $t = \infty$. Moreover, in order that the definition of $F(s)$ be meaningful, it is necessary that the integral converge and that $f(t)$ be defined for $t > 0$ and equal to zero for $t \le 0$. To assure convergence for the type of time functions encountered in practical feedback control systems (which are single-valued and piecewise continuous), it is usually sufficient that the real part of s be positive, i.e., that Re $(s) > 0$.† Imposing these conditions assures that ϵ^{-st}

† If the time function were of the form

$$f(t) = K\epsilon^{at} \qquad a > 0$$

then for $f(t)$ to be Laplace-transformable it is necessary that Re $(s) > a$. Such functions are rarely encountered in practical feedback control systems analysis.

approaches zero rapidly as time approaches infinity. The physical significance of t in the Laplace transform is *time* as it will be used in this book. Accordingly, this fixes s as a quantity having the dimensions of sec^{-1}. Combining this with the condition that Re $(s) > 0$ gives s the important significance of *complex frequency*. Furthermore, for our work here, it identifies the direct Laplace transform as a mathematical tool which permits solving time-domain problems in the frequency domain. This is a reasonable conclusion when it is realized that integrating the time function $f(t)$ in accordance with Eq. (3-2) usually results in an algebraic function of the complex-frequency variable $s = \sigma + j\omega$.

Once $r(t)$ in Eq. (3-1) is specified as a function of time, its corresponding direct Laplace transform $R(s)$ can be determined. The Laplace transform of the response $c(t)$ is $C(s)$, and $C(s)$ represents the desired solution in the transform domain, i.e., the s domain. A study of Eq. (3-1) reveals that, before $C(s)$ can be obtained, it is necessary to know how to Laplace-transform derivatives and integrals of a time function. In fact, a real test of the worth and usefulness of the definition of the Laplace transform as embodied in Eq. (3-2) lies in the manner in which it permits handling such operations of time. In order that the Laplace transformation be useful in solving integrodifferential equations, the Laplace integral must possess the property that when it is applied to the derivative or integral of a time function it gives a result which *preserves the transform of the original time function except for an algebraic operation*. In this way finding the solution $[c(t)]$ of an integrodifferential equation is reduced to the simpler operation of finding the solution $[C(s)]$ of an algebraic equation.

To demonstrate that the Laplace transform does possess this property, let us start with the Laplace transform of $c(t)$, namely,

$$C(s) = \mathcal{L}\, c(t) = \int_{0^+}^{\infty} c(t)\epsilon^{-st}\, dt \tag{3-3}$$

Although we do not know the explicit form of $c(t)$, we are assuming that it is a continuous function for $t > 0$ and that its Laplace transform can be identified as $C(s)$. The right side of Eq. (3-3) is of the form

$$\int u\, dv = uv - \int v\, du$$

Hence, letting

$$u = c(t) \qquad dv = \epsilon^{-st}\, dt$$
$$du = c'(t)\, dt \qquad v = -\frac{1}{s}\epsilon^{-st}$$

and applying integration by parts

$$\begin{aligned} C(s) &= -\left.\frac{c(t)}{s}\epsilon^{-st}\right]_{0^+}^{\infty} + \frac{1}{s}\int_{0^+}^{\infty} c'(t)\epsilon^{-st}\, dt \\ &= \frac{c(0^+)}{s} + \frac{1}{s}\int_{0^+}^{\infty} c'(t)\epsilon^{-st}\, dt \end{aligned} \tag{3-4}$$

Note that, by proceeding in the manner outlined, it is possible to identify in Eq. (3-4) the Laplace transform of the derivative of $c(t)$, namely,

$$\mathcal{L}\, c'(t) = \mathcal{L}\, \frac{dc(t)}{dt} = \int_{0^+}^{\infty} c'(t)\epsilon^{-st}\, dt \qquad (3\text{-}5)$$

Introducing Eq. (3-5) into Eq. (3-4) gives the result

$$\mathcal{L}\, c'(t) = sC(s) - c(0^+) \qquad (3\text{-}6)$$

Several important conclusions are derived from this equation. Perhaps first and foremost is the fact that the Laplace transform of the derivative of a time function is related to the transform of the time function in an algebraic fashion, namely, multiplication by s.† Accordingly, differentiation in the time domain transforms into the simpler operation of multiplication in the s domain. Furthermore, the presence of $c(0^+)$ permits the inclusion of initial conditions directly and formally in a single operation.

Extension of the Laplace transform to derivatives of higher order is readily accomplished by repeated application of the general procedure implied in Eq. (3-6). Thus the Laplace transform of the second derivative is

$$\begin{aligned}\mathcal{L}\, c''(t) &= s[sC(s) - c(0^+)] - c'(0^+) \\ &= s^2C(s) - sc(0^+) - c'(0^+)\end{aligned} \qquad (3\text{-}7)$$

Similarly, the Laplace transform of the nth derivative can be shown to be

$$\mathcal{L}\, c^n(t) = s^nC(s) - s^{n-1}c(0^+) - s^{n-2}c'(0^+) - \cdots - c^{n-1}(0^+) \qquad (3\text{-}8)$$

This equation is often referred to as the *real differentiation theorem*.

Returning to Eq. (3-1), we see that we are now in a position to Laplace-transform each term in the equation with the exception of the term involving the integral. How is this to be treated? Again we can proceed by investigating the usefulness of Eq. (3-2) as it applies to integration. The criterion will be the same, namely, to show that

$$\mathcal{L}\, c^{-1}(t) \equiv \int_{0^+}^{\infty} \left[\int_0^t c(t)\, dt \right] \epsilon^{-st}\, dt = \text{some algebraic function of } C(s)$$

The starting point is the same as for the derivative case, which is Eq. (3-3), except that here we let

$$u = \epsilon^{-st} \qquad dv = c(t)\, dt$$

$$du = -s\epsilon^{-st}\, dt \qquad v = \int c(t)\, dt = c^{-1}(t) = \int_{0^+}^t c(\tau)\, d\tau + c^{-1}(0^+)$$

† It should be clear that if the Laplace transform had been so defined that when applied to the derivative of the time function a derivative of the transform of the time function resulted, namely, $\mathcal{L}\, c'(t) = f[C'(s)]$, then its introduction would have been useless since it would have failed to simplify the analysis. In other words, the transformed equation would still have been a differential equation.

and again integrate by parts. This leads to

$$C(s) = \epsilon^{-st}c^{-1}(t) \Big]_{0^+}^{\infty} + s \int_{0^+}^{\infty} c^{-1}(t)\epsilon^{-st}\, dt \tag{3-9}$$

Simplifying yields

$$C(s) = -c^{-1}(0^+) + s\mathcal{L}\, c^{-1}(t)$$

or

$$\mathcal{L}\, c^{-1}(t) = \frac{C(s)}{s} + \frac{c^{-1}(0^+)}{s} \tag{3-10}$$

Inspection of this last equation points out that the Laplace transform of the integral of a time function is also algebraically related to the transform of the time function. More specifically, this relationship is one of division by s, which means that the process of integration in the time domain is replaced by the simpler operation of division in the s domain. Also, the initial condition associated with the energy-storing element responsible for the integrating property appears explicitly and therefore can be handled directly and formally in a single operation.

By applying the operation indicated by Eq. (3-10), the Laplace transform of integrals of higher order can be deduced. Thus, the Laplace transform of a double integral is

$$\mathcal{L}\, c^{-2}(t) = \frac{1}{s}\left[\frac{C(s)}{s} + \frac{c^{-1}(0^+)}{s}\right] + \frac{c^{-2}(0^+)}{s}$$

$$= \frac{C(s)}{s^2} + \frac{c^{-1}(0^+)}{s^2} + \frac{c^{-2}(0^+)}{s} \tag{3-11}$$

For an n-order integral the result becomes

$$\mathcal{L}\, c^{-n}(t) = \frac{C(s)}{s^n} + \frac{c^{-1}(0^+)}{s^n} + \frac{c^{-2}(0^+)}{s^{n-1}} + \cdots + \frac{c^{-n}(0^+)}{s} \tag{3-12}$$

Equation (3-12) is often called the *real integration theorem*.

This last equation, as well as Eq. (3-8), illustrates one of the advantages of using the Laplace-transform method of solution. It permits a systematic formulation of the problem, and this is especially desirable where a high-order integrodifferential equation is involved having many initial conditions. These equations show precisely how each of the initial-condition terms enters into the expressions for the higher-order derivatives and integrals.

We can now formally write the solution to Eq. (3-1), using the method of the Laplace transform. By introducing Eqs. (3-3), (3-6), (3-7), and (3-10) into Eq. (3-1) there results the following transformed equation:

$$\beta_2[s^2 C(s) - sc(0^+) - c'(0^+)] + \beta_1[sC(s) - c(0^+)] + \beta_0 C(s)$$

$$+ \beta_{-1}\left[\frac{C(s)}{s} + \frac{c^{-1}(0^+)}{s}\right] = R(s) \tag{3-13}$$

The left side of the integrodifferential equation, Eq. (3-1), has now been transformed into an algebraic equation. Accordingly, the solution to the differential equation as it is found in the transform domain (also called the intermediate result) is

$$C(s) = \frac{R(s) + \beta_2 sc(0^+) + \beta_2 c'(0^+) + \beta_1 c(0^+) - \dfrac{\beta_{-1} c^{-1}(0^+)}{s}}{\beta_2 s^2 + \beta_1 s + \beta_0 + \dfrac{\beta_{-1}}{s}} \tag{3-14}$$

Further evaluation of $C(s)$ in a form identifiable in available tables will permit performing the inverse operation, which means identifying the solution in the time domain, $c(t)$, corresponding to the s-domain solution $C(s)$. This evaluation involves finding the roots of the denominator of Eq. (3-14), which entails solving for the roots of a cubic equation. It is interesting to point out that solving this very same cubic equation is required whether the solution of the integrodifferential equation is obtained by the classical or the Laplace-transform method. To this extent both methods involve the same amount of labor. However, aside from this, the Laplace-transform method does offer the advantages of a systematic procedure which leads directly to the end result, and all this appears in a single equation such as Eq. (3-14). Thus, by introducing the proper algebraic expression for $R(s)$ both the driven and source-free solutions can be found simultaneously.

A cursory examination of the numerator of Eq. (3-14) should make us aware that the presence of the initial-condition terms are nothing more than driving functions of the same character as $R(s)$. In other words the dimensions of the initial-condition terms are the same as those of the Laplace-transformed applied forcing function $R(s)$. This feature is pointed out subsequently in an example.

3-3. Laplace Transforms of Common Driving Functions

In the preceding section we pointed out how the use of the Laplace transform converts an integrodifferential equation into an algebraic equation, thereby allowing a formal solution in the s domain to be found in terms of the system parameters, the initial conditions, and the Laplace transform of the driving function $R(s)$. This procedure leads to a result which is similar to that represented by Eq. (3-14). However, before a specific complete solution, $c(t)$, can be identified with $C(s)$, it is necessary first to stipulate the nature of $R(s)$. Consequently, attention is directed next to a consideration of the form of the Laplace transform for various types of time functions. These are readily obtained through a direct application of the Laplace integral as given by Eq. (3-2). Our concern here will be primarily with those functions which are common to feedback control systems.   For a more complete coverage one or more of the references listed at the end of this chapter should be consulted.

Unit-step Function $u(t)$.   Mathematically the unit-step function is defined as

$$u(t) = \begin{cases} 0 & t \le 0 \\ 1 & t > 0 \end{cases} \tag{3-15}$$

and is plotted in Fig. 3-1.   Physically, it refers to a steady input which is suddenly applied to a system in zero time, as, for example, in closing an ideal switch in an electric circuit.   Introducing Eq. (3-15) into Eq. (3-2) for $f(t)$ yields

$$F(s) = \mathcal{L}\, u(t) = \int_{0+}^{\infty} \epsilon^{-st}\, dt = \frac{1}{s} \tag{3-16}$$

The time function $u(t)$ and its Laplace transform $1/s$ constitute a Laplace-transform pair, and they may be put into a table for ready reference.   In fact, once the Laplace transform for any function $f(t)$ is determined and tabulated, it need never be derived again.   A tabulation of some of the more useful transform pairs appears in Table 3-1.

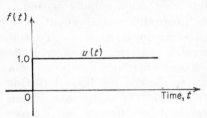

FIG. 3-1. Unit-step function occurring at $t = 0$.

A comparison of the form of Eqs. (3-15) and (3-16) reveals another interesting feature of the Laplace transform, which in some measure helps to account for its usefulness.   Because of its discontinuity at $t = 0$, the function $u(t)$ must be specified in segments, i.e., as a piecewise continuous function, as was done in Eq. (3-15).   However, the Laplace transform of $u(t)$ is represented by a well-behaved algebraic function which possesses a derivative at every point in the s plane with the exception of $s = 0$. In short the Laplace transform exhibits the additional property of yielding well-behaved algebraic functions of s for discontinuous time functions. This property is attributable to the integral definition of the Laplace transform.   Integration is always a smoothing process.   This is perhaps best illustrated by noting that the integral of the unit step is a well-behaved algebraic function t, namely, $\int_{0}^{t} u(t)\, dt = t$.   In contrast note that, if the derivative of $u(t)$ were to be taken, then the value at $t = 0$ would lead to difficulty.[1]

Exponential Decay, $f(t) = \epsilon^{-\alpha t}$.   Direct application of Eq. (3-2) yields

$$\mathcal{L}\, \epsilon^{-\alpha t} = \int_{0+}^{\infty} \epsilon^{-\alpha t}\epsilon^{-st}\, dt = \frac{1}{s + \alpha} \tag{3-17}$$

Again a well-behaved algebraic function results.

[1] See Sec. 3-8.

Sinusoidal Function, $f(t) = \sin \omega t$. It is convenient to use the exponential form of $\sin \omega t$. Thus

$$\sin \omega t = \frac{\epsilon^{j\omega t} - \epsilon^{-j\omega t}}{2j}$$

Substituting into Eq. (3-2) gives

$$\mathcal{L} \sin \omega t = \frac{1}{2j} \int_{0^+}^{\infty} (\epsilon^{-(s-j\omega)t} - \epsilon^{-(s+j\omega)t}) \, dt$$

$$= \frac{1}{2j} \left(\frac{1}{s - j\omega} - \frac{1}{s + j\omega} \right) = \frac{\omega}{s^2 + \omega^2} \tag{3-18}$$

Cosinusoidal Function, $f(t) = \cos \omega t$. This result is readily derived by use of the derivative theorem. We have $\cos \omega t = \dfrac{1}{\omega} \dfrac{d}{dt} \sin \omega t$. Laplace transforming both sides of this equation yields

$$\mathcal{L} \cos \omega t = \frac{1}{\omega} [sF(s) - f(0^+)]$$

But in this case $F(s) = \mathcal{L} \sin \omega t = \omega/(s^2 + \omega^2)$. Therefore,

$$\mathcal{L} \cos \omega t = \frac{1}{\omega} \left(\frac{s\omega}{s^2 + \omega^2} - 0 \right) = \frac{s}{s^2 + \omega^2} \tag{3-19}$$

Ramp Function, $f(t) = tu(t)$. The Laplace transform of the ramp function can be determined by direct application of Eq. (3-2) and requires integration by parts. However, it is simpler to use the real integration theorem, but it is necessary first to express t in terms of an integral as follows: $\int_0^t u(t) \, dt = tu(t)$. Thus

$$\mathcal{L} \, tu(t) = \mathcal{L} \int_0^t u(t) \, dt$$

But the Laplace transform of an integral is

$$\mathcal{L} \int_0^t u(t) \, dt = \frac{F(s)}{s} + \frac{f^{-1}(0^+)}{s} = \frac{F(s)}{s} + 0 \tag{3-20}$$

where $F(s) = \mathcal{L} \, u(t) = 1/s$. Substituting this result into Eq. (3-20) yields

$$\mathcal{L} \, tu(t) = \frac{1}{s^2} \tag{3-21}$$

Parabolic Function, $f(t) = t^2$. The same procedure is used here as in the foregoing case. First write t^2 in terms of an integral. Thus

$$\mathcal{L} \, t^2 = \mathcal{L} \int 2t \, dt$$

TABLE 3-1. TABLE OF LAPLACE-TRANSFORM PAIRS

Time function			Laplace transform
$f(t)$	$f(t)$ vs. t, where $f(t) = 0$ for $t \leq 0$	$F(s)$	Pole location in s plane
1. $u(t)$		$\dfrac{1}{s}$	
2. $\epsilon^{-\alpha t}$		$\dfrac{1}{s + \alpha}$	
3. $\sin \omega t$		$\dfrac{\omega}{s^2 + \omega^2}$	
4. $\cos \omega t$		$\dfrac{s}{s^2 + \omega^2}$	
5. t		$\dfrac{1}{s^2}$	Double pole at $s = 0$
6. t^2		$\dfrac{2}{s^3}$	Triple pole at $s = 0$
7. t^n		$\dfrac{n!}{s^{n+1}}$	$(n+1)$ multiple pole at $s = 0$
8. $\epsilon^{-\alpha t} t^n$		$\dfrac{n!}{(s + \alpha)^{n+1}}$	$(n+1)$ multiple pole at $s = -\alpha$

TABLE 3-1. TABLE OF LAPLACE-TRANSFORM PAIRS (*Continued*)

Time function		Laplace transform	
$f(t)$	$f(t)$ vs. t, where $f(t) = 0$ for $t \leq 0$	$F(s)$	Pole location in s plane
9. $\epsilon^{-\alpha t} \sin \omega t$		$\dfrac{\omega}{(s+\alpha)^2 + \omega^2}$	
10. $\epsilon^{-\alpha t} \cos \omega t$		$\dfrac{s+\alpha}{(s+\alpha)^2 + \omega^2}$	
11. $\dfrac{\epsilon^{-\alpha t} - \epsilon^{-\beta t}}{\beta - \alpha}$		$\dfrac{1}{(s+\alpha)(s+\beta)}$	
12. $\sinh \beta t$		$\dfrac{\beta}{s^2 - \beta^2}$	
13. $\cosh \beta t$		$\dfrac{s}{s^2 - \beta^2}$	
14. $u(t - T)$		$\dfrac{\epsilon^{-sT}}{s}$	
15. $(t - T)$ $u(t - T)$		$\dfrac{\epsilon^{-sT}}{s^2}$	Double pole at $s = 0$
16. $tu(t - T)$		$\dfrac{(1 + s)\epsilon^{-sT}}{s^2}$	Double pole at $s = 0$
17. $\delta(t)$		1	
18. $\delta(t - T)$		ϵ^{-sT}	

Then apply the integration theorem, viz., Eq. (3-10), to obtain

$$\mathcal{L} \int 2t \, dt = \frac{F(s)}{s} + \frac{f^{-1}(0^+)}{s} = \frac{F(s)}{s} + 0$$

where $F(s)$ now refers to the $\mathcal{L}$ transform of $2t$, namely, $F(s) = \mathcal{L} \, 2t = 2/s^2$. Inserting this result into the last equation gives

$$\mathcal{L} \, t^2 = \frac{2}{s^3} \tag{3-22}$$

$f(t) = t^n$. Extension of the analysis of the preceding case leads to the following general result:

$$\mathcal{L} \, t^n = \frac{n!}{s^{n+1}} \tag{3-23}$$

All the foregoing results are tabulated in Table 3.1 along with others. Use will now be made of these results by solving a simple problem in order to illustrate the procedure more clearly.

3-4. Example.   RC Circuit with Initial Charge

Let it be desired to find the total solution for the flow of current $i(t)$ in the circuit of

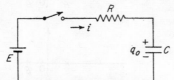

FIG. 3-2. RC circuit with initial charge q_0 on C.

Fig. 3-2 after the switch is closed. Assume that the initial charge on the capacitor is q_0, having the polarity shown.

The differential equation which describes the behavior of the system after the switch is closed is

$$Eu(t) = Ri(t) + \frac{1}{C} \int i(t) \, dt \tag{3-24}$$

where $Eu(t)$ means that the battery voltage E is applied at time $t = 0$. The first step is to Laplace-transform both sides of the differential equation. Thus

$$\mathcal{L} \, Eu(t) = R\mathcal{L} \, i(t) + \frac{1}{C} \mathcal{L} \int i(t) \, dt \tag{3-25}$$

The unknown quantity in the time domain is $i(t)$, and its corresponding unknown in the s domain is $I(s)$, that is,

$$\mathcal{L} \, i(t) = I(s) \tag{3-26}$$

Also,

$$\mathcal{L} \, Eu(t) = \frac{E}{s} \tag{3-27}$$

and

$$\mathcal{L} \int i(t) \, dt = \frac{I(s)}{s} + \frac{i^{-1}(0^+)}{s} = \frac{I(s)}{s} + \frac{q_0}{s} \tag{3-28}$$

Substituting Eqs. (3-26), (3-27), and (3-28) into Eq. (3-24) yields the algebraic equation

$$\frac{E}{s} = RI(s) + \frac{1}{C}\left[\frac{I(s)}{s} + \frac{q_0}{s}\right] \tag{3-29}$$

Rewriting gives

$$I(s)\frac{R}{s}\left(s + \frac{1}{RC}\right) = \frac{E}{s} - \frac{q_0}{sC} \tag{3-30}$$

There are several points worth noting in Eq. (3-30). (1) The expression on the right side has been so manipulated that the form permits immediate use of the table of transform pairs. (2) Note that the Laplace-transformed battery voltage has the dimensions of volts × seconds, and so, too, does the initial-condition term. In essence, then, the initial charge on the capacitor-energy-storing-element may be looked upon as an initial-condition generator having the same character as the forcing function. (3) Observe that the s in the denominator cancels out on both sides of the equation, which removes the pole at $s = 0$ associated with the applied battery voltage. The meaning which this conveys here is that the steady component of $i(t)$ is zero.

The transformed solution for the current as it follows from Eq. (3-30) is

$$I(s) = \frac{E}{R(s + 1/RC)} - \frac{q_0}{RC(s + 1/RC)} \tag{3-31}$$

The corresponding time solution is the inverse transform of $I(s)$.† Hence,

$$i(t) = \mathcal{L}^{-1} I(s) = \frac{E}{R} \mathcal{L}^{-1} \frac{1}{s + 1/RC} - \frac{q_0}{RC} \mathcal{L}^{-1} \frac{1}{s + 1/RC} \tag{3-32}$$

Since the term $1/(s + 1/RC)$ is recognizable as $1/(s + \alpha)$ in Table 3-1, it follows that the solution in the time domain is

$$i(t) = \frac{E}{R} \epsilon^{-t/RC} - \frac{q_0}{RC} \epsilon^{-t/RC} \tag{3-33}$$

This last step illustrates that the inverse Laplace transformation can be conveniently performed by means of an appropriate table of transform pairs.

3-5. Summary of the Outstanding Features of the Laplace Transform

On the basis of the foregoing material it should be apparent that the Laplace transform exhibits several outstanding features which are sufficiently important to be summarized for emphasis' sake. They are as follows:

1. Algebraical property. This refers to the ability of the Laplace transform to convert an integrodifferential equation into an algebraic equation. A moment's reflection reveals that this property is attributable to the presence of ϵ^{-st} in the definition of the Laplace transform.

2. Regularizing property. This refers to the fact that the Laplace transform enables discontinuous functions in the time domain to become well-behaved analytic functions in the s domain. The presence of the integral in the definition of the Laplace transform is responsible for this characteristic.

3. Wide range of application. By imposing the proper restrictions on the real part of s in order to assure convergence of the integral, the Laplace transform of many time functions can be determined. This applies even to time functions which increase exponentially with time.

4. Handles initial conditions directly. The presence of the lower limit 0^+ is the factor which accounts for this property of the Laplace transform.

5. Provides a systematic procedure for solving integrodifferential equations. The formulation associated with the Laplace transform is such

† The inverse Laplace transform of a function $I(s)$ is represented by $\mathcal{L}^{-1} I(s)$.

that it enables the steady-state solution, the transient solution, and the effect of all initial conditions to be treated in a single operation.

3-6. Translation Theorems

Frequently the control systems engineer needs to know the Laplace transform of two commonly encountered time functions, namely, $f(t - T)$ and $\epsilon^{-\alpha t}f(t)$. The theory of the Laplace transformation makes it possible to treat both these functions in a specific and systematic manner.

Time-displacement Theorem (Real Translation). The function $f(t - T)$, where T is a constant having the same dimensions as t, describes the function $f(t)$ in terms of a fixed displacement T in the time domain. This is illustrated in Fig. 3-3. Figure 3-3a shows the delayed unit step which is used to represent the transportation lag associated with feedback systems

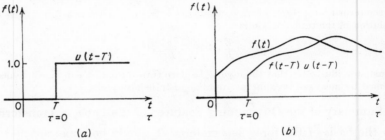

FIG. 3-3. (a) Delayed unit step; (b) delayed time function $f(t - T)$.

employing pneumatic devices and reset-type magnetic amplifiers. Figure 3-3b shows the function $f(t)$ and its time-displaced version $f(t - T)$. In order to emphasize that $f(t - T)$ is zero in the interval $0 < t < T$, it is necessary to multiply $f(t - T)$ by the term $u(t - T)$. However, for simplicity this policy will not be observed in this book. It will be understood that the use of the notation $f(t - T)$ implies that the function is zero for $t - T < 0$.

As has been the case before, the result we are seeking can be derived by resorting to the integral definition of the Laplace transform and applying it to the time-displaced function. But first let

$$\tau \equiv t - T \tag{3-34}$$

so that

$$f(t - T) = f(\tau)$$

Then,

$$\mathcal{L} f(\tau) = F(s) = \int_{0^+}^{\infty} f(\tau)\epsilon^{-s\tau}\, d\tau \tag{3-35}$$

By substituting Eq. (3-34) into the last equation we can write

$$F(s) = \int_{T}^{\infty} f(t - T)\epsilon^{-st}\epsilon^{sT}\, dt$$

Multiplying both sides by ϵ^{-sT} gives

$$\epsilon^{-sT}F(s) = \int_{T}^{\infty} f(t - T)\epsilon^{-st}\, dt$$

The lower limit may be changed to zero because by definition $f(t - T)$ is zero for $0 < t < T$ so that the inclusion of this interval does not affect the value of the integral. Accordingly,

$$\epsilon^{-sT}F(s) = \int_{0^+}^{\infty} f(t - T)\epsilon^{-st}\,dt = \mathcal{L}\,f(t - T) \qquad (3\text{-}36)$$

which is the desired result.

Equation (3-36) states that if a function $f(t)$ is Laplace-transformable and if the $\mathcal{L}\,f(t) = F(s)$ then $\mathcal{L}\,f(t - T) = \epsilon^{-sT}F(s)$. Thus, displacement in the time domain becomes multiplication by ϵ^{-sT} in the s domain.

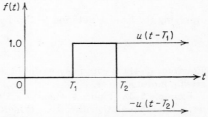

Example 3-1. The Laplace transform of the pulse shown in Fig. 3-4 is readily obtained by recognizing it as the superposition of two delayed unit-step functions. Thus,

Fig. 3-4. Pulse as the superposition of two delayed steps.

$$f(t) = u(t - T_1) - u(t - T_2)$$

Hence,

$$\mathcal{L}\text{ pulse} = \mathcal{L}\,u(t - T_1) - \mathcal{L}\,u(t - T_2)$$

$$= \frac{\epsilon^{-sT_1}}{s} - \frac{\epsilon^{-sT_2}}{s} \qquad (3\text{-}37)$$

Again note the regularizing property of the Laplace transform in yielding an analytical expression in the s domain.

Complex Translation. The effect of a displacement in the s domain upon the time function $f(t)$ also follows from the integral definition of the Laplace transformation. In general we can write

$$\int_{0^+}^{\infty} f(t)\epsilon^{-wt}\,dt = F(w)$$

where w is related to t in the manner indicated by the integral. Now introduce

$$w = s + \alpha$$

into the foregoing equation to get

$$\int_{0^+}^{\infty} f(t)\epsilon^{-(s+\alpha)t}\,dt = F(s + \alpha)$$

The quantity α is a positive real number, while s and w are of the same nature, viz., complex variables. Rearranging the last equation yields

$$\int_{0^+}^{\infty} \epsilon^{-\alpha t} f(t)\epsilon^{-st}\,dt = F(s + \alpha) \qquad (3\text{-}38)$$

Accordingly, it follows that

$$\mathcal{L}\,\epsilon^{-\alpha t}f(t) = F(s + \alpha) \qquad (3\text{-}39)$$

Equation (3-39) states that, if $f(t)$ is Laplace-transformable and has the transform $F(s)$, then multiplication of $f(t)$ by $\epsilon^{-\alpha t}$ becomes a displacement in the s domain. The significance and application of this result are demonstrated by some examples.

Example 3-2. Find the Laplace transform of $\epsilon^{-\alpha t}t^n$. Since, in accordance with Eq. (3-23), the $\mathcal{L} t^n = n!/s^{n+1}$, then by use of the complex translation theorem it follows that

$$\mathcal{L} \epsilon^{-\alpha t}t^n = \frac{n!}{(s+\alpha)^{n+1}} \tag{3-40}$$

Applying the inverse notation to this result enables us to write

$$\mathcal{L}^{-1} \frac{1}{(s+\alpha)^{n+1}} = \frac{1}{n!} \epsilon^{-\alpha t}t^n \tag{3-41}$$

Equation (3-41) is extremely useful in determining the time solution of systems possessing multiple poles.

Example 3-3. Find $\mathcal{L} \epsilon^{-\alpha t} \cos \omega t$. Use of the complex translation theorem permits us to write the solution directly. It merely requires replacing s by $s + \alpha$ in Eq. (3-19). Thus,

$$\mathcal{L} \epsilon^{-\alpha t} \cos \omega t = \frac{s+\alpha}{(s+\alpha)^2 + \omega^2} \tag{3-42}$$

3-7. Additional Laplace-transform Theorems

There are several other theorems which derive from the Laplace transform and which are useful to the control systems engineer. For convenience these will be just stated here.

Final-value Theorem. This theorem states that if the function $f(t)$ and its first derivative $f'(t)$ are Laplace-transformable and the

$$\mathcal{L} f(t) = F(s)$$

and if the poles of $sF(s)$ lie *inside* the left half of the s plane, then

$$\lim_{s \to 0} sF(s) = \lim_{t \to \infty} f(t) \tag{3-43}$$

The restriction on the poles of $sF(s)$ is required in order to assure that $f'(t)$ decreases exponentially with time, a condition which is absolutely necessary for the validity of the derivation leading to Eq. (3-43). Essentially, Eq. (3-43) says that it is possible to find the steady-state value of $f(t)$ by working with the intermediate result $F(s)$. Accordingly, if information concerning just the final value is desired, then direct use of the foregoing theorem avoids the need of performing the inverse operation to find the explicit form of $f(t)$. In a later chapter this theorem will be applied to form the basis upon which to classify feedback control systems.

To illustrate the application of the theorem, let us use it to find the steady-state solution for the current in the example of Sec. 3-4. The intermediate result in this case is the transformed solution for the current $I(s)$ as given by Eq. (3-31). Note that the theorem is applicable because the pole of $sI(s)$ lies inside the left-half s plane. Thus, by the final-value theorem we get

$$\lim_{s \to 0} sI(s) = \lim_{s \to 0} s \left[\frac{E}{R(s + 1/RC)} - \frac{q_0}{RC} \frac{1}{(s + 1/RC)} \right] = 0$$

This result is in agreement with the value obtained from Eq. (3-33), viz., $\lim_{t \to \infty} i(t) = 0$.

Initial-value Theorem. This theorem states that, if $f(t)$ and $f'(t)$ are Laplace-transformable, $\mathcal{L} f(t) = F(s)$, and $\lim_{s \to \infty} sF(s)$ exists, then

$$\lim_{s \to \infty} sF(s) = \lim_{t \to 0^+} f(t) \tag{3-44}$$

Application of this theorem permits evaluating the initial value of $f(t)$ at $t = 0^+$, assuming that the situation is such that only $F(s)$ is immediately available. Thus, the need for finding the inverse Laplace transform in order to obtain this information is avoided. Another interesting aspect of the theorem is that, when used in conjunction with Eq. (3-8), it can be made to provide the initial values of all the time derivatives of $f(t)$.

Example 3-4. The Laplace transform of a function $f(t)$ is $F_0(s) = (2s + 5)/[s(s^2 + 4s + 7)]$. Find the initial value of $f(t)$ and of its first and second derivatives.

Direct use of Eq. (3-44) yields

$$f(0^+) = \lim_{t \to 0^+} f(t) = \lim_{s \to \infty} sF_0(s) = \lim_{s \to \infty} s \frac{2s + 5}{s(s^2 + 4s + 7)} = 0$$

Before we can find the initial value of the first derivative, we must first find its Laplace transform. This is accomplished through use of Eq. (3-8). Thus,

$$\mathcal{L} f'(t) \equiv F_1(s) = sF_0(s) - f(0^+) = \frac{2s + 5}{s^2 + 4s + 7} - 0$$

Applying the initial-value theorem to this last equation gives

$$f'(0^+) = \lim_{s \to \infty} sF_1(s) = \lim_{s \to \infty} s \frac{2s + 5}{s^2 + 4s + 7} = 2$$

To find the initial value of the second derivative of $f(t)$ requires further use of Eq. (3-8). Hence

$$\mathcal{L} f''(t) \equiv F_2(s) = s^2 F_0(s) - sf(0^+) - f'(0^+)$$
$$= \frac{2s^2 + 5s}{s^2 + 4s + 7} - 0 - 2 = \frac{-3s - 14}{s^2 + 4s + 7}$$

Accordingly,

$$f''(0^+) = \lim_{s \to \infty} sF_2(s) = \lim_{s \to \infty} s \frac{-3s - 14}{s^2 + 4s + 7} = -3$$

A glance at the statement of this theorem reveals that no restriction on the location of the poles of $sF(s)$ appears as it did for the final-value theorem. In other words, this theorem is applicable generally, and the reason lies in the fact that it concerns itself with the initial value of the function $f(t)$. In this connection, for example, it should be apparent that the initial-value theorem is applicable to the Laplace-transformed cosine or sine function, whereas the final-value theorem is not.

Linearity Theorem. This follows from a direct application of the Laplace transform to the function $af(t)$. Thus,

$$\mathcal{L}\, af(t) = \int_{0+}^{\infty} af(t)\epsilon^{-st}\, dt = aF(s) \tag{3-45}$$

Furthermore, if $\mathcal{L}\, f_1(t) = F_1(s)$ and $\mathcal{L}\, f_2(t) = F_2(s)$, then

$$\mathcal{L}\, [f_1(t) \pm f_2(t)] = F_1(s) \pm F_2(s) \tag{3-46}$$

The inverse operations are equally valid.

3-8. Laplace Transform of the Unit-impulse Function

The unit impulse can be of considerable importance in analyzing the transient behavior of systems. For example, the transient response of a system to an arbitrary forcing function can be determined once the system's response to the unit impulse is established. This is an especially useful tool in light of the fact that the unit-impulse response of linear systems is related in a simple way to its transfer function.

One mathematical definition[1] of the impulse function is

$$\delta(t) \equiv \lim_{\Delta t \to 0} \frac{u(t) - u(t - \Delta t)}{\Delta t} \tag{3-47}$$

which will be recognized as the derivative of the unit-step function. In other words,

$$\delta(t) \equiv \frac{d}{dt}\, u(t) \tag{3-48}$$

Strictly speaking, therefore, Eq. (3-48) has the value zero for $t > 0$ and infinity at $t = 0$. Now, because the infinity value at $t = 0$ is unrealistic, we introduce a new function

$$g(t) = 1 - \epsilon^{-\alpha t} \tag{3-49}$$

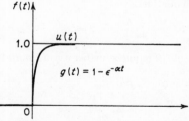

Fig. 3-5. Approximation of the unit-step function.

which can be made to represent the unit-step function very closely by choosing α very large (see Fig. 3-5). The use of $g(t)$ offers the advantage of dealing with a function which has a continuous first derivative. Specifically, its value is

$$g'(t) = \frac{d}{dt}\, g(t) = \alpha\epsilon^{-\alpha t} \tag{3-50}$$

[1] For other definitions see S. Goldman, "Transformation Calculus and Electrical Transients," p. 101, Prentice-Hall, Inc., Englewood Cliffs, N.J., 1953.

An important property of this last equation is that

$$\int_0^\infty g'(t)\,dt = \int_0^\infty \alpha \epsilon^{-\alpha t}\,dt = 1 \tag{3-51}$$

regardless of the value of α. Equations (3-49) to (3-51) can now be used to lead us to a more realistic interpretation of the impulse function. It will be observed that, by making $\alpha \to \infty$, $g(t)$ approaches $u(t)$. Furthermore, by Eq. (3-50) the ordinate intercept approaches infinity, and by Eq. (3-51) the area enclosed by $g'(t)$ remains equal to 1. It therefore follows that, as the ordinate intercept approaches infinity, the abscissa intercept approaches zero with the enclosed area always equal to unity. The impulse function therefore refers

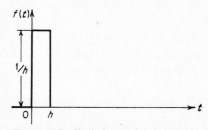

FIG. 3-6. Prelimit form of unit impulse in the form of a rectangular pulse.

to any quantity which has so large a value occurring in so negligibly small an interval of time that it causes a finite change in the state of the system.

The direct Laplace transform of the unit impulse is readily established from Eq. (3-50) as α is made to approach infinity. Thus,

$$\mathcal{L}\,\delta(t) = \lim_{\alpha \to \infty} \mathcal{L}\,g'(t) = \lim_{\alpha \to \infty} \mathcal{L}\,\alpha \epsilon^{-\alpha t} = \lim_{\alpha \to \infty} \frac{\alpha}{s + \alpha} = 1$$

The Laplace transform of a unit impulse may also be found by letting the height of a unit rectangular pulse approach infinity and the width approach zero in such a way as to maintain the enclosed area equal to unity as required by Eq. (3-51). This is illustrated in Fig. 3-6. The expression in the time domain for such a pulse is

$$f(t) = \frac{1}{h}\,[u(t) - u(t - h)] \tag{3-52}$$

The corresponding Laplace transform is

$$\mathcal{L}\,\text{pulse} = \frac{1}{h}\left(\frac{1}{s} - \frac{\epsilon^{-sh}}{s}\right) = \frac{1}{sh}\,(1 - \epsilon^{-sh}) \tag{3-53}$$

Inserting the power-series equivalent of ϵ^{-sh} yields

$$\mathcal{L}\,\text{pulse} = \frac{1}{sh}\left[1 - \left(1 - sh + \frac{s^2h^2}{2!} - \frac{s^3h^3}{3!} + \cdots + \right)\right]$$
$$= \left(1 - \frac{sh}{2!} + \frac{s^2h^2}{3!} - \cdots\right)$$

Accordingly, $\quad \mathcal{L}\,\text{unit impulse} = \mathcal{L}\,\delta(t) = \mathop{\mathcal{L}\,\text{pulse}}_{h \to 0} = 1 \tag{3-54}$

This same result is obtainable by direct application of the Laplace integral. Also, from the time-displacement theorem it follows that the Laplace transform of a delayed impulse function is

$$\mathcal{L} \, \delta(t - T) = \epsilon^{-sT} \tag{3-55}$$

Furthermore, in the case where the magnitude of the impulse is other than unity, it can be shown that

$$\int_{T-\epsilon}^{T+\epsilon} f(t) \, \delta(t - T) \, dt = f(T) \tag{3-56}$$

provided that $f(t)$ is a finite and continuous function of time, and where ϵ is a positive number.

3-9. Inverse Laplace Transformation.   Partial-fraction Expansion

The complete time solution of a differential equation cannot be obtained usually without some additional algebraic manipulation of the solution in the s domain. This is required in order that the solution be put in a form immediately recognizable in a table of Laplace-transform pairs such as Table 3-1. For example, Eq. (3-14) is the transformed solution of the integrodifferential equation (3-1). A little reflection indicates that the general form which Eq. (3-14) assumes as the solution of Eq. (3-1) for $F(s) = 1$ is

$$C(s) = \frac{a_2 s^2 + a_1 s + a_0}{s^3 + b_2 s^2 + b_1 s + b_0} \tag{3-14a}$$

The denominator is the characteristic equation of the system and is a cubic in this example. The numerator can be of second order at most and usually arises because of the presence of the initial-condition terms. To find directly the time solution corresponding to Eq. (3-14a) would require a table of Laplace-transform pairs where this form is explicitly identifiable. As a rule such tables are not made available for two reasons. (1) The required table would become endless if all cases were to be included. In fact, in the case of Eq. (3-14a) alone, there are seven distinct solutions which would have to be tabulated depending on the presence or absence of a_0, a_1, and a_2 and the combination in which these constants appear. (2) The algebraic manipulation needed to put Eq. (3-14a) into a directly usable form is simple and straightforward. It merely requires an application of the Heaviside expansion formula, which is more commonly known as the *partial-fraction expansion theorem*. Of course, this procedure assumes that the roots of the characteristic equation are available or can be found by any one of the standard methods. On recalling that the roots of the characteristic equation can occur in no more complicated form than as a pair of complex conjugate roots or as multiple roots, it should be apparent that a table such as Table 3-1 will be entirely sufficient for evaluating the inverse Laplace transformation. All that really remains now is to describe the techniques by which the time solution is determined from the partial-fraction expansion of the algebraic solution, with particular attention devoted to the manner of handling multiple roots as well as complex roots.

In general the transformed solution of an nth-order differential equation is of the form

$$C(s) = \frac{a_m s^m + a_{m-1} s^{m-1} + \cdots + a_1 s + a_0}{s^n + b_{n-1} s^{n-1} + \cdots + b_1 s + b_0} = \frac{N(s)}{D(s)} \qquad (3\text{-}57)$$

For physical systems the order of the denominator polynomial is very often greater than, sometimes equal to, but never less than that of the numerator. In the vast majority of the cases, therefore, the partial-fraction expansion is directly applicable since $n > m$. In those very few cases where $n = m$ it is necessary to perform longhand division of the denominator into the numerator in order that $C(s)$ be in the form of a proper fraction. Since this case occurs very infrequently, no further attention will be given to it. Consequently, in the material that follows, the transformed solution $C(s)$ is assumed to be a rational algebraic proper fraction, thus making the partial-fraction expansion immediately applicable. However, once this is done, the specific procedure employed in getting the time solution depends upon the nature of the roots of the characteristic equation. As a matter of convenience three distinct cases will be considered, although it should be understood that combinations of these are just as likely to occur as not.

$C(s)$ *Contains First-order Poles Only.* The zeros of the characteristic equation are the poles of $C(s)$. These are found by solving

$$D(s) = s^n + b_{n-1} s^{n-1} + \cdots + b_1 s + b_0 = 0 \qquad (3\text{-}58)$$

Assume that the roots of this equation are each real and distinct. Then Eq. (3-57) may be rewritten with the roots shown in literal form,

$$C(s) = \frac{N(s)}{(s - s_1)(s - s_2) \cdots (s - s_n)} \qquad (3\text{-}59)$$

Applying the partial-fraction expansion to this expression yields

$$\frac{N(s)}{(s - s_1)(s - s_2) \cdots (s - s_k) \cdots (s - s_n)} = \frac{K_1}{s - s_1} + \frac{K_2}{s - s_2}$$
$$+ \cdots + \frac{K_k}{s - s_k} + \cdots + \frac{K_n}{s - s_n} \qquad (3\text{-}60)$$

where the K's are undetermined coefficients. To evaluate any one of these coefficients requires isolating it in Eq. (3-60). For example, K_k is found by first multiplying both sides of Eq. (3-60) by $s - s_k$ and then substituting $s = s_k$ for each term. This leads to

$$K_k = \left[(s - s_k) \frac{N(s)}{D(s)} \right]_{s = s_k} \qquad (3\text{-}61)$$

By use of this expression each of the coefficients of the partial-fraction expansion is determined. It is interesting to note at this point that, since

$N(s)$ reflects the influence of all initial conditions in the system, the respective K's automatically take on the proper magnitudes to assure a smooth transition from the initial energy state to the final energy state of the system.

An alternative form of Eq. (3-61) is available upon recognizing that the denominator $D(s)$ may be written as

$$D(s) = (s - s_k)D_1(s) \tag{3-62}$$

Differentiating both sides and substituting $s = s_k$ gives

$$\left[\frac{d}{ds}D(s)\right]_{s=s_k} = [(s - s_k)D_1'(s)]_{s=s_k} + [D_1(s)]_{s=s_k} = [D_1(s)]_{s=s_k} \tag{3-63}$$

But from Eq. (3-62)

$$D_1(s)\Big|_{s=s_k} = \frac{D(s)}{s - s_k}\Big|_{s=s_k} = \frac{d}{ds}D(s)\Big|_{s=s_k} \tag{3-64}$$

Substituting Eq. (3-64) into Eq. (3-61) gives the alternative form for K_k:

$$K_k = \frac{N(s)}{d/ds\,D(s)}\Big|_{s=s_k} = \frac{N(s_k)}{D'(s_k)} \tag{3-65}$$

where $D'(s_k)$ is the derivative of $D(s)$ evaluated at $s = s_k$.

The transformed solution can now be written as

$$C(s) = \frac{N(s_1)}{D'(s_1)}\frac{1}{s - s_1} + \frac{N(s_2)}{D'(s_2)}\frac{1}{s - s_2} + \cdots + \frac{N(s_k)}{D'(s_k)}\frac{1}{s - s_k}$$
$$+ \cdots + \frac{N(s_n)}{D'(s_n)}\frac{1}{s - s_n} \tag{3-66}$$

which is in a form that readily lends itself to inverse Laplace transformation by using Table 3-1. It merely requires transform pair 2 of the table, which states that $\mathcal{L}^{-1}[1/(s - s_k)] = \epsilon^{s_k t}$. Accordingly, the time solution which corresponds to Eq. (3-66) is

$$c(t) = \mathcal{L}^{-1}\,C(s) = \sum_{k=1}^{n}\frac{N(s_k)}{D'(s_k)}\,\epsilon^{s_k t} \quad \text{for } t > 0 \tag{3-67}$$

Example 3-5. Find the inverse Laplace transform of

$$C(s) = \frac{(s + 1)}{(s + 2)(s + 3)}$$

By partial-fraction expansion $(s + 1)/(s + 2)(s + 3) = K_1/(s + 2) + K_2/(s + 3)$. From Eq. (3-61)

$$K_1 = \frac{s + 1}{s + 3}\Big|_{s=-2} = -1$$

$$K_2 = \frac{s + 1}{s + 2}\Big|_{s=-3} = 2$$

Therefore $c(t) = \mathcal{L}^{-1}\,C(s) = \mathcal{L}^{-1}\frac{-1}{s + 2} + \mathcal{L}^{-1}\frac{2}{s + 3} = -\epsilon^{-2t} + 2\epsilon^{-3t}$

C(s) Contains a Pair of Complex Poles plus First-order Poles. In this case $C(s)$ may be written as

$$C(s) = \frac{N(s)}{(s - s_1)(s - s_1^*)(s - s_2) \cdots (s - s_n)}$$

$$= \frac{K_1}{s - s_1} + \frac{K_1^*}{s - s_1^*} + \frac{K_2}{s - s_2} + \cdots + \frac{K_n}{s - s_n} \quad (3\text{-}68)$$

where s_1 and s_1^* are the complex conjugate roots and $s_2 \cdots s_n$ are the real and distinct roots of $D(s)$. Assume

$$s_1 = -\alpha + j\omega \qquad s_1^* = -\alpha - j\omega$$

Then, as was pointed out in Chap. 2, the coefficients K_1 and K_1^* must also be complex conjugate. Hence assume

$$K_1 \equiv a + jb \qquad \text{and} \qquad K_1^* \equiv a - jb$$

Inserting these quantities into Eq. (3-68) gives

$$C(s) = \frac{a + jb}{(s + \alpha) - j\omega} + \frac{a - jb}{(s + \alpha) + j\omega} + \frac{K_2}{s - s_2} + \cdots + \frac{K_n}{s - s_n} \quad (3\text{-}69)$$

Combining the first two terms on the right side and simplifying leads to

$$C(s) = \frac{2a(s + \alpha) - 2b\omega}{(s + \alpha)^2 + \omega^2} + \frac{K_2}{s - s_2} + \cdots + \frac{K_n}{s - s_n} \quad (3\text{-}70)$$

The values of a and b are found by determining K_1 in the usual manner; thus

$$K_1 \equiv a + jb = \frac{N(s)}{D'(s)}\bigg|_{s = -\alpha + j\omega} \quad (3\text{-}71a)$$

Since evaluation of the right side of Eq. (3-71a) will be in general a complex number, then from the definition of K_1 it follows that

$$\begin{aligned} a &= \text{Re}\,(K_1) \\ b &= \text{Im}\,(K_1) \end{aligned} \quad (3\text{-}71b)$$

Taking the inverse Laplace transformation of Eq. (3-70) yields

$$c(t) = \mathcal{L}^{-1}\,C(s) = 2a\mathcal{L}^{-1}\,\frac{s + \alpha}{(s + \alpha)^2 + \omega^2}$$

$$- 2b\mathcal{L}^{-1}\,\frac{\omega}{(s + \alpha)^2 + \omega^2} + \sum_{k=2}^{n} \frac{N(s_k)}{D'(s_k)}\,\epsilon^{s_k t}$$

By transform pairs 9 and 10 of Table 3-1, the final form of the solution is

$$c(t) = 2a\epsilon^{-\alpha t}\cos \omega t - 2b\epsilon^{-\alpha t}\sin \omega t + \sum_{k=2}^{n} \frac{N(s_k)}{D'(s_k)}\,\epsilon^{s_k t} \qquad t > 0 \quad (3\text{-}72a)$$

Upon combining the sine and cosine terms Eq. (3-72a) becomes

$$c(t) = 2 \sqrt{a^2 + b^2}\, \epsilon^{-\alpha t} \cos (\omega t + \psi) + \sum_{k=2}^{n} \frac{N(s_k)}{D'(s_k)}\, \epsilon^{s_k t} \qquad t > 0 \qquad (3\text{-}72b)$$

where $\psi = \tan^{-1}(b/a)$.

$C(s)$ *Contains Multiple Poles plus First-order Poles.* Let the multiple root be identified as s_0, and for the purposes of illustration and simplicity assume s_0 to be of third order. Consequently $C(s)$ may be written in literal form as

$$C(s) = \frac{N(s)}{(s - s_0)^3(s - s_1) \cdots (s - s_n)} = \frac{K_{01}}{(s - s_0)^3}$$
$$+ \frac{K_{02}}{(s - s_0)^2} + \frac{K_{03}}{s - s_0} + \frac{K_1}{s - s_1} + \cdots + \frac{K_n}{s - s_n} \qquad (3\text{-}73)$$

When a multiple root is involved, the partial-fraction expansion must be modified to include as many additional coefficients as the order of the multiplicity. The reasonableness of this procedure is apparent upon recalling that the Laplace transform of higher powers of t carries over in the s domain as higher powers of inverse s. Evaluation of the coefficients of the partial fraction expansion involves the same procedure as before, namely, isolation of the specific coefficient through appropriate algebraic manipulation. In the case of K_{01} this merely requires multiplying both sides of Eq. (3-73) by $(s - s_0)^3$. Thus

$$(s - s_0)^3 \frac{N(s)}{D(s)} = K_{01} + (s - s_0)K_{02} + (s - s_0)^2 K_{03}$$
$$+ (s - s_0)^3 \frac{K_1}{s - s_1} + \cdots + (s - s_0)^3 \frac{K_n}{s - s_n} \qquad (3\text{-}74)$$

Upon substituting $s = s_0$ all terms on the right side drop out with the exception of K_{01}, which takes on the value

$$K_{01} = (s - s_0)^3 \frac{N(s)}{D(s)} \bigg|_{s = s_0} \qquad (3\text{-}75)$$

To evaluate K_{02} requires that it, too, be made to stand alone. This is most readily accomplished by differentiating both sides of Eq. (3-74) with respect to s. Thus

$$\frac{d}{ds}\left[(s - s_0)^3 \frac{N(s)}{D(s)} \right] = 0 + K_{02} + 2(s - s_0)K_{03} + 3(s - s_0)^2 \frac{K_1}{s - s_1}$$
$$+ \cdots + 3(s - s_0)^2 \frac{K_n}{s - s_n} \qquad (3\text{-}76)$$

Inserting $s = s_0$ gives

$$K_{02} = \frac{d}{ds}\left[(s - s_0)^3 \frac{N(s)}{D(s)} \right]_{s = s_0} \qquad (3\text{-}77)$$

A similar procedure makes available the expression from which K_{03} is determined. Hence differentiating Eq. (3-76) and putting $s = s_0$ yields

$$K_{03} = \frac{1}{2} \frac{d^2}{ds^2} \left[(s - s_0)^3 \frac{N(s)}{D(s)} \right]_{s=s_0} \tag{3-78}$$

An extension of this reasoning can be used to provide the following general expression for coefficient K_{0m}, associated with a multiple pole occurring at $s = s_0$, having multiplicity p:

$$K_{0m} = \frac{1}{(m - 1)!} \frac{d^{m-1}}{ds^{m-1}} \left[(s - s_0)^p \frac{N(s)}{D(s)} \right]_{s=s_0} \tag{3-79}$$

With this last result, the inverse Laplace transformation of Eq. (3-73) may be taken to provide the time solution. Therefore,

$$c(t) = \mathcal{L}^{-1} C(s) = K_{01} \mathcal{L}^{-1} \frac{1}{(s - s_0)^3} + K_{02} \mathcal{L}^{-1} \frac{1}{(s - s_0)^2}$$

$$+ K_{03} \mathcal{L}^{-1} \frac{1}{s - s_0} + \sum_{k=1}^{n} \frac{N(s_k)}{D'(s_k)} \epsilon^{s_k t} \tag{3-80}$$

Reference to the table of Laplace-transform pairs quickly reveals that the time functions associated with the first three terms of the last expression are obtained from transform pair 8. Note that this result applies regardless of the order of the multiplicity of the repeated root. The complete time solution is then

$$c(t) = \frac{K_{01}}{2} \epsilon^{s_0 t} t^2 + K_{02} \epsilon^{s_0 t} t + K_{03} \epsilon^{s_0 t} + \sum_{k=1}^{n} \frac{N(s_k)}{D'(s_k)} \epsilon^{s_k t} \qquad t > 0 \tag{3-81}$$

It is appropriate and important at this point to emphasize the intimate relationship prevailing between the location of the poles of $C(s)$ in the s plane and the character of the corresponding solution $c(t)$ in the time domain. Each root, and perhaps this is especially true of the multiple roots, makes a contribution to $c(t)$. Clearly, if any of the roots of the characteristic equation $D(s)$ have a positive real part, then with increasing time it becomes the predominant mode and causes $c(t)$ to increase without bound, thereby indicating that the system is unstable. On the other hand, if the poles of $C(s)$ are all located inside the left-half s plane, then the system will be stable. In fact, since the exact location of each root is known once the roots of the characteristic equation have been determined, we can very closely describe the character of $c(t)$ in terms of only those roots which are closest to the origin. This follows from the fact that the roots which are far removed have such large negative real parts that the exponential ($\epsilon^{-\alpha t}$) decays very rapidly to zero leaving those centered about the origin as the only predominant terms in $c(t)$.

3-10. Graphical Evaluation of the Coefficients of the Partial-fraction Expansion

Analytical evaluation of the partial-fraction coefficients K_k as represented by Eq. (3-61) can be laborious especially when the order of the characteristic equation is high and nonmultiple roots are involved. In such cases a graphical procedure greatly simplifies the calculation and appreciably reduces the likelihood of making mistakes. The method will be outlined by means of the following example.

Example 3-6. The s-plane solution of the output quantity in a feedback control system for a step-input disturbance is found to be

$$C(s) = \frac{326(s + 4)}{s(s^2 + 2s + 11.6)(s^2 + 12.8s + 113.2)}$$

Find the corresponding time solution.

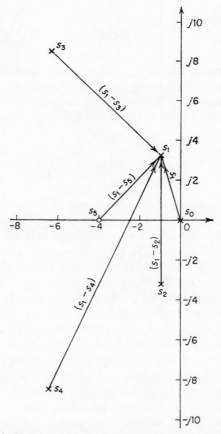

FIG. 3-7. Graphical evaluation of coefficients in partial-fraction expansion.

Begin by first locating the poles and zeros of $C(s)$ in the s plane as shown in Fig. 3-7. These are listed below for convenience:

Poles:
$$s_0 = 0$$
$$s_{1,2} = -\sigma_1 \pm j\omega_1 = -1 \pm j3.25$$
$$s_{3,4} = -\sigma_3 \pm j\omega_3 = -6.4 \pm j8.5$$

Zeros:
$$s_5 = -4$$

Applying the partial-fraction expansion, we have

$$C(s) = \frac{326(s+4)}{s(s-s_1)(s-s_2)(s-s_3)(s-s_4)} = \frac{K_0}{s} + \frac{K_1}{s-s_1} + \frac{K_2}{s-s_2} + \frac{K_3}{s-s_3} + \frac{K_4}{s-s_4}$$

and performing the inverse transformation then yields

$$c(t) = K_0 + K_1\epsilon^{s_1 t} + K_2\epsilon^{s_2 t} + K_3\epsilon^{s_3 t} + K_4\epsilon^{s_4 t}$$

All that remains in getting the explicit time-domain solution is the evaluation of the coefficients. Determining K_0 is simple since it proceeds directly from the final-value theorem. Thus,

$$K_0 = \lim_{s \to 0} sC(s) = \frac{326(4)}{11.6(113.2)} = 1.0$$

Note that this also follows from Eq. (3-61). Furthermore, applying Eq. (3-71) yields

$$K_1 = \left[\frac{326(s+4)}{s(s-s_2)(s-s_3)(s-s_4)} \right]_{s=s_1=-1+j3.25}$$

A moment's thought clearly indicates that a good deal of manipulation is needed to evaluate K_1 if a straight substitution of $s = s_1$ is made and carried out. However, in the graphical approach K_1 is written as $K_1 = \dfrac{326(s_1+4)}{s_1(s_1-s_2)(s_1-s_3)(s_1-s_4)}$, and by means of a protractor and ruler the magnitude and phase angle of each root factor are determined. Reference to Fig. 3-7 shows that $s_1 + 4$ is the phasor drawn from the zero located at -4 to s_1. The value of this phasor is readily found to be $4.4\underline{/47°}$. In a similar fashion each of the other factors can be properly identified so that K_1 may then be written as

$$K_1 \equiv a_1 + jb_1 = \frac{326(4.4)\underline{/47°}}{3.4\underline{/107°}\ 6.5\underline{/90°}\ 7.5\underline{/-45}\ 12.9\underline{/66°}}$$

$$= 0.67\underline{/-171} = -0.66 - j0.105$$

Hence,
$$a_1 = -0.66 \quad \text{and} \quad b_1 = -0.105$$

Also, since s_2 is the complex conjugate of s_1, it follows that K_2 is the complex conjugate of K_1. Accordingly, $K_2 = 0.67\underline{/+171}$.

Evaluating K_3 leads to

$$K_3 \equiv a_3 + jb_3 = \left[\frac{326(s+4)}{s(s-s_1)(s-s_2)(s-s_4)} \right]_{s=s_3} = \frac{326(s_3+4)}{s_3(s_3-s_1)(s_3-s_2)(s_3-s_4)}$$

$$= \frac{326(8.8)\underline{/106°}}{10.6\underline{/127}\ 7.5\underline{/136}\ 12.9\underline{/115}\ 17\underline{/90}} = 0.164\underline{/-2°}$$

$$= 0.164 + j0.0057$$

Therefore, $a_3 = 0.164$, and $b_3 \approx 0$.

The required time solution then follows from the inverse transformation as represented by Eq. (3-72)

$$
\begin{aligned}
c(t) &= 1 + 2a_1\epsilon^{-\sigma_1 t}\cos\omega_1 t - 2b_1\epsilon^{-\sigma_1 t}\sin\omega_1 t + 2a_3\epsilon^{-\sigma_3 t}\cos\omega_3 t - 2b_3\epsilon^{-\sigma_3 t}\sin\omega_3 t \\
&= 1 - 1.32\epsilon^{-t}\cos 3.25t + 0.21\epsilon^{-t}\sin 3.25t + 0.328\epsilon^{-6.4t}\cos 8.5t \\
&= 1 - 1.34\epsilon^{-t}\cos(3.25t + 9.1°) + 0.326\epsilon^{-6.4t}\cos 8.5t
\end{aligned}
$$

A study of the foregoing solution makes it clear that the contribution to the transient response of the complex conjugate roots $s_{3,4}$ is very small, for two reasons.   (1) The damping factor of this pair of complex roots is considerably greater than that of the first pair, which means that this part of the transient dies out rapidly.   (2) Because the roots $s_{3,4}$ are located farther from the origin than $s_{1,2}$, the amplitude of this transient term is appreciably smaller than that associated with the complex roots $s_{1,2}$. Therefore, in spite of the fact that the characteristic equation of this sytem is fourth-order, the dynamic behavior is essentially that of a second-order system since there is only one predominant pair of complex conjugate roots.

SUGGESTED READING

Gardner, M. F., and J. L. Barnes: "Transients in Linear Systems," chaps. 1, 3–6, 8, John Wiley & Sons, Inc., New York, 1942.

Murphy, G. F.: "Basic Automatic Control Theory," chap. 4, D. Van Nostrand Company, Inc., Princeton, N.J., 1957.

Nixon, F. E.: "Principles of Automatic Controls," chap. 3, Prentice-Hall, Inc., Englewood Cliffs, N.J., 1953.   Also, see Appendix B for an extensive table of Laplace-transform pairs.

Widder, D. V.: "The Laplace Transform," Princeton University Press, Princeton, N.J., 1941.

PROBLEMS

3-1. Obtain the Laplace transform of the following linear differential equations. Assume zero initial conditions except where noted.

(a) $\dfrac{d^2c}{dt^2} + 2\zeta\omega_n\dfrac{dc}{dt} + \omega_n^2 c = \omega_n^2 r$ (b) $m_2(t) = m_1(t) + \dfrac{1}{T}\int m_1(t)\,dt$

(c) $\dfrac{d^2m(t)}{dt^2} + \dfrac{dm(t)}{dt} = A\sin 2\omega t$

(d) $\dfrac{d^3m(t)}{dt^3} + a_2\dfrac{d^2m(t)}{dt^2} + a_1\dfrac{dm(t)}{dt} + a_0m(t) + a_{-1}\int m(t)\,dt = t\epsilon^{-\alpha t}$

(e) $\dfrac{d^2c}{dt^2} + 3\dfrac{dc}{dt} + 2c = t$ (initial conditions $dc/dt = 2$; $c = -1$)

3-2. Find the Laplace transform of the following functions:

(a) $f(t) = \sin(\omega t + \theta)$

(b) $f(t) = \epsilon^{-\alpha t}\sin(\omega t + \theta)$

(c) $f(t) = \dfrac{\epsilon^{-\alpha t} + \alpha t - 1}{\alpha^2}$

(d) $f(t) = \dfrac{1 - (1 + \alpha t)\epsilon^{-\alpha t}}{\alpha^2}$

(e) $f(t) = \dfrac{1}{2\beta} + \epsilon^{-\alpha t}\sin\beta t$

(f)

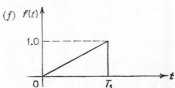

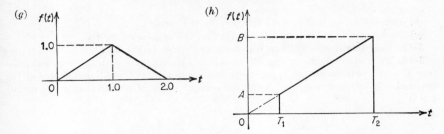

(g) $f(t)$ ... 1.0 ... 1.0 ... 2.0 ... t

(h) $f(t)$ ... B ... A ... O ... T_1 ... T_2 ... t

3-3. Find the current response in a series RL circuit to a unit step of voltage, assuming an initial coil current of i_0.

3-4. Using the Laplace-transform method, find the current response in a series RLC circuit to a unit-step voltage, assuming zero initial conditions.

3-5. Repeat Prob. 3-4 for a unit-impulse forcing function.

3-6. The circuit shown in Fig. P3-6 is in the steady state when at $t = 0$ the switch is thrown from position 1 to position 2. Obtain the expression for $i(t)$ for all $t > 0$. Assume $e(t) = 100tu(t)$.

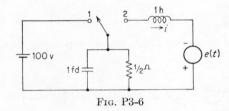

FIG. P3-6

3-7. Find the initial value (at $t = 0^+$) of the time function specified by

$$\mathcal{L}\,f(t) = F(s) = \frac{(2s + 5)(s + 4)}{(s + 6)^2(s + 2)}$$

3-8. Determine the initial value of the second derivative of $f(t)$ in Prob. 3-7.

3-9. The Laplace transform of the time function

$$f(t) = \frac{1}{ab^2} - \frac{\epsilon^{-at}}{a(a^2 + b^2)} + \frac{\cos bt}{b^2 \sqrt{a^2 + b^2}}$$

is $F(s) = 1/[s(s + a)(s^2 + b^2)]$. Find the final value of the time function by applying the final-value theorem to $F(s)$, and then check this with the result obtained from $f(t)$. Compare and discuss.

3-10. The input voltage shown in Fig. P3-10 is applied to an initially deenergized series RL circuit.

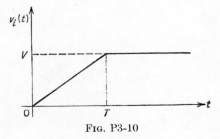

FIG. P3-10

(a) Find the Laplace transform of $v_i(t)$.

(b) Determine the transformed solution for the current.

(c) By inverse Laplace-transforming (b) find the expression for $i(t)$.

3-11. Find the inverse Laplace transform of $F(s) = 1/(s + 2)^3$.

3-12. The circuit shown in Fig. P3-12 is in the steady state with the switch at position 1. At $t = 0$ the switch is put to position 2 so that the additional source $e(t)$ is inserted. If $e(t) = \epsilon^{-t}u(t)$, determine the current supplied by the source $e(t)$ for all $t > 0$.

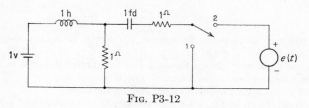

FIG. P3-12

3-13. A feedback control system is found to have a response which in the s plane is given by

$$\frac{C}{R}(s) = \frac{137(s + 0.56)(s + 4)}{(s^2 + 1.8s + 4.23)(s^2 + 14s + 85)}$$

Using partial-fraction expansion, find the corresponding time function $c(t)$ for $r(t) = u(t)$.

3-14. Show that

$$\mathcal{L}^{-1} \frac{as + b}{(s + \alpha)^2 + \beta^2} = a\epsilon^{-\alpha t}\left[\cos \beta t + \frac{1}{\beta}\left(\frac{b}{a} - \alpha\right)\sin \beta t\right]$$

3-15. Find the time function corresponding to

$$F(s) = \frac{s + 3}{(s + 1)(s + 2)^2}$$

II | Time-domain Approach

4 | Dynamic Behavior of Systems. Differential-equation Method

In the course of the development of the subject matter of this book the dynamic behavior of feedback control systems is analyzed by several different approaches, each of which has a definite place and purpose in the over-all composite picture. Obtaining the differential equation describing the system is a necessary starting point in each. The first method is concerned with a direct solution of the differential equation by using the procedures outlined in Chaps. 2 and 3 and constitutes the chief subject matter of this chapter. Primarily emphasis is put on the solution of the differential equation of the second-order system because the dynamic response of higher-order systems frequently can be established in terms of a single pair of predominant complex conjugate roots.

Usually, it is the complete solution of the differential equation which provides a maximum of information regarding the system's dynamic performance. Consequently, whenever it is convenient, the control system engineer attempts to establish such a solution first. Unfortunately, however, this is not easily accomplished for high-order systems, and, what is more, the design procedure which permits reasonably direct modification of the transient response is virtually impossible to realize. In such cases we are forced to seek out other, simpler, more direct methods, even though this means sacrificing some accuracy in the solution obtained.

The existence of transients is characteristic of systems which possess energy-storing elements and which are subjected to disturbances. Usually, the disturbance occurs at the input end or the output end or both. Often these transients are associated with oscillations, and, depending upon the magnitude of the system parameters, such oscillations may even be sustained. One purpose of this chapter is to provide an understanding of the role which the parameters of a second-order system play in establishing the nature of the dynamic response. Because of the insight to be gained, the response will be determined for a servomechanism which is subjected to a step-position input and a ramp input. The solutions are put in nondimensional form so that they may be readily interpreted as well as applied to second-order feedback control systems in general. The universality of the results and the identification of the transient response in terms of two figures of merit (viz., the damping ratio and natural frequency of the system) are aspects of the analysis which prove highly useful for work to follow in later chapters. The second significant objective of the material treated here is to describe two very important procedures for compensating the transient response of feedback control systems, while simultaneously satisfying the specifications on the steady-state performance. These procedures are applicable to higher-order systems as well.

4-1. Analysis of a Second-order System.   Step-Position Input

The system to be analyzed specifically is the servomechanism shown in Fig. 4-1.   It contains two energy-storing elements in the form of inertia

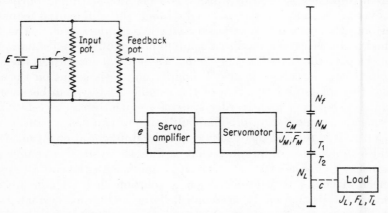

FIG. 4-1. A servomechanism showing gear reduction from motor shaft to load and to feedback potentiometer.

and shaft stiffness,[1] which thereby make it a second-order system. Note that the motor displacement angle c_M is reduced at the load and at the feedback potentiometer by appropriate gearing.   Figure 4-2 gives the block diagram[2] of the system with the gear ratios explicitly shown in terms of the following symbols:

[1] *Stiffness* refers to the torsional elasticity of the servoamplifier-servomotor combination which causes the system to act as though an elastic shaft connects the input to the inertial load.

[2] In this chapter the block diagrams will show only the gain factors of the system components.   In a subsequent chapter a more complete description will be given in terms of transfer functions.

N_M = number of teeth on motor gear

N_L = number of teeth on load gear

N_f = number of teeth on feedback potentiometer gear

In Chap. 1 it is carefully pointed out that the slope of the torque-speed curve of a motor is equivalent to a viscous-friction constant. Call this quantity F_M with the units of torque/radian/sec. Moreover, assume that the load itself is characterized by a viscous-friction constant F_L with the same units of measurement. Before it is possible to determine the dynamic behavior of the system, it is necessary to establish the manner in which the load's viscous friction makes itself felt at the motor shaft as a result of the gear ratio between them. Certainly, if this ratio were unity, the total viscous-friction constant would be merely the sum of

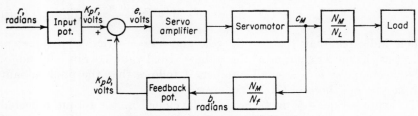

FIG. 4-2. Block diagram of Fig. 4-1.

the two quantities. A related problem is the manner in which the load inertia J_L reflects at the motor shaft. The answer to both problems is readily available from the following consideration. Using the symbolism shown in Fig. 4-1, we can write for the developed torque of the motor

$$T_d = J_M \frac{d^2 c_M}{dt^2} + F_M \frac{d c_M}{dt} + T_1 \qquad (4\text{-}1)$$

where T_d = motor developed torque

J_M = angular moment of inertia of motor

F_M = motor equivalent viscous friction

T_1 = total torque delivered to load as seen from motor shaft

Equation (4-1) is valid at all times, including the dynamic state, since it accounts for the torque components associated with the motor inertia and viscous friction. In virtually all servomechanisms the ratios N_M/N_L and N_M/N_f are less than unity. As a matter of convenience let $a = N_M/N_L$ and $h = N_M/N_f$. Then it follows that

$$T_1 = a T_2 \qquad (4\text{-}2)$$

Also, T_2 represents the applied torque on the load side, and it must be equal to the sum of the opposing torques, which leads to Eq. (4-3).

$$T_2 = J_L \frac{d^2 c}{dt^2} + F_L \frac{d c}{dt} + T_L \qquad (4\text{-}3)$$

where T_L is an externally applied load torque or may even represent the load coulomb friction where instrument-type servomechanisms are involved. Although the positive sign is used for T_L, it must be understood that T_L itself may be either positive or negative depending upon whether it acts in a direction to aid or oppose T_d. To put Eq. (4-3) in terms of the motor displacement angle c_M requires recognizing that

$$N_M c_M = N_L c$$

or

$$c = a c_M$$

Hence

$$T_2 = a J_L \frac{d^2 c_M}{dt^2} + a F_L \frac{d c_M}{dt} + T_L \qquad (4\text{-}4)$$

Substituting Eqs. (4-2) and (4-4) into Eq. (4-1) yields

$$T_d = (J_M + a^2 J_L) \frac{d^2 c_M}{dt^2} + (F_M + a^2 F_L) \frac{d c_M}{dt} + a T_L \qquad (4\text{-}5)$$

which indicates that the load-inertia and viscous-friction parameters reflect at the motor shaft as a^2 times the original values. Since for many servomechanisms a is a small number, it follows that the predominant parameters are those of the servomotor itself.

To express Eq. (4-5) in terms of a developed motor torque reflected to the load shaft requires dividing each term by a. If c_M is then replaced by its equivalent, viz., c/a, Eq. (4-5) becomes

$$\left[\frac{T_d}{a} \right] = \left(\frac{J_M}{a^2} + J_L \right) \frac{d^2 c}{dt^2} + \left(\frac{F_M}{a^2} + F_L \right) \frac{dc}{dt} + T_L \qquad (4\text{-}6)$$

which shows that the motor parameters J_M and F_M may be referred to the load side by dividing the original values by a^2. The foregoing results are summarized in the table below. We shall for the most part deal with the

Quantity	Equivalent quantity referred to motor shaft	Equivalent quantity referred to load shaft
Inertia	$J_M + a^2 J_L$	$\dfrac{J_M}{a^2} + J_L$
Viscous friction	$F_M + a^2 F_L$	$\dfrac{F_M}{a^2} + F_L$

quantities referred to the motor shaft. The reason for this preference lies in the fact that the stability of the system is associated with the closed loop and the feedback is taken from the *motor* shaft (see Fig. 4-2).

The arrangement of Fig. 4-2 can be represented by the simplified form shown in Fig. 4-3. Such a modification is always permissible provided that the input and feedback transducers are the same units. For the case being considered, it follows from Fig. 4-2 that the actuating signal input to the first amplifier stage expressed in volts is

$$e = K_p(r - b) \tag{4-7}$$

where K_p, the transducer constant, is in volts/radian and r and b are expressed in radians. If we now define the error in radians as

$$\varepsilon \equiv r - b \tag{4-8}$$

then clearly $e = K_p\varepsilon$ so that K_p may be looked upon as being an additional gain factor associated with the direct transmission path as depicted in Fig. 4-3.

To determine the response of the system to externally applied disturbances requires writing the correct differential equation. The solution of this equation then provides the description of the system's dynamic

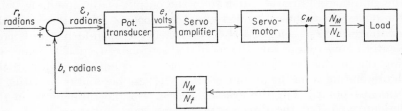

FIG. 4-3. Modified form of Fig. 4-2.

behavior. For the system of Fig. 4-3 the differential equation describing the motion is found by equating the developed motor torque to the sum of the opposing torques. The motor developed torque is found from the fact that, upon the application of an input of position, an error ε is created, which in turn manifests itself as an input to the servomotor and therefore as a developed torque. Accordingly, the differential equation expressing the torques in the system is

$$\varepsilon K_p K_A K_M = J\frac{d^2 c_M}{dt^2} + F\frac{dc_M}{dt} + T_L' \tag{4-9}$$

where J = equivalent inertia referred to motor shaft = $J_M + a^2 J_L$

F = equivalent viscous friction referred to motor shaft = $F_M + a^2 F_L$

T_L' = load disturbance referred to motor shaft = $a T_L$

K_M = motor developed torque constant = lb-ft/volt

K_A = amplifier gain factor, volts/volt

K_p = transducer constant, volts/radian

ε = $r - b$ = error, radians

c_M = motor output displacement angle, radians

a = N_M/N_L

h = N_M/N_f

The equation which describes the actuating signal expressed in radians is

$$\varepsilon = r - hc_M \tag{4-10}$$

Substituting c_M from this equation into Eq. (4-9) makes available the nonhomogeneous system differential equation involving ε and the applied external disturbances. Thus,

$$J\frac{d^2\varepsilon}{dt^2} + F\frac{d\varepsilon}{dt} + hK_pK_AK_M\varepsilon = J\frac{d^2r}{dt^2} + F\frac{dr}{dt} + hT'_L \tag{4-11a}$$

For simplicity define

$$K \equiv hK_pK_AK_M = \text{open-loop proportional gain} \tag{4-12}$$

This quantity is a very important parameter as regards both the steady-state and transient performance. Care must be exercised not to confuse this gain with the direct transmission gain, which is defined as the product of the gain factors in proceeding from the output of the summing point to the place where the controlled variable appears. Note that once the block diagram has been properly established the open-loop gain is conveniently found by opening the loop at the primary feedback point and taking the product of the gain factors of each component lying in the path originating from the output point of the summer and terminating at the opened point. For the system of Fig. 4-3 the ratio between the open-loop gain and the direct transmission gain is the feedback gain factor h.

Rewriting Eq. (4-11a) in terms of the foregoing substitution, it becomes

$$J\frac{d^2\varepsilon}{dt^2} + F\frac{d\varepsilon}{dt} + K\varepsilon = J\frac{d^2r}{dt^2} + F\frac{dr}{dt} + hT'_L \tag{4-11b}$$

The complete solution of Eq. (4-11b) will be found by using the Laplace-transform technique. Of course the classical method can be readily applied here, but for the sake of seeing both methods used this approach will be delayed until the next section, where it will be used to find the response of a second-order system subjected to a step velocity input. Before Laplace-transforming Eq. (4-11b), a description of the initial conditions at $t = 0^+$ is necessary. These are listed in the table below, and they correspond to a step input of magnitude r_0 at the command station with the system initially undisturbed (see Fig. 4-4). In this

	r	$\varepsilon = r - hc_M$	c_M
	r_0	r_0	0
$\dfrac{d}{dt}$	0	0	0

simple situation the initial conditions can be written by inspection once it is realized that the output position and velocity cannot change in infinitesimal time because of inertial effects. However, the procedures outlined in Sec. 2-12 can always be used to provide the correct information regarding initial conditions whenever there is doubt.

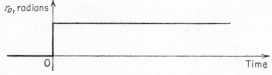

FIG. 4-4. Step position input command.

Let the unknown solution $\mathcal{E}(t)$ in the time domain be represented by $E(s)$ in the s domain, that is, $\mathcal{L} \, \mathcal{E}(t) = E(s)$. The Laplace-transformed differential equation then becomes

$$J\left[s^2 E(s) - s\mathcal{E}(0^+) - \frac{d\mathcal{E}}{dt}(0^+) \right] + F[sE(s) - \mathcal{E}(0^+)] + KE(s)$$

$$= J\left[s^2 R(s) - sr(0^+) - \frac{dr}{dt}(0^+) \right] + F[sR(s) - r(0^+)] + hT'_L(s) \quad (4\text{-}13)$$

Assume that T'_L is specifically a *step* load disturbance of magnitude T'_o. Inserting the initial conditions and $R(s) = r_0/s$, $T'_L(s) = T'_o/s$ and rearranging yields

$$E(s)(s^2 J + sF + K) = r_0(sJ + F) + \frac{hT'_o}{s}$$

Accordingly, the solution for the error as found in the s domain is

$$E(s) = \frac{(s + F/J)r_0}{s^2 + (F/J)s + K/J} + \frac{hT'_o/J}{s[s^2 + (F/J)s + K/J]} \quad (4\text{-}14)$$

Keep in mind that this solution applies to the situation where there is a simultaneous disturbance applied at the input and output ends and that the total solution is the superposition of the effect of each disturbance. A close inspection of Eq. (4-14) reveals some interesting facts about the solution in general. First of all, applying the final-value theorem shows that for just a step position input, that is, $T'_o = 0$, there is no steady-state position error, whereas a step load torque disturbance of constant value demands the existence of a lack of correspondence between the input shaft position and the feedback shaft position by an amount equal to hT'_o/K.† It will be recalled that this is the same conclusion arrived

† It is interesting to note that the larger the value of K the stiffer the system. This fact is made more apparent by rewriting the expression for the steady-state error as

$$\frac{\mathcal{E}_{ss}}{T'_o} = \frac{h}{K} = \frac{1}{K_p K_A K_M}$$

which is frequently called the *compliance* of the system. Note, too, that this form reveals a convenient way of measuring the direct transmission gain. It merely requires subjecting the system to a constant T'_L and then measuring the corresponding value of $\mathcal{E}_{ss}$.

at in Sec. 1-3 through physical reasoning, while here in Eq. (4-14) it is apparent because of the existence of the pole at $s = 0$. Second, it will be noticed that the denominator of both terms of this equation involves the same quadratic expression. As a matter of fact this quadratic is precisely the characteristic equation of the system which follows immediately from Eq. (4-11) when the external disturbances are set to zero. Consequently, the source-free modes are of the same character whether they are associated with a disturbance originating at the input or at the output end.

To determine the time-domain solution corresponding to the s-plane solution of Eq. (4-14), the roots of the characteristic equation must be found. Because of the frequent occurrence of such quadratic terms in control systems work, particular attention is directed to this case with a view toward generalizing the results in terms of appropriate figures of merit which are readily recognizable. Let us start with the characteristic equation as it appears in Eq. (4-14). Thus,

$$s^2 + \frac{F}{J} s + \frac{K}{J} = 0$$

The roots are

$$s_{1,2} = -\frac{F}{2J} \pm \sqrt{\left(\frac{F}{2J}\right)^2 - \frac{K}{J}}$$

Depending upon the radical term the response can be any one of the following: (1) overdamped if $(F/2J)^2 > K/J$; (2) underdamped if $(F/2J)^2 < K/J$; (3) critically damped if $(F/2J)^2 = K/J$. One desirable feature of a servomechanism is that it be fast-acting. Since an overdamped system by its very nature is sluggish, we shall omit this case from further consideration whenever discussing servomechanisms. However, in dealing with the other areas of feedback control systems this may very well be the important case, especially in situations involving low gains and high inertia, as, for example, in temperature control systems. Critical damping occurs whenever the damping term (in this case F) is related to the gain and inertia in accordance with

$$F_c = 2 \sqrt{KJ} \tag{4-15}$$

Because we shall be concerned more frequently with systems which are underdamped, attention is focused specifically on this case. Hence the roots may be written as

$$s_{1,2} = -\frac{F}{2J} \pm j \sqrt{\frac{K}{J} - \left(\frac{F}{2J}\right)^2} \tag{4-16}$$

To put these roots in a form which will have greater significance in terms of the resulting time response, introduce the following definition for the damping ratio, viz.,

$$\zeta \equiv \frac{\text{total damping}}{\text{critical damping}} \equiv \frac{F}{2 \sqrt{KJ}} \tag{4-17}$$

and the following definition for the system natural frequency, viz.,

$$\omega_n \equiv \sqrt{\frac{K}{J}} \tag{4-18}$$

Accordingly, $\qquad \dfrac{F}{2J} = \dfrac{\zeta F_c}{2J} = \dfrac{2\zeta \sqrt{KJ}}{2J} = \zeta \omega_n$

and $\qquad \sqrt{\dfrac{K}{J} - \left(\dfrac{F}{2J}\right)^2} = \sqrt{\omega_n{}^2 - \zeta^2 \omega_n{}^2} = \omega_n \sqrt{1 - \zeta^2}$

Therefore Eq. (4-16) may be written as

$$s_{1,2} = -\zeta \omega_n \pm j \omega_n \sqrt{1 - \zeta^2} \tag{4-19}$$

Introducing the substitution

$$\omega_d \equiv \omega_n \sqrt{1 - \zeta^2} \tag{4-20}$$

simplifies Eq. (4-19) to

$$s_{1,2} = -\zeta \omega_n \pm j \omega_d \tag{4-21}$$

The quantity ω_d is the damped frequency of oscillation, and $0 \leq \zeta \leq 1$. One distinguishing feature of Eq. (4-21) is that both the real and j parts have the dimensions of inverse seconds, which is frequency. This in fact gives rise to the term *complex frequency*. The practical interpretation is that the real part of the complex frequency represents the damping factor associated with the decaying transients, while the imaginary part refers to the actual frequency of oscillation at which the underdamped response decays.

In terms of the quantities ζ and ω_n Eq. (4-14) can be rewritten

$$E(s) = \frac{(s + 2\zeta\omega_n)r_0}{s^2 + 2\zeta\omega_n s + \omega_n{}^2} + \frac{hT'_o/J}{s(s^2 + 2\zeta\omega_n s + \omega_n{}^2)} \tag{4-22}$$

To determine the time solution which corresponds to Eq. (4-22), a partial-fraction expansion is introduced. However, to simplify the algebraic manipulations required, the assumption is made that there is no applied load disturbance, i.e., $T'_o = 0$. Thus

$$E(s) = \frac{(s + 2\zeta\omega_n)r_0}{(s - s_1)(s - s_2)} = \frac{K_1}{s - s_1} + \frac{K_1^*}{s - s_2} \tag{4-23}$$

where s_1 and s_2 are given by Eq. (4-21). Evaluating K_1, we have

$$K_1 = \frac{(s + 2\zeta\omega_n)r_0}{s - s_2}\Bigg|_{s = s_1} = \frac{\zeta\omega_n + j\omega_d}{j2\omega_d} r_0 \tag{4-24}$$

Since K_1^* must be the complex conjugate of K_1, it follows that

$$K_1^* = \frac{\zeta\omega_n - j\omega_d}{-j2\omega_d} r_0 \tag{4-25}$$

Substitution of Eqs. (4-24) and (4-25) into Eq. (4-23) yields

$$E(s) = \frac{\zeta\omega_n + j\omega_d}{j2\omega_d}\frac{r_0}{s - s_1} + \frac{\zeta\omega_n - j\omega_d}{-j2\omega_d}\frac{r_0}{s - s_2} \qquad (4\text{-}26)$$

which is in a form which lends itself to inverse Laplace transformation. Consequently, the time solution is

$$\begin{aligned}
\mathcal{E}(t) &= \frac{\zeta\omega_n + j\omega_d}{j2\omega_d} r_0\epsilon^{-\zeta\omega_n t}\epsilon^{j\omega_d t} + \frac{\zeta\omega_n - j\omega_d}{-j2\omega_d} r_0\epsilon^{-\zeta\omega_n t}\epsilon^{-j\omega_d t} \\
&= r_0\epsilon^{-\zeta\omega_n t}\left[\frac{\zeta\omega_n}{\omega_d}\frac{\epsilon^{j\omega_d t} - \epsilon^{-j\omega_d t}}{2j} + \frac{1}{2}(\epsilon^{j\omega_d t} + \epsilon^{-j\omega_d t})\right] \\
&= r_0\epsilon^{-\zeta\omega_n t}\left(\frac{\zeta\omega_n}{\omega_d}\sin \omega_d t + \cos \omega_d t\right)
\end{aligned} \qquad (4\text{-}27)$$

This last equation can be further simplified as outlined in Sec. 2-5 to

$$\mathcal{E}(t) = \frac{r_0\epsilon^{-\zeta\omega_n t}}{\sqrt{1 - \zeta^2}}\sin (\omega_d t + \phi) \qquad (4\text{-}28)$$

where $\phi = \tan^{-1}(\sqrt{1 - \zeta^2}/\zeta)$ and is valid for $0 \leq \zeta \leq 1$ and $T'_o = 0$.

Undamped Solution. One extreme of Eq. (4-28) corresponds to the situation where $\zeta = 0$. This makes $\phi = 90°$ so that

$$\mathcal{E}(t) = r_0 \sin (\omega_d t + 90°) = r_0 \cos \omega_n t \qquad (4\text{-}29)$$

The solution for the actuating signal is therefore a sustained oscillation

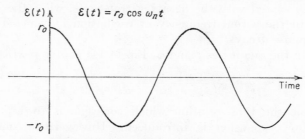

FIG. 4-5. Solution for the actuating signal for $\zeta = 0$.

which is entirely expected since the system has two energy-storing elements and no damping (see Fig. 4-5). The frequency of oscillation is

$$\omega_d = \omega_n = \sqrt{\frac{K}{J}}$$

which is the natural frequency of the system since it depends upon the two energy-storing elements K (stiffness) and J (inertia).

Critically Damped Response. The other extreme of Eq. (4-28) corresponds to the situation where $\zeta = 1$ and $\omega_d = 0$, which means that there are no oscillations. The form of $\mathcal{E}(t)$ which is more convenient to use here is Eq. (4-27). Thus

$$\mathcal{E}(t) = r_0 \epsilon^{-\zeta \omega_n t} \left(\cos \omega_d t + \frac{\zeta \omega_n}{\omega_n \sqrt{1 - \zeta^2}} \sin \omega_d t \right)$$

If the conditions $\zeta = 1$ and $\omega_d = 0$ are introduced, it will be noted that an indeterminate expression results. Use of L'Hopital's rule eliminates the difficulty so that the response reduces to

$$\mathcal{E}(t) = r_0 \epsilon^{-\omega_n t}(1 + \omega_n t) \tag{4-30}$$

It is interesting to note that the form of Eq. (4-30) is consistent with the fact that for critical damping the roots of the characteristic equation are identical, which means the existence of a double pole in the expression for the Laplace-transform solution.

Solution of the Output Displacement. When we set out to find the solution of Eq. (4-9), we chose to do so with the actuating signal $\mathcal{E}$ (expressed in radians) acting as the dependent variable. This led to Eq. (4-11b), the solution of which has now been found. Of course we could have modified Eq. (4-9) just as easily so that the dependent variable would have been c, viz., the output displacement angle at the load shaft. The method of solution would have been the same, leading to the same characteristic equation since the source-free response is dependent solely upon the system parameters and not at all upon the external disturbances. With the solution for $\mathcal{E}$ available the solution for the output displacement is easily obtained by first finding the motor shaft angle from Eq. (4-10); thus,

$$c_M = \frac{1}{h} (r - \mathcal{E})$$

and then, recognizing that the motor displacement angle differs from the load displacement angle by the gear ratio, $a = N_M/N_L$. Accordingly, the complete time response of the output angle c for a step input command of r_0 radians is

$$c = ac_M = \frac{a}{h} \left[r_0 - \frac{r_0}{\sqrt{1 - \zeta^2}} \epsilon^{-\zeta \omega_n t} \sin (\omega_d t + \phi) \right]$$

or

$$c = \frac{a}{h} r_0 \left[1 - \frac{\epsilon^{-\zeta \omega_n t}}{\sqrt{1 - \zeta^2}} \sin (\omega_d t + \phi) \right] \tag{4-31}$$

where ϕ is defined as in Eq. (4-28). Note that, if the gear ratio from motor shaft to load is the same as from motor shaft to feedback, then at steady state the output angle c equals the command angle r.

Universal Curves. It is both desirable and useful to represent the response of a second-order system graphically for specific values of damping ratios independently of the magnitude of the input step disturbance or system parameters. Consider, for example, the solution for the output displacement angle when the damping is critical, thus,

$$c = \frac{a}{h} r_0[1 - \epsilon^{-\omega_n t}(1 + \omega_n t)] \qquad (4\text{-}32)$$

To make the graph of this equation independent of the magnitude of the applied input, we plot the ratio $c(h/a)/r_0$. A little thought shows that $c(h/a)$ is really the output displacement referred to the feedback transducer shaft. This permits ready comparison with the input displacement. In this way a single curve represents the critically damped case for all values of the input r_0. Figure 4-6 shows the plot, but such a graph as it stands does not apply for a different second-order system in spite of the fact that it, too, may be critically damped. To illustrate, suppose

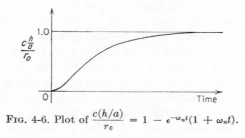

FIG. 4-6. Plot of $\dfrac{c(h/a)}{r_0} = 1 - \epsilon^{-\omega_n t}(1 + \omega_n t)$.

that one system has a natural frequency of $\omega_n = 1$ radian/sec and a second system a natural frequency of 2 radians/sec because of different values of gain and inertia. Suppose, too, that both systems are adjusted for a damping ratio of 1. After the lapse of 1 sec Eq. (4-32) reveals that $c(h/a)/r_0 = 1 - \epsilon^{-1}(1 + 1) = 0.264$ for the first system, while for the second system this same value is reached in $\frac{1}{2}$ sec. Accordingly, if the response were to be plotted as shown in Fig. 4-6, a different set of curves would be needed each time a system with a different natural frequency was considered. However, further thought reveals that, when the systems have the same value of output to input ratio, they also have the same value of $\omega_n t$. It therefore follows that if Fig. 4-6 is changed so that the abscissa axis is nondimensional time, viz., $\omega_n t$, then a single graph can be made to represent the response of any linear second-order system for a specific damping ratio. For obvious reasons such curves are referred to as *universal* curves, and these are represented in Fig. 4-7 for various values of damping ratio.

Figures of Merit Identifying the Transient Response. The dynamic behavior of any second-order linear system is readily described in terms of two figures of merit: ζ and ω_n. To understand what each quantity conveys about the transient response, let us first determine the time at which the maximum overshoot occurs. Differentiating Eq. (4-31) with respect

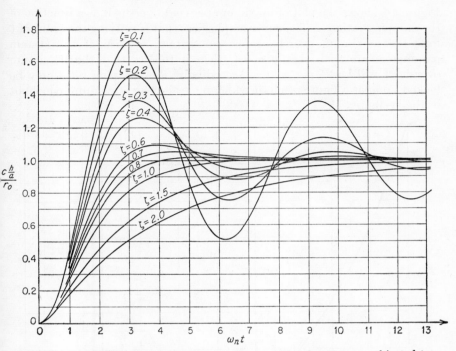

FIG. 4-7. Universal transient response curves for second-order systems subjected to a step input.

to time yields upon simplification

$$\frac{d}{dt} \frac{c}{(a/h)r_0} = \frac{\omega_n}{\sqrt{1 - \zeta^2}} \epsilon^{-\zeta\omega_n t} \sin \omega_d t \qquad (4\text{-}33)$$

Clearly, then, the first and therefore the peak overshoot occurs when

$$\omega_d t = \pi$$

or

$$\omega_n t = \frac{\pi}{\sqrt{1 - \zeta^2}} \qquad (4\text{-}34)$$

Substituting this result into Eq. (4-31) gives the expression for the maximum instantaneous value of the output. Thus

$$\left[\frac{c}{(a/h)r_0} \right]_{\max} = 1 + \epsilon^{-\zeta\pi/\sqrt{1-\zeta^2}} \qquad (4\text{-}35)$$

Moreover, it follows from Eq. (4-35) that the maximum per cent overshoot is

$$\frac{c_{\max} - c}{(a/h)r_0} = 100\epsilon^{-\zeta\pi/\sqrt{1-\zeta^2}} \% \qquad (4\text{-}36)$$

Figure 4-8 shows the plot of maximum per cent overshoot as a function of the damping ratio ζ.   The curve emphasizes that specifying the value of ζ fixes the maximum overshoot for the system.   Hence, if the system parameters are such that $\zeta = 0.4$, then it follows that the maximum overshoot will be 25 per cent.   Accordingly, the damping ratio may be looked upon as a figure of merit which identifies the maximum overshoot in the system.

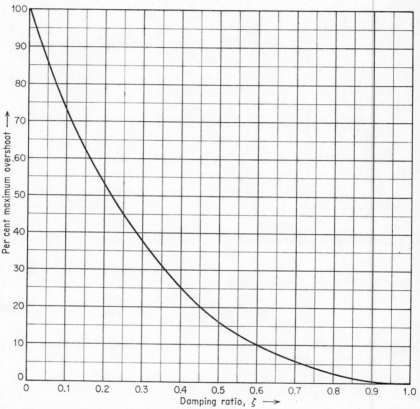

FIG. 4-8. Per cent maximum overshoot vs. damping ratio for linear second-order system.

The information which the natural frequency directly makes available in terms of the transient response is deduced from an inspection of output response to a step input for a given value of ζ plotted nondimensionally. Such a plot is shown in Fig. 4-9 along with the inclusion of an arbitrary tolerance band of ± 2 per cent.   The system is considered as having reached steady state once the response stays confined within the tolerance band.   The time required to do this is called the *settling time*.   As a practical matter the response time of all systems is necessarily gauged in terms of a tolerance band, however small or large, that the particular specifications demand. For the example illustrated in Fig. 4-9, it follows that the settling time is $t_s = k/\omega_n$. The important fact to recognize here is that the settling time is inversely proportional to the natural frequency of the system. Thus, if the response shown in Fig. 4-9 applies to two different systems having the same ζ, then clearly the one with the larger natural frequency will have a smaller settling time in responding to input commands or load disturbances. Consequently, the value of the natural frequency of the system may be interpreted as a figure of merit which provides a measure of the settling time.

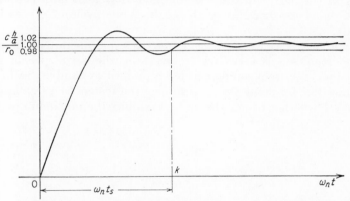

FIG. 4-9. Identification of settling time in terms of a ± 2 per cent tolerance band.

In the servomechanisms group of feedback control systems the value of the damping ratio frequently lies within the following limits:

$$0.3 \leq \zeta \leq 0.8$$

The reason for the upper bound lies in the fact that for values of ζ exceeding 0.8 the rate at which the response changes proceeds slowly in the first instants, thereby manifesting the characteristic of sluggishness. Or, expressed in other words, the *rise time* is large. The rise time is usually defined as the time required for the response to go from 10 to 90 per cent of its final value. On the other hand the lower limit is imposed in order to keep the settling time within reasonable values. A glance at Fig. 4-7 with tolerance bands superposed reveals clearly that with ζ much less than 0.3 the oscillations outside the tolerance-band limits persist for a long period of time.

Influence of Gain on Settling Time. An inspection of Eq. (4-31) indicates that the transient response decays with a time constant identified as $1/\zeta\omega_n = 2J/F$, a result which is obviously independent of the system gain K. The settling time can then be described as equivalent to three to five times the time constant. However, a more significant settling time is obtained when one is reasoning in terms of a tolerance band. Such a description leads to the conclusion that the settling time is influenced to some degree by the value of the open-loop gain. This is forcefully illustrated by measuring the settling time in terms of a ± 5 per cent tolerance band introduced upon the curves of Fig. 4-7 for each value of ζ specified. These results are shown in Fig. 4-10a. The inertia and damping coefficient are assumed constant, and ζ is varied by changing the gain. Thus, as the gain is increased beyond the value which makes $\zeta = 1$, the settling time at first decreases, reaches an optimum value around 0.7, and then increases for low values of ζ. The discontinuities in this curve are due to the fact that final entrance into the tolerance band can occur over the span of one cycle of the oscillation frequency.

Attenuation per Cycle Curves. Often in experimental or in analog-computer studies it is necessary to ascertain whether a specific second-order system or system component has a prescribed damping ratio. One quick procedure for doing this is to subject the system to a step input and check to see whether or not the output exhibits the maximum overshoot

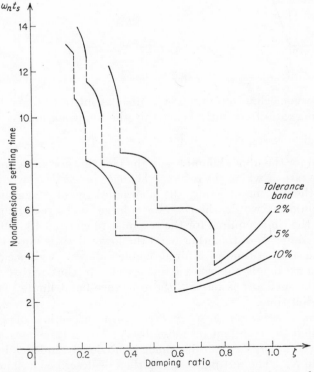

FIG. 4-10a. Settling time vs. damping ratio for several tolerance bands.

called for by Fig. 4-8. Another useful procedure is to apply an impulse to the system and compare the ratio of the amplitude of the second positive peak to the amplitude of the first. For a linear second-order system the attenuation which occurs during the first cycle starting with the time when the first peak occurs is determinable. Of course the degree of attenuation that occurs per cycle is dependent upon the damping ratio. Figure 4-10*b* plots these results as well as those which apply to the attenuation per half cycle measured as indicated in the figure.

4-2. Analysis of Second-order Servo System.   Step Velocity Input

The use of a pair of bridge-connected potentiometers as the error detector in a system which is to follow velocity commands is not as practical as using a pair of a-c synchros. This is due to the fact that the synchros are capable of continuous rotation (as contrasted to 1-turn and 10-turn potentiometers) and are virtually free of resolution difficulties and brush contact problems. Figure 4-11 shows the modified system. Before proceeding with an analysis of such a system let us first study the operating characteristics of the a-c synchro and in this way assure ourselves of a full understanding of the operation of the system.

Synchro Construction Features. The control transmitter consists of a stationary member called the *stator* and a rotating member called the

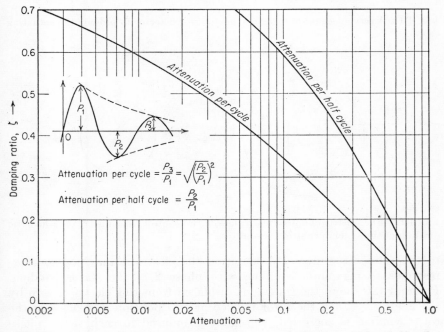

Fig. 4-10*b*. Damping ratio for second-order system vs. attenuation per cycle or half cycle.

rotor. The inner surface of the stator iron is slotted to accommodate a balanced three-phase winding, which is usually of the concentric-coil type. The rotor is of the dumbbell construction with many turns of wire wrapped round the stem as depicted in Fig. 4-12*a*. An a-c voltage is applied to the rotor winding through the slip rings, which causes an excitation current to flow, thus producing an alternating flux field with respect

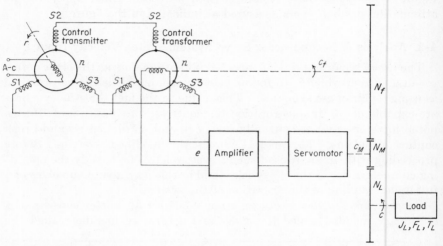

Fig. 4-11. A servomechanism using a synchro error detector to provide the actuating signal.

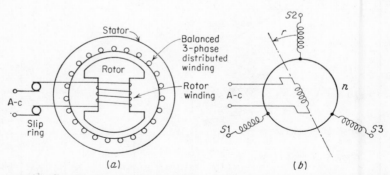

Fig. 4-12. (*a*) Construction features of the synchro control transmitter; (*b*) schematic diagram of the synchro control transmitter.

to the rotor structure. By definition the electrical zero position corresponds to maximum coupling with phase 2 of the stator winding. Figure 4-12*b* shows the rotor axis displaced from this electrical zero by the angle *r*. When the rotor is fixed at this position in space and the rotor winding is energized, voltages are induced in each stator phase because of transformer action. Since the flux is assumed sinusoidally distributed around the periphery of the air gap, it follows that the emf in phase 2 of the synchro is proportional to $\cos r$. Thus,

$$E_{n2} = E_m \cos r \tag{4-37}$$

where E_m is the rms voltage induced in phase 2 corresponding to a condition of maximum coupling. Also, since phase 3 is 120° displaced from phase 2 in a direction opposite to the assumed displacement of the rotor, the value of the rms voltage induced at this same position is

$$E_{n3} = E_m \cos (r + 120) \tag{4-38}$$

Similarly for phase 1 there results

$$E_{n1} = E_m \cos (r - 120) \tag{4-39}$$

The cosine factors essentially account for the variation of the coefficient of coupling between the rotor winding and the corresponding stator phase

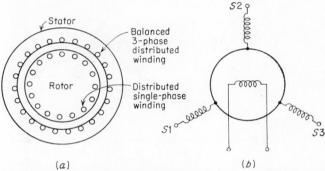

(a) (b)

FIG. 4-13. (a) Construction features of the synchro control transformer; (b) schematic diagram of the synchro control transformer with the rotor at electrical zero.

windings. The induced voltages are each in time phase since they are produced by the same flux.

The construction details of the synchro control transformer differ somewhat from those of the control transmitter. One important difference is that the air gap is uniform owing to the rotor's cylindrical construction (see Fig. 4-13a). This feature is included to keep the magnetizing current it draws from the transmitter to a minimum when used as shown in Fig. 4-11. Furthermore, the rotor winding is usually a distributed winding as contrasted to the concentrated winding used in the transmitter. Another difference is the definition of the electrical zero position. For the control transformer it is defined as that position of the rotor which makes the coupling with phase 2 of the stator zero. This condition is indicated in Fig. 4-13b. The stator winding is also a balanced three-phase winding; however, it differs from the transmitter in that it has a higher impedance per phase. This latter feature permits several control transformers to be fed from a single transmitter.

System Operation. By electrically connecting the stator terminals in the manner shown in Fig. 4-14 and exciting the rotor of the transmitter with an a-c voltage, the synchro combination can be used as a device which detects a lack of correspondence between the transmitter rotor shaft position and the transformer rotor shaft position in terms of an error voltage appearing across the rotor terminals of the control transformer. For example, assume that the rotor of the transmitter is displaced by $r = 30°$; then in accordance with Eqs. (4-37) to (4-39) the rms values of the phase-induced emfs are as indicated in Fig. 4-14. The axis of the alternating flux field coincides with the rotor axis position. Since the stator of the transmitter is connected to the stator of the transformer, the transmitter supplies magnetizing currents to the control-transformer

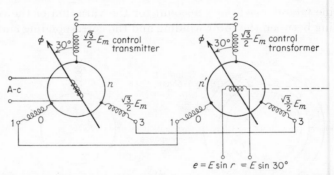

$$e = E \sin r = E \sin 30°$$

Fig. 4-14. Control-transmitter–control-transformer combination used as an error detector.

stator which in turn creates a pulsating field in its own air gap. The magnitude of the control-transformer stator phase currents must be such that the resulting air-gap flux induces voltages in each phase which are equal and opposite to those prevailing in the stator of the transmitter. This represents the equilibrium condition for the given value of r of the transmitter. Accordingly, the resultant flux field in the control transformer is forced to take a position which corresponds to that of the axis of the transmitter rotor. If the control-transformer rotor is assumed fixed at its electrical zero position, then clearly there is a voltage induced in the rotor winding which is given by

$$e = E \sin r \qquad (4\text{-}40)$$

where E is the maximum value of the rms voltage induced in the rotor winding of the control transformer when the coupling with the field is a maximum. The magnitude of this rotor voltage is therefore an indication of the lack of correspondence between the rotor positions of the transmitter and transformer. Now, if the transformer rotor were manually rotated counterclockwise by $r = 30°$ in Fig. 4-14, then clearly the rotor emf would become zero, thereby indicating exact correspondence between control-transmitter and control-transformer displacement. Of course, when used in a feedback control system as shown in Fig. 4-11, the output of the control transformer provides the actuating signal for the system and the actuating signal is nulled to zero through the feedback gearing for position-command inputs.

Let us now turn our attention to the operation of this system when the input is a velocity command, which means that the transmitter rotor is driven at a constant velocity. In the final state it is desired that the output also be driven at a constant velocity consistent with the command. To understand how the system of Fig. 4-11 accomplishes this, consider the actions which take place immediately upon the application of the step input velocity. Assume that initially the rotor is at its electrical zero position. Keep in mind, too, that the synchro combination is a *position-sensitive error detector* as is evident from Eq. (4-40). Thus, an actuating signal is created whenever there is a lack of correspondence in the position of the two shafts (irrespective of how this comes about), i.e., a rotor voltage exists whether the transmitter rotor is given a fixed displacement or whether it increases linearly with time (velocity input) or parabolically with time (acceleration input). Accordingly, to emphasize this point, Fig. 4-11 shows the input to the transmitter rotor as $r(= \omega_i t)$ rather than dr/dt. Now, as r increases with time, driving the transmitter rotor away from electrical zero, an actuating signal appears at the amplifier input terminals. Immediately after the application of the input, the rotor of the control transformer remains stationary because of the inertia connected at the output shaft. As time passes, the actuating signal increases, thus causing the servoamplifier-servomotor combination to develop sufficient torque to accelerate the load to the velocity of the input command. When this situation prevails, the velocity of the control-transformer shaft is identical to the command velocity at the transmitter shaft. However, there is a position phase lag existing between the two rotors; this is a condition which is absolutely necessary in order to assure the existence of an actuating signal for the purpose of generating sufficient torque to overcome the viscous-friction torque, thereby maintaining constant output velocity. Of course the magnitude of the actuating signal depends upon the value of the direct transmission gain. The greater this gain, the smaller the actuating signal and therefore the smaller the lag error in position.

The operation of this system may be understood better by keeping in mind that, as the transmitter rotor revolves at the command velocity, the axis of the flux field also rotates at the same velocity. Moreover, the corresponding magnetizing currents which are caused to flow in the control-transformer stator will be such as to create a resultant flux field which besides pulsating also rotates at the same value as the input velocity,

Hence, as the transmitter rotor moves away from the electrical zero position upon application of the input, the flux field in the transformer moves away from its electrical zero position, thereby inducing a voltage in its rotor winding. If the input displacement angle increases rapidly owing to a large command velocity, the actuating signal becomes correspondingly large, which in turn means ample developed torque to provide high acceleration for the purpose of establishing the commanded output velocity. Now, when the rotor of the transformer travels at the same velocity as the transmitter rotor, there is no relative motion between the transformer flux field and its rotor winding. However, under these circumstances, the axis of the rotor winding is not in quadrature with the axis of the flux field in order to assure sufficient coupling between the two so that through transformer action the actuating signal needed to generate the output will be maintained. It is interesting to note that, with such an arrangement, the output velocity is exactly related to the commanded value; i.e., the system operates, not with an error in velocity, but rather

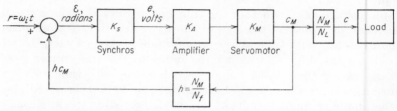

FIG. 4-15. Block diagram of Fig. 4-11, showing the gain factors of each component.

with an error in position. For example, if the feedback and load gear ratios were unity, then the output velocity would be identical to the input velocity in the final state. If this were not so, the actuating signal would then vary sinusoidally at a frequency proportional to the difference in speeds, which means that the system could not function properly since as the actuating signal reverses sign the output rotation would also reverse. The ability of the system to operate without an error in commanded velocity is attributable to the use of an error detector which is position-sensitive. If the synchros were replaced with velocity-sensitive devices such as a pair of tachometer generators, the system would be forced to operate with an error in velocity in order to develop the torque required to overcome viscous friction.

Mathematical Analysis. The block diagram for the system is shown in Fig. 4-15. For ease of handling the load torque T'_L is assumed zero so that the differential equation describing the system behavior is

$$\mathcal{E}K_sK_AK_M = J\frac{d^2c_M}{dt^2} + F\frac{dc_M}{dt} \tag{4-41}$$

where K_s is the synchro constant expressed in volts/radian and the other constants have the same identification as in the foregoing. The description of the input is shown in Fig. 4-16a and b. The variation of the input displacement expressed in radians is shown in Fig. 4-16a and represents a ramp position input having a slope of ω_i radians/sec. Since the error detector is position-sensitive, it is this description of the input which is important. Figure 4-16b shows the step velocity input, which merely indicates that at $t = 0^-$ the slope of the position vs. time curve is zero, while for $t = 0^+$ this slope changes to a finite value, viz., ω_i, and remains at this value. The actuating signal expressed in radians is

$$\varepsilon = r - hc_M \tag{4-42}$$

Again, because of greater ease, the dynamic behavior will be found by first solving for the actuating signal and then using Eq. (4-42) to obtain

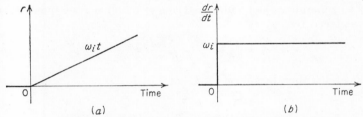

FIG. 4-16. Description of input to the system of Fig. 4-11.

the solution for the output. Substituting Eq. (4-42) into Eq. (4-41) yields

$$J \frac{d^2\varepsilon}{dt^2} + F \frac{d\varepsilon}{dt} + hK_sK_AK_M\varepsilon = J \frac{d^2r}{dt^2} + F \frac{dr}{dt} \tag{4-43}$$

Introducing

$$\frac{dr}{dt} = \omega_i \quad \text{and} \quad K = hK_sK_AK_M \tag{4-44}$$

enables us to write the last equation as

$$J \frac{d^2\varepsilon}{dt^2} + F \frac{d\varepsilon}{dt} + K\varepsilon = J \frac{d\omega_i}{dt} + F\omega_i \tag{4-45}$$

The classical approach will now be used to find the solution of this equation.

The driven or steady-state solution (ε_{ss}) is found by setting the time derivatives to zero in Eq. (4-45).[1] Thus

$$\varepsilon_{ss} = \frac{F}{K} \omega_i \quad \text{radians} \tag{4-46}$$

Keep in mind that this is an error in position due to a velocity input. For a system with fixed parameters, the larger the input velocity, the greater

[1] ε_{ss} is of the same form as the driving function, i.e., a constant.

the actuating signal required to generate the corresponding output velocity. Another way of arriving at Eq. (4-46) is to recognize that at steady state the motor developed torque must be just enough to supply the torque required to overcome the viscous-friction effect. Therefore, $\mathcal{E}_{ss}K_sK_AK_M = F\omega_M$. But

$$\omega_f = h\omega_M = \omega_i$$

where ω_f is the velocity at the feedback shaft. Hence

$$\mathcal{E}_{ss}K_sK_AK_M = F\frac{\omega_i}{h}$$

from which it follows that

$$\mathcal{E}_{ss} = \frac{F}{hK_sK_AK_M}\,\omega_i = \frac{F}{K}\,\omega_i$$

In order to generalize the results in terms of ζ and ω_n, the quantity F/K may be replaced by

$$\frac{F}{K} = \frac{\zeta F_c}{K} = \frac{2\zeta\sqrt{KJ}}{K} = \frac{2\zeta}{\omega_n} \tag{4-47}$$

Equation (4-46) then becomes

$$\mathcal{E}_{ss} = \frac{2\zeta}{\omega_n}\,\omega_i \tag{4-48}$$

The complementary function is found as the solution of the characteristic equation as outlined in Chap. 2. By setting the external disturbance equal to zero in Eq. (4-45), the characteristic equation takes the form $s^2 + (F/J)s + K/J = 0$, which is recognized as being the same as for the system of Fig. 4-1. This result is not unexpected because both error detectors are position-sensitive devices. The roots of this equation are of the same form as before, viz.,

$$s_{1,2} = -\zeta\omega_n \pm j\omega_d$$

Therefore, the complementary function is specifically

$$\mathcal{E}_c = \epsilon^{-\zeta\omega_n t}(k'\cos\omega_d t + k''\sin\omega_d t) \tag{4-49}$$

where k' and k'' are arbitrary constants which are to be determined from the initial conditions.

The total solution of Eq. (4-45) is the sum of Eqs. (4-48) and (4-49). Thus

$$\mathcal{E} = \frac{2\zeta}{\omega_n}\,\omega_i + \epsilon^{-\zeta\omega_n t}(k'\cos\omega_d t + k''\sin\omega_d t) \tag{4-50}$$

The initial conditions prevailing for the situation under study are summarized below and apply for $t = 0^+$. Figure 4-16a reveals that $r = 0$ and $dr/dt = \omega_i$ for $t = 0^+$, while because of inertial effects c_M and dc_M/dt

	r	ε	c_M
	0	0	0
$\dfrac{d}{dt}$	ω_i	ω_i	0

are each zero. The corresponding values of ε are established from Eq. (4-42). Substituting the first initial condition into the expression for the total solution gives

$$k' = -\frac{2\zeta}{\omega_n}\,\omega_i \qquad (4\text{-}51)$$

To use the second initial condition requires differentiating Eq. (4-50) first. This leads to

$$\frac{d\varepsilon}{dt} = -k'\zeta\omega_n\cos\omega_d t\,\epsilon^{-\zeta\omega_n t} - k'\omega_d\epsilon^{-\zeta\omega_n t}\sin\omega_d t$$
$$+\, k''\omega_d\epsilon^{-\zeta\omega_n t}\cos\omega_d t - k''(\zeta\omega_n)\sin\omega_d t\,\epsilon^{-\zeta\omega_n t}$$

Substitution of the initial conditions yields

$$k'' = \frac{\omega_i}{\omega_d}\,(1 - 2\zeta^2) \qquad (4\text{-}52)$$

Inserting the values of k' and k'' into Eq. (4-50) gives

$$\varepsilon = \frac{2\zeta}{\omega_n}\,\omega_i + \epsilon^{-\zeta\omega_n t}\left[-\frac{2\zeta}{\omega_n}\,\omega_i\cos\omega_d t + \frac{\omega_i}{\omega_d}\,(1-2\zeta^2)\sin\omega_d t\right]$$

Rearranging,

$$\varepsilon\frac{\omega_n}{\omega_i} = 2\zeta\left[1 - \epsilon^{-\zeta\omega_n t}\left(\cos\omega_d t + \frac{2\zeta^2-1}{2\zeta\sqrt{1-\zeta^2}}\sin\omega_d t\right)\right] \qquad (4\text{-}53)$$

Combining the sine and cosine terms leads to the simpler form

$$\varepsilon\frac{\omega_n}{\omega_i} = 2\zeta\left[1 - \frac{\epsilon^{-\zeta\omega_n t}}{2\zeta\sqrt{1-\zeta^2}}\sin(\omega_d t + \phi_d)\right] \qquad (4\text{-}54)$$

where
$$\phi_d = \tan^{-1}\frac{2\zeta\sqrt{1-\zeta^2}}{2\zeta^2-1}$$

These expressions for the actuating signal are valid for $0 \leq \zeta \leq 1.0$ and for $T'_L = 0$. Plots of this solution for several values of damping ratio ζ are shown in Fig. 4-17. The graphs indicate that as ζ is decreased the steady-state lag error also diminishes. This follows from the fact that a decrease in ζ entails an increase in gain, which in turn means a decrease in ε_{ss} as revealed by Eq. (4-46). It is assumed that F and J remain fixed.

Output Displacement Solution. From Eq. (4-42) the motor displacement angle is given by $c_M = (1/h)(r - \varepsilon)$. Also, the load displacement angle is related to c_M by $c = ac_M$, where a is the gear ratio from motor

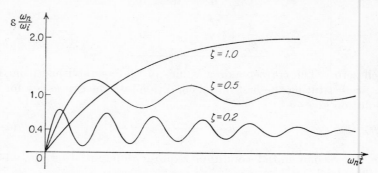

FIG. 4-17. Plot of Eq. (4-54) for several values of ζ.

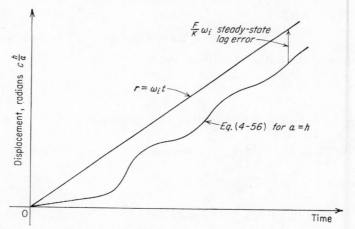

FIG. 4-18. Response of a second-order system to a step velocity input.

shaft to load shaft. Therefore the output displacement angle is

$$c = \frac{a}{h}(r - \varepsilon) \tag{4-55}$$

Inserting $r = \omega_i t$ and Eq. (4-54) in the last equation provides the desired result.

$$c\frac{h}{a} = \left[\omega_i t - \frac{2\zeta}{\omega_n}\omega_i \left(1 - \frac{\epsilon^{-\zeta\omega_n t}}{2\zeta\sqrt{1 - \zeta^2}}\sin(\omega_d t + \phi_d) \right) \right] \tag{4-56}$$

A graphical sketch of this solution appears in Fig. 4-18. Note that after the transient dies out the slope of the output displacement curve is the same as that of the input, which indicates that the two velocities are equal, but with a position lag error existing between the two shafts.

4-3. Meeting Performance Requirements

The design specifications of a second-order system which is used to provide velocity follow-up frequently limit the allowable position lag error during steady state as well as the maximum overshoot in the transient state. Attempting to satisfy both requirements with one set of parameters is usually impossible to accomplish. The steady-state performance is described by Eq. (4-46),

$$\mathcal{E}_{ss} = \frac{F}{K} \omega_i \tag{4-57}$$

while the description of the dynamic behavior is indicated by the damping ratio from Eq. (4-17),

$$\zeta = \frac{F}{2\sqrt{KJ}} \tag{4-58}$$

As a general rule, the viscous-friction and the inertia terms are kept as small as permissible so that the one adjustable variable in the system is the open-loop gain K. Equation (4-57) shows that for a specified F and ω_i the value of gain K needed to meet the specification on the allowable position lag error can be readily established. The difficulty, however, lies in the fact that the use of this gain in Eq. (4-58) may very well call for values of ζ which make it impossible to keep the maximum overshoot within the allowable limit. Accordingly, the need for a modification in the basic design of the second-order system presents itself.

This problem is present not only in the case of a velocity input, although certainly it is of great importance here, but exists, too, in those second-order systems which follow position-type commands in the presence of external load disturbances. In such instances the lack of correspondence between the output and the command is given by

$$\mathcal{E}_{ss} = \frac{T'_o}{K} h \tag{4-59}$$

where T'_o is the magnitude of the external load. Again, if this quantity is to be kept within reasonable limits, it is necessary to provide sufficiently large gains, which in turn result in low damping ratios, with a consequent deterioration in transient behavior.

This selfsame problem continues to be present even in those cases where there are no external disturbances to speak of, but where very high accuracy is to be maintained. Under such circumstances it is the imperfections of the system components which loom large, i.e., such imperfections as coulomb friction and bearing friction in potentiometers and synchros, dead-zone and slot-lock effects in servomotors, and so on. These effects, too, can be greatly minimized by the use of high gains.

The foregoing comments make it apparent that the need for high gains in accurate feedback control systems is imperative and that equally imperative is the need to preserve a satisfactory dynamic performance. Clearly, then, there exists the need for appropriate compensation schemes which will prevent the deterioration of the transient performance in spite of the use of high gains. Although there are several methods which can provide the type of control being sought, only two are truly practical and have accordingly gained widespread acceptance. The first of these makes use of error-rate damping to control the dynamic response, while the second employs output-rate damping. Consideration of both schemes constitutes the subject matter of the remainder of this chapter.

4-4. Second-order System with Error-rate Damping. Velocity Input

A system possesses error-rate damping when the generation of the output in some way depends upon the rate of change of the actuating signal.

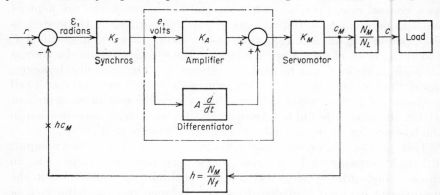

FIG. 4-19. Block diagram of a second-order system with error-rate damping.

For the system of Fig. 4-11 a simple way of introducing error-rate damping is to use an amplifier which provides an output signal containing a term proportional to the derivative of the input as well as one proportional to the input itself. Accordingly, the torque developed by the servomotor will be dependent not only upon the magnitude of the position error but also upon the rate at which it is changing with time. Such a control system is described as having a *proportional plus derivative controller*. When error-rate damping is not included, it is simply referred to as a *proportional controller*. The block-diagram representation of the error-rate-damped system is shown in Fig. 4-19. The proportional plus derivative outputs of the amplifier are shown as two parallel paths which are summed prior to being applied to the servomotor. The quantity A is the error-rate gain factor and is usually expressed in units of volts/volt/sec or more simply as seconds. It is one of the purposes of the following analysis to permit the evaluation of A for specified damping ratios.

Essentially, the operation of the system of Fig. 4-19 is the same as that of Fig. 4-11 with the sole exception that the damping ratio is now determined by the combined action of the equivalent motor viscous friction and the error-rate term. The precise manner in which this takes place physically will be discussed after the analytical solution has been found. The differential equation describing the system behavior in this case is

$$\mathcal{E}K_sK_AK_M + K_sK_MA\,\frac{d\mathcal{E}}{dt} = J\,\frac{d^2c_M}{dt^2} + F\,\frac{dc_M}{dt} \tag{4-60}$$

The left side of the equation represents the motor developed torque and differs from that of Eq. (4-41) by the presence of the derivative term. The actuating signal $\mathcal{E}$ expressed in radians is still given by Eq. (4-42). Inserting c_M from this equation into Eq. (4-60) yields

$$J\,\frac{d^2\mathcal{E}}{dt^2} + (F + hK_sAK_M)\,\frac{d\mathcal{E}}{dt} + hK_sK_AK_M\mathcal{E} = J\,\frac{d^2r}{dt^2} + F\,\frac{dr}{dt} \tag{4-61}$$

In Sec. 4-2 the proportional open-loop gain was identified as

$$K = hK_sK_AK_M \tag{4-62}$$

It has the same value for the system of Fig. 4-19. As a matter of further convenience, let us define the following additional quantity:

$$Q_\mathcal{E} \equiv hK_sAK_M = \text{error-rate open-loop gain} \tag{4-63}$$

An inspection of the dimensions of this equation reveals that $Q_\mathcal{E}$ is effectively a viscous-friction term whose amplitude can be independently adjusted by varying A. This dimensional character of $Q_\mathcal{E}$ is readily verified by glancing at Eq. (4-61), where it is seen to be combined with the viscous-friction term F. These expressions for K and $Q_\mathcal{E}$ can readily be obtained from the block diagram of Fig. 4-19. It merely requires opening the loop at the point of feedback and then forming the product of the gain factors of each block encountered in traversing the loop from the output point of the summer to the point where the loop is opened. Thus, to get K, open the loop at the X mark in Fig. 4-19, and take the product of the gain factors found in the *proportional* channel, which include the synchro (K_s), the amplifier (K_A), the servomotor (K_M), and the feedback (h) elements. To obtain $Q_\mathcal{E}$ requires traversing the *error-rate* channel, which includes the synchro (K_s), the differentiator (A), the servomotor (K_M), and the feedback (h) elements.

Upon introducing Eqs. (4-62) and (4-63) into Eq. (4-61) along with $dr/dt = \omega_i$, the system differential equation for a constant velocity input becomes

$$J\,\frac{d^2\mathcal{E}}{dt^2} + (F + Q_\mathcal{E})\,\frac{d\mathcal{E}}{dt} + K\mathcal{E} = J\,\frac{d\omega_i}{dt} + F\omega_i \tag{4-64}$$

Again by using the classical method to find the solution to this differential equation, it follows that the value of actuating signal needed at steady state is, as before, $\mathcal{E}_{ss} = (F/K)\omega_i$ (radians). The characteristic equation, however, is modified to

$$s^2 + \frac{F + Q_\varepsilon}{J} s + \frac{K}{J} = 0 \tag{4-65}$$

so that the roots identifying the character of the transient modes are

$$s_{1,2} = -\frac{F + Q_\varepsilon}{2J} \pm j \sqrt{\frac{K}{J} - \left(\frac{F + Q_\varepsilon}{2J}\right)^2} \tag{4-66}$$

for the case of underdamping. From this last equation it follows that the critical viscous friction is

$$(F + Q_\varepsilon)_c = 2 \sqrt{KJ} \tag{4-67}$$

Comparing Eq. (4-67) with Eq. (4-15) shows that, whether the system is just viscously damped or viscously damped plus error-rate-damped, the critical value of damping coefficient continues to be determined by $2\sqrt{KJ}$, which means that it remains dependent upon the open-loop proportional gain and the system inertia.

As pointed out in Eq. (4-17) the damping ratio of a second-order system is always expressed in terms of the ratio of the value of the total damping term to the critical value. Accordingly, in this case the damping ratio takes on the value,

$$\zeta = \frac{F + Q_\varepsilon}{2 \sqrt{KJ}} \tag{4-68}$$

A glance at the characteristic equation points out that the expression for the natural frequency remains unaltered, that is, $\omega_n = \sqrt{K/J}$. Written in terms of those two figures of merit, Eq. (4-66) now takes on the form

$$s_{1,2} = -\zeta\omega_n \pm j\omega_d$$

which will be recognized as being the same as Eq. (4-21). Of course there is a difference, and it lies in the make-up of ζ.

The complete expression for the actuating signal is

$$\mathcal{E} = \frac{F}{K}\omega_i + \epsilon^{-\zeta\omega_n t}(k' \cos \omega_d t + k'' \sin \omega_d t) \tag{4-69}$$

To put the steady-state error in terms of ζ and ω_n, we can proceed as before. However, in order to permit a quicker comparison of the response in this case with that of the system using no error-rate damping, let us introduce the quantity

$$\rho \equiv \frac{F}{F + Q_\varepsilon} \tag{4-70}$$

Such a factor allows a comparison to be made between the performance of a system which is just viscously damped and the performance of one which is viscously damped as well as error-rate-damped. Often F refers to the minimum viscous friction permissible, which frequently is determined by the servomotor selected on the basis of providing the output requirements. In order to continue to represent the steady-state error in terms of ζ and ω_n, we proceed as before. Thus

$$\frac{F + Q_\varepsilon}{K} = \frac{\zeta(F + Q_\varepsilon)_c}{K} = \frac{\zeta 2 \sqrt{KJ}}{K} = \frac{2\zeta}{\omega_n} \tag{4-71}$$

Substituting the expression for $F + Q_\varepsilon$ from Eq. (4-70) then yields

$$\frac{F}{K} = \frac{2\zeta}{\omega_n} \rho \tag{4-72}$$

This now makes it possible to express the steady-state solution for ε, not only in terms of ζ and ω_n, but also in terms of the comparison ratio ρ. Thus, Eq. (4-69) becomes

$$\varepsilon = \rho \frac{2\zeta}{\omega_n} \omega_i + \epsilon^{-\zeta\omega_n t}(k' \cos \omega_d t + k'' \sin \omega_d t) \tag{4-73}$$

The initial conditions here are the same as those appearing on page 121. Substituting these into Eq. (4-73) and proceeding in the usual manner yields the following values for the constants:

$$k' = - \rho \frac{2\zeta}{\omega_n} \omega_i \tag{4-74}$$

and

$$k'' = - \frac{\omega_i}{\omega_d} (2\rho\zeta^2 - 1) \tag{4-75}$$

Inserting the values of k' and k'' into Eq. (4-73) and rearranging terms provides the desired result, viz.,

$$\varepsilon \frac{\omega_n}{\omega_i} = 2\rho\zeta \left[1 - \epsilon^{-\zeta\omega_n t}(\cos \omega_d t + \frac{2\rho\zeta^2 - 1}{2\rho\zeta \sqrt{1 - \zeta^2}} \sin \omega_d t) \right] \tag{4-76}$$

This result is valid for $0 \leq \zeta \leq 1.0$ and $T_L = 0$. Of course, when $\rho = 1$, Eq. (4-76) reduces to Eq. (4-53).

The big advantage which error-rate damping has to offer in the way of improving system performance can be deduced by a careful study of the preceding expression. To facilitate matters, Eq. (4-76) is plotted in Fig. 4-20 for a fixed value of ζ and two different values of ρ. Curve (b) in this figure corresponds to a situation where the amount of error-rate damping (Q_ε) added is equal to the system's original viscous friction F. The steady-state level of this curve is accordingly one-half that of curve (a) as predicted by the right side of Eq. (4-76), which indicates that the steady-state error in position for a specific velocity input is decreased without sacrifice of a decrease in damping ratio. This comes about because an increase in open-loop gain is required in order to keep ζ the same in the presence of error-rate damping [see Eq. (4-68)]. Since the steady-state error is $\varepsilon_{ss} = (F/K)\omega_i$ and K has been increased, it follows that ε_{ss} must decrease. For the situation depicted in Fig. 4-20, to preserve the same ζ of 0.4 for $Q_\varepsilon = F$ requires an increase in open-loop gain of four times, a result which immediately follows from Eq. (4-68). Although the steady-state levels of Fig. 4-20 are different by a factor of $\frac{1}{2}$, it must be borne in mind that the ordinate quantity in this plot is now greater because the natural frequency is increased with the higher open-loop gain. Herein then lies the strength of error-rate damping—*it allows higher gains to be used without adversely affecting the damping ratio*

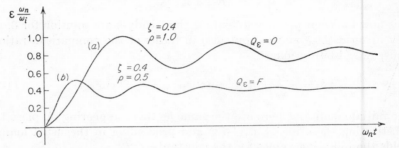

Fig. 4-20. Actuating-signal response of a second-order system to a velocity input ω_i: (a) system without error-rate damping; (b) system with error-rate damping.

and in this way makes it possible to satisfy the specifications on the magnitude of the damping ratio as well as the steady-state error. It offers the additional advantage of increasing the system's natural frequency, which in turn means smaller settling times. To better emphasize these beneficial aspects of error-rate damping, the foregoing results are summarized in Table 4-1.

Viscous damping is effective in controlling the oscillations to an input command because of a retarding force which it applies to the system in an amount proportional to the rate of change of the controlled variable. In those cases where a fixed output velocity is commanded, this very factor is also responsible for the existence of a steady-state error. It will be noted, however, that a significant feature of error-rate damping is that it in no way increases the amount of actuating signal needed to generate the commanded velocity because of its presence. This characteristic is attributable to the fact that error-rate damping derives its damping action from the changes in the actuating signal during the transient state of the error, which after all is the time when increased damping is needed. Once these oscillations cease, so too does the damping originating from this source. In this way there is no attendant adverse

TABLE 4-1. COMPARISON OF A VISCOUS-DAMPED SYSTEM AND A
VISCOUS- PLUS ERROR-RATE-DAMPED SYSTEM

Case 1†	Case 2‡	Comments§
$\varepsilon_{ss} = \dfrac{F}{K}\,\omega_i$	$\varepsilon'_{ss} = \dfrac{F}{K'}\,\omega_i$	For a given ω_i the value of K' needed to satisfy the steady-state specifications is computed
$\zeta = \dfrac{F}{2\sqrt{KJ}}$	$\zeta' = \dfrac{F + Q_\varepsilon}{2\sqrt{K'J}}$	For $\zeta = \zeta'$, find the required Q_ε
$\omega_n = \sqrt{\dfrac{K}{J}}$	$\omega'_n = \sqrt{\dfrac{K'}{J}}$	$\omega'_n > \omega_n$, hence faster response, i.e., smaller settling time
$\zeta\omega_n = \dfrac{F}{2J}$	$\zeta'\omega'_n = \dfrac{F + Q_\varepsilon}{2J}$	This is the damping factor, and it is greater for case 2, again indicating faster response

† Original viscous friction = F; open-loop gain = K; no error-rate damping.
‡ Original viscous friction = F; increased open-loop gain = K'; error-rate damping = Q_ε.
§ Comparison is made on basis of *same* damping ratio in both cases.

influence upon the steady-state performance.   To get a physical appreciation of how error-rate damping brings about the desired damping action, consider the manner in which the system of Fig. 4-19 behaves when subjected to a step position input.   (The latter is preferred in place of a step velocity command because of the greater simplicity.)   Assume that the

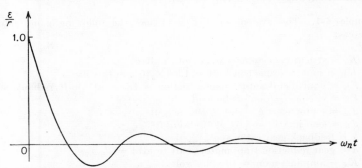

FIG. 4-21. Nondimensional step response curve for the actuating signal.

open-loop proportional gain is very high; then, upon application of a step position input r_0, there is generated, through the medium of the proportional channel, a very large developed torque which takes action to drive the output member rapidly to the commanded level.   However, as the output increases to its new value, there is produced a rate of change of output signal $d\varepsilon/dt$ which as the slope in Fig. 4-21 indicates is initially negative.   Accordingly, since the resultant developed torque is expressed as $\mathcal{E}K_sK_AK_M + K_sK_MA \, d\mathcal{E}/dt$, it follows that as movement of the output member takes place the large proportional torque component is diminished by the error-rate action. In this way large overshoots are prevented in spite of the large gain factors.

When a unit step input is applied to an error-rate-damped system which is initially at rest, it is interesting to note that at $t = 0^+$ there occurs an initial velocity of value $Q_\mathcal{E}/J$, as an examination of Eq. (4-61) reveals. Consequently, the step response of the error-rate-damped system is different from those depicted in Fig. 4-7. This comes about because of the inclusion of an additional term, namely, $(Q_\mathcal{E}/J\omega_d)\epsilon^{-\zeta\omega_n t}$ sin $\omega_d t$, which becomes part of the transient solution. Obviously, when $Q_\mathcal{E}$ is made very small, the step response approaches that of the uncompensated system.

Specification of Error-rate Constant and Amplifier Gain. The calculation of the error-rate constant needed to provide a particular transient performance and minimum steady-state error follows from Eq. (4-63) once the basic make-up of the system has been established. The selection of a suitable servomotor and feedback gearing along with the choice of synchros as the means of providing the actuating signal leaves only the error-rate constant to be determined. First the necessary open-loop gain is computed on the basis of meeting the specification on the minimum allowable value for $\mathcal{E}_{ss}$. Then the restriction on ζ together with Eq. (4-68) permits calculation of $Q_\mathcal{E}$, from which A is subsequently found. A little reflection reveals that the required amplifier gain K_A is similarly determined through use of Eq. (4-62).

Example 4-1. The system of Fig. 4-11 has the following gain factors and parameters:

K_s = synchro constant = 57.3 volts/radian
K_M = motor torque constant = 1.82 × 10^{-4} lb-ft/volt
F_M = equivalent motor viscous friction = 1.5 × 10^{-4} lb-ft/radian/sec
F_L = viscous friction of the load = 0
J_M = motor inertia = 4.0 × 10^{-6} slug-ft^2
J_L = load inertia = 8.64 × 10^{-4} slug-ft^2
h = feedback gear ratio = $\frac{1}{12}$
a = gear reduction from motor shaft to load = $\frac{1}{12}$
K_A = amplifier gain = 10 volts/volt
T'_L = load torque = 0

(a) With the loop open find the value of actuating signal needed to generate a motor velocity of 1,000 rpm. Express the result in volts and in radians.

(b) Compute the complete solution for the actuating signal expressed in radians when the loop is closed and subjected to a step input of 0.2 radian.

(c) Determine the complete solution for the output displacement corresponding to the conditions of part b.

(d) A command input velocity of 0.1 radian/sec is applied to the closed-loop system. Find the time solution for the actuating signal and the output.

(e) The amplifier is redesigned so that it includes an error-rate term in addition to a proportional term. Assuming no change in the proportional gain, calculate the value of error-rate constant needed to increase the damping ratio to 0.7.

(f) Determine the complete solution for the output displacement corresponding to the conditions of part e and for an input velocity of 0.1 radian/sec.

(g) Compute the power which would be dissipated by a viscous-friction damper placed on the motor shaft for the purpose of providing a damping ratio of 0.7 in place of error-rate damping. Assume a command input velocity of 10 radians/sec.

The solutions are as follows:

(a) Upon reaching steady-state velocity with the loop open, the motor must develop sufficient torque to overcome the viscous-friction torque. Thus,

$$eK_AK_M = F_M\omega_M \qquad \text{where } \omega_M = \frac{2\pi(1,000)}{60} = 104.6 \text{ radians/sec}$$

Therefore
$$e = \frac{1.5 \times 10^{-4} \times 104.6}{10 \times 1.82 \times 10^{-4}} = 8.63 \text{ volts}$$

The value of this actuating signal expressed in radians is

$$\frac{8.63}{57.3} = 0.151 \text{ radian}$$

(b) Since the load torque is zero, the desired solution is represented by Eq. (4-28). Therefore finding the solution merely requires identifying the values of the figures of merit ζ and ω_n.

The open-loop gain is

$$K = hK_sK_AK_M = \tfrac{1}{12} \times 57.3 \times 10 \times 1.82 \times 10^{-4} = 86.9 \times 10^{-4} \text{ lb-ft/radian}$$

Also needed is the equivalent inertia reflected to the motor shaft. Hence

$$J_{eM} = J_M + a^2J_L = 4 \times 10^{-6} + \frac{8.64 \times 10^{-4}}{144} = 10^{-5} \text{ slug-ft}^2$$

Accordingly, the system natural frequency is

$$\omega_n = \sqrt{\frac{K}{J}} = \sqrt{\frac{86.9 \times 10^{-4}}{10^{-5}}} = 29.5 \text{ radians/sec}$$

The damping ratio is

$$\zeta = \frac{F}{2\sqrt{KJ}} = \frac{1.5 \times 10^{-4}}{2\sqrt{86.9 \times 10^{-4} \times 10^{-5}}} = \frac{1.5 \times 10^{-4}}{5.88 \times 10^{-4}} = 0.254$$

Also, $\qquad \omega_d = 29.5\sqrt{1 - (0.254)^2} = 28.4 \text{ radians/sec}$

Inserting these quantities into Eq. (4-28) yields the solution

$$\mathcal{E}(t) = 0.20\epsilon^{-7.6t} \sin(28.4t + 75.2°)$$

(c) This immediately follows from Eq. (4-31); thus,

$$c(t) = 0.2[1 - 1.04\epsilon^{-7.6t} \sin(28.4t + 75.2°)]$$

(d) The solution for the actuating signal follows from Eq. (4-54). Substituting yields

$$\mathcal{E}(t) = 0.00174[1 - 2.03\epsilon^{-7.6t} \sin(28.4t + 150.5°)] \qquad \text{radians}$$

Equation (4-56) makes available the output solution.   Thus

$$c(t) = 0.1t - 0.00174[1 - 2.03\epsilon^{-7.6t} \sin{(28.4t + 150.5°)}] \qquad \text{radians}$$

(e) From Eq. (4-68) we have

$$Q_\varepsilon = \zeta(2\sqrt{KJ}) - F_M = 0.7(5.88 \times 10^{-4}) - 1.5 \times 10^{-4} = 2.62 \times 10^{-4}$$

Use of Eq. (4-63) then gives

$$A = \frac{Q_\varepsilon}{hK_sK_M} = \frac{2.62 \times 10^{-4}}{\frac{1}{12} \times 57.3 \times 1.82 \times 10^{-4}} = 0.302 \frac{\text{volt}}{\text{volt/sec}}$$

(f) The time solution is

$$c(t) = r(t) - \varepsilon(t)$$

where $\varepsilon(t)$ is given by Eq. (4-76).   More explicitly we have

$$c(t) = \omega_i t - \rho \frac{2\zeta}{\omega_n} \omega_i \left[1 - \epsilon^{-\zeta\omega_n t} \left(\cos{\omega_d t} + \frac{2\rho\zeta^2 - 1}{2\rho\zeta\sqrt{1 - \zeta^2}} \sin{\omega_d t} \right) \right]$$

From the results of part e

$$\rho = \frac{F}{F + Q_\varepsilon} = \frac{1.5 \times 10^{-4}}{(1.5 + 2.62) \times 10^{-4}} = 0.364$$

Hence

$$\rho \frac{2\zeta}{\omega_n} \omega_i = 0.364 \frac{2 \times 0.7}{29.4} \times 0.1 = 0.00174 \text{ radian}$$

As expected, this quantity remains unaffected by the inclusion of error-rate damping. Note that, if the appropriate quantities for ρ and ζ are introduced, the left side of the last equation reduces to $(F/K)\omega_i$.   Further,

$$\zeta\omega_n = 0.7 \times 29.4 = 20.6$$
$$\omega_d = 29.4\sqrt{1 - 0.49} = 21 \text{ radians/sec}$$

and

$$\frac{2\rho\zeta^2 - 1}{2\rho\zeta\sqrt{1 - \zeta^2}} = \frac{-0.644}{0.364} = -1.77$$

Substituting these values into the expression for $c(t)$ yields

$$c(t) = 0.1t - 0.00174[1 - 2.03\epsilon^{-20.6t} \sin{(21t + 150.5°)}] \qquad \text{radians}$$

(g) The external viscous damper must provide a viscous-damping coefficient equal to 2.62×10^{-4} lb-ft/radian/sec.   Accordingly, the power dissipated is

$$P_{\text{diss}} = F\omega_M^2 = 2.62 \times 10^{-4}(12 \times 10)^2$$
$$= 3.78 \frac{\text{lb-ft}}{\text{sec}} = 5.07 \text{ watts}$$

It is interesting to note that the use of error-rate damping eliminates the need for such a loss because it derives its damping action from the transient state rather than the steady state.

4-5. Meeting Performance Specifications by Using Output-derivative Feedback Damping

A system possesses derivative feedback damping when the generation of the output quantity in some way is made to depend upon the rate at which the controlled variable is changing. Its introduction often involves the creation of an auxiliary loop, thereby making the system multiloop. For the servomechanism group of feedback control systems a common way of obtaining output-derivative damping is by means of a tachometer generator which is driven from the servomotor shaft with or without appropriate gearing as the case warrants. In order to illustrate the general results and to demonstrate the method of analysis, this study will be developed with a particular system in mind, namely, that of a second-order servomechanism employing tachometric feedback damping. Although most of the derived results apply to this system specifically, it should be clearly understood that the procedures and conclusions apply to feedback control systems in general.

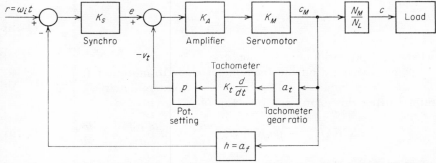

FIG. 4-22. Block diagram of Fig. 4-11 with tachometric feedback damping included.

The basic servomechanism to be studied is that of Fig. 4-11. The system is modified to the extent that a tachometer generator is assumed to be driven from the servomotor shaft through a gear ratio a_t and its output applied to a potentiometer and thence to a summing point in the servoamplifier, where it is then combined with the proportional signal. The tachometer generator is either the a-c or the d-c type depending upon the make-up of the remainder of the system. Most frequently it is of the two-phase induction type, which has a reference winding excited with alternating current and an output voltage directly proportional to the rotor velocity. The block diagram of this modified system showing the tachometric feedback loop appears in Fig. 4-22. The presence of the auxiliary loop does not alter the basic operation of the system. The manner of operation is still the same as that of the system of Fig. 4-11, which means that it still behaves as essentially a position-sensitive system. Hence, to follow a velocity command, the system continues to demand a position lag error in the steady state. Therefore, it is reasonable to expect that the tachometer damping is primarily effective in influencing the character of the transient response. This fact will be borne out by the following mathematical analysis.

The differential equation for the system represented in Fig. 4-22 is formulated in the usual manner. However, for reasons which will be apparent later, the signal coming from the tachometer generator must be introduced opposite in sign to that originating from the proportional term. With this precaution observed the system differential equation referred to the output of the motor shaft is

$$\mathcal{E} K_s K_A K_M - v_t K_A K_M = J \frac{d^2 c_M}{dt^2} + F \frac{dc_M}{dt} \tag{4-77}$$

where, of course, J and F refer to the equivalent inertia and viscous-friction quantities referred to the motor shaft, respectively. Furthermore, as long as the motor output displacement is changing with time, there exists a tachometer voltage v_t given by

$$v_t = p a_t K_t \frac{dc_M}{dt} \tag{4-78}$$

where p = potentiometer setting
a_t = gear ratio from tachometer shaft to motor shaft
K_t = tachometer voltage constant, volts/radian/sec
Substituting this expression into Eq. (4-77) gives

$$\mathcal{E} K_s K_A K_M - p a_t K_t K_A K_M \frac{dc_M}{dt} = J \frac{d^2 c_M}{dt^2} + F \frac{dc_M}{dt} \tag{4-79}$$

The left side of this equation represents the developed motor torque, and clearly it contains one component which is proportional to the actuating signal itself and a second component which is negative and proportional to the derivative of the output displacement. The actuating signal $\mathcal{E}$ still bears the identification shown by Eq. (4-42), and its insertion into the preceding expression yields the result

$$J \frac{d^2 \mathcal{E}}{dt^2} + (F + p a_t K_t K_A K_M) \frac{d\mathcal{E}}{dt} + h K_s K_A K_M \mathcal{E}$$
$$= J \frac{d^2 r}{dt^2} + (F + p a_t K_t K_A K_M) \frac{dr}{dt} \tag{4-80}$$

Again note that the open-loop proportional gain, which is the coefficient of $\mathcal{E}$, is the same as it was before. Refer to Eqs. (4-62) and (4-44). To simplify Eq. (4-80), introduce

$$Q_t \equiv p a_t K_t K_A K_M = \text{open-loop tachometer-rate gain} \tag{4-81}$$

As previously pointed out, this result is readily obtained by forming the product of the gain factors found in the loop we are concerned with, which here is the tachometer feedback loop. A check on the dimensions of Q_t indicates that it is analogous to F and accordingly provides a means of controlling the system damping. Rewriting Eq. (4-80), we have

$$J \frac{d^2\varepsilon}{dt^2} + (F + Q_t) \frac{d\varepsilon}{dt} + K\varepsilon = J \frac{d\omega_i}{dt} + (F + Q_t)\omega_i \qquad (4\text{-}82)$$

The system's characteristic equation is therefore

$$s^2 + \frac{F + Q_t}{J} s + \frac{K}{J} = 0 \qquad (4\text{-}83)$$

Comparison with Eq. (4-65) reveals that the presence of output-derivative control influences the transient response in precisely the same way as does error-rate damping. It follows then that the inclusion of the auxiliary loop does not change the order of the system but merely changes the effective damping coefficient. The damping ratio for the system of Fig. 4-22 is analogous to Eq. (4-68); thus

$$\zeta = \frac{F + Q_t}{2 \sqrt{KJ}} \qquad (4\text{-}84)$$

Of course, the expression for the natural frequency remains the same, viz., $\omega_n = \sqrt{K/J}$.

In so far as the mathematical description of the transient response is concerned, there is no difference in the effects which error-rate and output-derivative damping offer. This is not true, however, with regard to the magnitude of the actuating signal required to generate a commanded velocity. Setting the time derivatives equal to zero in Eq. (4-82) shows that the value of actuating signal at steady state is

$$\varepsilon_{ss} = \frac{F + Q_t}{K} \omega_i \qquad (4\text{-}85)$$

and a comparison with the result obtained by using error-rate damping makes it clear that for a given open-loop gain and commanded velocity the actuating signal must necessarily be greater. That this should be the situation is entirely reasonable when it is realized that in error-rate damping the damping action is derived from the transient state, whereas in output-derivative damping the source lies in the generation of the steady-state velocity. To illustrate this, assume that the gain factors of the system of Fig. 4-22 are such that, with the tachometer feedback loop removed, an actuating signal of 0.01 radian is needed to follow a command velocity of ω_i radians/sec. Expressed in volts, the actuating signal must have a value of 0.573 volt. If it is now assumed that the tachometer feedback loop is closed and steady state is reached corresponding to the command input of ω_i radian/sec, then since the tachometer generator will be rotating continuously it clearly introduces a voltage of $-v_t$ at the amplifier summing point. For purposes of illustration assume this value to be -1.0 volt. It follows therefore that, if the level of commanded output velocity is to be attained, the actuating signal must increase by a sufficient amount so that at steady state the effect of the -1.0 volt introduced by the tachometer generator is neutralized. Accordingly, the actuating signal expressed in volts must reach a new level of $+1.573$ volts, and this can happen only by an increase in the lack of correspondence between the input and output shaft positions.

The complete time solutions for the actuating signal and the output displacement corresponding to a step velocity input command for the case where there is negligible load torque and $0 \leq \zeta \leq 1$ are, respectively,

$$\varepsilon \frac{\omega_n}{\omega_i} = 2\zeta \left[1 - \frac{\epsilon^{-\zeta \omega_n t}}{2\zeta \sqrt{1 - \zeta^2}} \sin (\omega_d t + \phi_d) \right] \tag{4-86}$$

and

$$c = \frac{a}{h} \left[\omega_i t - \frac{2\zeta}{\omega_n} \omega_i \left(1 - \frac{\epsilon^{-\zeta \omega_n t}}{2\zeta \sqrt{1 - \zeta^2}} \sin (\omega_d t + \phi_d) \right) \right] \tag{4-87}$$

where

$$\phi_d = \tan^{-1} \frac{2\zeta \sqrt{1 - \zeta^2}}{2\zeta^2 - 1}$$

These results will be recognized as being equivalent to those represented by Eqs. (4-54) and (4-56). The difference of course lies in the values of the system parameters. As was the case with error-rate damping, the inclusion of tachometric feedback damping permits use of considerably greater open-loop gains with the attendant decrease in settling time. To better emphasize these distinctions, a comparison is presented in Table 4-2. Usually the values of K' and Q_t which are required to provide the

TABLE 4-2. COMPARISON OF A VISCOUS-DAMPED SYSTEM AND A VISCOUS- PLUS OUTPUT-RATE-DAMPED SYSTEM

Case 1†	Case 2‡	Comments§
$\varepsilon_{ss} = \dfrac{F}{K} \omega_i$ $\zeta = \dfrac{F}{2\sqrt{KJ}}$	$\varepsilon'_{ss} = \dfrac{F + Q_t}{K'} \omega_i$ $\zeta' = \dfrac{F + Q_t}{2\sqrt{K'J}}$	From these two expressions the value of K' and Q_t needed to provide the specified values of ε_{ss} and ζ may be determined
$\omega_n = \sqrt{\dfrac{K}{J}}$	$\omega'_n = \sqrt{\dfrac{K'}{J}}$	$\omega'_n > \omega_n$, hence faster settling
$\zeta \omega_n = \dfrac{F}{2J}$	$\zeta' \omega'_n = \dfrac{F + Q_t}{2J}$	The damping factor for case 2 is much greater, again indicating faster response

† Original viscous friction $= F$; open-loop gain $= K$; no output-rate damping.

‡ Original viscous friction $= F$; increased open-loop gain $= K'$; output-rate damping $= Q_t$.

§ Comparison is made on the basis of the same actuating signal and damping ratio for the same ω_i.

specified ε_{ss} and ζ are so large that considerable improvement in the transient behavior results. This is primarily due to the large damping factor that prevails. A typical response comparison is depicted in Fig. 4-23 along with the appropriate description.

The manner in which tachometric feedback asserts itself in controlling the transient response is most easily demonstrated by applying a step position input to the system of Fig. 4-22. Again assume a high proportional gain so that immediately upon application of the step input a large proportional developed torque exists, which in turn acts to quickly bring the output to the new steady-state level. However, in the process of doing so it simultaneously generates a large rate of change of output, which means that the tachometer generator inserts a corresponding signal opposing the proportional signal and thereby eliminates

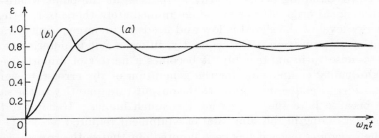

FIG. 4-23. Actuating-signal response to a velocity command. Curve (a), viscous damped system; curve (b), viscous- plus output-rate-damped system. Same damping ratio and steady-state error.

the tendency for an excessively oscillatory response. This discussion should also make clear why the sign of the tachometer output voltage must be correct. Certainly, greater overshoots and possible instability would result if the tachometer output were made to aid the proportional signal. Improper tachometer polarity reflects as a reversal in the sign of Q_t in Eq. (4-84), from which it then becomes obvious that the transient behavior deteriorates rather than improves.

Specification of the Output-rate Constant. Determination of the output-rate constant (tachometer-rate gain for the system of Fig. 4-22) which is required to provide a specific transient performance and minimum steady-state error follows from Eq. (4-81) once the basic design of the system has been established. Upon selection of a suitable servoamplifier and servomotor, the parameters K_A and K_M are essentially known. The output-rate-damping coefficient Q_t is computed as already outlined on the basis of meeting the performance specifications. Consequently, the value of output-rate constant must be

$$pa_t K_t = \frac{Q_t}{K_A K_M} \qquad (4\text{-}88)$$

The quantity p is the potentiometer setting, and so its magnitude lies between zero and one. The result of Eq. (4-88) provides the information by which the selection of a suitable tachometer generator and gear ratio can be made.

Error-rate vs. Output-rate Damping. On what basis does the designer make a choice leading to the preference of one method of damping over the other? Actually there are many factors which must be considered, among which are to be found such items as the specific make-up of the system, the availability of suitable components, the extent to which noise frequencies are present and the degree to which they are troublesome, the influence of nonlinearities in producing rate saturation, and the experience of the designer. Attention is confined here to just a few of the salient differences.

Error-rate damping is customarily introduced at the point where the actuating signal originates or the stage immediately thereafter. Hence the energy level of the signal is low and needs to undergo a considerable amount of amplification. Consequently, in order not to deteriorate the signal-to-noise ratio appreciably, it becomes a matter of importance to use high-quality components for the generation of the error-rate signal. This consideration does not apply to the output-rate quantity to the same degree because here the energy level is much higher. Generally, this reflects as a saving in the sum total of equipment required.

In the foregoing pages it has been pointed out that both error-rate and output-rate damping can be used to provide a definite damping ratio and a specified minimum steady-state error in position due to velocity input commands. Since the output-rate damping enters into the expression for the steady-state error, there must be a difference between the two and it lies in the required magnitude of the open-loop gain. This gain must necessarily be larger when output-rate damping is used, which in turn means a greater natural frequency for the system. For linear systems a high natural frequency can work to advantage or disadvantage depending upon the prevailing circumstances. One big advantage offered is the small settling time. On the other hand, if sufficient noise is present, then the larger natural frequency could very well be troublesome to the point where error-rate damping must be preferred as the means of meeting the performance specifications.

Throughout this discussion the implication has been that the system is capable of generating whatever rates are called for by the controller irrespective of the damping scheme used. For linear systems this is entirely valid. However, we must never lose sight of the fact that all practical systems have linearity limits. Accordingly, in those instances where error-rate or output-rate control is used, it is very important to check that system saturation does not prevent generation of the rates required to meet the specifications.

Example 4-2. The basic system of Example 4-1 is modified to include tachometric feedback damping in the manner indicated in Fig. 4-22.

(a) Compute the value of open-loop gain and output-rate damping required to give the same damping ratio of 0.7 and actuating signal of 0.00174 radian as found in part d of Example 4-1 for an input velocity of 0.1 radian/sec.

(b) Calculate the natural frequency of the system.

(c) Find the time solution for the output displacement, assuming linearity prevails. The solutions are as follows:

(a) Inserting the expression for $F + Q_t$ from Eq. (4-85) into Eq. (4-84) yields a single equation with the open-loop gain as the only unknown. Thus

$$\sqrt{K} = \frac{2\zeta \sqrt{J}}{\varepsilon_{ss}} \omega_i = \frac{2 \times 0.7 \sqrt{10^{-5}}}{0.00174} \times 0.1 = 0.254$$

Therefore $\qquad K = 0.0645$

Furthermore, the output-rate damping coefficient Q_t follows from Eq. (4-85),

$$F + Q_t = \frac{K\varepsilon_{ss}}{\omega_i} = \frac{0.0645 \times 0.00174}{0.1} = 11.2 \times 10^{-4}$$

Therefore $\qquad Q_t = 11.2 \times 10^{-4} - 1.5 \times 10^{-4} = 9.7 \times 10^{-4}$

Observe that the viscous damping is now only a small part of the total system damping. Note, too, that this value is considerably greater than was needed when error-rate damping was employed to meet the same specifications.

(b) The new value of the natural frequency is

$$\omega_n = \sqrt{\frac{0.0645}{10^{-5}}} = 80.2 \text{ radians/sec}$$

This value is exceptionally large and is $80.2/29.4 = 2.73$ times greater than the value corresponding to the case where error-rate damping is used. Such an excessive ω_n not only accentuates the noise components in the signal but also is unrealistic because of velocity saturation, which is almost certain to be present in the servomotor.

(c) To find the time solution of the output displacement merely requires calculating the new values of the damping factor $\zeta\omega_n$ and the damped frequency of oscillation. Thus

$$\zeta\omega_n = 0.7 \times 80.2 = 56.1 \text{ sec}^{-1}$$
$$\omega_d = 80.2 \sqrt{1 - (0.7)^2} = 57.1 \text{ radians/sec}$$

Hence

$$c(t) = 0.1t - 0.00174[1 - 2.03\epsilon^{-56.1t} \sin (57.1t + 150.5°)] \qquad \text{radians}$$

4-6. Second-order System with Integral Error Compensation. Velocity Input

A system is said to contain *integral compensation* when the generation of the output in some way depends upon the integral of the actuating signal. The inclusion of an integrating device in the direct transmission path of the system of Fig. 4-11 provides this kind of compensation. The block diagram for the modified system appears in Fig. 4-24. Since the signal applied to the output device, which in this case is the servomotor, consists of two components, viz., one originating from the proportional channel and another from the integral channel, it follows that the servomotor develops an output torque proportional to each component. Consequently the differential equation describing the behavior is

$$\varepsilon K_s K_A K_M + K_s B K_M \int \varepsilon \, dt = J \frac{d^2 c_M}{dt^2} + F \frac{d c_M}{dt} \qquad (4\text{-}89)$$

Introducing ε from Eq. (4-42) and replacing dr/dt by ω_i gives

$$J \frac{d^2\varepsilon}{dt^2} + F \frac{d\varepsilon}{dt} + h K_s K_A K_M \varepsilon + h K_s B K_M \int \varepsilon \, dt = J \frac{d\omega_i}{dt} + F\omega_i \qquad (4\text{-}90)$$

The open-loop proportional gain has the same value as in the foregoing systems. This is entirely expected since in each case the proportional loop consists of the same components. A glance at Eq. (4-90) further reveals the interesting fact that the integral term does not combine with

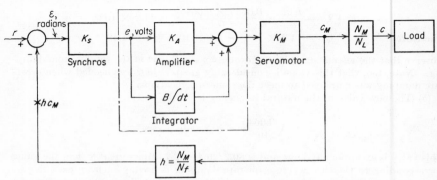

Fig. 4-24. A second-order system with integral compensation.

the viscous-friction term as was the case when error-rate and output-rate signals were introduced. Rather, the integral term stands alone in the differential equation, thereby manifesting its influence on system performance in a manner which differs basically from the previous compensation methods.

Let us call the gain factor associated with the integral term I. Then

$$I = h K_s B K_M \qquad (4\text{-}91)$$

as it applies to the system of Fig. 4-24. For other systems, of course, a different combination of gain factors identifies I, but the manner of establishing this value remains the same. Since B is expressed in $\sec^{-1}$, I has the units of torque/radian-sec. Rewriting Eq. (4-90), we have

$$J \frac{d^2\varepsilon}{dt^2} + F \frac{d\varepsilon}{dt} + K\varepsilon + I \int \varepsilon \, dt = J \frac{d\omega_i}{dt} + F\omega_i \qquad (4\text{-}92)$$

Differentiating then yields

$$J \frac{d^3\varepsilon}{dt^3} + F \frac{d^2\varepsilon}{dt^2} + K \frac{d\varepsilon}{dt} + I\varepsilon = J \frac{d^2\omega_i}{dt^2} + F \frac{d\omega_i}{dt} \qquad (4\text{-}93)$$

The form of the last equation makes it obvious that integral error compensation has changed the order of the system from second to third. Its inclusion therefore means that a third independent energy-storing element is present. This effect stands in sharp contrast to the influence which error rate or output rate exerts on the same basic proportional system. For the latter the effect is confined to altering the coefficient of the first derivative term, and for this reason it does not appear as an additional independent energy-storing element.

It follows from Eq. (4-93) that the system's characteristic equation is now a cubic, viz.,

$$s^3 + \frac{F}{J} s^2 + \frac{K}{J} s + \frac{I}{J} = 0 \qquad (4\text{-}94)$$

Finding the solution of this equation is more difficult and laborious than it is for the second-order system. The very fact that the system has an additional independent energy-storing element is reason enough to suspect that obtaining a satisfactory transient performance is more difficult. Furthermore, if standard time-domain procedures are used, it becomes considerably more difficult to design *directly* for a specific transient behavior. This is discussed in greater detail in the next section. A general form of the transient solution is not found here because of the complications involved. Also, because more direct and simpler procedures are available for accomplishing the same result, this aspect of the problem is delayed for consideration in a succeeding chapter.

Since it is apparent that integral error compensation does not show to advantage in controlling the behavior in the transient state, is there any advantage to be gained at all? The answer lies in the second part of the solution to Eq. (4-93), viz., the forced (or steady-state) solution. Setting the time derivatives equal to zero shows that

$$\varepsilon_{ss} \equiv 0 \qquad (4\text{-}95)$$

i.e., the value of the actuating signal required to generate the commanded output velocity is now reduced to zero. This indeed is a very significant contribution. In fact it is characteristic of integral error compensation that it permits either considerable reduction or elimination of steady-state errors. In this way a system can be made to meet very stringent accuracy requirements.

At first thought the result of Eq. (4-95) appears puzzling since effectively it says that the system of Fig. 4-24 is capable of generating a finite output velocity without an input signal. Clearly, this is an oversimplification of the situation. Returning for a moment to Eq. (4-89), we see that the motor developed torque consists of a component proportional to the magnitude of the error and another which depends upon the error as well as *time*. At steady state the right side of this equation is a constant, which means that a fixed torque of amount $F \, dc_M/dt$ is required to generate the output velocity. Therefore, as time increases, the integral component contributes more and more torque, but since only a fixed amount is needed, the actuating signal becomes increasingly smaller. In fact, if the integral gain factor I is made large enough, the actuating signal is reduced to zero in a relatively small period of time.

4-7. Difficulties of the Differential-equation Approach

Whenever the design of a feedback control system leads to a characteristic equation which is greater than second-order, the differential-equation method of analysis shows to disadvantage for several reasons. As already pointed out in the preceding section, one reason is that it involves

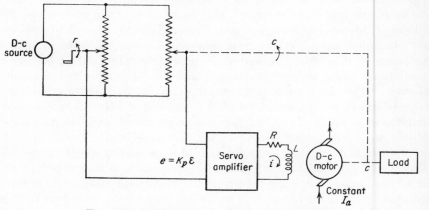

FIG. 4-25. A third-order feedback control system.

solving algebraic equations of orders higher than the second, which can readily become a long and tedious process. However, a more important reason, especially from the viewpoint of the designer, lies in the fact that it now becomes very difficult to specify system parameters *in a direct fashion* to yield a desired transient performance, as could be done with the second-order systems. As a matter of fact in such situations the designer is forced to resort to cut-and-try procedures before he can obtain a suitable response. And even when he succeeds in doing this, he often does not have the one which is optimum.

In order to illustrate this point more clearly, consider the system shown in Fig. 4-25. The servomotor in this case is a d-c type which is field-excited with constant armature current. We are considering the time delay associated with the inductance of the control field winding of the servomotor. Note, too, that for simplicity the gear ratio from the motor shaft to the load and from motor shaft to the feedback potentiometer are taken equal to unity. The three equations which describe the closed-loop system behavior are then

$$r - c = \varepsilon \tag{4-96}$$

$$K_p K_A \varepsilon = iR + L \frac{di}{dt} \tag{4-97}$$

and

$$K_f i = J \frac{d^2c}{dt^2} + F \frac{dc}{dt} \tag{4-98}$$

Equation (4-97) relates the output voltage of the amplifier to the sum of the voltage drops incurred in the control winding of the servomotor. Furthermore, R denotes the resistance in ohms and L the inductance in henrys of the control field winding, and i is the current in amperes which flows in this circuit. The left side of Eq. (4-98) denotes the developed motor torque expressed in terms of K_f, where K_f has the units of torque per unit field current. The right side of this equation represents the sum of the opposing torques, where J and F, of course, refer to the total quantities reflected to the motor shaft. Load torque is assumed equal to zero. Equations (4-97) and (4-98) may be rewritten as

$$K_p K_A \varepsilon = R \left(i + \tau_f \frac{di}{dt} \right) \tag{4-99}$$

where $\tau_f = \dfrac{L}{R}$ = time constant of control field winding $\qquad$ (4-100)

and

$$K_f i = F \left(\tau_m \frac{d^2c}{dt^2} + \frac{dc}{dt} \right) \tag{4-101}$$

where $\tau_m = \dfrac{J}{F}$ = mechanical motor time constant $\qquad$ (4-102)

Inserting the expression for ε from Eq. (4-99) into Eq. (4-96) yields

$$r = c + \varepsilon = c + \frac{R}{K_p K_A} \left(i + \tau_f \frac{di}{dt} \right) \tag{4-103}$$

Introducing i from Eq. (4-101) into the last equation and rearranging gives

$$r = c + \frac{RF}{K_p K_A K_f} \left[\tau_m \tau_f \frac{d^3c}{dt^3} + (\tau_m + \tau_f) \frac{d^2c}{dt^2} + \frac{dc}{dt} \right] \tag{4-104}$$

Now let

$$K = \frac{K_p K_A K_f}{RF} \tag{4-105}$$

Upon substitution into Eq. (4-104) there results the system differential equation

$$Kr = \tau_m \tau_f \frac{d^3c}{dt^3} + (\tau_m + \tau_f) \frac{d^2c}{dt^2} + \frac{dc}{dt} + Kc \tag{4-106}$$

from which it follows that the characteristic equation is

$$\tau_m \tau_f s^3 + (\tau_m + \tau_f) s^2 + s + K = 0 \qquad (4\text{-}107)$$

Examination of the last equation reveals two important conclusions. (1) It shows that the field-winding time constant has raised the system to that of third order. (2) Inspection of the coefficients of Eq. (4-107) makes it clear that the time constants τ_m and τ_f appear more often than once and in different combinations. Thus, for the foregoing system the coefficient of s^3 is the product of the two time constants, whereas the coefficient of s^2 involves these same quantities as a sum. Consequently, if the designer is interested in making a study of the effects of τ_m, τ_f, and K upon the dynamic behavior, it is apparent that this cannot be readily accomplished from a direct solution of Eq. (4-107). This is not to say that such procedures cannot be derived. They can be and have been derived for the third-order system. The resulting equations are considerably more complicated than for second-order systems. But more important than this is that for still higher-order systems the complexity of such results increases all the more, thereby negating the usefulness of such an approach as a design tool. The example of the third-order system has been used simply to underscore the nature of the difficulty involved. In summary, therefore, it can be said that, with the differential equation approach, it is not readily feasible to determine the immediate effect of changing a system parameter such as τ_f on the maximum overshoot, rise time, settling time, etc. In addition a good deal of labor is involved each time a new value is assigned to a particular parameter. Therefore the need for a more direct approach is clear.

The frequency-response approach for analyzing system behavior satisfies this need. Frequency-response techniques permit the study of time-domain behavior in such a manner that the effect of any parameter on the dynamic performance is made apparent almost at a glance. This feature is attributable primarily to two factors. The first is that the transient behavior of system components, as well as systems themselves, can be described in terms of transfer functions. The second is that information about the closed-loop transient response of the system can be derived in a simple and straightforward fashion from a study of the open-loop-system transfer function. The advantage which the latter representation offers is that each system parameter stands by itself, thus placing in evidence clearly the manner in which variation of the particular parameter influences over-all performance.

Unfortunately this ease of analysis and design is not obtained without a price. The cost is a sacrifice in accuracy. The performance is frequently identified in terms of appropriate figures of merit as they apply to the frequency domain rather than in terms of an exact time-domain solution.

SUGGESTED READING

Brown, G. S., and D. P. Campbell: "Principles of Servomechanisms," chap. 2, John Wiley & Sons, Inc., New York, 1948.

Lauer, H., R. Lesnick, and L. E. Matson: "Servomechanism Fundamentals," 2d ed., McGraw-Hill Book Company, Inc., New York, 1960.

Thaler, G. J.: "Elements of Servomechanism Theory," chaps. 2 and 3, McGraw-Hill Book Company, Inc., New York, 1955.

———— and R. G. Brown: "Servomechanism Analysis," 2d ed., chap. 4, McGraw-Hill Book Company, Inc., New York, 1960.

PROBLEMS

4-1. In the system shown in Fig. P4-1 the parameters are known as a result of experimental tests.

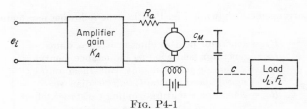

FIG. P4-1

K_T = motor torque constant K_n = back-emf constant
    = 0.0234 lb-ft/amp   = 0.2 volt/rev/sec
K_A = amplifier gain = 0.15 volt/volt
J_M = motor armature inertia = 1.0×10^{-6} slug-ft^2
J_L = load inertia = 225×10^{-6} slug-ft^2
F_L = load viscous-friction coefficient = 5.68×10^{-4} lb-ft/radian/sec
a = number of teeth on motor shaft gear to number of teeth on load shaft gear = $\frac{1}{15}$
R_a = motor armature resistance = 0.2 ohm

Write the differential equation of the system relating c_M to the input voltage, and solve for c_M and ω_M for a unit-step voltage applied to the input.

4-2. Measurements conducted on a servomechanism show the error response to be

$$\frac{\varepsilon}{r_0} = 1.66\epsilon^{-8t} \sin (6t + 37°)$$

when the input is given a sudden displacement r_0.

(a) Determine the natural frequency, the damping ratio, and the damped angular frequency of the system.

(b) The inertia of the output member is known to be 0.01 lb-ft sec^2, and the viscous coefficient is 0.16 lb-ft/radian/sec. What is the loop gain K?

(c) How much can the loop gain be increased if the damping ratio is to be not less than 0.4?

4-3. For the system of Fig. P4-3 assume that the reference and feedback tachometer are identical.

(a) Draw the block diagram of the system, identifying each component.

(b) Write the differential equation of the system, and solve for the velocity error ω_e when the reference motor is given a sudden constant angular velocity ω_i starting from standstill.

(c) Can any setting of the amplifier gain cause sustained oscillation of the system? Explain.

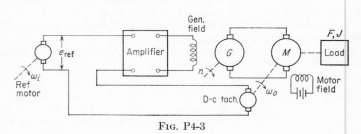

FIG. P4-3

4-4. The arrangement shown is Fig. P4-4 has the following parameters:

R_f = generator field-winding resistance, ohms
L_f = generator field-winding inductance, henrys
K_G = generator gain constant, volts/field amp
K_n = motor speed constant, volts/radian/sec
R_G = generator armature-winding resistance, ohms
R_M = motor armature-winding resistance, ohms
K_T = motor torque constant, lb-ft/armature amp
J_L = load moment of inertia, slug-ft^2
F_L = load viscous friction, lb-ft/radian/sec
a = motor-to-load gear ratio

Neglect motor inertia as well as the inductance of the generator and motor armatures.

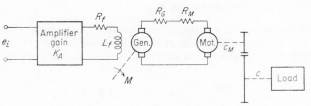

FIG. P4-4

(a) Using the letter symbols, determine the differential equation of the motor for a step input voltage e_i.

(b) Write the characteristic equation.

(c) If the arrangement shown is to be part of a velocity feedback control system operating without velocity error, indicate the changes required to accomplish this. Be specific.

4-5. The block diagram of a servomechanism is given in Fig. P4-5. The system parameters are

$K_s = 60$ volts/radian $K_A = 20$ volts/volt $K_M = 30 \times 10^{-6}$ lb-ft/volt
$J = 10 \times 10^{-6}$ slug-ft² $F = 161 \times 10^{-6}$ lb-ft/radian/sec

(a) Find the damping ratio.

(b) Compute the lack of correspondence between the input and feedback shaft positions for an input velocity of 2 radians/sec at steady state.

(c) The system specifications are revised so that they call for a steady-state actuating signal not exceeding 1° when the command velocity is 2 radians/sec. The damping ratio is to remain the same as in part a. To accomplish this, the amplifier is redesigned to yield an output given by $K_A + A\,d/dt$, and a value of 1.5 is assigned to A. Determine whether or not the specifications on ζ are met, assuming the specification on the steady-state actuating signal is satisfied.

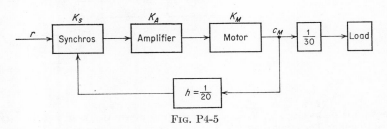

Fig. P4-5

(d) If tachometric feedback is used in place of error-rate damping in order to meet the specifications of part c, compute the value of open-loop proportional gain needed.

4-6. The fixed configuration of a 400-cps aircraft feedback control system consists of a synchro error detector, an amplifier, a 400-cps servomotor, and a geared load. The parameters are as follows:

$K_s =$ synchro constant $= 25$ volts/radian $h = a = \frac{1}{30}$
$K_M =$ motor torque constant $= 40 \times 10^{-6}$ lb-ft/volt
$F_M =$ motor viscous friction $= 9 \times 10^{-6}$ lb-ft/radian/sec
$F_L =$ load viscous friction $= 45 \times 10^{-4}$ lb-ft/radian/sec
$J_M =$ negligible $J_L =$ load inertia $= 9 \times 10^{-4}$ slug-ft² $K_A = 3$ volts/volt

(a) When the system is used as described above, compute the value of the steady-state velocity error as well as the steady-state actuating signal (ε in radians) for a command velocity of 1 radian/sec.

(b) Calculate the damping ratio for the condition of part a. What specific information does this quantity convey about the system's dynamic performance?

(c) It is desirable to reduce the magnitude of the steady-state actuating signal to 0.035 radian while maintaining ζ fixed. Compute the amount of error-rate damping to accomplish this.

(d) Repeat part c, using output-rate damping in place of error-rate damping.

(e) Assuming the settling time is correctly described by four times the system time constant, determine the settling time for both parts c and d.

(f) If noise frequencies exceeding 3 cps are to be attenuated even at the expense of an increased settling time, will either or both modified systems of parts c and d provide this? Explain.

4-7. In the proportional servo shown in Fig. P4-7 the synchros and gears have negligible inertia and friction. The feedback loop is opened by removing the gear from the control-transmitter shaft. The load shaft is then held fixed, and a 1.0-radian displacement is introduced between the two synchro shafts (assume linear synchros). The load shaft is next suddenly released and its rotation observed. It attains a steady speed of 20 radians/sec and reaches 63.2 per cent of this value in 0.1 sec (time measured from instant of release).

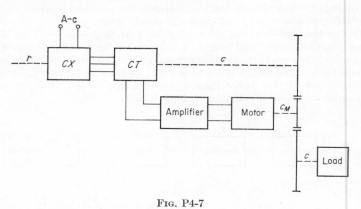

FIG. P4-7

The loop is then closed by replacing the control-transmitter gear and the servo is allowed to null. The input shaft is next given a step displacement (r). Compute the time required for the output variable (c) to reach within 2 per cent of its new steady-state value. (*Note:* Do not use four times the time constant in this problem.)

4-8. A servomechanism has the block diagram shown in Fig. P4-8. It makes use of both error-rate damping and tachometric feedback damping. The error detector

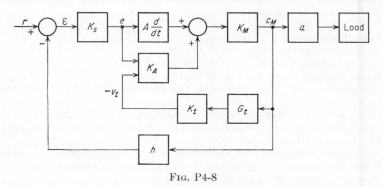

FIG. P4-8

is a synchro-transmitter–control-transformer combination. The following constants apply for the system:

$$J = 11 \times 10^{-6} \text{ slug-ft}^2 = \text{equivalent inertia at motor shaft}$$
$$F_M = 10 \times 10^{-6} \text{ lb-ft/radian/sec} = \text{motor viscous friction}$$
$$F_L = 0 \text{ (i.e., load viscous friction reduced to zero)}$$
$$A = 1.2 \text{ volts/volt/sec} \qquad K_A = 20$$

$K_M = 30 \times 10^{-6}$ lb-ft/volt $K_S = 1$ volt/deg = synchro constant

$K_t = 0.191$ volt/radian/sec $h = \frac{1}{20}$ = feedback gear ratio

G_t = tachometer gear ratio $a = \frac{1}{30}$ = load gear ratio

(a) Determine the characteristic equation for this system.

(b) Assuming that the system has the foregoing specified constants, find the value of G_t in order that the damping ratio be 0.7.

(c) Calculate the steady-state actuating signal when the input is a velocity of 10 radians/sec. Assume the conditions of part b prevailing.

(d) If the steady-state position lag error is to be no more than 6.5° for an input velocity of 10 radians/sec, what changes would you recommend, assuming that $\zeta = 0.7$ is to be maintained. Calculate the new value of parameter(s) you recommend be employed.

4-9. (a) What advantage results from representing the dynamic response of second-order systems in nondimensional form? Explain.

(b) The natural frequency of a second-order system is said to be a figure of merit which is indicative of the settling time of the servo. Explain.

4-10. (a) Explain why a feedback control system includes the following two features in its design: negative feedback and sign sensitivity.

(b) A servomechanism is represented by the following differential equation:

$$\frac{d^2 c_M}{dt^2} + 6.4 \frac{dc_M}{dt} = 160 \, \varepsilon$$

where $\varepsilon = r - 0.4 c_M$

c_M = motor output shaft position

Find the value of the damping ratio. What information does this convey about the transient performance?

4-11. Find the solution for the actuating signal for the system of Fig. P4-7 when it is subjected to a step load disturbance of magnitude T_0. Assume the system to be initially at null with a zero load torque and that $\zeta < 1$.

4-12. Given the servomechanism shown in Fig. P4-12a. The motor rotates an inertial load through a gear reduction of a, as shown. The following information is

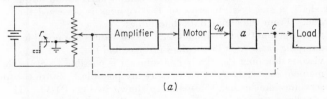

(a)

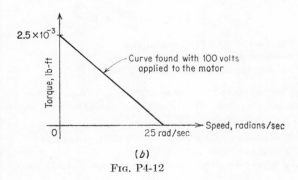

(b)

Fig. P4-12

also available for the system:

> Moment of inertia of load $= 0.05$ slug-ft^2
> Moment of inertia of motor $= 2 \times 10^{-5}$ slug-ft^2
> Load viscous friction negligible
> Error voltage $= a_1(r - c)$ where $a_1 = 20$ volts/radian
> Amplifier gain $= a_2 = 20$ volts/volt
> Gear ratio $= a = \frac{1}{100}$

The speed-torque characteristic of the motor is depicted in Fig. P4-12b (assume that intercepts on axes are proportional to applied voltage). Determine the differential equation for the system.

4-13. A servomechanism consists of a motor which produces a torque proportional to the error, an output load having inertia and viscous damping, and a position-sensitive error-measuring means. The system is pictured in Fig. P4-13a. The motor

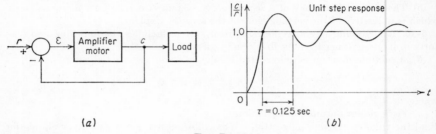

(a)   (b)

FIG. P4-13

torque $T = K\varepsilon$. The response of the system to a unit-step input is sketched in Fig. P4-13b. Only the time interval τ is known accurately.

When a constant velocity input of 1 radian/sec is put into the system, a position lag error of $1/8.333\pi$ radians is observed.

When the input shaft is held fixed so that it cannot move and a torque is applied to the output shaft, a steady-state error of $1/\pi^2$ radians is observed for each ft-lb of applied torque. From the above data determine:

    (a) The undamped natural frequency ω_n. (Two values are possible.)
    (b) The damping ratio ζ. (Two values are possible.)
    (c) The viscous damping F. (Only one solution is possible.) State the units.
    (d) The moment of inertia J. (Two values are possible.) State the units.

4-14. A servomechanism has the make-up shown in Fig. P4-14. The two-phase servomotor develops a torque in accordance with the equation

$$T_d = -D\frac{dc_M}{dt} + Be_o$$

where $D =$ constant $= 10^{-5}$ lb-ft/radian/sec
      $B =$ constant $= 1.5 \times 10^{-4}$ lb-ft/volt
      $e_o =$ voltage applied to motor control field

For the amplifier the output voltage is given by $e_o = K_A e_i + A\, de_i/dt$. The values of K_A and A are not specified. However, other constants of the system are:

> $J =$ load inertia $= 2.5 \times 10^{-5}$ slug-ft^2
> $F =$ load viscous friction $= 0.01$ lb-ft/radian/sec
> $a =$ gear ratio $= \frac{1}{40}$
> $K_p =$ potentiometer transducer constant $= 1.615$ volts/radian

(a) Determine the differential equation of the system relative to the motor shaft. The coefficients of the equations are to be in terms of the specified *letter* symbols.

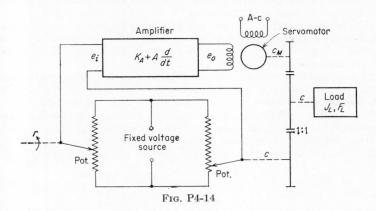

FIG. P4-14

(b) Using the numerical values of the system constants, calculate values of the gain K_A and error-rate damping coefficient A such that the system will have a steady-state position lag error of 0.01 radian for a velocity input of $r = \omega_i t$, where $\omega_i = 6$ radians/sec, and such that the servo will also be critically damped.

4-15. In the servo system shown in Fig. P4-15 the total friction coefficient F_1 measured at the motor shaft is 50×10^{-6} lb-ft/radian/sec. The damping ratio ζ is equal to 0.25. The moment of inertia J of the motor is 1×10^{-6} slug-ft² measured

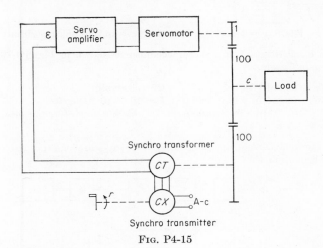

FIG. P4-15

at the motor shaft. The motor shaft is connected to the load through a reduction gear of 100:1 step-down ratio. The motor is controlled by the error voltage through an amplifier. The motor develops a torque T of 0.02 lb-ft when a voltage of 100 volts is applied to its terminals. The motor torque is proportional to the applied voltage, and the differential device produces a voltage of 1 volt/deg error voltage.

(a) Determine the amplifier gain.

(b) Compute the natural frequency ω_n and the damped frequency ω_d of the system.

(c) Calculate the value of the actuating signal expressed in radians when the input member is driven at a constant speed ω_i of 20 rpm.

(d) Calculate the steady-state error for a step input displacement of 1 radian.

4-16. Plot the locus of the roots $s_{1,2}$, as given in Eq. (4-19), in the complex plane as ζ varies from zero to infinity. Assume that ζ is varied by letting F go from zero to infinity. Consider ω_n to be constant.

4-17. Determine the complete response of the position servomechanism for $r(t) = 0$ and a load disturbance $T_L' = tu(t)$.

4-18. Refer to Fig. P4-18. For the amplifier $i_p = K_1 e_a$; for the motor $T = K_2 i_p$; for the generator $e_g = K_3 \, dc/dt$; for the potentiometers $\varepsilon_1 = K_4(r - c)$. Consider the motor load to be a moment of inertia J plus a fixed load T_L.

(a) Write the differential equation for the system.

(b) If r is held fixed, what is the value of c per unit of applied external torque T_L?

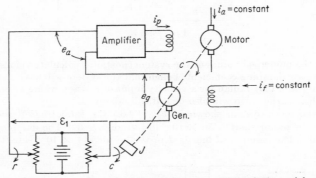

Fig. P4-18. r = input shaft position; c = output shaft position.

4-19. The block diagram of a servomechanism is shown in Fig. P4-19 with the appropriate gain factors.

$$K_s = 60 \text{ volts/radian} \qquad K_A = 20 \text{ volts/volt}$$
$$K_M = 30 \times 10^{-6} \text{ lb-ft/volt} \qquad J = 10 \times 10^{-6} \text{ slug-ft}^2$$
$$F = 161 \times 10^{-6} \text{ lb-ft/radian/sec} \qquad K_t = 0.25 \text{ volt/radian/sec}$$
$$a_t = 1.0 \qquad a = \tfrac{1}{30} \qquad h = \tfrac{1}{20}$$

(a) With the feedback loop open calculate the steady-state load speed corresponding to an input displacement of 1°.

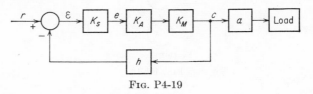

Fig. P4-19

(b) Find the value of the system damping ratio.

(c) Determine the amount of the total error-rate damping needed to make the damping ratio 0.7 while meeting the specification that the steady-state error as seen at the synchros is not to exceed 2° for an input velocity of 2 radians/sec.

(d) Compute the natural frequency of the system.

4-20. Tachometric damping is to be introduced into the system of Prob. 4-19, having the values listed there.

(a) Find the value of proportional open-loop gain required to make the damping ratio 0.7 while meeting the specification that the steady-state error as seen at the synchros is not to exceed 2° for an input velocity of 2 radians/sec.

(b) Calculate the total tachometric damping required to meet these specifications.

(c) Comparing the performance using error-rate damping as found in Prob. 4-19 with that of tachometric damping, which has the smaller settling time? Explain.

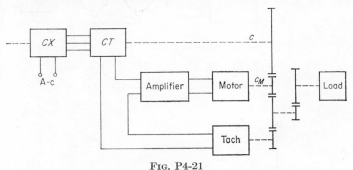

Fig. P4-21

4-21. The schematic diagram for a servomechanism using synchros as the error detector is shown in Fig. P4-21. The following information is available for this system:

Synchro constant: 1 volt/deg
Amplifier gain: 20 volts/volt
Motor torque constant: 30×10^{-6} lb-ft/volt
Effective motor inertia at motor shaft: 11×10^{-6} slug-ft^2
Effective motor viscous friction at motor shaft: 45×10^{-6} lb-ft/radian/sec
Tachometer constant: 0.2 volt/radian/sec
Gear ratio from motor shaft to load: 1 to 30 reduction
Gear ratio from motor shaft to tachometer: 1 to 1
Gear ratio from motor shaft to synchro: 1 to 60 reduction

(a) Find the frequency of oscillation of the motor output shaft corresponding to a step input disturbance, assuming that the tachometer is disconnected.

(b) Determine the value of the damping ratio when the tachometer is included as part of the system.

(c) State the change you would recommend in order that the damping ratio for the system of part b will be 0.5. Calculate the new value of this quantity, and give the advantage this method has over any other method for obtaining the required damping ratio.

(d) The tachometer is removed, and the amplifier is replaced by another which has the output voltage characteristic given by $e_o = A e_i + B \int e_i \, dt$. The output of the servo is operated at a velocity of ω_o radians/sec. Write the differential equation of the system, and comment about the steady-state error.

4-22. The system shown in Fig. P4-22 is used to control the speed of a heavy load. The system constants are

$$\text{Amplifier} - K_A = 10 \text{ field amp/volt}$$
$$\text{Generator} - K_G = 100 \text{ volts/field amp}$$
$$\text{Motor} - K_M = 0.5 \text{ lb-ft/volt}$$

The speed-torque curve for the motor is shown in Fig. P4-22b. Both the reference d-c magneto tachometer and the feedback tachometer are identical and have a constant of 0.01 volt/rpm.

(a) Find the speed at which the reference motor must turn (in rpm) in order that at no load the output speed of the controlled motor be 600 rpm.

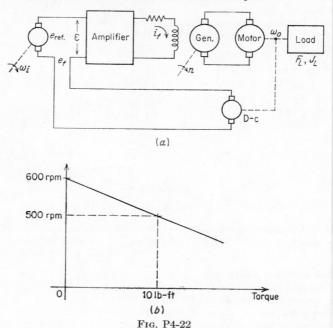

(a)

(b)

Fig. P4-22

(b) Determine the change in output speed which results when the load torque suddenly increases from zero to 12 lb-ft.

(c) If the system were operated open-loop (i.e., with the feedback tachometer removed), calculate the increase in reference tachometer voltage needed to restore the speed to 600 rpm after the load increase.

4-23. Assume that the error-detector portion of the system shown in Prob. 4-22 has been changed in such a way that now the controller output torque is proportional to position displacement error rather than velocity error. Assume $K_p = 1$ v/rad.

(a) Write the differential equation describing the behavior of the system.

(b) Compute the frequency (in radians/sec) at which the output will oscillate about its new value after a sudden change in requirement. The value of J is 5.0 lb-ft/sec².

(c) What recommendations could you make to improve the transient performance? Why?

4-24. For the system described by Eq. (4-9), determine the value of d^2c_M/dt^2 at $t = 0^+$, assuming a step input command of $r_o = 1$ and no load torque.

III | Frequency-domain Approach

5 | Frequency-response Analysis

The frequency-response method for the study of feedback control systems is one of the oldest and most useful tools available to the engineer. In general, it may be described as the study of system behavior with pure sinusoidal inputs. It is always assumed that the sinusoidal input has been applied for a long time so that the source-free response has decayed and the so-called sinusoidal steady-state condition has been reached. As was pointed out in Chap. 2, if the input to a linear system is sinusoidal, then the driven response throughout the system must be sinusoidal also and of the same frequency, differing only in amplitude and phase. The frequency-response approach consists in the study of the amplitude and phase angle of the response of a component or a system as a function of the sinusoidal frequency. Before proceeding to a discussion of frequency response it is worthwhile to review briefly why this method is of such practical importance. There are several major reasons.

First and foremost there is a definite correlation between the sinusoidal steady-state system response and all other modes of behavior. This relationship plays a major role in our considerations, but unfortunately it is not a simple one mathematically. However, qualitatively some useful and well-known examples may be cited. There is a relationship between a system's initial response to a sudden input (such as a step) and the highest sinusoidal frequency to which it will respond with any significant magnitude. There is also a relationship between the lowest frequency to which it will respond and the long-time or steady-state behavior. These ideas really follow from the initial- and final-value theorems of the Laplace transform. Another familiar example is the relationship between a resonant peak in the frequency domain and the damped sinusoidal frequency of the source-free response. At low values of damping the resonant frequency and the damped sinusoidal frequency are very close to each other. More is said about this later on, but for the

157

present it is sufficient to point out that relationships between the time and the frequency domains form the basis of most design procedures and criteria. A common procedure is to interpret desired time-domain behavior in terms of frequency-response characteristics. Design is usually carried out in the frequency domain, and afterward the frequency response is checked and translated back into the time domain. Thus there is a constant interplay of characteristics between the two domains, and the designer finds it advantageous to work in both.

Another important feature of the frequency-response approach is that it can be measured conveniently. Sine-wave generators and various types of measuring instruments and techniques are available for use in the laboratory and field. Thus theoretical results and characteristics, for both components and systems, can be calculated and measured. The mathematics of sinusoidal analysis is well known to most engineers, and it is a practical and useful tool. In this chapter we are concerned primarily with the mathematical techniques of the frequency-response approach so as to make it useful for both system analysis and synthesis.

5-1. The Sinusoidal Steady-state Transfer Function. Correlation with the Time Domain

In Secs. 2-9 to 2-11 the steady-state, or driven, response of a linear system to an exponential driving function was considered in detail. Let us now briefly review these results with particular attention to sinusoidal steady-state sources. It is recommended that the reader reread these sections in Chap. 2 if necessary.

If we start with a linear differential equation of the form

$$B_0 c + B_1 \frac{dc}{dt} + B_2 \frac{d^2 c}{dt^2} + \cdots + B_n \frac{d^n c}{dt^n} = A_0 r(t) + A_1 \frac{dr(t)}{dt}$$
$$+ A_2 \frac{d^2 r(t)}{dt^2} + \cdots + A_m \frac{d^m r(t)}{dt^m} \quad (5\text{-}1)$$

the steady-state solution to a driving function of the type $r(t) = \bar{R} \epsilon^{s_g t}$ (where in general $\bar{R}$ is a complex constant and $s_g = \sigma_g + j\omega_g$) is given by $c(t) = \bar{C} \epsilon^{s_g t}$, where

$$\frac{\bar{C}}{\bar{R}}(s_g) = \frac{A_0 + A_1 s_g + A_2 s_g^2 + \cdots + A_m s_g^m}{B_0 + B_1 s_g + B_2 s_g^2 + \cdots + B_n s_g^n} = \frac{A(s_g)}{B(s_g)} \quad (5\text{-}2)$$

Equation (5-2) is the transfer function of the system at the complex frequency $s = s_g$. It is seen to be identical to the result obtained by taking the Laplace transform of Eq. (5-1) for zero initial conditions, formulating the ratio $C(s)/R(s)$, and letting $s = s_g$. Also, as indicated in Chap. 3, we can expect in practical systems that $n \geq m$.

When the driving function is sinusoidal, then $r(t)$ is usually written as either the real or the imaginary part of an exponential source, $s_g = j\omega_g$, where ω_g is the radian frequency of the source.

Taking the real or the imaginary part of a system's response to an exponential driving function can be delayed to the very end of the problem solution. Thus for the sinusoidal steady state the transfer function of Eq. (5-2) becomes

$$\frac{\overline{C}}{\overline{R}}(j\omega_g) = \frac{\overline{C}}{\overline{R}}(s)\Big|_{s=j\omega_g} = \frac{A_0 + A_1 s + A_2 s^2 + \cdots + A_m s^m}{B_0 + B_1 s + B_2 s^2 + \cdots + B_n s^n}\Big|_{s=j\omega_g} \quad (5\text{-}3)$$

Equation (5-3) can also be written in factored form, in general, as follows:

$$\frac{\overline{C}}{\overline{R}}(j\omega_g) = \frac{\overline{C}}{\overline{R}}(s)\Big|_{s=j\omega_g}$$
$$= \frac{K'(s + 1/\tau_a) \cdots (s^2 + 2\zeta_b \omega_{nb} s + \omega_{nb}{}^2) \cdots}{s^N(s + 1/\tau_1) \cdots (s^2 + 2\zeta_2 \omega_{n2} s + \omega_{n2}{}^2) \cdots}\Big|_{s=j\omega_g} \quad (5\text{-}4)$$

where the K' is a constant and the numerator and denominator polynomials are factored into linear and quadratic factors. Thus the roots of the equation $A(s) = 0$ occur at $s = -1/\tau_a, \ldots, s = -\zeta_b \omega_{nb} \pm j\omega_{nb}\sqrt{1 - \zeta_b{}^2}$, where $\zeta_b \leq 1$; these roots are the zeros of the transfer function.

The roots of the equation $B(s) = 0$ yield the values of s which make $\frac{\overline{C}}{\overline{R}}(s) \to \infty$, and are referred to as the poles of the transfer function. They occur at $s = 0$ (of multiplicity N), $s = -1/\tau_1, \ldots, s = -\zeta_2 \omega_{n2} \pm j\omega_{n2}\sqrt{1 - \zeta_2{}^2}$, where $\zeta_2 \leq 1$.

When $s_g = j\omega_g$ is substituted into Eq. (5-4), the result is a complex number whose value can be represented graphically as shown in Fig. 5-1. Thus the term $j\omega_g + 1/\tau_a$ is represented by the phasor $\overline{AG}$. A quadratic term is represented by the product of two phasors as follows:

$$(s^2 + 2\zeta_b \omega_{nb} s + \omega_{nb}{}^2)\Big|_{s=j\omega_g} = (s + \zeta_b \omega_{nb} + j\omega_{nb}\sqrt{1 - \zeta_b{}^2})$$
$$(s + \zeta_b \omega_{nb} - j\omega_{nb}\sqrt{1 - \zeta_b{}^2})\Big|_{s=j\omega_g}$$
$$= (\overline{FG})(\overline{EG})$$

In view of the above, Eq. (5-4) can be expressed as

$$\frac{\overline{C}}{\overline{R}}(j\omega_g) = \frac{K'(\overline{AG})(\overline{FG})(\overline{EG})}{(\overline{HG})^N(\overline{BG})(\overline{DG})(\overline{CG})} \quad (5\text{-}5)$$

Since $\overline{C}/\overline{R}$ is a complex number, we may express it also in polar form as

$$\frac{\overline{C}}{\overline{R}}(j\omega_g) = \overline{T}(j\omega_g) = T(\omega_g)\epsilon^{j\phi(\omega_g)} = T(\omega_g)\underline{/\phi(\omega_g)} \qquad (5\text{-}6)$$

Thus we obtain from Eqs. (5-5) and (5-6)

$$\left|\frac{\overline{C}}{\overline{R}}\right| = T(\omega_g) = \frac{K'|\overline{AG}|\ |\overline{FG}|\ |\overline{EG}|}{|\overline{HG}|^N|\overline{BG}|\ |\overline{DG}|\ |\overline{CG}|} \qquad (5\text{-}7a)$$

and $\qquad \phi(\omega_g) = (\theta_a + \theta_b + \theta_c) - (90N° + \theta_1 + \theta_2 + \theta_3) \qquad (5\text{-}7b)$

If the frequency of the source is now considered as the variable, the behavior of $\overline{T}(j\omega_g)$ can be determined graphically by considering the

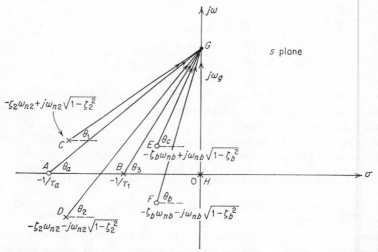

Fig. 5-1. Graphical evaluation of a sinusoidal steady-state transfer function in the s plane.

effects on Eqs. (5-7a) and (5-7b) of moving the point G along the $j\omega$ axis. Under these conditions it is no longer necessary to write the frequency of the source as $j\omega_g$, but it can be denoted simply by the expression $j\omega$, where the absence of the subscript indicates that the frequency can assume any value along the imaginary axis.

In order to make the preceding technique clearer and to illustrate the correlation between the sinusoidal frequency response and the time-domain response, let us consider two simple examples.

A First-order System. Consider the RL circuit of Fig. 5-2a, where e_i represents an input, or source, voltage and e_o is the output voltage. We are concerned with the behavior of this network from input to output.

The governing equations are

$$e_i = Ri + L\frac{di}{dt} \quad (5\text{-}8a)$$

$$e_o = Ri \quad (5\text{-}8b)$$

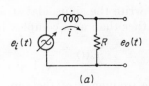

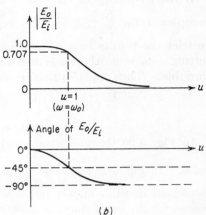

Let us consider the steady-state response of this network when e_i is a sinusoidal function:

$$e_i = E_i \sin \omega t = E_i \, \text{Im} \, (\epsilon^{j\omega t}) \quad (5\text{-}9)$$

Under these conditions Eqs. (5-8a) and (5-8b) become

$$E_i = (R + j\omega L)I \quad (5\text{-}10a)$$
$$E_o = RI \quad (5\text{-}10b)$$

where E_o and I are complex numbers representing the magnitude and phase of the output voltage and the loop current, respectively, with E_i taken as the reference phasor. Taking the ratio of Eqs. (5-10b) and (5-10a) yields the sinusoidal steady-state transfer function we are seeking. Thus

$$\frac{E_o}{E_i}(j\omega) = \frac{R}{R + j\omega L} = \frac{1}{1 + j\omega(L/R)}$$

$$= \frac{1}{1 + j\omega\tau} = \frac{1/\tau}{1/\tau + j\omega} \quad (5\text{-}11)$$

where $L/R = \tau$. τ of course is the time constant of the network and, as is demonstrated shortly, is directly involved in the network's transient response.

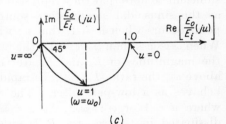

Fig. 5-2. Frequency-response characteristics for the transfer function of a simple RL circuit. (a) Simple RL circuit; (b) magnitude and phase angle of $\frac{E_0}{E_i}(ju)$ vs. u; (c) polar plot of $\frac{E_0}{E_i}(ju)$ with u as a parameter.

If we let $\omega_0 = 1/\tau$, Eq. (5-11) can be rewritten as

$$\frac{E_o}{E_i}(j\omega) = \frac{1}{1 + j(\omega/\omega_0)} = \frac{1}{\sqrt{1 + (\omega/\omega_0)^2}} \Big/ -\tan^{-1}\frac{\omega}{\omega_0} \quad (5\text{-}12)$$

This result gives the ratio of the output to the input voltage expressed as a complex number in terms of the network parameters and the frequency of the source. It is important to note that the network parameters appear in the term ω_0, which has the dimensions of radians/sec and is equal to the reciprocal of the network's time constant. From Eq. (5-12) we can write the sinusoidal steady-state output voltage as a function of time rather than as a complex number.　Thus

$$e_o(t) = \frac{E_i}{\sqrt{1 + (\omega/\omega_0)^2}} \sin\left(\omega t - \tan^{-1}\frac{\omega}{\omega_0}\right) \tag{5-13}$$

If the frequency of the source voltage is varied, the behavior of the complex ratio $\frac{E_o}{E_i}(j\omega)$ can be represented graphically.　Rather than restrict the results to a specific value of ω_0, they can be generalized by letting $\omega/\omega_0 = u$, where u is now a nondimensional, normalized frequency variable.　Thus Eq. (5-12) is rewritten as follows:

$$\frac{E_o}{E_i}(ju) = \frac{1}{1 + ju} = \frac{1}{\sqrt{1 + u^2}} \underline{/-\tan^{-1} u} \tag{5-14}$$

In Fig. 5-2b the magnitude and phase angle of $\frac{E_o}{E_i}(ju)$ are sketched vs. u.　In Fig. 5-2c the locus of the tip of the phasor representing $\frac{E_o}{E_i}(ju)$ is plotted in the complex plane with u as a variable parameter.　The reason for the exact shape of these curves is discussed presently; now it is sufficient to note that they represent the behavior of the transfer function as the sinusoidal steady-state source frequency is varied.　A critical point occurs when $u = 1$, that is, when the source frequency equals ω_0. When ω is less than $\omega_0(u < 1)$, the ratio $|E_o/E_i|$ is greater than 0.707 and the magnitudes of E_o and E_i are close to each other.　At frequencies above ω_0, the ratio $|E_o/E_i|$ falls rapidly toward zero.　Thus the network behaves as a low-pass filter.　The critical, or cutoff, frequency occurs where $u = 1$ or $\omega = \omega_0$.　At $\omega = \omega_0$, $|E_o| = 0.707|E_i|$, and the power dissipated in the resistor R is given by $E_o{}^2/R = \frac{1}{2}(E_i{}^2/R)$, which is exactly one-half of maximum power which can be developed across R (which occurs at direct current when $\omega = 0$).　Thus the frequency ω_0 is also called the *half-power frequency*.

The fact that the cutoff frequency is directly related to the network's time constant can be demonstrated by considering the transient behavior of the output voltage.　From Eqs. (5-8a) and (5-8b) we can write the differential equation relating e_o to e_i.　Thus

$$e_o + \frac{L}{R}\frac{de_o}{dt} = e_i$$

or

$$e_o + \tau\frac{de_o}{dt} = e_i \tag{5-15}$$

The characteristic equation is $1 + s\tau = 0$, so that the source-free response is given by

$$e_o = k\epsilon^{-t/\tau}$$

where k is an arbitrary constant to be determined from the initial conditions. Thus we have shown that the time constant of the transient response is given by $\tau = L/R = 1/\omega_0$.

Another important correlation between the time and the frequency domains may be illustrated by considering the network response when the source voltage is any Laplace-transformable input function applied at $t = 0$ with zero initial conditions in the network. Let $\mathcal{L} e_i(t) = E_i(s)$. Taking the Laplace transform of Eq. (5-15) yields the following simple result relating the Laplace transform of the output to the input:

$$\frac{E_o}{E_i}(s) = \frac{1}{1 + s\tau} = \frac{1}{1 + s/\omega_0} = \frac{1/\tau}{s + 1/\tau} \qquad (5\text{-}16)$$

Equation (5-16) is recognized as being identical to Eq. (5-11) with $j\omega$ replaced by s. Thus we see that the sinusoidal steady-state transfer function $\frac{E_o}{E_i}(j\omega)$ is the same as the ratio $\frac{E_o}{E_i}(s)$, with the variable s replaced by $j\omega$. Equating the denominator of Eq. (5-16) to zero yields the characteristic equation of the network.

The transfer function of Eq. (5-16) has a single pole located at

$$s = -\omega_0 = -\frac{1}{\tau}$$

Thus the sinusoidal steady-state behavior of Eq. (5-11) or (5-12) can be determined using the s-plane diagram of Fig. 5-3 from the relation

$$\frac{E_o}{E_i}(j\omega) = \frac{1/\tau}{|\overline{AG}|} \underline{/-\theta} \quad (5\text{-}17)$$

As the frequency increases, point G moves up the $j\omega$ axis; thus the graph of Fig. 5-2b can be readily correlated to Fig. 5-3.

Another important result is illustrated if we consider $e_i(t)$ to be a unit impulse: $e_i(t) = \delta(t)$. Since $E_i(s) = \mathcal{L} e_i(t) = \mathcal{L} \delta(t) = 1$, it follows that $E_o(s)$ is given by

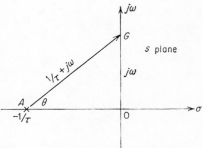

FIG. 5-3. Graphical representation of the sinusoidal steady-state transfer function of the network in Fig. 5-2a in the s plane.

$$E_o(s) = \frac{1}{1 + s\tau}$$

The inverse transform of this equation gives the network's impulse response. Thus

$$e_o(t) = \mathcal{L}^{-1} E_o(s)$$

$$= \mathcal{L}^{-1} \frac{1}{1 + s\tau} = \mathcal{L}^{-1} \frac{1/\tau}{1/\tau + s}$$

$$= \frac{1}{\tau} \epsilon^{-t/\tau} \qquad (5\text{-}18)$$

Examination of Eq. (5-18) reveals that it is identical, within a constant multiplier, to the source-free response represented by Eq. (5-15). Thus the impulse and the source-free responses are identical in character.

A Second-order System. Let us now consider the frequency response of the second-order system discussed in Chap. 4. For simplicity assume that $h = 1$ and $T'_L = 0$. The differential equation relating the output to the input is obtained from Eqs. (4-9) and (4-10). Thus we write

$$J \frac{d^2c(t)}{dt^2} + F \frac{dc(t)}{dt} + Kc(t) = Kr(t) \tag{5-19}$$

or

$$\frac{d^2c(t)}{dt^2} + 2\zeta\omega_n \frac{dc(t)}{dt} + \omega_n{}^2 c(t) = \omega_n{}^2 r(t) \tag{5-20}$$

where $\omega_n = \sqrt{K/J}$, the undamped natural frequency

$\zeta = F/2\sqrt{KJ}$, the damping ratio ≤ 1

The response of this system to a sinusoidal input is now found by following the usual steps. First take the Laplace transform of Eq. (5-20), assuming zero initial conditions. Thus,

$$(s^2 + 2\zeta\omega_n s + \omega_n{}^2)C(s) = \omega_n{}^2 R(s)$$

or

$$\frac{C(s)}{R(s)} = \frac{\omega_n{}^2}{s^2 + 2\zeta\omega_n s + \omega_n{}^2} \tag{5-21}$$

Upon replacing s by $j\omega$ the expression becomes

$$\overline{T}(j\omega) = \frac{\overline{C}(j\omega)}{\overline{R}(j\omega)} = \frac{\omega_n{}^2}{\omega_n{}^2 - \omega^2 + j2\zeta\omega_n\omega}$$

$$= \frac{1}{1 - (\omega/\omega_n)^2 + j2\zeta(\omega/\omega_n)} \tag{5-22}$$

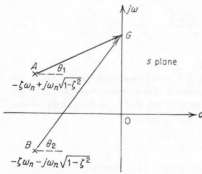

The above result can be correlated to the zero-pole pattern of Eq. (5-21) as depicted in Fig. 5-4. Equation (5-21) is seen to have a pair of complex conjugate poles for $\zeta < 1$. When $\zeta > 1$, these poles lie along the negative real axis, and when $\zeta = 1$, they coalesce at $s = -\omega_n$. In any case we may write from Fig. 5-4

$$\overline{T}(j\omega) = \frac{\omega_n{}^2}{(\overline{AG})(\overline{BG})} \underline{/-(\theta_1 + \theta_2)}$$

FIG. 5-4. Graphical representation of the sinusoidal steady-state transfer function

$$\overline{T}(j\omega) = \frac{\omega_n{}^2}{s^2 + 2\zeta\omega_n s + \omega_n{}^2}\bigg|_{s=j\omega}$$

where $\zeta \leq 1$, in the s plane.

Letting $u = \omega/\omega_n$, a new nondimensional normalized frequency variable equal to the ratio of the actual radian frequency of the source to the undamped natural frequency of the system, we obtain the following result:

$$\bar{T}(ju) = \frac{1}{1 - u^2 + j2\zeta u} = |\bar{T}(ju)|\epsilon^{j\phi(ju)} \tag{5-23}$$

The magnitude and phase angle of the transfer function are

$$|\bar{T}(ju)| = \frac{1}{\sqrt{(1 - u^2)^2 + 4\zeta^2 u^2}} \tag{5-24}$$

$$\phi(ju) = -\tan^{-1}\frac{2\zeta u}{1 - u^2} \tag{5-25}$$

For the sake of completeness it is worthwhile to review the meaning of Eqs. (5-24) and (5-25) in terms of the system's driven response to the sinusoidal input, $r(t) = R \sin(\omega t + \theta)$, where R is the peak amplitude and θ is an arbitrary phase angle. The system's steady-state response to this input is given by

$$c(t) = \frac{R}{\sqrt{(1 - u^2)^2 + 4\zeta^2 u^2}} \sin\left(\omega t + \theta - \tan^{-1}\frac{2\zeta u}{1 - u^2}\right) \tag{5-26}$$

with $u = \omega/\omega_n$, as defined previously. It is important that the foregoing use of complex numbers and their relationship to the steady-state sinusoidal response be understood clearly.

In Fig. 5-5a the magnitude of $\bar{T}(ju)$ is plotted vs. u, for different values of damping ζ, as given by Eq. (5-24). It is apparent from the curves that for values of $\zeta < \sqrt{2}/2 \approx 0.707$ there is a resonant peak in the characteristic. As ζ approaches zero, the magnitude of the resonant peak approaches infinity and the frequency at which it occurs approaches the undamped natural frequency of the system, i.e., $u = 1$. The equation for the location of the resonant peak may be determined by differentiating Eq. (5-24) with respect to u and equating to zero. Thus

$$u_{\text{resonance}} = \sqrt{1 - 2\zeta^2} \qquad \zeta \leq \sqrt{2}/2 \tag{5-27}$$

The magnitude of the resonant peak is found by substituting Eq. (5-27) into Eq. (5-24), yielding

$$|\bar{T}(ju)|_{\text{max}} = \frac{1}{2\zeta\sqrt{1 - \zeta^2}} \tag{5-28}$$

Both the foregoing expressions have physical significance only when $\zeta < 1/\sqrt{2}$ since, for values of damping greater than this, the slope of Eq. (5-24) is always negative and there is no resonant peak. The solid curve of Fig. 5-6 shows the magnitude of the resonant peak plotted for different values of ζ, and the solid curve of Fig. 5-7 shows the frequency at which resonance occurs, also plotted against ζ.

The correlation between the magnitude vs. frequency characteristics and the transient response may be found by considering the results of Chap. 4. The response to a unit step is redrawn in Fig. 5-5b for different values of ζ. For $\zeta < 0.707$ the response is seen to overshoot and return

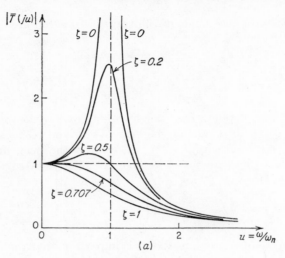

(a)

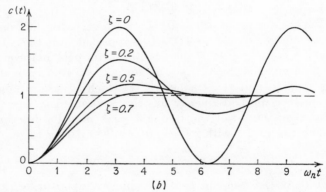

(b)

FIG. 5-5. Behavior of a second-order system. (a) Normalized frequency; amplitude vs. frequency characteristic of a second-order system,

$$\overline{T}(ju) = \frac{C(ju)}{R(ju)} = \frac{1}{\sqrt{(1 - u^2)^2 + 4\zeta^2 u^2}}$$

(b) response of second-order system to a unit-step input, for different values of damping ratio ζ.

to the steady-state value in a damped oscillation. The dotted curve of Fig. 5-6 shows the peak magnitude of the overshoot for different values of ζ. The frequency of the damped oscillation of the response was derived in Chap. 4 and is given by $\omega_d = \omega_n \sqrt{1 - \zeta^2}$. If this frequency is expressed in terms of the normalized frequency variable $u = \omega/\omega_n$, it becomes $u = \sqrt{1 - \zeta^2}$. The dotted curve of Fig. 5-7 shows the damped frequency of oscillation plotted vs. the damping ratio ζ. The curves of Figs. 5-6 and 5-7 point out graphically the relationship between the frequency-domain and the time-domain response. From Fig. 5-6 it is apparent that the resonant peak and the peak overshoot are very close to each other over a limited range of ζ. From Fig. 5-7 it is apparent that the resonant frequency and the damped frequency of oscillation are related to

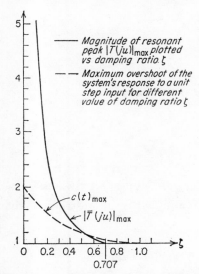

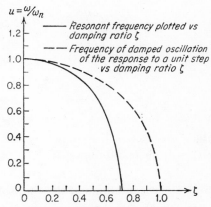

Fig. 5-6. A second-order system. Correlation between the resonant peak of the amplitude vs. frequency characteristic and the peak overshoot of the response to a unit-step input.

Fig. 5-7. A second-order system. Correlation between the resonant frequency (of the amplitude vs. frequency characteristic) and the damped frequency of oscillation of the response to a unit-step input.

each other for any particular value of ζ. Thus a definite and useful correlation has been established between the two domains. Of course the results presented apply specifically to the linear second-order system. For higher-order systems similar relationships exist, but they are more complex. In this respect the second-order system is quite useful as a general guide, but care must be exercised not to overextend the results to higher-order systems.

In this connection consider an unknown system whose unit-step respose is measured and found to be as depicted in Fig. 5-8. As a first approximation this step response may be considered as that of a second-order system of a particular damping ratio ζ and undamped resonant frequency ω_n. To the extent that this approximation holds, the system's transfer function and behavior are obviously dominated by a pair of complex conjugate poles in the s plane corresponding to the poles of the equivalent second-order system. Although this type of approximation seems somewhat naive, it is quite important in system design because of the simplicity of the correlation between the time and frequency domains which prevails for the second-order system.

The exact mathematical relationship between the time and frequency domains is expressed by the Laplace transform or the Fourier integral, the latter being identical to the Laplace transform with the condition

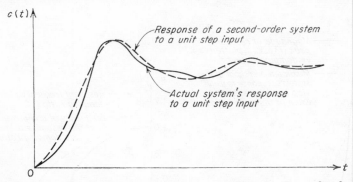

FIG. 5-8. Approximating a system's response by an equivalent second-order system.

that $s = j\omega$ (rather than $s = \sigma + j\omega$) and with the restriction that $f(t) = 0$ for $t < 0$ removed.

5-2. Representations of the Sinusoidal Transfer Function

Let us consider a general transfer function $\overline{T}(j\omega)$ between an input $\overline{R} = R/\underline{\theta}$ and a response $\overline{C}(j\omega)$. $\overline{T}(j\omega)$ is determined from the differential equation relating the output to the input and is of the form

$$\overline{T}(j\omega) = T(\omega)\epsilon^{j\phi(\omega)} = T(\omega)/\underline{\phi(\omega)}$$
$$= T(\omega) \cos \phi(\omega) + jT(\omega) \sin \phi(\omega)\dagger \qquad (5\text{-}29)$$

The relationship between time- and frequency-domain quantities is illustrated in Fig. 5-9.

Since $\overline{T}(j\omega)$ is a complex function of the variable ω, it may be represented graphically in many ways. The most common and useful of these are now discussed with the object of pointing out the particular advantages and disadvantages of each.

The Phasor Diagram and Polar Plot. At any particular frequency, $\overline{T}(j\omega)$ may be represented as a phasor[1] of a specific magnitude and phase

---

† When dealing with transfer functions the barred and unbarred notations are used synonymously, for example, $\overline{T}(j\omega) = T(j\omega)$. Also, $|T(j\omega)| = T(\omega)$.

[1] In many texts the term *vector* is used in place of the term *phasor*. Since we are talking about complex numbers, rather than vectors in the physical sense, the term phasor seems more appropriate.

angle as illustrated in Fig. 5-10.   The projections of $\overline{T}(j\omega)$ on the real and imaginary axes are its real and imaginary components.   As the frequency of the sinusoidal input varies (its peak magnitude R and arbitrary phase angle θ remaining constant) or as a particular parameter in the system varies, $\overline{T}(j\omega)$ changes in both amplitude and phase.   The tip of the phasor representing $\overline{T}(j\omega)$ traces out a locus in the complex plane, each

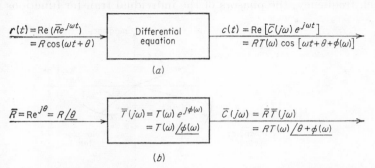

(a)

(b)

Fig. 5-9. Notation for sinusoidal steady-state representations of a transfer function. (a) Time domain; (b) frequency domain.

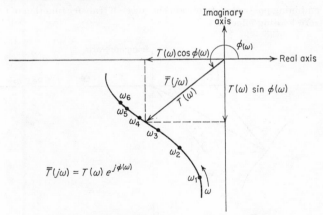

Fig. 5-10. Polar-plot representation for $\overline{T}(j\omega)$.

point on the locus representing the location of the phasor at any particular value of the varying parameter.   Usually the input frequency ω is the varying parameter, and the resulting locus is known as a *polar plot* of the transfer function.   In general, constant increments of frequency will not be separated by equal intervals along the polar plot, for their spacing depends upon how the transfer-function phasor has changed in the frequency interval.   The nonuniformity of frequency points along the polar plot is one of the disadvantages of the representation.   However, the polar plot does have the advantage of presenting the data over the entire frequency spectrum in a single diagram.

When two systems are connected in cascade or tandem so that the output of one becomes the input of the other, it being assumed that there is negligible loading effect (i.e., that the output of the first is unaffected by connection of the second), then the over-all transfer function of the combination is given by the complex product of the two individual transfer functions. On a polar-diagram representation this means that, at each frequency, the phasors of the individual transfer functions must

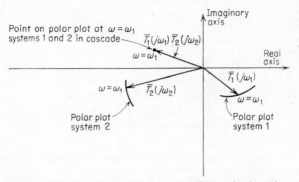

FIG. 5-11. Combining polar plots to obtain the over-all transfer function of two systems in cascade (zero loading effect).

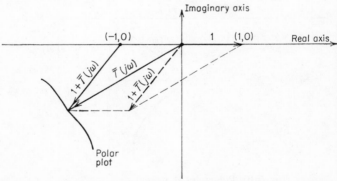

FIG. 5-12. Determining the function $1 + \overline{T}(j\omega)$ on a polar diagram.

be multiplied by using complex algebra multiplication to give the phasor of the over-all transfer function. This is illustrated in Fig. 5-11. It can be seen that such a combination is not particularly convenient with polar-diagram representations.

On the other hand, an operation such as determining the function $1 + \overline{T}(j\omega)$ is done easily with a polar diagram. As can be seen in Fig. 5-12, $1 + \overline{T}(j\omega)$ is simply the vector sum of the phasor for $+1$ and the phasor of $\overline{T}(j\omega)$. The resultant is identical to the phasor drawn from the point $(-1,0)$ to the original polar plot for $\overline{T}(j\omega)$. In other words, the polar plot for $1 + \overline{T}(j\omega)$ is identical to the polar plot for $\overline{T}(j\omega)$ with the origin of coordinates shifted to the point $(-1,0)$.

Magnitude and Phase vs. Frequency Characteristic. The transfer function may also be represented by two graphs, one giving the magnitude of $\overline{T}(j\omega)$ vs. frequency, the other the phase angle vs. frequency. Another possibility is a set of curves giving the real and imaginary parts of $\overline{T}(j\omega)$ vs. frequency. The latter representations are not often used to represent transfer functions, although they are sometimes used to represent impedance functions. The magnitude and phase-shift characteristics on the other hand are quite common, particularly in specifying the output-input characteristic of electrical components such as servo-amplifiers. It is interesting to note that the magnitude and phase-shift characteristics (as well as the real- and imaginary-part characteristics) are not independent. They are related to each other by a rather complicated integral formula so that one can be determined from the other.[1]

When the frequency range covered is large, $T(\omega)$ and $\phi(\omega)$ are often plotted vs. the logarithm of ω, that is, with frequency on a logarithmic rather than a linear scale. The magnitude vs. frequency characteristic is useful in that it points out the low- or high-pass characteristic of the transfer function. When two systems are connected in cascade with negligible loading effect of one upon the other, then the transfer function of the combination is found by multiplying the individual amplitude characteristics and adding the phase-shift characteristics at each frequency.

Log-modulus (Magnitude) and Phase vs. Frequency Plots. One of the most useful representations of a transfer function is the log-modulus plot in which the logarithm of $\overline{T}(j\omega)$ is plotted vs. the logarithm of frequency. Semilog graph paper is used, and the logarithmic scale is used for ω. The logarithm of $\overline{T}(j\omega)$ may be taken either to the base ϵ or to the base 10.[†] Let us consider the natural base ϵ first. Thus

$$\begin{aligned} \ln \overline{T}(j\omega) &= \ln \left[|\overline{T}(j\omega)| \epsilon^{j\phi(\omega)} \right] \\ &= \ln |\overline{T}(j\omega)| + j\phi(\omega) \end{aligned} \tag{5-30}$$

The real part of $\ln \overline{T}(j\omega)$ is the natural logarithm of its magnitude and is measured in a basic unit called the neper. The imaginary part of $\ln \overline{T}(j\omega)$ is simply the phase-shift characteristic.

The most common log-modulus plots are taken to the base 10. The standard procedure is to plot $20 \log |\overline{T}(j\omega)|$ and the phase angle vs. $\log \omega$, that is, frequency on a logarithmic scale. The basic unit for

---

[1] This relationship is not developed here but may be found in the book by H. W. Bode, "Network Analysis and Feedback Amplifier Design," D. Van Nostrand Company, Inc., Princeton, N.J., 1945.

[†] Logarithms to the base 10 are designated by log, and logarithms to the base ϵ by ln.

$20 \log |\overline{T}(j\omega)|$ is called the *decibel*, abbreviated db.   This type of characteristic is often called a Bode[1] plot.

Log-modulus plots have two advantages which will become more obvious as our work proceeds.   (1) When two systems are connected in cascade with negligible loading effect, their individual log-modulus and phase-shift plots can be added to give the over-all characteristic.   This is obviously true since multiplication of magnitudes is equivalent to adding the logarithms of their magnitudes.   (2) Log-modulus plots are easy to draw since they can often be approximated by a series of straight-line segments.   Another advantage of the log-modulus plot is the logarithmic-frequency scale which is used.   The contraction of this scale gives a representation which emphasizes equally all portions of the frequency characteristic.   This aids in the correlation between the frequency and time domains and greatly facilitates the design of compensation networks when these are required.

Log-modulus vs. Angle Plots.   Another representation used in feedback control theory is the log-modulus vs. phase-angle plot, often referred to as Nichol's charts in the literature.   In this representation $20 \log |\overline{T}(j\omega)|$ is plotted vs. the phase angle $\phi(\omega)$ on rectangular coordinates with frequency ω as a running parameter, similar to a polar plot.   This representation is quite practical and has been used in design procedure.

5-3. Transfer Characteristics of Basic Operational Functions

Prior to discussing the transfer characteristics of any specific control component or system let us first discuss the transfer characteristics associated with some basic operational functions.   The object is to illustrate the relationship between the operation and the corresponding sinusoidal transfer function and to point out the fundamental forms which make up the more complicated types.   The polar plot, the magnitude vs. frequency (linear scale), and the log-modulus and phase vs. log-frequency and the pole-zero representation are given for each.   The phase vs. linear frequency is not presented because of its similarity to the phase vs. log-frequency characteristic.   In general, the characteristics are drawn vs. a normalized frequency factor $u = \omega\tau = \omega/\omega_b$, so that the curves can be adapted to any frequency scale. τ is a constant with the dimensions of time, and $\omega_b = 1/\tau$ is a radian frequency known as the *breakpoint*, or *corner*, frequency.   The usefulness of this normalization becomes apparent as it is used.

Pure Differentiation.   In this case the output and input are related by differentiation.   Thus

$$c(t) = \tau \frac{dr(t)}{dt} \tag{5-31}$$

or
$$C(s) = \tau s R(s) \tag{5-32}$$

---

[1] Named after H. Bode, who did basic work in this area.   Consult Bode, *op. cit.*

where τ is a constant with the dimensions of time when $c(t)$ and $r(t)$ have the same units. The transfer function $\dfrac{C}{R}(s) = \tau s$ has a single zero at the origin as illustrated in Fig. 5-13d. The sinusoidal steady-state transfer function is given by

$$\overline{T} = j\omega\tau = \omega\tau\underline{/90^\circ}$$
$$= ju = u\underline{/90^\circ} \qquad (5\text{-}33)$$

where $u = \omega\tau = \omega/\omega_b$, a nondimensional frequency factor.

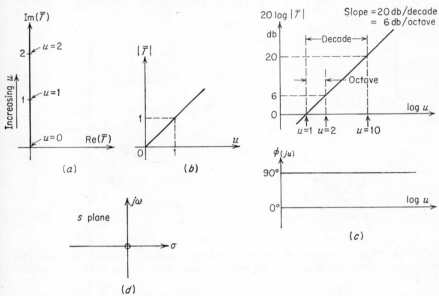

FIG. 5-13. Transfer-function representations for pure differentiations. $\overline{T} = ju$, where $u = \omega\tau$. (a) Polar plot; (b) magnitude vs. frequency; (c) log modulus and phase vs. log u; (d) zero location for $\overline{T}(s) = s\tau$.

The polar plot of Eq. (5-33) is a straight line along the ju axis as shown in Fig. 5-13a. The magnitude vs. frequency characteristic is a straight line and appears in Fig. 5-13b. The log modulus of Eq. (5-33) is given by

$$\text{db} = 20 \log |\overline{T}| = 20 \log u \qquad (5\text{-}34)$$

If the decibels are plotted vs. log u (that is, u on a logarithmic scale), then the result is a straight line, which passes through 0 db at $u = 1$ (that is, where $\omega = 1/\tau = \omega_b$). The slope of this line is 20 db/unit of log u. A unit increment of log u corresponds to increasing u (or ω) by a factor of 10 since log 10 = 1. Thus the slope is said to be 20 db/decade, where a decade corresponds to a factor of 10 in frequency. The slope is also often specified in terms of db/octave, where an octave corresponds to doubling the frequency. In this case the number of decibels is increased by 20 log 2 = 6.02 db each time the frequency is doubled so that the slope is specified as 6 db/octave. These slopes and multiples thereof appear again and again in transfer functions. The log-modulus and phase characteristics are drawn in Fig. 5-13c. The phase shift of Eq. (5-33) is obviously a constant 90° and is independent of frequency. The 90° phase lead associated with this transfer function in the frequency domain is indicative of pure differentiation in the time domain, and one can be inferred from the other.

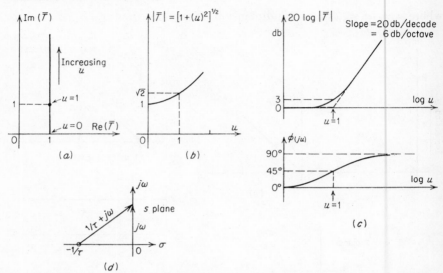

Fig. 5-14. Transfer characteristics of $\bar{T} = 1 + ju$, where $u = \omega\tau$. (a) Polar plot; (b) magnitude vs. frequency; (c) log modulus and phase vs. log u; (d) zero location for $\bar{T}(s) = 1 + s\tau$.

Proportional plus Derivative Control. In this case the output and input are related by the expression

$$c(t) = r(t) + \tau \frac{dr(t)}{dt} \tag{5-35}$$

or

$$C(s) = (1 + \tau s)R(s) \tag{5-36}$$

where τ is a constant with the units of time when $c(t)$ and $r(t)$ have the same units. The transfer function $\frac{C}{R}(s) = (1 + \tau s) = \tau\left(\frac{1}{\tau} + s\right)$ has a single zero located at $s = -1/\tau$ as indicated in Fig. 5-14d. The transfer function for sinusoidal inputs is given by

$$\bar{T} = 1 + j\omega\tau = 1 + ju$$
$$= \sqrt{1 + (\omega\tau)^2} \,\underline{/\tan^{-1} \omega\tau} = \sqrt{1 + u^2} \,\underline{/\tan^{-1} u} \tag{5-37}$$

where $u = \omega\tau = \omega/\omega_b$. The polar plot is a straight line parallel to the j axis as drawn in Fig. 5-14a. The magnitude vs. frequency characteristic is drawn in Fig. 5-14b. The log-modulus plot is given by

$$
\begin{aligned}
db &= 20 \log |\bar{T}| \\
&= 10 \log (1 + u^2)
\end{aligned} \tag{5-38}
$$

Equation (5-38) can be sketched easily by considering its behavior at extreme values of frequency. When $u \ll 1$ (i.e., when $\omega \ll \omega_b$), Eq. (5-38) becomes equal to $10 \log 1 = 0$. When $u \gg 1$ (i.e. when $\omega \gg \omega_b$), Eq. (5-38) becomes equal to $10 \log (\omega\tau)^2 = 20 \log u$. The latter is obviously a straight line, identical to the case of pure differentiation, which passes through 0 db when $u = 1$ (or $\omega = \omega_b$) and has a slope of 20 db/decade or 6 db/octave. These asymptotes are drawn dotted in Fig. 5-14c. The frequency where the high-frequency asymptote and the low-frequency asymptote (the 0-db line) intersect (i.e., when $u = 1$ or $\omega = 1/\tau = \omega_b$) is known by several names, including the *corner*, or *breakpoint*, frequency. When $u = 1$, Eq. (5-38) is actually equal to $10 \log 2 = 3.01$ db. Thus it can be seen that at the breakpoint frequency the log-modulus characteristic lies 3 db above the intersection of the asymptotes. The two asymptotes and the value at the breakpoint frequency are usually sufficient to sketch the log-modulus characteristic. Figure 5-15 is a graph of the decibel corrections to be applied to the asymptotes to obtain the actual curve for various values of frequency u. It should also be noted that at the breakpoint frequency the magnitude of the transfer function is equal to $\sqrt{2}$. The phase-shift characteristic of Eq. (5-37) is seen to lie between $\tan^{-1} 0 = 0°$ and $\lim_{u \to \infty} \tan^{-1} u = 90°$ as shown in Fig. 5-14c. The fact that the phase angle represents a phase lead between 0 and 90° is indicative of proportional plus derivative control. As the frequency increases and the phase angle approaches 90°, the differentiation term predominates.

Pure Integration. In this case the input and output are related by

$$
c(t) = \frac{1}{\tau} \int r(t) \, dt \tag{5-39}
$$

or

$$
C(s) = \frac{R(s)}{\tau s} \tag{5-40}
$$

where τ is a constant with the dimensions of time when $c(t)$ and $r(t)$ have the same units. The transfer function $\dfrac{C}{R}(s) = \dfrac{1}{\tau s}$ is seen to have a pole at the origin as indicated in Fig. 5-16d. The sinusoidal steady-state transfer function is given by

$$
\begin{aligned}
\bar{T} &= \frac{1}{j\omega\tau} = \frac{1}{\omega\tau} \underline{/-90°} \\
&= \frac{1}{ju} = \frac{1}{u} \underline{/-90°}
\end{aligned} \tag{5-41}
$$

where $u = \omega\tau = \omega/\omega_b$.

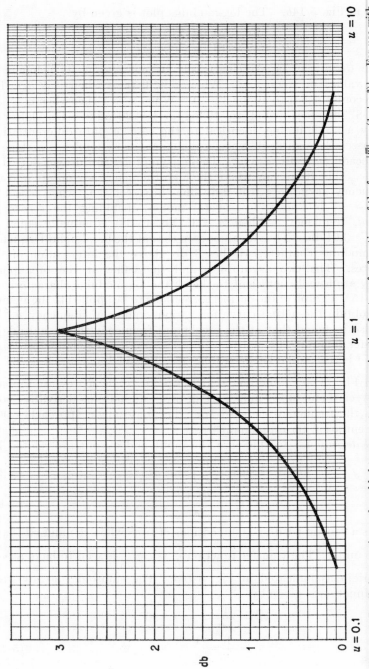

FIG. 5-15. Decibel correction to be added to asymptote approximation for transfer functions of the form $|\overline{T}| = (1 + u^2)^{\frac{1}{2}}$. For use with those of the form $|\overline{T}| = (1 + u^2)^{-\frac{1}{2}}$, the decibel correction given must be subtracted from the asymptotes.

The polar plot of Eq. (5-41) is obviously a straight line along the $-j$ axis as shown in Fig. 5-16a. The magnitude vs. frequency characteristic is hyperbolic as shown in Fig. 5-16b. The log-modulus curve is given by

$$\text{db} = 20 \log |\overline{T}| = 20 \log \frac{1}{u}$$

$$= -20 \log u \tag{5-42}$$

This characteristic is a straight line similar to pure differentiation except that the slope is negative, that is, -20 db/decade or -6 db/octave. These characteristics are shown in Fig. 5-16c. The 90° phase

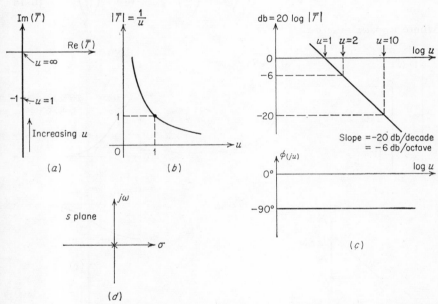

Fig. 5-16. Transfer-function representations for pure integration. $\overline{T} = 1/ju$, where $u = \omega\tau$. (a) Polar plot; (b) magnitude vs. frequency; (c) log modulus and phase vs. log u; (d) pole pattern for $T(s) = 1/\tau s$.

lag is indicative of pure integration, and one can be inferred from the other.

Proportional plus Integral Control. In this case the output and input are related by the equations

$$c(t) = r(t) + \frac{1}{\tau} \int r(t)\, dt \tag{5-43}$$

or

$$C(s) = \left(1 + \frac{1}{\tau s}\right) R(s) \tag{5-44}$$

where τ is a constant having the dimension of time when $c(t)$ and $r(t)$ have the same units. The transfer function

$$\frac{C}{R}(s) = 1 + \frac{1}{\tau s} = \frac{1 + \tau s}{\tau s} = \frac{1/\tau + s}{s}$$

is seen to have a zero at $s = -1/\tau$ and a pole at $s = 0$, as indicated in Fig. 5-17d. The sinusoidal steady-state transfer function is given by

$$\overline{T}(j\omega) = 1 + \frac{1}{j\omega\tau} = \sqrt{1 + \left(\frac{1}{\omega\tau}\right)^2} \bigg/ - \tan^{-1}\frac{1}{\omega\tau}$$

$$= 1 + \frac{1}{ju} = \sqrt{1 + \left(\frac{1}{u}\right)^2} \bigg/ - \tan^{-1}\left(\frac{1}{u}\right) \qquad (5\text{-}45)$$

where $u = \omega\tau = \omega/\omega_b$.

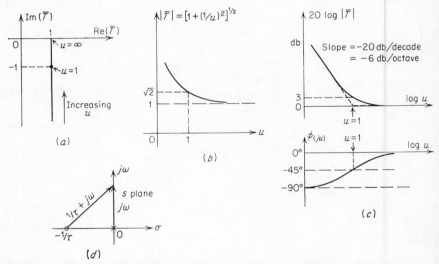

Fig. 5-17. Transfer characteristic of $\overline{T} = 1 + 1/ju$, where $u = \omega\tau$. (a) Polar plot; (b) magnitude vs. frequency; (c) log modulus and phase vs. log u; (d) zero-pole pattern for $\overline{T}(s) = 1 + 1/\tau s = (1 + \tau s)/\tau s$.

The polar plot is a straight line parallel to the j axis as drawn in Fig. 5-17a. The magnitude vs. frequency characteristic is drawn in Fig. 5-17b. The log-modulus plot is given by

$$\mathbf{db} = 20 \log \sqrt{1 + \left(\frac{1}{u}\right)^2}$$

$$= 10 \log\left[1 + \left(\frac{1}{u}\right)^2\right] = 10 \log(1 + u^2) - 10 \log u^2 \qquad (5\text{-}46)$$

Equation (5-46) can be sketched easily by considering its behavior at extreme values of frequency. When $u \gg 1$, Eq. (5-46) becomes equal to 0 db. When $u \ll 1$, Eq. (5-46) becomes equal to

$$10 \log \left(\frac{1}{u}\right)^2 = -20 \log u$$

This is a straight line of slope -20 db/decade or -6 db/octave, which intersects the 0-db asymptote at $u = 1$ (or $\omega = 1/\tau = \omega_b$). At $u = 1$, Eq. (5-46) is equal to $10 \log 2 = 3.01$ db, so that the actual curve lies 3 db above the intersection of the asymptotes at the corner frequency $u = 1$.

The correction curve of Fig. 5-15 can also be used to determine the actual characteristic with respect to the asymptotes. For this particular case the decibel correction must be added to the asymptotes. The phase angle of Eq. (5-45) varies from $-90°$ when $\omega = 0$ to $0°$ when $\omega = \infty$. These characteristics are pictured in Fig. 5-17c. The fact that the phase represents a lag between 90° and 0° is indicative of proportional plus integral behavior with the integral term predominating at the lower frequencies.

5-4. The Repeated Application of Basic Operational Forms

The transfer functions of the previous section often appear in the following general forms, where $u = \omega\tau$:

$$\overline{T} = (ju)^{\pm n} = (u)^{\pm n} \underline{/\pm 90n°} \tag{5-47}$$

$$\overline{T} = (1 + ju)^{\pm n} = (1 + (u)^2)^{\pm n/2} \underline{/\pm n \tan^{-1} u} \tag{5-48}$$

$$\overline{T} = \left(1 - \frac{j}{u}\right)^{\pm n} = \left[1 + \left(\frac{1}{u}\right)^2\right]^{\pm n/2} \underline{\bigg/ \mp n \tan^{-1}\frac{1}{u}} \tag{5-49}$$

where n may be any positive integer.

Equation (5-47) represents successive differentiation or integration depending upon whether the exponent is positive or negative. The polar plot for Eq. (5-47) is seen to lie along the $\pm j$ or the ± 1 axis depending upon the particular value for n and the sign of the exponent, as illustrated in Fig. 5-18a. The log-modulus representation for Eq. (5-47) is obtained from the equation $20 \log u^{\pm n} = \pm 20n \log u$. This is seen to be a straight line passing through 0 db at $u = 1$ with a slope of $\pm 20n$ db/decade or $\pm 6n$ db/octave. These characteristics are pictured in Fig. 5-18.

The transfer characteristics of Eq. (5-48) depend upon whether the exponent is positive or negative. The polar plot is no longer a straight line and thus becomes more difficult to draw. When n is positive, the polar plot for $\overline{T}$ approaches infinity as u gets larger. When n is negative,

TABLE 5-1. VALUES OF 20 LOG N

N	0	1	2	3	4	5	6	7	8	9
0.0		−40.00	−33.98	−30.46	−27.96	−26.02	−24.44	−23.10	−21.94	−20.92
0.1	−20.0	−19.17	−18.32	−17.72	−17.08	−16.48	−15.92	−15.39	−14.89	−14.42
0.2	−13.98	−13.56	−13.15	−12.77	−12.40	−12.04	−11.70	−11.37	−11.06	−10.76
0.3	−10.46	−10.17	− 9.90	− 9.63	− 9.37	− 9.12	− 8.87	− 8.64	− 8.40	− 8.18
0.4	− 7.96	− 7.74	− 7.54	− 7.33	− 7.13	− 6.94	− 6.74	− 6.56	− 6.36	− 6.20
0.5	− 6.02	− 5.85	− 5.68	− 5.51	− 5.35	− 5.19	− 5.04	− 4.88	− 4.73	− 4.58
0.6	− 4.44	− 4.29	− 4.15	− 4.01	− 3.88	− 3.74	− 3.61	− 3.48	− 3.35	− 3.22
0.7	− 3.10	− 2.97	− 2.85	− 2.73	− 2.62	− 2.50	− 2.38	− 2.27	− 2.16	− 2.05
0.8	− 1.94	− 1.83	− 1.72	− 1.62	− 1.51	− 1.41	− 1.31	− 1.21	− 1.11	− 1.01
0.9	− 0.92	− 0.82	− 0.72	− 0.63	− 0.54	− 0.45	− 0.35	− 0.26	− 0.18	− 0.09
1.0	− 0.00	0.09	0.17	0.26	0.34	0.42	0.51	0.59	0.67	0.75
1.1	0.83	0.91	0.98	1.06	1.14	1.21	1.29	1.36	1.44	1.51
1.2	1.58	1.66	1.73	1.80	1.87	1.94	2.01	2.08	2.14	2.21
1.3	2.28	2.3b	2.41	2.48	2.54	2.61	2.67	2.73	2.80	2.86
1.4	2.92	2.98	3.05	3.11	3.17	3.23	3.29	3.35	3.41	3.46
1.5	3.52	3.58	3.64	3.69	3.75	3.81	3.86	3.92	3.97	4.03
1.6	4.08	4.14	4.19	4.24	4.30	4.35	4.40	4.45	4.51	4.56
1.7	4.61	4.66	4.71	4.76	4.81	4.86	4.91	4.96	5.01	5.06
1.8	5.11	5.15	5.20	5.25	5.30	5.34	5.39	5.44	5.48	5.53
1.9	5.58	5.62	5.67	5.71	5.76	5.80	5.85	5.89	5.93	5.98
2.0	6.02	6.44	6.85	7.23	7.60	7.96	8.30	8.63	8.94	9.25
3.0	9.54	9.83	10.10	10.37	10.63	10.88	11.13	11.36	11.60	11.82
4.0	12.04	12.26	12.46	12.67	12.87	13.06	13.26	13.44	13.62	13.80
5.0	13.98	14.15	14.32	14.49	14.65	14.81	14.96	15.12	15.27	15.42
6.0	15.56	15.71	15.85	15.99	16.12	16.26	16.39	16.52	16.65	16.78
7.0	16.90	17.03	17.15	17.27	17.38	17.50	17.62	17.73	17.84	17.95
8.0	18.06	18.17	18.28	18.38	18.49	18.59	18.69	18.79	18.89	18.99
9.0	19.08	19.18	19.28	19.37	19.46	19.55	19.65	19.74	19.82	19.91

the polar plot approaches zero as u gets larger. For the particular
case when $n = -1$ the polar plot becomes a semicircle[1], but the other

[1] It can be demonstrated that the polar plot of all functions of the form

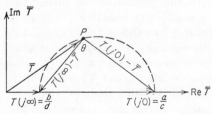

$$\bar{T}(j\omega) = \frac{(a + j\omega b)}{(c + j\omega d)}$$

are semicircles, where a, b, c, and d are real
constants. Consider the following:

$$\bar{T}(j0) = \frac{a}{c} \qquad \bar{T}(j\infty) = \frac{b}{d}$$

$$\bar{T}(j0) - \bar{T} = \frac{a}{c} - \frac{a + j\omega b}{c + j\omega d} = \frac{j\omega(ad - bc)}{c(c + j\omega d)}$$

$$\bar{T}(j\infty) - T = \frac{b}{d} - \frac{a + j\omega b}{c + jwd} = \frac{-(ad - bc)}{d(c + j\omega d)}$$

Now

$$|\theta| = |\; \angle \,[\bar{T}(j\infty) - \bar{T}] - \angle \,[\bar{T}(j0) - \bar{T}]|$$

$$= \left| \; \angle \, \frac{\bar{T}(j\infty) - \bar{T}}{\bar{T}(j0) - \bar{T}} \right| = \left| \; \angle \, \frac{-(ad - bc)}{d(c + j\omega d)} \frac{c(c + j\omega d)}{j\omega(ad - bc)} \right| = 90°$$

Hence the interior angle θ, at point P, is 90° for all values of ω. It therefore follows
from the inscribed angle of a semicircle that the locus of point P is a semicircle.

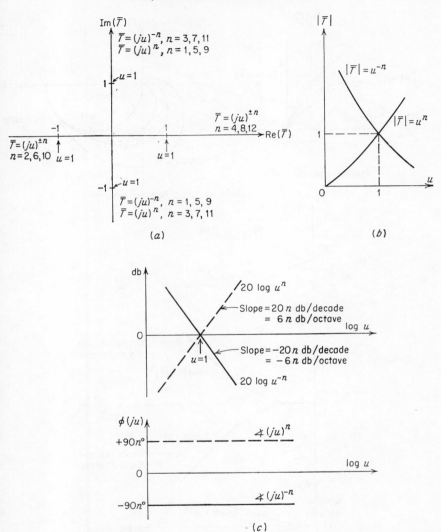

FIG. 5-18. Transfer characteristics for $\overline{T} = (ju)^{\pm n}$, where $u = \omega\tau$. (a) Polar plot; (b) magnitude vs. frequency; (c) log modulus and phase vs. log u.

cases are not simple curves as can be seen from Fig. 5-19a. However the log-modulus plot still retains its simplicity since the asymptotes may be found readily. Thus

$$20 \log (1 + u^2)^{\pm n/2} = \pm 10n \log (1 + u^2) \qquad (5\text{-}50)$$

When $u \ll 1$, Eq. (5-50) becomes the 0-db line. When $u \gg 1$, Eq. (5-50) becomes $\pm 20n \log u$. This is a straight line on the log-modulus

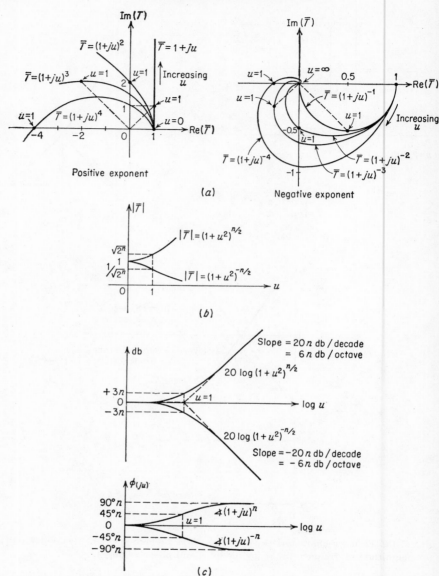

FIG. 5-19. Transfer characteristic for $\overline{T} = (1 + ju)^{\pm n}$, where $u = \omega\tau$.   (a) Polar plot of $(1 + ju)^{\pm n}$; (b) magnitude vs. frequency; (c) log modulus and phase angle vs. log u.

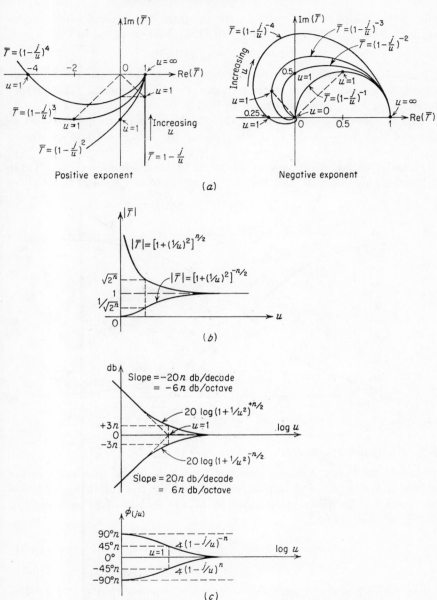

FIG. 5-20. Transfer characteristic for $\overline{T} = (1 + 1/ju)^{\pm n} = (1 - j/u)^{\pm n}$, where $u = \omega\tau$. (a) Polar plot of $(1 - j/u)^{\pm n}$; (b) magnitude vs. frequency; (c) log modulus and phase angle vs. log u.

plot, with a slope of $\pm 20n$ db/decade (or $\pm 6n$ db/octave), which passes through 0 db when $u = 1$. At $u = 1$, Eq. (5-50) is equal to

$$\pm 10n \log 2 = \pm 3.01n \text{ db}$$

Thus the actual point lies either above or below the breakpoint frequency by $3n$ db depending upon the sign of the original exponent. The characteristics for Eq. (5-48) are drawn in Fig. 5-19.

The transfer characteristics of Eq. (5-49) are seen to be identical to those of Eq. (5-48) except that u is replaced by $-1/u$. These are drawn in Fig. 5-20.

In order to facilitate accurate drawing of these characteristics, Table 5-1 lists $20 \log N$ vs. N, and Fig. 5-21 is a plot of $\tan^{-1} x$ and $\tan^{-1} (1/x)$ vs. x.

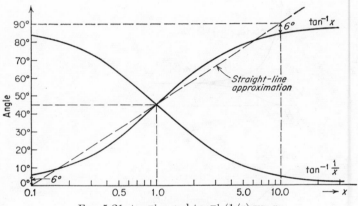

FIG. 5-21. $\tan^{-1} x$ and $\tan^{-1} (1/x)$ vs. x.

5-5. The Quadratic Factor

One of the most common transfer functions is the quadratic factor in which the input and output are related by the following equation [identical to the differential equation of the second-order system, Eq. (5-20), with $\tau = 1/\omega_n$]:

$$\tau^2 \frac{d^2 c(t)}{dt^2} + 2\zeta\tau \frac{dc(t)}{dt} + c(t) = r(t) \tag{5-51}$$

or $$(\tau^2 s^2 + 2\zeta\tau s + 1)C(s) = R(s) \tag{5-52}$$

where τ and ζ are real numbers with the restriction that $\zeta < 1$.† The zero-pole pattern for this transfer function is illustrated in Fig. 5-4. The sinusoidal steady-state transfer function is given by

$$\begin{aligned} \overline{T}(j\omega) &= [\tau^2(j\omega)^2 + 2\zeta\tau j\omega + 1]^{-1} \\ &= [(j\omega\tau)^2 + 2\zeta\omega\tau j + 1]^{-1} \end{aligned} \tag{5-53}$$

† If $\zeta \geq 1$, the quadratic can be factored into two linear factors involving real roots.

If $u = \omega\tau = \omega/\omega_n$, then

$$\overline{T}(ju) = [(ju)^2 + j2\zeta u + 1]^{-1}$$

$$= [(1 - u^2) + j2\zeta u]^{-1} \qquad (5\text{-}54)$$

The polar plot and log-modulus and phase characteristics are drawn in Fig. 5-22. The log-modulus characteristic is given by

$$db = 20 \log [(1 - u^2)^2 + 4\zeta^2 u^2]^{-\frac{1}{2}} \qquad (5\text{-}55)$$

When $u \ll 1$, the curve approaches the 0-db line. When $u \gg 1$, the curve approaches the line, $20 \log (u^4)^{-\frac{1}{2}} = -40 \log u$, which has a slope of -40 db/decade or -12 db/octave. These asymptotes are independent of the value of ζ. However, the damping ratio ζ determines the

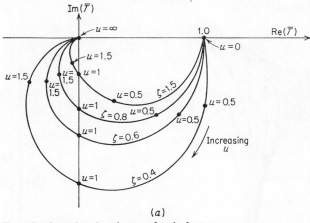

(a)

Fig. 5-22a. Transfer function for the quadratic factor

$$\overline{T} = \frac{1}{(ju)^2 + j2\zeta u + 1} = \frac{1}{1 - u^2 + j2\zeta u}$$

where $u = \omega\tau$. Polar plot.

magnitude of the resonant peak in the neighborhood of $u = 1$, and at low values of ζ these corrections are large and cannot be neglected.

5-6. The Phase-lag Characteristic

One of the more important types of transfer function is the phase-lag characteristic in which the input and output are related by the following differential equation,

$$c(t) + \alpha\tau \frac{dc(t)}{dt} = r(t) + \tau \frac{dr(t)}{dt} \qquad (5\text{-}56)$$

or

$$(1 + \alpha\tau s)C(s) = (1 + \tau s)R(s) \qquad (5\text{-}57)$$

where τ is a constant with the dimension of time if $c(t)$ and $r(t)$ have the

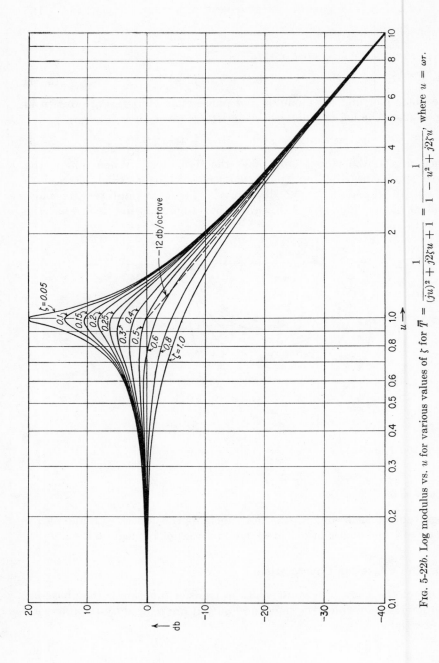

Fig. 5-22b. Log modulus vs. u for various values of ζ for $\overline{T} = \dfrac{1}{(ju)^2 + j2\zeta u + 1} = \dfrac{1}{1 - u^2 + j2\zeta u}$, where $u = \omega\tau$.

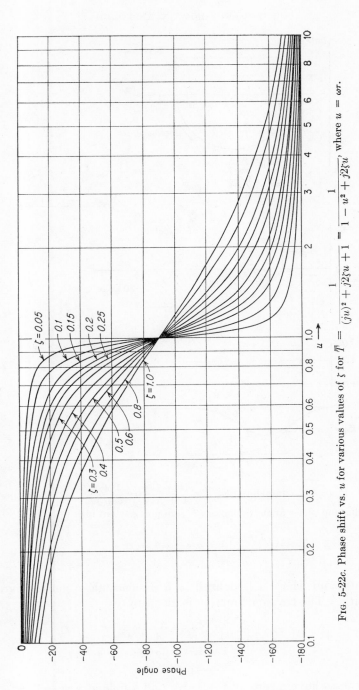

Fig. 5-22c. Phase shift vs. u for various values of ζ for $\bar{T} = \dfrac{1}{(ju)^2 + j2\zeta u + 1} = \dfrac{1}{1 - u^2 + j2\zeta u}$, where $u = \omega\tau$.

187

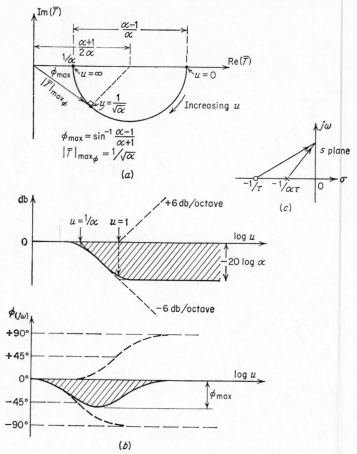

FIG. 5-23. Phase-lag characteristics $\bar{T} = \dfrac{1 + j\omega\tau}{1 + j\alpha\omega\tau} = \dfrac{1 + ju}{1 + j\alpha u}$. (a) Polar plot; (b) log modulus and phase angle vs. log u; (c) zero-pole pattern for

$$\bar{T}(s) = \frac{1 + \tau s}{1 + \alpha\tau s} = \frac{1}{\alpha}\frac{1/\tau + s}{1/\alpha\tau + s}$$

same units and where α is defined as a dimensionless constant greater than unity. The transfer function is given by

$$\frac{C}{R}(s) = \frac{1 + \tau s}{1 + \alpha\tau s} = \frac{1}{\alpha}\frac{1/\tau + s}{1/\alpha\tau + s}$$

and is seen to have a zero at $s = -1/\tau$ and a pole at $s = -1/\alpha\tau$. The zero-pole pattern is illustrated in Fig. 5-23c. The sinusoidal steady-state transfer function for Eq. (5-57) is given by

$$\overline{T} = \frac{1 + j\omega\tau}{1 + j\alpha\omega\tau} = \frac{1 + ju}{1 + j\alpha u} \tag{5-58}$$

where $u = \omega\tau = \omega/\omega_b$.

The polar plot for Eq. (5-58) may be determined most easily by reduction to the polar form

$$\overline{T}(ju) = \frac{\sqrt{1 + u^2}}{\sqrt{1 + \alpha^2 u^2}} \underline{/\tan^{-1} u - \tan^{-1} \alpha u}$$

$$= \sqrt{\frac{1 + u^2}{1 + \alpha^2 u^2}} \underline{/\tan^{-1} \frac{u - \alpha u}{1 + \alpha u^2}} \tag{5-59}$$

The polar plot is sketched in Fig. 5-23a and is seen to be a semicircle with its center at $\left(\dfrac{1 + \alpha}{2\alpha}, 0\right)$.† The maximum lag angle which this transfer function can introduce is denoted by ϕ_{max} and occurs at $u = 1/\sqrt{\alpha}$. From the geometry of Fig. 5-23a it can be shown that

$$\phi_{max} = \sin^{-1} \frac{\alpha - 1}{\alpha + 1} \tag{5-60}$$

The magnitude of $\overline{T}$ when $u = 1/\sqrt{\alpha}$ is denoted by $|\overline{T}|_{\phi max}$ and is given by

$$|\overline{T}|_{\phi max} = \frac{1}{\sqrt{\alpha}} \tag{5-61}$$

ϕ_{max} and $|\overline{T}|_{\phi max}$ are plotted vs. α in Fig. 5-25a and b. These curves are of value later in the text.

It is apparent from the foregoing equations that, as α is increased to introduce more phase lag, $|\overline{T}(ju)|$ decreases so that phase lag is obtained at the expense of introducing more attenuation into the transfer function.

The log modulus vs. frequency of Eq. (5-59) is given by

$$\begin{aligned} db &= 20 \log (1 + u^2)^{\frac{1}{2}} - 20 \log (1 + \alpha^2 u^2)^{\frac{1}{2}} \\ &= 10 \log (1 + u^2) - 10 \log (1 + \alpha^2 u^2) \end{aligned} \tag{5-62}$$

Equation (5-62) is seen to be made up of two terms. The first, representing the numerator of Eq. (5-59), is a proportional plus derivative type of term whose log-modulus curve has a breakpoint frequency at $u = 1$, $(\omega = 1/\tau)$. The second, representing the denominator of Eq. (5-58), is a term of the form $(1 + j\alpha u)^{-1}$ (see Fig. 5-19c) and has a breakpoint frequency at $u = 1/\alpha$, $(\omega = 1/\alpha\tau)$. These two terms are plotted in Fig.

† See footnote, page 180, for proof.

5-23*b* and their sum is the log-modulus characteristic of Eq. (5-59). Note the relationship between the breakpoint frequencies and the zero-pole pattern of Fig. 5-23*c*. If $\alpha \gg 1$, the two breakpoint frequencies are far enough apart so that the actual curve is 3 db away from the intersection of the asymptotes at the breakpoints.

The phase characteristic is similarly given by

$$\phi(ju) = \tan^{-1} u - \tan^{-1} \alpha u$$
$$= \tan^{-1} \frac{u - \alpha u}{1 + \alpha u^2} = -\tan^{-1} \frac{(\alpha - 1)u}{1 + \alpha u^2} \qquad (5\text{-}63)$$

This is the sum of the phase characteristics associated with each of the terms and is sketched in Fig. 5-23*b*.

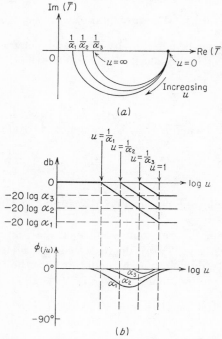

FIG. 5-24. Phase-lag characteristic of Fig. 5-23 for different values of α, where $\alpha_1 > \alpha_2 > \alpha_3 > 1$.   (*a*) Polar plot; (*b*) log modulus and phase angle vs. log u.

Figure 5-24 illustrates the polar and log-modulus and phase-angle plots for various values of α.   Figure 5-28 is included to provide accurate determination of the phase-angle curve and is used later in the text. Figure 5-29 is a Nichol's-chart representation for both phase-lag and phase-lead transfer functions.

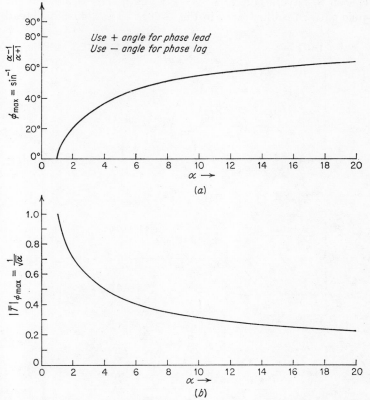

FIG. 5-25. Plot of maximum phase angle ϕ_{max}, and $\left|\bar{T}\right|_{\phi_{max}}$ vs. α for phase-lag or -lead transfer functions. (a) ϕ_{max} vs. α; (b) $\left|\bar{T}\right|_{\phi_{max}}$ vs. α.

5-7. The Phase-lead Characteristic

The counterpart of the phase-lag transfer function of the previous section is the phase lead in which the input and output are related by the differential equation

$$\alpha c(t) + \alpha\tau \frac{dc(t)}{dt} = r(t) + \alpha\tau \frac{dr(t)}{dt} \tag{5-64}$$

or $$\alpha(1 + \tau s)C(s) = (1 + \alpha\tau s)R(s) \tag{5-65}$$

where τ is a constant with the dimension of time if $c(t)$ and $r(t)$ have the same units and where α is again a dimensionless constant greater than unity. The transfer function is given by

$$\frac{C}{R}(s) = \frac{1 + \alpha\tau s}{\alpha(1 + \tau s)} = \frac{1/\alpha\tau + s}{1/\tau + s}$$

and is seen to have a pole at $s = -1/\tau$ and a zero at $s = -1/\alpha\tau$. The zero-pole pattern is illustrated in Fig. 5-26c. The sinusoidal steady-state

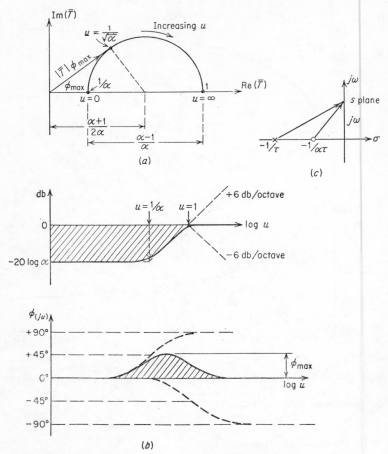

FIG. 5-26. Phase-lead characteristic $\bar{T} = \dfrac{1}{\alpha}\dfrac{1 + j\omega\alpha\tau}{1 + j\omega\tau} = \dfrac{1}{\alpha}\dfrac{1 + j\alpha u}{1 + ju}$, where $u = \omega\tau$ and $\alpha > 1$. (a) Polar plot; (b) log modulus and phase angle; (c) zero-pole pattern for $\bar{T}(s) = (1 + \alpha\tau s)/[\alpha(1 + \tau s)]$.

transfer function for Eq. (5-65) is given by

$$\bar{T} = \frac{1}{\alpha}\frac{1 + j\omega\alpha\tau}{1 + j\omega\tau} = \frac{1}{\alpha}\frac{1 + j\alpha u}{1 + ju} \tag{5-66}$$

where $u = \omega\tau$.

The polar plot for Eq. (5-66) is sketched in Fig. 5-26a and is seen to be a semicircle with its center located at $\left(\dfrac{\alpha + 1}{2\alpha},\ 0\right)$. The geometry of this case is identical to that of the phase-lag characteristic so that the same equations for ϕ_{max} and $|T|_{\phi max}$ apply as in the previous section. The log modulus of Eq. (5-66) is given by

$$
\begin{aligned}
db &= -20 \log \alpha + 20 \log \sqrt{1 + \alpha^2 u^2} - 20 \log \sqrt{1 + u^2} \\
&= -20 \log \alpha + 10 \log (1 + \alpha^2 u^2) - 10 \log (1 + u^2) \quad (5\text{-}67)
\end{aligned}
$$

This characteristic is drawn term by term in a similar manner to the phase-lag case and is shown in Fig. 5-26b. The phase characteristic is given by

$$
\begin{aligned}
\phi(ju) &= \tan^{-1} \alpha u - \tan^{-1} u \\
&= \tan^{-1} \frac{\alpha u - u}{1 + \alpha u^2} = \tan^{-1} \frac{u(\alpha - 1)}{1 + \alpha u^2} \quad (5\text{-}68)
\end{aligned}
$$

This characteristic is similar to the phase-lag case except that a positive angle is involved. The phase angle also appears in Fig. 5-26b. Figure

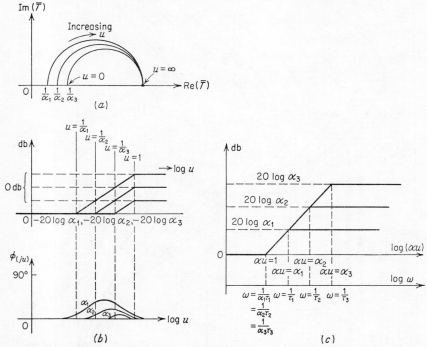

FIG. 5-27. Phase-lead characteristic of Fig. 5-26 for different values of α, where $\alpha_1 > \alpha_2 > \alpha_3 > 1$. (a) Polar plot; (b) log modulus and phase vs. log u; (c) log modulus plotted vs. log αu and log ω with a preamplifier gain of α included.

5-28 may be used for accurate determination of the phase angle, and Fig. 5-29 presents a Nichol's-chart representation of the function. The behavior of the transfer characteristic for different values of α may be seen in Fig. 5-27.

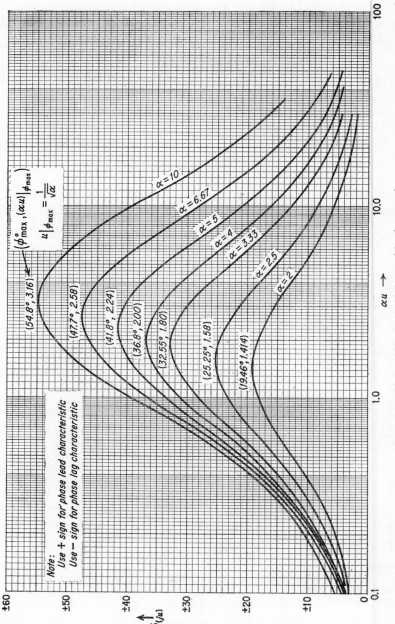

FIG. 5-28. Phase shifts for both lag and lead networks.

Note:
Use + sign for phase lead characteristic
Use — sign for phase lag characteristic

$\left(\overset{\circ}{\phi}_{max}, (\alpha u)\left|_{\phi_{max}}\right.\right)$

$u\left|_{\phi_{max}} = \dfrac{1}{\sqrt{\alpha}}\right.$

(54.8°, 3.16)
(47.7°, 2.58)
(41.8°, 2.24)
(36.6°, 2.00)
(32.55°, 1.80)
(25.25°, 1.58)
(19.46°, 1.414)

$\alpha = 10$
$\alpha = 6.67$
$\alpha = 5$
$\alpha = 4$
$\alpha = 3.33$
$\alpha = 2.5$
$\alpha = 2$

$\alpha u \longrightarrow$

$\phi_{(j u)}$

194

Examination of the log-modulus plots of Fig. 5-27b reveals that they are inconvenient as drawn because the exact location of the 0-db axis depends upon the specific value of α.   For this reason, and also because of the manner in which the phase-lead characteristics are used in practice, these curves are usually redrawn as shown in Fig. 5-27c.   In this diagram the characteristic is plotted vs. log αu as the abscissa.   Here (αu) is the nondimensional frequency ω/ω_b, where ω_b is the lower-corner frequency of

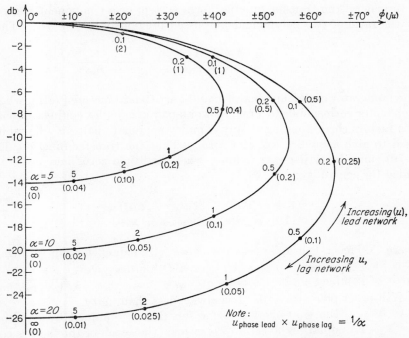

Fig. 5-29. Nichols chart, log modulus (decibels) vs. phase angle for phase-lag and phase-lead networks, with u as a parameter.   Use $+$ angle and values of u within parentheses for phase lead.   Use $-$ angle and values of u without parentheses for phase lag.

the lead network, namely, $1/\alpha\tau$.   In order to sketch the log-modulus asymptotes it is desirable to rewrite Eq. (5-67) as follows:

$$ \text{db} = -20 \log \alpha + 10 \log (1 + \alpha^2 u^2) - 10 \log\left(1 + \frac{\alpha^2 u^2}{\alpha^2}\right) \quad (5\text{-}69)$$

When (αu) is taken as the variable, the second term is seen to have a breakpoint frequency at $\alpha u = 1$ and the last term is seen to have a breakpoint frequency at $(\alpha u) = \alpha$.   The asymptotes are drawn in Fig. 5-27c for different values of α.   The lower breakpoint frequency occurs at $\alpha u = 1$, which is the same point for all values of α.   The upper breakpoint frequency occurs at $(\alpha u) = \alpha_1, \alpha_2, \alpha_3, \ldots$, where $\alpha_1, \alpha_2, \alpha_3, \ldots$ are the specific values of α for which each of the phase-lead characteristics is drawn. In Fig. 5-27c the 0-db ordinate point is located so that it is the same for all the curves. This means that a constant term equal to 20 log α has been added to the expression of Eq. (5-69) before plotting.

5-8. The Generalized Transfer Function

In general the transfer function for a system or a component is given by the ratio of two polynomials discussed previously in Sec. 5-1. Thus

$$T(s) = \frac{A_0 + A_1 s + A_2 s^2 + \cdots + A_m s^m}{B_0 + B_1 s + B_2 s^2 + \cdots + B_n s^n} \tag{5-70}$$

The numerator and denominator may be written in factored form, where each factor corresponds to a real root or a pair of complex conjugate roots. The factors corresponding to any complex conjugate pair may be multiplied to give a quadratic-factor term. Thus the transfer function, Eq. (5-70), may be written as follows, where multiple zeros and poles are added for generality:

$$T(s) = \frac{(1 + s\tau_a)^P (s^2 + 2\zeta_b \omega_{nb} s + \omega_{nb}^2) \cdots}{s^N (1 + s\tau_1)^Q (s^2 + 2\zeta_2 \omega_{n2} s + \omega_{n2}^2) \cdots} \tag{5-71}$$

where $T(s)$ has a Pth-order zero at $s = -1/\tau_a$, a pair of complex conjugate zeros at $s = -\zeta_b \omega_{nb} \pm j\omega_{nb} \sqrt{1 - \zeta_b^2}$, a Qth-order pole at $s = -1/\tau_1$, a pair of complex conjugate poles at $s = -\zeta_2 \omega_{n2} \pm j\omega_{n2} \sqrt{1 - \zeta_2^2}$, and an Nth-order pole at $s = 0$. ζ is always less than unity.

As before, the sinusoidal transfer function is obtained by equating $s = j\omega$. Examination of Eq. (5-71) reveals that each of the factors corresponds to one of the basic transfer functions of the previous section. Thus the generalized transfer function may be represented by combining these basic functions. For this purpose the log-modulus representation is particularly useful. Thus, if $|\overline{T}(j\omega)|$ of Eq. (5-71) is expressed in decibels,

$$\begin{aligned}
20 \log |\overline{T}(j\omega)| = {} & 20 \log (1 + \omega^2 \tau_a^2)^{P/2} - 20 \log (1 + \omega^2 \tau_1^2)^{Q/2} \\
& + 20 \log [(\omega_{nb}^2 - \omega^2)^2 + 4\zeta_b^2 \omega^2 \omega_{nb}^2]^{\frac{1}{2}} \\
& - 20 \log [(\omega_{n2}^2 - \omega^2) + 4\zeta_2^2 \omega^2 \omega_{n2}^2]^{\frac{1}{2}} \\
& \qquad\qquad - 20 \log \omega^N + \cdots \\
= {} & 10P \log (1 + \omega^2 \tau_a^2) - 10Q \log (1 + \omega^2 \tau_1^2) \\
& + 10 \log [(\omega_{nb}^2 - \omega^2)^2 + 4\zeta_b^2 \omega^2 \omega_{nb}^2] \\
& - 10 \log [(\omega_{n2}^2 - \omega^2)^2 + 4\zeta_2^2 \omega^2 \omega_{n2}^2] \\
& \qquad\qquad - 20N \log \omega + \cdots \tag{5-72}
\end{aligned}$$

Similarly the phase of $\overline{T}(j\omega)$ is given by

$$\phi(j\omega) = P \tan^{-1} \omega\tau_a - Q \tan^{-1} \omega\tau_1 + \tan^{-1} \frac{2\omega\omega_{nb}\zeta_b}{\omega_{nb}{}^2 - \omega^2}$$
$$- \tan^{-1} \frac{2\omega\omega_{n2}\zeta_2}{\omega_{n2}{}^2 - \omega^2} - 90°N + \cdots \quad (5\text{-}73)$$

Equations (5-72) and (5-73) may be represented graphically by combining the log-modulus and phase-angle characteristics of each of the terms. This procedure may be demonstrated by means of some simple examples.

Example 5-1. Consider a transfer function given by

$$T(s) = \frac{(1 + s\tau_a)(1 + s\tau_b)}{(1 + s\tau_1)(1 + s\tau_2)} \quad (5\text{-}74)$$

where $\tau_1 > \tau_a > \tau_b > \tau_2$. Draw the asymptotic log-modulus and phase-shift characteristics.

For the sinusoidal steady state this becomes

$$\overline{T}(j\omega) = \frac{(1 + j\omega\tau_a)(1 + j\omega\tau_b)}{(1 + j\omega\tau_1)(1 + j\omega\tau_2)} \quad (5\text{-}75)$$

The log-modulus characteristic is given by

$$20 \log |\overline{T}(j\omega)| = 20 \log (1 + \omega^2\tau_a{}^2)^{\frac{1}{2}} - 20 \log (1 + \omega^2\tau_1{}^2)^{\frac{1}{2}}$$
$$+ 20 \log (1 + \omega^2\tau_b{}^2)^{\frac{1}{2}} - 20 \log [1 + \omega^2\tau_2{}^2]^{\frac{1}{2}} \quad (5\text{-}76)$$

The phase-angle characteristic is given by

$$\phi(j\omega) = \tan^{-1} \omega\tau_a - \tan^{-1} \omega\tau_1 + \tan^{-1} \omega\tau_b - \tan^{-1} \omega\tau_2 \quad (5\text{-}77)$$

Each term corresponds to a linear factor with corner frequencies at $\omega_a = 1/\tau_a$, $\omega_1 = 1/\tau_1$, $\omega_b = 1/\tau_b$, $\omega_2 = 1/\tau_2$, and slopes of ± 6 db/octave, depending upon whether the factor is in the numerator or denominator, respectively. Thus the transfer function of Eq. (5-75) may be represented as illustrated in Fig. 5-30. When there are quadratic factors present in the original transfer function, the procedure is identical. It should be remembered that the actual log-modulus characteristic lies either above or below the asymptotes. This becomes particularly important when the corner frequancies are close to each other.

Example 5-2. Consider a transfer function of the form given by Eq. (5-78), where a, b, c, d, e, and f are positive real numbers.

$$T(s) = \frac{A(s + a)}{(s + b)(cs + d)(s^2 + es + f)} \quad (5\text{-}78)$$

Draw the asymptotic log-modulus and phase-shift characteristics.

It is assumed that the quadratic factor has a pair of complex conjugate roots. Equation (5-78) is rewritten as follows:

$$T(s) = \frac{Aa}{bdf} \frac{1 + s/a}{(1 + s/b)(1 + sc/d)[s^2/f + (e/f)s + 1]} \quad (5\text{-}79)$$

For the sinusoidal steady state this becomes

$$\bar{T}(j\omega) = \frac{Aa}{bdf} \frac{1 + j\omega/a}{(1 + j\omega/b)(1 + j\omega c/d)[(j\omega)^2/f + (e/f)j\omega + 1]}$$ (5-80)

The log modulus is given by

$$20 \log T(\omega) = 20 \log \frac{Aa}{b\,df}$$
$$+ 20 \log \left(1 + \frac{\omega^2}{a^2}\right)^{\frac{1}{2}}$$
$$+ 20 \log \left(1 + \frac{\omega^2}{b^2}\right)^{-\frac{1}{2}}$$
$$+ 20 \log \left(1 + \frac{w^2 c^2}{d^2}\right)^{-\frac{1}{2}}$$
$$+ 20 \log \left[\left(1 - \frac{\omega^2}{f}\right)^2 + \frac{\omega^2 e^2}{f^2}\right]^{-\frac{1}{2}}$$ (5-81)

The first term is a numeric. The next three terms are linear factors with corner frequencies at $\omega = a$, $\omega = b$, $\omega = d/c$ and slopes of ± 6 db/octave, depending upon whether the factor is in the numerator or denominator, respectively. The quadratic factor is seen to correspond to the form of Eq. (5-53) or (5-54). Comparison with

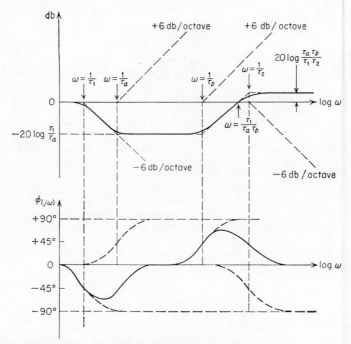

FIG. 5-30. Log-modulus and phase-angle representation for

$$\bar{T}(j\omega) = \frac{(1 + j\omega\tau_a)(1 + j\omega\tau_b)}{(1 + j\omega\tau_1)(1 + j\omega\tau_2)}$$

where $\tau_1 > \tau_a > \tau_b > \tau_2$.

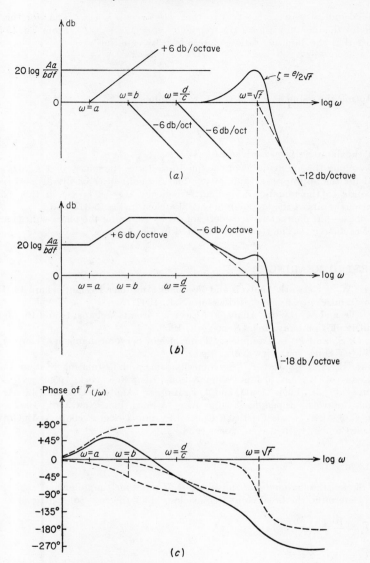

Fɪɢ. 5-31. Asymptotic log-modulus plot of

$$\overline{T}(j\omega) = \frac{Aa}{bdf} \frac{1 + j\omega/a}{\left(1 + \dfrac{j\omega}{b}\right)\left(1 + j\omega\,\dfrac{c}{d}\right)\left[\dfrac{(j\omega)^2}{f} + \dfrac{e}{f}(j\omega) + 1\right]}$$

$$= \frac{A(j\omega + a)}{(j\omega + b)(j\omega c + d)[(j\omega)^2 + j\omega e + f]}$$

(a) **Asymptotic log-modulus plot of each term;** (b) final asymptotic log-modulus plot;
(c) phase-shift characteristic of $\overline{T}(j\omega)$.

Eq. (5-55) indicates that $u^2 = \omega^2/f$ so that $u = \omega\tau = \omega\sqrt{1/f}$. Thus for this quadratic factor the undamped resonant frequency $\omega_n = 1/\tau = \sqrt{f}$. From Eq. (5-55) we also note that the damping ratio is determined by equating

$$4\zeta^2 u^2 = \omega^2 \frac{e^2}{f^2}$$

Substituting the value of $u = \omega\sqrt{1/f}$, we obtain

$$4\zeta^2 \frac{\omega^2}{f} = \omega^2 \frac{e^2}{f^2}$$

so that the damping ratio is given by $\zeta = e/2\sqrt{f}$.

In sketching the log modulus of the quadratic term, the curves of Fig. 5-22 should be used for the appropriate value of ζ. The resonant peak occurs at $u = 1$, which corresponds to the undamped resonant frequency $\omega = \omega_n = \sqrt{f}$ in this example. The various terms of the log modulus are sketched in Fig. 5-31a and b.

The phase-shift characteristic is determined by summing the phase-shift characteristics of each term. The result is illustrated in Fig. 5-31c.

SUGGESTED READING

Bode, H. W.: "Network Analysis and Feedback Amplifier Design," chap. 14, D. Van Nostrand Company, Inc., Princeton, N.J., 1947.

Brenner, E., and M. Javid: "Analysis of Electric Circuits," chaps. 14 and 15, McGraw-Hill Book Company, Inc., New York, 1959.

Brown, G. S., and D. P. Campbell: "Principles of Servomechanisms," chap. 4, John Wiley & Sons, Inc., New York, 1948.

Chestnut, H., and R. Mayer: "Servomechanisms and Regulating System Design," 2d ed., vol. 1, chap. 5, John Wiley & Sons, Inc., New York, 1959.

Newton, G. C., Jr., L. A. Gould, and J. F. Kaiser: "Analytic Design of Linear Feedback Controls," appendix C, John Wiley & Sons, Inc., New York, 1957.

Savant, C. J., Jr.: "Basic Feedback Control System Design," chap. 5, McGraw-Hill Book Company, Inc., New York, 1958.

PROBLEMS

5-1. Sketch the log-modulus and phase-shift plots for the following transfer functions. Determine the breakpoint frequencies. Plot the zero-pole patterns for $T(s)$.

(a) $\bar{T} = \dfrac{10(1 + ju)}{(ju)^2}$ (b) $\bar{T} = \dfrac{1}{3 + 2ju}$

(c) $\bar{T} = \dfrac{(1 + ju)^2}{2 + \sqrt{2}\,ju + (ju)^2}$ (d) $\bar{T} = \dfrac{(ju)^3}{1 + j5u + 6(ju)^2 + (ju)^3}$

(e) $\bar{T} = \dfrac{1}{(1 + ju)(1 + \alpha ju)}$ where $\alpha > 1$ (f) $\bar{T} = \dfrac{a(ju)^2 + g}{\beta(ju)^2 + g}$ where $\beta > a$

5-2. Draw the polar-plot representation for each of the transfer functions of Prob. 5-1.

5-3. If a phase lead and phase lag have the same value of α, show that the frequencies at which their log moduli have the same value are related by the formula

$$(u_{\text{phase lag}})(u_{\text{phase lead}}) = \frac{1}{\alpha}$$

5-4. The asymptotic log-modulus curves for various transfer functions are drawn in Fig. P5-4. Sketch the corresponding phase-shift characteristic and the polar-plot representation for each case. Determine the transfer function for each.

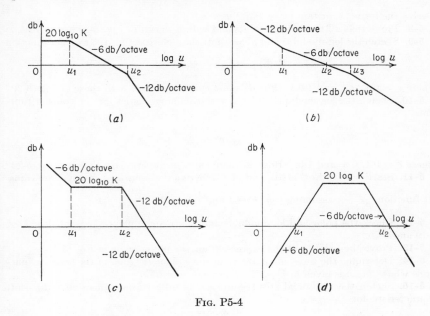

Fig. P5-4

5-5. Given the three transfer functions whose asymptotic log-modulus characteristics are drawn in Fig. P5-5, determine the log-modulus, phase-shift, and polar-plot representations for the following combined transfer function T_4: $T_4(j\omega) = T_1T_2/(1 + T_2T_3)$. (*Hint:* Write the expressions for each transfer function first, and then combine algebraically to get the desired result.)

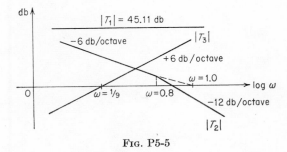

Fig. P5-5

5-6. Draw the log-modulus vs. phase-angle representation for the following transfer functions:

(*a*) Pure differentiation   (*b*) Proportional plus derivative

(*c*) Pure integration   (*d*) Proportional plus integral

5-7. Prove that

$$\tan^{-1} x \, - \, \tan^{-1} y \, = \, \tan^{-1} \frac{x - y}{1 + xy}$$

Derive the formula for $\tan^{-1} x + \tan^{-1} y$.

5-8. Prove that all the critical points and values shown in Fig. 5-30 are correct.

5-9. Sketch the log-modulus and phase-shift characteristics for the transfer function

$$\bar{T}(ju) \, = \, (ju)^2 + j2\zeta u + 1$$

where $\zeta = 0.1, 0.3,$ and 1.0. How do these curves compare with those of Fig. 5-22?

5-10. Sketch the log-modulus and phase-shift characteristics for the transfer function

$$\bar{T}(ju) \, = \, \frac{(ju)^2}{(ju)^2 + j2\zeta u + 1}$$

where $\zeta = 0.1, 0.3,$ and 1.0. How do these curves compare with those of Fig. 5-22?

5-11. Starting with Eqs. (4-10) and (4-11), derive the sinusoidal steady-state transfer function $\dfrac{C(j\omega)}{T'_L(j\omega)}$, assuming that $h = 1$ and $r(t) = 0$.

5-12. Check the polar and log-modulus and phase-angle plots represented in Figs. 5-19 and 5-20.

5-13. Prove the validity of the expression for the phase angle in Eq. (5-59).

5-14. Determine the zero-pole patterns in the s plane for each of the transfer functions whose $\bar{T}(j\omega)$ is given in Eqs. (5-47), (5-48), and (5-49).

5-15. Sketch the sinusoidal steady-state asymptotic log-modulus and phase-shift characteristic for

$$T(s) \, = \, \frac{20(2s + 8)}{s(4s^2 + 4s + 5)}$$

6 | Transfer Functions of Control System Components

In this chapter the transfer functions of various types of components and simple systems are derived in order to demonstrate the procedure involved and to illustrate how some of the basic mathematical forms of the previous chapter are realized physically. The object of determining a transfer function is to obtain an expression which describes the dynamic behavior of a component so that the effects of its operation can be included in the over-all analysis of a system's dynamic behavior. In general every component fits into the basic control system block diagram of Fig. 1-1. Its transfer function thus becomes part or all of the transfer function for one of the major blocks of this diagram. In particular, attention is directed to some typical components which fit into the control-elements block (g_1), the controlled-system block (g_2), and the feedback-element block (h). The reader should realize that the use of the components discussed is not necessarily restricted to the blocks indicated but that they can appear in other parts of a feedback control system.

The components discussed are chosen for several other reasons. (1) They are typical of those found in practice and thus provide a background in commonly used control system components. (2) The derivation of the transfer function is illustrative of the basic procedures involved. (3) The transfer functions derived are available for use later in the text as well as for use in other control systems which the reader may encounter. It should be realized that any discussion presented must necessarily be limited in both detail and scope. The literature and manufacturer's catalogues are the best sources of detailed information on commercially available components. It is by keeping up with these sources that the engineer can be abreast of developments in the field.

6-1. Control Elements (g_1).   Electrical Networks

In the control-element portion of a feedback control system it is often necessary to operate upon the actuating signal in order to stabilize the

203

system or make it conform with performance specifications. From the time-domain point of view this may involve differentiation or integration or both. From the frequency-domain point of view this involves reshaping the frequency-response characteristic. Actually both these approaches are merely different aspects of the same problem, and the transfer function serves as the starting point for both.

Integrating Networks. Phase Lag. As a first example let us consider the problem of performing an integration by using an electrical network.

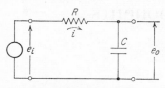

FIG. 6-1. A phase-lag, or integrating, network.

The use of such a network is convenient from the point of view of size, availability, and simplicity of operation. One obvious possibility is the simple RC circuit shown in Fig. 6-1. Roughly, its operation as an integrator is based upon the fact that the voltage across a capacitor is proportional to the integral of the current through it. In order to determine the actual behavior of the network, it is necessary to determine the transfer function between the output and input voltages. The differential equations describing the behavior of the network are

$$e_i = Ri + \frac{1}{C} \int i \, dt \tag{6-1a}$$

$$e_o = \frac{1}{C} \int i \, dt \tag{6-1b}$$

Taking the Laplace transform of the foregoing equations and assuming $e_o(0^+) = 0$ yields the following result:

$$\frac{E_o}{E_i}(s) = \frac{1}{1 + RCs} \tag{6-2}$$

One property of the foregoing network can be seen by considering its sinusoidal steady-state behavior at high frequencies. Thus, if $s = j\omega$ in Eq. (6-2), then

$$\lim_{\omega \to \infty} \left| \frac{E_o}{E_i}(j\omega) \right| = \lim_{\omega \to \infty} \left| \frac{1}{1 + j\omega RC} \right| = 0 \tag{6-3}$$

Physically it can be seen that the impedance of the capacitor approaches a short circuit as the frequency gets higher so that eventually there is zero output voltage. The network therefore acts as a low-pass filter, and if the RC time constant has been chosen large to improve the integrating property, the cutoff frequency is quite low. If such a network were introduced into the direct transmission path of a system, it would reduce the high-frequency response excessively. In practice, therefore, it is necessary to modify the circuit of Fig. 6-1 so that the attenuation at high frequencies is limited. This can be done easily by including an additional resistor R_2, as shown in Fig. 6-2. At high frequencies the capacitor approaches a short circuit as before, but now the transfer function becomes

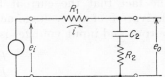

$$\lim_{\omega \to \infty} \left| \frac{E_o}{E_i}(j\omega) \right| = \frac{R_2}{R_1 + R_2} \qquad (6\text{-}4)$$

FIG. 6-2. A phase-lag network with fixed high-frequency attenuation.

The exact sinusoidal steady-state transfer function for the circuit of Fig. 6-2 may be obtained by using the transform impedance $1/Cs$ for the capacitor and the voltage-divider theorem of network theory for impedances in series. Thus

$$\frac{E_o}{E_i}(s) = \frac{R_2 + 1/C_2 s}{R_1 + R_2 + 1/C_2 s} \qquad (6\text{-}5)$$

Upon substituting $s = j\omega$ and rearranging, the sinusoidal steady-state transfer function becomes

$$T = \frac{E_o}{E_i}(j\omega) = \frac{1 + j\omega R_2 C_2}{1 + j\omega C_2 (R_1 + R_2)}$$

$$= \frac{1 + j\omega\tau}{1 + j\omega\alpha\tau} \qquad (6\text{-}6)$$

where

$$\tau = R_2 C_2 \qquad (6\text{-}7)$$

$$\alpha = \frac{R_1 + R_2}{R_2} = 1 + \frac{R_1}{R_2} \qquad (6\text{-}8)$$

It is interesting to note that, as $R_2 \to 0$, $\tau \to 0$ and $\alpha\tau \to R_1 C_2$. The circuit and the corresponding transfer function therefore approach those of Fig. 6-1.

The form of Eq. (6-6) is identical to Eq. (5-58) for a phase lag. Thus this transfer function is represented graphically in Fig. 5-23 and 5-19. In normal design procedures values for α and τ are determined from the characteristics of Figs. 5-25 and 5-28, as required by the system specification. Specific values for R_1, R_2, and C_2 are then chosen to give the correct values for α and τ. Since there are three elements (R_1, R_2, C_2) and only two defining equations [Eqs. (6-7) and (6-8)] relating them to the required values of α and τ, many solutions are possible for the individual element values. In fact the designer is free to choose any one element value arbitrarily, and the others may be derived in terms of it and α and τ by using Eqs. (6-7) and (6-8). Thus, if R_2 is chosen, C_2 is given by τ/R_2 and R_1 by $R_2(\alpha - 1)$. The specific choice of R_2 depends upon such factors as practical element values and the impedance level at which it is desired to operate the network (which in turn depends upon the part of the system into which the network is placed).

Differentiating Networks. Phase Lead. Figure 6-3 represents an electrical differentiating network. Its operation is roughly based upon the fact that the current through a capacitor is proportional to the derivative of the voltage across it. The transfer function between the output and input voltages is given by

$$\frac{E_o}{E_i}(s) = \frac{RCs}{1 + RCs} \tag{6-9}$$

A serious limitation to the use of this simple RC differentiator occurs because with a constant input signal there is zero signal transmitted through the network. In general the circuit behaves as a high-pass filter. This means that the inclusion of such a network in the direct transmission path of a control system would result in zero steady-state response.

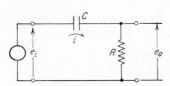

FIG. 6-3. A phase-lead, or differentiating, network.

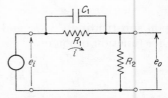

FIG. 6-4. A phase-lead network with fixed steady-state (d-c) attenuation.

This, of course, is impractical for many situations, and it is necessary to modify the circuit in accordance with Fig. 6-4 in order to obtain direct transmission. With a constant input the ratio of output to input voltages is then given by $R_2/(R_1 + R_2)$.

The exact transfer function for the circuit of Fig. 6-4 is given by

$$\frac{E_o}{E_i}(s) = \frac{R_2}{R_2 + \dfrac{1}{1/R_1 + C_1 s}} = \frac{R_2}{R_2 + R_1} \frac{1 + R_1 C_1 s}{1 + \dfrac{R_1 R_2}{R_1 + R_2} C_1 s}$$

or

$$\frac{E_o}{E_i}(s) = \frac{1}{\alpha} \frac{1 + \alpha \tau s}{1 + \tau s} \tag{6-10}$$

where

$$\alpha = \frac{R_2 + R_1}{R_2} = 1 + \frac{R_1}{R_2} \tag{6-11}$$

and

$$\tau = \frac{R_1 R_2}{R_1 + R_2} C_1 \tag{6-12}$$

As $R_1 \to \infty$ (an open circuit), then Fig. 6-4 reduces to Fig. 6-3 and $\alpha \to \infty$ while $\tau \to R_2 C_1$.

In the sinusoidal steady state Eq. (6-10) becomes

$$T = \frac{E_o}{E_i}(j\omega) = \frac{1}{\alpha} \frac{1 + j\omega \alpha \tau}{1 + j\omega \tau} \tag{6-13}$$

This result is recognized as being identical to Eq. (5-66), a phase lead. Consequently the transfer function is represented graphically in Figs. 5-26 and 5-27. In normal design procedures α and τ are again determined from the requirements of the system, and the specific values for R_1, C_1, and R_2 are chosen to give the correct values for α and τ. As in the case of the lag network it is possible to choose one of the element values and determine the value of the other two in terms of this element and α and τ. The specific choice of the arbitrary element again depends upon practical values and the impedance level at

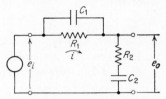

FIG. 6-5. A lag-lead network.

which it is desired to operate the network. The resistor shunting capacitor C_1 should be chosen to be much less than the normal leakage resistance of the capacitor.

A Phase Lag-Lead Network. In many situations it is desired to incorporate a phase lag-lead network into a system, combining the effects of the two networks considered previously. Figure 6-5 illustrates such a network. The transfer function between output and input voltages is given by

$$\frac{E_o}{E_i}(s) = \frac{R_2 + 1/C_2 s}{R_2 + \dfrac{1}{C_2 s} + \dfrac{1}{1/R_1 + C_1 s}} \tag{6-14}$$

After some algebraic manipulation this transfer function may be put into the form

$$T(s) = \frac{E_o}{E_i}(s) = \frac{(1 + s\tau_a)(1 + s\tau_b)}{\tau_a \tau_b s^2 + (\tau_a + \tau_b + \tau_{ab})s + 1} \tag{6-15}$$

where

$$\tau_a = R_1 C_1 \tag{6-16a}$$

$$\tau_b = R_2 C_2 \tag{6-16b}$$

$$\tau_{ab} = R_1 C_2 \tag{6-16c}$$

Before this transfer function can be represented graphically, it is necessary to investigate the quadratic factor of the denominator to determine whether it can be factored into two real root factors or two complex conjugate root factors. The roots of the quadratic are located at

$$
\begin{aligned}
s &= \frac{-(\tau_a + \tau_b + \tau_{ab}) \pm \sqrt{(\tau_a + \tau_b + \tau_{ab})^2 - 4\tau_a \tau_b}}{2\tau_a \tau_b} \\
&= \frac{-(\tau_a + \tau_b + \tau_{ab}) \pm \sqrt{(\tau_a - \tau_b)^2 + 2(\tau_a + \tau_b)\tau_{ab} + \tau_{ab}^2}}{2\tau_a \tau_b} \tag{6-17}
\end{aligned}
$$

Examination of the radical of Eq. (6-17) indicates that it is real for all positive real values of τ_a, τ_b, and τ_{ab}, so that the quadratic can always be factored into two linear real root terms. Thus Eq. (6-15) may be written as

$$T(s) = \frac{(1 + s\tau_a)(1 + s\tau_b)}{(1 + s\tau_1)(1 + s\tau_2)} \qquad (6\text{-}18)$$

where

$$\tau_1\tau_2 = \tau_a\tau_b \qquad (6\text{-}19a)$$

and

$$\tau_1 + \tau_2 = \tau_a + \tau_b + \tau_{ab} \qquad (6\text{-}19b)$$

The last two equations serve to identify τ_1 and τ_2 in terms of τ_a, τ_b, and τ_{ab}, the time constants defined for the network. In particular, examination of Eq. (6-19a) reveals that

$$\frac{\tau_a}{\tau_1} = \frac{\tau_2}{\tau_b} \qquad (6\text{-}20)$$

Let us now assume that $\tau_1 > \tau_a$ so that we may define a number $\alpha > 1$ such that

$$\tau_1 = \alpha\tau_a \qquad (6\text{-}20a)$$

From Eq. (6-20) it follows that

$$\tau_b = \alpha\tau_2 \qquad (6\text{-}20b)$$

Thus Eq. (6-18) becomes

$$T(s) = \frac{(1 + s\tau_a)(1 + s\tau_b)}{(1 + s\alpha\tau_a)[1 + s(\tau_b/\alpha)]} \qquad (6\text{-}20c)$$

In the sinusoidal steady state Eq. (6-20c) becomes

$$T(j\omega) = \frac{[1 + j(\omega/\omega_a)][1 + j(\omega/\omega_b)]}{\left[1 + j\left(\dfrac{\omega}{\omega_a/\alpha}\right)\right]\left[1 + j\left(\dfrac{\omega}{\alpha\omega_b}\right)\right]} \qquad (6\text{-}21)$$

where $\omega_a = 1/\tau_a$ and $\omega_b = 1/\tau_b$.

The form of this equation is identical to that of Eq. (5-75). The log-modulus representation is therefore similar to that of Fig. 5-30 with the added restriction of Eqs. (6-20). This restriction means that the asymptotic characteristic returns to 0 db at $\omega = 1/\tau_2$. This is verified physically by inspecting the transfer function as $\omega \to \infty$. At high frequencies the capacitors become short circuits, and the output voltage equals the input voltage, which corresponds to 0 db. The log-modulus and phase-shift characteristics for the lag-lead network are drawn in Fig. 6-6.

An additional useful relationship may be derived from the phase-shift characteristic. If ω_0 denotes the frequency of zero phase shift, then the following formula holds:

$$\omega_0 = \frac{1}{\sqrt{\tau_a\tau_b}} \qquad (6\text{-}22)$$

The proof of this equation is left as an exercise for the reader.

It is interesting to note that here there are four circuit parameters but only three defining time constants. Thus it is possible to define one of

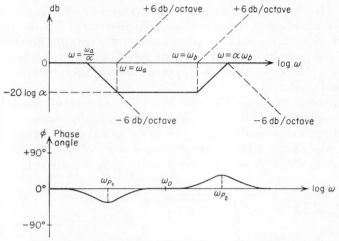

FIG. 6-6. Log-modulus and phase-angle representation of a lag-lead network

$$T = \frac{(1 + j\omega\tau_a)(1 + j\omega\tau_b)}{(1 + j\omega\tau_1)(1 + j\omega\tau_2)}$$

where $\tau_1\tau_2 = \tau_a\tau_b$ and $\tau_1 = \alpha\tau_a$, $\alpha > 1$.

the circuit parameters arbitrarily and find the others in terms of the arbitrarily chosen element and the required time constants.

6-2. Control Elements (g_1). Amplifiers

In all closed-loop systems it is necessary to amplify the actuating signal, which, by the very nature of the feedback, is small. This amplification may be provided in many forms. Often the shaping networks of the previous section are an integral part of the amplifier. Many times the amplifier is so closely related to the controlled system that the two cannot be conveniently separated in the derivation of a transfer function. Several different types are discussed in some detail to illustrate this point and to indicate the type of transfer function which results.

Electronic and Magnetic Amplifiers. The vacuum tube and solid-state amplifier provide a very common and practical way to obtain amplification. In general the time constants associated with these circuits are very small compared with the major time constants of the entire system. For this reason the transfer function associated with them can often be represented as a constant gain factor K. Of course there are many exceptions to this rule. The engineer should always be aware of this fact and should check to see that the time constants are truly negligible before assigning a constant gain factor. This is particularly true of magnetic amplifiers. In the case of a saturable reactor-type magnetic amplifier the transfer function is similar to that of a linear RL circuit. In the case of a reactor-rectifier type of magnetic amplifier time delays of one cycle of the excitation voltage occur. For the purposes of this text we shall make the assumption that the transfer function for any amplifier is represented by a constant gain factor. If this is not true in any particular case, then the appropriate transfer function must be found and used.

The Rotary Amplifier (Amplidyne). The amplidyne has gained considerable prominence in those servomechanism applications demanding high output levels ranging from $\frac{1}{2}$ to 50 kw and above. Often the amplidyne serves as the power stage driving a d-c motor. The control field winding (of which there are several sections) is usually driven from the

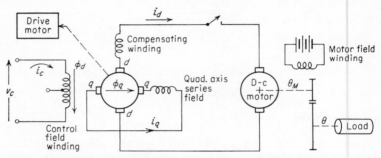

FIG. 6-7. An amplidyne generator showing windings and connected d-c motor load.

output stage of an electronic amplifier. During World War II this unit was extensively used in control systems which positioned the gun turrets of war vehicles. Nowadays it is used a great deal in performing many difficult industrial as well as military tasks.

The amplidyne is basically a d-c generator. It is driven at constant speed by means of a suitable motor which serves as the source of power for the unit. The magnitude of the output voltage is controlled by the amount of field current flowing through the control winding. Usually, the armature winding of a d-c motor is placed across the amplidyne output terminals, and, accordingly, it is important to account for its loading effect in deriving the amplidyne transfer function. This loading effect must properly take into consideration the inertia and viscous friction of the motor as well as the connected mechanical load.

The principle of operation of the amplidyne is straightforward. A small current flowing through the control winding is made to create a flux ϕ_d directed as illustrated in Fig. 6-7. Since the armature winding is rotating at full speed, a voltage e_q is induced and it appears across the brushes q-q. By short circuiting these brushes and using an armature-winding resistance of low value, very large values of armature current can be made to flow.   For example, if e_q is 1 volt and the armature-winding resistance is 0.01 ohm, a current of 100 amp flows through the armature winding.   As a result of the armature reaction associated with such large currents, a very strong flux field ϕ_q is produced and is directed in quadrature to the original field ϕ_d.   Upon placing a second set of brushes d-d normal to the ϕ_q field, there is made available a high-level voltage source which can be applied to the d-c motor, which in turn provides the desired output at the mechanical load.   In practice it is customary to short-circuit the brushes q-q through a series field.   This enables the required value of ϕ_q to be established with smaller quadrature-axis armature current.   Another modification involves the inclusion of a compensating winding placed in the direct-axis circuit.   Its function is to prevent the armature reaction flux produced by the output current i_d from diminishing the original field ϕ_d.   The compensating winding is designed to provide 100 per cent compensation, a condition which is absolutely necessary in view of the small values which ϕ_d assumes during normal operation.

The transfer function of the amplidyne as an isolated unit, i.e., without its connected load, is found by considering the direct-axis induced voltage e_d as the output quantity and the applied control-winding voltage v_c as the input.   The derivation which follows is based on the assumption that there is zero coupling between the flux in the direct axis and the flux in the quadrature axis and that saturation of the magnetic circuit is negligible.   The differential equation for the field winding is as usual

$$v_c = i_c R_c + L_c \frac{di_c}{dt} \tag{6-23}$$

where R_c = control-winding resistance, ohms
      L_c = control-winding inductance, henry
      v_c = applied control-winding voltage, volts
      i_c = control-winding current, amp
Expressed in transformed form, this equation becomes

$$\frac{I_c}{V_c}(s) = \frac{1}{R_c(1 + s\tau_c)} \tag{6-24}$$

where $\tau_c = \dfrac{L_c}{R_c}$ = control-field-winding time constant (sec)   (6-25)

Moreover, $e_q = K_q \phi_d \tag{6-26}$

where K_q is a factor which includes the amplidyne armature-winding factor and its speed of rotation.   A more convenient form of Eq. (6-26) results by recalling that ϕ_d is proportional to i_c so that we can write

$$e_q = K_1 i_c \tag{6-27}$$

where K_1 is a proportionality factor relating the number of volts induced in the q axis per unit control field current in amperes. Furthermore, writing Kirchhoff's voltage law as it applies to the quadrature axis, we have

$$e_q = i_q R_q + L_q \frac{di_q}{dt} \tag{6-28}$$

where R_q = total resistance in quadrature-axis circuit, ohms
       L_q = total inductance in quadrature-axis circuit, henry
       i_q = current flowing in quadrature-axis circuit, amp
Transforming the last equation after combining with Eq. (6-27) gives

$$\frac{I_q}{I_c}(s) = \frac{K_1}{R_q(1 + s\tau_q)} \tag{6-29}$$

where
$$\tau_q = \frac{L_q}{R_q} \tag{6-30}$$

Finally, with the amplidyne output circuit open it follows that the output voltage is proportional to i_q. Thus,

$$e_d = K_2 i_q \tag{6-31}$$

where K_2 is a generator constant which expresses the number of volts induced in the direct-axis circuit per ampere in the quadrature axis. Expressed in terms of Laplace notation Eq. (6-31) is simply

$$\frac{E_d}{I_q}(s) = K_2 \tag{6-32}$$

Multiplying Eqs. (6-24), (6-29), and (6-32) yields the unloaded transfer function. Thus,

$$\frac{E_d}{V_c}(s) = \left[\frac{I_c}{V_c}(s)\right]\left[\frac{I_q}{I_c}(s)\right]\left[\frac{E_d}{I_q}(s)\right] = \frac{K_1 K_2}{R_c R_q}\frac{1}{(1 + s\tau_c)(1 + s\tau_q)} \tag{6-33}$$

The usefulness of this result is restricted to those applications where the output load current of the amplidyne i_d is negligible. This is certainly not the case in an application such as depicted in Fig. 6-7.

The transfer function for this arrangement must be found by considering the d-c motor as part of the direct-axis circuitry of the amplidyne and in this way accounting for the loading effect. The resulting transfer function then provides the correct description of the dynamics of the amplidyne-motor combination. For this derivation the additional assumption is made that the output circuit is compensated perfectly, thereby assuring that the load current i_d has no effect on the control flux ϕ_d.

Two more equations are needed to complete the analysis. The first of these is obtained by applying Kirchhoff's voltage law to the direct-axis circuit. Thus,

$$e_d = K_2 i_q = i_d R_d + K_n \frac{d\theta_M}{dt} \tag{6-34}$$

The amplidyne armature-winding inductance in the direct axis contributes very little in Eq. (6-34). Transformed, Eq. (6-34) becomes

$$K_2 I_q(s) = I_d(s) R_d + K_n(s\theta_M) \tag{6-35}$$

In these equations R_d represents the total direct-axis resistance, which for our configuration includes the resistances of the amplidyne armature and compensating windings as well as the armature winding of the d-c motor. The last term on the right side of Eq. (6-34) denotes the counter emf produced by the rotating motor armature, where K_n has the units of volts/radian/sec. The second equation results upon writing the torque equation as it applies at the motor shaft. Thus,

$$K_T i_d = J \frac{d^2\theta_M}{dt^2} + F \frac{d\theta_M}{dt} \tag{6-36}$$

where K_T = motor torque constant, torque/direct-axis amp, lb-ft/amp
     J = total inertia reflected to motor shaft, slug-ft^2
     F = total viscous-friction coefficient reflected to motor shaft, lb-ft/radian/sec

Rewriting in transformed form, we have

$$\frac{\theta_M}{I_d}(s) = \frac{K_T}{F} \frac{1}{s(1 + s\tau_m)} \tag{6-37}$$

where

$$\tau_m = \frac{J}{F} \tag{6-38}$$

The form of Eq. (6-37) points out that the output quantity of the amplidyne-motor combination is taken to be the motor displacement.

Inserting $s\theta_M$ as found from Eq. (6-37) into Eq. (6-35) leads to

$$\frac{I_d}{I_q}(s) = \frac{K_2(1 + s\tau_m)}{R_d(1 + s\tau_m) + K_T K_n/F} \tag{6-39}$$

Thus,

$$\frac{I_d}{I_q}(s) = \frac{K_2(1 + s\tau_m)}{R_d[(1 + K_T K_n/F R_d) + s\tau_m]} = \frac{K_2}{R_d(1 + K_T K_n/F R_d)} \frac{1 + s\tau_m}{1 + s\tau'_m} \tag{6-40}$$

where

$$\tau'_m = \frac{\tau_m}{1 + K_T K_n/F R_d} \tag{6-41}$$

The combined amplidyne-motor transfer function then follows from the relationship

$$\frac{\theta_M}{V_e}(s) = \left[\frac{I_c}{V_c}(s)\right]\left[\frac{I_q}{I_c}(s)\right]\left[\frac{I_d}{I_q}(s)\right]\left[\frac{\theta_M}{I_d}(s)\right] \tag{6-42}$$

Equations (6-24), (6-29), (6-40), and (6-37) may be introduced here directly since all loading effects have been accounted for. Therefore,

$$\frac{\theta_M}{V_c}(s) = \frac{K_1 K_2}{R_c R_q} \frac{K_T}{FR_d + K_T K_N} \frac{1}{s(1 + s\tau_c)(1 + s\tau_q)(1 + s\tau_m')} \quad (6\text{-}43)$$

A comparison of this equation with Eq. (6-33) reveals the precise manner in which the presence of the motor modifies the transfer function. It introduces a change in gain along with pure integration and a simple time lag as represented by τ_m'. Note that, if the loading effect of the motor were neglected, the result would be a larger time constant and a somewhat different gain.

The magnitudes of the amplidyne time constants τ_c and τ_q vary with the size of the unit. Although for any given size machine τ_c and τ_q have the same order of magnitude, the values vary from 0.05 sec for $\frac{1}{2}$-kw units to 0.4 sec for 50-kw units. The value of τ_m', of course, depends upon the size of the motor and the nature of the connected load, but it easily can be of the order of several seconds. The use of such a combination in a control system leads to stability problems because of the four time lags associated with the composite transfer function.

6-3. Control Elements (g_1). Actuators

The final control element in many systems involves a power component for the conversion of the electrical actuating signal (after shaping and amplification) into a mechanical output motion. There are many components used for this purpose, including electrical solenoids, hydraulic rams, and electrical motors. The latter are particularly common, and for this reason we shall spend some time discussing the transfer function of both the d-c and the a-c motor.

The D-C Motor. The d-c motor is an excellent example of an electromechanical device, and we shall investigate its transfer function in several situations. The d-c motor is used as a servomotor in many applications, although a-c servomotors are to be preferred from the point of view of brush and commutator, amplifier drift, and related problems. However, on the basis of output-power to motor-volume ratio, the d-c motor shows to advantage. The principles of d-c motor operation are applicable to many situations, and several special devices, such as the accelerometer (see Sec. 6-5) and various types of electromechanical actuators, have been built utilizing these principles.

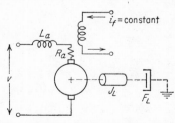

Fig. 6-8. A constant-field d-c motor with inertial load and viscous-friction damper.

The D-C Motor as a Servomotor. Let us first consider the d-c motor when used as a constant-field motor with the input voltage applied to the armature as shown in Fig. 6-8. The motor's developed torque is given by

$$T_L = K_T I_a = \frac{V - K_n \dot\theta_M}{R_a + L_a s} K_T \tag{6-44}$$

where T_L = load torque delivered by the motor, lb-ft

K_T = motor's torque constant, lb-ft/amp

R_a = armature resistance, ohms

L_a = armature, inductance, henrys

K_n = motor's back-emf constant, volts/radian/sec

$\dot\theta_M = d\theta_M/dt$ = motor's angular velocity, radians/sec

V = applied armature voltage, volts

If the motor has a rotor inertia of J_M (slug-ft^2) and drives an inertial load J_L (slug-ft^2) and a viscous-friction damper F_L (ft-lb/radian/sec), then its equation of motion is given by

$$\frac{K_T(V - K_n \dot\theta_M)}{R_a + L_a s} = (J_M + J_L) s \dot\theta_M + F_L \dot\theta_M \tag{6-45}$$

Combining terms, and letting the total inertia be denoted by the letter $J = J_M + J_L$, with $\tau_a = L_a/R_a$, yields

$$\frac{K_T}{R_a} V = \left[\frac{K_n K_T}{R_a} + Js(1 + \tau_a s) + F_L(1 + \tau_a s) \right] \dot\theta_M \tag{6-46a}$$

Also, $K_T V = [K_n K_T + Js(R_a + L_a s) + F_L(R_a + L_a s)] \dot\theta_M \tag{6-46b}$

Equation (6-46b) is of particular interest when $L_a = 0$ and $R_a = 0$, which corresponds to a lossless motor. The transfer function becomes

$$\frac{\theta_M}{V}(s) = \frac{1}{s} \frac{1}{K_n} \tag{6-47}$$

The angular position thus becomes proportional to the *integral* of the applied voltage. The motor approaches an ideal integrator as its internal resistance is reduced. It is important to note that it is not necessary for the external viscous friction F_L to become zero for perfect integration. Physically making R_a approach zero means that the motor's back emf becomes equal to the applied voltage. Since the back emf is proportional to the motor's angular velocity, it follows that its angular position is proportional to the integral of V. It is this property which enables a motor to be used for integration.

Equation (6-46a) may be expressed in more concise form by defining a total viscous-damping coefficient $F = F_L + K_T K_n/R_a$ and a motor constant $K_M = K_T/R_a$. Thus

$$K_M V = [F + Js(1 + \tau_a s) + F_L \tau_a s] \dot\theta_M \tag{6-48}$$

If we now define $\tau_a^* = (F_L/F)\tau_a$, Eq. (6-48) can be rewritten as

$$K_M V = [Js(1 + \tau_a s) + F(1 + \tau_a^* s)]\dot{\theta}_M$$

Solving for the ratio $\dot{\theta}_M/V$, we obtain the motor's transfer function when the angular velocity is taken as the output.

$$\frac{\dot{\theta}_M}{V} = \frac{K_M}{F\left[\dfrac{J}{F} s(1 + \tau_a s) + 1 + \tau_a^* s\right]}$$

$$= \frac{K}{\tau\tau_a s^2 + (\tau + \tau_a^*)s + 1]} \tag{6-49}$$

where $K = K_M/F$ and $\tau = J/F$.

When the armature inductance is neglected, we let $L_a = 0$ so that $\tau_a = \tau_a^* = 0$ and the transfer function becomes

$$\frac{\dot{\theta}_M}{V}(s) = \frac{K}{1 + s\tau} \tag{6-50}$$

or

$$\frac{\dot{\theta}_M}{V}(s) = \frac{K}{s(1 + s\tau)} \tag{6-51}$$

In terms of the sinusoidal steady-state response, the transfer function of Eqs. (6-51) and (6-50) becomes

$$\frac{\dot{\theta}_M}{V}(j\omega) = \frac{K}{j\omega(j\omega\tau + 1)} \tag{6-52a}$$

or

$$\frac{\dot{\theta}_M}{V}(j\omega) = \frac{K}{j\omega\tau + 1} \tag{6-52b}$$

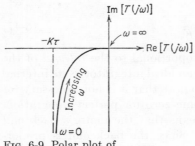

FIG. 6-9. Polar plot of

$$\bar{T}(j\omega) = \frac{K}{j\omega(1 + j\omega\tau)}$$

The transfer function which applies in any given situation depends upon whether the angular position or angular velocity of the motor is used as the output.

Equation (6-52b) is identical to one of the basic forms of Sec. 5-4 so that it is graphically represented in Fig. 5-19.

Equation (6-52a) is a form which has not been discussed previously. Its polar plot is sketched in Fig. 6-9.

The behavior of this characteristic may be checked by rationalizing Eq. (6-52a). Thus

$$\frac{\dot{\theta}_M}{V}(j\omega) = \frac{K}{j\omega(j\omega\tau + 1)} = \frac{-K\tau}{1 + \omega^2\tau^2} - j\frac{K}{\omega(1 + \omega^2\tau^2)} \tag{6-53}$$

As ω approaches infinity, both the real and imaginary parts of Eq. (6-53) approach zero but it can be seen that the imaginary part approaches zero faster than the real part because of the ω factor in the denominator of the imaginary part.   Thus, as ω approaches infinity, the polar plot approaches the origin along the negative real axis.   As ω approaches zero, Eq. (6-53) approaches the value $-K - j\infty$ as depicted on the polar plot (Fig. 6-9).   For intermediate values of ω the characteristic is seen to lie in the quadrant between -90 and $-180°$.

The log-modulus representation of Eq. (6-52a) is given by

$$20 \log \left| \frac{\theta_M}{V} \right| = 20 \log K - 20 \log \omega - 20 \log (1 + \omega^2 \tau^2)^{\frac{1}{2}} \quad (6\text{-}54)$$

The first two terms represent a straight line with a slope of -6 db/octave which passes through 0 db at $\omega = K$.   The third term represents a broken

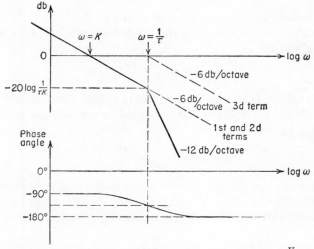

Fig. 6-10. Log-modulus and phase angle of $\overline{T}(j\omega) = \dfrac{K}{j\omega(1 + j\omega\tau)}$.

line with a slope of -6 db/octave occurring after the corner frequency of $\omega = 1/\tau$ and zero slope before.   These terms are drawn in Fig. 6-10 and are combined to give the over-all transfer function.

The phase-shift representation of Eq. (6-52a) is given by

$$\phi(j\omega) = -90° - \tan^{-1} \omega\tau \qquad (6\text{-}55)$$

This characteristic appears in Fig. 6-10 also.

In some applications, such as for speed control, the d-c motor may also be used as a constant-armature-current controlled field device (see

Fig. 6-11) provided that its magnetic circuit is operated unsaturated, i.e., equal changes in field current produce equal changes in flux. Upon assuming a linear saturation characteristic the developed torque T_d is given by

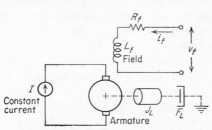

FIG. 6-11. A field-controlled d-c motor.

$$T_d = K_{T_f}I_f \qquad (6\text{-}56)$$

where K_{T_f} is a torque constant giving the developed torque per unit of field current with constant armature current.

If the motor drives the same load as previously, its equation of motion is given by

$$K_{T_f}i_f = J\frac{d^2\theta_M}{dt^2} + F_L\frac{d\theta_M}{dt} \qquad (6\text{-}57)$$

where F_L denotes the viscous friction of the load.

The transfer function relating the output angular position to the field current is given by

$$\frac{\theta_M}{I_f}(s) = \frac{K_{T_f}}{s(Js + F_L)} \qquad (6\text{-}58)$$

Equation (6-58) is similar to Eq. (6-51) except that the constants are different. Now the field current is related to the voltage applied to the field winding by the equation

$$I_f(s) = \frac{V_f(s)}{R_f + L_f s} \qquad (6\text{-}59)$$

where R_f and L_f are the field-winding resistance and inductance, respectively. Substituting Eq. (6-59) into Eq. (6-58) yields the over-all transfer function from field voltage to angular position. Thus,

$$\begin{aligned}
\frac{\theta_M}{V_f}(s) &= \frac{K_{T_f}}{s(Js + F_L)(L_f s + R_f)} \\
&= \frac{K_{T_f}/F_L R_f}{s[(J/F_L)s + 1][(L_f/R_f)s + 1]}
\end{aligned} \qquad (6\text{-}60)$$

This equation indicates how the constants of the field winding are reflected in the over-all transfer function. If the time constant (L_f/R_f) of the field winding may be neglected, Eq. (6-60) reduces to

$$\frac{\theta_M}{V_f}(s) = \frac{K_{T_f}/F_L R_f}{s[(J/F_L)s + 1]} \qquad (6\text{-}61)$$

The sinusoidal steady-state transfer functions may be derived from Eqs. (6-60) and (6-61) and the results represented graphically by using the rules outlined previously. This is left as an exercise for the reader.

The Two-phase Servomotor. Instrument-type servomechanisms requiring output devices which can provide anywhere from $\frac{1}{2}$ to 100 watts output most frequently use the two-phase a-c servomotor. It is not too frequently used where larger output power is involved because of its inherently poor efficiency.

The two-phase servomotor consists of a stator and a rotor. The stator is built up of sheet-steel laminations which are slotted to accommodate the two-phase distributed winding. The winding for each phase is distributed so that the axes are in space quadrature, a condition which permits the motor to develop greater useful torque than if this condition were not satisfied. The rotor construction is any one of three types, viz., the squirrel cage, the solid, and the dragcup type. The most commonly used is the squirrel cage; however, for high-performance fast-responding instrument servomechanisms which require relatively small output power,

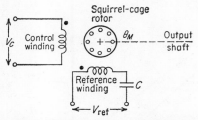

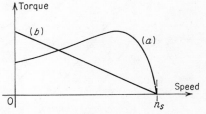

FIG. 6-12. Schematic diagram of the two-phase squirrel-cage servomotor.

FIG. 6-13. (*a*) Torque-speed curve of conventional two-phase motor; (*b*) torque-speed curve of servomotor.

the dragcup type is commonly used. The chief reason lies in the very small rotor inertia which can be realized with this construction.

In normal operation one of the two phase windings has a fixed, rated voltage applied to it at all times. For this reason it is called the *reference winding*. The excitation for the second phase is obtained from the preceding stage in the control loop, which often is the output stage of the servoamplifier. This winding is called the *control winding*. Of course, to produce torque efficiently, not only must the axes of the phase windings be in space quadrature, but the phase voltages must be in time quadrature. Usually, the latter condition is provided in one of two ways. Either a series capacitor is included in the reference-winding circuit as shown in Fig. 6-12, or the 90° phase shift is obtained in the servoamplifier by means of suitable phase-shifting circuits.

The torque-speed curve of a conventional two-phase motor is shown as curve *a* in Fig. 6-13. Such a motor characteristic is entirely unsuitable for control system applications owing to the fact that the slope is not negative over the entire speed range. It will be recalled that it is this drooping characteristic which provides the necessary damping in many servomechanisms. A positive slope means a negative damping coefficient and hence can easily lead to a condition of instability. To provide the servomotor with a negative slope over the entire speed range, the rotor winding is designed for very high resistance. The torque-speed curve then looks like (b) in Fig. 6-13. The torque-speed characteristics of a typical servomotor appear in Fig. 6-14, for various fixed values of control-winding voltage 90° out of time phase with the fixed reference voltage.

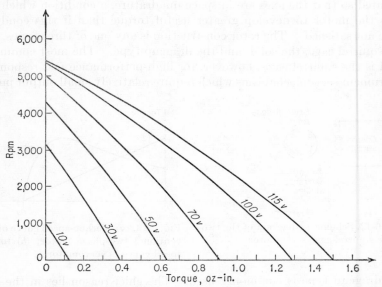

FIG. 6-14. Actual torque-speed curves. Speed-torque voltage characteristics: **115** volts, 2ϕ, 400 cps. Tested with 115 volts on fixed phase and varying excitation on control phase as indicated.

The servomotor transfer function is found readily once these external characteristics are available. Since the transfer function relates an output quantity to an input quantity, we must identify these first. There is no doubt as to what the input quantity is, viz., the control-winding voltage, but there is some question about what the output quantity of the motor is. Is it velocity, or is it displacement? Certainly from the arrangement in Fig. 6-12 it is apparent that the application of a control voltage manifests itself as an output velocity. However, this is not necessarily the controlling factor. More important is the function which the motor output is to perform in terms of the complete control system. To be sure, if the output of the system is to be a velocity, then it is appropriate to derive a transfer function relating output velocity to control-winding voltage. On the other hand, if the motor output is to be used to drive a *position-sensitive* feedback transducer element, then clearly the appropriate motor output quantity is displacement. Because the transfer function for velocity output is derived readily from the transfer function by using displacement as the output, attention is focused on the latter.

The general form of the servomotor transfer function is of primary concern at the moment. Consequently, the torque-speed curves shown in Fig. 6-14 are assumed linear for simplicity. A study of these plots reveals that an increased motor developed torque comes about either by an increase in control-winding voltage v_c or by a decrease in speed for fixed v_c. Expressed mathematically we have

$$\text{Motor developed torque} = K_M v_c - F_M \frac{d\theta_M}{dt} \qquad (6\text{-}62)$$

where K_M = motor torque constant, developed torque/voltage

F_M = motor equivalent-viscous-friction constant, torque/radian/sec

θ_M = angular displacement of motor, radians

v_c = magnitude of a-c voltage applied to control winding, volts

Equating this torque to the sum of the opposing load torques yields

$$K_M v_c - F_M \frac{d\theta_M}{dt} = J \frac{d^2\theta_M}{dt^2} + F_L \frac{d\theta_M}{dt} \qquad (6\text{-}63)$$

where $J = J_M +$ load inertia reflected to motor shaft

F_L = reflected-load viscous-friction coefficient

Equation (6-63) does not consider the presence of a fixed load torque T_L because it does not affect the generality of the result. Rearranging and taking the Laplace transform of Eq. (6-63) gives

$$K_M V_c(s) = (Js^2 + Fs)\theta_M(s) \qquad (6\text{-}64)$$

where
$$F = F_M + F_L \qquad (6\text{-}65)$$

Hence the desired transfer function becomes

$$\frac{\theta_M}{V_c}(s) = \frac{K_m}{s(1 + s\tau_m)} \qquad (6\text{-}66)$$

where
$$K_m = \frac{K_M}{F}\left(\frac{1}{\text{volt-sec}}\right) \qquad (6\text{-}67)$$

$$\tau_m = \frac{J}{F}\ (\text{sec}) \qquad (6\text{-}68)$$

Very often the motor time constant τ_m plays an important role in establishing the character of the dynamic performance of the control system of which it is a part. This is attributable to the fact that its magnitude is established in terms of the inertia of physical elements such as the size of the servomotor rotor and reflected load inertia. These elements are such that although they may be appreciably reduced (for example, by using a dragcup rotor where small output power is involved) they cannot be reduced to negligence primarily because the size of J goes hand in hand with the required level of output power. Thus in many cases the motor inertia is the determining factor which establishes

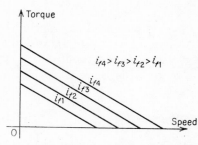

to what extent the system will be capable of following variations of the command signal with time.

Effect of the Control-winding Time Constant. The result of Eq. (6-66) is approximate because it neglects the time lag caused by the inductance of the control winding. A more exact description of the servomotor transfer function is obtained by recognizing that the control-winding voltage really produces a field current i_f, which in turn produces the flux that enables the motor to develop torque. The

FIG. 6-15. Servomotor torque-speed curves using field current as the parameter where i_f is the control field current at zero speed.

parameter for the torque-speed curves therefore should be field current rather than control-winding voltage as depicted in Fig. 6-15.

When analyzed on this basis, the transfer function describing the motor displacement per unit control-winding voltage can be shown to be given by

$$\frac{\theta_M}{V_c}(s) = \frac{K_m}{s(1 + s\tau_m)(1 + s\tau_f)} \tag{6-69}$$

where τ_f is the time constant of the control winding. Comparison of this result with that of Eq. (6-66) indicates that the difference lies in the field-winding time constant, as originally suspected. Therefore, strictly speaking, the transfer function of the servomotor really involves a denominator with s to the third power. However, since the value of τ_f is very low, i.e., of the order of 0.001 to 0.005 sec, the transfer function involves s in a practical sense only to the second power.

Variation of Servomotor Torque Parameters with Control-winding Voltage. The torque parameter K_M is defined as the change in torque per unit change in control-winding voltage at constant speed and fixed reference winding voltage, i.e.,

$$K_M = \frac{\Delta T}{\Delta v_c}\bigg|_{\text{constant speed}} \tag{6-70}$$

Similarly the motor speed constant F_M is defined as the change in torque per unit change in speed at constant control-winding voltage. Reference winding voltage, of course, is at the rated value. Thus

$$F_M = \frac{\Delta T}{\Delta n}\bigg|_{v_c = \text{constant}} \tag{6-71}$$

An examination of the curves plotted in Fig. 6-14 makes it clear that both quantities vary appreciably over the operating range of the motor. In other words neither K_m nor τ_m as they appear in Eqs. (6-67) and (6-68) are constant quantities but really vary with the operating point.

The nature of this variation is established easily in the following manner: Operate the motor open loop as shown in Fig. 6-12, and apply a fixed voltage v_{c1} to the control winding. When steady state is reached, the output is a velocity and the governing equation is

$$K_M v_{c1} = (F_M + F_L)\omega_M \qquad (6\text{-}72)$$

where $\omega_M = d\theta_M/dt$ = motor velocity. Rearranging yields

$$\frac{\omega_M}{v_{c1}} = \frac{K_M}{F_M + F_L} = K_m \qquad (6\text{-}73)$$

This equation states that the value of K_m may be found by measuring the steady-state velocity attained by the motor for a specific control-winding voltage and formulating the ratio of the two quantities. Figure 6-16 shows the results of such a series of measurements carried out for a 400-cps 115-volt Kearfott R111 servomotor. It is to be noted that there is a change in K_m of more than 2:1. Since K_m is one of the gain factors making up the over-all open-loop gain, such a change can be troublesome. This increase in loop gain, as the system drives toward null (i.e., as $v_c \to 0$), may cause a highly oscilla-

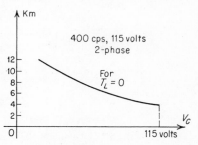

FIG. 6-16. Variation of servomotor torque parameters with operating point.

tory response and even result in instability in some extreme cases.

A similar variation can be shown to occur in τ_m; that is, as the control voltage nulls toward zero, the motor time constant increases by an appreciable factor. Here, too, the change is in a direction which causes the transient performance to deteriorate.

Hydraulic Amplifier. Hydraulically operated components are quite common in control systems which are either all hydraulic feedback systems or combined electromechanical hydraulic systems. Hydraulic elements use relatively noncompressible fluids, such as petroleum-base oils or certain noninflammable synthetic fluids, for the transmission of power through the action of fluid flow and pressure. This may be contrasted to pneumatic elements which use compressible fluids, i.e., gases such as air. In general hydraulic elements are economical and show to advantage over electrical components from the point of view of horsepower per unit volume and torque-to-inertia ratio. They also can be used to produce precise linear motion more easily than electrical units. On the other hand hydraulic systems have inherent problems of sealing against foreign particles and leaks, operating noise, and the tendency to become sluggish at low temperatures owing to the increased viscosity of the fluid. Common hydraulic control operations include power steering and brakes in automobiles, the steering mechanisms of large ships, and the control of large machine tools.

Since the study of hydraulic components is a specialized field, only a few of the fundamentals of operation, illustrated by some examples, are presented here. These examples will also illustrate how it is possible to obtain a transfer function from the published characteristics of a device

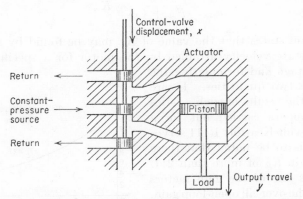

FIG. 6-17. A control valve and piston. A hydraulic actuator.

without detailed knowledge of why these characteristics occur. In the ensuing analysis it is assumed that the hydraulic fluid is available from a constant-pressure source and that fluid compressibility is negligible. A more complete analysis must take these factors into account.

Consider the simple control-valve and piston-actuator system shown in Fig. 6-17. Constant-pressure hydraulic fluid is provided at the center of the control valve. When the control valve is moved downward, hydraulic fluid passes through the upper portion of the valve into the main piston cylinder. This produces a differential pressure across the piston, and it moves down, pushing the hydraulic fluid in front of it through the lower portion of the valve to the return line. When the control valve is moved upward, the same action takes place in the opposite direction.

The dynamic behavior may be derived from the control-valve characteristics drawn in Fig. 6-18. These characteristics relate the volumetric fluid flow Q to the main piston actuator and the differential pressure P across the actuator for different values of valve displacement x. The curves are idealized as straight lines, which is permissible for small valve displacements. Thus from the given data we write the expression

$$Q = k_v \left(x - \frac{P}{k_p} \right) \tag{6-74}$$

where Q = volumetric fluid flow to actuator, in.^{3}/sec
$\quad P$ = differential pressure across actuator piston, psi
$\quad x$ = valve displacement, in.
$\quad k_v$ = valve flow gradient, in.^{2}/sec
$\quad k_p$ = valve pressure gradient, lb/in.^{3}

In this system, k_v and k_p are constants. The change in volumetric flow per unit valve displacement, at constant differential pressure, is given by

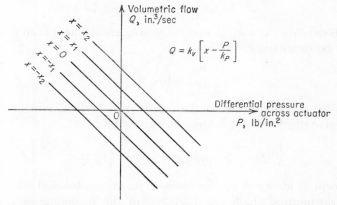

Fig. 6-18. Actuator-valve characteristics.   Constant pressure supply.

k_v; that is, $\partial Q/\partial x = k_v$. Similarly the change in differential pressure per unit valve displacement, at constant volumetric flow, is given by k_p; that is, $\partial P/\partial x = k_p$. These constants can be measured for any given hydraulic system. It is interesting to note that Q, P, and x are analagous to the quantities T, n, and v_c, respectively, in the case of the torque-speed curves of the electric servomotor.

To illustrate the use of the valve characteristics in obtaining a transfer function, consider the case where the actuator piston moves a load of mass M with a viscous friction F. Let A denote the area of the actuator piston. The force developed by the actuator piston is given by the differential pressure multiplied by the piston area. Thus, with the aid of Eq. (6-74)

$$\text{Developed force} = AP = Ak_p \left(x - \frac{Q}{k_v} \right) \tag{6-75}$$

This force is applied to the mechanical load so that the following equation holds,

$$A k_p \left(x - \frac{Q}{k_v} \right) = M \frac{d^2y}{dt^2} + F \frac{dy}{dt} \tag{6-76}$$

where y = output displacement of the actuator piston.

An additional relationship is available from the fact that (for an incompressible fluid) the volumetric fluid flow must be equal to the rate at which the actuator piston displaces hydraulic fluid. Thus

$$Q = A \frac{dy}{dt} \tag{6-77}$$

Substituting Eq. (6-77) into Eq. (6-76) and rearranging gives the following result:

$$x = \frac{M}{A k_p} \frac{d^2y}{dt^2} + \frac{F}{A k_p} \frac{dy}{dt} + \frac{A}{k_v} \frac{dy}{dt} \tag{6-78}$$

If the constants $C_1 = k_v/A$ and $C_2 = A k_p$ are defined, then this equation may be rewritten as follows:

$$x = \frac{M}{C_2} \frac{d^2y}{dt^2} + \left(\frac{1}{C_1} + \frac{F}{C_2} \right) \frac{dy}{dt} \tag{6-79}$$

The transfer function between the output piston displacement and the control-valve displacement is therefore given by

$$\frac{Y}{X}(s) = \frac{1}{s[(M/C_2)s + (1/C_1 + F/C_2)]} \tag{6-80}$$

This form is identical to the transfer function obtained for either of the electric motors which are discussed in the preceding sections. If $M = 0$, that is, if the load mass is negligible, then Eq. (6-80) reduces to

$$\frac{Y(s)}{X(s)} = \frac{1}{s(1/C_1 + F/C_2)} \tag{6-81}$$

Equation (6-81) corresponds to a transfer function of an ideal integrator.

As a further extension of a hydraulic control system, consider a system similar to the power-steering mechanism illustrated in Fig. 1-9. The essentials of this system are reproduced in Fig. 6-19. The linkage between the power-ram output y and the movable-sleeve displacement x_s is specified as shown. They are related by the formula

$$\frac{x_s}{y} = \frac{a}{b} < 1 \tag{6-82}$$

In this application the opening between the valve spool and the movable sleeve serves the same function as the control-valve displacement x in the previous case. Let x_i represent the displacement of the valve spool. Then Eq. (6-78) may be rewritten as

$$x_i - x_s = \frac{M}{C_2}\frac{d^2y}{dt^2} + \left(\frac{1}{C_1} + \frac{F}{C_2}\right)\frac{dy}{dt} \tag{6-83}$$

Substituting Eq. (6-82) into Eq. (6-83) yields the following differential equation:

$$x_i = \frac{M}{C_2}\frac{d^2y}{dt^2} + \left(\frac{1}{C_1} + \frac{F}{C_2}\right)\frac{dy}{dt} + \frac{a}{b}y \tag{6-84}$$

This equation relates the power-ram displacement y to the control-valve spool displacement x_i. It is seen to be similar to the typical

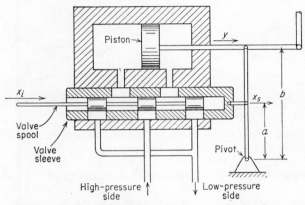

FIG. 6-19. A hydraulic power-steering mechanism.

second-order system equation discussed previously so that all the comments made about these systems and their transfer functions apply to this case as well.

6-4. The Controlled System (g_2)

The transfer functions associated with the controlled-system block (g_2), referred to in Fig. 1-1, can range from simple to complex in form. For example, in the case of a servomechanism where the controlled system is the bedplate of a milling machine or of a gun turret, the influence of the bedplate upon the system dynamics is readily accounted for by combining its inertia and viscous-friction effects with those of the output actuator. In such a case the transfer function of the controlled system is unalterably related to that of the output device. However, there are many situations where the dynamics of the controlled system appears in explicit form, as in the case where a process or an aircraft is involved. Of course, the basic approach in establishing the transfer function remains the same, viz., to identify the governing differential equations.

Transfer Function of a Missile in the Pitch Axis. Consider the case where the controlled system is a cruciform missile as depicted in Fig. 6-20. This example is particularly worthwhile because (1) it leads to an explicit transfer function for the controlled system and (2) it illustrates a situation where derivation of the transfer function is dependent upon more than one differential equation. For simplicity attention is confined to the manner in which the pitch angles θ, α, and γ vary with changes in the wing-flap deflection δ_e. The pitch axis is perpendicular to the longitudinal x axis and is directed out of the paper at the center of gravity of the missile. The description of θ as a function of wing deflection δ_e is of

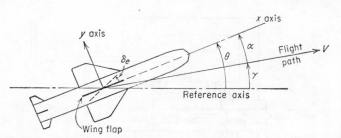

FIG. 6-20. Cruciform missile showing angular relationships in pitch axis. θ = attitude angle; α = angle of attack; γ = flight-path angle.

particular importance in connection with the design of an autopilot for the missile.

The derivation is made with NACA[1] approved notation as used in the study of aerodynamics. The symbols are as follows:

V = velocity of air past aircraft
ρ = density of air
L = lift or force normal to velocity vector
S = wing area
c = wing chord
C_L = dimensionless aerodynamic lift coefficient
$C_{L\alpha} = dC_L/d\alpha$ = change in lift coefficient with angle of attack
$C_{M\alpha}$ = change in moment coefficient due to change in angle of attack
$C_{M\delta e}$ = change in moment coefficient due to a change in wing-flap deflection
C_{MQ} = change in moment coefficient with pitching velocity
M = mass of missile
a = acceleration normal to flight path
I_{vv} = missile moment of inertia about the y axis
c' = damping coefficient

[1] National Advisory Committee for Aeronautics.

The appropriate differential equations must be identified.   One equation is obtained by equating the applied moments of force due to changes in angle of attack α and wing-flap position δ_e to the opposing torque.   Thus,

$$I_{yy}\frac{d^2\theta}{dt^2} + c'\frac{d\theta}{dt} = \sum \text{ applied moments of force}$$
$$= M_\alpha\alpha + M_{\delta e}\delta_e \tag{6-85}$$

$M_\alpha = \frac{1}{2}\rho V^2 C_{M\alpha}Sc$ = aerodynamic coefficient denoting moment about pitch axis due to change in α (6-86)

$M_{\delta e} = \frac{1}{2}\rho V^2 C_{M\delta e}Sc$ = aerodynamic coefficient denoting moment about pitch axis due to change in wing-flap position (6-87)

and $c' = -\frac{1}{2}\rho V^2 C_{MQ}Sc$ = drag coefficient, which opposes change in pitch velocity (6-88)

A second equation results upon recognizing that motion normal to the flight path is due to the lift forces.   Accordingly,

$$ma = L_\alpha\alpha + L_{\delta e}\delta_e \tag{6-89}$$

where $L_\alpha = \frac{1}{2}\rho V^2 C_{L\alpha}S$ = lift-force coefficients associated with α (6-90)

$L_{\delta e} = \frac{1}{2}\rho V^2 C_{L\delta e}S$ = lift-force coefficients associated with δ_e (6-91)

Moreover, it can be shown from the theory of aerodynamics that the acceleration normal to the flight path is described by

$$a = V\frac{d\dot\gamma}{dt} \tag{6-92}$$

Substituting Eq. (6-92) into Eq. (6-89) gives

$$mV\frac{d\gamma}{dt} - L_\alpha\alpha - L_{\delta e}\delta_e = 0 \tag{6-93}$$

Equations (6-85) and (6-93) are not sufficient to provide the desired transfer function because they involve three angles, viz., θ, δ_e, and γ. Therefore a third equation is required, and it is

$$\theta = \alpha + \gamma \tag{6-94}$$

which is apparent from a glance at Fig. 6-20.

Upon rearranging terms and applying the Laplace transformation, Eqs. (6-85) and (6-93) become

$$\frac{s^2\theta}{\omega_a{}^2} - \frac{s\theta}{\omega_b} - C_{M\alpha}\alpha - C_{M\delta e}\delta_e = 0 \tag{6-95}$$

and

$$\frac{s\gamma}{\omega_c} - C_{L\alpha}\alpha - C_{L\delta e}\delta_e = 0 \tag{6-96}$$

where $\omega_a{}^2 = \dfrac{M_\alpha}{C_{MQ}I_{yy}}$ $\omega_b = \dfrac{1}{C_{MQ}}$ $\omega_c = \dfrac{L_\alpha}{mVC_{L\alpha}}$

Equations (6-94), (6-95), and (6-96) may now be manipulated to provide any one of three transfer functions as they relate to the pitch axis. The transfer function describing the behavior of θ per unit change in δ_e is given by

$$\frac{\theta}{\delta_e}(s) = \frac{1}{As^2 + Bs + 1}\left(1 + \frac{s}{\omega_d}\right)\frac{K_2\omega_c}{s} \qquad (6\text{-}97)$$

where

$$A = -\frac{1}{\omega_a^2[(\omega_c/\omega_b)C_{L\alpha} + C_{M\alpha}]}$$

$$B = \frac{1}{(\omega_c/\omega_b)C_{L\alpha} + C_{M\alpha}}\left(\frac{1}{\omega_b} - \frac{\omega_c C_{L\alpha}}{\omega_a^2}\right)$$

$$\omega_d = -\frac{\omega_c K_1}{C_{M\delta e}}$$

$$K_1 = C_{M\alpha}C_{L\delta e} - C_{M\delta e}C_{L\alpha}$$

$$K_2 = \frac{K_1}{(\omega_c/\omega_b)C_{L\alpha} + C_{M\alpha}}$$

A glance at Eq. (6-97) indicates that the composite log-modulus and phase characteristics are made up of the standard forms treated in the preceding chapter. However, here is a situation which requires three of these standard forms to properly describe the dynamic characteristics of the controlled system.

6-5. Feedback Elements (h)

The components associated with the feedback-element block of Fig. 1-1 are usually of a classification known as *transducers*. Their primary function is to convert the controlled variable (which may be anything from an angular position to a controlled temperature) to the primary feedback signal, which may be of a completely different nature. Of course the use of transducers is not limited to the feedback element, and they often appear in other parts of the system. Usually there is no power required for the signal conversion. In Chap. 4 the feedback transducer was either a potentiometer or a synchro. In the power-steering mechanism of Sec. 6-3 the feedback element was the simple linkage connecting the output power ram to the valve spool. The transfer functions for these devices are constants and relatively simple to derive. However, this is not always the case, and several examples of more complicated transducer types are now discussed.

The Linear Accelerometer. The linear accelerometer has gained widespread use in high-speed-aircraft and guided-missile applications. In either case it can be made to serve a twofold purpose. It can be employed as a measuring device which provides valuable data regarding the extent to which the missile or jet aircraft is subjected to vibrations and shock. Or else it can be incorporated as an important part of the missile or aircraft guidance system.

Our attention is directed here to a linear accelerometer having a single degree of freedom as shown in Fig. 6-21. The frame of the accelerometer is assumed attached to the missile frame. Let

$$y = \text{motion of } M \text{ relative to inertial space[1]}$$
$$M = \text{accelerometer mass}$$
$$x_i = \text{motion of frame relative to inertial space}$$

and $$x_o = y - x_i = \text{motion of } M \text{ relative to frame} \qquad (6\text{-}98)$$

The quantity x_o is considered the output of the accelerometer. The input quantity may be taken to be either the displacement x_i or the input

acceleration $s^2 x_i$. The equation of motion for the system is found by equating to zero the sum of the forces associated with an assumed displacement of the mass and the frame. Thus,

$$M \frac{d^2 y}{dt^2} + F\left(\frac{dy}{dt} - \frac{dx_i}{dt}\right)$$
$$+ K(y - x_i) = 0 \qquad (6\text{-}99)$$

There is a total of three transfer functions which can be identified for the accelerometer. One of these follows directly from Eq. (6-99). Thus, rearranging and taking the Laplace transform yields

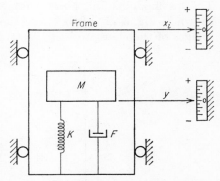

FIG. 6-21. Construction features of a linear accelerometer constrained for a single degree of freedom.

$$s^2 Y + \frac{F}{M} s Y + \frac{K}{M} Y = \frac{F}{M} s X_i + \frac{K}{M} X_i \qquad (6\text{-}100)$$

Introducing $$\frac{F}{M} = 2\zeta\omega_n$$

and $$\omega_n = \sqrt{\frac{K}{M}}$$

and formulating the ratio of output to input results in the expression

$$\frac{Y}{X_i}(s) = \frac{1 + (2\zeta/\omega_n)s}{(s/\omega_n)^2 + (2\zeta/\omega_n)s + 1} \qquad (6\text{-}101)$$

The transfer function of Eq. (6-101) applies whenever the output is measured relative to inertial space.

A more useful form of the output of the accelerometer, however, occurs when the displacement of the mass M is measured relative to the frame and not to the inertial space. To provide this transfer function, Eq.

[1] See footnote, p. 240.

(6-98) is inserted into Eq. (6-99) to yield

$$\frac{d^2x_o}{dt^2} + 2\zeta\omega_n\frac{dx_o}{dt} + \omega_n{}^2 x_o = -\frac{d^2x_i}{dt^2} \tag{6-102}$$

Upon taking the Laplace transform and formulating the ratio of output to input, the desired result is obtained. Thus

$$\begin{aligned}
\frac{X_o}{X_i}(s) &= -\frac{s^2}{s^2 + 2\zeta\omega_n s + \omega_n{}^2} \\
&= -\frac{1}{\omega_n{}^2}\frac{s^2}{(s/\omega_n)^2 + (2\zeta/\omega_n)s + 1}
\end{aligned} \tag{6-103}$$

The log-modulus and phase characteristics of this transfer function are shown in Fig. 6-22. It is interesting to note that these curves are mirror images of the characteristics plotted in Fig. 5-22.

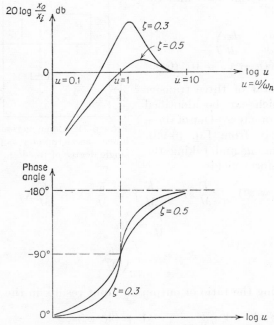

FIG. 6-22. Log modulus and phase of x_o/x_i vs. frequency for a linear accelerometer.

Examination of Eq. (6-103) or of its corresponding Bode plots reveals some useful information about the application limitations of linear accelerometers. For example, the question may arise regarding the advisability of using the accelerometer as a measuring device for detecting low-frequency oscillations in the missile air frame. Equation (6-103) shows that the transfer function under such circumstances is approximately

$$\frac{X_o}{X_i} \approx -\frac{1}{\omega_n^2} s^2 \qquad (6\text{-}104)$$

However, the accelerometer's natural frequency is designed to be very high by virtue of a small mass and a very stiff spring. Accordingly, there is very little observable output displacement if it is used for such a purpose. In fact the output signals may very well fall within the noise level of the system, thereby making such measurements unreliable. By the same token, however, it follows that to detect and measure an oscillation having a frequency comparable with that of the natural frequency of the accelerometer, the use of the accelerometer is satisfactory.

Of most importance is the transfer function which relates the output displacement to input acceleration. The right side of Eq. (6-102) represents the input acceleration, which we shall now call a_x. Consequently the desired transfer function becomes

$$\frac{X_o}{a_x} = -\frac{1}{s^2 + 2\zeta\omega_n + \omega_n^2} = -\frac{1}{\omega_n^2}\frac{1}{(s/\omega_n)^2 + (2\zeta/\omega_n)s + 1} \qquad (6\text{-}105)$$

which is readily recognized as the standard quadratic form. Since the input quantity is acceleration, it follows that the output displacement X_o is proportional to input acceleration. Recalling the nature of the second-order response curves, it is easy to understand why the damping ratio in these units is kept between 0.4 and 0.7. In this way large overshoots and therefore false indications of peak accelerations are avoided. Furthermore, the large natural frequency is designed into the system to assure the ability of the accelerometer to measure acceleration pulses with a high degree of accuracy.

Since the magnitude of X_o provides the means of measuring missile acceleration, the accelerometer serves an important function in the missile autopilot. Through the inclusion of an accelerometer in a feedback path of the missile air frame, it follows that, whenever the missile output acceleration deviates from the command value, an actuating signal arises which acts to remove this lack of correspondence. Thus, high performance is assured.

A Motor Accelerometer. The principle of motor operation is often used in the design of special-purpose devices. One such application is shown in Fig. 6-23. The object is to obtain a device which is sensitive to accelerations and produces an output which is proportional to either the acceleration or, preferably, the integral of acceleration (velocity) or the double integral of acceleration (distance). Such a component is essential to the operation of an inertial guidance system, which is discussed in Chap. 7.

In Fig. 6-23 a d-c motor is mounted with its axis vertical. The motor case, containing a constant magnetic field, is mounted so that it can also rotate about this vertical axis.   The case is also provided with an eccentric mass M, as shown.   When the entire assembly (i.e., the platform reference frame upon which the motor is mounted) is accelerated in the x direction, the eccentric mass and the motor case are displaced by an angle θ_c, owing to the inertia of the eccentric mass.   This displacement causes a signal to be picked up from the error-measuring potentiometer. This error signal is amplified and converted into an armature current i_a for the motor.   The armature current results in a developed motor

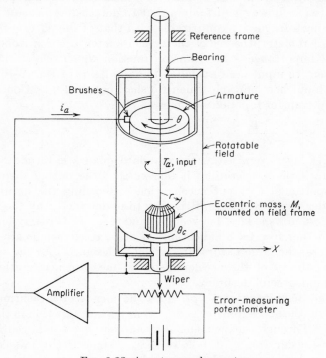

FIG. 6-23. A motor accelerometer.

torque which acts as an action-reaction pair (Newton's third law of motion), involving the motor armature and the field windings.   The direction of the current is arranged so that the reaction torque on the case opposes the original displacement of the case and tends to restore it to its null position.   The developed torque thus becomes a measure of the original acceleration, and since it also acts upon the motor armature, the angular displacement of the armature is related to the acceleration also.   The transfer function for this system is to be developed, but first the following quantities are defined:

θ = angular displacement of armature, radians
θ_c = angular displacement of case, radians

M = eccentric mass of case, slugs

r = radial eccentricity of mass M, ft

Mr^2 = moment of inertia of case, slug-ft^2

K_p = potentiometer constant, volts/radian

G_m = amplifier gain, amp/volt

I_a = motor armature current, amp

T_m = torque developed by the motor, lb-ft

K_m = motor torque constant, ft-lb/amp

T_a = external torque applied to case

J = moment of inertia of armature

F_c = viscous friction of case

F = viscous friction of rotor

$\ddot{x}$ = acceleration in x direction, perpendicular to radial line from motor axis to eccentric mass, ft/sec^2

$\ddot{X}$ = $s^2 x$

In order to simplify the analysis, let us first consider the behavior of the system when it is at rest and an external torque T_a is applied to the case as shown. At any instant the net torque acting on the case is given by $T_a - T_m$. Thus, if it is assumed that the case has viscous friction, its motion is given by the equation

$$T_a - T_m = (Mr^2s^2 + F_cs)\theta_c \qquad (6\text{-}106)$$

The motor torque T_m is given by $K_m I_a$ and may be written in terms of the case displacement θ_c, as follows:

$$\begin{aligned} T_m &= K_m I_a \\ &= K_m G_m K_p \theta_c \end{aligned} \qquad (6\text{-}107)$$

If the value of θ_c in Eq. (6-107) is substituted into Eq. (6-106), the following formula results:

$$T_a - T_m = \frac{(Mr^2s^2 + F_cs)T_m}{K_m G_m K_p} \qquad (6\text{-}108)$$

Combining terms,

$$T_m = \frac{T_a}{(Mr^2/K_m G_m K_p)s^2 + (F_c/K_m G_m K_p)s + 1} \qquad (6\text{-}109)$$

Equation (6-109) relates the developed motor torque to the applied torque.

The applied torque T_a may be related to an acceleration $\ddot{x}$ by Newton's laws of motion. Thus an acceleration $\ddot{x}$ is equivalent to applying a force $M\ddot{x}$ to the eccentric mass. This force produces a torque through the moment arm r. Thus

$$T_a = Mr\ddot{x} \qquad (6\text{-}110)$$

Combining Eq. (6-110) with Eq. (6-109) gives the desired relationship between the motor torque and system acceleration,

$$T_m = \frac{Mr\ddot{X}}{(Mr^2/K_mG_mK_p)s^2 + (F_c/K_mG_mK_p)s + 1} \qquad (6\text{-}111)$$

It is interesting to note that the motor armature current can be used as a direct measure of the applied acceleration since

$$I_a = \frac{T_m}{K_m} = \frac{Mr\ddot{X}}{K_m[(Mr^2/K_mG_mK_p)s^2 + (F_c/K_mG_mK_p)s + 1]} \qquad (6\text{-}112)$$

If G_m is very large, then $I_a \approx Mr\ddot{X}/K_m$.

In many applications the output of this device is taken as the angular displacement of the motor armature. The transfer function for this output variable is obtained by equating the motor torque to the armature load, i.e.,

$$T_m = (Js^2 + Fs)\theta \qquad (6\text{-}113)$$

Combining this equation with Eq. (6-111) yields the transfer function between the angular position of the armature and the input acceleration.

$$\frac{\theta}{\ddot{X}} = \frac{Mr}{(Js^2 + Fs)[(Mr^2/K_mG_mK_p)s^2 + (F_c/K_mG_mK_p)s + 1]} \qquad (6\text{-}114)$$

If G_m is made very large, the resulting equation becomes

$$\frac{\theta}{\ddot{X}} = \frac{Mr}{Js^2 + Fs} \qquad (6\text{-}115)$$

If the motor's viscous friction is ideally zero, the preceding equation reduces to

$$\frac{\theta}{\ddot{X}} = \frac{Mr}{Js^2} \qquad (6\text{-}116)$$

Since $\ddot{X} = s^2x$, it follows that

$$\theta = \frac{Mr}{J}x \qquad (6\text{-}117)$$

Thus the angular position of the motor armature at any instant is proportional to the distance traveled in the x direction. If a rotation counter were placed on the motor armature shaft, its reading would be equal to the distance traveled, similar to the mileage reading of an automobile odometer. This is particularly important in view of the fact that we now have a mileage indication without any reference to an outside source of information. For the purposes of this chapter we have succeeded in deriving a transfer function for a rather intricate device and are now in a position to investigate its operation in detail and to include it as part of a still larger system, as, for example, the entire control system of a space vehicle.

The Gyroscope. The gyroscope has achieved wide use in the aircraft industry as an indicating instrument and as a component in fire control, automatic flight control, and navigational systems. The principle of the gyroscope is well known and is based upon the law of conservation of angular momentum.

When this instrument is used as a practical component, the motion of the spinning wheel of the gyroscope is usually restrained by mounting it in a set of bearings called *gimbals*. It is customary to classify gyroscopes in terms of the number of degrees of freedom of angular motion of the spinning wheel. Figure 6-24a shows a system with one degree of freedom

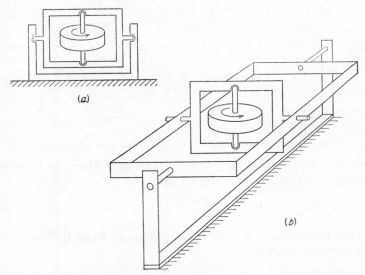

(a)

(b)

FIG. 6-24. Gyroscope degrees of freedom. (a) One-degree-of-freedom gyroscope; (b) two-degrees-of-freedom gyroscope.

and Fig. 6-24b a system with two degrees of freedom. There are many types of gyroscopes used in practice, including the rate gyro, the integrating rate gyro, and the directional gyro of the one-degree-of-freedom class and the displacement gyro, the vertical gyro, and the gyrocompass of the two-degree-of-freedom class. Because of the general complexity of the subject and the limited treatment possible here, only the transfer functions of some simple one-degree-of-freedom components are derived.

Figure 6-25 illustrates a general one-degree-of-freedom system with an elastic restraint (spring K) and a viscous damper (dashpot F) about the free, or output, axis x. If the gyro case is rotated about the z axis with an angular velocity Ω_i, then a torque $T = H\Omega_i$ is developed as shown, which tends to rotate the gyro through an angle θ about the gimbal axis x. The unit tends to rotate so as to align its angular-momentum vector

H with the input angular-velocity vector Ω_i.   This torque is opposed by
the inertia of the system about the output x axis, the spring restraint K,
and the viscous damping F.   If the moment of inertia about the x axis is

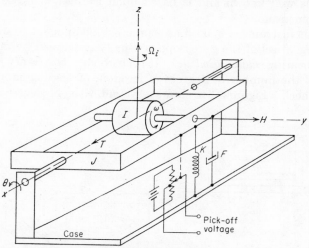

FIG. 6-25. A generalized one-degree-of-freedom gyroscope.

denoted by J and the angular displacement by θ, then the equation for
the dynamic balance of the system is given by

$$H\Omega_i = J\frac{d^2\theta}{dt^2} + F\frac{d\theta}{dt} + K\theta \tag{6-118}$$

The transfer function between the output angle θ and the input angular
velocity is therefore given by

$$\frac{\theta}{\Omega_i} = \frac{H}{Js^2 + Fs + K} \tag{6-119}$$

Mathematically this equation is similar in form to Eq. (5-52), and the
sinusoidal steady-state characteristics are as shown in Fig. 5-22.   Usually
the output angle is transformed to a voltage by means of a "pick-off"
transducer, which is pictured as a potentiometer in Fig. 6-25 although
differential transformers and other types of pick-offs are also used.

This type of gyro, described by Eq. (6-118), is known as a *rate gyro*
and is commonly used for measuring aircraft motion and for computing
rates of turn for use in autopilots and gunfire control systems.   The
application of this device as a rate-of-turn indicator may be illustrated by
considering the steady-state output deflection for a constant angular
velocity Ω_{io} input.   The steady-state deflection about the output axis is
therefore given by

$$\theta_{ss} = \frac{H}{K}\Omega_{io} \tag{6-120}$$

Thus the output angular displacement is proportional to the constant input angular velocity. Some damping is always necessary in this gyroscope to prevent an oscillatory response.

It is important to note that a constant deflection θ_{ss} introduces an error into the system because it causes the H vector to move away from the y axis, and the input vector Ω_i is therefore no longer in line with the z axis. The resulting error in angular-rate measurement is said to be due to *geometric cross coupling*. In order to keep its effect to a minimum, the angular rotation about the output axis must be restrained to small values by increasing the spring constant K. This requires that the pick-off transducer be extremely sensitive, which in turn gives rise to problems of drift and noise. The effects of frictional torques in the output bearings and pick-off transducer are also a major source of error in the system. Thus designing a precision gyroscope becomes a difficult engineering problem.

If the elastic restraint of the rate gyro is removed, then the instrument becomes an *integrating rate gyro*. This unit is also known as an integrating gyro or HIG (hermetically sealed integrating gyro). In this case the equation for dynamic balance about the output axis is given by

$$H\Omega_i = J\frac{d^2\theta}{dt^2} + F\frac{d\theta}{dt} \qquad (6\text{-}121)$$

The transfer function corresponding to Eq. (6-121) depends on how the input and output variables are defined, which, of course, depends upon the particular application. If the output pick-off transducer is sensitive to angular deflection about the output axis, then θ becomes the output variable. Usually the input to the instrument is taken as the angular displacement about the input z axis (denoted by the letter θ_i) rather than the input angular velocity Ω_i (note that $\Omega_i = d\theta_i/dt$). For these variables the transfer function becomes

$$\frac{\theta}{\theta_i} = \frac{H}{Js + F} \approx \frac{H}{F} \qquad \text{for negligible } J \qquad (6\text{-}122)$$

This transfer function is identical to one of the forms of Eq. (5-48) and is pictured in Fig. 5-19.

If the gyroscope input consists of a constant angle θ_{io}, then the steady-state deflection about the output axis is given by

$$\theta_{ss} = \frac{H}{F}\theta_{io} \qquad (6\text{-}123)$$

Thus the steady-state output angular displacement is proportional to the input angular displacement. The problem of geometric cross coupling also exists in the integrating rate gyro. Typical values for H/F are of the order of 1 to 10 so that the problem cannot be neglected. Because of this, integrating rate gyros are usually restricted to applications such as stabilized platforms, where the output angle is returned close to the zero position by feedback.

As an example of the use of a gyroscope let us consider the problem of obtaining a stable reference plane for a moving vehicle. This need arises because of the high maneuverability and speed of present-day aircraft

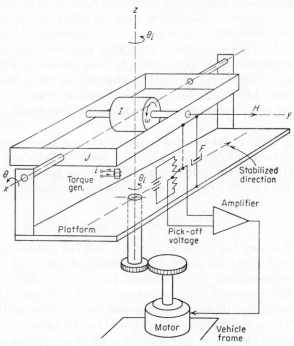

FIG. 6-26. Single axis of a stabilized platform using an integrating rate gyroscope.

and missiles and the lack of reliable outside reference points. It becomes necessary to provide the vehicle with a stable reference plane which maintains its position fixed in space regardless of maneuvers. Such a plane is called a stable platform, and it is said to maintain its position constant with respect to *inertial space*.[1] When integrating rate gyros are used to obtain a stable platform, one integrating rate gyro must be used for each axis to be stabilized. Figure 6-26 illustrates one axis of such a system;

[1] "Inertial space is defined as the space in which Newton's Law of Inertia is valid, that is, the reference frame in which a force-free body is unaccelerated. For many purposes, the celestial space determined by the 'fixed stars' acts as an inertial space." This definition has been taken from the paper The Floating Integrating Gyro and Its Application to Geometrical Stabilization Problems on Moving Bases by C. S. Draper, W. Wrigley, and L. R. Grohe, published by the Institute of Aeronautical Sciences, Jan. 27, 1955.

stabilization is in angular position about the z axis. Imagine this platform initially aligned so that the x axis is along the longitudinal axis of an airplane. The angle θ_i is measured with respect to inertial space, the xyz axes. The stator of the drive motor is rigidly connected to the aircraft frame. If the airplane changes its direction of flight, then there is a rotation θ_i of the airplane and the platform about the z axis. The gyro senses this change and precesses about its gimbals through the angle θ. This produces a pick-off voltage, which, after being amplified, is applied to the motor. The motor then drives the platform relative to the air frame in such a direction that the angle θ_i is returned to its initial value relative to inertial space and the pick-off voltage returns to zero.

The transfer function of this system may be determined by considering the relationship between the angle θ_i and a disturbing torque T_a applied to rotate the platform about the z axis away from its stable position. The ideal result would be to have the angle remain constant, independent of T_a. Let us define the following quantities:

T_a = applied external torque about z axis

T_m = developed motor torque, platform side

F_p = viscous friction of motor and platform on platform side

J_p = moment of inertia of motor and platform about z axis, platform side

K = combined gain of pick-off, amplifier, and motor torque constant giving developed motor torque (on platform side) per radian of pick-off angle θ

The torque balance equation for the platform is given by

$$T_a - T_m = J_p \frac{d^2\theta_i}{dt^2} + F_p \frac{d\theta_i}{dt} \qquad (6\text{-}124)$$

The transfer function between the angle θ_i and the pick-off angle θ is given by Eq. (6-122).

$$\frac{\theta}{\theta_i}(s) = \frac{H}{Js + F} \approx \frac{H}{F} \qquad (6\text{-}125)$$

where J denotes the moment of inertia about the x axis, which is usually small and may be neglected. The developed motor torque T_m is given by

$$T_m = K\theta \qquad (6\text{-}126)$$

Laplace-transforming and combining Eqs. (6-124) to (6-126) gives the following results:

$$\frac{T_m}{T_a} = \left[1 + \frac{s(J_p s + F_p)F}{HK} \right]^{-1} \qquad (6\text{-}127)$$

and

$$\frac{\theta_i}{T_a} = \frac{F}{s(J_p s + F_p)F + HK} \qquad (6\text{-}128)$$

If the gain factor K is made very large, it can be seen that T_m approaches T_a and θ_i approaches zero so that the platform tends to maintain its alignment in the x direction regardless of applied torques which tend to disturb it from that position. One important aspect of this system is that the platform can be made to precess about the z axis by applying a current to the small torque generator shown in the figure. The magnetic attraction of the torque generator on the gimbal mounting tends to produce rotation about the x axis, which produces a pick-off voltage and causes the motor to rotate the platform. The motor rotates the platform at an angular velocity which is just sufficient to generate a precession torque about the x axis equal and opposite to that developed by the torque generator. This constant rotation rate is necessary in inertial guidance systems in order to keep the stable platform (upon which the accelerometers are mounted) tangent to the earth's sphere as the vehicle rotates about the earth. More is said about this in the next chapter.

As mentioned previously, the design of a gyroscope is an exacting engineering problem. Drift rates of 1°/hr cause errors of 60 nautical miles per hour in an inertial navigational system. Some gyroscopes have drift rates as low as 0.02°/hr. Problems such as mass unbalance, bearing deformation under acceleration, convection currents in lubricating fluids, and even the elasticity of lead in wires must be taken into account in any careful design.

SUGGESTED READING

Ahrendt, W. R.: "Servomechanism Practice," chaps. 6, 7, 9, 11–13, McGraw-Hill Book Company, Inc., New York, 1954.

Brown, G. S., and D. P. Campbell: "Principles of Servomechanisms," chap. 5, John Wiley & Sons, Inc., New York, 1948.

Bruns, R. A., and R. M. Saunders: "Analysis of Feedback Control Systems," pt. 1, McGraw-Hill Book Company, Inc., New York, 1955.

Gibson, J. E., and F. B. Tuteur: "Control System Components," chaps. 1, 4, 7, 10, 11, McGraw-Hill Book Company, Inc., New York, 1958.

Savant, C. J., Jr.: "Basic Feedback Control System Design," chaps. 8 and 9, McGraw-Hill Book Company, Inc., New York, 1958.

Truxal, J. G.: "Control Engineer's Handbook," Secs. 6–18, McGraw-Hill Book Company, Inc., New York, 1958.

PROBLEMS

6-1. Show that for the network given in Fig. P6-1

$$\frac{E_o}{E_i}(s) = \frac{1}{\tau_1\tau_2 s^2 + (\tau_1 + \tau_2 + \tau_{12})s + 1}$$

where $\tau_1 = R_1C_1$, $\tau_2 = R_2C_2$, $\tau_{12} = R_1C_2$.

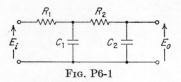

FIG. P6-1

6-2. Determine the transfer function for the circuit shown in Fig. P6-2. Under what conditions does the transfer function of Prob. 6-1 reduce to the same form as this problem?

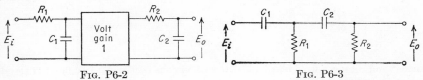

FIG. P6-2   FIG. P6-3

6-3. Determine the transfer function for the network shown in Fig. P6-3. Put your answer in a form similar to Prob. 6-1.

6-4. Derive the transfer functions for the networks shown in Fig. P6-4. In each case put the result in the form of either a phase lag or a phase lead, and define α and τ in terms of the components.

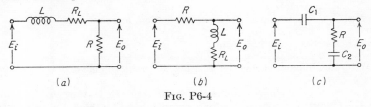

(a)   (b)   (c)

FIG. P6-4

6-5. Derive the transfer function $\dfrac{X_o}{X_i}(s)$ for the mechanical systems shown in Fig. P6-5. In each case put the transfer function in the form of either a phase lag or a phase lead, and define α and τ in terms of the mechanical parameters.

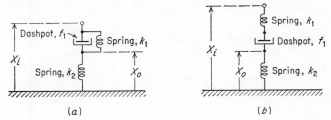

(a)   (b)

FIG. P6-5

6-6. Determine the transfer function $\dfrac{X_o}{F}$ for Fig. P6-6. To which one of the basic forms discussed in the chapter does this transfer function correspond?

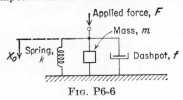

FIG. P6-6

6-7. See Fig. P6-7. The input voltage e_i is applied to the generator field (R_F = 100 ohms; L_F = 0 henry). The generator is turned by a constant-rpm prime mover. The generator output is connected to the motor input. The motor has a fixed field

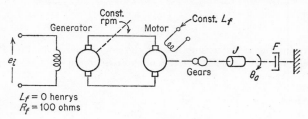

L_f = 0 henrys
R_f = 100 ohms

FIG. P6-7

current and rotates a fixed inertial load J with viscous friction F through a 2:1 speed-reduction gear ratio.

For the generator: Induced emf = 100 volts/amp field current
                      Armature resistance = 5 ohms
For the motor: Back-emf constant = 100 volts/rpm
                      Torque constant = 10 lb-ft/amp
                      Armature resistance = 5 ohms
For the load: Gear ratio = 2:1, speed reduction, motor to load
                      J = 200 slug-ft²
                      F = 100 lb-ft/rpm

(*a*) Write the differential equation relating the input voltage e_i to the output shaft position θ_o at the load.

(*b*) Sketch the log-modulus and phase-shift characteristic for the θ_o/e_i characteristic.

6-8. The following low-inertia motor is manufactured by the Eclipse-Pioneer Division of the Bendix Aviation Corporation: Type No. CK-1048-24-A1; two-phase motor.

Voltage:
  Fixed phase = 18 volts
  Control phase = 18 volts
Frequency = 400 cps
Current (at stall with rated voltage applied to each phase):
  Fixed phase = 95 ma
  Control phase = 95 ma
At stall with rated voltage applied to each phase:
  Impedance, fixed phase = 158 + j104 ohms
  Impedance, control phase = 158 + j104 ohms
  Power input (total) = 3 watts
Stall torque = 0.15 oz-in.
No-load speed = 6,300 rpm
Rotor moment of inertia = 0.5 g-cm²
Weight = 1.5 oz
Operating temperature = −55 to +85°C

Assuming that the torque-speed characteristic for this motor is a straight line, how long will it take for the motor to reach full no-load speed from rest when rated voltage is applied to the control winding? Assume that the fixed winding is already excited. *Note:* 28.35 g = 1 oz.

6-9. The following permanent-magnet d-c motor is manufactured by the Barber-Colman Company. BYLM 70001 motor specification:

Maximum output = 56 millihp	Rated output = 37 millihp
Voltage = 26 volts d-c	Current at rated output = 1.8 amp
Speed at rated output = 11,200 rpm	

Duty cycle (based on rated output + 200°F ambient) = $1\frac{1}{2}$ min on, 8 min off
Moment of inertia = 11.77 × 10^{-3} lb-m²

Weight = 9.4 oz	Stall torque = 0.95 lb-in.

Assuming that the torque-speed characteristic for this motor is a straight line, how long will it take for the motor to reach full no-load speed from rest when rated voltage is applied to the motor? What is the no-load speed? (*Note:* hp = [T(lb-ft) N(rpm)]/5,250).

6-10. Draw the polar plot for the transfer function for the phase lag-lead network of Fig. 6-5.

6-11. Derive a consistent set of units for all the constants in Eq. (6-43). Check the units for τ_c, τ_q, and τ'_m in terms of their defining equations to see that they properly come out to be seconds.

6-12. To the armature of a constant-field-current d-c motor 100 volts is suddenly applied. Measurements indicate that it takes the motor $\frac{1}{2}$ sec (three time constants) to get to its full load speed of 2,000 rpm. There is no external viscous-friction load on the motor, and armature inductance is negligible. The motor's stall torque is measured at 20 lb-ft when 100 volts is applied to the armature. $Ra = 1$ ohm. From these data calculate K_m, F, J, and K_n for the motor. Write the transfer function $\frac{\theta_M}{V}$ ($j\omega$) for this motor, and sketch its log-modulus characteristic, labeling all critical points.

6-13. Sketch the log-modulus and phase-shift characteristic for Eq. (6-60). Let $\tau_m = J/F_L$, $\tau_f = L_f/R_f$, and $K = K_{Tf}/F_L R_f$. Determine the breakpoint and 0-db crossover frequencies in terms of these constants.

6-14. Derive the differential equation relating the angular displacement θ_M to the applied field voltage v_f for a field-controlled d-c motor whose armature is fed from a constant voltage source. Assume that the field-circuit constants are R_f and L_f. Also assume that the field flux is given by $\phi = K_1 i_f$, the developed torque by the equation $T = K_2 \phi I_a$, and the back emf by $E = K_3 \phi \theta_M$. The armature resistance is R_a, and the constant applied armature voltage is V. Neglect the inductance of the armature circuit. The motor load is inertial of value J. What kind of differential equation results?

6-15. Design a lag network such that $\alpha = 10$, $\tau = 0.2$, and the impedance level is such that at very high frequencies the input impedance seen by the source is 100 kilohms.

6-16. Design a lead network such that $\alpha = 10$, $\tau = 0.2$ and the d-c input impedance is 100 kilohms.

6-17. Design a lag-lead network with the first three breakpoint frequencies at $\omega = 3$, 9, and 15 radians/sec. The very-high-frequency input impedance should be 50 kilohms.

6-18. Prove Eq. (6-22). Also show that, if $\omega_b \gg \omega_a$, $\omega_{p1} = \omega_a/\sqrt{\alpha}$ and $\omega_{p2} = \omega_b \sqrt{\alpha}$, where ω_{p1} and ω_{p2} are the frequencies where maximum phase shift occurs, as indicated in Fig. 6-6. Under these conditions show that $\omega_0 = \sqrt{\omega_{p1}\omega_{p2}}$.

6-19. For the stabilized platform of Fig. 6-26 determine the precession rate θ_i when the torque generator produces a constant angle of rotation θ_c of the gyroscope about the x axis.

6-20. Starting from Eqs. (6-94) to (6-96), derive Eq. (6-97) with the constants defined as given. Also derive the appropriate transfer functions for $\frac{\alpha}{\delta_e}$ (s) and $\frac{\gamma}{\delta_e}$ (s).

6-21. For the hydraulic system of Fig. 6-19, which is described by Eq. (6-84), determine the damping ratio and the undamped resonant frequency in terms of the system constants.

6-22. From Eq. (6-115) derive the exact expression for the transfer function $\frac{\theta}{X}$ (s) for the motor accelerometer. Investigate the steady-state output for θ when $x(t)$ is a unit step, a unit ramp, and a unit parabola.

6-23. Given the electromechanical transducer shown in Fig. P6-23. When the solenoid is energized, the lower arm of the lever, P, moves to the left and the upper arm Q moves to the right. The coil has resistance R and inductance L. The solenoid pull is given by the constant K newtons/amp of coil current. Determine the transfer function $\frac{X}{e}$ (s). Neglect all inertia, and consider the effects of the spring k and viscous damper F only.

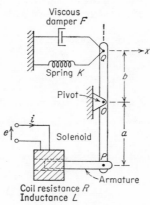

FIG. P6-23

6-24. The diagram in Fig. P6-24 is identical to that of Fig. 6-19 except that a spring K and a viscous-friction dashpot F have been added as shown. Calculate the transfer function $\frac{Y}{X_i}$ (s).

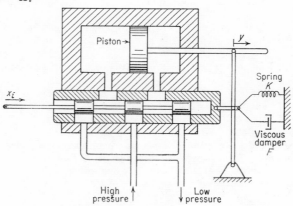

FIG. P6-24

6-25. Determine the transfer function $\dfrac{E_2}{E_i}(j\omega)$ for the system shown in **Fig. P6-25**.

Generator:
$$L_f = 50 \text{ henrys}$$
$$R_f = 50 \text{ ohms}$$
$$R_a = 1 \text{ ohm}$$
$$L_a = 1 \text{ henry}$$
Emf constant: $K_g = 200 \text{ volts/amp}$
Low-pass filter: $L = 1 \text{ henry}$
$$R = 1 \text{ ohm}$$

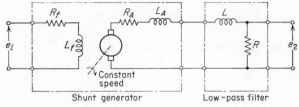

Shunt generator   Low-pass filter

FIG. P6-25

6-26. The sketch in Fig. P6-26 shows a pneumatic transducer. When the input pressure is applied, the bellows expand and move the lever. K_s and F represent a spring constant and viscous friction, respectively. Determine the transfer function between P and the output motion X. Assume that all motions are small.

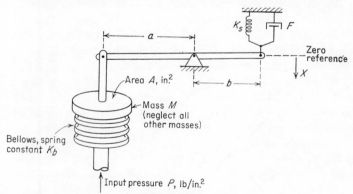

FIG. P6-26

6-27. Show that when $L_a = R_a = 0$ the torque vs. speed characteristics for a d-c constant-field servomotor become vertical lines and the motor behaves as an ideal integrator for the transfer function between applied armature voltage and the output shaft angle; that is, $\theta_M/V = 1/K_n s$.

7 | Transfer Functions of Systems and Their Behavior

In this chapter we are concerned with the over-all behavior of complete feedback control systems. In practice such systems are usually complicated, involving a variety of components, several feedback loops, and multiple inputs. The first task then is to learn how to handle the block diagram for these systems and reduce them to convenient, manageable forms. The second task is to be able to use the block diagram and the transfer functions of the individual components to predict the over-all performance of the system. The engineer must also be able to relate system performance to the behavior of individual components so that the system can be designed to meet specifications. For this reason a major portion of our attention is directed toward determining the *closed-loop* system characteristics (steady-state, transient, and sinusoidal) from the sinusoidal *open-loop* transfer function. Since the open-loop transfer function is directly related to the transfer functions of individual components, we have a procedure for controlling the design of a system.

Many of the techniques developed and the results quoted are approximate for the purposes of design. There are two reasons for this. First of all, it is difficult to generalize without making some simplifying assumptions. Second, we are restricted because most of our design procedures are carried out in the frequency domain for system requirements specified in the time domain, and the correlation between the two is not simple.

7-1. The Basic Block Diagram

The basic block diagram of a negative feedback control system is shown in Fig. 7-1a. The following quantities are defined for this system:

$$G(s) = \text{direct transfer function}$$

In general $G(s)$ denotes an operational transfer function and includes a constant gain factor K.

$$H(s) = \text{feedback transfer function}$$

In general $H(s)$ denotes an operational transfer function in the feedback path. In many cases $H(s)$ is equal to unity or a numerical constant.

$$G(s)H(s) = \text{(open)-loop transfer function}[1]$$

This transfer function is obtained by multiplying the transfer functions encountered as one proceeds round the feedback loop, starting at the output of the summing point and ending at the primary feedback point.

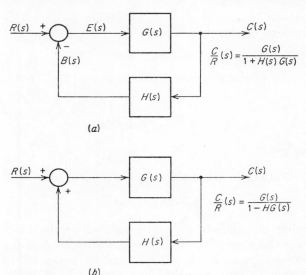

(a)

(b)

Fig. 7-1. Basic block diagram for a feedback system. (a) Negative feedback; (b) positive feedback.

In accordance with this block-diagram notation the following equations hold between the variables $R(s)$, $C(s)$, and $E(s)$.

$$E(s) = R(s) - B(s) \qquad (7\text{-}1a)$$
$$C(s) = G(s)E(s) \qquad (7\text{-}1b)$$
$$B(s) = H(s)C(s) \qquad (7\text{-}1c)$$

From these equations the following formulas are derived, relating the output and error signals to the input command:

[1] The terms *loop transfer function* and *open-loop transfer function* are used synonymously in this text.

$$\frac{C}{R}(s) = \text{closed-loop transfer function}$$

$$= \frac{G(s)}{1 + HG(s)} = \frac{\text{direct transfer function}}{1 + \text{loop transfer function}} \qquad (7\text{-}2a)$$

$$\frac{E}{R}(s) = \text{actuating-signal ratio} \qquad (7\text{-}2b)$$

$$= \frac{1}{1 + HG(s)} = \frac{1}{1 + \text{loop transfer function}}$$

The characteristic equation for the system may be identified by rewriting Eq. (7-2a) as follows:

$$[1 + HG(s)]C(s) = G(s)R(s)$$

The characteristic equation is obtained by setting the input signal to zero. Thus it is given by the expression

$$1 + HG(s) = 0 \qquad (7\text{-}3)$$

For the particular case of unity feedback, $H(s) = 1$; Eqs. (7-2a) and (7-2b) become

$$\frac{C}{R}(s) = \frac{G(s)}{1 + G(s)} \qquad (7\text{-}4a)$$

and

$$\frac{E}{R}(s) = \frac{1}{1 + G(s)} \qquad (7\text{-}4b)$$

When $H(s) = 1$, the characteristic equation reduces to

$$1 + G(s) = 0 \qquad (7\text{-}5)$$

The foregoing equations are directly related to the block diagram of Fig. 7-1a for the particular algebraic signs stipulated at the summing point, i.e., for negative feedback with $G(s)$ and $H(s)$ nominally assumed to be positive. When $H(s)$ is negative, Eqs. (7-2a) and (7-2b) become

$$\frac{C}{R}(s) = \frac{G(s)}{1 - HG(s)} \qquad (7\text{-}6a)$$

$$\frac{E}{R}(s) = \frac{1}{1 - HG(s)} \qquad (7\text{-}6b)$$

This corresponds to a condition of positive feedback, and the block diagram of Fig. 7-1a becomes equivalent to that of Fig. 7-1b. The characteristic equation is then given by the expression

$$1 - HG(s) = 0 \qquad (7\text{-}6c)$$

For this case the system is often unstable, for, with positive feedback, the feedback signal has the correct phase for regeneration to take place round the feedback loop, and if the amplitude of the feedback is sufficient, sustained oscillations result. The condition of instability is always indicated by the presence of roots of the characteristic equation on the $j\omega$ axis or in the right-half complex plane. Obviously $G(s)$ and $H(s)$ may occur with other sign combinations than those discussed here. The evaluation of the closed-loop transfer function and the characteristic equation for these cases is left as an exercise for the reader. Negative feedback always occurs when the feedback signal has the opposite sign to the input signal, and positive feedback occurs when they both have the same sign.

An important property of feedback theory is obtained by considering the closed-loop transfer function of Fig. 7-1a when the gain factor K, associated with the direct transmission function, becomes very large. As K approaches infinity, the closed-loop transfer function approaches $[H(s)]^{-1}$; that is, the closed-loop system transfer function becomes independent of the direct transmission path. This property is used extensively in feedback amplifier design in order to obtain stable gain which is independent of amplifier parameter variations and drift. It also affords a useful approach to the synthesis of certain operational forms, as is discussed in a later chapter.

7-2. Block-diagram Reduction

In general the block diagram of a practical system is complicated, often involving multiple feedback loops and several inputs. Multiple loops are introduced by the very nature of the control problem itself, and the engineer must be prepared to analyze and design such systems. By means of block-diagram reduction[1] every multiple-loop system can be reduced to the basic form of Fig. 7-1a and studied in the light of general feedback theory. Any parameter of a transfer function, such as a time constant, may be isolated so that its effect on system performance can be studied in detail. Multiple inputs are inherent in all control systems because of the presence of extraneous inputs, such as noise (random inputs) or drift variations, which may occur anywhere within the system. Here again block-diagram reduction affords a technique for isolating the effect so that it can be studied in terms of general feedback theory.

The process of block-diagram reduction is carried out in terms of several simple block-diagram transformation theorems. Some of the most useful of these are illustrated in Fig. 7-2.[2] Figure 7-2a illustrates the reduction formula for two transfer functions in cascade. It is assumed that the

[1] An equivalent procedure referred to as *signal-flow diagrams* is described by S. J. Mason in Feedback Theory—Some Properties of Signal Flow Graphs, *Proc. IRE*, vol. 41, no. 9, September, 1953.

[2] A more complete listing may be found in a paper by T. D. Graybeal, Block Diagram Network Transformation, *Elec. Eng.*, vol. 70, pp. 985–990, 1951.

Transformation	Original diagram	Equivalent diagram	Equation
(a) Combining blocks in cascade	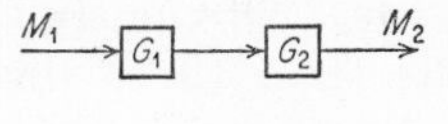 $M_1 \to G_1 \to G_2 \to M_2$	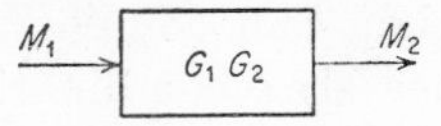 $M_1 \to \boxed{G_1 G_2} \to M_2$	$M_2 = M_1 G_1 G_2$
(b) Eliminating a feedback loop	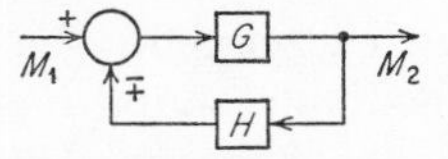	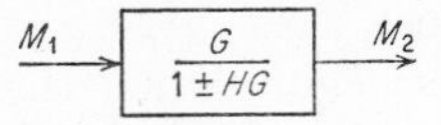	$M_2 = M_1 \dfrac{G}{1 \pm HG}$
(c) Eliminating a forward loop	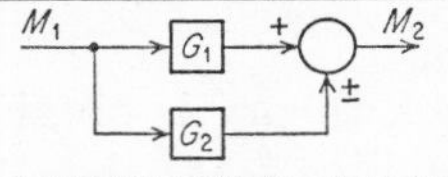	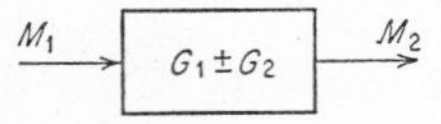	$M_2 = M_1 (G_1 \pm G_2)$
(d) Removing a block from a feedback loop	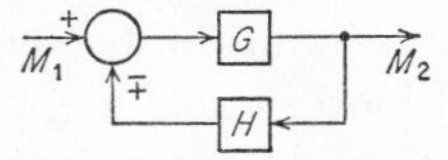	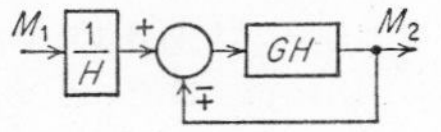	$M_2 = M_1 \left(\dfrac{G}{1 \pm HG} \right)$
(e) Removing a block from a forward path	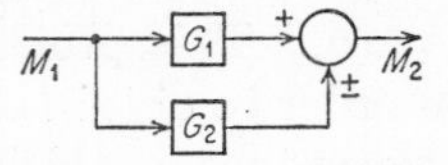	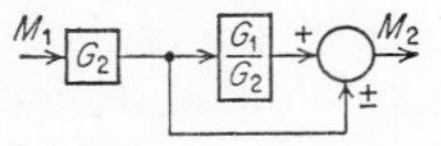	$M_2 = M_1 (G_1 \pm G_2)$
(f) Moving a pick-off point ahead of a block	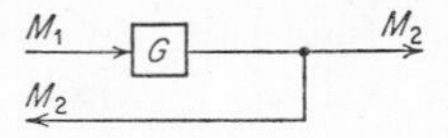	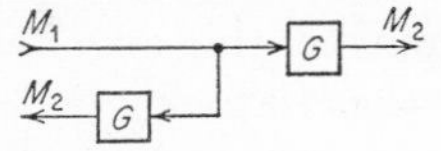	$M_2 = M_1 G$
(g) Moving a pick-off point beyond a block	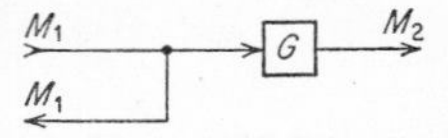	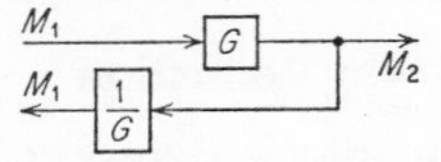	$M_2 = M_1 G$
(h) Moving a summing point ahead of a block	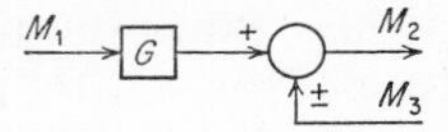	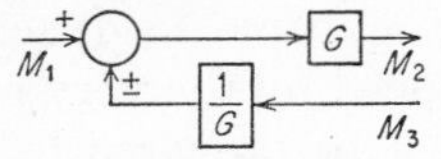	$M_2 = M_1 G \pm M_3$
(i) Moving a summing point beyond a block	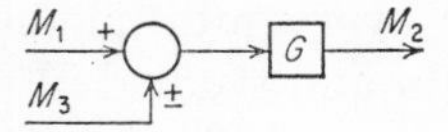	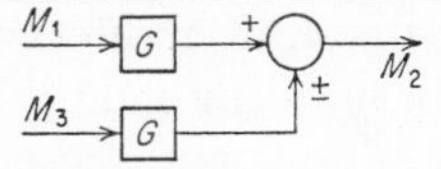	$M_2 = [M_1 \pm M_3] G$
(j) Moving a pick-off point ahead of a summing point	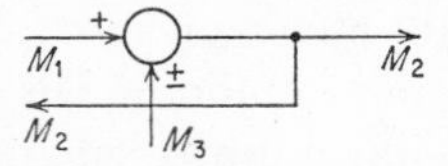	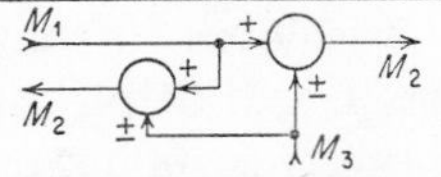	$M_2 = M_1 \pm M_3$
(k) Moving a pick-off point beyond a summing point	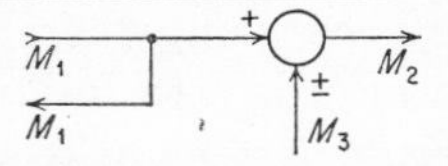	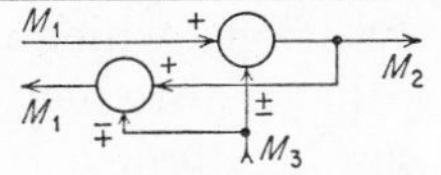	$M_2 = M_1 \pm M_3$
(l) Rearranging summing points	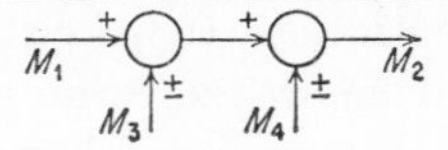	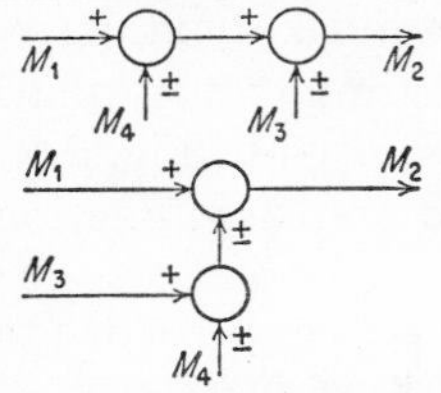	$M_2 = M_1 \pm M_3 \pm M_4$

FIG. 7-2. Block-diagram transformation theorems.

loading effects of one transfer function upon the other have been taken into account in the derivation of the transfer functions. Figure 7-2b illustrates the reduction formula for a simple feedback loop and is identical to Fig. 7-1a and b. Figure 7-2c serves to define a forward loop and illustrates its reduction formula. Figure 7-2d and e gives reduction diagrams for removing a component from either a feedback or a forward loop. The equivalent diagram is readily derived by an appropriate manipulation of the equation relating input and output for the original diagram. To illustrate this, consider case d of Fig. 7-2. The equation which describes this relationship for the original diagram is

$$(M_1 \mp HM_2)G = M_2$$

If it is desirable to modify the original block diagram in terms of a unity feedback system, an examination of the foregoing equation reveals that this is equivalent to removing H from the term HM_2. Thus, the modified equation becomes

$$\left(\frac{M_1}{H} \mp M_2\right) HG = M_2$$

Interpretation of this equation in block-diagram form results in the equivalent diagram appearing in Fig. 7-2d.

Figure 7-2d is particularly useful for cases where $H(s)$ is a constant, for it enables the feedback system to be reduced to an equivalent system involving a unity feedback loop. Figure 7-2i through l illustrates some block-diagram transformations which are used to reduce multiple-loop systems to simpler forms. Proof of the equivalence of these transformations is left to the reader. The use of these reduction diagrams is demonstrated in several examples. It is important to note that the equivalent diagrams result simply from a modified form of the equation relating input to output for the original block diagram.

When multiple inputs are present, each may be treated independently of the other inputs. The signs at each summing point correspond to the way in which each input is introduced into the system. By superposition, the individual outputs, due to each input by itself, are added to give the output when all inputs are present simultaneously. For example, consider the multiple-input system of Fig. 7-3a. Particular attention is directed to the signs at the summing points. They define the following relationships:

$$E_1(s) = R_1(s) - B(s)$$
$$E_2(s) = M_1(s) + R_2(s)$$
$$E_3(s) = M_2(s) - R_3(s)$$

In order to determine the output due to each input by itself, the diagram of Fig. 7-3a is redrawn in Fig. 7-3b to d for each input alone. By using the block-diagram reduction formulas of Fig. 7-2, the following transfer functions may be written for Fig. 7-3b to d:

$$\frac{C_1(s)}{R_1(s)} = \frac{G_1 G_2 G_3}{1 + H G_1 G_2 G_3}$$

$$\frac{C_2(s)}{R_2(s)} = \frac{G_2 G_3}{1 + H G_1 G_2 G_3}$$

$$\frac{C_3(s)}{R_3(s)} = \frac{-G_3}{1 + H G_1 G_2 G_3}$$

The denominators of each of the foregoing expressions must be identical. This is true because when each of the denominators is equated to

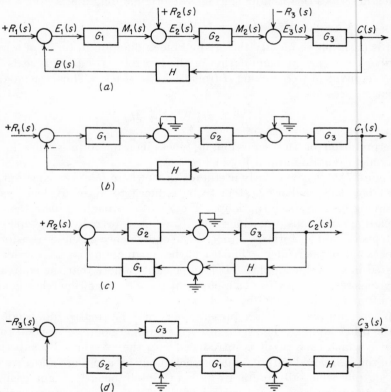

FIG. 7-3. Reducing a multiple-input system $C(s) = C_1(s) + C_2(s) + C_3(s)$. (a) A multiple-input system; (b) input $R_1(s)$ alone; (c) input $R_2(s)$ alone; (d) input $R_3(s)$ alone.

zero it becomes the characteristic equation for the system, and the latter is independent of any input signal. When all inputs are present simultaneously, the output is given by the expression

$$C(s) = C_1(s) + C_2(s) + C_3(s)$$
$$= \frac{G_1 G_2 G_3 R_1(s) + G_2 G_3 R_2(s) - G_3 R_3(s)}{1 + H G_1 G_2 G_3}$$

This result may be obtained in another way by considering Fig. 7-4, which is a reduced form of Fig. 7-3 in which the summing points have been moved ahead of the transfer functions G_1, G_2, and G_3 in accordance with the theorem of Fig. 7-2h. The interesting result of Fig. 7-4 is that it converts each input to an equivalent input at R_1. To obtain the equivalent input, the original is multiplied by the reciprocal of the direct transmission factors which precede it in the direct transmission path from R_1

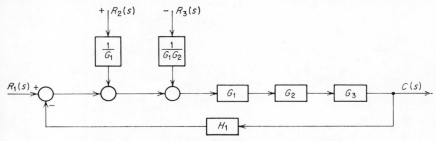

FIG. 7-4. Equivalent block diagram for Fig 7-3a.

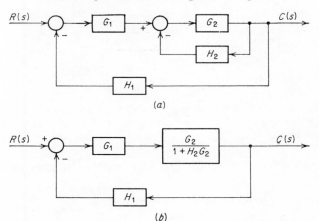

(a)

(b)

FIG. 7-5. Reducing a multiloop system, isolating $H_1(s)$. (a) Original; (b) reducing the inner feedback loop.

to the input in question. This result is useful in comparing the effects of noise signals introduced at various points in a system. Thus, if G_2 is a constant gain factor and $R_2(s)$ and $R_3(s)$ are equal input noise signals, then it follows that the magnitude of the noise output due to $R_3(s)$ is $1/G_2$ times the output due to $R_2(s)$.

Another example of the use of block-diagram reduction is illustrated in Fig. 7-5a and b. Here the theorem of Fig. 7-2b is used to eliminate minor feedback loops in the diagram. The steps involved should be obvious from the diagram. Figure 7-6 illustrates an alternate way to reduce Fig. 7-5a. Comparison of Figs. 7-5b and 7-6c illustrates that in the former $H_1(s)$ has been preserved intact, while in the latter case $H_2(s)$ has been preserved. The usefulness of this result is demonstrated by considering the loop transfer function for both cases.

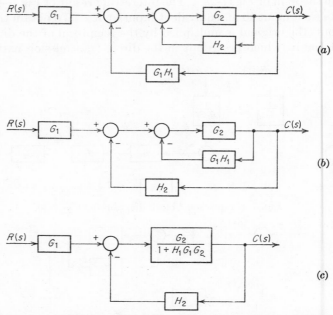

FIG. 7-6. Alternative method for reducing Fig. 7-5a, isolating $H_2(s)$. (a) Moving the first summing point beyond G_1; (b) interchanging summing points; (c) reducing the inner feedback loop.

The loop transfer function for Fig. 7-5b is given by the expression

$$\text{Loop transfer function} = \frac{G_1 G_2 H_1}{1 + H_2 G_2} \qquad (7\text{-}7a)$$

The loop transfer function for Fig. 7-6c is given by the expression

$$\text{Loop transfer function} = \frac{G_2 H_2}{1 + H_1 G_1 G_2} \qquad (7\text{-}7b)$$

Comparison of Eq. (7-7a) with Eq. (7-7b) illustrates that in the first case H_1 appears isolated, whereas in the second case H_2 appears as the isolated quantity. Of course the characteristic equation for both cases is identical and is obtained by equating 1 plus the loop transfer function to 0. Thus it is given by the expression

$$1 + H_1 G_1 G_2 + H_2 G_2 = 0 \qquad (7\text{-}7c)$$

Similarly the closed-loop transfer function in both cases reduces to the

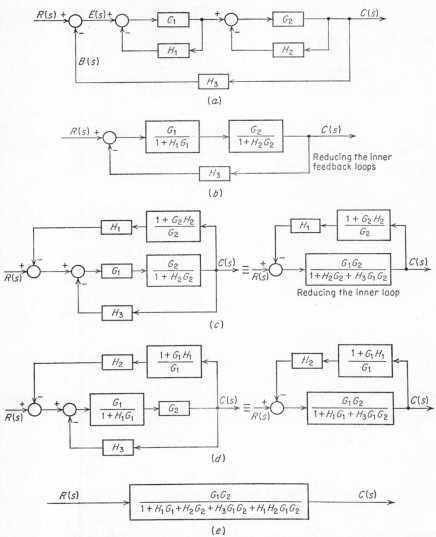

Fig. 7-7. Example of block-diagram reduction. Three-loop system. (a) Original block diagram; (b) isolating H_3; (c) isolating H_1: reducing the second inner feedback loop, shifting the pick-off point for H_1, and interchanging summing points; (d) isolating H_2: reducing the first inner feedback loop, shifting the summing point for H_2, and interchanging summing points; (e) the closed-loop transfer function.

same relationship, namely,

$$\frac{C}{R}(s) = \frac{G_1 G_2}{1 + H_1 G_1 G_2 + H_2 G_2} \qquad (7\text{-}7d)$$

Figure 7-7 illustrates the reduction of a block diagram for a three-loop system isolating components H_1, H_2, and H_3.

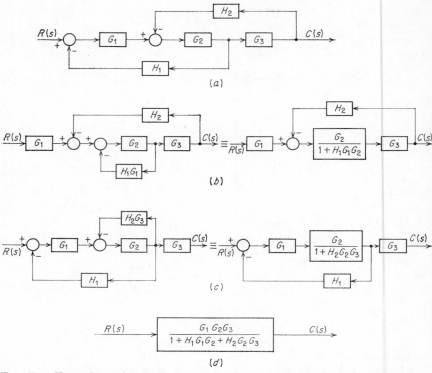

FIG. 7-8. Example of block-diagram reduction. (a) Original block diagram; (b) isolating H_2: moving the summing point for H_1 beyond G_1, interchanging summing points, and reducing the inner loop; (c) isolating H_1: moving the pick-off point for H_2 ahead of G_3, and reducing the inner loop; (d) the closed-loop transfer function.

Figure 7-8 is still another example of alternate ways of reducing a multiloop system.

7-3. Examples of System Transfer Functions

In this section the transfer functions of several systems are studied in order to demonstrate the use of the block-diagram technique.

An Elementary Voltage Control System. As a first example let us consider the elementary voltage control system of Fig. 1-11. In spite of its simplicity this example illustrates the technique involved in deriving a block diagram as well as the ease with which it leads to results. All quantities are as defined in Fig. 1-13. The system block diagram of Fig. 7-9 may be drawn by inspection of Figs. 1-11 and 1-13. Thus E_R and hV (the feedback voltage) are combined at a summing point, with the signs indicated to give the error voltage E. This, upon multiplying by the amplifier gain factor K_A, yields the voltage applied to the generator field winding. The transfer function between the applied field-winding voltage and the generator induced emf is of the form $K_G/(1 + s\tau_f)$, where K_G is a numerical constant and $\tau_f = L_f/R_f$ is the time constant of the field winding. This transfer function is represented in the second

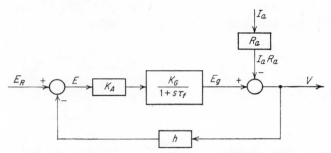

FIG. 7-9. Block diagram for the elementary voltage regulator of Fig. 1-11.

box of the direct transmission path. The remainder of the diagram represents the equation which gives the terminal voltage V in terms of the generator induced emf E_G and its internal voltage drop I_aR_a, namely,

$$V = E_G - I_aR_a \tag{7-8}$$

The feedback loop is completed by returning V to the first summation point through the feedback factor h. Reducing Fig. 7-9 as a multiple-input system gives the following result for the terminal voltage:

$$V = \frac{E_{R(s)}K_AK_G - I_{a(s)}R_a(1 + s\tau_f)}{1 + K_AK_Gh + s\tau_f} \tag{7-9}$$

This equation is identical to the results obtained in Chap. 1 except that the transfer function of the field winding has been taken into account. Equation (7-9) may now be converted into the time domain for study as a differential equation or into the frequency domain for study in the sinusoidal steady state.

An Elementary Servomechanism. As a second example, let us consider the servomechanism of Fig. 4-1. All the symbols are as defined in Sec. 4-1. The block diagram of Fig. 7-10a is identical to the block diagram of the system as drawn in Fig. 4-1 with the exception of the motor and load. In Fig. 7-10a the motor and load are combined into a single transfer function with all quantities referred to the motor shaft. The effects of an external load disturbance T_L are taken into account by means of the second summing point. The T_L input is shown as $\pm$ depending upon whether it acts in the same direction as or opposite to the developed motor torque T_d. Figure 7-10b and c illustrates the block diagram for inputs $R(s)$ and T_L alone. The equation for the motor's angular output when both inputs are present is given by the expression

$$C_M(s) = \frac{K_P K_A K_M R(s) \pm T_L}{J s^2 + F s + K_P K_A K_M h} \qquad (7\text{-}10)$$

The reader should derive this result for himself and pay particular attention to the handling of the $\pm$ sign associated with T_L. The fore-

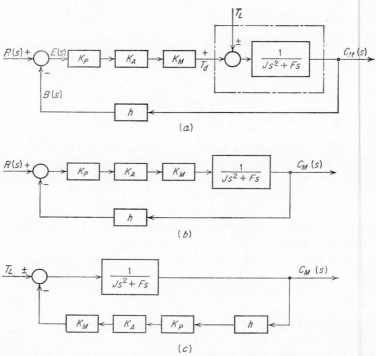

Fig. 7-10. Block diagram for the servomechanism of Fig. 4-1. $C_M(s)$ is the output. (a) Original system; (b) input $R(s)$ alone; (c) input T_L alone.

going result may be rewritten in differential equation form as follows:

$$J \frac{d^2 c_M}{dt^2} + F \frac{d c_M}{dt} + h K_P K_A K_M c_M = K_P K_A K_M r \pm T_L \qquad (7\text{-}11)$$

The equation relating the actuating signal to the two inputs may also be obtained by block-diagram reduction. For this purpose Fig. 7-10a is redrawn in Fig. 7-11. When $R(s)$ is the sole input, $E(s)$ is given by the equation

$$E(s) = \frac{R(s)}{1 + K_A K_P K_M h / (J s^2 + F s)} \qquad (7\text{-}12a)$$

When T_L is the sole input, $E(s)$ is given by

$$E(s) = \frac{-[h/(Js^2 + Fs)](\pm T_L)}{1 + K_A K_P K_M h/(Js^2 + Fs)} \qquad (7\text{-}12b)$$

Superimposing these two outputs and clearing fractions yields the following equation:

$$(Js^2 + Fs + K_P K_A K_M h)E(s) = (Js^2 + Fs)R(s) - (\pm T_L)h \quad (7\text{-}13)$$

Equation (7-13) may be rewritten as a differential equation,

$$J \frac{d^2\mathcal{E}}{dt^2} + F \frac{d\mathcal{E}}{dt} + K_P K_A K_M h \mathcal{E} = J \frac{d^2r}{dt} + F \frac{dr}{dt} - h(\pm T_L) \quad (7\text{-}14a)$$

For comparison of this result with Eq. (4-11) the reader should recall that in Chap. 4, T_L was assumed to be a retarding torque (opposing T_d) so

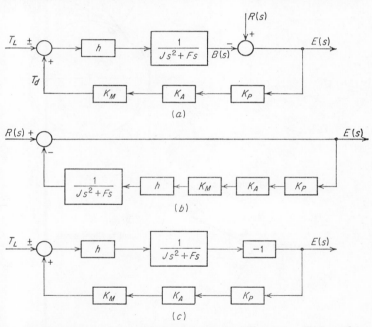

FIG. 7-11. Block diagram for the servomechanism of Fig. 4-1. $E(s)$ as the output. (a) Original system; (b) input $R(s)$ alone; (c) input T_L alone.

that, for this case, T_L is negative in Eq. (7-14) and the final equation becomes

$$J \frac{d^2\mathcal{E}}{dt^2} + F \frac{d\mathcal{E}}{dt} + K_P K_A K_M h \mathcal{E} = J \frac{d^2r}{dt^2} + F \frac{dr}{dt} + h T_L \qquad (7\text{-}14b)$$

An Inertial-guidance System. As a final example, let us consider an inertial-guidance system. This application is an interesting example of a multiloop system and illustrates the power of the block diagram as an aid in analyzing a difficult problem.

Inertial guidance is a self-contained navigational system which does not require any outside data (such as radio signals, magnetic compass,

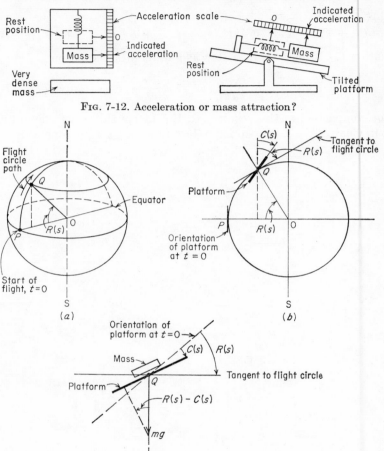

FIG. 7-12. Acceleration or mass attraction?

FIG. 7-13. The great-circle flight of an inertial navigator about a fixed sphere along a line of constant longitude from the equator to the North Pole. (a) Flight path; (b) detail of flight circle; (c) detail of conditions at the platform.

ocean currents, etc.) for the calculation of position. It is primarily a system of "dead reckoning" in which the movement of the vehicle is measured with respect to inertial space.[1] Any motion with respect to inertial space is measured by means of accelerometers which detect

[1] See footnote, p. 240.

vehicle accelerations. These accelerometer outputs are doubly integrated, starting at time $t = 0$, to yield the distance traveled in the direction in which the acceleration is measured. In an aircraft or missile, three accelerometers are usually required, one to detect north-south acceleration, one to detect east-west accelerations, and one to detect up and down motion. For navigation on a sphere only two accelerometers are required. The north-south and east-west accelerometers are usually aligned at the beginning of a flight. If the system is to operate properly, it is necessary for them to maintain this orientation despite any maneuvers of the vehicle. Thus the accelerometers must be mounted on a stable platform which keeps them pointing in the N-S, E-W directions. Another complication arises because accelerometers cannot distinguish between vehicle accelerations and gravity (see Fig. 7-12). Therefore, as the vehicle moves round the earth's surface, it is necessary to maintain the plane of the stable platform so that it is always tangent to the earth's sphere, i.e., perpendicular to the pull of gravity. Any platform tilt gives rise to accelerometer outputs which are interpreted erroneously as vehicle accelerations. In order to draw the block diagram for an inertial navigation system, let us consider the simple case of a great-circle flight about a fixed sphere, from the equator to the North Pole along a line of constant longitude.[1] The following quantities are defined (see Fig. 7-13):

$R(s)$ = input angle, radians of latitude, through which vehicle has flown since $t = 0$. $R(s)$ is the input signal to the system.

$C(s)$ = angle, about E-W axis, in radians through the which stable platform is rotated during flight. $C(s)$ is measured with respect to its original orientation at $t = 0$, that is, tangent to the earth's sphere at the equator. If $C(s) = R(s)$ at all times, then the platform remains tangent to the flight sphere and the accelerometers measure true vehicle accelerations.

a = radius of flight sphere, ft. Nominally a is assumed to be the earth's radius.

K_1/s^2 = transfer function of N-S accelerometer and integrators. K_1 is measured in volts/ft so that the output from the accelerometer-integrator combination is obtained in volts when the input acceleration is measured in ft/sec^2.

K_2 = transfer function for remainder of system which acts to rotate platform about E-W axis through an angle of K_2 radians for each volt input from the N-S accelerometer-integrator combination. The units for K_2 are therefore radians/volt.

---

[1] In this way the effects of the earth's rotation may be neglected and only the N-S accelerometer considered. The results obtained in this section are quite general in spite of these simplifications.

The block diagram for the system is drawn in Fig. 7-14. There are two inputs to the accelerometer-integrator combination.

1. The true vehicle acceleration which is given by the formula $a[s^2R(s)]$, where $s^2R(s)$ is the angular acceleration of the vehicle due to its flight $R(s)$. The factor a converts this angular acceleration to a linear acceleration.

2. An erroneous acceleration, due to gravity, which is given by the expression $g[R(s) - C(s)]$. The angle $[R(s) - C(s)]$ represents the amount of tilt which the accelerometer platform has from being tangent to the

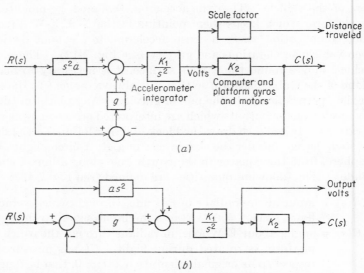

FIG. 7-14. Block diagram for an inertial-guidance system. (a) Basic system; (b) block diagram redrawn.

flight sphere (see Fig. 7-13c). This tilt gives rise to a component of gravity, $mg \sin [R(s) - C(s)] \approx mg[R(s) - C(s)]$, which acts on the mass m of the accelerometers and causes an output signal. This component of output signal is interpreted erroneously as being due to a linear vehicle acceleration of magnitude $g[R(s) - C(s)]$.

The two foregoing inputs act upon the accelerometer-integrator combination to produce an output voltage as shown in the diagram. The remainder of the system is represented by the transfer K_2, which converts the accelerometer-integrator output into a platform rotation of $C(s)$ radians. Physically K_2 includes a computer and the gyros and motors of the stable platform. Hence the factor K_2 is obviously a simplified transfer function.

The transfer function between $C(s)$ and $R(s)$ is obtained by block-diagram reduction. Figure 7-14a is redrawn in Fig. 7-14b to assist in this process.   The reduction leads to the following result:

$$C(s) = \frac{R(s)K_1K_2(as^2 + g)}{s^2 + gK_1K_2} \tag{7-15}$$

For the system to operate as a navigator, it is necessary that

$$C(s) = R(s)$$

Examination of Eq. (7-15) reveals that this is true if $K_1K_2a = 1$, that is, if K_1K_2 are equal to $1/a$, the reciprocal of the earth's radius!   Under these conditions the characteristic equation for the system may be written as

$$s^2 + gK_1K_2 = s^2 + \frac{g}{a} = 0 \tag{7-16}$$

The roots are located at $s = \pm j \sqrt{g/a}$, and the source-free system response is given by the equation

$$c(t) \bigg|_{\text{source-free}} = A \sin\left(\sqrt{\frac{g}{a}}\, t + B\right) \tag{7-17}$$

where A and B are constants to be evaluated from initial conditions. This source-free response is an undamped sinusoid with a period of $2\pi \sqrt{a/g}$ sec.   Substituting numerical values for a and g reveals that the period is 84 min.   Therefore the platform tends to oscillate as an 84-min undamped pendulum.   The length of such a pendulum is a, the radius of the earth.   It is interesting to note that the source-free response of the platform is truly a pure sinusoid with an 84-min period.   In fact, it can be shown that the only way to damp this system is to introduce additional navigational information to it from an outside source.   The effect of the source-free response is to introduce navigational errors which propagate with an 84-min period.   Fortunately these errors are bounded and can be kept small in practice.

7-4. System Classification.   Error Coefficients

All control systems can be classified in accordance with their ability to follow input commands such as steps, ramps, parabolas, etc., in the steady state.   This classification becomes a basic figure of merit which identifies the system's final-state performance.   Each of the inputs mentioned is the integral of the previous one and is more difficult for the system to follow.   Consider, for example, an automatically controlled contour-reproducing machine in which the motion of the cutting tool is to follow the motion of an input stylus as it traces out the contour of a master pattern (see Fig. 7-15).   As a minimum requirement the cutting tool should be able to follow a constant velocity motion of the input stylus with zero error between the position of the cutting tool and the position of the input stylus. In fact the performance of the system is limited by its ability to follow higher-order inputs with zero position error. In contrast let us consider a simple control system which is used to reproduce the constant setting of an input dial at a remote location. This system needs only to reproduce the constant angular position of the input dial with zero position error and does not have any steady-state velocity requirement.

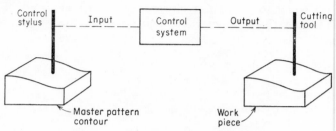

FIG. 7-15. A contour-reproducing machine.

The final-value theorem of the Laplace transform provides a convenient way to study the steady-state performance of any system for various input signals. Consider the basic feedback system of Fig. 7-1a. The relationship between the input command and the actuating signal is given by the equation

$$E(s) = \frac{R(s)}{1 + HG(s)} \tag{7-18}$$

The steady state is defined by conditions as $t \to \infty$. Thus, upon using the final-value theorem, it follows that the steady-state actuating signal is given by the equation

$$\mathcal{E}(t)\Big|_{ss} = \lim_{t \to \infty} \mathcal{E}(t) = \lim_{s \to 0} \frac{sR(s)}{1 + HG(s)} \tag{7-19}$$

We are interested in the following types of inputs:
1. $r(t) = r_0 u(t)$, a step. Thus, $R(s) = r_0/s$.
2. $r(t) = r_1 t u(t)$, a ramp. Thus, $R(s) = r_1/s^2$.
3. $r(t) = \frac{1}{2} r_2 t^2 u(t)$, a parabola. Thus, $R(s) = r_2/s^3$.

The loop transfer function is assumed to be available in the following factored form:

$$HG(s) = \frac{K(1 + s\tau_a) \cdots [(s\tau_{nb})^2 + 2\zeta_b \tau_{nb}s + 1]}{s^N(1 + s\tau_1) \cdots [(s\tau_{n2})^2 + 2\zeta_2 \tau_{n2}s + 1]} \tag{7-20}$$

In Eq. (7-20) K is a constant gain factor, and the bracketed terms represent linear and quadratic factors. The term s^N in the denominator represents a pole of multiplicity N at the origin, i.e., where $s = 0$. The exponent N is used to classify the system. Thus a type 0 system has a loop transfer function of the form of Eq. (7-20) with $N = 0$. A type 1 system has $N = 1$, a type 2 system has $N = 2$, a type 3 system has $N = 3$, etc. The reader is cautioned that the system classification is different from the order of the system. The latter refers to the order of the differential equation which describes the system's operation. The system classification refers to the order of the pole of the loop transfer function at $s = 0$; that is, it depends upon the number of *ideal integrations* with which the system is furnished.

Let us consider the steady-state actuating signal for each of the system classifications for three inputs, the step, ramp, and parabola.

Consider the step input first. $R(s) = r_0/s$. The steady-state actuating signal is denoted by the symbol $\mathcal{E}_{ss}$ and is given by the following equation

$$\mathcal{E}_{ss} = \lim_{s \to 0} \frac{s(r_0/s)}{1 + HG(s)}$$

$$= \frac{r_0}{1 + \lim_{s \to 0} HG(s)} = \frac{r_0}{1 + K_p} \tag{7-21a}$$

The quantity K_p is known as the *position error coefficient* and is defined by the equation

$$K_p = \lim_{s \to 0} HG(s) \tag{7-21b}$$

Substituting the value of $HG(s)$ for the various system types into Eq. (7-21b) yields the value of K_p for each case. Thus for a type 0 system

$$K_p = \lim_{s \to 0} \frac{K(1 + s\tau_a) \cdots}{(1 + s\tau_1) \cdots} = K \tag{7-21c}$$

For a type N system, when $N > 0$

$$K_p = \lim_{s \to 0} \frac{K(1 + s\tau_a) \cdots}{s^N(1 + s\tau_1) \cdots} = \infty \tag{7-21d}$$

Substituting the appropriate value for K_p into Eq. (7-21a) yields the following results for the steady-state actuating signal for a step input:

Type 0:

$$\mathcal{E}_{ss} = \frac{r_0}{1 + K} \tag{7-21e}$$

Type N system, where $N > 0$:

$$\mathcal{E}_{ss} = 0 \tag{7-21f}$$

Let us consider the ramp input next. $R(s) = r_1/s^2$. The steady-state actuating signal is again denoted by the symbol $\mathcal{E}_{ss}$ and is given by the equation

$$\mathcal{E}_{ss} = \lim_{s \to 0} \frac{s(r_1/s^2)}{1 + HG(s)}$$

$$= \frac{r_1}{\lim_{s \to 0} sHG(s)} = \frac{r_1}{K_v} \tag{7-22a}$$

The quantity K_v is known as the *velocity error coefficient* and is defined by the equation

$$K_v = \lim_{s \to 0} sHG(s) \tag{7-22b}$$

Substituting the value of $HG(s)$ for the various system types into Eq. (7-22b) yields the value of K_v for each case. Thus

Type 0 system: $K_v = \lim_{s \to 0} s \dfrac{K(1 + s\tau_a) \, \cdots}{(1 + s\tau_1) \, \cdots} = 0$ $\tag{7-22c}$

Type 1 system: $K_v = \lim_{s \to 0} s \dfrac{K(1 + s\tau_a) \, \cdots}{s(1 + s\tau_1) \, \cdots} = K$ $\tag{7-22d}$

Type N system, when $N > 1$:

$$K_v = \lim_{s \to 0} s \frac{K(1 + s\tau_a) \, \cdots}{s^N(1 + s\tau_1) \, \cdots} = \infty \tag{7-22e}$$

Substituting these values for K_v into Eq. (7-22a) yields the following results for the steady-state actuating signal for the ramp input:

Type 0 system: $\varepsilon_{ss} \to \infty$ $\tag{7-22f}$

Type 1 system: $\varepsilon_{ss} = \dfrac{r_1}{K}$ $\tag{7-22g}$

Type N system, where $N > 1$:

$$\varepsilon_{ss} = 0 \tag{7-22h}$$

Equation (7-22f) shows that a type 0 system requires an infinite actuating signal to follow a ramp input in the steady state. Obviously such a system would saturate in trying to follow this input signal so that a type 0 system is incapable of following a ramp input in the steady state. On the other hand the type 1 system can follow a ramp input with a finite actuating signal, and type 2 and higher-order systems can follow ramp inputs with zero actuating signals. A physical explanation of how this comes about is presented shortly.

Let us now consider a parabolic input signal. $R(s) = r_2/s^3$. Let ε_{ss} again denote the steady-state actuating signal. ε_{ss} is given by the equation

$$\begin{aligned} \varepsilon_{ss} &= \lim_{s \to 0} \frac{s(r_2/s^3)}{1 + HG(s)} \\ &= \frac{r_2}{\lim_{s \to 0} s^2 HG(s)} = \frac{r_2}{K_a} \end{aligned} \tag{7-23a}$$

K_a is known as the *acceleration error coefficient* and is defined by the equation

$$K_a = \lim_{s \to 0} s^2 HG(s) \tag{7-23b}$$

Substituting the value of $HG(s)$ for the various system types into Eq. (7-23b) yields the value of K_a in each case.

Type 0 system:

$$K_a = \lim_{s \to 0} s^2 \frac{K(1 + s\tau_a) \cdots}{(1 + s\tau_1) \cdots} = 0 \qquad (7\text{-}23c)$$

Type 1 system:

$$K_a = \lim_{s \to 0} s^2 \frac{K(1 + s\tau_a) \cdots}{s(1 + s\tau_1) \cdots} = 0 \qquad (7\text{-}23d)$$

Type 2 system:

$$K_a = \lim_{s \to 0} s^2 \frac{K(1 + s\tau_a) \cdots}{s^2(1 + s\tau_1) \cdots} = K \qquad (7\text{-}23e)$$

Type N system, when $N > 2$:

$$K_a = \lim_{s \to 0} s^2 \frac{K(1 + s\tau_a) \cdots}{s^N(1 + s\tau_1) \cdots} = \infty \qquad (7\text{-}23f)$$

Substituting these values for K_a into Eq. (7-23a) yields the following results for the steady-state actuating signal for a parabolic input:

Type 0 and 1 systems: $\qquad \mathcal{E}_{ss} \to \infty$ $\qquad\qquad\qquad (7\text{-}23g)$

Type 2 system: $\qquad\qquad \mathcal{E}_{ss} = \dfrac{r_2}{K}$ $\qquad\qquad\quad (7\text{-}23h)$

Type N system, where $N > 2$: $\quad \mathcal{E}_{ss} = 0$ $\qquad\qquad\quad (7\text{-}23i)$

Equation (7-23g) indicates that both the type 0 and type 1 systems are incapable of following a parabolic input in the steady state without saturating. The type 2 system follows a parabolic input with a finite actuating signal, whereas the type 3 and higher systems require zero actuating signals.

In order to compare the preceding results, they are tabulated in Table 7-1. Examination of the table will establish its pattern so that the reader can extend it to other system classifications and input functions. In each case the steady-state actuating signal is either zero, a finite number inversely proportional to the constant gain factor K, or infinite for the specified inputs. As mentioned before, an infinite actuating signal is impossible to achieve, so that the system cannot follow such inputs in the steady state and soon saturates.

It is important to realize that the results appearing in Table 7-1 are general and therefore applicable to all types of systems. The step, ramp, and parabolic inputs refer to commands which call for corresponding time variations of the *controlled variable* independently of the particular form it takes. Thus, if the controlled variable is mechanical (i.e., position), a step command calls for a position follow-up of the output. However, if the controlled variable is velocity (see Prob. 7-7), then a step command calls for a step change in velocity. Similarly, in the first case, a ramp input command calls for a controlled output variation in the

TABLE 7-1. TABULATION OF THE STEADY-STATE ACTUATING SIGNAL ε_{ss} FOR VARIOUS SYSTEM CLASSIFICATIONS AND INPUTS

$$K_p = \lim_{s\to 0} HG(s) \qquad K_v = \lim_{s\to 0} sHG(s) \qquad K_a = \lim_{s\to 0} s^2HG(s)$$

Input type / System type	A step $r(t) = r_0 u(t)$. $R(s) = \dfrac{r_0}{s}$	A ramp $r(t) = r_1 t u(t)$. $R(s) = \dfrac{r_1}{s^2}$	A parabola $r(t) = \frac{1}{2} r_2 t^2 u(t)$. $R(s) = \dfrac{r_2}{s^3}$
$N = 0$ $HG(s) = \dfrac{K(1 + s\tau_a)\cdots}{(1 + s\tau_1)\cdots}$	$\varepsilon_{ss} = \dfrac{r_0}{1 + K_p} = \dfrac{r_0}{1 + K}$ Step output with constant actuating signal	Actuating signal increases with time	Actuating signal increases with time
$N = 1$ $HG(s) = \dfrac{K(1 + s\tau_a)\cdots}{s(1 + s\tau_1)\cdots}$	Step output with zero actuating signal	$\varepsilon_{ss} = \dfrac{r_1}{K_v} = \dfrac{r_1}{K}$ Ramp output with constant actuating signal	Actuating signal increases with time
$N = 2$ $HG(s) = \dfrac{K(1 + s\tau_a)\cdots}{s^2(1 + s\tau_1)\cdots}$	Step output with zero actuating signal	Ramp output with zero actuating signal	$\varepsilon_{ss} = \dfrac{r_2}{K_a} = \dfrac{r_2}{K}$ Parabolic output with constant actuating signal
$N = 3$ $HG(s) = \dfrac{K(1 + s\tau_a)\cdots}{s^3(1 + s\tau_1)\cdots}$	Step output with zero actuating signal	Ramp output with zero actuating signal	Parabolic output with zero actuating signal

steady state which is a ramp. In particular it is a ramp of position, which is velocity. In the second case, where the controlled variable is specifically velocity, a ramp command calls for a ramp of velocity, which is acceleration. This distinction is important to keep in mind when the controlled variable is not mechanical. To cite still another example, consider a pressure control system. A ramp command calls for a ramp of the controlled variable, which is rate of change of pressure. In this connection it should be apparent that the names given to the error coefficients are really special because they offer a correct description only in the case where the feedback control system is a servomechanism. Accordingly, a more fitting title for the position error coefficient would be the *step* error coefficient. Similarly, the velocity error coefficient is better described as the *ramp* error coefficient, and the acceleration error coefficient as the *parabolic* error coefficient.

The results of Table 7-1 lead to some very important conclusions concerning the steady-state behavior of systems, particularly when the feedback factor is a numerical constant. When $H(s) = 1$, the actuating signal $E(s)$ is a direct measure of the lack of correspondence, i.e., the error, between the input and output signals. When $H(s) = h_0$, a constant other than unity, the system can be reduced to an equivalent unity-feedback case by use of the reduction theorem of Fig. 7-2d. The following remarks then apply to the error between the input divided by h_0 and the output.

When $H(s) = 1$, the steady-state error for a constant input command r_0 is given by $r_0/(1 + K_p)$. For a type 0 system K_p is finite, whereas for higher-order systems K_p is infinite. Thus, if a system is to respond to a constant input with zero error, it must be at least a type 1 system or higher.

The steady-state error for a constant ramp input command $r(t) = r_1 t$ is given by r_1/K_v so that the steady-state output $c_{ss}(t)$ is given by the formula

$$c_{ss}(t) = r_1 t - \frac{r_1}{K_v} \qquad (7\text{-}24a)$$

For a type 0 system K_v approaches zero so that error increases with time and the output lags further and further behind the input until the system saturates. For a type 1 system K_v approaches a finite number so that the output lags the input by a constant amount. For this particular case Eq. (7-24a) becomes

$$c_{ss}(t) = r_1 t - \frac{r_1}{K} \qquad (7\text{-}24b)$$

Thus the steady-state output is seen to be a ramp function with the same slope as the input except that at any instant of time it lags behind the input ramp by a fixed amount equal to r_1/K. In terms of a type 1 servomechanism this means that, in the steady state, the system responds to a constant velocity input (a ramp position input) by reproducing the input velocity at the output shaft except that the angular position of the output shaft lags behind the input shaft by a fixed number of degrees. The amount of position lag is proportional to the angular velocity of the input signal and inversely proportional to the constant gain factor K.

For a type 2 or higher system K_v is infinite so that the output is identically equal to the input. Thus a type 2 or higher servomechanism can follow a constant velocity input with zero position lag error.

When the input command is a parabola $r(t) = \frac{1}{2}r_2t^2$, the steady-state output is given by the formula

$$c_{ss}(t) = \frac{1}{2}r_2t^2 - \frac{r_2}{K_a} \tag{7-25}$$

For type 0 and type 1 systems K_a is zero so that the output lags further and further behind the input until the system saturates. On the other hand K_a approaches a finite number for a type 2 system so that it can follow a parabolic input with a constant error. In order to follow a parabolic input with zero steady-state error, at least a type 3 system is required.

From Table 7-1 it follows that the contour-reproducing machine should be at least a type 2 system for the cutting head to follow a constant velocity motion of the input stylus with zero position error. On the other hand the system required to reproduce a constant dial setting needs to be only a type 1 in order to have zero error. If a constant error can be tolerated, then a type 0 system is permissible provided that the gain factor K is large enough to make the steady-state error small. Of course too large a K factor may lead to difficulty in the transient response.

As a further example of the use of error coefficients, let us consider the steady-state response of the type 0, 1, and 2 unity feedback systems to a polynomial input of the form $r(t) = r_0 + r_1t + \frac{1}{2}r_2t^2$. By means of superposition the response for each term of the input may be treated independently and the results added. Thus by using Table 7-1 the following results are obtained for the steady-state error.

Type 0 system: $\mathcal{E}_{ss} = \dfrac{r_0}{1 + K} + (\to \infty) + (\to \infty)$

The first term represents the steady-state error due to the constant input term r_0, and the next two terms represent the steady-state errors due to the ramp and parabolic input terms. Thus this system would lag further and further behind and soon saturate in attempting to follow the input function specified.

Type 1 system: $\mathcal{E}_{ss} = 0 + \dfrac{r_1}{K} + (\to \infty)$

The first term indicates zero error due to the constant input term r_0. The second term indicates a finite error due to the ramp input term. The third term indicates a steady-state error which approaches infinity owing to the parabolic input term so that, here again, the system would lag further and further behind until saturation occurred.

Type 2 system: $$\varepsilon_{ss} = 0 + 0 + \frac{r_2}{K}$$

The first two terms indicate zero error for the constant and ramp input terms. The last term indicates a finite error due to the parabolic input. Since the output signal is equal to the input minus the error, it follows that the steady-state output is given by the equation

$$c_{ss}(t) = r(t) - \varepsilon_{ss}$$
$$= r_0 + r_1 t + \tfrac{1}{2} r_2 t^2 - \frac{r_2}{K}$$

Thus the type 2 system follows the input specified except that the output lags behind the input by a fixed amount. In terms of a servomechanism this means that there is a fixed *positional* error due to a parabolic (constant-acceleration) input term.

Clearly the results of Table 7-1 can be used to predict the steady-state response of higher-order systems to higher-order polynomial-type input functions.

The results of Table 7-1 lead to some important physical interpretations. Since the factor $1/s$ means integration, it follows that a type 1 system has one integration in the loop and that a type 2 system has two integrations. Examination of the examples of Sec. 7-3 reveals that the elementary voltage regulator is a type 0 system. For a constant output voltage V, there must always be an error signal, and $V \neq E_R$. On the other hand the servomechanism is an example of a type 1 system. The ideal integration occurs because of the transfer function of the servomotor and because the feedback transducer is sensitive to the motor-shaft angular position. The actuating signal causes the motor to rotate at a proportionate angular velocity. Since angular position is the integral of angular velocity, it follows that the feedback voltage is proportional to the integral of the actuating signal. If the feedback transducer were sensitive to the motor's angular velocity instead, then the transfer function would not involve an ideal integration and the system would be of the type 0 variety. Thus higher-order systems are obtained by adding integrators to the loop transmission path. It should be noted, however, that each integration brings additional stability problems with it.

From a physical point of view an integrator is a device which is capable of producing an output with zero instantaneous input. This is because an integrator "remembers" and produces an output proportional to the

274   FREQUENCY-DOMAIN APPROACH

time integral of all previous inputs. Thus, when a step function is applied to a type 1 system, it produces a constant steady-state output with zero actuating signal by integrating the error signal which occurs during the transient period prior to reaching the steady state. For an input step of magnitude r_0, the net shaded area under the curve for the transient actuating signal from $t = 0$ to $t = \infty$ can be shown to equal r_0/K (see Fig. 7-16a). This may be proved by writing, in operational form,

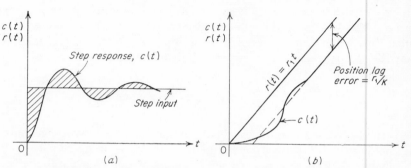

Fig. 7-16. Complete response of type 1 system to step and ramp input signals for unity feedback. (a) Step response (shaded area $= r_0/K = r_0/K_v$); (b) ramp response.

the differential equation relating $E(s)/s$ to $R(s)$ for a type 1 system. From Eq. (7-18) it follows that $E(s)[1 + HG(s)] = R(s)$. Substituting the value for $HG(s)$ from Eq. (7-20) with $N = 1$ and clearing fractions yields the result

$$[(1 + s\tau_1) \cdots (s^2\tau_{n2}{}^2 + 2\zeta_2\tau_{n2}s + 1)]R(s)$$
$$= [s(1 + s\tau_1) \cdots (s^2\tau_{n2}{}^2 + 2\zeta_2\tau_{n2}s + 1)$$
$$+ K(1 + s\tau_a) \cdots (s^2\tau_{nb}{}^2 + 2\zeta_b\tau_{nb}s + 1)]\frac{E(s)}{s} \quad (7\text{-}26)$$

Rewriting this equation in the time domain for $t > 0$, letting $r(t) = r_0$, yields the following result

$$r_0 = K \int_0^t e(t)\,dt + k_1e(t) + k_2\frac{de(t)}{dt} + \cdots \quad (7\text{-}27)$$

where $k_1, k_2, \ldots$ are numerical constants derived from multiplying the factors of Eq. (7-26). In the steady state, as $t \to \infty$, $e(t)$ and all its derivatives approach zero. Therefore it follows that as $t \to \infty$ Eq. (7-27) becomes

$$\int_0^\infty e(t)\,dt = \frac{r_0}{K} \quad (7\text{-}28)$$

It is also possible to relate a system's response from one type of input to another by use of the related-sources theorem of Chap. 2. Since a ramp input is the integral of the step, it follows that a system's ramp response is the integral of its step response. Assume that a system is initially at rest. Let $c_{step}(t)$ denote the complete response to a unit-step input $r(t) = u(t)$. It follows that the system response to a unit-ramp input $r(t) = tu(t)$ is given by the formula

$$c_{ramp}(t) = \int_0^t c_{step}(t)\, dt \qquad (7\text{-}29)$$

This result leads to an interesting conclusion in terms of a type 2 system. Typical step and ramp responses for this system are drawn in Fig. 7-17.

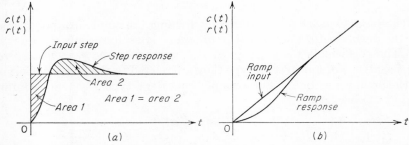

FIG. 7-17. Response of a type 2 system to input step and ramp functions for unity feedback. (a) Step response; (b) ramp response.

If the ramp response is to have zero steady-state error, it follows that, as $t \to \infty$, the area under the step-response curve must be equal to the area under a step function. Hence the shaded area above the input step in Fig. 7-17a must be equal to the shaded area below it. In other words a type 2 system must exhibit at least one overshoot in its step-response characteristic. It would be impossible to prevent this overshoot without changing the system's classification. This is not so surprising when one recognizes that the characteristic equation for a type 2 system must be at least of the second degree and its source-free response involves more than one time constant.

7-5. Generalized Error Coefficients

When $H(s) = 1$, it is possible to define a set of system error coefficients which are more general than those of the previous section. This is accomplished by writing Eq. (7-20) in unfactored form as the ratio of two polynomials in s.

$$HG(s) = \frac{K(1 + A_1s + A_2s^2 + \cdots + A_ms^m)}{s^N(1 + B_1s + B_2s^2 + \cdots + B_ns^n)} \qquad (7\text{-}30)$$

Substituting into Eq. (7-18) with $H(s) = 1$ yields the result

$$
\begin{aligned}
\frac{E(s)}{R(s)} &= \frac{1}{1 + G(s)} \\
&= \frac{s^N(1 + B_1 s + B_2 s^2 + \cdots + B_n s^n)}{s^N(1 + B_1 s + B_2 s^2 + \cdots + B_n s^n) + K(1 + A_1 s + A_2 s^2 + \cdots + A_m s^m)}
\end{aligned}
$$

$$(7\text{-}31)$$

If like powers of s in the numerator and denominator are grouped together, then Eq. (7-31) can be written

$$
\frac{E(s)}{R(s)} = \frac{\alpha_0 + \alpha_1 s + \alpha_2 s^2 + \cdots}{\beta_0 + \beta_1 s + \beta_2 s^2 + \cdots} = C_0 + C_1 s + C_2 s^2 + C_3 s^3 + \cdots
$$

$$(7\text{-}32)$$

The series expansion is obtained by dividing the numerator polynomial by the denominator polynomial to obtain a series in ascending powers of s. The coefficients C_0, C_1, C_2, C_3, ... are called the *generalized error coefficients*. For any system type they are related to the error coefficients of the previous section. For example, consider a type 0 system such that Eq. (7-31) becomes

$$
\begin{aligned}
\frac{E(s)}{R(s)} &= \frac{1 + B_1 s + B_2 s^2 + \cdots}{(1 + K) + (B_1 + KA_1)s + (B_2 + KA_2)s^2 + \cdots} \\
&= \frac{1}{1 + K} + \frac{1}{1 + K}\left(B_1 - \frac{B_1 + KA_1}{1 + K}\right)s + \cdots
\end{aligned}
$$

$$(7\text{-}33)$$

Comparison of Eq. (7-33) with Eq. (7-32) reveals that $C_0 = 1/(1 + K)$ and that the values of the other generalized error coefficients C_1, C_2, ... depend upon the numerical coefficients of Eqs. (7-33). From Eq. (7-21c) we note that for a type 0 system $K = K_p$ so that we may write

$$
C_0 = \frac{1}{1 + K_p}
$$

$$(7\text{-}34)$$

Equation (7-34) relates C_0 to the position error coefficient of a type 0 system. Similarly for a type 1 system Eq. (7-31) becomes

$$
\begin{aligned}
\frac{E(s)}{R(s)} &= \frac{s + B_1 s^2 + B_2 s^2 + \cdots}{K + (1 + KA_1)s + (B_1 + KA_2)s^2 + \cdots} \\
&= \frac{1}{K}s^2 + \frac{1}{K}\left(B_1 - \frac{1 + KA_1}{K}\right)s + \cdots
\end{aligned}
$$

$$(7\text{-}35)$$

Comparison with Eq. (7-32) reveals that $C_0 = 0$ and $C_1 = 1/K$. Comparing with Eq. (7-22d), we note that for a type 1 system

$$
C_1 = \frac{1}{K_v}
$$

$$(7\text{-}36)$$

Thus for a type 1 system C_1 is the reciprocal of the velocity error coefficient K_v.

If the foregoing procedure is followed for higher-order systems, it can be shown that for a type N system the generalized error coefficients C_ν (where $\nu = 0, 1, 2, 3, \ldots$) are given as follows:

$$C_\nu = 0 \qquad \text{for } \nu < N \qquad (7\text{-}37a)$$

$$C_\nu = \frac{1}{\lim\limits_{s \to 0} s^N G(s)} \qquad \text{for } \nu = N \qquad (7\text{-}37b)$$

The values of C_ν for $\nu > N$ depend upon the numerical results of the division process as indicated in Eq. (7-32).

The advantage of the generalized error coefficients becomes more obvious when Eq. (7-32) is rewritten as follows:

$$E(s) = C_0 R(s) + C_1 s R(s) + C_2 s^2 R(s) + \cdots \qquad (7\text{-}38)$$

Rewriting this expression in the time domain, neglecting all initial conditions and impulses at $t = 0$, yields

$$\mathcal{E}_{ss}(t) = C_0 r(t) + C_1 r'(t) + C_2 r''(t) + \cdots \qquad (7\text{-}39)$$

Thus the generalized error coefficients can be used to relate the steady-state system error to the *input function* and its *successive derivatives*. It is also important to note that the generalized error coefficients can be expected to be finite numbers.

As an illustration of the use of the generalized error coefficients, consider a simple unity-feedback type 2 system whose loop transfer function is given by

$$G(s) = \frac{10(1 + s)}{s^2(1 + 5s)}$$

Substituting into Eq. (7-31) after multiplying through by $R(s)$ yields

$$\begin{aligned} E(s) &= \frac{R(s)}{1 + G(s)} = \frac{s^2(1 + 5s)}{s^2(1 + 5s) + 10(1 + s)} R(s) \\ &= (\tfrac{1}{10}s^2 + \tfrac{2}{5}s^3 + \cdots)R(s) \end{aligned}$$

In the time domain for the steady state we get

$$\mathcal{E}_{ss}(t) = \tfrac{1}{10}r''(t) + \tfrac{2}{5}r'''(t) + \cdots$$

so that the generalized error coefficients become

$$C_0 = C_1 = 0 \qquad C_2 = \tfrac{1}{10} \qquad C_3 = \tfrac{2}{5} \qquad \cdots$$

If $r(t)$ is a polynomial-type input of the form $r(t) = r_0 + r_1 t + \tfrac{1}{2}r_2 t^2$, it follows that $r'(t) = r_1 + r_2 t$, $r''(t) = r_2$, $r'''(t) = r''''(t) = \cdots = 0$. Thus the steady-state error is given by

$$\mathcal{E}_{ss}(t) = \frac{r_2}{10}$$

7-6. Predicting System Performance from the Open-loop Transfer Function

In this section we are concerned with the general problem of predicting the transient and steady-state performance of a closed-loop system from the open-loop transfer function. Part of this problem has already been treated in Table 7-1, where the closed-loop steady-state response for step, ramp, and parabolic inputs is listed in terms of the error coefficients K_p, K_v, and K_a. In this section these coefficients are identified on the graphical representation of the sinusoidal loop transfer function $HG(j\omega)$.

Predicting a system's closed-loop transient behavior from the frequency response of the open-loop transfer function is a much more formidable task. Exact mathematical techniques to do this are available, but they involve a great deal of work, and usually the closed-loop frequency-response characteristic must be found first. More important, however, is the fact that these techniques do not directly relate the transient response to system parameters, and thus they are of limited value in design. However, it is possible to correlate certain characteristics of the transient response to the sinusoidal loop transfer function, and some very useful generalizations and design rules can be made. In order to clarify the principles involved, let us consider the sinusoidal open-loop transfer function for the type 0, 1, and 2 systems.

The Type 0 System. As a first example, consider the open-loop transfer function for a type 0 system. In terms of Eq. (7-20) $HG(j\omega)$ is given by the formula

$$HG(j\omega) = \frac{K(1 + j\omega\tau_a) \cdots [1 - (\omega\tau_{nb})^2 + j2\zeta_b\tau_{nb}\omega]}{(1 + j\omega\tau_1) \cdots [1 - (\omega\tau_{n2})^2 + j2\zeta_2\tau_{n2}\omega]} \quad (7\text{-}40)$$

When $\omega = 0$, $HG(j\omega) = K$, so that the polar plot always starts at the finite point $(K,0)$. The steady-state actuating signal for a step input function, as defined in Table 7-1, may be determined from this starting point. In terms of the log-modulus and phase-shift plots it is easy to show that as $\omega \to 0$ the log-modulus characteristic approaches the constant value of $20 \log K$ db and the phase-shift characteristic approaches $0°$. Thus the system type and the value of K may be determined from these characteristics. At intermediate and high frequencies the transfer function behaves in accordance with the specific terms present in the loop transfer function. This is illustrated best by a simple example.

A SECOND-ORDER TYPE 0 SYSTEM. Consider that $HG(jw)$ is given by the formula

$$HG(j\omega) = \frac{K}{(1 + j\omega\tau_1)(1 + j\omega\tau_2)}$$
$$= \frac{K(1 - \omega^2\tau_1\tau_2) - j\omega(\tau_1 + \tau_2)K}{(1 - \omega^2\tau_1\tau_2)^2 + \omega^2(\tau_1 + \tau_2)^2} \quad (7\text{-}41)$$

The polar plot has the form illustrated in Fig. 7-18. As the frequency gets higher, the transfer function is given by

$$\lim_{\omega \to \infty} HG(j\omega) = \lim_{\omega \to \infty} \frac{K}{-\omega^2 \tau_1 \tau_2} = 0/180° \qquad (7\text{-}42)$$

Thus the polar plot approaches the origin along the negative real axis.

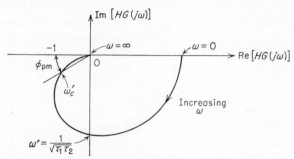

FIG. 7-18. Polar plot of a type 0 open-loop transfer function:

$$HG(j\omega) = \frac{K}{(1 + j\omega\tau_1)(1 + j\omega\tau_2)}$$

From Eq. (7-41) it is obvious that there is a frequency at which the transfer function is a pure imaginary; that is, $-90°$ phase shift occurs at a frequency $\omega = \omega'$, which is given by the formula

$$\omega' = \frac{1}{\sqrt{\tau_1 \tau_2}} \qquad (7\text{-}43)$$

The frequency ω' is indicated on the polar plot.

In order to relate the closed-loop transient response of this system to its open-loop frequency-response characteristic, it is necessary to investigate how close the system is to being unstable. System stability is one of the major considerations of control system analysis and design. In general the question to be answered is not merely whether a system is absolutely stable or not but how close the system is to instability. The term used to describe this state of the system is *relative stability*. Relative stability is important because it enables us to correlate the closed-loop transient response to the open-loop frequency-response characteristics. Of course the question of how relative stability is measured and its exact relationship to the transient response is a matter we have to investigate in detail. In general it is reasonable to expect that the closer a system is to being unstable the larger the maximum overshoot of its transient response and the longer it takes to decay. In a sense an unstable system is one whose transient response never disappears. On the other hand, if a system is far from being unstable, its transient response might be expected to be sluggish. In Chap. 2 it is pointed out that the requirement for absolute stability is that the roots of the characteristic equation

$1 + HG(s) = 0$ lie within the left-half complex plane. The boundary condition between stability and instability occurs where the roots lie on the $j\omega$ axis. Thus, if we let $s = j\omega$, a borderline condition exists if there is a frequency ω which satisfies the equation $HG(j\omega) + 1 = 0$ or if $HG(j\omega) = \dfrac{B}{E}(j\omega) = -1 = 1\underline{/180°}$. Thus, if the open-loop transfer function $HG(j\omega)$ were to pass through the point $(-1,0)$, a condition of sustained oscillations would exist. From this discussion it is reasonable to infer that the closer the open-loop frequency-response characteristic comes to passing through the point $(-1,0)$ in Fig. 7-18 the closer the

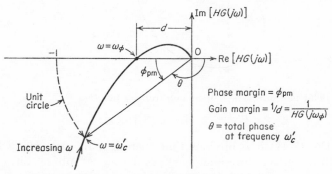

FIG. 7-19. Definitions of gain and phase margins on a polar plot.

closed-loop system is to being unstable. Proximity to the $(-1,0)$ point is measured by means of two quantities, phase margin and gain margin. These are defined as illustrated in Fig. 7-19 for the polar plot of a type 1 loop transfer function. *Gain margin* is defined as the reciprocal of the open-loop transfer function evaluated at the frequency ω_ϕ at which the phase shift is $-180°$. Thus

$$\text{Gain margin} = \frac{1}{d} = |HG(j\omega_\phi)|^{-1}$$

Gain margin is a measure of the factor by which the gain of a system would have to be increased for the locus of the loop transfer function to pass through the $(-1,0)$ point, i.e., for the system to be in a state of sustained oscillations.

Phase margin ϕ_{pm} is 180° plus the phase angle at unity gain. It is a measure of how much additional phase lag is required to make a system unstable if the gain is unchanged. Phase and gain margin can also be defined on the log-modulus and phase-shift characteristics for a loop transfer function as shown in Fig. 7-20. Phase margin is measured on the phase-shift characteristic at the frequency where the log-modulus characteristic crosses the 0-db line, i.e., where the magnitude equals unity. In practice this crossover frequency is often taken as the frequency at which the asymptotic straight-line approximation crosses the 0-db line rather than the crossover frequency of the actual log-modulus curve itself.   This saves drawing the actual characteristic and usually does not introduce excessive design errors, as illustrated in Chap. 9. Gain margin is measured in decibels on the log-modulus characteristic at the point where the phase-shift characteristic crosses the $-180°$ line.

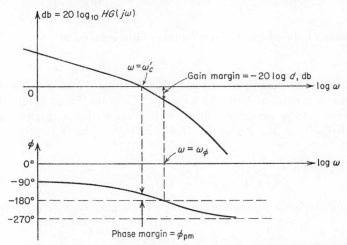

FIG. 7-20. Phase and gain margins on log-modulus and phase-shift characteristics.

The fact that the polar plot of the loop transfer function of Fig. 7-19 lies to the right of the $(-1,0)$ point means that the log-modulus characteristic crosses the 0-db line at a lower frequency than where the phase-shift characteristic crosses the $-180°$ line.

With these definitions for phase and gain margin in mind let us now return to the second-order type 0 system of Fig. 7-18 and see how they are related to the closed-loop transient response.

The gain margin for this system is infinite since the polar plot does not cross the negative real axis.   It would require infinite gain to make the polar plot pass through the point $(-1,0)$.   Thus gain margin appears to be of little value for our present purpose.

Prior to discussing the phase margin for this system, it is worthwhile to determine the characteristic equation for the closed-loop system.   If s replaces $j\omega$ in Eq. (7-41), the characteristic equation is given by

$$1 + HG(s) = 1 + \frac{K}{(1 + s\tau_1)(1 + s\tau_2)} = 0 \qquad (7\text{-}44)$$

Clearing fractions and multiplying gives the following result:

$$s^2\tau_1\tau_2 + s(\tau_1 + \tau_2) + 1 + K = s^2 + \frac{\tau_1 + \tau_2}{\tau_1\tau_2}s + \frac{1 + K}{\tau_1\tau_2} = 0 \quad (7\text{-}45)$$

The system is obviously of the second order so that Eq. (7-45) may be written in the following form,

$$s^2 + 2\zeta\omega_n s + \omega_n{}^2 = 0 \tag{7-46}$$

where
$$\omega_n{}^2 = \frac{1 + K}{\tau_1\tau_2} \approx \frac{K}{\tau_1\tau_2} \qquad \text{if } K \gg 1 \tag{7-47}$$

and
$$2\zeta\omega_n = \frac{\tau_1 + \tau_2}{\tau_1\tau_2} = \frac{1}{\tau_1} + \frac{1}{\tau_2} \approx \frac{1}{\tau_2} \qquad \text{if } \tau_1 \gg \tau_2 \tag{7-48}$$

The roots of the characteristic equation are located at

$$s_{1,2} = -\zeta\omega_n \pm j\omega_n \sqrt{1 - \zeta^2}$$

where ζ is the damping ratio and ω_n is the undamped resonant frequency.[1]

With these results at hand let us now determine the phase margin for this system. It is necessary first to determine the frequency $\omega = \omega_c'$, where $|HG(j\omega_c')| = 1$. From Eq. (7-41) it follows that ω_c' is given by the equation

$$\frac{K}{\sqrt{1 + (\omega_c')^2\tau_1{}^2} \, \sqrt{1 + (\omega_c')^2\tau_2{}^2}} = 1 \tag{7-49}$$

After some algebraic manipulations Eq. (7-49) may be written as follows:

$$(\omega_c')^4 + (\omega_c')^2 \left(\frac{1}{\tau_1{}^2} + \frac{1}{\tau_2{}^2} \right) - \frac{K^2 - 1}{\tau_1{}^2\tau_2{}^2} = 0 \tag{7-50a}$$

or
$$(\omega_c')^4 + 4\zeta^2\omega_n{}^2(\omega_c')^2 - \omega_n{}^4 = 0 \qquad \text{if } K \gg 1 \text{ and } \tau_1 \gg \tau_2 \tag{7-50b}$$

Equation (7-50a) is a quadratic equation which can be easily solved for ω_c', particularly when numerical values for τ_1, τ_2, and K are given. The phase margin ϕ_{pm} is determined from Eq. (7-41) and Fig. 7-18. Thus ϕ_{pm} is given by the equation

$$\phi_{\mathrm{pm}} = \tan^{-1} \left| \frac{\mathrm{Im}\, [HG(j\omega_c')]}{\mathrm{Re}\, [HG(j\omega_c')]} \right| = \tan^{-1} \left| \frac{\omega_c'(\tau_1 + \tau_2)}{1 - (\omega_c')^2\tau_1\tau_2} \right|$$
$$\approx \tan^{-1} \left| 2\zeta \left(\frac{\omega_n}{\omega_c'} \right) \right| \qquad \text{if } \omega_c'^2 \gg 1/\tau_1\tau_2 \tag{7-51}$$

The inequality holds for large values of K.

Substituting the value of ω_c' from Eq. (7-50b) into Eq. (7-51) enables ϕ_{pm} to be calculated in terms of ζ. The result is plotted in Fig. 7-21.

Before leaving this particular example let us investigate its open-loop log-modulus and phase-shift characteristic. The log-modulus character-

---

[1] Since $\zeta = \dfrac{1}{2\,\sqrt{1 + K}} \dfrac{\tau_1 + \tau_2}{\sqrt{\tau_1\tau_2}}$, it follows that the system is underdamped when

$$1 + K > \frac{(\tau_1 + \tau_2)^2}{4\tau_1\tau_2} = \frac{1}{4} \left(\frac{\tau_1}{\tau_2} + \frac{\tau_2}{\tau_1} + 2 \right)$$

We shall consider the underdamped state only.

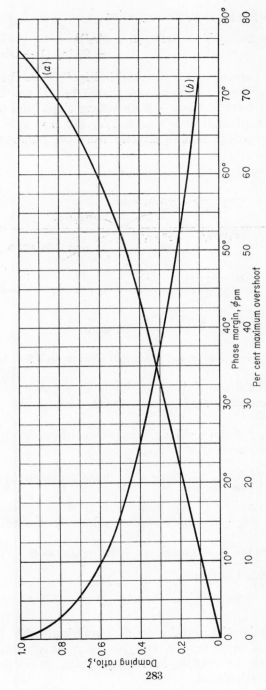

FIG. 7-21. (a) Damping ratio vs. phase margin, second-order system; (b) damping ratio vs. per cent maximum overshoot, second-order system step response.

istic for Eq. (7-41) is given by the equation

$$20 \log |HG(j\omega)| = 20 \log K - 20 \log (1 + \omega^2\tau_1^2)^{\frac{1}{2}}$$
$$- 20 \log (1 + \omega^2\tau_2^2)^{\frac{1}{2}} \quad (7\text{-}52)$$

The asymptotic characteristic is sketched in Fig. 7-22 for the case where the 0-db crossover frequency is greater than $1/\tau_2$. It consists of three terms, a constant term and two -6 db/octave slope lines occurring at the breakpoint frequencies of $\omega = \omega_1 = 1/\tau_1$ and $\omega = \omega_2 = 1/\tau_2$. The phase-shift characteristic follows directly from the phase-angle curves

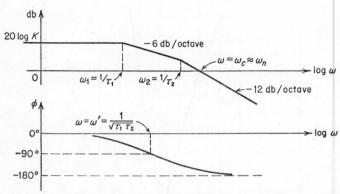

FIG. 7-22. Asymptotic log-modulus and phase-shift characteristic for a type 0 system.

associated with the log modulus. It should be apparent to the reader that these characteristics may be drawn with much less effort than the polar plot.

The expression for the -12 db/octave asymptote is given by Eq. (7-52) for $\omega \gg 1/\tau_2$, namely,

$$20 \log \left|HG(j\omega)\right|_{\omega \gg 1/\tau_2} = 20 \log K - 20 \log \omega\tau_1 - 20 \log \omega\tau_2 \quad (7\text{-}53)$$

Equating this expression to zero enables us to solve for the frequency $\omega = \omega_c$ at which the -12 db/octave asymptote crosses the 0-db line. Thus

$$20 \log K - 20 \log \omega_c\tau_1 - 20 \log \omega_c\tau_2 = 0$$

Solving for ω_c yields the result

$$\omega_c = \sqrt{\frac{K}{\tau_1\tau_2}} \approx \omega_n \quad (7\text{-}54)$$

where the approximation results from comparison with Eq. (7-47); thus the undamped frequency for the system may be estimated from the frequency at which the -12 db/octave asymptote crosses the 0-db axis for the conditions stipulated.

The Type 1 *System.* Consider the sinusoidal loop transfer function for a type 1 system. In terms of Eq. (7-20), $HG(j\omega)$ is given by the expression

$$HG(j\omega) = \frac{K(1 + j\omega\tau_a) \cdots [1 - (\omega/\omega_{nb})^2 + j2\zeta_b(\omega/\omega_{nb})]}{j\omega(1 + j\omega\tau_1) \cdots [1 - (\omega/\omega_{n2})^2 + j2\zeta_2(\omega/\omega_{n2})]} \quad (7\text{-}55)$$

As $\omega \to 0$, Eq. (7-55) gives the following results:

$$\lim_{\omega \to 0} |HG(j\omega)| = \lim_{\omega \to 0} \frac{K}{\omega} = \infty \quad (7\text{-}56)$$

$$\phi = -90° \quad (7\text{-}57)$$

Equations (7-56) and (7-57) do not contain sufficient information to locate the polar plot for the loop transfer functions as $\omega \to 0$. The reason for this is that Eqs. (7-56) and (7-57) merely define a line parallel to the $-j$ axis. The intersection of this line with the negative real axis is undefined. The exact behavior of the polar plot at low frequencies is obtained by rationalizing Eq. (7-55) into its real and imaginary parts and examining them when $\omega \to 0$. This is done in a general way at the end of this section and leads to the following result,

$$\lim_{\omega \to 0} \text{Re}\,[HG(j\omega)] = K[(\tau_a + 2\zeta_b\tau_{nb} + \cdots) - (\tau_1 + 2\zeta_2\tau_{n2} + \cdots)]$$

$$(7\text{-}58)$$

where $\tau_{nb} = 1/\omega_{nb}$, $\tau_{n2} = 1/\omega_{n2}$, ...

This equation locates the intersection of the low-frequency asymptote of the polar plot with the real axis.

The log-modulus and phase-angle plot for Eq. (7-55) at low frequencies is given by the following expressions:

$$20 \log_{\omega \to 0} |HG(j\omega)| = 20 \log \frac{K}{\omega} = 20 \log K - 20 \log \omega \quad (7\text{-}59)$$

$$\phi \Big|_{\omega \to 0} = -j = -90° \quad (7\text{-}60)$$

Thus the log-modulus characteristic has an initial slope of -6 db/octave. If extended, this line cuts the 0-db axis at $\omega = K$. From Table 7-1 $K_v = K$ so that K_v may be determined directly from the log-modulus characteristic by extending the initial -6 db/octave slope to the 0-db line. It is interesting to note that K is not available conveniently on the polar plot.

At other than low frequencies the exact behavior of the loop transfer function depends upon the exact nature of the specific terms in the transfer function. Accordingly, let us consider some specific examples.

A SECOND-ORDER TYPE 1 SYSTEM. As an example of a type 1 system, consider the simple second-order servomechanism of Chap. 4. The loop transfer function may be determined from the block diagram of Fig. 7-10 and is given by the expression

$$HG(s) = \frac{K_p K_A K_M h}{Js^2 + Fs} \qquad (7\text{-}61)$$

Substituting the values for ζ and ω_n from Chap. 4, namely,

$$\zeta = \frac{F}{2\sqrt{K_p K_A K_M h J}}$$

and $\omega_n{}^2 = K_p K_A K_M h / J$, enables Eq. (7-61) to be rewritten as follows:

$$HG(s) = \frac{\omega_n{}^2}{s(s + 2\zeta\omega_n)} \qquad (7\text{-}62)$$

This is obviously a type 1 system and the sinusoidal loop transfer function is given by

$$HG(j\omega) = \frac{\omega_n{}^2}{j\omega(j\omega + 2\zeta\omega_n)} = \frac{\omega_n/2\zeta}{j\omega(1 + j\omega/2\zeta\omega_n)} \qquad (7\text{-}63)$$

The loop transfer function is identical to the transfer function of Eq. (6-52a), which is sketched in Figs. 6-9 and 6-10. For convenience these sketches are redrawn in Fig. 7-23.

The phase margin is determined by following the procedure used for the second-order type 0 system of the previous section. From Eq. (7-63) the frequency ω_c', where $|HG(j\omega_c')| = 1$, is given by the expression

$$(\omega_c')^4 + 4\zeta^2\omega_n{}^2(\omega_c')^2 - \omega_n{}^4 = 0 \qquad (7\text{-}64)$$

Solving for ω_c' gives the result

$$\frac{(\omega_c')^2}{\omega_n{}^2} = \sqrt{4\zeta^4 + 1} - 2\zeta^2 \qquad (7\text{-}65)$$

A study of Eq. (7-63) and Fig. 7-23a indicates that the phase margin ϕ_{pm} is given by the equation

$$\phi_{pm} = \tan^{-1}\left|\frac{\text{Im}\,[HG(j\omega_c')]}{\text{Re}\,[HG(j\omega_c')]}\right| = \tan^{-1} 2\zeta\,\frac{\omega_n}{\omega_c'} \qquad (7\text{-}66)$$

under the assumption that the system is stable so that the damping ratio ζ corresponds to a positive phase margin. Substituting the value for ω_c' from Eq. (7-65) yields the result

$$\phi_{pm} = \tan^{-1} 2\zeta\left[\frac{1}{(4\zeta^4 + 1)^{1/2} - 2\zeta^2}\right]^{1/2} \qquad (7\text{-}67)$$

Figure 7-21 illustrates ϕ_{pm} plotted vs. ζ. Since Eqs. (7-64) and (7-65) are identical with Eqs. (7-50b) and (7-51) of the previous section, it follows that the plot of Fig. 7-21 also holds for the underdamped second-order type 0 system for the conditions stated. When $0 < \phi_{pm} < 40°$, the curve

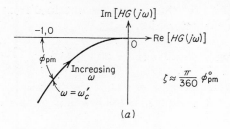

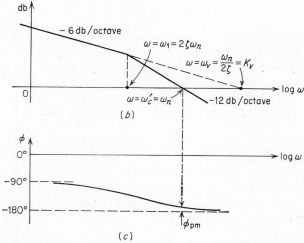

FIG. 7-23. Loop transfer characteristics for a type 1 servomechanism:

$$HG(j\omega) = \frac{\omega_n{}^2}{j\omega(j\omega + 2\zeta\omega_n)}$$

(a) Polar plot; (b) log modulus; (c) phase shift.

is linear so that in this range the damping ratio is related to the phase margin by the equation

$$\zeta = \frac{\pi}{360}\,\phi_{pm}{}^{\circ} \tag{7-68a}$$

where $\phi_{pm}{}^{\circ}$ is measured in degrees. Expressing ϕ_{pm} in radians gives the result

$$\zeta = \tfrac{1}{2}\phi_{pm} \tag{7-68b}$$

Although this formula is derived for a second-order type 1 system, it is also useful for higher-order systems, based on the assumption that the transient response is determined usually by a predominant pair of complex conjugate roots of the characteristic equation for the closed-loop system. These roots may then be considered as belonging to an equivalent second-order system in so far as the transient response is concerned. The limitations of this approximation are obvious, but nonetheless it is a useful and practical concept.

Several other relationships for this system are obtained from the equation for the log-modulus characteristics,

$$20 \log |HG(j\omega)| = 20 \log \frac{\omega_n}{2\zeta} - 20 \log \omega - 20 \log \left(1 + \frac{\omega^2}{4\zeta^2 \omega_n^2}\right)^{\frac{1}{2}} \quad (7\text{-}69)$$

The initial -6 db/octave slope line intersects the 0-db axis at the frequency $\omega = \omega_v = \omega_n/2\zeta$. Accordingly it follows that K_v is given by the formula

$$K_v = \frac{\omega_n}{2\zeta} = \omega_v \quad (7\text{-}70)$$

The breakpoint frequency for the linear term occurs at $\omega = \omega_1 = 2\zeta\omega_n$. The geometric mean between ω_v and ω_1 is ω_n, that is, $\omega_n = \sqrt{\omega_v\omega_1}$. If extended, the -12 db/octave line crosses 0 db at $\omega = \omega_c$, where ω_c is determined from the equation

$$20 \log \frac{\omega_n}{2\zeta} - 20 \log \omega_c - 20 \log \frac{\omega_c}{2\zeta\omega_n} = 0 \quad (7\text{-}71)$$

Solving this equation yields $\omega_c = \omega_n$. Thus, as in the second-order type 0 system, the undamped frequency may be determined by extending the -12db/octave asymptote until it crosses 0 db.

NUMERICAL EXAMPLE. A THIRD-ORDER TYPE 1 SYSTEM. As a numerical example, consider a third-order type 1 system whose loop transfer function is given by the equation

$$HG(s) = \frac{5}{s(1 + s/2)(1 + s/6)} \quad (7\text{-}72)$$

The sinusoidal loop transfer function is given by

$$HG(j\omega) = \frac{5}{j\omega (1 + j \omega/2)(1 + j \omega/6)} \quad (7\text{-}73)$$

The polar plot for this expression is sketched in Fig. 7-24a. In terms of Eq. (7-55), $K = 5$, $\tau_1 = 0.5$, and $\tau_2 = 0.167$. From Eq. (7-58) the low-frequency asymptote is located at $-5(0.5 + 0.167) = -3.33$ units from the $j\omega$ axis. At high frequencies the loop transfer function behaves according to the formula

$$\lim_{\omega \to \infty} HG(j\omega) = \lim_{\omega \to \infty} \frac{5}{0.5(0.167)(j\omega)^3} = 0\underline{/-270°} \quad (7\text{-}74)$$

Thus the polar plot approaches the origin along the $+j\omega$ axis. The polar plot crosses the negative real axis (180° phase shift) at the frequency $\omega = \omega_\phi$, given by the formula

$$\tan^{-1} \frac{\omega_\phi}{2} + \tan^{-1} \frac{\omega_\phi}{6} = \tan^{-1} \frac{0.5\omega_\phi + 0.167\omega_\phi}{1 - 0.5\omega_\phi(0.167\omega_\phi)} = 90° \quad (7\text{-}75)$$

Thus $0.5(0.167)\omega_\phi^2 = 1$, and $\omega_\phi = \sqrt{1/[0.5(0.167)]} = 3.46$. At $\omega = \omega_\phi$

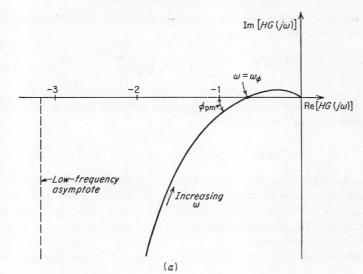

(a)

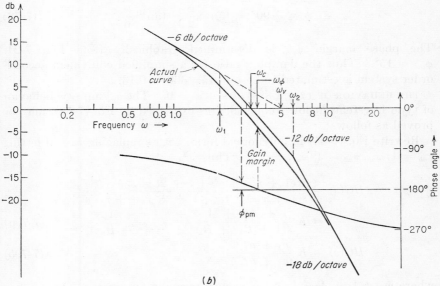

(b)

FIG. 7-24. (a) Polar plot for $HG(j\omega) = \dfrac{5}{j\omega(1 + 0.5j\omega)(1 + 0.167j\omega)}$; (b) log-modulus

and phase-shift plot for $HG(j\omega) = \dfrac{5}{j\omega(1 + 0.5j\omega)(1 + 0.167j\omega)}$.

the magnitude of $HG(j\omega)$ is given by

$$|HG(j\omega_\phi)| = \frac{5}{3.46 \sqrt{1 + (1.73)^2} \sqrt{1 + (0.575)^2}}$$
$$= 0.624 \tag{7-76}$$

Thus the gain margin is $1/0.624 = 1.6$.

The asymptotes for the log modulus of Eq. (7-73) are given by the following equation:

$$\mathbf{db} = 20 \log 5 - 20 \log \omega - 20 \log \left[1 + \left(\frac{\omega}{2}\right)^2 \right]^{\frac{1}{2}} - 20 \log \left[1 + \left(\frac{\omega}{6}\right)^2 \right]^{\frac{1}{2}}$$

(7-77)

The initial -6 db/octave slope passes through 0 db at $\omega = \omega_v = 5$. The corner frequencies occur at

$$\omega = \omega_1 = \frac{1}{0.5} = 2 \quad \text{and} \quad \omega = \omega_2 = \frac{1}{0.167} = 6$$

The log-modulus and phase-shift curves are drawn in Fig. 7-24b. The extension of the -6 db/octave slope to 0 db gives the value of $\omega_v = K_v = 5$. The geometric mean between ω_v and ω_1 is given by $\omega = \sqrt{10} = 3.16$, which is identical with ω_c, the frequency at which the -12 db/octave line crosses 0 db.

The phase angle for Eq. (7-73) is given by the following equation:

$$\phi = -90° - \tan^{-1}\frac{\omega}{2} - \tan^{-1}\frac{\omega}{6}$$

(7-78)

The phase margin ϕ_{pm} is determined graphically from Fig. 7-24. $\phi_{\mathrm{pm}} = 15°$. Thus the damping ratio for a simplified equivalent second-order system is estimated to be $\zeta = 15\pi/360 = 0.13$.

THE BEHAVIOR OF TYPE 1 SYSTEMS AS $\omega \to 0$. The asymptotic behavior of type 1 systems at low frequencies, as expressed by Eq. (7-58), may be proved as follows:

Rewrite Eq. (7-55) in polynomial form, with s replacing $j\omega$ and letting $\tau_{nb} = 1/\omega_{nb}$, $\tau_{n2} = 1/\omega_{n2}$, ... Thus

$$HG(s) = \frac{K(1 + \tau_a s) \cdots [(1 + 2\zeta_b \tau_{nb} s + \tau_{nb}^2 s^2)]}{s(1 + \tau_1 s) \cdots [(1 + 2\zeta_2 \tau_{n2} s + \tau_{n2}^2 s^2)]}$$

$$= K \frac{1 + A_1 s + A_2 s^2 + \cdots + A_m s^m}{s(1 + B_1 s + B_2 s^2 + \cdots + B_n s^n)}$$

(7-79a)

$$HG(s) = K \frac{m_1 + n_1}{m_2 + n_2}$$

(7-79b)

where $m_1 = 1 + A_2 s^2 + \cdots = $ even terms in numerator
$n_1 = A_1 s + A_3 s^3 + \cdots = $ odd terms in numerator
$m_2 = B_1 s^2 + B_3 s^4 + \cdots = $ even terms in denominator
$n_2 = s + B_2 s^3 + \cdots = $ odd terms in denominator

Now, if Eq. (7-79b) is multiplied by $(m_2 - n_2)/(m_2 - n_2)$, it becomes

$$HG(s) = K \frac{m_1 + n_1}{m_2 + n_2} \frac{m_2 - n_2}{m_2 - n_2} = K \frac{m_1 m_2 - n_1 n_2}{m_2^2 - n_2^2} + K \frac{m_2 n_1 - m_1 n_2}{m_2^2 - n_2^2}$$

(7-80)

The first term of Eq. (7-80) contains only even powers of s, whereas the second term contains only odd powers of s. Thus

$$\text{Re } [HG(j\omega)] = \frac{K(m_1 m_2 - n_1 n_2)}{m_2{}^2 - n_2{}^2}\bigg|_{s=j\omega} \tag{7-81a}$$

and

$$\text{Im } [HG(j\omega)] = \frac{K(m_2 n_1 - m_1 n_2)}{m_2{}^2 - n_2{}^2}\bigg|_{s=j\omega} \tag{7-81b}$$

From Eqs. (7-81a) and (7-81b) it follows that

$$\lim_{\omega \to 0} \text{Re } [HG(j\omega)] = \frac{K(m_1 m_2 - n_1 n_2)}{m_2{}^2 - n_2{}^2}\bigg|_{s=0} \tag{7-82a}$$

$$\lim_{\omega \to 0} \text{Im } [HG(j\omega)] = \frac{K(m_2 n_1 - m_1 n_2)}{m_2{}^2 - n_2{}^2}\bigg|_{s=0} \tag{7-82b}$$

If the values for m_1, m_2, n_1, and n_2 of Eq. (7-79b) are substituted into Eqs. (7-82a) and (7-82b), the following results are obtained:

$$\lim_{\omega \to 0} \text{Re } [HG(j\omega)] = K(A_1 - B_1) \tag{7-83a}$$

$$\lim_{\omega \to 0} \text{Im } [HG(j\omega)] = -\infty \tag{7-83b}$$

If A_1 and B_1 are referred back to the time constants of the systems, it can be shown that

$$\begin{align} A_1 &= \tau_a + 2\zeta_b \tau_{nb} + \cdots \\ B_1 &= \tau_1 + 2\zeta_2 \tau_{n2} + \cdots \end{align} \tag{7-84}$$

Thus Eq. (7-83a) may be written as

$$\lim_{\omega \to 0} \text{Re } [HG(j\omega)] = K[(\tau_a + 2\zeta_b \tau_{nb} + \cdots) - (\tau_1 + 2\zeta_2 \tau_{n2} + \cdots)] \tag{7-85}$$

The Type 2 System. The loop transfer function for a type 2 system is given by the expression

$$G(j\omega) = \frac{K(1 + j\omega\tau_a) \cdots [1 - (\omega/\omega_{nb})^2 + j2\zeta_b(\omega/\omega_{nb})]}{(j\omega)^2(1 + j\omega\tau_1) \cdots [1 - (\omega/\omega_{n2})^2 + j2\zeta_2(\omega/\omega_{n2})]} \tag{7-86}$$

As $\omega \to 0$, Eq. (7-86) indicates that

$$\lim_{\omega \to 0} |G(j\omega)| = \lim_{\omega \to 0} \frac{K}{-\omega^2} = \infty \underline{/180°} \tag{7-87}$$

The log-modulus and phase-angle plot for Eq. (7-86), at low frequencies, is given by

$$\lim_{\omega \to 0} 20 \log KG(j\omega) = 20 \log \frac{K}{\omega^2} = 20 \log K - 20 \log \omega^2 \tag{7-88}$$

$$\lim_{\omega \to 0} \measuredangle KG(j\omega) = 180° \tag{7-89}$$

The log-modulus characteristic therefore has an initial slope of -12 db/octave. If we consider steady-state performance, then we are interested in the decibel plot as $\omega \to 0$, that is, the low-frequency portion of Eq. (7-88). If extended, this line intersects the 0-db line at $\omega = \omega_a = \sqrt{K}$. Hence K_a may be determined by finding this point of intersection, viz., $K_a = K = \omega_a{}^2$.

A SECOND-ORDER TYPE 2 SYSTEM. Let us consider a second-order type 2 system with the following open-loop transfer function:

$$HG(j\omega) = \frac{K(1 + j\omega\tau)}{(j\omega)^2} \tag{7-90}$$

If s replaces $j\omega$ in Eq. (7-90), the characteristic equation is given by

$$1 + HG(s) = 1 + \frac{K(1 + s\tau)}{s^2} = 0$$

Clearing fractions yields the result

$$s^2 + K\tau s + K = 0 \tag{7-91}$$

Equation (7-91) may be expressed in the following form,

$$s^2 + 2\zeta\omega_n s + \omega_n{}^2 = 0$$

where
$$\omega_n{}^2 = K \tag{7-92a}$$
and
$$2\zeta\omega_n = K\tau \tag{7-92b}$$

The phase margin for this system is determined by first evaluating the frequency $\omega = \omega_c'$ where $|HG(j\omega_c')| = 1$. From Eq. (7-90) it therefore follows that ω_c' is given by the equation

$$\frac{K\sqrt{1 + (\omega_c')^2\tau^2}}{(\omega_c')^2} = 1$$

Clearing fractions, squaring, and rearranging terms yields

$$(\omega_c')^4 - K^2\tau^2(\omega_c')^2 - K^2 = 0$$

By means of Eqs. (7-92a) and (7-92b) the coefficients of the previous equation may be expressed in terms of ζ and ω_n. Thus we get

$$(\omega_c')^4 - (2\zeta\omega_n)^2(\omega_c')^2 - \omega_n{}^4 = 0$$

Solving for ω_c' yields the result

$$\frac{(\omega_c')^2}{\omega_n{}^2} = \sqrt{4\zeta^4 + 1} + 2\zeta^2 \tag{7-93a}$$

By using Eq. (7-90) the phase margin can be expressed by the equation

$$\phi_{\text{pm}} = \tan^{-1}\left|\frac{\text{Im}\,[HG(j\omega_c')]}{\text{Re}\,[HG(j\omega_c')]}\right| = \tan^{-1} 2\zeta\,\frac{\omega_c'}{\omega_n} \tag{7-93b}$$

Substituting Eq. (7-93a) into (7-93b) yields the result

$$\phi_{pm} = \tan^{-1} 2\zeta[(4\zeta^2 + 1)^{\frac{1}{2}} + 2\zeta^2]^{\frac{1}{2}} \tag{7-94}$$

A plot of Eq. (7-94) vs. ζ gives a curve which for all practical purposes is identical with that drawn in Fig. 7-21. This result comes from the fact that for $\zeta \leq 1$ the bracketed expression in Eqs. (7-94) and (7-67) are almost equal numerically. The reader can readily prove this to his satisfaction.

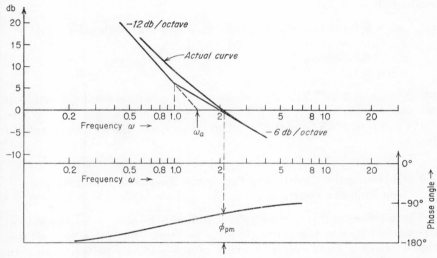

Fig. 7-25. Log-modulus and phase-shift plot for $HG(j\omega) = \dfrac{2(1 + j\omega)}{(j\omega)^2}$.

As an example of a type 2 system, let us consider the following loop transfer function:

$$HG(s) = \frac{2(s + 1)}{s^2}$$

The sinusoidal loop transfer function is given by the equation

$$HG(j\omega) = \frac{2(1 + j\omega)}{(j\omega)^2} = \frac{2(1 + j\omega)}{-\omega^2}$$

The log-modulus and phase-shift characteristics for this system are drawn in Fig. 7-25. The log-modulus and phase-shift characteristics are given by the following equations:

$$db = 20 \log 2 - 20 \log \omega^2 + 20 \log (1 + \omega^2)^{\frac{1}{2}}$$
$$\phi = -180° + \tan^{-1} \omega$$

At high frequencies the function behaves as follows:

$$\lim_{\omega \to \infty} HG(j\omega) = \lim_{\omega \to \infty} \frac{j2\omega}{(j\omega)^2} = 0\underline{/-90°}$$

At low frequencies the function behaves as follows:

$$\lim_{\omega \to 0} HG(j\omega) = \lim_{\omega \to 0} \frac{2}{(j\omega)^2} = \infty \underline{/-180°}$$

From the graphical representation the following quantities are evaluated:

ω_a = intersection of -12 db/octave line with 0-db axis = 1.41
$K_a = \omega_a^2 = (1.41)^2 = 2 = \omega_n^2$
$\phi_{pm} = 65.5°$
$\zeta = 0.71$

using ϕ_{pm} and Fig. 7-21. The characteristic equation for the closed-loop system is given by $s^2 + 2s + 2 = 0$. From this equation $\omega_n = \sqrt{2} = 1.414$ and $\zeta = 2/2\sqrt{2} \approx 0.707$. The values agree well with the graphical results.

7-7. Obtaining the Closed-loop Frequency Response from the Open-loop Transfer Function

There are several reasons why it is desirable to obtain the closed-loop frequency-response characteristic for a system. The primary reason is that it gives a good over-all picture of the system's performance. In general the closed-loop frequency-response characteristic for a control system is similar to that of a low-pass filter. From this point of view it is possible to relate the bandwidth of the system to the rise time for a unit-step response. Consider the ideal low-pass filter of Fig. 7-26a. The unit-step response is sketched in Fig. 7-26b. The rise time τ_r is related to the bandwidth ω_c by the formula

$$\tau_r = \frac{1}{2}\frac{2\pi}{\omega_c} = \frac{\pi}{\omega_c} \tag{7-95}$$

where τ_r and ω_c are defined in Fig. 7-26. The rise time is defined by the slope of the response function as it passes through the value of $\frac{1}{2}$.† Equation (7-95) will not be proved, but it may be derived by the use of the Fourier integral. Its usefulness lies in the general correlation it provides between the time and frequency domains. Thus, if a system is to respond

---

† Other formulas for the rise time are available, based upon the definition for rise time. In general $\tau_r = k(2\pi)/\omega_c$, where k may be specified as between 0.3 and 0.6, depending upon the definition used. Equation (7-95) is easy to remember since the rise time is given as one-half the period of the highest frequency the filter can pass.

to a unit step with a rise time of 0.1 sec, it should have a bandwidth of at least 5 cps.

This correlation, of course, is approximate and does not take into account such considerations as maximum overshoot and settling time.

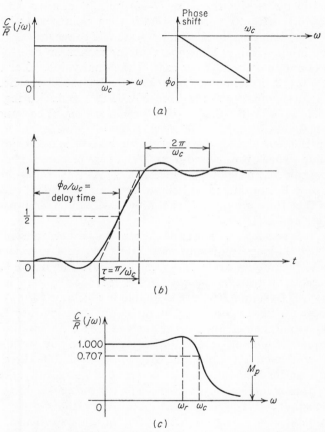

FIG. 7-26. Response of an ideal filter to a step input. (a) Ideal filter; (b) step response; (c) closed-loop frequency-response characteristic for an underdamped second-order system.

Its chief advantage is that it provides a simple rule which can be applied to many situations.

If the system to be designed is approximated by a simple underdamped second-order system, a more realistic estimate of the required bandwidth can be made. From the results of Chap. 4 it is known that the time constant of the transient response for this system is given by the equation $\tau = 1/\zeta\omega_n$. Thus ω_n, the undamped frequency, is related to the time constant τ and the damping ratio ζ by the formula

$$\omega_n = \frac{1}{\zeta\tau} \tag{7-96}$$

If the maximum overshoot is specified in terms of ζ and the settling time is specified in terms of τ, then Eq. (7-96) may be used to determine ω_n. The bandwidth of the required system is then estimated to be equal to $\omega_c \approx \omega_n$. For example, assume that a system is to reach steady state for a unit-step input within 0.1 sec and that the maximum overshoot of the transient is not to exceed 31 per cent of the final value. For these conditions $\tau = 0.1/3$ (it being assumed that steady state is reached in three time constants) and $\zeta = 0.35$ (from Fig. 4-8). Substituting into Eq. (7-96) yields $\omega_n = 3/[0.1(0.35)] = 85.6$ radians/sec. The bandwidth of the system should be approximately $85.6/2\pi = 13.6$ cps.

Some further correlations between the time and the frequency domains are possible when the closed-loop frequency-response characteristic exhibits a peak M_p, as shown in Fig. 7-26c. As a useful approximation the peak may be considered as being due to an equivalent second-order system so that the formulas derived in Sec. 5-1 can be used to advantage in relating ζ and ω_n to M_p.

Finally, it is possible to determine the system's exact transient response from the closed-loop frequency characteristics. As mentioned previously, these techniques are cumbersome and are not useful in design.[1]

The closed-loop transfer function for a feedback system is given by Eq. (7-2a). If $G(s)$ and $H(s)$ are available in algebraic form, the closed-loop transfer function is obtained by direct substitution into Eq. (7-2a). The result is a polynomial and may be analyzed as a differential equation or in the frequency domain. On the other hand, if the polar or log-modulus and phase-shift plots for $G(j\omega)$ and $HG(j\omega)$ are available, the closed-loop sinusoidal transfer function may be determined graphically. In general this is a rather complicated process except for the particular case where $H(s) = $ constant. When this constant is other than unity, Fig. 7-2d is used to reduce the system to a condition of unity feedback.

Figure 7-27 illustrates the polar plot for a typical unity-feedback loop transfer function, $HG(j\omega) = G(j\omega)$. The closed-loop transfer function for this feedback system is determined directly from this diagram by using the following equation:

$$\frac{C}{R}(j\omega) = \frac{G(j\omega)}{1 + G(j\omega)} \tag{7-97}$$

As shown in Chap. 5, the polar plot for the denominator is simply the polar plot for $G(j\omega)$ with the origin shifted to the point $(-1,0)$. Hence

[1] One method is attributed to G. F. Floyd. See G. S. Brown and D. Campbell, "Principles of Servomechanisms," chap. 11, John Wiley & Sons, Inc., New York, 1948.

at any frequency it follows that

$$\left| \frac{C}{R}(j\omega) \right| = \left| \frac{G(j\omega)}{1 + G(j\omega)} \right| = \frac{0B}{AB} \tag{7-98a}$$

$$\phi(j\omega) = \measuredangle G(j\omega) - \measuredangle[1 + G(j\omega)]$$
$$= -(\theta_1 - \theta_2) = -\measuredangle AB0 \tag{7-98b}$$

At each frequency on the loop transfer function, Eqs. (7-98) are used to derive the magnitude and phase angle of the closed-loop transfer function. For example, consider the type 1 loop transfer function sketched in Fig.

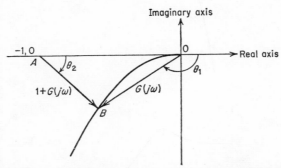

FIG. 7-27. Determining the closed-loop transfer function–unity feedback case.

7-28a. Figure 7-28b illustrates the frequency-response characteristics for the closed-loop system. At $\omega = 0$, the ratio of $0B/AB$ approaches unity (both phasors are very large). As ω increases, AB is smaller than $0B$ so that the ratio $0B/AB > 1$, reaching a maximum value at some frequency $\omega = \omega_r$. At the frequency $\omega = \omega_2$, $AB = 0B$. For $\omega > \omega_2$, AB is greater than $0B$ and the ratio $0B/AB < 1$. The phase-shift characteristic may be reasoned in a similar way. At $\omega = 0$, the phase angle $AB0$ is equal to zero. As the frequency gets larger, $\measuredangle AB0$ increases to 180° at $\omega = \omega_\phi$ and a maximum value of 270° at $\omega = \infty$. Thus the closed-loop phase-angle characteristic behaves as sketched in Fig. 7-28b.

Lines of Constant Magnitude (M Circles). Rather than calculate the magnitude of the closed-loop transfer function at each frequency, it is possible to read this magnitude directly from the polar plot. This is accomplished by drawing, on the same graph paper, a set of curves representing the locus of all points at which the ratio $0B/AB$ is a constant denoted by the letter M. These lines are then lines of constant magnitude for the closed-loop transfer function. Obviously the locus for $M = 1$ is a vertical line passing through the point $(-\frac{1}{2},0)$ since for any point on the line $0B = AB$. The locus for lines of constant M are a set of circles. Their equation is derived as follows:

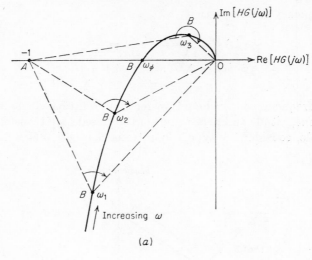

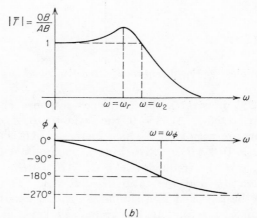

Fig. 7-28. Obtaining the frequency-response characteristics from the loop transfer function. (a) Polar plot of a loop transfer function; (b) frequency-response characteristic of closed-loop system.

Let x, y be the coordinates of a point on the desired locus (see Fig. 7-29). Thus

$$\frac{0B}{AB} = \sqrt{\frac{x^2 + y^2}{(1 + x)^2 + y^2}} = M \qquad (7\text{-}99)$$

This equation can be rearranged as follows:

$$\left[x - \left(\frac{M^2}{1 - M^2} \right) \right]^2 + y^2 = \left(\frac{M}{1 - M^2} \right)^2 \qquad \text{for } M < 1 \quad (7\text{-}100a)$$

$$\left[x + \left(\frac{M^2}{M^2 - 1} \right) \right]^2 + y^2 = \left(\frac{M}{M^2 - 1} \right)^2 \qquad \text{for } M > 1 \quad (7\text{-}100b)$$

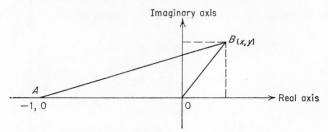

FIG. 7-29. Derivation of M and N circles.

Thus the lines of constant magnitude of $\dfrac{C}{R}(j\omega)$ are recognized as circles with radii of $|M/(M^2 - 1)|$ and centers located at:

$$y = 0 \qquad x = -\frac{M^2}{M^2 - 1} \qquad \text{for } M > 1 \qquad (7\text{-}101a)$$

$$y = 0 \qquad x = \frac{M^2}{1 - M^2} \qquad \text{for } M < 1 \qquad (7\text{-}101b)$$

A set of constant-M circles is drawn in Fig. 7-30.

Some further information concerning M circles is derived from Fig. 7-31, in which a single M circle is drawn. From the geometry of the diagram the following relationships are proved:

$$0C = 1 \qquad (7\text{-}102a)$$

$$\psi = \sin^{-1}\frac{1}{M} \qquad (7\text{-}102b)$$

Figure 7-32 illustrates the use of M circles for determining a closed-loop frequency-response characteristic. It is important to note that the maxi-mum magnitude of $\dfrac{C}{R}(j\omega)$, denoted

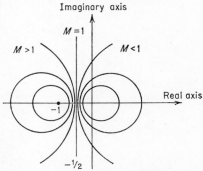

FIG. 7-30. Lines of constant magnitude. M circles.

by M_p, occurs where one of the M circles is tangent to the $G(j\omega)$ polar plot. This corresponds to the "resonant" peak of the frequency-response characteristic of the closed-loop system.

Lines of Constant Phase Angle (N Circles). By use of Eq. (7-98b) it is also possible to draw a set of lines of constant phase angle for the closed-loop transfer function. These are called N circles, where N is a constant defined by the equation

$$\angle \frac{C}{R}(j\omega) = \tan^{-1} N \qquad (7\text{-}103)$$

Let x, y be a point on the desired locus.   From Fig. 7-29 it follows that

$$\measuredangle T(j\omega) = \tan^{-1} N = \tan^{-1} \frac{y}{x} - \tan^{-1} \frac{y}{1+x}$$

$$= \tan^{-1} \frac{y/x - y/(1+x)}{1 + (y/x)[y/(1+x)]} \qquad (7\text{-}104)$$

Simplifying this equation yields the result

$$\left(x + \frac{1}{2}\right)^2 + \left(y - \frac{1}{2N}\right)^2 = \frac{1}{4} \frac{N^2 + 1}{N^2} \qquad (7\text{-}105)$$

These are also a set of circles which are drawn in Fig. 7-33.   The use of the

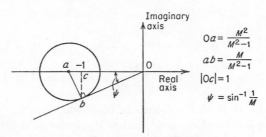

$$Oa = \frac{M^2}{M^2 - 1}$$

$$ab = \frac{M}{M^2 - 1}$$

$$|Oc| = 1$$

$$\psi = \sin^{-1} \frac{1}{M}$$

Fig. 7-31. Properties of an M circle.

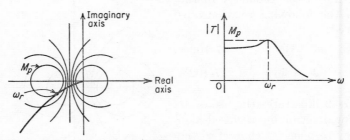

Fig. 7-32. Use of M circles to determine the closed-loop transfer function.

N circle in reading the phase angle of the closed-loop transfer function is identical to the use of M circles in reading the magnitude.

Example of the Use of M Circles.   *Setting the Gain Factor.*   As an example of the use of M circles, let us consider the case where it is desired to adjust the gain factor K of a unity feedback system so that it has a specified resonant peak $M = M_p$.   The effect of adjusting the gain factor on the polar plot is shown in Fig. 7-34, where $G(j\omega)$ is sketched for two values of K, where $K_2 > K_1$.   If the M circle which corresponds to the desired value of M_p is drawn, the problem reduces to one of determining the value of K required to make the plot of $G(j\omega)$ tangent to the M_p circle. Rather than drawing the M_p circle first and then trying to locate the

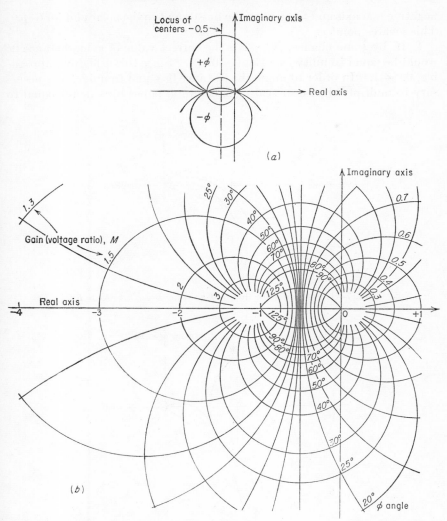

FIG. 7-33. (a) Lines of constant-phase-angle N circles; (b) lines of constant magnitude and phase angle superimposed on the same coordinate axes.

tangent $G(j\omega)$ function, it would be much easier to draw the loop transfer function first and then try to locate the position of the tangent M_p circle. The following is a procedure which enables us to do just this (refer to Fig. 7-35):

1. Draw the polar plot for the loop transfer function with $K = 1$.

2. For the given value of M_p determine the angle ψ_p, using Eq. (7-102b), namely, $\psi_p = \sin^{-1}(1/M_p)$. This determines line $0e$.

3. By means of a compass draw the M_p circle with its center on the

negative real axis and tangent to the line $0e$ and to the polar plot for $G(j\omega)$. This locates point c.

4. If, by some chance, $K = 1$ is the correct value of gain, distance $0c$ would be equal to unity [see Eq. (7-102a)]. Since this is highly improbable, $0c \neq 1$. In order to make the distance $0c$ equal to unity, it is necessary to multiply the linear scales of the graph paper by a factor equal to

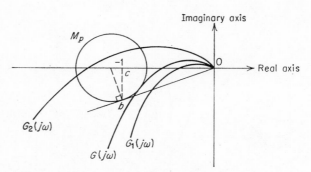

Fig. 7-34. Polar plot for different gain factors $K_2 > K > K_1$.

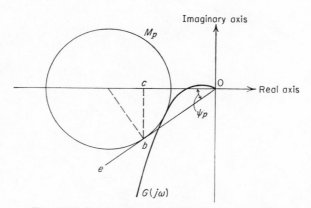

Fig. 7-35. Setting the gain factor for a given M_p.

$1/0c$. If this were done, any point on the polar plot which was originally located at coordinates (x,y) would now be located at coordinates $\left(\dfrac{x}{0c}, \dfrac{y}{0c}\right)$. Thus the original plot for $G(j\omega)$ is transformed to a plot of the function $\left(\dfrac{1}{0c}\right)G(j\omega)$. Since this transformed plot is tangent to the M_p circle, it has the gain factor we are seeking. Thus the required gain for the desired M_p is given by $1/0c$.

SUGGESTED READING

Brown, G. S., and D. P. Campbell: "Principles of Servomechanisms," chap. 6, John Wiley & Sons, Inc., New York, 1948.

Bruns, R. A., and R. M. Saunders: "Analysis of Feedback Control Systems," chap. 13, McGraw-Hill Book Company, Inc., New York, 1955.

Chestnut, H., and R. Mayer: "Servomechanisms and Regulating System Design," 1st ed., vol. 1, chaps. 8 and 9, John Wiley & Sons, Inc., New York, 1951.

Savant, C. J., Jr.: "Basic Feedback Control System Design," chap. 3, McGraw-Hill Book Company, Inc., New York, 1958.

PROBLEMS

7-1. Prove each of the block-diagram reduction formulas of Fig. 7-2.

7-2. Reduce the block diagrams of Fig. P7-2a and b, isolating H_1, H_2, and H_3, respectively.

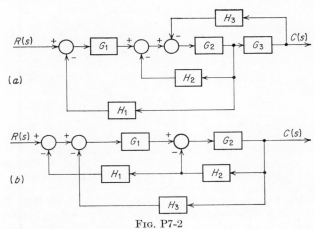

Fig. P7-2

7-3. Determine the system output for each of the inputs given in Fig. P7-3a and b.

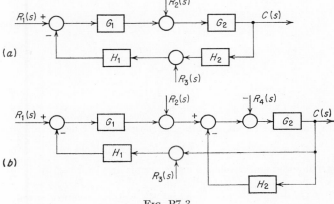

Fig. P7-3

7-4. A type 1 system used for static position has a transfer function

$$HG = \frac{10}{j\omega(1 + j0.07\omega)(1 + j0.03\omega)}$$

(a) Draw the asymptotic logarithmic plot, and determine the phase and gain margins.

(b) Determine the closed-loop system response to unit-step-, -ramp, and parabolic inputs.

7-5. Identify the system type for the systems presented in the following problems: 1-5, 1-9, 1-10, 4-3, 4-5.

7-6. The block diagram of a simple automatic control system used in controlling airplanes is shown in Fig. P7-6.

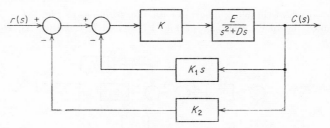

FIG. P7-6

(a) Find the system transfer function $\dfrac{C}{R}(s)$.

(b) If $E = 25$, $D = 0.8$, and $K_2 = 1$, determine K_1 and K so that the natural frequency of the system will be 6 radians/sec and the damping ratio will be 0.8.

(c) A more refined analysis shows that the box labeled K actually should be labeled $(K \times a)/(s + a)$, where $a = 12$ and K has the previous value. Determine the phase and gain margin for this system.

7-7. A speed control servomechanism is represented by the block diagram of Fig. P7-7. The generator field winding has resistance R_f and inductance L_f. Let R represent the armature circuit resistance of both the motor and the generator. Assume no-load

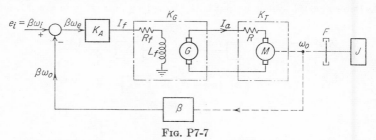

FIG. P7-7

torque. Furthermore, the output voltage of the generator is described by the equation

$$K_G I_f = I_a R + K_1 \omega_0 \qquad \text{where } K_G = \text{volts/field amp}$$

and the output speed and developed motor torque are described by

$$K_T I_a = J \frac{d\omega_0}{dt} + F \omega_0 \qquad \text{where } K_T = \text{lb-ft/armature current}$$

(a) Find the open-loop transfer function ω_0/ω_e.

(b) Simplify the result so that it is in a form similar to the general transfer function, and identify the type system.

7-8. Given are two positioning servos (employing motors) with transfer functions as specified:

Servo 1: $\qquad HG(j\omega) = \dfrac{8}{j\omega(j\omega 0.125 + 1)}$

Servo 2: $\qquad H'G'(j\omega) = \dfrac{16 + j\omega 0.414}{j\omega(j\omega 0.125 + 1)}$

Do the following for *each* servo:

(a) Draw a block diagram, identifying all components.

(b) Determine the damping ratio and the damped and undamped natural frequencies.

(c) Draw clearly on one set of axes to scale the error in radians as a function of time in seconds if a displacement of 1 radian is applied to each servo.

7-9. The circuit diagram of a voltage control system is given in Fig. P7-9.

$$T_{\text{ft-lb}} = AV_{in} - B\frac{d\theta}{dt} \qquad \text{where } A = 10^{-4} \text{ ft-lb/volt, } B = 10^{-5} \text{ ft-lb/radian/sec}$$

The moment of inertia of the motor and its load may be neglected. The frictional load on the motor is given by $F = 10^{-5}$ ft-lb/radian/sec.

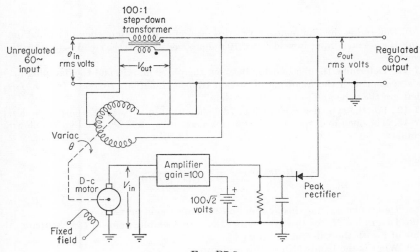

Fig. P7-9

The output of the variac may be assumed to be given by $V_o = (50/\pi)\theta$, where θ is given in radians.

(a) Draw a block diagram for the system, including the transfer function for each block.

(b) Write the system differential equation relating e_o and e_i directly from the block diagram.

(c) What is the regulated steady-state output voltage from the system?

(d) What is the time constant of this system?

7-10. The block diagram of a servomechanism system is shown in Fig. P7-10a. The asymptotic attenuation characteristics for G_1, G_2, G_3 are given in Fig. P7-10b.

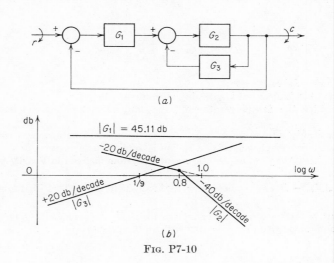

(a)

(b)

FIG. P7-10

(a) Determine the damping ratio of this system and the frequency of oscillation.

(b) If r is a step input in velocity of 10 radians/sec, what is the steady-state position error?

7-11. Determine the relationship between the phase margin and the damping ratio for a system with the following open-loop transfer function: $HG(s) = (s + K)/s^2\tau_1$. What are the type and order of this system?

7-12. For the type 0 system of Fig. 7-22 show that $\omega_c = \sqrt{\omega_0\omega_2}$, where $\omega_0 = K/\tau_1$.

7-13. The open-loop transfer function for a control system is given by the following formula:

$$HG(s) = \frac{10}{s(1 + s/4)(1 + s/16)}$$

(a) Determine ϕ_{pm} for this system and the corresponding value of ζ.

(b) Determine M_p for this system and the corresponding value of ζ. Compare this value of ζ with the value of ζ obtained in (a).

(c) What is the bandwidth of this system?

7-14. Determine the complete response of an inertial-guidance system which is initially at rest to the following input accelerations:

(a) A unit impulse

(b) A unit step

(c) A unit ramp

7-15. Prove Eqs. (7-100) and (7-105).

7-16. The polar plot $G(j\omega)$ of a unity-feedback control system is sketched in Fig. P7-16.

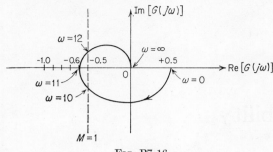

FIG. P7-16

(a) Sketch $\left|\dfrac{C}{R}(j\omega)\right|$ for the closed-loop system vs. ω. Label the values at $\omega = 0$, 10, 11, 12, and ∞.

(b) What type of system is this?

(c) Sketch the phase angle of $\dfrac{C}{R}(j\omega)$ vs. ω.

8 | Stability

In this chapter we are concerned with the topic of system stability. The possibility of unstable operation is present in all feedback systems because of the very nature of feedback itself. If certain undesirable conditions exist, the closed-loop system becomes unstable and it is impossible for it to perform the control task which is required of it. An unstable system either oscillates violently or saturates, and often some of the components are damaged. As engineers, we must be able to answer two important questions. First, under what conditions will a system become unstable? Second, what design changes can be made to prevent instability, and how do these changes affect the closed-loop performance of the system? The second question is really the subject of the next chapter. In the present chapter we are primarily concerned with the first question. Unfortunately the answer is not simple, particularly for multiloop systems, and it is necessary to devote an entire chapter to the subject even though the basic premise is quite simple and has been stated many times before, namely, that a system is absolutely stable if and only if all the roots of the characteristic equation lie in the left half portion of the s plane. In this way all the terms of the source-free response decay exponentially with time, and the system attains stable steady-state operation. This concept is the starting point for all discussions of system stability.

8-1. The Routh Stability Criterion

The Routh test is a mathematical technique for determining how many roots of an algebraic equation have positive real parts. When applied to the characteristic equation of a control system it provides a simple test for absolute stability because a stable system cannot have any roots of the characteristic equation with positive real parts. The Routh stability criterion is presented here without proof. The interested reader may find a complete discussion of the topic in other sources.[1] The procedure involved follows a simple pattern which may be mastered easily.

Let the following equation represent the characteristic equation for a system:

$$B_n s^n + B_{n-1} s^{n-1} + B_{n-2} s^{n-2} + \cdots + B_0 = 0 \qquad (8\text{-}1)$$

Arrange the coefficients of the characteristic equation in the first two rows of an array as shown.

$$
\begin{array}{llll}
Row\ 1: & B_n & B_{n-2} & B_{n-4} & \cdots \\
Row\ 2: & B_{n-1} & B_{n-3} & B_{n-5} & \cdots \\
 & a_1 & a_2 & a_3 & \cdots \\
 & b_1 & b_2 & b_3 & \cdots \\
 & c_1 & c_2 & c_3 & \cdots
\end{array}
\qquad (8\text{-}2)
$$

The other terms $(a_1, a_2, \ldots , b_1, b_2, \ldots)$ of the array in any row are obtained by cross multiplying the terms of the two previous rows as follows:

$$
\begin{aligned}
a_1 &= \frac{B_{n-1}B_{n-2} - B_n B_{n-3}}{B_{n-1}} & a_2 &= \frac{B_{n-1}B_{n-4} - B_n B_{n-5}}{B_{n-1}} \\[2mm]
b_1 &= \frac{a_1 B_{n-3} - B_{n-1} a_2}{a_1} & b_2 &= \frac{a_1 B_{n-5} - B_{n-1} a_3}{a_1} \\[2mm]
c_1 &= \frac{b_1 a_2 - a_1 b_2}{b_1} & c_2 &= \frac{b_1 a_3 - a_1 b_3}{b_1}
\end{aligned}
\qquad (8\text{-}3)
$$

When there are missing coefficients in the original characteristic equation, they are replaced by zeros in the array. For a finite polynomial the array of Eq. (8-2) always terminates with a finite number of terms, the number of terms in each row decreasing as the array is generated. In developing the array all the terms in a row may be multiplied or divided by a positive number without altering the results. This often simplifies the numerical work of finding the coefficients of a succeeding row.

After the complete table is determined, the following rule is applied. *The number of changes in sign for the terms in the first column of the table equals the number of roots with positive real parts.* Thus for a system to be absolutely stable there cannot be any changes in the sign of the terms in the first column.

Let us consider a numerical example of a system whose characteristic equation is given by the following:

$$s^5 + 2s^4 + s^3 + 3s^2 + 4s + 5 = 0 \qquad (8\text{-}4)$$

[1] E. J. Routh, "Dynamics of a System of Rigid Bodies," 3d ed., Macmillan & Co., Ltd., London, 1877.

The array of coefficients is calculated as follows:

$$
\begin{array}{lll}
1 & 1 & 4 \\
2 & 3 & 5 \\
-1 & 3 & \qquad \text{after multiplication by 2} \\
9 & 5 \\
32 & & \qquad \text{after multiplication by 9} \\
5
\end{array}
$$

Examination of the first column reveals that there are two changes in sign, from $+2$ to -1 and from -1 to $+9$. Therefore the characteristic equation has two roots with positive real parts, and the system is not stable.

In some cases the first column term in a row is zero, while the remaining terms in the row are finite. If the table expansion process is continued, the next row is infinite and the usefulness of the table collapses. In order to avoid this difficulty, the zero term may be replaced by a small number ϵ and the process continued as usual. Consider the following characteristic equation:

$$s^4 + 2s^3 + s^2 + 2s + 1 = 0 \tag{8-5}$$

The Routh array is (substituting ϵ for zero):

$$
\begin{array}{lll}
1 & 1 & 1 \\
2 & 2 \\
\epsilon & 1 \\
2 - \dfrac{2}{\epsilon} \\
1
\end{array}
$$

When ϵ approaches zero, the term $2 - 2/\epsilon$ approaches a large negative number so that there are two changes of sign in the first column, indicating two roots of the characteristic equation with positive real parts. The system is therefore unstable. The preceding technique may be used to demonstrate that a system is absolutely unstable if a zero appears anywhere in the first column of the Routh array. Similarly the Routh test can be used to demonstrate that a system is absolutely unstable if any of the terms in the characteristic equation are missing or if they do not have identical signs.

For a system of any given order it is possible to use the Routh criterion to determine the conditions which must exist between the coefficients of the characteristic equation for the system to be absolutely stable. For example, consider the characteristic equation for a third-order system where the coefficients are positive numbers different from zero.

$$B_3 s^3 + B_2 s^2 + B_1 s + B_0 = 0 \tag{8-6}$$

The table of coefficients is given below

$$
\begin{array}{cc}
B_3 & B_1 \\
B_2 & B_0 \\
\dfrac{B_2 B_1 - B_3 B_0}{B_2} & \\
B_0 &
\end{array}
$$

For this system to be absolutely stable it is necessary and sufficient that

$$B_2 B_1 > B_3 B_0 \tag{8-7}$$

Similarly let us consider the characteristic equation for a fourth-order system.

$$B_4 s^4 + B_3 s^3 + B_2 s^2 + B_1 s + B_0 = 0 \tag{8-8}$$

Application of the Routh stability criterion indicates that this system is

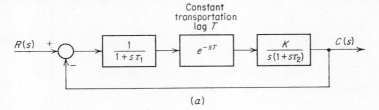

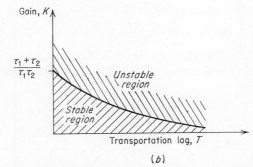

(b)

FIG. 8-1. Absolute-stability analysis for a control system with a constant transportation lag in the direct transmission path. (a) Block diagram; (b) stability diagram.

absolutely stable if the following condition holds between the coefficients:

$$B_1(B_3 B_2 - B_4 B_1) - B_3{}^2 B_0 > 0 \tag{8-9}$$

As a final example, let us investigate the absolute stability of a process control system in which there is a constant transportation lag, or dead time,[1] in the direct transmission path (see Fig. 8-1).

[1] A dead time might be due to many causes, such as, for example, the time that it takes for a fluid to flow through a pipe in a chemical-process system.

The transfer function corresponding to a constant transportation lag can be taken into account readily.   Consider that the output from the fixed delay component is equal to the input delayed by T sec.   Mathematically this can be expressed as follows

$$c_o(t) = c_i(t - T) \tag{8-10}$$

Taking the Laplace transform of both sides and using Eq. (3-36) reveals that

$$\frac{C_o(s)}{C_i(s)} = \epsilon^{-sT} \tag{8-11}$$

Thus the transfer function for a constant transportation lag is given by ϵ^{-sT}, as indicated in Fig. 8-1.

Let us now investigate the absolute stability of the system of Fig. 8-1 in terms of the direct transmission gain K, the time constants τ_1 and τ_2, and the time delay T.   The characteristic equation for this system is given by

$$1 + \frac{K\epsilon^{-Ts}}{s(1 + s\tau_1)(1 + s\tau_2)} = 0 \tag{8-12}$$

The Routh criterion applies for finite polynomials in s so that as a first approximation we write, for small T and low frequency,

$$\epsilon^{-sT} \approx 1 - Ts \tag{8-13}$$

Thus the characteristic equation becomes

$$\tau_1\tau_2 s^3 + (\tau_1 + \tau_2)s^2 + (1 - KT)s + K = 0 \tag{8-14}$$

This is a cubic equation so that the condition for absolute stability in terms of the coefficients is given by Eq. (8-7).   Thus the system is stable if the following holds:

$$(1 - KT)(\tau_1 + \tau_2) > K\tau_1\tau_2 \tag{8-15}$$

Rearranging Eq. (8-15) yields the condition for stability as

$$K < \frac{1}{\tau_1\tau_2/(\tau_1 + \tau_2) + T} \tag{8-16}$$

The boundary between stability and instability occurs when

$$K = \left(\frac{\tau_1\tau_2}{\tau_1 + \tau_2} + T\right)^{-1} \tag{8-17}$$

Equation (8-17) is drawn in Fig. 8-1b, where K is plotted vs. T for constant τ_1 and τ_2.   For any given value of dead time T the system is stable if the gain K lies below the marginal curve and unstable if K lies above it. The closer K lies to the curve, the more likely the system is to become unstable for any unfavorable variations of the time constants τ_1 and τ_2

which might be caused by temperature variations or the tolerance distribution of components.

It is worthwhile to point out that the stability condition of Eq. (8-16) depends upon the accuracy of the approximation of Eq. (8-13). If the exponential is expanded to include more terms of the series and the Routh criterion is then applied, a more exact statement of the stability condition is obtained. Comparison of this result with the previous one indicates whether the first approximation is adequate for the results required.

8-2. The Nyquist Stability Criterion

The Routh stability criterion of the previous section has two major disadvantages. First, it provides information only about the absolute stability of systems and tells us very little about their relative stability. Second, the Routh criterion assumes that the characteristic equation is available in polynomial form. This may not be the case, particularly when the loop transfer function is available from sinusoidal steady-state experimental data. In order to apply the Routh criterion in this case, it is necessary to approximate the data by an algebraic expression so that the characteristic equation may be derived in polynomial form.

The disadvantages of the Routh criterion are avoided by the Nyquist stability criterion. The Nyquist stability test is basically a graphical method that can be applied to experimental data of the sinusoidal open-loop transfer function or to computed results. Thus it enables us to predict a system's *closed-loop stability* from *open-loop data*, i.e., from data taken prior to closing the loop. If the system is going to be unstable when the loop is closed, we know about it ahead of time. In fact stability can be checked with pencil and paper even before purchasing specific components. Furthermore, the Nyquist plot provides information about relative stability. In the case of unstable systems it indicates how to stabilize the system by means of compensating networks and obtain the desired closed-loop system specifications.

Since the Nyquist criterion is so useful, it is important that the engineer have some insight into its mathematical basis so that the technique may be used intelligently as a design tool. The next part of the discussion is therefore devoted to a presentation of the mathematical background for the Nyquist criterion.

Two Plotting (Mapping) Theorems. In general the loop transfer function of a system is a function of the complex variable s, where $s = \sigma + j\omega$. Representing such a function graphically is a more difficult problem than representing a function of a real variable. Consider, for example, a function of the real variable x, such as $F(x) = x^2$. In order to represent this function graphically, we can use a single sheet of graph paper with cartesian coordinates and plot $F(x)$ as the ordinate vs. x as the abscissa (see Fig. 8-2a). Let us now consider the same function as a function of the complex variable s, that is,

$$\begin{aligned} F(s) &= s^2 = (\sigma + j\omega)^2 \\ &= (\sigma^2 - \omega^2) + j2\sigma\omega \end{aligned}$$

This function cannot be represented on a single set of coordinates, for two reasons. First, the complex variable $s = \sigma + j\omega$ depends upon the value

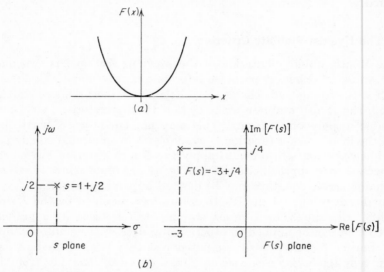

FIG. 8-2. Comparison of the graphical representation of a function of a real variable with the graphical representation of a function of a complex variable. (*a*) Plotting a function of a real variable $F(x) = x^2$; (*b*) plotting a function of a complex variable $F(s) = s^2$ for the point where $s = 1 + j2$.

of two independent quantities σ and ω. Second, for any given value of s, $F(s)$ is a complex number so that it must be represented by a point in a complex plane. In order to plot this function, two graphs are necessary. The first represents the s plane with axes σ and $j\omega$. The second represents the $F(s)$ plane with axes of Re $[F(s)]$ and Im $[F(s)]$. For any point on the s plane there is a corresponding point on the $F(s)$ plane. For example, if $s = 1 + j2$, then $F(s) = s^2 = (1 + j2)^2 = -3 + j4$. As shown in Fig. 8-2b, the point $s = 1 + j2$ in the s plane plots into the point $-3 + j4$ in the $F(s)$ plane. From the foregoing it is obvious that, for any given locus of point s in the s plane, there is a corresponding locus of points in the $F(s)$ plane. Thus the representation of a function of a complex variable depends upon the assumed locus in the s plane. Since an infinite number of possible paths exist in the s plane, it would seem to be almost fruitless to try to represent a function of a complex variable graphically and obtain some general results. This is not quite the case, and some very useful plotting theorems and generalizations may be obtained if the function $F(s)$ is an *analytic function*. The study of analytic functions is part of the mathematical theory of functions of a complex variable, and the reader is referred to any text for a full development of the subject.[1] For our purposes it is sufficient to point out that the transfer functions of all practical systems are analytic, so that this theory applies to them.

Attention is first directed to a simple plotting theorem, which is presented without proof. Consider that the assumed path in the s plane

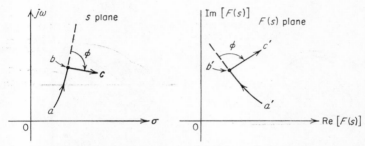

FIG. 8-3. Preservation of angles for plotting functions of a complex variable.

consists of the broken line abc, as shown in Fig. 8-3, which does not pass through any singularity points of $F(s)$, that is, points in the s plane for which $F(s) = \infty$. The corresponding contour in the $F(s)$ plane is indicated by the broken line $a'b'c'$. By the property of *conformal mapping* the angle ϕ is the same, in both magnitude and direction, in the s plane and the $F(s)$ plane. If the angle ϕ in the s plane were counterclockwise, the angle in the $F(s)$ plane would also be of the same magnitude in a counterclockwise direction. We shall use this conformal-mapping property as an aid in plotting loop transfer functions.

The second plotting theorem to be considered forms the basis of the Nyquist stability criterion. Let us consider this theorem first and then proceed to prove it and gain some insight into its application. Broadly speaking, it applies to any assumed closed contour in the s plane and relates the location and direction of this contour with respect to the zeros and poles of the $F(s)$ function to the corresponding $F(s)$-plane plot. The zeros and poles of $F(s)$ are points in the s plane for which the value of $F(s)$ becomes equal to either zero or infinity. Assume that the path in the s plane is a closed contour S_1 as shown in Fig. 8-4. The variable s starts at some arbitrary point a on the contour and assumes successive values round S_1 in a clockwise direction, returning to the starting point. If

[1] For example see E. A. Guillemin, "The Mathematics of Circuit Analysis," chap. 6, John Wiley & Sons, Inc., New York, 1951.

the area to the right of the contour, as one proceeds in a clockwise direction, is considered "inside," and the area to the left is considered "outside," then the shaded area is "enclosed" by S_1. The mapping theorem relates the difference between the number of zeros and poles of $F(s)$ which S_1 encloses to the number of encirclements of the origin of the $F(s)$ function in the $F(s)$ plane. The $F(s)$ locus, corresponding to the assumed s-plane path S_1, starts at point a', corresponding to the value of $F(s)$ when $s = a$. As the variable s takes on successive values around S_1, $F(s)$ changes in complex value and a locus of points F_1 is obtained in the $F(s)$ plane. The F_1 locus is closed if S_1 is closed since it eventually returns

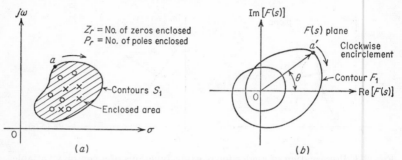

Fig. 8-4. A mapping theorem. Net clockwise encirclements of origin by $F(s) = Z_r - P_r = 2$. (a) s plane; (b) $F(s)$ plane.

to the starting point at a' when $s = a$. The number of encirclements of the origin by the closed curve F_1 is measured by considering the angular rotation of a radial line drawn from the origin to the $F(s)$ curve as s varies. When $s = a$, this line is given by $0a'$. As s takes on successive values on the S_1 contour, proceeding in a clockwise direction, the tip of the radial line in the $F(s)$ plane moves along the F_1 curve. A *positive encirclement* of the origin is obtained each time this radial line rotates through 360° in a *clockwise direction*, and a *negative encirclement* is obtained each time this line rotates through 360° in a *counterclockwise direction*.[1] The reader should note that since the $F(s)$ contour is closed the radial line must make an integral number of rotations in going completely round the path. In Fig. 8-4b there are two positive (clockwise) encirclements of the origin by the contour F_1. The plotting theorem states that the total number of encirclements of the origin by the F_1 contour in the $F(s)$ plane equals the difference between the number of zeros and poles of $F(s)$ enclosed by the S_1 contour in the s plane. The two encirclements of the origin by the F_1 contour of Fig. 8-4b follow from the fact that the S_1 contour of Fig. 8-4a encloses six zeros and four poles. If N denotes the

---

[1] In feedback control system literature this rotation is defined contrary to the usual mathematical definition of counterclockwise rotation being positive. This definition is arbitrary and does not affect the application of the plotting theorem as long as we are consistent in its use.

number of encirclements of the origin in the $F(s)$ plane, it follows that

$$N = Z_r - P_r \tag{8-18}$$

where Z_r = total number of zeros of $F(s)$ enclosed by assumed path in
        s plane, including orders of multiplicity
    P_r = total number of poles of $F(s)$ enclosed by assumed path in
        s plane, including orders of multiplicity

To reiterate, an enclosed zero or pole in the s plane is one which lies within the area to the right of the s-plane path as it is traversed in a clockwise direction. Encirclements of the origin in the $F(s)$ plane are measured by counting the number of 360° rotations (clockwise + and counterclockwise −) of a radial line drawn from origin to the curve in the $F(s)$ plane as $F(s)$ is plotted for successive values of s proceeding round the s-plane contour in a clockwise direction.

As an example of the use of Eq. (8-18), consider the curves of Fig. 8-4. The $F(s)$-plane contour F_1 encircles the origin twice in a clockwise direction. Thus it follows that the S_1 contour encloses two more zeros than poles of $F(s)$, that is, $Z_r - P_r = 2$. Nothing can be concluded about specific numbers for Z_r and P_r; only their difference is known. Also, the exact shapes of both S_1 and F_1 are immaterial to the result because only enclosures and encirclements are important. Figure 8-5 illustrates some other examples of $F(s)$-plane contours drawn for an unspecified contour in the s plane. The $F(s)$ plot is assumed to be traversed in the direction of the arrow as s assumes values round the s-plane contour. In each case the number of encirclements of the origin is calculated, and this tells us the difference between the number of zeros and poles enclosed by the s-plane contour even though we do not know exactly what this contour looks like. The number of encirclements of the origin for Fig. 8-5a to c should be obvious to the reader without further discussion. The number of encirclements for Fig. 8-5d and e is not quite so obvious. Let us consider Fig. 8-5d in detail. Assume that the $F(s)$-plane contour is traversed, starting at point a', in the direction of the arrows as shown: $a'b'c'd'e'f'g'd'c'a'$. The following table lists the total number of degrees (clockwise +, counterclockwise −) that the radial line from the origin to the curve rotates as the indicated portion of the $F(s)$ curve is traversed.

$$a'b' : 180°$$
$$a'b'c' : 270°$$
$$a'b'c'd' : 270°$$
$$a'b'c'd'e' : 180°$$
$$a'b'c'd'e'f' : 90°$$
$$a'b'c'd'e'f'g' : 0°$$
$$a'b'c'd'e'f'g'd' : -90°$$
$$a'b'c'd'e'f'g'd'c' : -90°$$
$$a'b'c'd'e'f'g'd'c'a' : 0°$$

Thus there are zero net encirclements of the origin in traversing the $F(s)$ plot. Hence $Z_r - P_r = 0$ for the number of zeros and poles enclosed by the s-plane path.

The following table is a similar listing for the $F(s)$ plot of Fig. 8-5e.

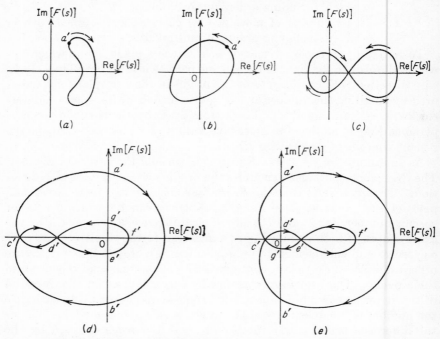

FIG. 8-5. Examples of $F(s)$-plane contours. (a) Number of encirclements of origin = $Z_r - P_r = 0 = N$; (b) number of encirclements of origin = $Z_r - P_r = -1 = N$; (c) number of encirclements of origin = $Z_r - P_r = 1 = N$; (d) number of encirclements = $Z_r - P_r = 0 = N$; (e) number of encirclements = $Z_r - P_r = 2 = N$.

This curve is identical to Fig. 8-5d except that the origin of coordinates is shifted.

$$a'b' : 180°$$
$$a'b'c' : 270°$$
$$a'b'c'd' : 360°$$
$$a'b'c'd'e' : 450° = 360° + 90°$$
$$a'b'c'd'e'f' : 450°$$
$$a'b'c'd'e'f'e' : 450°$$
$$a'b'c'd'e'f'e'g' : 540° = 450° + 90°$$
$$a'b'c'd'e'f'e'g'c' : 630° = 540° + 90°$$
$$a'b'c'd'e'f'e'g'c'a' : 720° = 630° + 90°$$

Thus for this case there are two net clockwise encirclements

$$720° = 2 \times 360°$$

Hence $Z_r - P_r = 2$ for the zeros and poles enclosed by the s-plane path.

Before proceeding with the use of the plotting theorem as a stability criterion, let us develop a heuristic proof which should throw additional light on its application.

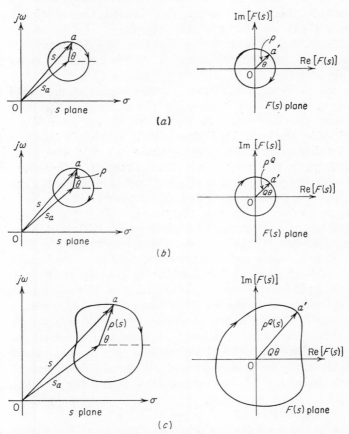

FIG. 8-6. Plotting the function $F(s) = (s - s_a)^Q$. (a) Plotting the function $F(s) = s - s_a$, where $s = s_a + \rho \epsilon^{j\theta}$; (b) plotting the function $F(s) = (s - s_a)^Q$, where $s = s_a + \rho \epsilon^{j\theta}$; (c) plotting the function $F(s) = (s - s_a)^Q$, where $s = s_a + \rho(s)\epsilon^{j\theta}$.

Proof of the Plotting Theorem. A heuristic proof of the theorem is presented here by considering some simple examples first and then extending the results to more general situations.

Assume that $F(s)$ is a polynomial with a simple zero at the point $s = s_a$; that is, $F(s)$ is given by the expression $F(s) = s - s_a$. It is desired to plot $F(s)$ for all values of s round a circular contour of radius ρ, with a center at the point s_a (see Fig. 8-6a). For this path in the s plane the variable s is defined by the equation $s = s_a + \rho \epsilon^{j\theta}$, where θ is an angle which varies through 2π radians in a clockwise direction as the path is traversed starting from point a. The zero of $F(s)$ at $s = s_a$ is obviously enclosed by the circular s-plane contour. The corresponding contour in the $F(s)$ plane is obtained by substituting $s = s_a + \rho\epsilon^{j\theta}$ into the equation for $F(s)$. Hence the $F(s)$ contour is given by $F(s) = s - s_a = \rho\epsilon^{j\theta}$. Examination of this expression indicates that it is the equation of a circle of radius ρ about the origin in the $F(s)$ plane. As the angle θ varies through 2π radians in a clockwise direction, the $F(s)$ contour encircles the origin once in a clockwise direction. Thus Eq. (8-18) is verified for this simple example.

If the assumed polynomial for $F(s)$ has a zero of multiplicity Q at the point s_a, its equation is given by the expression $F(s) = (s - s_a)^Q$. For the same circular contour in the s plane, the corresponding $F(s)$ contour is given by the equation $F(s) = \rho^Q\epsilon^{jQ\theta}$. Obviously this is a circle of radius ρ^Q which encircles the origin Q times in a clockwise direction as θ varies through 2π radians in a clockwise direction. Thus the mapping theorem is extended to the case of a multiple zero by simply considering the multiple zero as Q zeros located at the same point.

Let us now consider plotting the function $F(s) = (s - s_a)^Q$ for any *noncircular* closed contour in the s plane which encloses the point s_a as shown in Fig. 8-6c. For this contour s may be expressed by the equation $s = s_a + \rho(s)\epsilon^{j\theta}$, where $\rho(s)$ is now a variable distance from s_a to the contour. $\rho(s)$ changes as the contour is traversed. θ again varies through 2π radians as shown. Substitution of this equation into the expression for $F(s)$ gives the resulting contour in the $F(s)$ plane, namely, $F(s) = \rho^Q(s)\epsilon^{jQ\theta}$. Examination of the result reveals that the $F(s)$ curve again encircles the origin Q times in a clockwise direction as θ varies through 2π radians in a clockwise direction. We can draw the following conclusion from the foregoing example. When *any* closed s-plane contour encloses the point $s = s_a$, the corresponding plot of the function

$$F(s) = (s - s_a)^Q$$

in the $F(s)$ plane encircles the origin Q times in a clockwise direction. Thus in so far as the application of Eq. (8-18) is concerned, all closed s-plane contours which enclose the zero at $s = s_a$ give the same result as the simple circular path of Fig. 8-6a.

A little thought also reveals that, if the assumed closed s-plane contour *does not* enclose the zero at $s = s_a$, the corresponding plot of the function $F(s) = (s - s_a)^Q$ *does not* encircle the origin. Consider the case illustrated in Fig. 8-7. Here again s may be expressed by the equation $s = s_a + \rho(s)\epsilon^{j\theta}$, but this time θ does not vary through 2π radians as the contour is traversed. Thus the resulting $F(s)$-plane curve, given by the equation $F(s) = \rho^Q(s)\epsilon^{jQ\theta}$, never encircles the origin since θ does not change through 2π radians.

The fact that all closed s-plane contours which enclose the zero at $s = s_a$ produce the same number of encirclements of the origin in the $F(s)$ plane as a circular path may be proved in still another way by use of the results of the previous paragraph. Figure 8-8a illustrates a contour in the s plane which consists of several parts: an arbitrary clockwise path S_1, line segments AB and CD, and a circular counterclockwise path S_2'. If $F(s) = (s - s_a)^Q$ is plotted for this complete path, the number of encirclements of the origin in the $F(s)$ plane must be zero since the s-plane path does not enclose the zero of $F(s)$ (see the shaded area). In Fig. 8-8b the path of Fig. 8-8a is redrawn so that the line segments AB and CD coincide. For this s-plane contour the number of

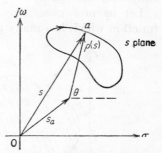

FIG. 8-7. An s-plane contour which does not enclose the point $s = s_a$.

encirclements of the origin for the $F(s)$-plane plot is still zero. In other words, it follows that

$$N_{S_1} + N_{S_2'} = 0$$

where N_{S_1} = number of encirclements of origin in $F(s)$ plane due to path S_1

$N_{S_2'}$ = number of encirclements of origin in $F(s)$ plane due to path S_2'.

Path S_2' is a circle traversed in a counterclockwise direction. Substituting this locus for s into the expression for $F(s) = (s - s_a)^Q$ yields the result that the number of encirclements due to path S_2' equals $-Q$, where the $-$ sign denotes a counterclockwise encirclement of the origin. Substitution of this value into the previous equation yields the following result:

$$N_{S_1} + (-Q) = 0$$

Rewriting this equation gives the previously stated result for any arbitrary closed path S_1, namely, $N_{S_1} = Q$.

The foregoing analysis may be applied equally well to a simple polynomial having an Mth-order *pole* at the point $s = s_1$, that is,

$$F(s) = (s - s_1)^{-M}$$

Here, because of the minus sign in the exponent, it follows that, for any closed path which encloses the pole at $s = s_1$ (clockwise rotation), the corresponding $F(s)$-plane contour encircles the origin M times in a *counterclockwise direction*, opposite to the direction of the encirclement due to an enclosed zero. Thus the plotting theorem is extended to include a multiple pole by simply considering the multiple pole as M

poles located at the same point.   Also, it can be shown that all closed s-plane contours which enclose the point $s = s_1$ give the same result as a simple circular path.

Let us now generalize the previous results by considering an $F(s)$ function which has many poles and zeros.   Multiple poles and zeros are

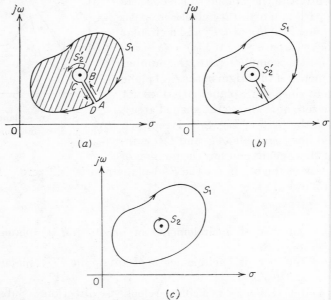

FIG. 8-8. Proof that any closed s-plane path may be contracted into an equivalent circular path in so far as the plotting theorem is concerned.   (a) $N = 0$; (b) $N_{S_1} + N_{S_2'} = 0$; (c) $N_{S_1} = N_{S_2}$; S_2, clockwise rotation; S_2', counterclockwise rotation.

taken into account by considering them as simple singularities repeated as many times as their multiplicity.   Thus assume the following $F(s)$:

$$F(s) = \frac{K(s - s_a)(s - s_b)\ \cdot\ \cdot\ \cdot}{(s - s_1)(s - s_2)\ \cdot\ \cdot\ \cdot} \tag{8-19}$$

The zeros and poles are located in the s plane as shown in Fig. 8-9a. Consider the path S_1', which encloses several poles and zeros of $F(s)$.   In Fig. 8-9b an s-plane path S_2' is drawn, which consists of S_1' plus several line segments and counterclockwise circular paths as shown.   Path S_2' does not enclose any zeros and poles of $F(s)$.   Thus the total number of $F(s)$-plane encirclements of the origin corresponding to path S_2' is zero. It follows that the number of encirclements of the origin in the $F(s)$ plane due to path S_1' is equal to the number of encirclements of the origin in the $F(s)$ plane due to path S_3', where path S_3' is drawn in Fig. 8-9c.   Let us consider S_3' in detail.   It is made up of many small clockwise circles connected by straight-line segments, which are traversed twice in opposite directions. The small circles may be reduced in radius and made as small as we like so that as s varies round any one of these circles all the factors comprising $F(s)$ in Eq. (8-19) remain substantially constant except for the one factor which contains the zero or pole of $F(s)$ at the center of the

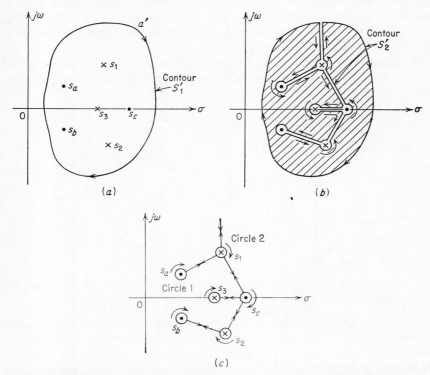

FIG. 8-9. Demonstration of Nyquist plotting theorem. (a) Original s-plane contour; (b) contour S_2' = contour S_1' plus counterclockwise circular paths plus connecting lines; (c) contour S_3'.

circle in question. For example, for variations of s about circle 1, $F(s)$ is given by the expression

$$F(s) = (\text{constant})(s - s_a) \qquad (8\text{-}20)$$

Similarly, for variations of s about circle 2, $F(s)$ is given by the expression

$$F(s) = (\text{constant}) \frac{1}{s - s_1} \qquad (8\text{-}21)$$

Thus the mapping theorem, which was demonstrated for the case of a single zero or pole function, may be applied independently to each of the smaller circular contours. The net number of encirclements due to path S_1' is given by the sum of the number of encirclements calculated for each circular path by itself. Obviously circle 1 contributes a clockwise encirclement of the origin in the $F(s)$ plane, whereas circle 2 contributes a counterclockwise encirclement. By extending these results to include the circular paths round the other zeros and poles of $F(s)$, we arrive at the general statement of the mapping theorem, namely, that the total number of encirclements N of the origin in the $F(s)$ plane equals $Z_r - P_r$, where Z_r equals the total number of zeros enclosed and P_r equals the total number of poles enclosed by S_1'.

Application of the Mapping Theorem to Control Systems. The Nyquist Path. With the previous plotting theorem firmly in mind, its application

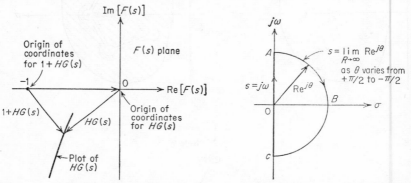

FIG. 8-10. Obtaining the graph of $1 + HG(s)$ from the graph of $HG(s)$.

FIG. 8-11. An s-plane path which encloses the entire right-half s plane.

as a stability criterion follows readily. In order to determine a system's absolute stability, we must check to see if there are any roots of the characteristic equation in the right-half s plane. That is, for absolute stability the expression $F(s) = 1 + HG(s)$ must not have any zeros in the right-half s plane, zeros being values of s for which $1 + HG(s) = 0$. Let us assume that the function $F(s) = 1 + HG(s)$ does not have any poles in the right-half s plane. We shall consider the effect of poles in the right half plane shortly, but, for the time being, it is worthwhile to consider the situation when they are absent. Thus, if we consider an s-plane contour which encloses the entire right-half s plane, it follows that $P_r = 0$ and the total number of encirclements of the origin by the function $F(s) = 1 + HG(s)$ equals the number of zeros of $1 + HG(s)$ in the right-half s plane. Hence, for this system to be absolutely stable, the function $F(s) = 1 + HG(s)$ cannot have any net encirclements of the *origin*. As shown in Fig. 8-10, the plot of the function $1 + HG(s)$ is simply the plot of the function $HG(s)$ with the origin of coordinates shifted to the point $(-1,0)$. Thus checking encirclements of the origin for the function $1 + HG(s)$ is equivalent to checking encirclements of the point $(-1,0)$ for the $HG(s)$ function. In other words, we can test the *closed-loop* stability of a system by considering the encirclements of the $(-1,0)$

point for the *open-loop* transfer function $HG(s)$. If the $(-1,0)$ point is not encircled, the system is stable.

Figure 8-11 shows an s-plane contour which encloses the entire right-half complex plane. It consists of the entire $j\omega$ axis, from $\omega = -\infty$ to $\omega = +\infty$, plus a semicircular path of infinite radius as shown. This path is called the *Nyquist path*. Plotting the function $HG(s)$ for this path is straightforward. The portion corresponding to segment $0A$ is obtained by letting $s = j\omega$. Hence for this part we must plot $HG(j\omega)$ for $\omega = 0$ to $\omega = \infty$. This is obviously the frequency-response characteristic for the open-loop transfer function. The portion of the characteristic corresponding to the infinite semicircle is obtained by letting $s = \lim_{R \to \infty} R\epsilon^{j\theta}$, as θ varies from $+\pi/2$ radians to $-\pi/2$ radians. Usually this part of the s-plane contour plots into a single point at the origin in the $F(s)$ plane so that it presents no particular difficulty. This is demonstrated in some examples in the next section. The portion of the characteristic corresponding to segment $C0$ is obtained by letting $s = -j\omega$ as ω varies from infinity to zero. Fortunately $HG(-j\omega) = HG^*(j\omega)$; that is, the plot of $HG(-j\omega)$ is the complex conjugate of the plot for $HG(j\omega)$. Graphically this means that the plot for $HG(-j\omega)$ is the mirror image about the real axis of the plot for $HG(j\omega)$, so that it is drawn readily once the latter is known.

Before illustrating the use of the Nyquist criterion with some typical examples, let us reconsider the earlier assumption that the function $1 + HG(s)$ does not have any poles in the right-half complex plane. If $1 + HG(s)$ has poles in the right half plane, application of the Nyquist plotting theorem gives information only about the difference between the number of zeros and poles in the right-half s plane, i.e., the value of $Z_r - P_r$, where the subscript r refers to the right half plane. If $Z_r = P_r$, the $HG(s)$ function has zero encirclements of the $(-1,0)$ point even though Z_r is finite. Thus it is possible to arrive at an erroneous conclusion that the system is closed-loop stable. The stability criterion of zero encirclements of the $(-1,0)$ point can be used directly only if we check first to see whether or not $P_r = 0$. In other words, it is necessary to check the function $1 + HG(s)$ for the existence of right-half s-plane poles before the plotting theorem is applied as a stability test. Fortunately the determination of poles of $1 + HG(s)$ in the right half plane is relatively easy, and in most cases $P_r = 0$. Consider the physical interpretation of the absence of poles of $1 + HG(s)$ in the right-half s plane. Write $HG(s)$ as the ratio of two polynomials $P(s)$ and $Q(s)$. Thus

$$F(s) = 1 + HG(s) = 1 + \frac{P(s)}{Q(s)} \qquad (8\text{-}22)$$

where
$$HG(s) = \frac{B}{E}(s) = \frac{P(s)}{Q(s)} \qquad (8\text{-}23)$$

From Eq. (8-22) it is obvious that the poles of $F(s)$ occur at values of s for which $Q(s) = 0$. Equation (8-23) expresses $HG(s)$ in terms of the actuating signal $E(s)$ and the primary feedback signal $B(s)$ for the open-loop system. Thus for the open-loop system

$$Q(s)B(s) = E(s)P(s) \tag{8-24}$$

If the actuating signal $E(s)$ is made zero, then Eq. (8-24) becomes the characteristic equation for the *open-loop* system, namely, $Q(s) = 0$. If the open-loop system is absolutely stable, its characteristic equation

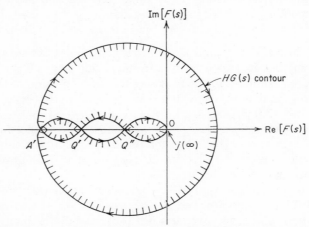

FIG. 8-12. Technique for determining which regions of the negative real axis are encircled by the $HG(s)$ contour.

does not have any roots in the right-half complex plane, i.e., there are no points in the right-half s plane for which $Q(s) = 0$. If this is true, it follows that the function $1 + HG(s) = 1 + P(s)/Q(s)$ does not have any poles in the right-half s plane. Thus we have arrived at the conclusion that if a system is open-loop stable then the function $1 + HG(s)$ for the closed-loop system does not have any poles in the right-half s plane. In such cases the Nyquist stability criterion can be applied with the knowledge that $P_r = 0$. Of course, if a system is unstable when the loop is open, the Nyquist test can still be applied except that the value of P_r must be taken into account. There are many cases where a system is open-loop unstable and becomes stable when the primary feedback loop is closed. These require special care when the Nyquist stability test is used. The Routh test can be applied to the polynomial $Q(s)$ to determine the number of roots in the right half plane. In this case the number of changes of sign for the terms in the first column of the Routh array for $Q(s)$ is equal to the value of P_r.

Determination of encirclements of the $(-1,0)$ point by the $HG(s)$ plot becomes troublesome when the plot is complicated.   Consider, for example, an $HG(s)$ plot as drawn in Fig. 8-12.   Let us determine whether the $(-1,0)$ point is encircled if it is located between points $A'Q'$, $Q'Q''$, and $Q''0$.   Rather than counting rotations of a radial line as outlined previously, it is possible to determine the regions where the $(-1,0)$ point is encircled by the following technique, known as the *shaded-area rule*.[1]   Starting at any point on the $HG(s)$ contour, one shades the area

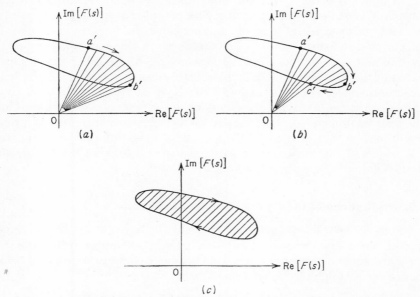

(a)   (b)

(c)

FIG. 8-13. Demonstration of the shaded-area rule for determining encirclements. (*a*) Line $0a'$ rotated to position $0b'$; (*b*) line $0a'$ rotated to position $0c'$; (*c*) shaded area after complete contour is swept through.

to the right of the curve as one proceeds round the curve in the direction of the arrow, i.e., in the direction of increasing frequency.   This is done in Fig. 8-12.   It can be seen that the portions of the negative real axis which lie between points $Q'Q''$ fall within an unshaded area.   The shaded-area rule states that if the $(-1,0)$ point lies in an unshaded area (i.e., within the interval $Q'Q''$) it is not encircled by the curve and the closed-loop system is stable.   If the point $(-1,0)$ lies within a shaded area, it is encircled by the curve and the system is unstable.   The reasoning behind the shaded-area rule is illustrated in Fig. 8-13.   Consider that the radial line $0a'$ is such that as it rotates in a *clockwise* direction it *shades* all the area through which it sweeps.   See Fig. 8-13*a*, in which line $0a'$ is rotated

[1] See L. S. Dzung, The Stability Criteria, in "Automatic and Manual Control" (papers contributed to the conference at Cranfield, 1951), pp. 13–23, Butterworth & Co. (Publishers) Ltd., London, 1952.

in a clockwise direction from position $0a'$ to $0b'$. When the radial line rotates in a *counterclockwise* direction, it is assumed that it *erases* the shading in the area through which it sweeps. This is illustrated in Fig. 8-13b, where the radial line has rotated to position $0c'$. When the tip of the radial line sweeps round the contour several times, it can be seen that the shaded area remaining is given by the area which lies to the right of the contour as one proceeds round it in the direction of the arrow (see Fig. 8-13c). A little thought reveals that if any point is encircled by the contour it must lie within the shaded area because the radial line from it to the contour has made at least one full net clockwise rotation in traversing the periphery of the contour. The usefulness of the shaded-area rule for determining stable regions for the location of the $(-1,0)$ point is illustrated in the next section. For the control systems engineer the shaded-area rule reduces the application of the Nyquist stability criterion to a simple procedure for type 3 systems or lower, which is as follows: Plot the sinusoidal open-loop transfer function for increasing frequency, from $\omega = 0$ to $\omega = \infty$. If the $(-1,0)$ point lies to the right of the contour as it is traversed, the system is unstable; if the $(-1,0)$ point lies to the left of the contour, the system is stable.

8-3. Applications of the Nyquist Stability Criterion

Let us now consider the Nyquist stability criterion as applied to some typical open-loop transfer functions. These examples will serve to illustrate some common Nyquist contours as well as to outline the procedure for sketching these contours.

Example 8-1. *Type 0 Systems.* Consider the open-loop transfer function given by the expression

$$HG(s) = \frac{K}{(1 + s\tau_1)(1 + s\tau_2)} \tag{8-25}$$

The poles of this function occur at $s = -1/\tau_1$ and $s = -1/\tau_2$, which are within the left-half s plane. The s-plane contour is as drawn in Fig. 8-14a. The corresponding plot for $HG(s)$ is sketched in Fig. 8-14b. Let us consider this plot for various sections of the s-plane contour.

Section 0A: $s = j\omega$ for $0 \leq \omega \leq \infty$

Hence $$HG(j\omega) = \frac{K}{(1 + j\omega\tau_1)(1 + j\omega\tau_2)} \tag{8-26}$$

At extreme values of ω we have
1. $HG(j0) = K$
2. $\lim_{\omega \to \infty} HG(j\omega) = 0/\underline{180°}$

At intermediate values of ω the plot passes through the third and fourth quadrants as each one of the linear factors in the denominator of Eq. (8-26) contributes a phase lag up to but never exceeding 90° as ω increases.

Section ABC: $\qquad\qquad s = \lim_{R\to\infty} R\epsilon^{j\theta} \qquad$ for $\pi/2 \leq \theta \leq -\pi/2$

The magnitude of $HG(s)$ is given by the expression

$$|HG(j\infty)| = \lim_{R\to\infty} \left| \frac{K}{(1 + R\tau_1\epsilon^{j\theta})(1 + R\tau_2\epsilon^{j\theta})} \right| = 0$$

Thus the semicircle ABC again plots into the point $0'$ in the $F(s)$ plane.

Section C0: $\qquad\qquad s = -j\omega \qquad$ for $0 \leq \omega \leq \infty$

This plot is the mirror image of the plot for $HG(j\omega)$ and is drawn dotted in Fig. 8-14b.

Examination of the complete Nyquist plot reveals that the $(-1,0)$ point is never encircled so that the closed-loop system is stable. Increasing K can never make the system unstable, but it will reduce the phase margin.

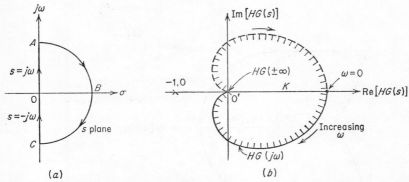

(a)   (b)

Fig. 8-14. Nyquist stability plots for some type 0 systems.   (a) s-plane contour; (b) $F(s)$-plane contour for $HG(s) = \dfrac{K}{(1 + s\tau_1)(1 + s\tau_2)}$.

Example 8-2. *Type 1 Systems.* Consider a system whose open-loop transfer function is

$$HG(s) = \frac{K}{s(1 + s\tau_1)} \qquad\qquad (8\text{-}27)$$

The poles of this function occur at $s = 0$ and $s = -1/\tau_1$. A little thought reveals that difficulties arise if the s-plane contour of Fig. 8-14a is used for the Nyquist path. The difficulty arises because of the pole at $s = 0$. If we permit s to become zero, $HG(s)$ becomes infinite. In order to avoid having to plot $HG(s)$ through this singularity point, it is necessary to modify the s-plane contour as shown in Fig. 8-15a. This contour also encircles the entire right-half s plane but avoids passing through the pole of $HG(s)$ at $s = 0$ by means of the semicircle EFA. Semicircle EFA is defined mathematically by the equation $s = \lim_{R\to 0} R\epsilon^{j\theta}$ as θ varies from $-\pi/2$ to $+\pi/2$. The modified s-plane contour of Fig. 8-15a does not enclose any poles of the $HG(s)$ so that this system is closed-loop stable if there are zero encirclements of the $(-1,0)$ point in the $F(s)$ plane.[1] Of course the semicircular indentation EFA must be taken into

---

[1] Another possibility is to modify the s-plane contour so that the small semicircle detours to the left instead of going to the right from point E to point A. In this case the pole at the origin would be enclosed by the s-plane contour, and the Nyquist criterion would require inserting $P_r = 1$.

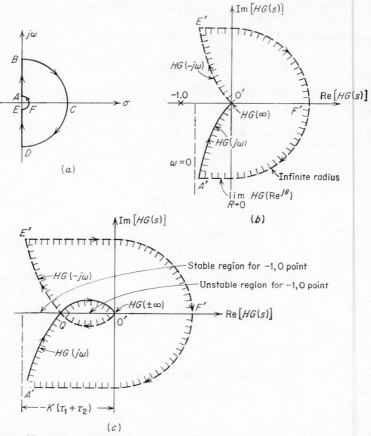

FIG. 8-15. Nyquist stability plots for some type 1 systems. (a) s-plane contour with indentation to avoid a pole of $HG(s)$ at $s = 0$; (b) $F(s)$-plane contour for $HG(s) = \dfrac{K}{s(1 + s\tau_1)}$; (c) $F(s)$-plane contour for $HG(s) = \dfrac{K}{s(1 + s\tau_1)(1 + s\tau_2)}$.

account in obtaining the Nyquist plot. Let us consider the Nyquist plot for Eq. (8-27) in detail. It is sketched in Fig. 8-15b.

Section AB: $s = j\omega$ where $0 < \omega \leq \infty$

Hence $$HG(j\omega) = \frac{K}{j\omega(1 + j\omega\tau_1)} \qquad (8\text{-}28)$$

At extreme values for ω we have the following:

1. $\lim\limits_{\omega \to 0} HG(j\omega) = \infty \underline{/-90^\circ} = -K\tau_1 - j\infty$

2. $\lim\limits_{\omega \to \infty} HG(j\omega) = 0\underline{/180^\circ}$

At intermediate values of ω the phase angle varies from -90° (due to the $j\omega$ term in the denominator) to -180° (the $1 + j\omega\tau_1$ adds a maximum of an additional 90° phase lag) as ω increases from zero to infinity.

Semicircle BCD: $s = \lim_{R \to \infty} R \epsilon^{j\theta}$ where $-\pi/2 \le \theta \le \pi/2$

Here again substitution into Eq. (8-27) reveals that the large semicircle plots into point $0'$.

Section DE: $s = -j\omega$ for $0 < \omega \le \infty$

This section yields the dotted mirror image of the plot for section AB.

Semicircle EFA: $s = \lim_{R \to 0} R \epsilon^{j\theta}$ where $-\pi/2 \le \theta \le \pi/2$

Substituting this value for s into Eq. (8-27) gives the following result:

$$\lim_{R \to 0} HG(R\epsilon^{j\theta}) = \lim_{R \to 0} \frac{K}{R\epsilon^{j\theta}(1 + R\tau_1\epsilon^{j\theta})}$$

$$= \lim_{R \to 0} \frac{K}{R\epsilon^{j\theta}} = \infty \, \epsilon^{-j\theta} \qquad \text{where } -\pi/2 \le \theta \le \pi/2 \qquad (8\text{-}29)$$

Equation (8-29) is that of a semicircle of infinite radius. At point E in the s plane $\theta = -\pi/2$ so that the phase angle of Eq. (8-29) is $\pi/2$. Hence point E plots into point E'. At point F in the s plane, $\theta = 0$ so that the corresponding phase angle of Eq. (8-29) is zero and point F plots into point F'. At point A in the s plane, $\theta = \pi/2$ so that the corresponding phase angle of Eq. (8-29) is $-\pi/2$ and point A plots into point A'. This portion of the graph is drawn dashed in Fig. 8-15b. Conformal mapping can be used as an aid in obtaining contour $E'F'A'$. In proceeding round the s-plane contour from D to E to F there is a 90° clockwise change in direction at point E. This angle must be preserved in the $F(s)$-plane plot so that in proceeding from $0'$ to E' to F' there is also a 90° clockwise change in direction at point E'. This establishes the direction in which the semicircle $E'F'A'$ closes without having to evaluate $HG(s)$ at point F as was done in the previous paragraph.

The Nyquist plot of Fig. 8-15b is seen to be a closed contour which under no circumstance encloses the $(-1,0)$ point, so that we are assured that the closed-loop system is unconditionally stable.

Example 8-3. Let us now consider a type 1 system whose open-loop transfer function is given by the expression

$$HG(s) = \frac{K}{s(1 + s\tau_1)(1 + s\tau_2)} \qquad (8\text{-}30)$$

Here again $HG(s)$ has a pole at $s = 0$ so that the modified s-plane contour of Fig. 8-15a must be used. There are no poles in the right-half s plane for this contour. Breaking the Nyquist plot into sections, we proceed as follows:

Section AB: $s = j\omega$ where $0 < \omega \le \infty$

$$HG(j\omega) = \frac{K}{j\omega(1 + j\omega\tau_1)(1 + j\omega\tau_2)} \qquad (8\text{-}31)$$

At extreme values for ω we have the following:

1. $\lim_{\omega \to 0} HG(j\omega) = \infty \underline{/-90°} = -K(\tau_1 + \tau_2) - j\infty$

2. $\lim_{\omega \to \infty} HG(j\omega) = \lim_{\omega \to \infty} \frac{K}{\tau_1\tau_2(j\omega)^3} = 0 \underline{/-270°}$

At intermediate values of ω the phase angle varies from $-90°$ (owing to the $j\omega$ term in the denominator) to $-270°$ as each one of the linear factor, in the denominator of Eq. (8-31) contributes a maximum of $-90°$ to the over-all phase angle. Thus the characteristic crosses the negative real axis as shown.

Semicircle BCD: $s = \lim_{R \to \infty} R\epsilon^{j\theta}$ where $-\pi/2 \leq \theta \leq \pi/2$

Here again substitution into Eq. (8-30) reveals that the large semicircle plots into point $0'$.

Section DE: $s = -j\omega$ for $0 < \omega \leq \infty$

This section yields the dotted mirror image of the plot for section AB.

Semicircle EFA: $s = \lim_{R \to 0} R\epsilon^{j\theta}$ where $-\pi/2 \leq \theta \leq \pi/2$

Substitution of this value for s yields the result

$$\lim_{R \to 0} HG(R\epsilon^{j\theta}) = \lim_{R \to 0} \frac{K}{R\epsilon^{j\theta}} = \infty\, \epsilon^{-j\theta}$$

where $-\pi/2 \leq \theta \leq \pi/2$. Clearly this is an infinite semicircle which closes the contour from point E' to point A', as drawn dotted in Fig. 8-15c. The semicircle must close to the right since there is a 90° change in direction to the right at point E in the s plane which must be preserved at point E' in the $F(s)$ plane.

Examination of this Nyquist plot reveals that if the $(-1,0)$ point lies to the right of point Q it is encircled by the plot and the system is closed-loop unstable. On the other hand, if the $(-1,0)$ point lies to the left of point Q, it is not encircled and the closed-loop system is stable. If we start with the stable closed-loop system and increase the gain factor K, the Nyquist plot expands and the point Q moves to the left. If the gain is made sufficiently large, the $(-1,0)$ point falls to the right of point Q and the system becomes unstable. When point Q coincides with the point $(-1,0)$, we have a condition of marginal stability. The value of K required to produce marginal stability may be calculated either from the Nyquist diagram or by use of the Routh criterion. The determination of K for marginal stability is left as an exercise for the reader.

Example 8-4. *Type 2 Systems.* Determine the Nyquist stability diagram for a system with the following open-loop transfer function:

$$HG(s) = \frac{K}{s^2(1 + s\tau_1)} \tag{8-32}$$

$HG(s)$ has a second-order pole at $s = 0$ so that the s-plane contour of Fig. 8-15a must be used. When $s = j\omega$, Eq. (8-32) becomes

$$HG(j\omega) = \frac{K}{(j\omega)^2(1 + j\omega\tau_1)} \tag{8-33}$$

At extreme values of ω we have the following:

1. $\lim_{\omega \to 0} HG(j\omega) = \infty\,\underline{/-180°}$

2. $\lim_{\omega \to \infty} HG(j\omega) = \lim_{\omega \to \infty} \frac{K}{(j\omega)^3\tau_1} = 0\,\underline{/-270°}$

These points are labeled A' and $0'$ in Fig. 8-16a. At intermediate values of ω the phase angle varies continuously from -180 to $-270°$ owing to the linear term $1 + j\omega\tau_1$ in the denominator of Eq. (8-33).

For values of s round the large semicircle of Fig. 8-15a, the plot for $HG(s)$ remains at point $0'$. When $s = -j\omega$, the dotted portion $0'E'$ of Fig. 8-16a is obtained. When s assumes values along the semicircle EFA, Eq. (8-32) becomes

$$\lim_{R \to 0} HG(R\epsilon^{j\theta}) = \lim_{R \to 0} \frac{K}{(R\epsilon^{j\theta})^2} = \infty\, \epsilon^{-j2\theta} \tag{8-34}$$

where θ varies from $-\pi/2$ to $+\pi/2$. Equation (8-34) is that of an infinite circle which closes in a clockwise direction in going from point E' to A'. This curve is drawn dashed in Fig. 8-16a. The fact that this circle closes in a clockwise direction follows from the property of conformal mapping and the fact that a 90° change of direction which occurs in the s plane at point E is preserved at point E'. The total rotation in the path $E'F'A'$ is $2(180°) = 360°$ clockwise. Examination of Fig. 8-16a reveals that the $(-1,0)$ point is always encircled by the contour. Thus this system is always closed-loop unstable. The only way to stabilize this system is to reshape the $HG(s)$ locus by adding other factors. Such an example is considered next.

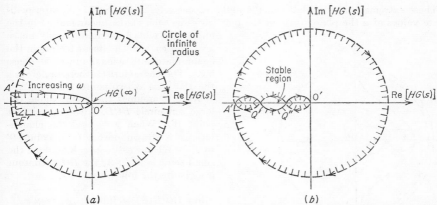

FIG. 8-16. Nyquist stability plots of some type 2 systems. (a) $F(s)$-plane contour for $HG(s) = \dfrac{K}{s^2(1 + s\tau_1)}$; (b) $F(s)$-plane plot for $HG(s) = \dfrac{K(1 + s\tau_a)(1 + s\tau_b)}{s^2(1 + s\tau_1)(1 + s\tau_2)(1 + s\tau_3)}$.

Example 8-5. Consider the loop transfer function of the previous example with linear factors added to both the numerator and the denominator. Thus $HG(s)$ is given by the equation

$$HG(s) = \frac{K(1 + s\tau_a)(1 + s\tau_b)}{s^2(1 + s\tau_1)(1 + s\tau_2)(1 + s\tau_3)} \qquad (8\text{-}35)$$

Examination of this equation indicates that at extremly low and high values of s (either when $s = j\omega$ or when s varies round the semicircles) Eq. (8-35) reduces to the same result as Example 8-4. Along the $j\omega$ axis, however, the two systems behave quite differently (see Fig. 8-16).

Examination of the plot of Fig. 8-16b reveals that the closed-loop system is stable if the $(-1,0)$ point lies within the interval $Q'Q''$. For all points within this interval there are zero net encirclements. If the $(-1,0)$ point lies elsewhere along the 180° axis, it is encircled by the plot and the system is closed-loop unstable. It should be apparent that if the system is operating closed-loop stable either increasing or decreasing the gain factor K beyond a point can cause the system to become unstable. The system is then said to be operating in a state of *conditional stability*.

Example 8-6. *Type 3 Systems.* Consider the Nyquist plot for a system whose open-loop transfer function is

$$HG(s) = \frac{K(1 + s\tau_a)(1 + s\tau_b)}{s^3(1 + s\tau_1)(1 + s\tau_2)} \qquad (8\text{-}36)$$

This function has a third-order pole at the origin so that the s-plane contour of Fig. 8-15a must be used. When $s = j\omega$, Eq. (8-36) becomes

$$HG(j\omega) = \frac{K(1 + j\omega\tau_a)(1 + j\omega\tau_b)}{(j\omega)^3(1 + j\omega\tau_1)(1 + j\omega\tau_2)} \tag{8-37}$$

At extreme values of ω we have the following:

1. $\lim\limits_{\omega \to 0} HG(j\omega) = \lim\limits_{\omega \to 0} \dfrac{K}{(j\omega)^3} = \infty \underline{/-270°}$

2. $\lim\limits_{\omega \to \infty} HG(j\omega) = \lim\limits_{\omega \to \infty} \dfrac{K(j\omega)^2\tau_a\tau_b}{(j\omega)^5\tau_1\tau_2} = 0\underline{/90°}$

These extreme points are labeled A' and $0'$, respectively, in Fig. 8-17. At intermediate values of ω the phase angle of the plot varies as each of the linear factors in the numerator adds a maximum of 90° phase lead and each of the linear factors in the denominator adds a maximum of 90° phase lag. The characteristic therefore crosses the 180° axis at two points Q' and Q''.

When s assumes the values along the large semicircle BCD, $HG(s)$ remains at point $0'$. When $s = -j\omega$, the characteristic is drawn dotted from points $0'$ to E'. When s assumes values along the small semicircle EFA, the $HG(s)$ contour is given by the following,

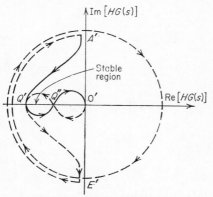

$$\lim\limits_{R \to 0} HG(R\epsilon^{j\theta}) = \lim\limits_{R \to 0} \frac{K}{(R\epsilon^{j\theta})^3} = \infty\,\epsilon^{-j3\theta} \tag{8-38}$$

Fig. 8-17. Nyquist stability plot for

$$HG(s) = \frac{K(1 + s\tau_a)(1 + s\tau_b)}{s^3(1 + s\tau_1)(1 + s\tau_2)}$$

where θ varies through 180° from $-\pi/2$ to $+\pi/2$. Thus Eq. (8-38) represents an infinite circular arc of $3(180°) = 540°$ in a clockwise direction in proceeding from point E' back to point A'. This portion of the plot is drawn dashed in Fig. 8-17. Examination of the complete plot reveals that the system is stable if the $(-1,0)$ point lies between the points $Q'Q''$. If the gain factor K were to be either increased or decreased so that the $(-1,0)$ point fell outside this region, the system would become unstable. Thus we have another example of a conditionally stable system.

Systems Which Are Open-loop Unstable. Let us now consider some examples of systems which have poles of the open-loop transfer function in the right-half s plane.

Consider that $HG(s)$ is given by the following equation:

$$HG(s) = \frac{K}{s(-1 + s\tau_1)} \tag{8-39}$$

The poles of $HG(s)$ are located at the points $s = 0$ and $s = 1/\tau_1$, the latter pole indicating that the open-loop system is unstable. The Nyquist plot for this system is drawn for the s-plane contour of Fig. 8-15a in Fig. 8-18a. The details of drawing this plot are left to the reader. Examination reveals that the $(-1,0)$ point is encircled once. Hence

$N_s = 1 = Z_r - P_r$. P_r is known to be equal to unity since the pole at $s = 1/\tau_1$ is enclosed by the s-plane contour of Fig. 8-15a. Hence it follows that $Z_r = 2$; that is, the characteristic equation for the closed-loop system has two roots in the right-half s plane. Obviously the closed-loop system is unstable. These results may be verified readily either by solving for the roots of the characteristic equation or by application of Routh's criterion. It is interesting to note that the shaded-area rule also reveals that the closed-loop system is unstable since the $(-1,0)$

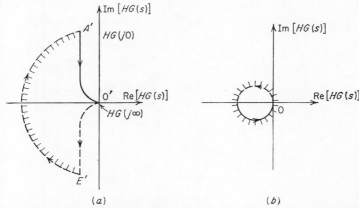

(a)   (b)

Fig. 8-18. Nyquist stability plots for systems which are open-loop unstable. (a) Nyquist stability plot for $HG(s) = \dfrac{K}{s(-1 + s\tau_1)}$; (b) Nyquist stability plot for

$$HG(s) = \frac{K}{-1 + s\tau_1}$$

point lies within the shaded area. As a matter of fact the shaded-area rule can always be used to predict the stability of a closed loop-system. To illustrate this point, let us consider another example of an open-loop transfer function which is given by the equation

$$HG(s) = \frac{K}{-1 + s\tau_1} \tag{8-40}$$

The open-loop system is unstable with a pole at $s = 1/\tau_1$. The Nyquist plot for this $HG(s)$ function is drawn in Fig. 8-18b. It is seen to be a circle which is traversed in a counterclockwise direction. If the $(-1,0)$ point is inside the circle (that is, $K > 1$), it is encircled -1 times so that $N = -1$. Applying the formula $N = Z_r - P_r$ indicates that $Z_r = 0$ and the system is closed-loop stable. Thus, if the gain K is greater than unity, we have the case of an unstable open-loop system which becomes stable when the loop is closed. If the $(-1,0)$ point lies outside the circle (that is, $K < 1$), then $N = 0$ and $Z_r = 1$, so that the closed-loop system remains unstable. If we examine Fig. 8-18 from the point of view of the shaded-area rule, it bears out the previous statement that a system is closed-loop stable if the $(-1,0)$ point lies within an unshaded area.

8-4. Alternate s-plane Paths

The Nyquist plotting theorem can be used with other types of s-plane contours than those of Figs. 8-11 and 8-15a. Two such contours are shown in Fig. 8-19.

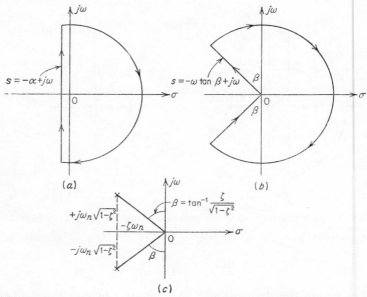

FIG. 8-19. Alternate s-plane contours for Nyquist plot. (a) Constant α contour; (b) constant-damping-ratio (ζ) contour; (c) location of a pair of complex conjugate roots on the s plane.

The first of these consists of a line parallel to the $j\omega$ axis and an infinite semicircle enclosing the entire right-half s plane and that part of the left-half s plane between the vertical line and the $j\omega$ axis. For the straight-line portion $s = -\alpha + j\omega$, where α is a constant and ω varies from $-\infty$ to $+\infty$. Assume that $HG(s)$ is plotted for this path and that the resulting plot does not encircle the $(-1,0)$ point. If $HG(s)$ does not have any poles enclosed by this s-plane contour, it follows that the characteristic equation for the closed-loop system does not have any zeros enclosed by the contour. Thus all the roots of the characteristic equation for the closed-loop system lie to the left of the vertical line. The reader should now recall that the roots of the characteristic equation decay with a time constant equal to the reciprocal of the negative real part of the roots. Since the real parts in this case lie to the left of the vertical line, it follows that all time constants are less than $1/\alpha$; that is, all the terms of the source-free response decay faster than $\epsilon^{-\alpha t}$. Thus this type of s-plane contour is useful for determining if a system has a settling time less than a specified amount. Unfortunately the plot does not provide any information about the damping ratio for the system, and it is possible that the system may have a very large transient overshoot even though its settling time is satisfactory.

An s-plane path which provides information about the damping ratio is drawn in Fig. 8-19b. The radial lines are given by a constant angle β. Along the radial lines s is given by the following formula,

$$s = -\omega \tan \beta \pm j\omega \qquad (8\text{-}41)$$

where β is a constant and ω varies from 0 to ∞. If this s-plane contour encloses no poles of $HG(s)$ and if the resulting plot in the $HG(s)$ plane does not encircle the $(-1,0)$ point, it follows that the characteristic equation for the closed-loop system does not have any roots within the specified s-plane contour. The significance of this result becomes obvious when one recognizes that all roots of the characteristic equation which have the same damping ratio lie on radial lines. Consider a pair of complex conjugate roots located at $s = -\zeta\omega_n \pm j\omega_n \sqrt{1 - \zeta^2}$ (see Fig. 8-19c). The angle β which the radial line from the origin to these roots makes with the $j\omega$ axis is given by the equation

$$\beta = \tan^{-1} \frac{\zeta}{\sqrt{1 - \zeta^2}} \qquad (8\text{-}42)$$

Thus, if β is constant, we have the locus of all roots which have the same damping ratio ζ. As β gets smaller, the corresponding value for ζ gets smaller. To return to the s-plane locus of Fig. 8-19b, it follows that, if there are no roots enclosed by this s-plane contour, then the roots of the characteristic equation must have a damping ratio greater than the value given by Eq. (8-42) for the assumed value of β in the s-plane contour. Unfortunately this path does not provide any information about settling time, so that it is possible for a system to have a satisfactory damping ratio and still have an exceptionally long settling time. This is the case for roots of the characteristic equation which lie close to the origin but outside the contour of Fig. 8-19b. Thus by use of both the foregoing s-plane contours it is possible to investigate the maximum time constant and minimum damping ratio of roots of the characteristic equation of a closed-loop system in terms of the open-loop transfer function.

SUGGESTED READING

Bowers, J. L., and P. M. Schultheiss: "Introduction to the Design of Servomechanisms," chaps. 4 and 5, John Wiley & Sons, Inc., New York, 1952.

Brown, G. S., and D. P. Campbell: "Principles of Servomechanisms," chap. 6, art. 8, John Wiley & Sons, Inc., New York, 1948.

Chestnut, H., and R. Mayer: "Servomechanisms and Regulating System Design," 2d ed., vol. 1, John Wiley & Sons, Inc., New York, 1960.

James, H. M., N. B. Nichols, and R. S. Phillips: "Theory of Servomechanisms,"
Massachusetts Institute of Technology Radiation Laboratories Series, vol. 25,
chap. 2, McGraw-Hill Book Company, Inc., New York, 1947.

PROBLEMS

8-1. Check the following characteristic equations for right-half-plane roots, using
the Routh criterion:

(a) $5s^3 + 2s^2 + 12s + 6 = 0$ (b) $4s^3 + 3s^2 + 2s + 5 = 0$
(c) $s^5 + 6s^4 + 3s^3 + 2s^2 + s + 1 = 0$

8-2. Prove Eq. (8-9) for the stability conditions for a fourth-order system.

8-3. Sketch Nyquist and Bode plots for the following transfer functions and determine whether or not they represent stable systems:

(a) $HG(j\omega) = \dfrac{200}{j\omega(j\omega + 5)}$ (b) $HG(j\omega) = \dfrac{200}{j\omega(j\omega + 5)(j\omega + 10)}$

(c) $HG(j\omega) = \dfrac{200}{(j\omega)^2(j\omega + 5)}$ (d) $HG(j\omega) = \dfrac{10(j\omega + 1)}{(j\omega)^2}$

8-4. The open-loop transfer function of a feedback control system is $(1 + 4s)/
s^2(1 + s)(1 + 2s)$.

(a) Using the Nyquist criterion, determine whether the closed-loop system is
stable or unstable.

(b) Does the polar plot of the open-loop transfer function cross the real axis? If
so, find the frequency at which the cross occurs.   If not, explain why not.

8-5. The open-loop transfer function for the control system of Fig. P8-5a has the
asymptotic log-modulus and phase-shift characteristic drawn in Fig. P8-5b.

(a) Determine the Nyquist stability plot for this system.

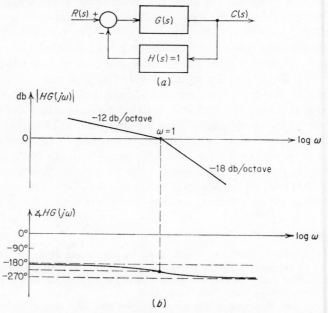

Fig. P8-5. (a) System; (b) log-modulus and phase-shift characteristic.

(b) Is this system always stable, always unstable, or conditionally stable?

(c) Write the characteristic equation for the closed-loop system.

(d) Repeat the previous parts when $H(s) = 10$.

(e) Repeat the previous parts when $H(s) = 1 + 4s$.

8-6. Write the simplest $HG(s)$ function which can have the Nyquist plots drawn in Fig. P8-6a and b.

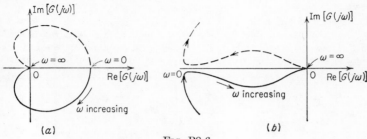

FIG. P8-6

8-7. Given the control system drawn in Fig. P8-7:

(a) Investigate the stability of the inner closed-loop system by itself. Show that if $\tau_0 > \tau_m$ the Nyquist plot for the inner loop intersects the negative real axis at the frequency $\omega_0 \approx \dfrac{1}{\sqrt{3}} \dfrac{1}{\tau_0}$ and that the inner loop is unstable if $\frac{1}{8}K_1K_2 > 1$.

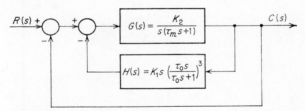

FIG. P8-7

(b) Sketch the Nyquist plot for the complete closed-loop system. Indicate the section (s) of the negative real axis where the $(-1,0)$ point can lie for the over-all system to be stable even though the inner loop system is unstable by itself.

8-8. Examine the stability of the open-loop transfer functions of Examples 8-3 to 8-5, assuming the s-plane contour of Fig. P8-8, where the singularity at the origin is encircled by the s-plane contour.

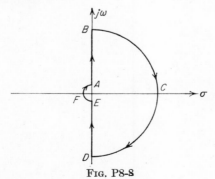

FIG. P8-8

8-9. Draw the Nyquist plots for the following open-loop transfer functions, which involve a time delay in the direct transmission path as indicated by the exponential term. Comment upon the closed-loop stability of these systems, using the shaded-area rule.

(a) $HG(s) = \dfrac{\epsilon^{-2s}}{s + 5}$ (b) $HG(s) = \dfrac{\epsilon^{-2s}}{s(s + 5)}$

(c) The system of Fig. 8-1a

8-10. A system has an open-loop transfer function described by $HG(s) = 25/(s^2 + 25)$. Draw the Nyquist diagram. Indicate the assumed contour in the s plane and label the sections in the $HG(j\omega)$ plane with the corresponding sections in the s plane.

9 | System Design. Frequency-domain Approach

In control systems engineering it is frequently necessary to introduce compensation networks, not only to provide absolute stability, but more importantly to meet specifications on the steady-state and transient performance. Usually the characteristics of the controlled systems are established in terms of providing the desired output quantity as well as the output velocity[1] and acceleration when such requirements are called for. At the outset the control systems engineer often starts out with a fixed configuration over whose transfer function he has little or no control. For example, in a given situation it may well be that to provide the required output torque, velocity, and acceleration an amplidyne driving a d-c motor is needed. In such a case the characteristics of the controlled system are represented by means of the transfer function of the fixed elements, which for this example takes the form[2]

$$G_f(s) = \frac{K}{s(1 + s\tau_c)(1 + s\tau_q)(1 + s\tau_m')} \tag{9-1}$$

Generally, if a feedback path is put round such a system, not only is it likely that the specifications on the transient-response and steady-state behavior will not be met but there is a strong possibility that the system will be absolutely unstable. Clearly, then, there is a need for inserting appropriate compensation networks which permit satisfying the specifications as well as providing an absolutely stable system. Figure 9-1 illustrates the single-loop feedback control system with the fixed elements separated from the compensation elements. The primary objective of this chapter is to describe a procedure for designing the networks

---

[1] Throughout this chapter output velocity is to be interpreted as meaning the first derivative of the output controlled variable, whether it be displacement, temperature, pressure, etc.

[2] See p. 214.

341

which cause the system to behave in the specified manner. The design method is carried out entirely in the frequency domain, and throughout the emphasis is placed on electrical compensation networks, with particular attention focused on the lag, lead, and lag-lead networks treated in Chap. 6. In the case of all-pneumatic control systems analogous compensation schemes can be derived. The techniques of design are the same. Placing emphasis on just these three standard compensation networks offers the decided advantage of dealing with realizable RC circuits.

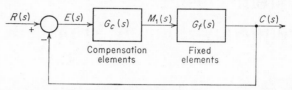

FIG. 9-1. A feedback control system with series compensation.

Other procedures than those dealt with in this chapter are possible, but often realization of the resulting compensation transfer functions requires a more extensive background than is assumed here.

9-1. Design Considerations

We are already aware of the existence of a correlation between the steady-state frequency response of a system and its corresponding time response. This is treated at length in Sec. 5-1 for the second-order system. Because of the complexity of the mathematical description, this correlation is made by using graphs, so that only an approximate correlation is possible. As previously pointed out, this is a limitation of the frequency-domain approach; it sacrifices an exact description of the time-domain performance for ease of analysis and design. Accordingly, in dealing with the problem of stabilizing and compensating control systems by using the frequency-domain technique, control over the time-domain behavior is most conveniently secured in terms of appropriate figures of merit such as phase margin and gain margin, which although defined in the frequency domain are used as indications of the performance in the time domain. For the second-order system the relationship between a time-domain figure of merit, viz., damping ratio (which is a measure of the maximum overshoot), and a frequency-domain figure of merit, viz., phase margin, is relatively simple and appears in Fig. 7-21. However, for higher-order systems the relationship is more complicated and usually requires a whole series of design charts[1] in order to cover most of the systems as well as to provide a satisfactory correlation. For

[1] See H. Chestnut and R. Mayer, "Servomechanisms and Regulating System Design," 2d ed., vol. 1, chap. 15, John Wiley & Sons, Inc., New York, 1960.

our purposes control of the transient response of control systems is achieved in terms of the phase margin, with Fig. 7-21 as a guide, as well as in terms of bandwidth. This policy is followed even for systems higher than second-order and is justifiable for two reasons. (1) Most higher-order systems behave as second-order systems because of the predominance of a pair of complex conjugate roots in the solution of the characteristic equation. (2) Since the practical correlation between frequency response and time-response behavior is approximate at best, the design must necessarily be approximate. Therefore, the object is to design a system which when put together is found to work fairly well in spite of the fact that the specifications are not exactly met. This latter aspect of the problem can then readily be resolved by fine adjustments in amplifier gains and circuit parameters once a workable system is attained. This is certainly a reasonable approach, especially in view of the fact that even if an exact, practical correlation were available final adjustments are still needed because of the influence of the inherent system nonlinearities.

As a result of working in the pure frequency domain, the procedures outlined in this chapter necessarily involve *design by analysis*. Basically this stems from the lack of having direct control over the roots of the characteristic equation. Design of compensation by analysis constitutes an indirect approach to the problem of providing the control system with satisfactory dynamic behavior. It is indirect because it first requires estimating the compensation transfer function which will provide the required phase margin and then analyzing the modified system to check whether or not it does. If it fails to do so, a modified transfer function is designed and the analysis repeated. Usually no more than two or three attempts are necessary before arriving at a compensation transfer function which yields the specified phase margin, and the amount of calculation needed is relatively little provided that the design is carried out on the db vs. log ω plots (Bode diagrams). In fact the use of such representations of the open-loop transfer function and of the corrective networks makes it almost obvious as to what time constants are needed for these circuits to furnish the required compensation.

Design by analysis stands in sharp contrast to design by synthesis. In the former the designer is concerned with modifying the open-loop transfer function $G_c(s)G_f(s)$ until he finally reaches a point where the system behaves in the manner desired with the loop closed. However, in design by synthesis the designer specifies the form of the closed-loop transfer function directly from the specifications. Then he works his way inward toward a corresponding, suitable open-loop transfer function and finally the appropriate compensation network.

In addition to the advantages of simplicity and ease of analysis (because it uses mathematics that are familiar to most engineers), the frequency-domain design technique offers several others worth noting. One important point is the fact that this method places the figures of merit identifying the steady-state performance clearly in evidence in the Bode plots. Thus, for the type 1 system the value of velocity constant is merely the value of the frequency corresponding to the intersection of the initial -6 db/octave slope line with the 0-db coordinate axis (see Fig. 7-24b). A similar scheme prevails for identifying the acceleration constant (refer to Fig. 7-25). Another feature of the frequency-response method is that it provides a very good indication of system bandwidth, which often appears explicitly in the specifications and can only be approximated with some of the other methods of design. Still another feature lies in the fact that the influence of lead and lag networks on system bandwidth is made clearly evident. This together with the explicit identification of K_v and K_a makes the design of suitable compensation networks a relatively simple matter.

9-2. How Compensation is Achieved through Use of Standard Lead and Lag Networks

The success or failure of a compensation network in providing a feedback control system with suitable phase margin depends upon the selection of appropriate time constants for the circuit. Unfortunately, not too much leeway is permissible. If the time constants are chosen too large or too small, the desired phase margin will not be achieved. There is only a restricted portion of the frequency spectrum over which the lag and lead networks are effective in establishing the relative stability called for in the specifications. A clear demonstration of this point is revealed from a study of the db vs. log ω plots of the standard lag and lead networks (refer to Fig. 9-2a and b). The function of the lead network is primarily to provide sufficient phase-lead angle to offset the phase-lag angular contributions associated with the fixed system elements. Figure 9-2a shows that the portion of the frequency spectrum over which this is possible is restricted to the region lying between the two breakpoint frequencies. Below the first breakpoint frequency the lead network behaves merely as an attenuator with very little angular phase-lead contribution. On the other hand beyond the second breakpoint frequency the circuit manifests neither attenuation nor phase shift and so exhibits negligible effect. Note that the region in which phase-lead angular contributions are realized is also the region in which the log modulus is changing slope. In fact these statements are nothing more than a recognition of Bode's[1] two important network theorems for linear systems. A glance at Fig. 9-2b reveals a similar situation existing

[1] H. W. Bode, "Network Analysis and Feedback Amplifier Design," D. Van Nostrand Company, Inc., Princeton, N.J., 1945.

for the lag network, except, of course, that the effects at the high- and low-frequency ends are reversed.

A comparison of these characteristics of the lead and lag network should make it clear that the manner of achieving the desired compensation cannot be the same for both methods. For example, if a control system exhibits poor dynamic behavior owing to the excessive lag angles of the fixed elements, then certainly using the lag network in the region

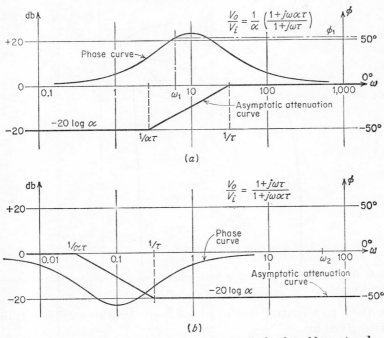

FIG. 9-2. (a) Bode plot of lead network; (b) Bode plot of lag network.

lying between the two breakpoint frequencies (as is done with the lead network) can serve only to aggravate the situation because, as Fig. 9-2b illustrates, it introduces still more lag and not enough attenuation. As is demonstrated presently, it is not this region of the lag network which is useful, but rather that portion, lying much beyond the second breakpoint, which is characterized by attenuation and practically no phase lag. It is important to appreciate that this attenuation feature of the lag network is effective only in the dynamic state, which is when it is needed. In the steady state, i.e., when $\omega \to 0$ (or $s \to 0$; see final-value theorem in Chap. 3) there is no attenuation introduced by the lag network so that such quantities as the velocity constant or acceleration constant remain intact. In summary, therefore, it can be said that *the lead network achieves the desired compensation by virtue of its phase-lead characteristic, whereas the lag network accomplishes it by virtue of its attenuation property.* Of course, it follows, too, that, if the lag network parameters are chosen so that this attenuation does not occur in the vicinity of the $-1 + j0$ point of the polar plot of $G_f(s)$, it will fail to provide the required compensation.

To understand better the way in which the lag and lead networks are capable of providing compensation in the manner already outlined, let us

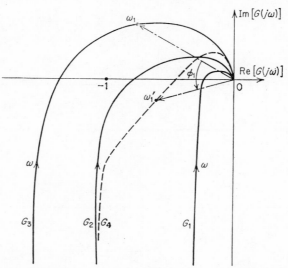

Fig. 9-3. Illustrating the effect of a lead network on a gain-compensated open-loop transfer function.

apply them to a control system whose fixed elements exhibit a transfer function given by

$$G_f(j\omega) = \frac{K_f}{j\omega(1 + j\omega\tau_1)(1 + j\omega\tau_2)} \qquad (9\text{-}2)$$

where K_f denotes the gain factor associated with the fixed elements. A clearer picture of how this transfer function is influenced by the insertion of compensation networks is possible by using the polar-plot representations of the transfer function. This has the advantage of placing in view the entire frequency spectrum, going from very low values of frequency to infinite frequency on any standard-sized sheet of paper. A little thought points out that a db vs. log ω representation could show only four or five cycles on the same size of sheet. In other words, the polar plot gives a macroscopic view which is ideal for the generalities to be demonstrated here. Of course, when it comes to the matter of design, the microscopic view is the desirable one, and Bode plots on three-cycle paper are used for this purpose.

Compensation by Using a Lead Network.   Type 1 System.   The object here is to demonstrate the ideas involved in selecting a lead network such that it provides the specified steady-state performance as well as suitable dynamic behavior.   The latter is identified in terms of an appropriate

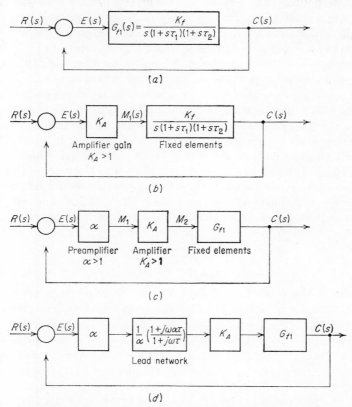

FIG. 9-4. Lead-network compensation.   (a) Uncompensated system G_1; (b) gain-compensated system to meet steady-state performance G_2; (c) unstable system G_3; (d) final, compensated system which meets specifications G_4.

phase margin and a predominant time constant.   Assume that the controlled system is represented by Eq. (9-2) and that its polar plot appears as G_1 in Figs. 9-3 and 9-4. G_1 is intentionally drawn so that it exhibits two undesirable characteristics.   (1) It is sluggish in responding to command signals.   This is deduced from the fact that it has a very large phase margin.   It can also be deduced from the fact that the maximum M circle associated with the G_1 plot is clearly less than unity.   (2) It has a small velocity constant.   This conclusion is consistent with the fact that the G_1 plot for low frequencies is close to the $j\omega$ axis.

To meet the specification on the velocity constant, assume that a gain of $K_A K_f$ is necessary, where $K_A > 1$ by the required amount. The modified open-loop transfer function now becomes $G_2(j\omega)$ and appears in Figs. 9-3 and 9-4b. As is frequently the case, the gain value which satisfies the steady-state requirement usually does not yield a satisfactory transient response. The plot of G_2 in Fig. 9-3 reflects this situation by manifesting a small phase margin, thereby implying excessive overshoots and high oscillations. For reasons which are described below, assume that the open-loop gain is further increased by a factor of $\alpha(>1)$ beyond the value required to meet the specification on the velocity constant. Accordingly, the system takes on the configuration shown in Fig. 9-4c, and the corresponding polar plot is represented by curve G_3 in Fig. 9-3. Note that this system is absolutely unstable because there is an enclosure of the $-1 + j0$ point. The reason for increasing the gain by the additional factor α becomes apparent when a lead network is inserted in the direct transmission path of system $G_3(j\omega)$ to yield $G_4(j\omega)$, which is shown in Fig. 9-4d. Now, if the time constant as well as the attenuation factor $1/\alpha$ of the lead network is properly selected, then it should be possible to meet the specifications on both the value of the velocity constant and the dynamic performance. To demonstrate how the lead network permits this, consider the expression for $G_4(j\omega)$. Thus,

$$G_4(j\omega) = K_A \alpha \left(\frac{1}{\alpha} \frac{1 + j\omega\alpha\tau}{1 + j\omega\tau} \right) \frac{K_f}{j\omega(1 + j\omega\tau_1)(1 + j\omega\tau_2)} \tag{9-3}$$

The shape of the polar plot of G_4 is readily determined in terms of the previous plots by investigating first the form which $G_4(j\omega)$ takes under conditions where the frequency of the actuating signal ω is very high, and then when it is very low, and finally when it is intermediate. Of course the terms "very high" and "very low" are relative and must be reckoned in terms of the breakpoint frequencies of the selected lead network.

When the frequency is high, the transfer function of the lead network reduces to unity so that Eq. (9-3) becomes

$$G_4(j\omega) \Big|_{\omega \text{ large}} = K_A \alpha \frac{K_f}{j\omega(1 + j\omega\tau_1)(1 + j\omega\tau_2)} \tag{9-4}$$

Comparison with $G_3(j\omega)$ shows that the two are practically identical so that the polar plots at high frequency are almost coincident. In the low end of the frequency spectrum Eq. (9-3) reduces to

$$G_4(j\omega) \Big|_{\omega \text{ small}} = K_A \frac{K_f}{j\omega(1 + j\omega\tau_1)(1 + j\omega\tau_2)} \tag{9-5}$$

which is recognized as being equivalent to $G_2(j\omega)$. Hence the polar plot of $G_4(j\omega)$ for low frequencies must virtually coincide with the polar plot of $G_2(j\omega)$. Note that in this portion of the frequency spectrum the lead network behaves merely as an attenuator of value $1/\alpha$. This now makes clear the reason for introducing the additional gain factor α in $G_3(j\omega)$. It eliminates the attenuation associated with the lead network. If this were not done, the required velocity constant could not be realized.

The behavior of $G_4(j\omega)$ in the intermediate portion of the frequency spectrum is best illustrated by considering how a radius vector to a point on G_3 is modified by the presence of the lead network in G_4. Assume that ω_1 is a frequency which falls somewhere between the two breakpoint frequencies as depicted in Fig. 9-2a. Since the lead network appears in tandem with G_3, the radius vector $0\omega_1$ is modified both in magnitude and phase. As indicated in Fig. 9-2a, at the frequency ω_1 the lead network introduces a lead angle of ϕ_1 and some degree of attenuation. This has the total effect of relocating the open-loop radius vector from position $0\omega_1$ to a much more favorable position $0\omega_1'$. By repeating this procedure for a sufficient number of points the polar plot G_4 appearing in Fig. 9-3 is obtained. The net result is an increased phase margin with the gain adjusted to give the desired velocity constant. Thus the presence of the lead network enables both specifications to be met. A little reflection recalls to mind the great similarity this bears to the method of improving the steady-state and transient performance by using error-rate and output-rate damping, discussed in Chap. 4. Actually, these procedures are the same. The difference is that in Chap. 4 the design was carried out in terms of time-domain considerations, whereas here it is carried out in terms of the corresponding frequency-domain counterparts. This is immediately apparent upon recalling that a phase-lead characteristic in the frequency domain derives from an equation containing derivatives in the time domain. Note that either approach leads to the same result, viz., that the introduction of rate control (lead network) permits increasing the open-loop gain without adversely affecting the transient behavior.

In some situations it could very well happen that the fixed elements of a control system lead directly to a polar plot similar to G_3 in Fig. 9-3. The insertion of a lead network in such a case is sometimes described as not only performing compensation but providing stabilization as well. Therefore these circuits are sometimes referred to as stabilization networks.

Compensation by Using a Lag Network. Type 1 System. In order to provide a basis of comparison, the controlled system of Eq. (9-2) is again considered. For convenience the polar plot is repeated in Fig. 9-5 and is denoted by G_1. As is the case with lead compensation, the first step is to adjust the gain to meet the steady-state performance specification, which in our example means providing the required velocity constant. To do this involves increasing the gain by the factor K_A and thus producing a modified system which, so far, is the same as $G_2(j\omega)$ in Fig. 9-4b. This polar plot is also reproduced in Fig. 9-5. Introducing a lag network changes the configuration of Fig. 9-4b to that shown in Fig. 9-6. The expression for the loop transfer function of this compensated system is therefore,

$$G_5(j\omega) = K_A \frac{1 + j\omega\tau}{1 + j\omega\alpha\tau} \frac{K_f}{j\omega(1 + j\omega\tau_1)(1 + j\omega\tau_2)} \qquad (9\text{-}6)$$

It has already been pointed out that lag-network compensation results from the attenuation ability of the network in the high-frequency portion

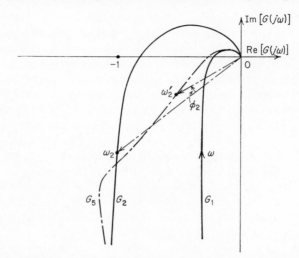

FIG. 9-5. Illustrating the effect of lag compensation on an open-loop transfer function G_5.

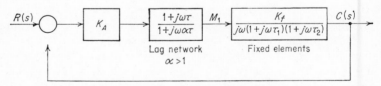

FIG. 9-6. Lag-network compensation.

of the spectrum. The fact that the G_2 plot in Fig. 9-5 passes so close to the $-1 + j0$ point is the reason why the transient behavior is unsatisfactory. If the lag network is to be effective in improving this situation, it must do so by relocating that portion of the polar plot which lies in the vicinity of the $-1 + j0$ point away from it toward the right. Such action has the effect of increasing the phase margin, which in turn means satisfactory dynamic performance. A little thought indicates that the lag network can readily accomplish this function provided that the attenuation characteristic of the network unmistakably predominates in that portion of the frequency spectrum beginning with ω_2 (see also Fig 9-2b) and continuing on to very large values.

Let us first establish the nature of the polar plot of $G_5(j\omega)$ at both the very low and very high end of the frequency spectrum. For very low sinusoidal frequency variation of the actuating signal Eq. (9-6) becomes

$$G_5(j\omega)\bigg|_{\omega \text{ small}} = \frac{K_A K_f}{j\omega(1 + j\omega\tau_1)(1 + j\omega\tau_2)} \tag{9-7}$$

Here "very low" is interpreted in terms of the first breakpoint frequency of the lag network. Thus, when ω is low compared with $1/\alpha\tau$ in Eq. (9-6), the transfer function of the lag network is unity for all practical purposes so that the polar plot of G_5 essentially coincides with that of G_2. It is interesting to note that, unlike the situation with the lead network, there is no additional increase in gain required to preserve the original adjustment because of the nonattenuating property of the lag network at steady state. For those frequencies which are large compared with the upper breakpoint frequency of the lag network, viz., $\omega \gg 1/\tau$, Eq. (9-6) reduces to

$$G_5(j\omega)\bigg|_{\omega \text{ large}} = \frac{K_A}{\alpha}\frac{K_f}{j\omega(1 + j\omega\tau_1)(1 + j\omega\tau_2)} \tag{9-8}$$

Thus, if K_A and α are of the same order of magnitude, the polar plot of G_5 coincides with that of G_1 at the high-frequency end.

Finally, in the frequency spectrum lying between the "low" and "high" ends, the polar plot of G_5 must make the transition from G_2 to G_1. The manner of making this transition is best illustrated by taking a typical point on G_2, such as ω_2. The lag network operates on this radius vector in two ways, viz., magnitude and phase. For a properly designed lag network the frequency ω_2 is located sufficiently far above the upper breakpoint frequency, as illustrated in Fig. 9-2b. Accordingly, the radius vector $0\omega_2$ is modified to one which is much smaller, viz., $0\omega_2'$, and which is slightly more lagging than $0\omega_2$ by the amount ϕ_2. Clearly the phase characteristic is of no consequence here; it is the attenuation characteristic which is responsible for providing the modified system with ample phase margin. The angular phase-lag contribution of the network manifests itself only in the very-low-frequency end of the spectrum, where it is usually unable adversely to influence the dynamic behavior. The kink that appears in the low-frequency part of the G_5 plot in Fig. 9-5 is attributable to the phase-lag angles. Note, however, how far removed it is from the $-1 + j0$ point.

Reduction of Steady-state Error by Using a Lag Network. Type 0 System. Consider next a type 0 system having fixed elements, the combined function of which is

$$G_f(j\omega) = \frac{K_p}{(1 + j\omega\tau_1)(1 + j\omega\tau_2)} = G_1(j\omega) \tag{9-9}$$

Assume that with the loop closed round this system, as illustrated in Fig.

9-7a, a satisfactory transient performance results but the steady-state error is too large. In this case the acceptable transient behavior is conveyed in Fig. 9-8 by noting that $G_1(j\omega)$ is tangent to the $M = 1.4$ circle. The problem confronting the designer is to reduce the steady-state error by increasing the position constant while essentially preserving the transient response. As is customary, the first step of the solution is to increase the gain by the required amount. The system then takes the

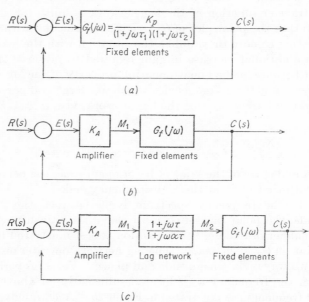

FIG. 9-7. (a) A system containing only fixed elements G_1; (b) a system modified to meet steady-state specification G_2; (c) a system modified to meet specifications on steady-state and transient performance G_3.

form shown in Fig. 9-7b and has a polar plot identified as $G_2(j\omega)$ in Fig. 9-8. Again note that satisfying the specification on the gain upsets the transient performance as revealed by the fact that the $G_2(j\omega)$ plot is tangent to the $M = 2$ circle. Hence the system of Fig. 9-7b is unsatisfactory because it exhibits excessive overshoots during the transient state. A little thought makes it apparent that what is needed is a device which attenuates in the high-frequency portion of the spectrum (i.e., in the vicinity about the M circles) and which introduces no attenuation at the low-frequency end of the spectrum. The lag network is just such a device. It provides the simplest solution to the problem of compensation. The final system configuration which meets all the specifications is shown in Fig. 9-7c, and the corresponding polar plot appears as $G_3(j\omega)$ in Fig. 9-8.

In several places in the preceding chapters it is pointed out that introduction of integration in the direct transmission path leads to a reduction of errors in the steady state. In fact in the case where pure integration is inserted by using an active element such as a servomotor, steady-state errors can even be entirely eliminated. The use of a lag network, which is a passive device, cannot accomplish this, but as illustrated in the foregoing discussion it can be effectively used to bring about a considerable reduction in the error. This limited ability of the lag network is entirely consistent with the fact that it is really an "impure integrator," as an inspection of its transfer function reveals.

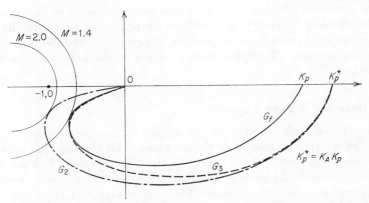

FIG. 9-8. Increasing the position constant with phase-lag compensation.

Comparison. In those situations involving the use of type 1 and type 0 systems, appropriate compensation for the purpose of meeting the specifications can usually be realized with either a lag or a lead network. Since each accomplishes essentially the same result but in a somewhat different manner, it is worthwhile to summarize these distinctions.

1. The lead network achieves compensation through the merits of its phase-lead angular contributions, whereas the lag network does it through the merits of its attenuation property, which prevails in the high-frequency portion of its spectrum.

2. To meet stringent steady-state performance specifications, either compensation method requires an increase in gain. However, because of the attenuation introduced by the lead network at steady state, it requires a greater increase in gain than is called for by the lag network. Sometimes this additional gain must come from a preamplifier, which means an increase in the number of components needed for the control system. Where space and weight are of prime importance, as is frequently the case with aircraft applications, this could be a definite drawback.

3. The bandwidth for a system using lead compensation is always greater than that for a system using lag compensation. From the viewpoint of reducing the settling time a large bandwidth is desirable. However, this advantage must be weighed against susceptibility to noise. The greater the bandwidth, the easier it is for the system to respond to spurious high-frequency noise disturbances. In fact, if the control system is to be used in an environment beset with intolerable vibrations occurring at frequencies within the bandwidth of the uncompensated control system, there is no choice but to use lag compensation.

4. The use of lag compensation in some applications may lead to time constants which are so large as to be impractical to realize. This undesirable aspect of the lag network stems from the need to introduce the first breakpoint frequency at a sufficiently low value to assure the effectiveness of the attenuation property of the circuit in the frequency range where it is needed. In such instances lead or lag-lead compensation must be used.

9-3. Design of a Type 2 System

Attention is now directed to the design of a type 2 system starting from just a paper statement of the problem. All the material appearing in the book up to this point serves as the background. Our concern is not only to select the basic make-up of the system but also to design the appropriate compensation should this be necessary. A type 2 system is considered first because the type of compensation needed is clear-cut.

Statement of the Problem. It is desired to design a feedback control system for a reproducing contour cutting tool (see Fig. 7-15) which is capable of following a constant velocity command signal in the steady state without the presence of a lag error. Moreover, in order to keep the position errors during the dynamic state within reasonable limits, an acceleration constant of at least 10 is deemed necessary.

The transient performance is to be consistent with a phase margin of $45° \pm 3°$, which is selected to keep the maximum overshoot in the vicinity of 25 per cent. Furthermore, the predominant time constant describing the time-domain response is to be better than 1 sec.

The statement of the problem is nothing more than a listing of the specifications which the final configuration of the control system must satisfy to be satisfactory in the application for which it is intended. Also, as previously explained, because of the lack of simple and exact correlation criteria between the time- and frequency-domain behavior, meeting the specifications is tested in terms of appropriate figures of merit of the frequency response characteristics.

Basic System Components. A study of that portion of the specifications dealing with the steady-state performance usually makes clear the type of control system required.   In this case it must be a type 2 system, which means that the basic composition of the system must include two pure integrations.   Since the controlled variable is position, it follows that two servomotors together with their driving amplifiers are needed. The function of the first servomotor is to apply the appropriate input signal to the amplifying source supplying the second servomotor.   Often this merely involves positioning the slider arm of a potentiometer or a variac.   The second servomotor, of course, drives the load, which in this case is the cutting tool.   This first stage in the development of the control system is shown in Fig. 9-9 in block form.

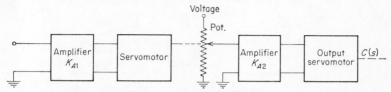

FIG. 9-9. The first stage in the development of a type 2 system.

The factors controlling the size of the servomotors depend upon the particular application.   The selection of the output actuator depends on the magnitude of the load torque as well as the maximum velocity and acceleration desired.   Use of a hydraulic motor is not uncommon in such applications.   The supplying amplifier is then frequently an electrohydraulic type.   Another possibility, of course, is to use an amplidyne–d-c motor combination, as discussed in Chap. 6.   However, when the output power requirements are not excessive, it is sufficient to use a two-phase a-c servomotor along with the proper electronic amplifier. In such a case the transfer function of the amplifier–output servomotor combination is merely

$$G_{M2}(j\omega) = \frac{K_{A2}K_{M2}}{j\omega(1 + j\omega\tau_2)} \tag{9-10}$$

where K_{A2} denotes the amplifier gain and K_{M2} is the motor gain constant. Because this transfer function is simpler in form than that of the amplidyne-motor or hydraulic amplifier–motor combinations, the solution is continued under the assumption that the electronic amplifier–two-phase servomotor unit adequately provides the required output performance. As for the first servomotor, it needs to be selected only large enough to furnish the torque required to position the slider arm of the potentiometer. Since there is no doubt about the low power level involved here, this combination can certainly be an electronic amplifier–two-phase servomotor combination with the transfer function

$$G_{M1}(j\omega) = \frac{K_{A1}K_{M1}}{j\omega(1 + j\omega\tau_1)} \tag{9-11}$$

where K_{A1} = amplifier gain constant

K_{M1} = motor gain constant

At this point it is helpful to note that, because of the small size of the first servomotor and its connected load, the time constant τ_1 will be very small and in fact may be entirely neglected when compared with τ_2, which is

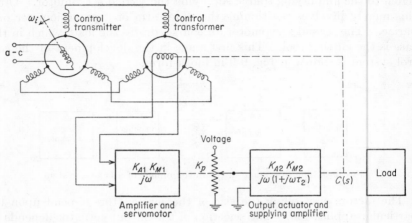

Fig. 9-10. Illustrating the second stage in the design of a type 2 system.

many times larger because of the nature of the load. Accordingly, Eq. (9-11) may be simplified to

$$G_{M1}(j\omega) = \frac{K_{A1}K_{M1}}{j\omega} \quad (9\text{-}12)$$

The combined transfer function of the first stage of the system as it appears in Fig. 9-9 is therefore

$$G_{M1}K_pG_{M2} = \frac{K_{A1}K_{M1}K_pK_{A2}K_{M2}}{(j\omega)^2(1 + j\omega\tau_2)} \quad (9\text{-}13)$$

where K_p denotes the potentiometer transducer constant expressed in volts/radian.

The second stage in the development of the control system involves the selection of a suitable error detector. The command signal which supplies the velocity input is assumed to originate from a reference motor. Hence the form of the command is mechanical, and this mechanical output may be used to drive a potentiometer, which is then paired with a similar potentiometer in the feedback path, or a synchro transmitter, which is paired with a control transformer in the feedback path. For reasons which are pointed out in Sec. 4-2 the synchro error detector is preferred. Consequently, the system now takes on the appearance illustrated in Fig. 9-10 and represents the basic composition of the feedback control system. Denoting the transducer constant as K_s, expressed in units of volts/radian, the open-loop transfer function of this system uncompensated is

$$G_f(j\omega) = \frac{K_s K_{A1} K_{M1} K_p K_{A2} K_{M2}}{(j\omega)^2(1 + j\omega\tau_2)} \tag{9-14a}$$

Need for Compensation. The basic components of the system are now identified, and we can begin the second part of the design. The next stage in the development is to investigate whether or not compensation is needed. One way of getting the answer is to determine whether the system as it stands in Fig. 9-10 is, first of all, stable and, second,

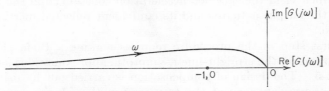

FIG. 9-11. Polar plot of the open-loop transfer function for the system of Fig. 9-10.

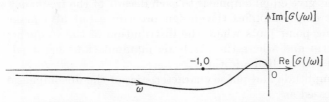

FIG. 9-12. Reshaped polar plot of Fig. 9-11 upon inserting lead compensation.

capable of meeting the specifications. A glance at the polar plot of Eq. (9-14a) makes the answer to both questions apparent: the system is absolutely unstable. Figure 9-11 shows that the polar plot over the real frequency range is located entirely inside the second quadrant, which means that the solutions to the characteristic equation contain roots with positive real parts no matter how small the open-loop gain is made. This bears out a fact which has been mentioned several times, viz., that, the higher the type of system (i.e., the greater the number of integrations), the more difficult it is to keep the system stable. Consequently, the system of Fig. 9-10 must be equipped with the proper compensation networks.

Examination of Fig. 9-11 should make it clear that the only type of compensation which works in this case is the lead type. A lag network fails to be useful here because no degree of attenuation can make this system stable, and this is all that the lag network can furnish in a constructive sense. Of course, a lead circuit is effective because, by virtue of its phase-lead angular contributions, it takes that portion of the polar plot in the vicinity of $-1 + j0$ and reshapes it in the manner shown in Fig. 9-12. Since the Nyquist point is no longer enclosed, the system is made stable. In fact, if sufficient reshaping is permitted by proper design of the lead network, not only is absolute stability assured but good relative stability as well.

Compensation Design Procedure. In order to illustrate the design procedure quantitatively, it is assumed that Eq. (9-14a) takes on the specific form

$$G_f(j\omega) = \frac{10}{(j\omega)^2(1 + j0.2\omega)} \tag{9-14b}$$

i.e., the amplifier gains K_{A1} and K_{A2} are considered to be adjusted to the values which yield the specified acceleration constant; and the time constant of the output actuator and its equivalent reflected inertia is taken as 0.2 sec.

The first step in the procedure requires making a Bode plot of Eq. (9-14b) by using the straight-line asymptotic approximations as outlined in Chap. 5. The design of compensation is carried out by using the db vs. log ω representations of the transfer functions because such representations give equal emphasis to each decade of the frequency spectrum. This not only simplifies the design procedure but also makes it easier than using polar plots where the distribution of the frequency values is nonuniform and where the algebraic manipulations involved are multiplication rather than addition.

The amplitude and phase characteristics of the uncompensated system are expressed as

$$\text{db} = 20 \log G_f(j\omega) = 20 \log 10 - 40 \log |j\omega| - 20 \log |1 + j0.2\omega| \tag{9-15}$$
$$\angle G_f(j\omega) = -180 - \tan^{-1} 0.2\omega = \phi \tag{9-16}$$

For our purposes it suffices merely to make a Bode plot of the magnitude characteristic. The equation for the phase angle is used solely in connection with calculating the phase margin. A plot of Eq. (9-15) appears in Fig. 9-13 as curve *a*. Note that this curve intersects the 0-db coordinate axis at approximately 3.2 radians/sec. Let us call this frequency the *crossover frequency* and denote it by ω_c.

Next compute the phase margin. This simply requires finding the total phase shift at the crossover frequency and adding 180° to it. Thus, at $\omega_c = 3.2$

$$\phi = -180 - \tan^{-1} 0.2(3.2) = -180 - 32.6$$

Hence the phase margin is

$$\phi_{\text{pm}} = -180 - 32.6 + 180 = -32.6°$$

Of course the negative phase margin corroborates a conclusion already arrived at from the polar plot, viz., that the system of Eq. (9-14b) is absolutely unstable. The absolute instability of this system could also have been deduced from the Bode plot without the help of the foregoing

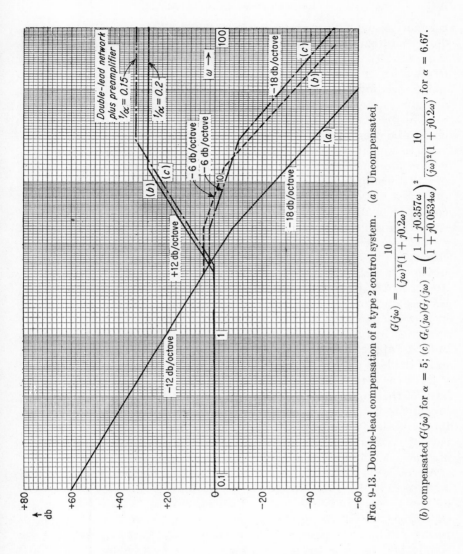

Fig. 9-13. Double-lead compensation of a type 2 control system. (a) Uncompensated,

$$G(j\omega) = \frac{10}{(j\omega)^2(1 + j0.2\omega)}$$

(b) compensated $G(j\omega)$ for $\alpha = 5$; (c) $G_c(j\omega)G_f(j\omega) = \left(\dfrac{1 + j0.357\omega}{1 + j0.0534\omega}\right)^2 \dfrac{10}{(j\omega)^2(1 + j0.2\omega)}$, for $\alpha = 6.67$.

calculation by noting at what slope the decibel curve intersects the 0-db coordinate axis. When systems are described with transfer functions that contain simple factors with fairly widely separated corner frequencies or quadratic factors with large values of ζ, there exists a simple relationship between the phase angle and the slope of the log modulus curve. In such cases if the slope of the log modulus curve is -12 db/octave or greater when it crosses the 0-db axis, the system can usually be considered absolutely unstable.

At this point we are in a position to estimate the extent to which the lead network must provide compensation. The computed phase margin of the uncompensated system is $-32.6°$. The specifications, however, call for a value of $45° \pm 3°$, which indicates the need for a phase-lead correction of about $78°$. Reference to Fig. 5-28 reveals that this degree of correction could be furnished by using two standard lead networks connected in cascade and having an attenuation factor of $1/\alpha = 0.2$. The corresponding maximum phase-lead contribution is then $2(41.8°) = 83.6°$, which is just slightly more than the $78°$ computed above. Actually this design is not enough to meet the specifications on the phase margin because the excess of $5.6°$ of lead angle is not sufficient to offset the increased phase lag of the fixed elements in the system due to the increased crossover frequency caused by the presence of the lead networks. In order to appreciate this better, the design is nevertheless continued by using the lead networks with the 0.2 attenuation factor.

Once the attenuation factor of the lead network is established on the basis of the required phase-lead angle, the next step is to choose the first breakpoint frequency of the compensation circuit in a manner which puts the phase-lead characteristic to optimum use. This is an important part of the design procedure because selecting this point too low or too high means failure in meeting the specifications.

An indispensable aid in assuring that the lead network is used to best advantage is this rule: *Choose the first or lower break-point frequency of the lead network in such a way that it makes the compensated db vs. log ω curve cross the 0-db coordinate axis at a slope of -6 db/octave.* This rule works well in many cases especially when the transfer function contains simple factors with widely separated corner frequencies or quadratic factors with large damping ratios. Thus, to realize a phase shift of $-180°$ requires an associated slope of -12 db/octave, that is, $-90°$ for each -6 db/octave of slope. Hence, if a slope of at least -12 db/ octave does not prevail, the phase shift likewise cannot be as much as $-180°$ but must be something less negative. As a matter of fact this explains why it is that a system which crosses the 0-db line at a -12 db/octave slope and then improves to -6 db/ octave is absolutely stable. The answer lies in the fact that the actual decibel curve (not the asymptotic approximation) has a value somewhat less negative than -12 db/octave and therefore a phase lag less negative than $-180°$.

By applying the foregoing criterion we can readily see why choosing the lower corner frequency too low or too high proves to be ineffective. Thus, selecting the first breakpoint frequency at any value greater than 3.2 radians/sec results in a slope of -12 db/octave for the asymptotic curve and something slightly less than this for the actual curve in the vicinity of the 0-db line. Hence the phase margin is either negative or very small if it is positive. On the other hand choosing the lower breakpoint frequency too low, such as at 1 radian/sec, completely fails since it causes the modified db vs. log ω curve to intersect the 0-db coordinate axis at a slope of -18 db/octave, which is definitely unstable in spite of the presence of the lead networks.

Therefore, keeping in mind the necessity of obtaining a -6 db/octave crossing of the 0-db coordinate line, choose the first breakpoint frequency of the selected lead network at 2.5 radians/sec. This results in the decibel curve identified as b in Fig. 9-13. Note that the Bode plot of the lead network is drawn with the assumption that a preamplifier is inserted for the purpose of eliminating the attenuation introduced by the lead circuits. Note, too, that since a double circuit is involved the slope increases at a rate of $+12$ db/octave up to a level of 28 db.

The new phase margin may now be computed. The lead networks cause the crossover frequency to increase from 3.2 radians/sec to 7.6 radians/sec. Again note the consistency with the same result arrived at from a study of the polar plots, viz., that a lead network increases the system bandwidth. The crossover frequency is often used as a measure of the bandwidth.[1] The expression for the phase angle of the compensated system is

$$\phi = -180° - \tan^{-1} 0.2\omega + 2\phi_{cn}$$

where ϕ_{cn} denotes the phase-lead angular contribution of a single network as obtained from the nondimensional plots of Fig. 5-28. To find ϕ_{cn} corresponding to a frequency of 7.6 radians, first calculate the ratio of this frequency to the lower breakpoint frequency, that is, $7.6:2.5 = 3.04$, then enter the appropriate phase curve corresponding to this nondimensional frequency, and read a value of $\phi_{cn} = 40.5°$. The total lead angle is therefore 81°. The closeness of this figure to 83.6° indicates that the lead networks are being efficiently used, which means that the lower breakpoint frequency of the network was well chosen. Total phase angle is

$$\phi = -180 - \tan^{-1} 0.2(7.6) + 2(40.5)$$
$$= -180 - 56.6 + 81 = -155.6°$$

yielding a phase margin of 24.4°, which fails to meet the specification.

[1] See Appendix E.

As pointed out at the beginning of this design, the failure to anticipate the increase in crossover frequency and its attendant increase in the phase-lag contributions of the fixed elements is responsible for not achieving a design which meets the specifications. This point is made clear by noting that at 3.2 radians/sec the lag angle associated with the 0.2-sec term is $-32.6°$, whereas at 7.6 radians/sec it is $-56.6°$. This represents a difference of $24°$, which in turn represents the amount by which the design falls short of meeting the specification.

The solution evidently lies in selecting a lead network with greater low-frequency attenuation, which in turn furnishes more phase-lead angle. Accordingly, select an attenuation factor of $1/\alpha = 0.15$, corresponding to which is a maximum phase-lead angle of $47.7°$. For a double network this represents a maximum contribution of $95.4°$, which should prove sufficient provided that the first breakpoint frequency is now chosen at a slightly higher value than before. This has the advantage of causing the attenuation curve to cross the 0-db axis closer to the beginning of the -6 db/octave slope, which in turn results in more phase margin. This is evident from a glance at the new compensated curve identified as c in Fig. 9-13. First of all, it gives a slightly lower crossover frequency, which means smaller phase-lag contributions from the fixed elements. Second, optimum use of the phase-lead characteristic of the lead network is realized. Recall that in the preceding calculation the nondimensional frequency of 3.04 put operation to the right of the peak phase angle of the lead network.

The asymptotic plot of curve c in Fig. 9-13 shows crossover taking place at 6.2 radians/sec. This value is not a reliable one here because it lies much too close to a breakpoint where the error between the actual curve and the straight-line asymptotic approximation is a maximum. This can be easily verified by checking the magnitude of the compensated open-loop transfer function at this frequency. Of course, it should be unity, that is, 0 db, but actually it will be found to be less than unity. Consequently, the crossover frequency of the actual decibel curve occurs below 6.2 radians/sec. A simple way to find this is to guess at one or two points and check for unity. Before checking this, it is helpful to write the expression for the compensated transfer function for the modified design. Thus

$$G(j\omega) = G_c(j\omega)G_f(j\omega) = \left(\frac{1 + j0.357\omega}{1 + j0.0534\omega}\right)^2 \frac{10}{(j\omega)^2(1 + j0.2\omega)} \quad (9\text{-}17)$$

Try $\omega_c = 5.2$ radians/sec. Then Eq. (9-17) becomes

$$G(j5.2) = \frac{4.2\underline{/123°}}{1.08\underline{/31°}} \frac{10}{27\underline{/180°}(1.45\underline{/44°})}$$

$$= \frac{42}{42.2}\underline{/-255° + 123°} = 1.0\underline{/-132°}$$

This calculation also reveals the phase margin to be 48° and so meets the specification.

There is one final item to be checked before accepting the design of the compensation network shown in Eq. (9-17). Does the time response of the system represented by this equation behave with a predominant time constant of less than 1 sec? We are not prepared here to give an exact answer to this question, but we can estimate an approximate one. First it should be appreciated that in spite of the fact that the characteristic equation is of fifth order the system's dynamic behavior very much resembles that of a second-order system with a pair of complex conjugate roots as the solution to its characteristic equation. In terms of the frequency domain this point is borne out by the existence of a positive phase margin of 48°. A perhaps crude but nonetheless useful expression for estimating the time constant can be deduced from the fact that for the straight underdamped second-order system the time constant is simply $1/\zeta\omega_n$. If we now replace ω_n by the crossover frequency ω_c and ζ by $\frac{1}{2}\phi_{pm}$, where ϕ_{pm} is the phase margin expressed in radians, there results

$$T = \frac{1}{\frac{1}{2}\phi_{pm}\omega_c} = \text{time constant, sec} \qquad (9\text{-}18a)$$

Expressing the phase margin in degrees permits writing

$$T = \frac{1}{(\phi_{pm}/360)\pi\omega_c} \qquad (9\text{-}18b)$$

Inserting the values which apply for our design yields

$$T = \frac{1}{\frac{48}{360}\pi(5.2)} = \frac{1}{2.18} = 0.46 \text{ sec}$$

To check that this result is not completely out of line, the roots of the characteristic equation were determined for this system and the predominant pair of complex roots was found to have a real part of -2.2. Indeed this compares favorably with the figure of -2.18 found above. Of course, the reason for making the comparison is to demonstrate that Eq. (9-18b) can be used to furnish an order of magnitude for the predominant time constant.

If this part of the specification had not been met, it would have been necessary to redesign the lead compensation in such a way as to provide the specified phase margin at an increased crossover frequency. The solution would then probably call for two nonidentical lead networks in order to realize the greater freedom of control necessary.

Figure 9-14 illustrates the compensation required to make the system of Fig. 9-10 operate essentially in accordance with the specifications. Undoubtedly, when the components are physically combined, adjustments will be needed. But this is only a minor consideration in comparison with the big job of having assembled a workable system. Note that for complete specification of the compensation network the values of R_1, R_2, and C need to be established. These elements must be chosen such that they satisfy the relations

$$\alpha = \frac{R_1 + R_2}{R_2} = (0.15)^{-1} = 6.67 \tag{9-19}$$

and

$$\tau = \frac{R_1 C}{\alpha} = R_1 C(0.15) = 0.357(0.15) = 0.0534 \tag{9-20}$$

Consequently, any one parameter may be arbitrarily selected. The values of the remaining two then follow from Eqs. (9-19) and (9-20).

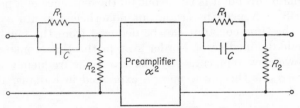

Fig. 9-14. Final design for the phase-lead compensation. $\alpha = \dfrac{R_1 + R_2}{R_2} = (0.15)^{-1}$;

$$\tau = 0.0534 = \frac{R_1 R_2}{R_1 + R_2} C = R_1 C(0.15)$$

The preamplifier shown in Fig. 9-14 serves two purposes. (1) It eliminates the attenuation of the lead networks at steady state; and (2), it provides the isolation needed to prevent the second RC network from loading the first one. The selection of the arbitrary parameter is made with the view of dealing with easily obtainable circuit elements and of minimizing the loading problem on the stages which precede and follow the network in the direct transmission path.

Combining the lead compensation with the system of Fig. 9-10 in the manner illustrated in Fig. 9-15 represents the final stage in the development of the feedback control system called for in the specifications. A study of this configuration affords the opportunity of commenting on an important point. It is this. The compensation networks treated here as well as in Chap. 6 are so-called "d-c corrective networks," which means that they operate upon the signal information as it exists in the low-frequency range, i.e., within the bandwidth of the system. The synchro error detector is an a-c carrier-type device, which often operates at a reference (carrier) frequency of 60 or 400 cps. If the output signals of the synchro are applied directly to the lead networks, the compensation would be ineffective because these circuits then respond to the carrier frequency and not to the modulation frequency, which contains the signal information. Therefore, whenever synchros are used, a demodulator must precede the d-c type of compensation network. Also, if a-c servo-motors are used, then the network must be followed by a modulator to convert the signals to the modulated carrier form required by the servomotors.

Description of Operation at Steady State. In order to gain increased insight into the system operation, it is worthwhile to describe how the output quantity in the steady state can be made to follow the constant velocity input command without a lag error in position. Assume that

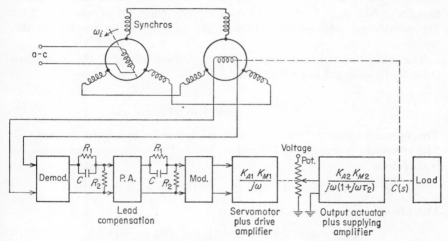

FIG. 9-15. Final configuration of the type 2 control system.

the system of Fig. 9-15 is initially in a quiescent state. So, upon application of the constant velocity command at the rotor of the synchro transmitter, a large actuating signal appears at the input terminals of the demodulator and thence to the first servomotor. The torque developed by this servomotor moves the slider arm of the potentiometer, thereby applying an input to the output servomotor, which in turn begins to accelerate the load. As the load velocity increases during the transient state, the magnitude of the actuating signal decreases. This means that the slider arm of the potentiometer, which feeds the driving amplifier of the output actuator, is being readjusted by smaller and smaller amounts. Finally, when the output velocity has reached the commanded value, the actuating signal which originates from the synchro control transformer becomes zero, which in turn means that the first servomotor ceases to generate an output. However, before this torque is allowed to be zero, the potentiometer slider arm is placed at such a position that the magnitude of the input signal is sufficient to generate the commanded output velocity. If for a moment this were not so, an actuating signal would exist for a sufficient period of time to permit the first servomotor to generate the torque required to place the slider arm at the necessary level. It is this integration feature represented by the first servomotor which eliminates the need for a lag error in position. This stands in sharp contrast to the type 1 system, which has just one integration and so requires a finite value of actuating signal in order to supply an input signal to the output actuator, thus enabling it to generate the output velocity.

MODIFIED PROBLEM. Assume that the specifications of the original problem are modified so that an acceleration constant of unity, a phase margin of $35° \pm 2°$, and a predominant time constant of less than 2 sec are considered satisfactory. Design the compensation needed in this case.

The reduction in the acceleration constant changes the open-loop transfer function of Eq. (9-14b) to

$$G_f(j\omega) = \frac{1}{(j\omega)^2(1 + j0.2\omega)} \tag{9-21}$$

The corresponding attenuation plot is shown in Fig. 9-16 as curve a. The crossover frequency is 1.0 radian/sec. The corresponding phase lag is therefore

$$\phi = -180° - \tan^{-1} 0.2(1) = -180° - 11.3 = -191.3°$$

The phase margin is therefore

$$\phi_{pm} = \phi + 180° = -191.3 + 180 = -11.3°$$

As expected, even with a reduced gain, the original system is still absolutely unstable. Accordingly, lead compensation is needed.

Selection of the attenuation constant of that lead network depends upon the maximum phase-lead angle required. Since a phase margin of 35° is called for, the total correction required is $35° + 11.3° = 46.3°$. However, an allowance must be made for the increased lag associated with the fixed elements at the higher crossover frequency which results when the lead compensation is present. This is why choosing a lead network with an attenuation factor of 0.15, thus making available a maximum phase-lead angle of 47.7°, does not work. The use of a single lead network having an attenuation of 0.1 and a maximum phase lead of 54.8°, however, looks promising and therefore worthy of investigation.

As a first try select the lower breakpoint frequency of the lead network at a value of 0.5 radian/sec. This has the effect of changing the slope of the uncompensated decibel curve from -12 db/octave to -6 db/octave over the frequency range from 0.5 radian/sec to 5 radians/sec and thereby assures that the compensated attenuation characteristic crosses the 0-db axis at a slope of -6 db/octave (see curve b in Fig. 9-16). This also means that the system is now absolutely

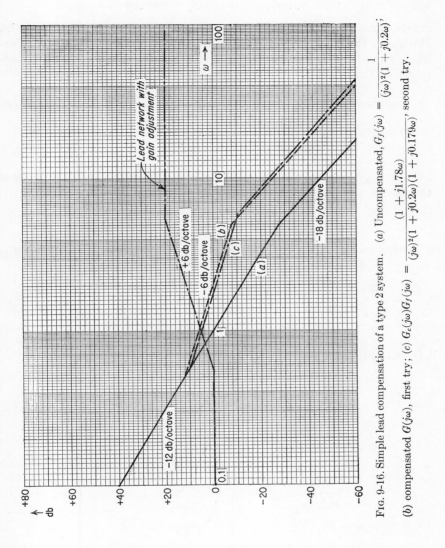

FIG. 9-16. Simple lead compensation of a type 2 system. (a) Uncompensated, $G_f(j\omega) = \dfrac{1}{(j\omega)^2(1 + j0.2\omega)}$;

(b) compensated $G(j\omega)$, first try; (c) $G_c(j\omega)G_f(j\omega) = \dfrac{(1 + j1.78\omega)}{(j\omega)^2(1 + j0.2\omega)(1 + j0.179\omega)}$, second try.

stable, but whether it provides the required phase margin remains to be checked. Once the attenuation factor and the lower breakpoint frequency of the lead network are selected, the transfer function is determined. Thus

$$G_c(j\omega) = \frac{1}{\alpha}\frac{1 + j\omega\alpha\tau}{1 + j\omega\tau} = \frac{1}{\alpha}\frac{1 + j(\omega/\omega_b)}{1 + j(\omega/\alpha\omega_b)} = 0.1\frac{1 + j(\omega/0.5)}{1 + j(\omega/5)} \quad (9\text{-}22a)$$

where ω_b = lower breakpoint frequency

$\alpha\omega_b$ = upper breakpoint frequency

$1/\alpha$ = attenuation ratio

Furthermore, accounting for the increase in gain which is made to offset the attenuation factor, this expression becomes

$$G_c(j\omega) = \frac{1 + j(\omega/0.5)}{1 + j(\omega/5)} \quad (9\text{-}22b)$$

To check the phase margin, we must first account for the lead angle introduced by Eq. (9-22b). Thus the new expression for the phase angle is

$$\phi = -180 - \tan^{-1} 0.2\omega + \phi_{cn}$$

where ϕ_{cn} denotes the angular contribution of the compensation network. The new crossover frequency is 2.0 radians/sec, as shown in Fig. 9-16. To find ϕ_{cn}, first compute $\omega/\omega_b = 2/0.5 = 4$, and then read the value of 54° from Fig. 5-28. Hence the total phase shift is

$$\phi = -180 - \tan^{-1} 0.2(2) + 54 = -180 - 21.8 + 54 = -147.8°$$

which makes the phase margin

$$\phi_{pm} = \phi + 180 = +32.2°$$

which falls just short of the specification.

A slight improvement can be effected by choosing the lower breakpoint frequency ω_b slightly higher. Hence as a second try take $\omega_b = 0.56$ radian/sec. The resulting attenuation curve appears also in Fig. 9-16 and is identified as curve c. The corresponding crossover frequency is 1.7 radians/sec, which leads to a total phase shift of

$$\phi = -180 - \tan^{-1} 0.2(1.7) + \phi_{cn} = -180 - 19.9 + 55 = -144.9°$$

and a phase margin of 35.1°, which is satisfactory.

The transfer function of the final lead network design is therefore

$$G_c(j\omega) = \frac{1 + j(\omega/0.56)}{1 + j(\omega/5.6)} = \frac{1 + j1.78\omega}{1 + j0.178\omega} \quad (9\text{-}23)$$

The expression for the compensated open-loop transfer function then becomes

$$G(j\omega) = G_c(j\omega)G_f(j\omega) = \frac{1 + j1.78\omega}{(j\omega)^2(1 + j0.2\omega)(1 + j0.178\omega)} \quad (9\text{-}24)$$

The use of Eq. (9-18*b*) for approximating the predominant time constant yields

$$T = \frac{1}{\frac{35}{360}\pi(1.7)} = \frac{1}{0.52} = 1.92 \text{ sec}$$

so that this condition is satisfied too.

9-4. Compensation of a Type 1 Control System

The choice of compensation for a type 1 control system is more sophisticated than it is for the type 2 system. This is because a given phase margin and velocity constant can be realized by using any one of the three standard circuits, viz., lag, lead, or lag-lead. The particular choice depends upon other factors, and it is the purpose of this section to bring these factors to light.

Statement of the Problem. A control system is required which is capable of meeting the following specifications:

On the steady-state performance: (1) It must be capable of following a command signal of constant velocity without an error in velocity. (2) At the maximum command velocity of π radians/sec the corresponding lag error in position is not to exceed 1°.

On the transient performance: (1) The transient behavior is to be that corresponding to a phase margin of $45° \pm 3°$. (2) Moreover, the predominant time constant of the response is to be less than 1 sec.

It should be appreciated that these specifications are restricted to the performance behavior of the control system, which is our chief interest here. In any practical situation the specifications cover a wider area, dealing with such items as temperature, environment, vibrations, etc.

Basic System Composition. A study of the specifications fixing the steady-state performance makes it clear that a type 1 system is called for. Thus there must be at least one component which furnishes pure integration in the system. Moreover, the gain must be high enough to provide the required velocity constant. From the statement of the problem and the use of Eq. (7-22*a*) this value is

$$K_v = \frac{\omega_i}{\mathcal{E}_{ss}} = \frac{\pi}{1°/(180/\pi)} = 180 \text{ sec}^{-1}$$

It is here assumed that the output variable is mechanical so that the required pure integration can be furnished by the servomotor selected to drive the load. Again, depending upon the particular circumstances, this output actuator may be a d-c or a-c motor, an amplidyne-motor combination, a hydraulic motor, or even a pneumatic device. For the sake of illustration, let us consider that the required output actuator together with its driving amplifier has a transfer function given by

$$G_f(j\omega) = \frac{K_A K_M}{j\omega(1 + j\omega\tau_1)(1 + j\omega\tau_2)} = \frac{K_A K_M}{j\omega[1 + j(\omega/6)][1 + j(\omega/2)]} \quad (9\text{-}25)$$

where τ_2 denotes the time constant associated with the output motor plus its connected load and τ_1 the time lag associated with the supplying amplifier. Thus Eq. (9-25) is a description of the fixed elements of the system without which the required power and specifications on the load side cannot be met. To complete the basic composition of the system requires merely specifying an appropriate type of error detector.

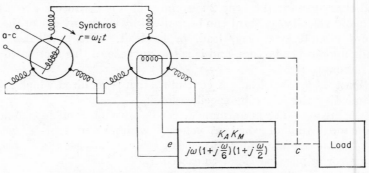

FIG. 9-17. Basic composition of a type 1 system.

Although in a practical situation many considerations can enter into this selection, we are simplifying the problem by again specifying synchros. Figure 9-17 illustrates the basic composition of the system to solve the problem at hand. Keep in mind, however, that so far the system is capable of satisfying specifications only on the steady-state performance and the load requirements. Whether it ever reaches the steady-state condition is a problem which remains to be investigated. Before proceeding it is helpful to have the complete expression for the transfer function of the uncompensated open-loop system which is made up solely of the fixed elements. Thus

$$G(j\omega) = K_s \frac{K_A K_M}{j\omega(1 + j\omega\tau_1)(1 + j\omega\tau_2)} = \frac{180}{j\omega[1 + j(\omega/6)][1 + j(\omega/2)]} \quad (9\text{-}26)$$

where K_s is the synchro transducer constant.

Compensation Design. The Bode diagram for the gain characteristic of Eq. (9-26) appears in Fig. 9-18 as curve a. An extension of the initial -6 db/octave slope intersects the 0-db axis at a frequency of 180 radians/ sec, which corresponds to the value of the velocity constant. It is in this manner, of course, that the Bode diagram puts the velocity constant clearly in evidence. The uncompensated attenuation curve intersects

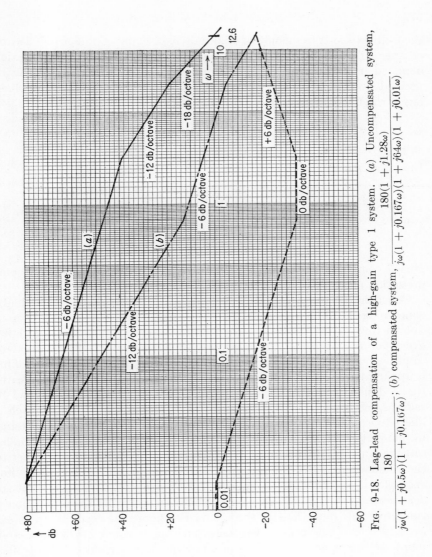

FIG. 9-18. Lag-lead compensation of a high-gain type 1 system. (a) Uncompensated system,
$$\frac{180}{j\omega(1+j0.5\omega)(1+j0.167\omega)};\ (b)\ \text{compensated system,}\ \frac{180(1+j1.28\omega)}{j\omega(1+j0.167\omega)(1+j64\omega)(1+j0.01\omega)}.$$

371

the 0-db axis at a frequency of 12.6 radians/sec and at a slope of -18 db/octave.   This large negative slope makes it obvious that the configuration depicted in Fig. 9-17 is absolutely unstable, a conclusion which can be verified by computing the phase margin.   The expression for the phase lag of the uncompensated system follows from Eq. (9-26).   Thus,

$$\phi = -90 - \tan^{-1}\frac{\omega}{6} - \tan^{-1}\frac{\omega}{2}$$

Inserting $\omega = 12.6$ yields

$$\phi = -90 - \tan^{-1} 2.12 - \tan^{-1} 6.3 = -235.7$$

which gives a phase margin of

$$\phi_{pm} = -235.7 + 180 = -55.7°$$

Hence compensation is clearly necessary.   However, the type of compensation network to use is not nearly so apparent.

Consider first the use of lead compensation.   There should be no doubt concerning the ability of the lead network not only to stabilize the system but to furnish the desired phase margin.   Further investigation, however, points out some rather serious shortcomings of this method of solution.   For one thing the bandwidth becomes excessively large.   This is apparent from an inspection of the db vs. log ω curve, which indicates that a double-lead network with a lower breakpoint frequency beyond 10 radians/sec must be used.   In turn this results in a bandwidth which is likely to exceed 25 radians/sec.   Generally, a large bandwidth is a desirable characteristic, primarily because it means faster response, i.e., smaller settling time.   But care must be taken not to overextend this matter to the point where it either is meaningless or leads to other difficulties.   For example, if in the case at hand a bandwidth of 25 radians/sec were designed into the system, Eq. (9-18b) shows roughly that the predominant time constant is less than 0.1 sec.   Now this figure can easily be meaningless if the lead networks generate output signals which apply such large inputs to the actuator that saturation occurs.   As a result the controlled variable in the actual system would not change in accordance with the computed commands, thus leading to a deterioration in performance. In other words, the lead compensation is calling for rates of change which are beyond the capabilities of the output actuator.   This is an important consideration, and one which the designer must be aware of, especially in designing on the basis of linear analysis.   The use of lead compensation in any system should always be accompanied by a check which assures that the output actuator can reasonably well follow the output commands of the compensation network.   Now if, for argument's sake, we assume the actuator of our example to have this capability, then there is strong reason for believing that the system is overdesigned. Essentially, it gives a response time ten times better than what is called for in the specifications. In addition to all this the unnecessarily large bandwidth makes the system a good deal more susceptible to annoyances arising from the presence of noise. A lower bandwidth can readily eliminate or reduce to negligibility such diffiulties. Then, too, with lead compensation there is the need for additional hardware in the form of the preamplifiers required to overcome the attenuation associated with the lead networks. Finally there is the possibility that the given compensation will cause the system to be conditionally stable. This is possible because the corrective phase action of the lead networks is introduced, as a result of other considerations, at a point beyond the region where a slope of -18 db/octave prevails. Hence a sharp dip in the resultant phase curve will occur in the region between 3 and 8 radians/sec. If the dip is severe enough to cause the total phase lag to be worse than $-180°$, then conditional stability[1] results. Therefore in view of these facts lead compensation is an unwise choice for the solution of this problem.

Consider next the use of lag compensation. Compensating the system for a phase margin of 45° can be effected in the manner illustrated in Fig. 9-5. However, using the lag network to provide the necessary compensation in high-performance systems such as the one under study often leads to two very serious disadvantages which can easily rule it out as a solution to the problem. One shortcoming is that very large time constants may be needed. In fact, the higher the velocity constant, the greater the required time constant. The truth of this statement is readily demonstrated by referring to curve a of Fig. 9-18. The lag network effectively compensates this system by introducing an amount of attenuation to lower the magnitude characteristic so that that portion of the curve having a slope of -6 db/octave is made to cross the 0-db axis. Clearly this would require a crossing somewhere in the vicinity of 1 radian/sec or less. Furthermore, in order to prevent the lag-angle characteristic from being troublesome, it is necessary to select the lower breakpoint frequency of the lag network at a sufficiently small value. A glance at Fig. 9-18 indicates that this could easily be in the vicinity of 0.001 radian/sec, which means that the required time constant of the lag network is of the order of 1,000 sec. Indeed this is an unrealistic figure, and so this approach must be abandoned, at least for our example. Let us suppose, however, that in some situations realizable time constants are obtained; then there is a second shortcoming. It has to do with the fact that, since the lag network can materially reduce the bandwidth, the resulting time response can suffer to the point where the specification on the predominant time constant cannot be met. In short, the com-

---

[1] *Conditional stability* refers to that state during which an increase or decrease in gain causes sustained oscillations.

pensated system is made too sluggish. A rough check for the example of Fig. 9-18 shows that the time constant exceeds two seconds.

The foregoing considerations demonstrate that simple lead compensation as well as simple lag compensation results in unsatisfactory compensation. This naturally turns the designer's thoughts to the possibility of meeting the specifications by means of the lag-lead network. As a matter of fact, for the present situation, this approach is the one which proves fruitful because, by its very nature, the lag-lead compensation

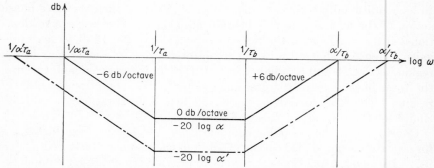

FIG. 9-19. Bode diagram for lag-lead network for two values of the attenuation constant.

network contains all the advantages of both the lag and the lead network and only a minimum of their undesirable aspects.

Before proceeding with the specific design, it is helpful to recall the transfer function of the lag-lead network, which is repeated here for convenience.

$$G_c(j\omega) = \frac{(1 + j\omega\tau_a)(1 + j\omega\tau_b)}{(1 + j\omega\tau_1)(1 + j\omega\tau_2)} \tag{9-27}$$

Although four time constants appear in this expression, only three are independent, as pointed out in Sec. 6-1. To emphasize this, Eq. (9-27) is rewritten as

$$G_c(j\omega) = \frac{(1 + j\omega\tau_a)(1 + j\omega\tau_b)}{(1 + j\omega\alpha\tau_a)\left(1 + j\omega\dfrac{\tau_b}{\alpha}\right)} = \frac{[1 + j(\omega/\omega_a)][1 + j(\omega/\omega_b)]}{\left(1 + j\dfrac{\omega}{\omega_a/\alpha}\right)\left(1 + j\dfrac{\omega}{\alpha\omega_b}\right)} \tag{9-28}$$

where $\qquad \tau_1 = \alpha\tau_a \qquad$ and $\qquad \tau_2 = \dfrac{\tau_b}{\alpha}$

and $\qquad \dfrac{1}{\alpha} =$ attenuation factor $\qquad \omega_a = \dfrac{1}{\tau_a} \qquad \omega_b = \dfrac{1}{\tau_b}$ $\tag{9-29}$

Thus Eq. (9-28) now contains just three independent quantities, viz., τ_a, τ_b, and α. Note that for both ω very small and ω very large this ratio is unity, as it should be. A Bode diagram of the attenuation characteristic showing the breakpoint frequencies appears in Fig. 9-19.   Two cases are illustrated, each having the same middle breakpoint frequencies $1/\tau_a = \omega_a$ and $1/\tau_b = \omega_b$ but a different attenuation constant.   Note that the lower the level of the 0 db/octave slope of the lag-lead network the greater the attenuation.   For example, for a level of -20 db the attenuation factor is $1/\alpha = 0.1$, a fact with which we are familiar.   Observe, too, that the smaller the attenuation factor, the greater the spread between the first and the last breakpoint frequencies.   This conclusion immediately follows from the fact that for the linear factors involved in Eq. (9-28) the magnitude characteristic can change only at a rate of ± 6 db/octave when we are reasoning in terms of the asymptotic approximations.

The design of the lag-lead compensation network essentially consists of three steps as here outlined:

1. Select τ_b or its corresponding breakpoint frequency ω_b.   Keeping in mind the fact that the slope of the lag-lead network beyond this break-point frequency is $+6$ db/octave, the designer can usually take advantage of this by permitting it to operate on that portion of the uncompensated decibel-curve which has a -12 db/octave slope.   The result is an extension of the -6 db/octave slope.   Examination of Fig. 9-18 makes it apparent that by choosing

$$\omega_b = 2 \text{ radians/sec}$$

the -12 db/octave slope of curve a is altered to the more favorable -6 db/octave value.

2. Select the proper level for the 0 db/octave slope line of the lag-lead network.   The first factor to keep in mind in making this choice is that the compensated decibel-curve should cross the 0-db axis at a slope of -6 db/octave.   Because of the influence of the lag-lead network beyond 2 radians/sec, a -6 db/octave slope is virtually guaranteed up to 6 radians/sec, after which the effect of the $\tau_1{}'$ time constant of the fixed elements enters the picture.   Consequently it is necessary to provide sufficient attenuation to assure that the extended portion of the original -6 db/octave slope intersects the 0-db axis at a frequency below 6 radians/sec.   The particular attenuation constant depends upon the specific value of crossover frequency which the designer chooses, which in turn is strongly guided by the necessity of meeting not only the specification on the phase margin but that on the predominant time constant as well.   Of course, the smaller this crossover frequency, the greater the settling time.   With these factors in mind let us choose a crossover frequency for the compensated system of 3.5 radians/sec.   The extended portion of -6 db/octave slope of curve a indicates that at 3.5 radians/sec the gain is $+34$ db.   Hence, to offset this, the lag-lead network must introduce an attenuation of -34 db.   Accordingly, the level of the 0 db/octave slope line of the lag-lead network is established.   The

figure of -34 db corresponds to an attenuation factor of 0.02, that is, $\alpha = 50$.

3. Solve for the value of ω_a in Eq. (9-28), which yields the desired phase margin. This quantity may be directly solved for because all other pertinent information is known. For example, the uppermost breakpoint frequency of the lag-lead network is determined once steps 1 and 2 are completed. The value here is $\alpha\omega_b = 100$ radians/sec. Before proceeding further, let us write the expression for the compensated open-loop-system transfer function. Thus

$$G_cG_f(j\omega) = \underbrace{\frac{180}{j\omega[1 + j(\omega/2)][1 + j(\omega/6)]}}_{\text{Fixed elements}} \underbrace{\frac{[1 + j(\omega/\omega_a)][1 + j(\omega/2)]}{[1 + j\alpha(\omega/\omega_a)][1 + j(\omega/100)]}}_{\text{Lag-lead network}}$$

(9-30)

The total phase angle is then

$$\phi = -90 - \tan^{-1}\frac{\omega}{6} + \tan^{-1}\frac{\omega}{\omega_a} - \tan^{-1}\alpha\frac{\omega}{\omega_a} - \tan^{-1}\frac{\omega}{100}$$

Since the crossover frequency is known to be 3.5 radians/sec, the last expression reduces to

$$\phi = -122.4° + \tan^{-1}\frac{\omega_c}{\omega_a} - \tan^{-1}\alpha\frac{\omega_c}{\omega_a}$$

Because $\alpha\omega_c = 50(3.5) = 175$ is such a large quantity, very little error is made by replacing $\tan^{-1}(\alpha\omega_c/\omega_a)$ by 90°. Also, since

$$\phi_{\text{pm}} = \phi + 180$$

combining the last two equations leads to

$$\phi_{\text{pm}} = -32.4 + \tan^{-1}\frac{\omega_c}{\omega_a}$$

Therefore
$$\tan^{-1}\frac{\omega_c}{\omega_a} = 45 + 32.4 = 77.4°$$

from which it follows that $\omega_a = \omega_c/4.48 = 3.5/4.48 = 0.78$. This makes the lowermost breakpoint frequency

$$\frac{\omega_a}{\alpha} = \frac{0.78}{50} = 0.0156 \text{ radian/sec}$$

Before declaring the design complete, it is necessary to ascertain the existence of a suitable settling time. In accordance with Eq. (9-18b) we have

$$T = \frac{1}{\frac{4.5}{360}\pi(3.5)} = \frac{1}{1.37} = 0.73 \text{ sec}$$

which meets the specification on the predominant time constant. This result is on the pessimistic side because the crossover frequency is usually less than the bandwidth or, for that matter, the natural frequency associated with the predominant pair of complex conjugate roots. A check of the actual roots of the characteristic equation of the system equipped with the foregoing compensation design shows the time constant of the predominant complex roots to be about half the value computed above. The natural frequency is found to be approximately twice as large as the crossover frequency.

The final design of the lag-lead-network compensation transfer function is summarized below. The Bode diagram is shown in Fig. 9-18.

$$\omega_a = 0.78 \text{ radian/sec} \qquad \tau_a = 1.28 \text{ sec}$$

$$\frac{\omega_a}{\alpha} = 0.0156 \text{ radian/sec} \qquad \alpha\tau_a = 64 \text{ sec}$$

$$\omega_b = 2.0 \text{ radian/sec} \qquad \tau_b = 0.5 \text{ sec}$$

$$\alpha\omega_b = 100 \text{ radian/sec} \qquad \frac{\tau_b}{\alpha} = 0.01 \text{ sec}$$

$$G_c(j\omega) = \frac{(1 + j1.28\omega)(1 + j0.5\omega)}{(1 + j64\omega)(1 + j0.01\omega)} \tag{9-31}$$

The complete expression for the compensated transfer function now becomes

$$G_cG_f(j\omega) = \frac{180(1 + j1.28\omega)}{j\omega(1 + j0.167\omega)(1 + j64\omega)(1 + j0.01\omega)} \tag{9-32}$$

The Bode plot of the magnitude characteristic of this function appears in Fig. 9-18 as curve b. It is interesting to note the manner by which the lag-lead network accomplishes the required compensation. Figure 9-18 shows that at the frequency of 0.0156 radian/sec the lag-lead network is first of all effective in increasing the slope to -12 db/octave for the purpose of providing the needed attenuation of -34 db. Upon accomplishing this, the slope must then return to -6 db/octave, and it stays there over a sufficient range of frequency to assure a -6 db/octave crossing of the 0-db axis. This feature is furnished by both the 0 and $+6$ db/octave portions of the lag-lead network. A comparison with the simple lag compensation or simple lead compensation reveals that the lag-lead network is really the happy medium in this case. It permits satisfying the specifications without the need of either a large bandwidth or excessive time constants. Although the largest time constant of the lag-lead design is 64 sec, it is realizable by using temperature-sensitive devices. The same cannot be as easily said for a time constant ten times as great.

There is an alternative procedure for the design of lag-lead networks which often results in smaller time constants. The method is outlined below.

1. On the basis of providing the desired predominant time constant as well as the phase margin, obtain a suitable value of crossover frequency

with the help of Eq. (9-18). This leads to

$$\omega_c = 3.5 \text{ radians/sec}$$

2. Choose $\omega_b < \omega_c$. Then draw a line having a slope of -6 db/octave and passing through the crossover frequency of 3.5 radians/sec. Continue this line until the next higher breakpoint frequency of the uncompensated system is encountered, which in this case is 6 radians/sec. This straight line is part of the attenuation characteristic of the compensated system. The extension of this attenuation characteristic beyond 6 radians/sec is a straight line having a slope of -12 db/octave. Since the slope of the uncompensated system beyond 6 radians/sec is -18 db/octave, it follows that the attenuation curves of the compensated and uncompensated systems will intersect. Beyond this point of intersection the two characteristics become identical because no further effect of the lag-lead network occurs. In other words the point of intersection of the compensated and uncompensated attenuation curves corresponds to the frequency $\alpha\omega_b$ of the lag-lead network (see Fig. 9-18). For the example at hand the point of intersection is found to be 100 radians/sec. Thus,

$$\alpha\omega_b = 100$$

3. Compute the value of the remaining parameters of the lag-lead network so that it furnishes the desired phase margin. The compensation network provides a total phase contribution at the crossover frequency given by

$$\phi_{\text{cn}} = \tan^{-1}\frac{\omega_c}{\omega_a} + \tan^{-1}\frac{\omega_c}{\omega_b} - \tan^{-1}\frac{\omega}{\omega_a/\alpha} - \tan^{-1}\frac{\omega_c}{\alpha\omega_b}$$

The quantity $\tan^{-1}\omega_c/\alpha\omega_b$ is exactly computed to be $\tan^{-1} 3.5/100$, or 2 degrees. Moreover, the quantity $\tan^{-1}\omega/(\omega_a/\alpha)$ has a value very close to 90 degrees, so that the total phase contribution of the lag-lead network can be written as

$$\phi_{\text{cn}} = \tan^{-1}\frac{\omega_c}{\omega_a} + \tan^{-1}\frac{\omega_c}{\omega_b} - 92°$$

Upon choosing $\omega_a = \omega_b$ as a matter of convenience, the expression for ϕ_{cn} is simplified to

$$\phi_{\text{cn}} = 2\tan^{-1}\frac{3.5}{\omega_b} - 92°$$

It therefore follows that the total phase angle of the compensated system at ω_c equal to 3.5 radians/sec is

$$\phi = -90° - \tan^{-1}\frac{3.5}{6} - \tan^{-1}\frac{3.5}{2} + 2\tan^{-1}\frac{3.5}{\omega_b} - 92°$$

or

$$\phi = -272.5° + 2\tan^{-1}\frac{3.5}{\omega_b}$$

For a phase margin of 45°, ϕ must have a value of $-135°$, which, upon insertion into the last equation, leads to

$$\omega_b = \omega_a = 1.35 \text{ radians/sec}$$

These are two of the three parameters needed for the lag-lead network design. The third parameter, which is the attenuation constant α, follows from

$$\alpha = \frac{100}{\omega_b} = \frac{100}{1.35} = 74$$

It is interesting to note that the lowest breakpoint frequency of the lag-lead network is ω_b/α, or $\frac{1}{55}$ radians/sec, corresponding to which is a time constant of 55 sec. This compares favorably with the value of 64 sec found in the preceding design.

Selection of Circuit Elements for the Lag-Lead Network. In the preceding pages the design procedure for determining the compensation transfer function of a lag-lead network which enables the system to meet the specifications in a high-performance application is outlined. Now attention is directed to the selection of the circuit elements which yield the desired values of τ_a, τ_b, and α as specified in the design. The circuit configuration corresponding to the lag-lead compensation transfer function is illustrated in Fig. 6-5 and is repeated in Fig. 9-20. For this circuit the time constants τ_a and τ_b as they appear in Eq. (9-28) are defined by Eqs. (6-16a) and (6-16b) as

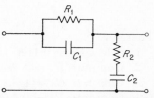

FIG. 9-20. Circuit configuration of a lag-lead network.

$$\tau_a = R_1 C_1 \tag{9-33}$$
$$\tau_b = R_2 C_2 \tag{9-34}$$

The third independent quantity is defined in Chap. 6, not as α, but as τ_{ab} and is given by Eq. (6-16c) as

$$\tau_{ab} = R_1 C_2 \tag{9-35}$$

The functional relationship between these three time constants and α follows from Eq. (6-19b). Thus,

$$\alpha\tau_a + \frac{\tau_b}{\alpha} = \tau_a + \tau_b + \tau_{ab}$$
$$= \tau_a + \tau_b + R_1 C_2$$

Rearranging leads to

$$R_1 C_2 = \frac{\alpha - 1}{\alpha} (\alpha\tau_a - \tau_b) \tag{9-36}$$

Equations (9-33), (9-34) and (9-36) are all that is needed to specify completely the circuit elements of Fig. 9-20 once the values of τ_a, τ_b, and α are established by the designer. The procedure follows:

1. Select C_1 arbitrarily, using reasonable values.
2. Compute R_1 from Eq. (9-33); that is, $R_1 = \tau_a/C_1$.
3. With R_1 known compute C_2 from Eq. (9-36). Thus,

$$C_2 = \frac{1}{R_1} \frac{\alpha - 1}{\alpha} (\alpha\tau_a - \tau_b)$$

If a reasonable value does not result for C_2, it may be necessary to reselect C_1.

4. Compute R_2 from Eq. (9-34), that is, $R_2 = \tau_b/C_2$.

For the purpose of illustration, let us apply this procedure to the design of the lag-lead compensation transfer function represented by Eq. (9-31). This design led to the following values of the parameters involved:

$$\tau_a = 1.28 \text{ sec}$$
$$\tau_b = 0.50 \text{ sec}$$
$$\alpha = 50$$

Therefore

1. Select $C_1 = 0.1$ μf.
2. Compute $R_1 = 1.28/0.1\mu f = 12.8$ megohms.
3. Compute $C_2 = 1/12.8(\frac{49}{50})(63.5) = 4.86$ μf.
4. Compute $R_2 = 0.5/4.86 = 0.103$ megohm.

The values of R_1 and C_2 are not in an especially desirable range. A capacitance of 4.86 μf is fairly large and should be avoided if possible. In aircraft applications where space is at a premium such a design may not be allowed, in which case the required high time constants are obtained from much smaller-sized units which work on temperature changes. The computed value of C_2 would be still worse had C_1 been chosen equal to 1 μf.

When a set of element values proves to be unsatisfactory, a new set can be readily determined by multiplying all the R values by a suitable constant and dividing all the C values by the same constant. This process of impedance-level shifting preserves the frequency-response characteristic because the time constants remain intact.

9-5. Design Procedure for Lag Compensation

In the preceding two sections the methods of designing simple lead compensation and lag-lead compensation are outlined. In this section attention is directed to the techniques of designing simple lag compensation. In general lag compensation is appropriate in furnishing satisfactory performance in those situations where the following conditions prevail: (1) There is need for a low bandwidth in order to discriminate against disturbing noise frequencies.   (2) An exceptionally fast response is not called for.   (3) There is need for high gain in order to provide high accuracy.

Statement of the Problem.   A specific application calls for a type 1 system with a velocity constant of 5 sec^{-1}.   The transient behavior is to be consistent with a phase margin of 45° so that excessive peak overshoots are avoided.   Also, the predominant time constant of the time response is to be less than 4 sec.   Moreover, compensation is to be restricted to the lag type in order to minimize the effect of troublesome noise frequencies which are known to exist in a frequency range beyond 2 cps.

Design Procedure.   Assume that on the basis of meeting the specifications on the steady-state performance as well as satisfying the output load requirements, the open-loop transfer function is

$$G_f(j\omega) = \frac{5}{j\omega[1 + j(\omega/2)][1 + j(\omega/6)]} \qquad (9\text{-}37)$$

The appropriate adjustment in gain to provide the velocity constant of 5 is already reflected in this expression.   A Bode diagram of the magnitude characteristic of Eq. (9-37) is illustrated in Fig. 9-21.

Where type 1 (or type 0) systems are involved, it is helpful to begin by first investigating how far the basic system is from meeting the specifications on the dynamic performance.   In this connection both the phase margin and an approximation of the predominant time constant are needed.   The phase margin is computed in the usual manner.   Figure 9-21 reveals the crossover frequency to be 3.15 radians/sec.   Inserting this value into the expression for the phase lag of Eq. (9-37) yields

$$\phi = -90 - \tan^{-1} 0.5(3.15) - \tan^{-1} 0.167(3.15) = -175.3°$$

Thus the phase margin is found to be

$$\phi_{\text{pm}} = \phi + 180 = +4.7°$$

This positive value of the phase margin indicates that the system is absolutely stable.   However, it is the relative stability which is important, and clearly the relative stability of the system of Eq. (9-37) is unsatisfactory.   Recalling that the phase margin essentially furnishes an indication of the maximum per cent overshoot of the time response, it is reasonable to expect that with such a small phase margin the peak overshoot is very likely in the vicinity of 90 per cent.   Of course zero phase margin corresponds to 100 per cent overshoot, which is merely another way of describing a condition of sustained oscillations.

Since the phase margin is positive, its value may be used to get an approximate indication of the predominant time constant by inserting

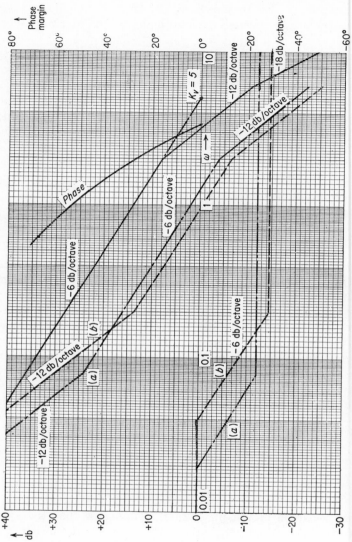

FIG. 9-21. Design of lag compensation for type 1 system.

it into Eq. (9-18b).   Thus,

$$T = \frac{1}{(4.7/360)\pi(3.15)} = 7.6 \text{ sec}$$

Because Eq. (9-18b) is over pessimistic, especially for type 1 and type 0 systems, it should not be concluded that the specification on the settling time cannot be met.   As a matter of fact a solution of the third-order characteristic equation corresponding to $K_v = 5$ reveals the actual value of the predominant time constant to be about 3.5 sec.   Accordingly, these considerations lead to the conclusion that compensation of the system of Eq. (9-37) is needed primarily to prevent excessive overshoots in the time response by furnishing ample phase margin.

Several methods of designing the necessary lag compensation are available, including a simple cut-and-try procedure which often is preferred by designers proficient in the application of frequency-domain techniques.   Our attention, however, is confined to two straightforward procedures which lead directly to the result.   A little more computation is involved than in the cut-and-try method because a portion of the phase characteristic of the uncompensated system needs to be calculated and drawn.   Actually the two methods discussed below are essentially the same method except for a modification which is introduced for the express purpose of reducing the magnitude of the time constants involved.

The design procedure consists fundamentally of four steps as outlined here:

1. Compute the phase of the original, uncompensated system.   For our example the expression for the uncompensated phase lag is

$$\phi = -90 - \tan^{-1}\frac{\omega}{2} - \tan^{-1}\frac{\omega}{6}$$

Upon inserting appropriately selected values of ω into this equation and then adding 180° to each computed value, the curve shown in Fig. 9-21 results.

2. Choose the crossover frequency of the compensated decibel-curve to correspond to the specified phase margin as obtained from the curve plotted in step 1.   For the system depicted in Fig. 9-21 this value is 1.25 radians/sec.   It should be realized that the validity of this operation is based upon the assumption that the phase-lag contribution associated with the lag network at this frequency is negligibly small.   Therefore, to assure this, it is necessary to select the upper breakpoint frequency of the lag network well below the new crossover frequency.

3. Select the upper breakpoint frequency of the lag network 4 octaves below the new crossover frequency.   A study of the normalized phase characteristics of the lag networks reveals that for a frequency 4 octaves

above the upper breakpoint frequency the phase lag is practically insignificant. If we call the upper breakpoint frequency ω_2 as illustrated in Fig. 9-22, its value is specified as

$$\omega_2 = \frac{\omega_c^*}{(2)^4} = \frac{\omega_c^*}{16} \tag{9-38}$$

where ω_c^* denotes the crossover frequency of the compensated magnitude curve. The figure $(2)^4$ is the mathematical representation of 4 octaves.

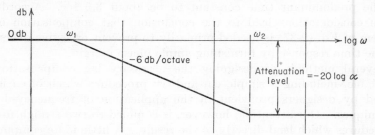

Fig. 9-22. Bode diagram for the magnitude characteristic of a lag network.

By definition a frequency ω_2 is said to be 1 octave higher than ω_1 if ω_2 is twice as large as ω_1; that is, $\omega_2/\omega_1 = 2 = 1$ octave. Similarly, $\omega_2/\omega_1 = 4 = 2$ octaves and $\omega_2/\omega_1 = 8 = 3$ octaves. Or expressed in general terms

$$\frac{\omega_2}{\omega_1} = 2^{(\text{number of octaves})} \tag{9-39}$$

Thus, for ω_2 to be 4 octaves higher than ω_1, its numerical value must be 16 times as large as ω_1.

Upon applying Eq. (9-38) to the example under study there results

$$\omega_2 = \frac{1.25}{16} = 0.078 \text{ radian/sec}$$

The establishment of this quantity furnishes one of the two independent parameters which is needed to specify the lag-network design. The other, of course, is the attenuation factor $1/\alpha$, which is computed in step 4.

The time constant corresponding to ω_2 is

$$\tau = \frac{1}{\omega_2} = 12.8 \text{ sec}$$

4. Select the attenuation level of the lag network equal to the amount the uncompensated decibel-curve lies above the 0-db axis at the new crossover frequency ω_c^*. The necessity of this step in the procedure is apparent; it guarantees that the compensated decibel curve intersects the 0-db axis at ω_c^*. Since the attenuation level of the lag network is specifically equal to 20 log α, the second independent quantity is determined and so the design is completed.

For the example at hand Fig. 9-21 indicates that at $\omega_c^* = 1.25$ radians/sec the original magnitude characteristic lies 12 db above the 0-db axis. Therefore

$$20 \log \alpha = 12$$

which gives

$$\alpha = 4$$

Once ω_2 and α are calculated, ω_1 is readily determined because it is a dependent quantity.   Graphically it may be obtained by drawing a line of -6 db/octave slope starting at the frequency ω_2 located at the proper decibel level until it intersects the ω axis.   The point of intersection identifies ω_1.   Otherwise it may be computed directly by recognizing that

$$\omega_1 = \frac{\omega_2}{\alpha} = \frac{0.078}{4} = 0.0195 \text{ radian/sec}$$

The corresponding time constant is

$$\alpha\tau = 4(12.8) = 51.2 \text{ sec}$$

Thus the final expression of the lag compensation transfer function is

$$G_c(j\omega) = \frac{1 + j\omega\tau}{1 + j\omega\alpha\tau} = \frac{1 + j(\omega/\omega_2)}{1 + j(\omega/\omega_1)} = \frac{1 + j12.8\omega}{1 + j51.2\omega} \qquad (9\text{-}40)$$

A study of this result shows that the time constants are fairly appreciable in magnitude and therefore undesirable from the viewpoint of using circuit elements of reasonably small size.

These large time constants are really a result of the conservative approach employed in the foregoing design procedure.   The selection of the upper breakpoint frequency of the lag network at a value so far below the new crossover frequency is what leads to the large time constants. This aspect of the design can be considerably improved upon by permitting the upper corner frequency to occur at a higher value and then making an allowance for the phase lag the network introduces at the new crossover frequency.   With the method just outlined the emphasis was put on simplicity at the expense of large time constant.   A study of the situation, however, makes it apparent that the degree of simplicity gained is trivial when compared with the disadvantages associated with the large time constants.   Accordingly, a modified design procedure yielding smaller time constants is next outlined and illustrated.   The system of Eq. (9-37) continues to be used for the illustration.

The modified design procedure involves five steps as outlined below:

1. Compute and plot the phase-margin characteristic of the uncompensated system.

2. Select the new crossover frequency to correspond to the desired phase margin plus an allowance to account for the lag angle introduced by the lag network.   As a first try, an allowance of 10° is reasonable.   Thus, for our example, the new crossover frequency is found on the phase-

margin curve corresponding to a value of

Desired phase margin + allowance = $45° + 10° = 55°$

which gives

$$\omega_c^* = 0.94 \text{ radian/sec}$$

3. Select the upper breakpoint frequency of the lag device 4 octaves below the crossover frequency of the uncompensated system. This manner of choosing ω_2 necessarily leads to a larger value than before, because the original crossover frequency always exceeds the crossover frequency of the compensated system when lag compensation is employed. Hence,

$$\omega_2 = \frac{\omega_c}{(2)^4} = \frac{3.15}{16} = 0.195$$

To round off the figure, use $\omega_2 = 0.2$ radian/sec. The corresponding time constant is then $\tau = 1/\omega_2 = 5$ sec, which represents a considerable improvement over the previous value obtained.

4. Select the attenuation level of the lag device equal to the amount the uncompensated decibel-curve lies above the 0-db axis of the new crossover frequency ω_c^*. As before, this step permits calculation of the appropriate attenuation constant. Thus

$$20 \log \alpha = 14.5$$

which yields

$$\alpha = 5.31$$

For convenience select $\alpha = 5.0$.

With α and ω_2 determined the value of the lower breakpoint frequency of the lag device is established as

$$\omega_1 = \frac{\omega_2}{\alpha} = \frac{0.2}{5} = 0.04 \text{ radian/sec}$$

The associated time constant is then

$$\alpha\tau = 5(5) = 25 \text{ sec}$$

Accordingly, the expression for the transfer function of the lag compensation becomes

$$G_c(j\omega) = \frac{1 + j\omega\tau}{1 + j\omega\alpha\tau} = \frac{1 + j(\omega/\omega_2)}{1 + j(\omega/\omega_1)} = \frac{1 + j5\omega}{1 + j25\omega} \tag{9-41}$$

5. Check that the phase-lag angle of the designed compensation transfer function at the new crossover frequency ω_c^* corresponds to the allowance provided for in step 2 within a tolerance equal to that specified for the phase margin. This step is necessary before accepting the design as final.

For the particular design of Eq. (9-41) the phase lag introduced by the lag device at 0.94 radian/sec is

$$\phi_c = + \tan^{-1} 5(0.94) - \tan^{-1} 25(0.94) = 78 - 87.6 = -9.6°$$

Since this figure compares favorably with the assumed value of $-10°$, the design is acceptable and the specification on the phase margin is satisfied.

The Bode diagrams for the magnitude characteristics of the two lag compensation designs as well as the corresponding compensated open-loop transfer functions are illustrated in Fig. 9-21. The original design is identified as a and the modified design as b.

A check on the predominant time constant as estimated by Eq. (9-18b) gives a value of 2.7 sec. Because this figure is pessimistic, the designer can rest assured that the settling time is satisfactory. A solution of the characteristic equation by using the techniques of Chap. 10 reveals the predominant time constant to be 1.4 sec.

Since either design of the lag compensation leads to satisfactory dynamic performance, a comparison of Eqs. (9-40) and (9-41) makes it apparent that the modified design of Eq. (9-41) is to be preferred. The basis of this preference, of course, lies in the fact that smaller time constants require physically smaller and less costly elements.

SUGGESTED READING

Chestnut, H., and R. Mayer: "Servomechanisms and Regulating System Design," 2d ed., vol. 1, chaps. 12 and 14, John Wiley & Sons, Inc., New York, 1960.

Murphy, G. J.: "Basic Automatic Control Theory," chap. 8, D. Van Nostrand Company, Inc., Princeton, N.J., 1957.

Thaler, G. J.: "Elements of Servomechanism Theory," chap. 9, McGraw-Hill Book Company, Inc., New York, 1955.

PROBLEMS

9-1. For the plot of the $HG(j\omega)$ shown in Fig. P9-1, explain whether or not this system may be made stable through the use of only a lag network or lead network. Sketch what the new $HG(j\omega)$ plot will look like with the inserted network.

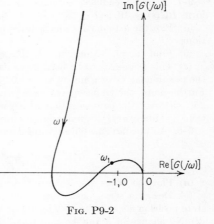

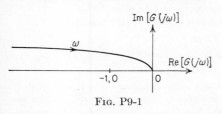

FIG. P9-1

FIG. P9-2

9-2. The $HG(j\omega)$ plot shown in Fig. P9-2 represents an unstable system.

(a) Why?

(b) A lead network is introduced to stabilize the system. Sketch the new locus, and indicate the position of ω_1 on the new locus.

(c) Can this system be stabilized by means of gain adjustment? Explain.

(d) If the answer to (c) is "yes," can you give a reason why this method of stabilization may not be preferred?

9-3. In order to meet the steady-state performance required of it, a servomechanism has an open-loop transfer function given by $HG(s) = 200/[s(1 + 0.1s)]$. Design a compensation network which will give a phase margin of 45°.

9-4. The open-loop transfer function of a servomechanism is given by

$$HG(j\omega) = \frac{7}{j\omega(1 + j0.5\omega)[1 + j(\omega/6)]}$$

Design a lag network which as a series compensator will give the system a phase margin of 40° ± 2°. Be sure to specify both the time constant and the attenuation factor of the network. The velocity constant must remain intact, and the gain crossover frequency shall have a minimum of 1 radian/sec.

9-5. A feedback control system has the following open-loop transfer function:

$$HG(j\omega) = \frac{200}{j\omega[1 + j(\omega/20)][1 + j(\omega/100)]}$$

(a) Determine the phase margin of the uncompensated system.

(b) Design a compensation network which will yield a phase margin of 40 to 50° while providing an open-loop gain of 40.

9-6. A servomechanism has an uncompensated open-loop transfer function given by $HG(j\omega) = 10/[(j\omega)^2(1 + j0.5\omega)]$. It is required that the system meet the following specifications: The actuating signal is not to exceed 0.1 radian for a maximum input acceleration of 10 radians/sec²; the transient behavior is to correspond to that of a phase margin of approximately 45° ± 3°.

Modify this system so that it meets the specifications. Be sure to indicate clearly the type of compensation used as well as the values of all time constants, attenuation factors, and preamplifier gains recommended. In order to avoid poor signal-to-noise ratios, it is recommended that attenuation factors of compensation networks be kept above a minimum of 0.05. Also, do not overdesign!

Estimate the settling time of this system.

9-7. A unity-feedback servomechanism has an open-loop transfer function of the form $HG(s) = 10/[s(1 + 2s)(1 + 0.1s)^2]$.

(a) Plot the attenuation characteristic of this system, using asymptotic approximations.

(b) Find the phase margin. Is this system absolutely stable?

(c) This system is to be used to control velocity. The specifications require that the position lag error is not to exceed 0.02 radian for an input velocity of 1 radian/sec. Furthermore, the transient response is to be that corresponding to a phase margin of 25°. Design the compensation which will permit this system to meet the specifications. Moreover, the predominant time constant is not to exceed 3 sec.

9-8. An uncompensated servomechanism has a direct transfer function

$$G(j\omega) = \frac{126}{j\omega[1 + j(\omega/10)][1 + j(\omega/60)]}$$

(a) Plot the db vs. log ω characteristic.

(b) Design a series compensator to meet the following specifications: (1) Steady-state position lag error to be $\frac{1}{126}$ radian (or less) for an input velocity of 1 radian/sec. (2) No change of amplifier gain permitted. (3) The phase margin of the compensated system is to satisfy the condition $\phi_{pm} = 30° ± 2°$.

Specify the numerical transfer function of the compensation network, and identify its circuit elements with the aid of a circuit diagram of the network.

(c) Sketch a polar plot of the uncompensated open-loop system as well as the compensated system, indicating clearly the manner in which the compensation network changes the original system to provide the proper stabilization.

(i) Estimate the settling time for the compensated system.

9-9. A type 0 system has the transfer function $HG(s) = K/[(1 + 0.1s)^2(1 + 0.01s)]$.

(a) Draw the asymptotic db vs. log ω characteristic as well as the phase curve.

(b) Determine the value of gain needed to yield a phase margin of 40°.

9-10. Shown in Fig. P9-10 are three compensation characteristics which are recommended for stabilizing a system having an open-loop transfer function $HG(s) = 400/[s^2(1 + 0.01s)]$.

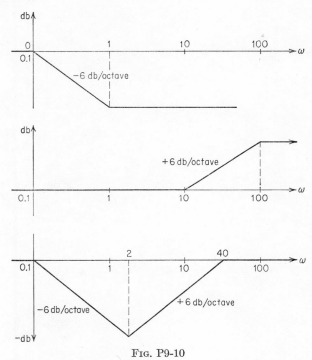

FIG. P9-10

(a) Determine which of these compensators will make the system absolutely stable.

(b) If the specifications require that the compensated system have a predominant time constant of better than 0.1 sec, which compensation scheme would you specify?

(c) If the maximum overshoot is not to exceed approximately 25 per cent, which compensation would you recommend?

(d) If it is imperative that the system attenuate sinusoidal noise beyond 12 cps even at the expense of increased settling time and greater maximum overshoot, which compensation would you specify?

(e) For the compensated system of part d compute the approximate value of the maximum overshoot as well as the predominant time constant.

IV | Root-locus Approach

10 | Dynamic Behavior of Systems. Root-locus Method

In Sec. 4-7 it is pointed out that the analysis and design of a third-order system or higher by the differential-equation approach is a laborious cut-and-try process, because the effect of changing a single system parameter cannot be studied directly. Examination of the characteristic equation reveals that the parameters of the system appear in several of the coefficients, thereby making a straightforward study impossible with this approach. The situation is significantly improved by the frequency-response approach, as pointed out in the preceding chapters. With the latter the effect of any one or several system parameters is investigated readily by using Bode-plot representations. The alteration of any parameter is studied in terms of the effect on the over-all attenuation and phase-shift characteristics of the open-loop transfer function and the manner in which figures of merit such as phase and gain margin are influenced. To illustrate this basic difference in the two approaches, let us return to the system of Sec. 4-7. Analysis by the differential-equation method leads to the characteristic equation identified as Eq. (4-107). A glance at this equation makes it clear that a direct study of how a change in τ_m or τ_f alters the source-free response can be made neither directly nor conveniently. However, analysis using frequency-response techniques leads to an open-loop transfer function of the form

$$\frac{C}{E}(s) = \frac{K_p K_A K_f}{RF} \frac{1}{s(1 + s\tau_f)(1 + s\tau_m)} = \frac{K}{s(1 + s\tau_f)(1 + s\tau_m)} \quad (10\text{-}1)$$

Clearly, the factored form of this equation makes it an easy matter to study the effect of a change in τ_f and/or τ_m by using Bode-plot representations. For example, doubling the value of τ_f merely means halving the corner frequency of the attenuation characteristic of this factor in Eq. (10-1). The subsequent effect on the gain and phase margins is then determined without any difficulty. Of course, one big limitation of this

393

procedure is that the exact time-domain solution is not obtained. However, the root-locus method developed by Walter R. Evans[1] not only eliminates this shortcoming and others but makes available to the control system engineer a truly powerful method of analysis as well as synthesis.

10-1. Transition from Pure-frequency to Complex-frequency Domain

A fuller grasp of the strength of the root-locus method may be had by investigating what happens as the values assigned to s in the expression for the open-loop transfer function are allowed to move off the $j\omega$ axis into the complex-frequency plane. In order to illustrate the transition, we continue with the example of the third-order system cited in Sec. 4-7. The general form of the closed-loop-system transfer function is

$$\frac{C}{R}(s) = \frac{G(s)}{1 + HG(s)} \tag{10-2}$$

For the configuration appearing in Fig. 4-25 the open-loop transfer function is

$$HG(s) = \frac{K}{s(1 + s\tau_f)(1 + s\tau_m)} \tag{10-3}$$

Upon setting the input signal equal to zero in Eq. (10-2), it follows that the characteristic equation may be expressed simply as

$$1 + HG(s) = 0 \tag{10-4}$$

which makes it clear that it is identified in terms of the open-loop transfer function. (Again note the recurrent important role which the open-loop transfer function continues to play in systems analysis.) Equation (10-4) is expressed alternatively as

$$HG(s) = -1 = \underline{/180°(2k + 1)} \qquad k = 0, \pm1, \pm2, \ldots \tag{10-5}$$

For sinusoidal-frequency studies (i.e., the values of s are restricted to the $j\omega$ axis) the open-loop transfer function becomes

$$HG(j\omega) = \frac{K}{j\omega(1 + j\omega\tau_m)(1 + j\omega\tau_f)} \tag{10-6}$$

Now, if at a given frequency, say, ω_1, the total phase shift is $-180°$, then by the proper choice of the open-loop gain the system can be made to be unstable; i.e., it goes into a state of sustained oscillations at the frequency ω_1. From Eq. (10-6) the expression for the total phase angle at this frequency ω_1 is clearly

$$\phi = -90 - \tan^{-1}\omega_1\tau_m - \tan^{-1}\omega_1\tau_f = -180°$$

[1] Graphical Analysis of Control Systems, *Trans. AIEE*, vol. 67, pp. 547–551, 1948; see also "Control-system Dynamics," McGraw-Hill Book Company, Inc., New York, 1954.

Each of the angles associated with the factors of the open-loop transfer function is shown in Fig. 10-1. Note that to form graphically the linear factors requires formulating the product $j\omega\tau$ and then adding 1 to it vectorially.

A more convenient procedure for identifying these angles in the complex plane results when Eq. (10-6) is rewritten as

$$HG(j\omega) = \frac{K}{\tau_m\tau_f} \frac{1}{j\omega(j\omega + 1/\tau_m)(j\omega + 1/\tau_f)}$$

This modification offers the advantage of terminating each phasor (or

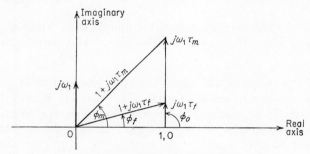

Fig. 10-1. Phasors of Eq. (10-6).

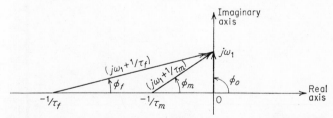

Fig. 10-2. Alternative representation of the phasors of Eq. (10-6).

vector) at the same point on the $j\omega$ axis. Of course, to do so also requires locating the critical frequencies[1] of $HG(s)$ as shown in Fig. 10-2. For convenience let

$$j\omega_1 + \frac{1}{\tau_m} = r_m \underline{/\phi_m}$$

$$j\omega_1 + \frac{1}{\tau_f} = r_f \underline{/\phi_f}$$

$$j\omega_1 = r_0 \underline{/\phi_0}$$

where r denotes the magnitude of each phasor and ϕ the corresponding phase angle. Then the gain needed to cause sustained oscillations to

---

[1] *Critical frequencies* is a term used to denote the poles and zeros of the open-loop transfer function.

occur at that frequency for which the phase shift is $-180°$ is clearly found by satisfying the condition

$$\frac{K_1}{\tau_m \tau_f} \frac{1}{r_0 r_m r_f} = 1$$

where K_1 denotes the desired gain value. Thus,

$$K_1 = r_0 r_m r_f \tau_m \tau_f$$

The expression for the characteristic equation as obtained from Eqs. (10-4) and (10-3) is

$$s^3 + \frac{\tau_m + \tau_f}{\tau_m \tau_f} s^2 + \frac{1}{\tau_m \tau_f} s + \frac{K}{\tau_m \tau_f} = 0 \tag{10-7}$$

On the basis of the foregoing material it follows that, when $K = K_1$, two of the roots of Eq. (10-7) are purely imaginary and specifically given by

$$s_{1,2} = \pm j\omega_1$$

where ω_1 is the frequency at which the total phase shift is $-180°$. An appropriate question to ask at this point is: What happens to the roots of this characteristic equation when the open-loop gain is changed from the value K_1 to some smaller or larger value?   In accordance with the laws of algebra the roots of a polynomial such as Eq. (10-7) are a continuous function of the constant term K.[†]   Thus, if a slightly larger gain is used

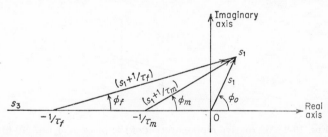

FIG. 10-3. Location of the phasors of the system of Fig. 10-2 for a complex frequency s_1.

three other different and distinct roots can be found, and it is reasonable to expect that the two purely imaginary roots now become complex conjugate roots.   Furthermore, since these new roots satisfy Eq. (10-7), they must also satisfy Eq. (10-5).   In fact, if these roots are solved for by any one of the standard methods available and the resulting pair of complex roots are located in the s plane (as illustrated in Fig. 10-3) and the angles of each phasor of the open-loop transfer function are measured and summed, the resultant phase angle would be found to add up to $-180°$.   This is entirely expected in view of the fact that any solution to Eq. (10-7) is also a solution of Eq. (10-5).   The value of the gain K which makes the magnitude of the open-loop transfer function unity is

[†] See Maxime Bocher, "Introduction to Higher Algebra," The Macmillan Company, New York, 1907.

found in the same manner as before, viz.,

$$K_2 = r_0 r_m r_f \tau_m \tau_f$$

The transition from the $j\omega$ axis to the entire complex plane is significant indeed. By confining attention to just the $j\omega$-axis as is done in the frequency-response approach, control over such things as velocity and acceleration constants, absolute and relative stability, and bandwidth is readily had, but direct control over the corresponding time-domain response does not exist. The latter must be accomplished in terms of appropriate figures of merit. However, the use of the entire complex plane provides the control systems designer with the tools which enable him to exert direct influence upon the frequency-domain as well as the time-domain response. By the judicious location of the poles and zeros of compensation devices, the designer can see almost at a glance the manner in which both the transient response and the frequency response of the closed-loop system are affected.

10-2. Criteria of the Root-locus Method

The essence of the root-locus method consists in finding the locus of points in the complex-frequency plane which are solutions of the characteristic equation for values of the open-loop gain varying from zero to infinity; this means satisfying the condition

$$HG(s) = -1 = 1\underline{/180°(2k + 1)} \qquad k = 0, \pm 1, \pm 2, \ldots$$

By seeking out those points in the s plane which cause the open-loop transfer function to satisfy the foregoing condition, exact information concerning the closed-loop time-domain response is made available.

In all practical control systems the form of the open-loop transfer function involves a gain factor, a numerator polynomial in factored form, and a denominator polynomial in factored form. The order of the denominator is greater than or at least equal to that of the numerator. The factored form exists because the loop transfer function is formulated as the product of the individual component transfer functions which make up the system. Upon inserting a specific value of the complex-frequency variable in $HG(s)$, the result is in general a complex number having a magnitude R and a total phase angle ϕ. Thus,

$$HG(s) = R\underline{/\phi}$$

Now when the value of s is a root of the characteristic equation, then

$$R = 1$$

and $\qquad \phi = (2k + 1)\pi \qquad$ where $k = 0, \pm 1, \pm 2, \pm 3, \ldots$

which is another way of stating that Eq. (10-5) is satisfied.

In order to put these conclusions into a more general form, consider the following expression for the open-loop transfer function:

$$HG(s) =$$
$$\frac{K(1 + s\tau_a)(1 + s\tau_b)(1 + s\tau_c) \ \cdot \ \cdot \ \cdot \ [(s/\omega_{na})^2 + (2\zeta_a/\omega_{na})s + 1]}{s^N(1 + s\tau_1)(1 + s\tau_2)(1 + s\tau_3) \ \cdot \ \cdot \ \cdot}$$
$$[(s/\omega_{n1})^2 + (2\zeta_1/\omega_{n1})s + 1][(s/\omega_{n2})^2 + (2\zeta_2/\omega_{n2})s + 1] \quad (10\text{-}8)$$

In making a frequency-response analysis of such a system, this form of $HG(s)$ is the most desirable since it leads directly to the identification of the breakpoint frequency and the two straight-line asymptotes which closely approximate the frequency characteristics of each factor. However, for the purposes of a root-locus study, such a form is not convenient because the root factors do not all terminate on the particular point in question in the s plane. Consequently, the procedure involved in measuring the angular contribution of each factor of $HG(s)$ to the total phase shift is more complicated. This disadvantage, however, is eliminated by writing the open-loop transfer function in the following modified form:

$$HG(s) = \frac{K\tau_a\tau_b\tau_c \ \cdot \ \cdot \ \cdot \ \omega_{n1}^2\omega_{n2}^2}{\tau_1\tau_2\tau_3 \ \cdot \ \cdot \ \cdot \ \omega_{na}^2}$$
$$\left[\frac{(s + 1/\tau_a)(s + 1/\tau_b) \ \cdot \ \cdot \ \cdot \ (s^2 + 2\zeta_a\omega_{na}s + \omega_{na}^2)}{s^N(s + 1/\tau_1)(s + 1/\tau_2)(s + 1/\tau_3) \ \cdot \ \cdot \ \cdot \ (s^2 + 2\zeta_2\omega_{n2}s + \omega_{n2}^2)} \right] \quad (10\text{-}9)$$

A little thought reveals that a linear factor such as $s + 1/\tau_a$ can be

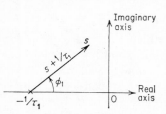

located on the s plane. The critical frequency $s = -1/\tau_1$ can be located to the left of the origin as shown in Fig. 10-4. For a particular s-plane point s it is noted that the vector $s + 1/\tau_1$ is located by simply *drawing a line from the critical frequency to the point in question.* A representation such as that of Fig. 10-4 is significant in that it gives the correct location of the poles and zeros of the open-loop transfer function, viz., Eq. (10-9),

FIG. 10-4. Representation of the linear factor $s + 1/\tau_1$.

and what is more the phasors associated with each of these critical frequencies terminate on the same point in the s plane.

To simplify the expression of Eq. (10-9), introduce the following substitutions:

$$z_1 = \frac{1}{\tau_a} \qquad z_2 = \frac{1}{\tau_b} \qquad \cdot \ \cdot \ \cdot$$
$$p_1 = \frac{1}{\tau_1} \qquad p_2 = \frac{1}{\tau_2} \qquad \cdot \ \cdot \ \cdot \qquad\qquad (10\text{-}10)$$

and
$$K' = \frac{K\tau_a\tau_b\tau_c \ \cdot \ \cdot \ \cdot \ \omega_{n1}^2\omega_{n2}^2}{\tau_1\tau_2\tau_3 \ \cdot \ \cdot \ \cdot \ \omega_{na}^2} \qquad\qquad (10\text{-}11)$$

The quantity K' is the gain factor used in root-locus studies because of the form of Eq. (10-9). Also, a little thought indicates that it is frequently the constant term present in the normalized form of the characteristic equation corresponding to the particular open-loop transfer function. Care should be taken not to confuse K' with the system open-loop gain K. The distinction is clearly indicated in Eq. (10-11). In any given situation the ω^2 terms appearing in Eq. (10-11) will or will not be present depending upon whether or not quadratic factors appear in the numerator and/or denominator of the open-loop transfer function.

As already pointed out, each factor of Eq. (10-9) has a magnitude and phase angle for each value of s. In terms of a polar representation we can write

$$s + z_1 = r_{z1}\underline{/\phi_{z1}}$$
$$s + z_2 = r_{z2}\underline{/\phi_{z2}}$$

$$s^N = r_{p0}{}^N\underline{/N\phi_{p0}}$$
$$s + p_1 = r_{p1}\underline{/\phi_{p1}}$$
$$s + p_2 = r_{p2}\underline{/\phi_{p2}}$$

$$(10\text{-}12)$$

The same representation also applies for the two complex roots associated with the underdamped quadratic terms.[1] Equation (10-12) replaces each phasor in terms of its magnitude r_{z1} and the angle ϕ_{z1}. The z and p notations are used to represent zeros and poles of the open-loop transfer function.

Upon inserting Eq. (10-12) into Eq. (10-9) and assuming that the order of the numerator polynomial is Z and that of the denominator P there results

$$HG(s) = \frac{K'r_{z1}r_{z2}\ \cdots\ r_{zZ}}{r_{p0}{}^N r_{p1}\ \cdots\ r_{p(P-N)}}$$
$$\underline{/(\phi_{z1} + \phi_{z2} + \cdots + \phi_{zZ}) - (N\phi_0 + \phi_{p1} + \cdots + \phi_{p(P-N)})} \quad (10\text{-}13)$$

or

$$HG(s) = K'\frac{\displaystyle\prod_{i=1}^{Z} r_{zi}}{r_{p0}{}^N\displaystyle\prod_{i=1}^{P-N} r_{pi}}\ \underline{\bigg/\ \sum_{i=1}^{Z}\phi_{zi} - \bigg(N\phi_0 + \sum_{i=1}^{P-N}\phi_{pi}\bigg)} \quad (10\text{-}14)$$

[1] If the quadratic terms are not underdamped, they would appear as two linear terms.

where Π denotes the product of the magnitudes of all indicated phasors.

The generalized criterion for finding the root loci of the characteristic equation of a control system can now be deduced from Eq. (10-14). As already demonstrated, a point in the s plane is a solution of the characteristic equation if, first of all, it satisfies the phase criterion. Since $HG(s)$ must be equal to -1, it follows that two phase criteria are possible depending upon the sign of the open-loop transfer function. Thus, if K' is positive, then, in order for Eq. (10-14) to be equal to -1, the resultant phase angle must be 180°. If K' is negative, the resultant phase angle must be 0°. A negative K' means that, with the feedback loop open and a positive actuating signal applied to the system, the output of the feedback transducer is negative. In such cases it should be apparent that the normal negative-feedback connection of the feedback transducer output to the input transducer no longer can be used; otherwise positive feedback results. Attention is directed to this situation because it is common in flight control systems. Once the phase condition is satisfied, then the particular value of gain needed to satisfy the unity-magnitude condition follows readily from Eq. (10-14). Summarizing these criteria, we have

Phase criterion:

$$\sum_{i=1}^{Z} \phi_{zi} - \left(N\phi_0 + \sum_{i=1}^{P-N} \phi_{pi} \right) = 180° \pm \text{multiples of } 360° = (2k+1)\pi$$

$$k = 0, \pm 1, \ldots \text{ for } K' \text{ positive} \qquad (10\text{-}15)$$

$$\sum_{i=1}^{Z} \phi_{zi} - \left(N\phi_0 + \sum_{i=1}^{P-N} \phi_{pi} \right) = 0° \pm \text{multiples of } 360° = 2k\pi$$

$$k = 0, \pm 1, \pm 2, \ldots \text{ for } K' \text{ negative}$$

Magnitude criterion:

$$K' \frac{\displaystyle\prod_{i=1}^{Z} r_{zi}}{r_{p0}{}^{N} \displaystyle\prod_{i=1}^{P-N} r_{pi}} = 1 \qquad (10\text{-}16)$$

The phase criterion is merely a statement of the fact that, for any point in the s plane to be a root of the characteristic equation, the sum of the angles of the phasors drawn from the zeros to s minus the sum of the angles of the phasors drawn from the poles to s must add up to a resultant of 180° or 0° depending upon the sign of the open-loop transfer function.

10-3. Application to a Second-order System

The advantages which the root-locus method offers as a tool for analysis and design are demonstrated simply and effectively by the second-order system illustrated in Fig. 10-5. The open-loop transfer function is

$$HG(s) = \frac{K'}{(s+1)(s+3)} \qquad (10\text{-}17)$$

The corresponding closed-loop transfer function is, for $h = 1$,

$$\frac{C}{R}(s) = \frac{K'/[(s+1)(s+3)]}{1 + K'/[(s+1)(s+3)]} = \frac{K'}{(s+1)(s+3) + K'} \qquad (10\text{-}18)$$

The system characteristic equation is

$$s^2 + 4s + (3 + K') = 0 \qquad (10\text{-}19)$$

Equation (10-19) may be solved by the standard algebraic method or by

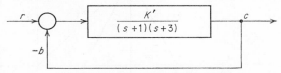

FIG. 10-5. A second-order system.

direct application of the Evans criteria as described by Eqs. (10-15) and (10-16). To emphasize that each method leads to the same result, the roots are first found algebraically for various values of K', thus leading to the appropriate loci. Then these loci are shown to satisfy Eqs. (10-15) and (10-16).

Because Eq. (10-19) is second-order, the roots may be written directly as

$$s_{1,2} = -2 \pm \sqrt{4 - (3 + K')} = -2 \pm \sqrt{1 - K'} \qquad (10\text{-}20)$$

Accordingly the following results are obtained for the specified values of K':

$K' = 0$	$s_{1,2} = -1, -3$	
$K' = \frac{3}{4}$	$s_{1,2} = -1.5, -2.5$	
$K' = 1$	$s_{1,2} = -2, -2$	a double root
$K' = 5$	$s_{1,2} = -2 \pm j2$	
$K' = 10$	$s_{1,2} = -2 \pm j3$	

Complex conjugate roots exist for any value of K' greater than unity as indicated by Eq. (10-20). These roots are shown plotted in Fig. 10-6 with the value of K' indicated alongside the point. Several items are worth noting. First, the roots of the characteristic equation for $K' = 0$ are the same as the poles of the open-loop transfer function. This conclusion is not restricted to second-order systems but is true generally. Second, the roots of the closed-loop transfer function migrate away from the poles of the open-loop transfer function as the gain is increased. Moreover, the migration is such that the sum of the roots remains equal to -4. Again, this is a general result which applies to any open-loop transfer function in which the order of s in the denominator is at least 2 greater than the order of s in the numerator. In such instances the sum of the roots is equal to the negative value of the coefficient of the s^{P-1} term in the normalized form of the characteristic equation regardless of

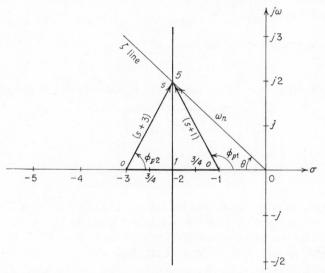

Fig. 10-6. Root-locus diagram of the second-order system of Fig. 10-5.

the value of K'. Third, as K' increases from 0 to 1, the roots migrate from the poles in opposite directions in order to keep the sum invariant. However, at $K' = 1$ the two roots coalesce, and any further increase in K' causes the roots to break away from the real axis, thus becoming complex. Consequently, $K' = 1$ represents the case of critical damping with underdamping resulting whenever K' exceeds unity. Accordingly, once a picture such as Fig. 10-6 is established, the nature of the transient-response modes is determined almost upon inspection. For positive values of K' the locus of roots of the characteristic equation is confined to the portion of the negative real axis lying between -1 and -3 (where the response is overdamped) and to the entire ordinate line passing through the -2 abscissa value (where the response is underdamped).

Although the loci of Fig. 10-6 could be constructed very simply by direct application of Eq. (10-15), this procedure is delayed until after the discussion dealing with rules of construction is treated in the next section.

Instead we now confine attention to showing that any point on the locus of Fig. 10-6 does satisfy the phase criterion. Calculation of the corresponding value of K' is also indicated.

The open-loop transfer function contains no explicit zeros so that the total phase angle of 180° must come from the phasors originating from the open-loop poles. Clearly, when a test point is taken anywhere between -1 and -3, the phasor $s + 1$ has a 180° phase angle, while the phasor $s + 3$ necessarily has a 0° phase angle. The resultant is therefore 180°, which satisfies the phase criterion. On the other hand, note that, if a test point were taken between 0 and -1, then both phasors would have zero angles. A test point selected to the left of -3 gives both phasors drawn from the poles an angle of 180° or a resultant of zero, so that this portion of the real axis cannot be part of the locus either. Consider next a test point s lying along the perpendicular passing through -2. The phasor from the pole at -1 makes the angle ϕ_{p1}, while that from the pole at -3 makes the angle ϕ_{p2}. But since an isosceles triangle is involved here for any point along the ordinate line, it follows that

$$\phi_{p1} + \phi_{p2} = \pm 180° \qquad \begin{cases} + \text{ for points above real axis} \\ - \text{ for points below real axis} \end{cases}$$

Once a point such as $s = -2 + j2$ has been identified as a root on the basis of the phase criterion, the required value of K' is determined from the magnitude criterion of Eq. (10-16). Thus, for this case

$$r_{p1} = |s + 1| = \sqrt{(2)^2 + 1} = \sqrt{5}$$
$$r_{p2} = |s + 3| = \sqrt{(2)^2 + 1} = \sqrt{5}$$

and

$$\frac{K'}{r_{p1}r_{p2}} = 1$$

Therefore

$$K' = 5$$

which checks with the value found analytically.

It is important to realize that the roots lying on the root locus are the solutions of the characteristic equation of the *closed-loop system*. It is for this reason that the control system designer has direct control over the time-domain response. For example, if the designer of the system of Fig. 10-5 wished to calculate the value of gain needed to give a damping ratio of 0.707, he could immediately do so by constructing in Fig. 10-6 a line from the origin at an angle of $\pm 45°$ with the negative real axis. The resulting points of intersection with the loci make available the roots characterizing the transient modes, while the gain is calculated as outlined above. Such a procedure can be applied to any pair of complex conjugate roots whether the system is second-order or higher.

The proof of this construction is straightforward when it is recalled that any pair of complex conjugate roots can be expressed as

$$s_{1,2} = -\zeta\omega_n \pm j\omega_n \sqrt{1 - \zeta^2}$$

Since each root is a complex number, it has a magnitude and phase angle which can be expressed generally as

$$s_{1,2} = \omega_n \; \underline{/\pm\theta}$$

where

$$\theta = \tan^{-1} \frac{\sqrt{1 - \zeta^2}}{\zeta}$$

Therefore

$$\cos\theta = \frac{\zeta\omega_n}{\omega_n} = \zeta \tag{10-21}$$

10-4. General Procedure for Constructing the Root Loci

The direct application of the Evans criteria [Eqs. (10-15) and (10-16)] yields the roots of the system characteristic equation; however, it might appear at this point that the determination of such loci is not a simple matter. Actually, this is not so, because the search for those points in the complex plane which satisfy Eq. (10-5) is not an aimless one. As a matter of fact, by the application of a few rules, the general form of the loci is placed clearly in evidence even with only a cursory examination of the open-loop transfer function. Moreover, this is true even for high-order systems, where $HG(s)$ contains many zeros and poles. Indeed, it is in such cases that the root-locus method shows to advantage over the previously treated methods of analysis and design. The general procedure for constructing the root loci is embodied in the eight steps described below.

Step 1. Locate the poles and zeros of $HG(s)$ in the complex-frequency plane. It is of the utmost importance to use the *same scale* for the abscissa and ordinate axes; otherwise the resulting root-locus plots are meaningless.

Step 2. Mark off those sections of the real axis which lie to the left of an odd number of critical frequencies when the positive sign appears before K' in Eq. (10-9). When K' is negative, the locus lies to the left of an even number of critical frequencies.

The validity of this statement is readily demonstrated by considering an open-loop transfer function of the following form

$$HG(s) = K' \frac{(s + z_1)(s + z_2)}{s(s + p_2)(s^2 + 2\zeta_3\omega_{n3}s + \omega_{n3}{}^2)} \tag{10-22}$$

A typical location of these poles and zeros is illustrated in Fig. 10-7a. Consider a point s located to the left of an even number of critical frequencies (Fig. 10-7a). If we turn our attention first to the angular contribution associated with the phasors originating from the complex conjugate poles, it is apparent that the net contribution is zero. This conclusion holds whenever s is located anywhere along the real axis. Therefore in this case the phase angle of $HG(s)$ must come from the phasors of the real poles and zeros.   Further examination reveals that all critical frequencies lying to the left of s have phasors with zero phase angle, while all those lying to the right of s have phasors with angles of 180°.   It follows then that the only phasors that can be of importance in meeting the phase criterion are those located to the right of s.   If an even number of these phasors originate to the right of s, the net phase angle is clearly 0°.   Hence such a section cannot be part of the root locus of the system of Eq. (10-9).   If s is placed now so that it is located to the left of an *odd* number of poles and/or zeros as shown in Fig. 10-7b, then the net

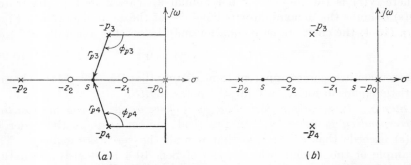

FIG. 10-7. (a) Demonstration that complex poles make no phase-angle contribution for a point along the real axis; (b) identifying those sections of the real axis which are part of the locus.

phase angle is 180°.   Consequently, such a point identifies a section of the real axis which is part of the locus.   In Fig. 10-7 those portions constituting part of the locus are the sections lying between $-p_2$ and $-z_2$ and also between $-z_1$ and $-p_0$.

On the basis of the foregoing considerations it should be clear that the sections of the real axis which are part of the locus extend over the range from one critical frequency to the next.

Step 3.   *Look for a number of separate loci equal to the number poles of* $HG(s)$.   From Eqs. (10-4) and (10-9) it follows that the characteristic equation is a polynomial of s having the same order as the denominator of $HG(s)$.   By the fundamental theorem of algebra, there are as many roots as the order of the polynomial.   If the order is assumed equal to P, then for each value of K' used in the characteristic equation, there are found P different roots.   If it is assumed further that these roots are determined analytically for many values of K' and then plotted, it should be apparent that P distinct[1] and separate loci will result.

---

[1] In some systems double roots will exist for a specific value of gain, in which case distinct loci are not readily apparent.   The loci start out separately but then coalesce at the double root and break away again.

Step 4. Begin sketching the loci by starting at the poles of the open-loop transfer function corresponding to $K' \to 0$. *These poles are the starting points of the locus.* The reasonableness of this step is demonstrated in the example of the second-order system treated in Sec. 10-3, where it is shown that for $K' = 0$ the roots of the characteristic equation are identical to the poles of $HG(s)$. The open-loop transfer function can be written as

$$HG(s) = K' \frac{N(s)}{D(s)} \tag{10-23}$$

where $N(s)$ is the numerator polynomial appearing in Eq. (10-9) and $D(s)$ denotes the denominator polynomial of the same equation. From Eq. (10-4) the characteristic equation may be written generally as

$$D(s) + K'N(s) = 0 \tag{10-24}$$

whereupon it becomes apparent immediately that the roots of the characteristic equation for $K' = 0$ are the poles of $HG(s)$.

Step 5. Terminate the loci at the zeros of the open-loop transfer function corresponding to $K' \to \infty$. In practical control systems the order of $D(s)$ exceeds that of $N(s)$ so that not all the zeros are explicit. The example of the second-order system of Sec. 10-3 illustrates a situation where there are no explicit zeros. The transfer function of Eq. (10-22), on the other hand, represents a case where there are two explicit zeros, viz., $-z_1$ and $-z_2$. It is interesting to note that, in those instances where the explicit zeros are located on the real axis, the combination of step 5 and step 2 establishes one or more of the loci. Thus in Fig. 10-7 two of the four loci are established by recognizing that, as K' increases from zero to infinity, one root of the characteristic equation is located on the locus extending from $-p_0$ to $-z_1$ and a second root on the locus extending from $-p_2$ to $-z_2$.

The existence of the explicit zeros is deduced from Eq. (10-24) upon introducing values of K' approaching infinity. This makes $D(s)$ negligible in comparison with $K'N(s)$, subject to the restriction, of course, that s is finite.[1]   Thus,

$$K'N(s) = 0 \qquad \text{for } K' \to \infty \tag{10-25}$$

Hence Eq. (10-25) is satisfied upon insertion of the zeros of $N(s)$, which now are also the roots of the characteristic equation for K' approaching infinity. The explicit zeros bring into evidence one or more of the required number of loci, as already pointed out. However, if the order of $D(s)$ is P and that of $N(s)$ is Z, then there are still $P-Z$ loci to be determined. In other words, there are $P-Z$ implicit zeros.

These implicit zeros cannot be revealed from Eq. (10-25), because to

[1] The explicit zeros are located in the finite s plane.

deduce them requires that s be very large, i.e., approach infinity. Under such circumstances the $D(s)$ is no longer negligible especially in view of the fact that it is of higher order than $N(s)$. Accordingly, information concerning the implicit zeros must come from another source, which accounts for the presence of both $N(s)$ and $D(s)$. This suggests Eq. (10-23). Introducing the appropriate condition on s modifies Eq. (10-23) to

$$\lim_{s \to \infty} HG(s) = \frac{K'}{s^{P-Z}} \tag{10-26}$$

The graphical representation of this equation appears in Fig. 10-8, which

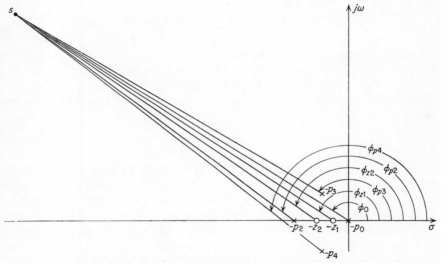

FIG. 10-8. Graphical representation of the implicit zeros of $HG(s)$.

is specifically drawn for the transfer function of Eq. (10-22). When the point s is far removed from the origin, the poles and explicit zeros appear so bunched together that the explicit zeros are neutralized by a corresponding number of poles of $HG(s)$ leaving what seems to be a pole of multiplicity $P-Z$. The only question which now remains to be answered is under what conditions Eq. (10-26) will yield a result of $1\underline{/180°}$, thereby assuring that these points are solutions of the system characteristic equation. The answer is provided by direct application of the Evans phase criterion which, for points a great distance from the origin, may be written as

$$\sum_{i=1}^{P-Z} \phi_{pi} = (2k+1)\pi \qquad \text{for } K' +$$

$$= 2k\pi \qquad \text{for } K' - \tag{10-27}$$

The form of this equation accounts for the cancellation of the explicit zeros with poles by permitting i to take on values only from 1 to $P - Z$, where the latter quantity denotes the number of excess poles of $HG(s)$ over explicit zeros. Moreover, inspection of Fig. 10-8 makes it clear that each of the angles of the phasors from the excess poles over zeros is equal and denoted by ϕ_{asymp}, so that Eq. (10-27) may be simplified to

$$(P - Z)\phi_{asymp} = (2k + 1)\pi \qquad \text{for } K' +$$
$$= 2k\pi \qquad \text{for } K' -$$

or, more explicitly,

$$\phi_{asymp} = \frac{(2k + 1)\pi}{P - Z} \qquad \text{for } K' + \text{ and } k = 0, \pm 1, \ldots$$
$$= \frac{2k\pi}{P - Z} \qquad \text{for } K' - \text{ and } k = 0, \pm 1, \ldots \qquad (10\text{-}28)$$

As many values of k are used as will yield distinct solutions. A little thought reveals that the number of distinct solutions equals $P - Z$.

Direct application of the Evans magnitude criterion establishes the appropriate value of K' corresponding to a point s far removed from the origin of the s plane. Thus

$$\frac{K'}{r^{P-Z}} = 1 \qquad (10\text{-}29)$$

Since r^{P-Z} is very large, K', too, must be very large to keep the ratio equal to unity.

Let us apply the result of Eq. (10-28) to the system of Eq. (10-22). It has been established already that associated with the explicit zeros two loci exist on the negative real axis. Since there are four open-loop poles, it follows that there are two implicit zeros located at $s \to \infty$ along the direction specified by Eq. (10-28), which in this case is

$$\phi_{asymp} = \frac{2k + 1}{2}\pi = \frac{\pi}{2} \qquad \text{for } k = 0$$
$$= \tfrac{3}{2}\pi \qquad \text{for } k = +1$$

The number of separate and distinct asymptotes is always equal to $P - Z$, which here is 2.

In summary, therefore, it can be said that step 5 provides the designer with information about the end points of the root loci as K' is increased to very large values.

Step 6. Locate the intersection point of the asymptotes from

$$\sigma_c = \frac{\Sigma \text{ poles} - \Sigma \text{ zeros}}{P - Z} \qquad (10\text{-}30)$$

Equation (10-28) provides information concerning the angles which the loci make with the positive real axis for large values of s. To be useful, this must be combined with knowledge of the point of origin of the asymptotes in the finite s plane. To an observer remotely located from the origin, the pole-zero configuration appears concentrated at a point along the real axis which we call the *centroid* because of the analogy to the center of gravity of a system of masses. In fact the location of this centroid is found in the same way as the center of gravity of distributed masses. All that is needed is that we arbitrarily assign a $+1$ to each pole and a -1 to each finite zero to denote equivalent masses. The moments produced about the origin are then proportional to the locations of these critical frequencies. The moment produced about the abscissa axis by complex conjugate zeros or poles is zero because the effects due to each conjugate zero or pole are equal and opposite. Hence only the real parts of complex critical frequencies influence the location of the centroid. Also, since each pole has an equivalent mass of $+1$ and each zero an equivalent mass of -1, it follows that the net moment about the origin is simply the sum of the locations of the poles minus the sum of the locations of the zeros. Thus,

Net moment of pole-zero configuration $= \Sigma$ poles $- \Sigma$ zeros (10-31)

Equation (10-31) is a statement of conditions as they appear to an observer in the finite s plane. But to an observer far removed from the origin, the specific "microscopic" details of the individual poles and zeros are lost. All that can be seen is a pole of multiplicity $P - Z$ located at some point from the origin σ_c. However, the net moment of this "apparent" multiple pole must be identical to the actual pole-zero configuration. Accordingly, we have

$$\sigma_c(P - Z) = \Sigma \text{ poles} - \Sigma \text{ zeros}$$

Hence to the remote observer the asymptotes seem to originate from

$$\sigma_c = \frac{\Sigma \text{ poles} - \Sigma \text{ zeros}}{P - Z} \qquad (10\text{-}30)$$

Applying Eq. (10-30) to the second-order system of Sec. 10-3, we get

$$\sigma_c = \frac{-1 - 3 + 0}{2} = -2$$

which checks with the result shown in Fig. 10-6.

The combination of the results of Eqs. (10-28) and (10-30) is instrumental not only in establishing the shape of the root loci for large values of s but also in serving as a guide in determining the paths which the root loci take in the region about the origin. This latter aspect is made clearer in the examples which follow.

Step 7. When the form of HG(s) is such that $P - Z \geq 2$, as certain loci branches move toward the left with increasing values of K' other loci *branches must move toward the right.* This statement follows immediately from that law of algebra which states that if the characteristic equation is in normalized form, that is, $s^P + bs^{P-1} + \cdots + K' = 0$, then the negative sum of the roots is a constant provided that $P - Z \geq 2$. Specifically, it is equal to the coefficient of the s^{P-1} term, viz., b, which is independent of the value of K'. This step is useful particularly in establishing at a glance the directions in which the loci originating from complex poles of $HG(s)$ are likely to move. Also, it provides a good estimate of the region where two loci are apt to coalesce and break away.

Step 8. *Use the spirule[1] to complete the locus.* The foregoing seven steps primarily serve the purpose of identifying those sections of the real axis which are part of the complete locus and of providing general information and construction guides concerning the manner in which the remainder of the locus will behave. Generally the important part of the locus lies neither on the real axis nor on the asymptotes, but rather in the finite portion of the s plane around the origin. Consequently, it is the finding of this part of the locus which is of chief concern to the designer. Fortunately, this search is greatly facilitated by the use of the spirule, which is essentially a device that permits the net phase angle of the phasors drawn from the poles and zeros to any point s to be determined in a matter of seconds. In fact, in combination with the steps already outlined, the complete root locus of a system can be determined in a relatively short time. Before illustrating these procedures with examples, let us discuss the spirule and its use.

But first let it be said that it is possible to learn the root-locus method without introducing the spirule. To do so, however, detracts appreciably from the strength of the method. Learning to use the spirule is easy, and it requires comparatively little time to become proficient at it. Once this is mastered, the location of critical points of the locus where, for example, loci break away from the real axis, or cross the ordinate s-plane axis, or depart from complex poles can be easily established upon making a few trial checks of the phase angle. Moreover, the procedure is no more complicated for higher-order systems. This cannot be said for some of the analytical procedures employed to locate these same points. This matter is discussed further in subsequent sections, and additional construction rules are accordingly developed.

10-5. The Spirule and Its Applications

The spirule consists of a disk, an arm, and two eyelets, as illustrated in Fig. 10-9. The disk is 3 in. in diameter and is provided with an angular

[1] The spirule was developed by W. R. Evans and is available from the Spirule Company, Whittier, Calif.

scale graduated every 5°. The arm measures 7½ in. from the pivot and has a linear scale on its edge and a logarithmic spiral on the face as shown in Fig. 10-9a. The standard eyelet serves to hold the arm and disk together because of the friction-fit design. The pivot is a special eyelet mounted inside the standard eyelet and is free to rotate. If the thumb is placed on the pivot and the arm moved, the arrangement is such that both the arm and disk rotate. However, if in addition to placing the

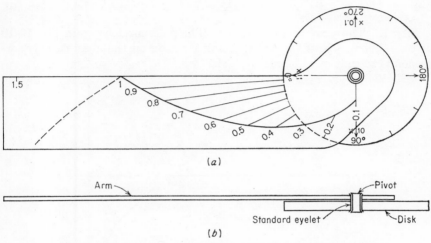

Fig. 10-9. (a) Top view of the spirule; (b) side view of the spirule.

thumb on the pivot, pressure is applied to the disk also by means of the forefinger, then just the arm rotates.

The best way to describe the use of the spirule in establishing the root loci is to apply it to a specific example. This also affords the opportunity of applying the steps outlined in the preceding section.

Example 10-1. A feedback control system has an open-loop transfer function given by

$$HG(s) = \frac{K}{s(1 + s/2)(1 + s/6)}$$

(a) Find the root locus as K is varied from small values to very large values.

(b) Compute the value of open-loop gain needed to give a time-domain response to a unit step corresponding to $\zeta = 0.5$ for the complex roots.

(c) Compute the value of open-loop gain which just makes the system absolutely unstable, that is, $\zeta = 0$.

The solutions are as follows:

(a) Before applying the general procedure, $HG(s)$ must be put in a form corresponding to Eq. (10-9).   Thus

$$HG(s) = 2(6)K \frac{1}{s(s+2)(s+6)} = \frac{K'}{s(s+2)(s+6)}$$

The relationship between the open-loop gain K and K' is therefore

$$12K = K'$$

Step 1.   There are no finite zeros.   The poles are located in Fig. 10-10 at 0, -2, -6.   Note, too, that a unit division on the abscissa axis corresponds to that on the ordinate axis.

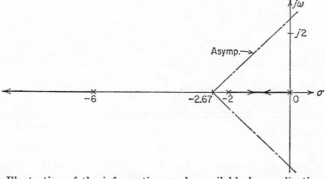

FIG. 10-10. Illustration of the information made available by application of steps 1 through 6.

Step 2.   Sections of the real axis between 0 and -2 and between -6 and $-\infty$ are part of the locus.

Step 3.   There are three loci.   The section from -6 to $-\infty$ along the real axis is one of these.

Step 4.   Of the remaining two loci, one originates from the pole at -2 and the other from the pole at the origin.   Also, as K' increases, the roots of the characteristic equation must migrate from the -2 pole toward the right and from the pole at the origin toward the left.

Step 5.   There are no finite zeros and three poles of $HG(s)$.   Hence there must be three implicit zeros at infinity, which means that the loci originating from the open-loop poles must terminate at infinity and they must do so along the prescribed asymptotes in order to assure that the s-plane points are solutions of the characteristic equation as s approaches infinity.   By Eq. (10-28) the angles of the asymptotes are

$$\phi_{\text{asymp}} = \frac{(2k+1)\pi}{P-Z} = \frac{(2k+1)\pi}{3} = \pm 60°, -180°$$

There are three asymptotes because $P - Z = 3$.

Step 6. The point of origin of the asymptotes is given by Eq. (10-30). Thus,

$$\sigma_c = \frac{(0 - 2 - 6) - 0}{3} = -2.67$$

The asymptotes are shown in Fig. 10-10. It should be understood that, although the asymptotes are part of the loci only for large values of s† (and therefore beyond the range of values for which Fig. 10-10 is drawn), they provide an excellent guide in defining how the locus behaves in the region about the origin.

Step 7. This step is applied usually simultaneously with step 8 since it provides guidance in seeking out points with the spirule which are solutions of the characteristic equation. For example, as K' is increased, there is a migration of the roots from the pole at -6 toward the left. There must also be a migration from the pole at the origin toward the left. Now, since the sum of the roots must be invariant, it follows that the rate of migration of the roots from the pole at -2 toward the right is greater than it is from the pole at the origin toward the left. This fact can be used to advantage in searching (with the spirule or otherwise) for the point where these two loci will break away from the origin and move on toward the two remaining asymptotes.

Step 8. Use the spirule to complete the locus. The explanation of how to use the spirule can now be considered, with attention focused upon location of the *breakaway point*, which in this case refers to that point where the branch from the origin and that from the pole at -2 depart from the abscissa axis. This is one of several important points that need to be established.

On the basis of the information conveyed by step 7 we should expect to find the breakaway point somewhere to the right of $(-1,0)$. As a first trial let us check whether or not the angular sum of the phasors originating from the open-loop poles to trial point s_a in Fig. 10-11 is equal to 180°. This summing of angles is accomplished by means of the spirule as described below.

Step 8A. *Locate points off the real axis which satisfy the phase criterion.* Set the edge of the arm so that it coincides with the 0° mark on the disk. Place the pivot over the trial point, which in this case is s_a in Fig. 10-11, and align the arm so that it passes through the pole located farthest to the right. Holding the disk fixed, rotate the arm until it points horizontally toward the left. The disk reading for this arm position is 206° or $-154°$. Figure 10-12 shows that the angle from the pole at the origin to the trial point s_a is $\phi_{p0} = 154°$; and in accordance with the phase-angle criterion this angle must be added with a negative

† Except, of course, for those loci lying on the real axis.

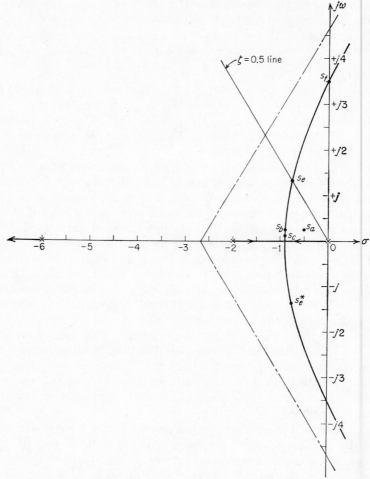

FIG. 10-11. Root-locus plot of $HG(s) = \dfrac{K'}{s(s+2)(s+6)}$.

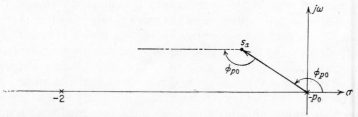

FIG. 10-12. The angular contribution of a phasor originating from a pole at the origin to an s-plane point s_a.

sign.   In measuring ϕ_{p0} by placing the pivot at s_a rather than at the pole, not only is the negative sign accounted for, but the contributions from the other critical frequencies can be readily obtained since the phasors drawn from these points terminate at the trial point.   Thus, to add the contribution made by the phasor originating from the pole at -2, start with the arm in the horizontal position of the previous measurement, keep the thumb on the pivot with pressure removed from the disk, and rotate the edge of the arm counterclockwise until it is aligned with the pole at -2.   Then fix the disk, and rotate the arm clockwise to the

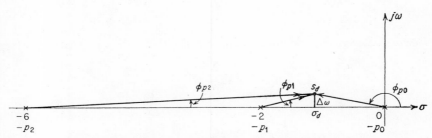

FIG. 10-13. Trial-and-check method of finding the breakaway point.

horizontal position, giving a disk reading of 198° (or $-162°$).   The contribution from the phasor originating at the pole at -6 is found by releasing the disk, rotating the arm to align it with the pole at -6, fixing the disk, and finally rotating the arm once again clockwise to the horizontal position.   The net phase angle is the final disk reading which for point s_a is 195° (or $-165°$).   Since this value differs from $\pm180°$, the trial point s_a is not on the locus.

A little thought reveals that s_a was selected too far to the right.   To introduce more phase lag, therefore, select a second trial point, located at s_b.   Repeating the angle-measuring procedure then shows the net phase angle to be 180°, which makes s_b a point on the locus.   Since s_b is a complex root, it must have a complex conjugate located below it. This brings out another fact about root-locus plots, viz., *that they are symmetrical about the abscissa axis.*

Step 8B.   Locate the breakaway points.   Checking the resultant phase angle for a point such as s_c located immediately below s_b identifies it, too, as part of the locus.   Hence, it is reasonable to conclude that the loci break away from the real axis at this point.   For the example cited the value is $\sigma_b = -0.9$.

The breakaway point can also be found without use of the spirule. However, a trail-and-check method still is necessary.   To illustrate, consider a trial point such as s_d in Fig. 10-13 which has a very small j part, viz., $\Delta\omega$.   The three phasors are also shown, and the respective phase angles are clearly

$$\phi_{p0} = \pi - \tan^{-1}\left|\frac{\Delta\omega}{\sigma_d + p_0}\right|$$

$$\phi_{p1} = \tan^{-1}\left|\frac{\Delta\omega}{\sigma_d + p_1}\right| \qquad (10\text{-}31)$$

$$\phi_{p2} = \tan^{-1}\left|\frac{\Delta\omega}{\sigma_d + p_2}\right|$$

Satisfying the Evans phase criterion requires that

$$\pi - \tan^{-1}\left|\frac{\Delta\omega}{\sigma_d + p_0}\right| + \tan^{-1}\left|\frac{\Delta\omega}{\sigma_d + p_1}\right| + \tan^{-1}\left|\frac{\Delta\omega}{\sigma_d + p_2}\right| = \pi \quad (10\text{-}32)$$

Because $\Delta\omega$ is a very small quantity, Eq. (10-32) may be written as

$$\left|\frac{\Delta\omega}{\sigma_d + p_1}\right| + \left|\frac{\Delta\omega}{\sigma_d + p_2}\right| = \left|\frac{\Delta\omega}{\sigma_d + p_0}\right|$$

which simplifies to

$$\frac{1}{|\sigma_d + p_1|} + \frac{1}{|\sigma_d + p_2|} = \frac{1}{|\sigma_d + p_0|} \qquad (10\text{-}33)$$

Upon selecting σ_d such that Eq. (10-33) is satisfied, it becomes the break-away point σ_b. Several trials are required normally just as is the case with the spirule. Upon inserting the value of $\sigma_b = -0.9$ previously found there result

$$\frac{1}{|-0.9 + 6|} + \frac{1}{|-0.9 + 2|} = \frac{1}{|-0.9 + 0|}$$
$$1.106 = 1.11$$

which check closely enough.

A general rule for determining the breakaway point can be deduced from Eq. (10-33). In equation form it is

$$\sum \frac{1}{|\sigma_b + p_{li}|} + \sum \frac{1}{|\sigma_b + z_{ri}|} = \sum \frac{1}{|\sigma_b + z_{li}|} + \sum \frac{1}{|\sigma_b + p_{ri}|} \qquad (10\text{-}34)$$

where p_{li} denotes the ith pole located to *left* of trial point

p_{ri} denotes the ith pole located to *right* of trial point

z_{li} denotes the ith zero located to *left* of trial point

z_{ri} denotes the ith zero located to *right* of trial point

The presence of complex poles and/or zeros does alter the validity of Eq. (10-34), because they do contribute to the resultant phase angle for a point slightly off the real axis. Furthermore, Eq. (10-34) is restricted to those situations where just two loci are involved in coalescing and breaking away. In fact the general rule[1] states that, when two loci are about to

[1] For proof see pp. 425–428.

coalesce, the loci arrive along 180° paths and depart along new paths which are 90° related to the arrival directions. In the case where three loci coalesce, the arrival paths are spaced 120° apart and the departure paths 60° from these. For the coalescence of four paths, the separation of the path angles is 90° for arrival, with departure occurring 45° from the arrival paths.

Once points such as s_b and s_c in Fig. 10-11 are established, the remainder of the locus is readily found by testing trial points located reasonably above and to the right of each preceding point found to be part of the locus. Such a procedure was used to determine the complete locus appearing in Fig. 10-11.

(b) The spirule is provided with a damping-ratio scale, and it applies to any pair of complex conjugate roots. The scale, of course, is determined from Eq. (10-21). To draw the $\zeta = 0.5$ line in Fig. 10-11, set the spirule arm to coincide with the 180° disk line, and place the pivot at the origin of Fig. 10-11 with the arm pointing toward the left. Next fix the disk, and rotate the arm clockwise until it coincides with the 0.5 marking on the damping-ratio scale. Draw a line along the arm intersecting the root-locus plot at s_e. Since this root is complex, it has a complex conjugate located at s_e^*.

Step 8C. Evaluate the gain parameter on the root-locus plot. The value of gain needed to make s_e and s_e^* roots of the characteristic equation can be found in one of two ways by using the spirule. One method involves applying the magnitude criterion of Eq. (10-16) directly. For our example this becomes

$$\frac{K'}{r_{p0}r_{p1}r_{p2}} = 1$$

or

$$K' = r_{p0}r_{p1}r_{p2}$$

Since the arm of the spirule is provided with a linear scale, r_{p0} may be found by placing the pivot at s_e and noting the scale reading for the distance to the pole at the origin. Thus, a scale reading of 0.3 is found for r_{p0}.† A scale-factor adjustment is needed now to get the true value of r_{p0}, because one unit on the spirule arm corresponds to five units on the plot of Fig. 10-11. Hence the proper value of r_{p0} is 0.3(5) = 1.5. A similar procedure is followed for r_{p1}, which of course denotes the length between s_e and the pole at -2. This value is found to be 1.8. The proper value of r_{p2} is found to be 5.4. Therefore, the magnitude criterion yields a value of K' which is

$$K' = 1.5(1.8)(5.4) = 14.6$$

† This reading as well as those which follow were determined from a plot drawn on an 8½- by 11-in. graph sheet. For the reader who is interested in checking these numbers, it is recommended that Fig. 10-11 be redrawn on such a sheet.

so that the required open-loop gain is

$$K = \frac{14.6}{12} = 1.22$$

A more direct and faster procedure for computing the gain employs the logarithmic spiral appearing on the face of the spirule arm. Essentially the logarithmic spiral permits the multiplication or division of phasors by the addition or subtraction of angles, respectively. The linear and angular scales of the spirule are selected so that rotation of the arm through 90° means multiplication or division by a factor of 10. For this reason the disk of the spirule has the 0° radial line also marked X1, the 90° radial line marked X10, and the −90° radial line marked X0.1. Computing the gain requires identifying the appropriate reading on the logarithmic spiral scale together with the appropriate quadrant multiplier (that is, X1, X10, or X0.1) and the scale-factor adjustment. To obtain the proper reading on the spiral curve, proceed as follows: Align the arm with the X1 marker, and place the pivot at the point in question, viz., s_e. Align the edge of the arm with the pole at the origin. Fix the disk, and rotate the arm until the pole lies on the spiral curve. Release the disk, and align the arm with the pole at −2. Again fix the disk, and rotate the arm until this pole lies on the spiral curve. Release the disk, and align the arm with the pole at −6. Note that the true spiral curve should lie above the radial edge of the arm beyond 1.0 on the scale. As a matter of convenience it is the mirror image of the true curve which is drawn, and the direction of rotation of the arm should be in the sense determined by the true curve. Hence, to assure this in the case of the pole at −6, it is necessary to align the spiral curve (not the arm edge) with the pole at −6. Then fix the disk, and rotate the arm until the pole lies on the radial edge. One of the four radial lines on the disk is observed to intersect the spiral curve. Identify this reading along with the multiplying factor of the radial line. For the example being considered, the spiral curve reading is 0.12, corresponding to the X1 radial line. Since the scale factor has already been established as 5:1 it follows that

$$K' = 0.12(5)^3 = 15$$

which compares favorably with 14.6.

Put into a more general formulation, the gain as computed with the help of the spirule is given by

$K' = $ (spiral-curve reading) (quadrant-multiplying factor)

$$\text{(scale factor)}^{P-Z} \quad (10\text{-}35)$$

where the *scale factor* denotes the number of units on the root-locus plot which corresponds to unity on the spirule. The spirule is constructed so that the unity marking is equal to a length of 5 in. The reason for raising the scale factor to the $(P - Z)$th power should be apparent from the magnitude criterion.

Step 8D. Evaluate the gain for sustained oscillations ($\zeta = 0$).

(c) Once the root-locus plot is drawn, the value of the open-loop gain which makes ζ equal to zero is determined by applying the foregoing procedure to the point where the locus intersects the $j\omega$ axis, i.e., at s_f in Fig. 10-11. This leads to a spiral-curve reading of 0.775 so that the open-loop gain becomes

$$K = \frac{K'}{12} = \frac{0.775(1)(5)^3}{12} = \frac{97}{12} = 8.1$$

Of course the frequency of the sustained oscillation resulting from this gain is the ordinate value corresponding to the point of intersection. Figure 10-11 shows this to be 3.5 radians/sec.

An analytical procedure is available for determining this same information, and the work involved is reasonably small provided that the characteristic equation is not of high order (e.g., not greater than the third or fourth). These points of intersection are found with the aid of the Routh criterion upon recognizing that such points are not only roots of the characteristic equation but, being purely imaginary, are also roots of a subsidiary equation. The subsidiary equation is identified as that associated with the row which precedes the first vanishing row of the Routh array. It is found in the following manner: First, formulate the complete Routh array as it applies to the characteristic equation. Second, choose the gain K' so as to cause the vanishing of *all* elements of a row. As a matter of fact this gain is the one responsible for the sustained oscillation. Third, using this value of K' formulate the subsidiary equation, and solve for the points of intersection with the $j\omega$ axis. Applying this procedure to the example under consideration, we get the following Routh array as derived from the characteristic equation: Thus,

Characteristic equation: $s^3 + 8s^2 + 12s + K' = 0$

Routh array:

$$\begin{array}{c|cc} s^3 & 1 & 12 \\ s^2 & 8 & K' \\ s & \dfrac{96 - K'}{8} & \end{array}$$

Clearly the third row can be made to vanish by choosing

$$\frac{96 - K'}{8} = 0$$

or

$$K' = 96$$

Note that this value compares favorably with the value of 97 found by using the spirule. Finally, from the second row of the Routh array the subsidiary equation is found to be

$$8s^2 + K' = 0$$

But $K' = 96$

Hence $s^2 + 12 = 0$

from which $s_{1,2} = \pm j3.46 \text{ radians/sec}$

which compares well with the graphically determined value of 3.5 radians/sec.

10-6. Additional Examples

Now that the basic ideas concerning the construction of the root loci are understood, we can proceed to a few more sophisticated examples in order to bring out additional information about these plots.

Example 10-2. Consider a system which is described by the open-loop transfer function

$$HG(s) = \frac{K'(s + 3)}{s(s + 2)(s^2 + 2s + 2)}$$

The presence of a finite zero as well as two complex conjugate poles represents the degree to which this case differs from the previous one. For one thing the search for points in the s plane which satisfy the phase criterion must account for the lead angle associated with the phasor originating from the finite zero. Moreover, the presence of open-loop poles located off the real axis requires identifying appropriate *angles of departure* from these poles in order to facilitate the construction of the root loci. Once again the root loci are drawn by following the outlined step-by-step procedure.

Step 1.   1 finite zero located at $s = -3$

4 poles located at $s = 0, -2, -1 \pm j1$

These are located in the s plane as shown in Fig. 10-14.

Step 2.   Sections of the real axis lying between 0 and -2 and -3 to $-\infty$ are part of the locus.

Step 3.   There are four loci. In this case the section of the real axis from -3 to $-\infty$ does not constitute one of these loci. Rather it is part of two loci, because both terminals of this locus are zeros, one of which is finite at -3 and the other infinite at $-\infty$.

Step 4.   There are four separate loci originating at the four poles of the open-loop transfer function. Two of these loci necessarily must enter the locus lying between -3 and $-\infty$ and thence proceed to the respective zeros as K' is increased indefinitely. The remaining two loci move on to the appropriate asymptotes.

Step 5. Since $P - Z = 3$, there are three asymptotes located by the angles

$$\phi_{\text{asymp}} = \frac{(2k + 1)\pi}{3} = \pm 60°, \ -180°$$

Step 6. The point of origin of these asymptotes is

$$\sigma_c = \frac{-4 + 3}{3} = -\frac{1}{3}$$

The results of steps 5 and 6 also appear in Fig. 10-14.

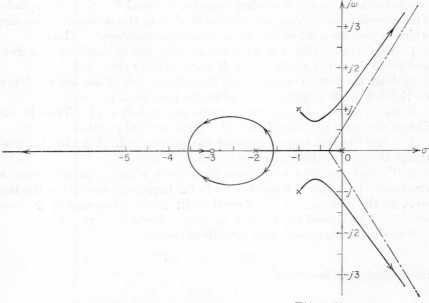

FIG. 10-14. Root-locus plot of $HG(s) = \dfrac{K'(s + 3)}{s(s + 2)(s^2 + 2s + 2)}$.

Step 7. It is not immediately obvious which way the loci originating from the complex poles turn as the gain is increased. Of course this information can be established readily by taking a few trial points round the complex pole and checking for a 180° phase shift. However, a somewhat faster procedure results upon finding the angle of departure directly and leads us to the following auxiliary step.

Step 7A. *Compute the angle of departure for complex poles.* The procedure merely requires determining the angular contributions of the phasors originating from each critical frequency (other than the one in question) for a trial point located very close to the complex pole. The angle of departure then is the difference between this net phase angle and

180°.   To illustrate, consider that the angle of departure ϕ_d is to be found for the complex pole located at $-1 + j1$. For a trial point which is displaced only slightly from the complex pole, find the angles associated with each phasor, and equate to 180°.   In equation form we have

$$- \underbrace{/s - /s + 2 - /s + 1 + j1 + /s + 3}_{\text{Determined by spirule}} - \phi_d = 180° \qquad (10\text{-}36)$$

where ϕ_d denotes the angle of the phasor originating from the complex pole in question to the trial point.   The angular contribution of the bracketed term in the foregoing equation is found by using the spirule. The procedure is outlined once again, in view of the presence of the zero which represents a situation not previously encountered.   Thus:

1. Align the spirule arm to coincide with the 0° mark on the disk, and place the pivot at the $-1 + j1$ point or very close to it.

2. Align the arm so that it passes through the pole at the origin.   Then fix the disk while rotating the arm to the horizontal position.

3. Align the arm to pass through the pole at $-1 - j1$.   Then fix the disk while again rotating the arm to the horizontal position.

4. Align the arm to pass through the pole at -2.   Fix the disk, and rotate the arm to the horizontal position.

5. To add the lead angle associated with a zero, the procedure is reversed.   Hence start with the arm in the horizontal position of the last step, fix the disk, and then rotate the arm counterclockwise to the zero at -3.   This should yield a disk reading of about 116° or $-244°$.

Introducing this result into Eq. (10-36) gives

$$-244° - \phi_d = 180°$$

from which it follows that

$$\phi_d = -64°$$

Therefore the locus originating from the pole at $-1 + j1$ departs toward the right in a downward direction.   With this information established, a search for successive points which satisfy the phase criterion is made.

Step 8.   Complete the locus, using the spirule.   Once the angle of departure is known and several successive points found, it becomes readily apparent that the two loci originating from the complex poles move on toward the $\pm 60°$ asymptotes as illustrated in Fig. 10-14.   It must follow therefore in accordance with step 7 that the remaining loci originating from the real poles must break away from the real axis, move into the complex plane toward the left, and reenter somewhere beyond -3.   All this is readily determined by means of the spirule, and the results appear in Fig. 10-14.

Inspection of the plot indicates that there is a value of gain K' beyond which the system is absolutely unstable.   By using the procedure previously outlined, this gain is found to be

$$K' = 0.19(0.1)(5)^3 = 2.4$$

Example 10-3.   Consider next a system having the open-loop transfer function

$$HG(s) = \frac{K'}{s(s + 2)(s^2 + 2s + 5)}$$

which is similar in form to that of Example 10-2 with the exception that no finite zero appears.   Accordingly, the only section of the real axis

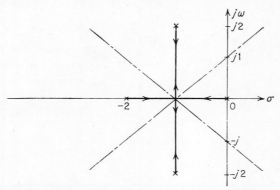

FIG. 10-15. The asymptotes and straight-line portion of the root locus of $HG(s) = \dfrac{K'}{s(s + 2)(s^2 + 2s + 5)}$.

which is part of the locus is that lying between 0 and -2.   Also, since $P - Z = 4$, there are now four asymptotes located along the directions given by

$$\phi_{\text{asymp}} = \frac{(2k + 1)\pi}{4} = \pm 45°, \pm 135°$$

and they intersect at

$$\sigma_c = \frac{-4}{4} = -1$$

Furthermore, because the complex poles are symmetrically located with respect to the real poles, the vertical line drawn between the two complex poles is part of the locus (see Fig. 10-15).   Any point on this line clearly satisfies the phase criterion.   If the complex roots were located a little to the right or to the left of the locations shown in Fig. 10-15, there would be no vertical-line locus.

To complete the root locus of the system requires answering one important question.   Where do the loci originating at the four poles break away from the partial locus illustrated in Fig. 10-15?   A little thought indicates that it is reasonable to assume that the loci from the poles at the origin and at -2 move toward each other, coalesce at -1, and then break away along the vertical part of the locus. Moreover, it is likewise reasonable to expect that the loci originating at the complex poles initially move along this same vertical locus. Thus, the situation is such that there are two loci approaching each other on the upper half of the vertical-line locus of Fig. 10-15 as well as on the lower half. Therefore, it follows that at some point on each half of the vertical locus the two loci coalesce and then break away and move on toward the respective asymptotes as

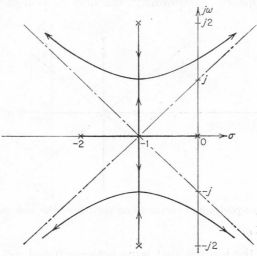

FIG. 10-16. Sketch of the complete root locus for $HG(s) = \dfrac{K'}{s(s+2)(s^2+2s+5)}$.

the gain is further increased. Although analytical methods are available for finding this breakaway point, the procedure is not simple. The point is found more quickly by checking the phase angle for a few trial points by means of the spirule. This was done for the example under consideration, and the complete results appear sketched in Fig. 10-16.

Example 10-4. An interesting modification of the root-locus plot of Fig. 10-16 results upon relocating the complex poles of Example 10-3 so that each pole of the open-loop transfer function is equidistant from the point of intersection of the asymptotes. In order to satisfy this condition, the complex poles must be placed at the locations they have in Example 10-2. Thus the open-loop transfer function becomes

$$HG(s) = \frac{K'}{s(s+2)(s^2+2s+2)}$$

The corresponding root-locus plot is illustrated in Fig. 10-17. Note that all four loci originating at the open-loop poles arrive at the point of coalescence along paths spaced 90° apart, and they depart along new paths spaced 45° apart from the former. At $s = -1$ a root of multiplicity 4 occurs. The order of the multiplicity is the same as that of the characteristic equation. In such cases the root locus is composed solely of straight lines.

The general criterion for establishing the angles of arrival and departure at a multiple root is treated in greater detail below.

Angles of Departure and Arrival of the Root Loci in the Vicinity of a Multiple Root of the Characteristic Equation. For simplicity attention

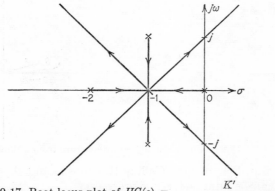

FIG. 10-17. Root-locus plot of $HG(s) = \dfrac{K'}{s(s + 2)(s^2 + 2s + 2)}$.

is directed first to the case where two loci coalesce at some point along the real axis and subsequently break away with further increase in the open-loop gain. For the sake of illustration, let us return to the example of Fig. 10-11, where it is demonstrated that the roots of the characteristic equation migrate from the open-loop poles located at the origin and at -2 and then break away at $\sigma_b = -0.9$. The plot shows that this breakaway occurs along lines of departure which are in quadrature with the directions of arrival. The proof of this result is easy to establish provided that the open-loop transfer function is written in such a way as to bring into evidence that value of the gain which is responsible for the existence of the double root at -0.9. Identifying this gain as K_0, the expression for the open-loop transfer function may be written as

$$HG(s) = \frac{K_0 + \Delta K}{s(s + 2)(s + 6)} \tag{10-37}$$

The corresponding expression for the characteristic equation becomes

$$[s(s + 2)(s + 6) + K_0] + \Delta K = 0 \tag{10-38}$$

The advantage which such a representation offers should be apparent. Thus by setting $\Delta K = 0$ the solution of the characteristic equation yields

the double root located at -0.9.   By making the gain take on a positive
increment from the value K_0, information concerning the departure of the
loci from the double root can be obtained, while by assigning a negative
value to ΔK similar information concerning the arrival routes can be had.
In this connection the open-loop transfer function may be even more
advantageously expressed upon recognizing that the bracketed part of
Eq. (10-38) can be replaced by a polynomial formed by the product of the
three roots corresponding to the gain K_0.   Two of these roots are of course
located at the breakaway point, and the third is located on the locus to

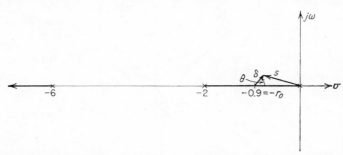

FIG. 10-18. Determining the angle of departure from a double root.

the left of -6 in Fig. 10-11.   Calling this root r_3 and the double root r_0,
Eq. (10-38) can be alternatively expressed as

$$(s + r_0)^2(s + r_3) + \Delta K = 0 \qquad (10\text{-}39)$$

Rearranging terms gives

$$\frac{\Delta K}{(s + r_0)^2(s + r_3)} = -1 \qquad (10\text{-}40)$$

Equation (10-40) can now be treated as a modified open-loop transfer
function having open-loop poles which are roots of the characteristic
equation for $\Delta K = 0$.   Note that when ΔK is assigned a positive value
the loci move away from the double root, while for negative values the
loci are moving toward it.

Since in this example there is no doubt about the directions of arrival
at the double root, attention is directed just to positive increments of
the gain.   In Fig. 10-18 an assumed arbitrary direction of the locus is
depicted as it breaks away from the double root corresponding to an
incremental increase in gain ΔK.   The corresponding value of s is

$$s = -r_0 + \bar{\delta} \qquad (10\text{-}41)$$

where $\bar{\delta} = \delta \underline{/\theta}$ and represents the increment in s associated with the increment in gain.   It is the value of θ which is of interest here.   Clearly, it
must be of such a value that, as the loci move off the real axis for $\Delta K > 0$,
they take on such positions as to continue to satisfy the phase criterion.

An examination of Eq. (10-40) makes apparent what value θ needs to assume in order to satisfy the phase condition under the given circumstances. Thus inserting Eq. (10-41) into Eq. (10-40) yields

$$\frac{\Delta K}{(-r_0 + \bar{\delta} + r_3)(-r_0 + \bar{\delta} + r_0)^2} = -1$$

Because $\bar{\delta}$ is confined to infinitesimal values about the point $-r_0$, it follows that neither the magnitude nor the phase of the left side of the last equation is affected by the root factor $-r_0 + \bar{\delta} + r_3$. Accordingly, we may write

$$\frac{\Delta K}{|r_3 - r_0|\bar{\delta}^2} = \frac{\Delta K}{|r_3 - r_0|\delta^2/2\theta} = -1$$

or

$$\frac{\Delta K}{|r_3 - r_0|\delta^2/2\theta} = 1/-\pi - 2k\pi \qquad (10\text{-}42)$$

where $k = 0, \pm 1, \pm 2, \ldots$. Inspection of Eq. (10-42) reveals that to satisfy the phase criterion for $\Delta K > 0$ requires that

$$-2\theta = -\pi - 2k\pi$$

or

$$\theta = \frac{\pi}{2} + k\pi \qquad \text{where } k = 0, \pm 1, \pm 2, \ldots \qquad (10\text{-}43)$$

For the example at hand, the angles of departure are found to be

$$\theta = \frac{\pi}{2} \qquad \text{for } k = 0$$

$$\theta = -\frac{\pi}{2} \qquad \text{for } k = -1$$

It should be appreciated that these results are valid only in the immediate vicinity of the double root. As points in the s plane are considered which are farther removed from the double root, Eq. (10-43) is no longer valid simply because the angular contribution of the third root factor, viz., $s + r_3$, is no longer negligible. In fact this is the reason why the loci move toward the right as movement away from the double root occurs for larger and larger values of $\bar{\delta}$.

The same approach is now used to verify the results depicted in Fig. 10-17. Because of the symmetry, it is apparent that a pole of multiplicity 4 occurs at $-1, 0$. Upon calling the multiple root $-r_0$ and proceeding as in the foregoing, the modified expression for the open-loop transfer function becomes

$$\frac{\Delta K}{(s + r_0)^4} = 1 \left/ \begin{array}{ll} \pm(2k + 1)\pi & \text{for } \Delta K > 0 \\ \pm 2k\pi & \text{for } \Delta K < 0 \end{array} \right. \qquad (10\text{-}44)$$

where $k = 0, \pm 1, \pm 2, \pm 3, \ldots$. Again, if the assumption is made that departure from the multiple pole occurs along a path described by

$s = -r_0 + \bar{\delta}$ for $\Delta K > 0$, there results

$$\frac{\Delta K}{\delta^4/4\theta} = 1\underline{/-(2k + 1)\pi} \qquad \text{for } \Delta K > 0$$

Hence $-4\theta = -(\pi + 2k\pi)$

Therefore $\theta = \dfrac{\pi}{4} + \dfrac{k\pi}{2}$ for $k = 0, \pm1, \pm2, \ldots$

For the case at hand

$$\theta = \frac{\pi}{4} \qquad \text{for } k = 0$$
$$= \tfrac{3}{4}\pi \qquad \text{for } k = 1$$
$$= -\frac{\pi}{4} \qquad \text{for } k = -1$$
$$= \tfrac{5}{4}\pi \qquad \text{for } k = +2$$

No further values of k need be used since they provide no additional information.

To ascertain the validity of the angles of approach as they appear in Fig. 10-17 (and which in this example were determined from other considerations), it is necessary merely to let ΔK take on negative values. Thus

$$\frac{-\Delta K}{(s + r_0)^4} = -1 = 1\underline{/-2k\pi}$$

Corresponding to the negative value of the gain parameter, the phase criterion is

$$-4\theta = -2k\pi$$

or $\theta = k\dfrac{\pi}{2}$ for $k = 0, \pm1, \pm2, \ldots$

Thus $\theta = 0$ for $k = 0$

$$= \frac{-\pi}{2} \qquad \text{for } k = -1$$
$$= +\frac{\pi}{2} \qquad \text{for } k = +1$$
$$= \pi \qquad \text{for } k = 2$$

It is interesting to note that in this example the equations for the angles of approach and departure are valid even for points in the s plane which are far removed from the location of the multiple pole. The reason is that there are no other factors in the expression for the transfer function [see Eq. (10-44)] which at values of s removed from the point of multiplicity would ordinarily influence the phase relationship. In fact this should make it even more apparent why the root loci in such a case consist of straight lines only.

10-7. The Source-free Time-domain Response

One of the outstanding features of the root-locus approach in analyzing the dynamic behavior of feedback control systems is that the particular time-domain response is determined once the parameters of the system are specified. In fact the nature of the source-free response can be fairly accurately identified even without computing the expression for the complete time solution. It merely requires knowledge of the location of the roots of the characteristic equation in the s plane, which, after all, is precisely the information made available by the root-locus method. This stands in sharp contrast to the frequency-response approach, where the

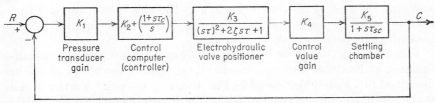

Fig. 10-19. Block diagram of supersonic wind-tunnel pressure control system. $K =$ appropriate gain factor; $\tau =$ time constant, sec.

dynamic performance in the time domain is approximated usually in terms of figures of merit such as phase margin and gain margin.

Although the root-locus method provides a more accurate description of the transient behavior, it is worthwhile to note that this is not done at the sacrifice of frequency-response information. On the contrary, much frequency-response information is available. For example, information concerning the bandwidth of a closed-loop system can be deduced readily once the roots of the characteristic equation are found from the root loci of the system. Primarily, however, our concern here is to describe the manner in which the time-domain solution is computed from a knowledge of the root loci.

Attention in this regard is directed to two cases: those feedback control systems employing unity feedback, and those in which frequency-sensitive elements appear in the feedback path.

Unity Feedback Systems, $H(s) = 1$. The system to be analyzed is that of the high-speed wind tunnel discussed in Sec. 1-4 and illustrated in Figs. 1-4 and 1-5. The intelligent design of the controller of such a system often depends upon an analysis such as is outlined in the following pages. The simplified block diagram for this pressure control system is illustrated in Fig. 10-19. The control computer is designed to provide proportional plus integral outputs. The proportional signal, of course, is responsible for generating the desired level of the output quantity, which here is pressure, while the integral term helps to keep this level at the commanded value as time passes.

Assume that, upon insertion of the system parameters, the open-loop transfer function of the system depicted in Fig. 10-19 is found to be

$$HG(s) = \frac{K'(s + 4)}{s(s + 0.16)(s^2 + 14.6s + 149)} \qquad (10\text{-}45)$$

Using the root-locus method, let us find the complete time response for the settling chamber pressure c corresponding to a normalized step input command when the value of K' is 326. The method of solution consists first in finding the root loci of Eq. (10-45), then locating the four roots on these loci corresponding to the specified open-loop gain, and finally applying the partial-fraction expansion to the closed-loop transfer function for the purpose of performing the inverse transformation, thus obtaining the time response.

Because Eq. (10-45) is identical in form to the open-loop transfer function of Example 10-2, the mechanics of finding the root loci are not described but merely presented in Fig. 10-20. One point worthy of note is the usefulness of the angle of departure in establishing an appreciable portion of the locus as it emanates from the complex poles. This angle was found to be $-53°$. Determining this portion of the locus provides a clue revealing whether the locus migrates into the real axis or toward the asymptotes. Identification of the remainder of the locus is thereby facilitated. In order to find the four specific roots located on the four root loci which are solutions of the characteristic equation when $K' = 326$, it is necessary to choose trial points on the loci and to compute the corresponding gain values. This needs to be repeated several times to arrive at the specified value of K'. Herein lies a disadvantage of the root-locus procedure; it does not place clearly in evidence the open-loop gain as does the frequency-response method using the log-modulus representation. However, when compared with its outstanding features, this is really a trivial point. Figure 10-20 shows specifically those four points on each of the root loci which correspond to the specified gain. Keep in mind that the search for a point on a locus corresponding to the given K' must be made for as many loci as there are roots of the characteristic equation, because each locus yields a root. In our example there are four loci, but the search is made on only two loci because the roots for the gain of interest are complex conjugates.

It is worthwhile to pause a moment and consider the significance of the results appearing in Fig. 10-20. The root loci are obtained in a fairly easy manner from the open-loop transfer function upon satisfying the Evans phase criterion. Subsequent application of the magnitude criterion then determines for any point on the locus the value of open-loop gain which makes the point a root of the resulting characteristic equation.

But the characteristic equation is associated always with the closed-loop situation, and, as a matter of fact, the roots of this equation provide an exact description of the source-free response. Thus, *from the open-loop transfer function the root-locus method makes available precise information about the closed-loop transient (time-domain) performance.* For the case

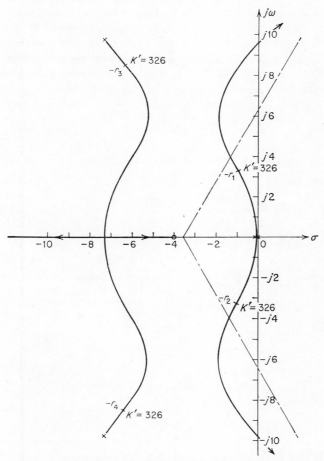

FIG. 10-20. Root-locus plot of the system of Fig. 10-19.

being studied the characteristic equation is of fourth order. Hence there are four loci, each yielding a root of the characteristic equation for the given value of K'. In Fig. 10-20 the four roots, which are solutions of the characteristic equation when $K' = 326$, are found to be

$$s_{1,2} = -r_{1,2} = -1 \pm j3.25 \qquad \text{for which } \zeta = 0.29$$

and $\qquad s_{3,4} = -r_{3,4} = -6.4 \pm j8.5 \qquad \text{for which } \zeta = 0.60 \qquad (10\text{-}46)$

The alternative form of representing the roots in terms of the symbol $-r$ is introduced because it avoids confusion in writing the closed-loop transfer function. The roots of Eq. (10-46) are those of a fourth-order polynomial. Doubtless, one is impressed by the simplicity with which they are obtained. Even more impressive, however, is the fact that roots of a fourth-order polynomial are available, not just for one or several values of the constant term, but for an almost unlimited number.

The first step in the process of calculating the source-free time-domain response is accomplished. Next the closed-loop transfer function in a form ready for partial-fraction expansion must be determined. To do this, recognize that, since $H(s)$ is unity, the expression for the closed-loop transfer function of the system of Fig. 10-19 is

$$\frac{C}{R}(s) = \frac{G(s)}{1 + G(s)} = \frac{\dfrac{K'(s + 4)}{s(s + 0.16)(s^2 + 14.6s + 149)}}{1 + \dfrac{K'(s + 4)}{s(s + 0.16)(s^2 + 14.6s + 149)}}$$

Simplifying yields

$$\frac{C}{R}(s) = \frac{K'(s + 4)}{s(s + 0.16)(s^2 + 14.6s + 149) + K'(s + 4)} \qquad (10\text{-}47)$$

The denominator polynomial of Eq. (10-47) is the system characteristic equation the roots of which appear in Fig. 10-20. For any specific value of K' this denominator polynomial may be replaced by the product of the root factors. If such roots are called $-r_1$, $-r_2$, $-r_3$, and $-r_4$, it follows that Eq. (10-47) may be rewritten as

$$\frac{C}{R}(s) = \frac{K'(s + 4)}{(s + r_1)(s + r_2)(s + r_3)(s + r_4)} \qquad (10\text{-}48)$$

For the instance when K' takes on the value of 326, the roots are those specified in Eq. (10-46). The first pair of these complex conjugate roots yields the quadratic factor

$$(s + 1)^2 + (3.25)^2 = s^2 + 2s + 11.6$$

and the second pair yields

$$(s + 6.4)^2 + (8.5)^2 = s^2 + 12.8s + 113.2$$

Consequently Eq. (10-48) becomes

$$\frac{C}{R}(s) = \frac{326(s + 4)}{(s^2 + 2s + 11.6)(s^2 + 12.8s + 113.2)} \qquad (10\text{-}49)$$

The form of this last equation lends itself to a partial-fraction expansion.

Assuming the command input to be a step of magnitude r_0, the normalized s-domain response is

$$\frac{C}{r_0}(s) = \frac{326(s+4)}{s(s^2+2s+11.6)(s^2+12.8s+113.2)}$$
$$= \frac{K_0}{s_0} + \frac{K_1}{s-s_1} + \frac{K_2}{s-s_2} + \frac{K_3}{s-s_3} + \frac{K_4}{s-s_4} \quad (10\text{-}50)$$

Upon evaluating the coefficients of the partial-fraction expansion, the inverse transformation is performed, and the complete time solution is

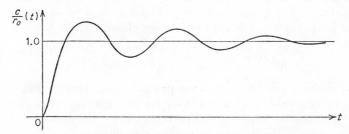

FIG. 10-21. Sketch of Eq. (10-51).

found.   All this is worked out in Example 3-6.   Application of the spirule in graphically evaluating the coefficients of the partial-fraction expansion is another illustration of its usefulness.   The resulting time solution was there found to be

$$\frac{c}{r_0}(t) = 1 - 1.34\epsilon^{-t}\cos(3.25t + 9.1°) + 0.326\epsilon^{-6.4t}\cos 8.5t \quad (10\text{-}51)$$

The comments given in Example 3-6 concerning this solution are worth reviewing at this point.   A plot of Eq. (10-51) appears in Fig. 10-21.

By properly modifying Eq. (10-48) the closed-loop transfer function can be put into a form which conveniently permits a frequency-response study to be made.   Rearranging leads to

$$\frac{C}{R}(s) = \frac{4K'(1+0.25s)}{r_1r_2r_3r_4(1+s/r_1)(1+s/r_2)(1+s/r_3)(1+s/r_4)}$$

In this case, because the roots are all complex, it is convenient to rearrange Eq. (10-49).   Thus

$$\frac{C}{R}(s) = \frac{4K'(1+0.25s)}{11.6(113.2)\left[\left(\frac{s}{3.4}\right)^2 + \frac{2(0.29)}{3.4}s + 1\right]\left[\left(\frac{s}{10.6}\right)^2 + \frac{2(0.6)}{10.6}s + 1\right]}$$

A little thought reveals that the quantity 11.6(113.2) is actually the product of the four roots of the characteristic equation for K' equal to 326. Also, from the laws of algebra the product of the roots of a polynomial is equal to its constant term, which here is $4K'$. Accordingly, the closed-loop transfer function reduces to

$$\frac{C}{R}(s) = \frac{1 + 0.25s}{\left[\left(\frac{s}{3.4}\right)^2 + \frac{2(0.29)}{3.4}s + 1\right]\left[\left(\frac{s}{10.6}\right)^2 + \frac{2(0.6)}{10.6}s + 1\right]} \tag{10-52}$$

and can be sketched readily in the log-modulus vs. frequency plane.

As already pointed out in connection with the discussion of Example 3-6, the effects of the second pair of complex conjugate roots in the denominator of Eq. (10-52) on the time solution is so small that for all practical purposes Eq. (10-52) may be simplified to

$$\frac{C}{R}(s) = \frac{1 + 0.25s}{(s/3.4)^2 + [2(0.29)/3.4]s + 1} \tag{10-53}$$

A glance at this equation reveals the presence of a zero, so that an important query to make here is whether or not the presence of the zero adversely influences the dynamic performance of the system. If it does not, then clearly the transient response is appropriately described in terms of the value of $\zeta = 0.29$ (corresponding to which is a maximum overshoot of 39 per cent) and $\omega_n = 3.4$ radians/sec (from which the corresponding settling time may be found). If it does influence the result, then it is important to know to what extent.

To illustrate more effectively the nature of the problem, let us consider the manner in which a second-order system with and without a zero responds to a step input of magnitude r_0. The normalized solution for the controlled variable without a zero is

$$\frac{C}{r_0}(s) = \frac{1}{s}\frac{\omega_n^2}{s^2 + 2\zeta\omega_n s + \omega_n^2} \tag{10-54}$$

The maximum per cent overshoot in such a case is correctly described by Fig. 4-8. When a zero is present, the solution becomes

$$\frac{C}{r_0}(s) = \frac{1}{s}\frac{1 + s/z_1}{(s/\omega_n)^2 + (2\zeta/\omega_n)s + 1} = \frac{1}{s}\frac{\omega_n^2}{s^2 + 2\zeta\omega_n s + \omega_n^2}\frac{s + z_1}{z_1} \tag{10-55}$$

A comparison of Eqs. (10-54) and (10-55) makes it clear that neither the damping ratio nor the natural frequency of the complex roots of the characteristic equation can be altered by the presence of the zero. However, the amplitudes of the transient modes will or will not be affected depending upon the relative importance of z_1. Thus, examination of the last equation reveals that, if z_1 is large compared with the values of s which are predominant in characterizing the time solution (i.e., that portion of the frequency spectrum up to ω_n of the prevailing complex roots), then the influence is very small because $(s + z_1)/z_1$ is not appreciably larger than unity. On the other hand, in those situations where the magnitude of z_1 is small compared with the ω_n of the predominant complex roots, the effect may be quite significant depending upon the value ζ. The precise manner in which the presence of the zero influences the value of the maximum per cent overshoot is depicted in Fig. 10-22 for three values of the damping ratio. Note that, because both ω_n and ζ are involved in determining the importance of the zero, the abscissa quantity is plotted as $z_1/\zeta\omega_n$. It is of interest to note, too, that when $z_1/\zeta\omega_n \geq 10$ the maximum overshoot of the corresponding time solution is correctly

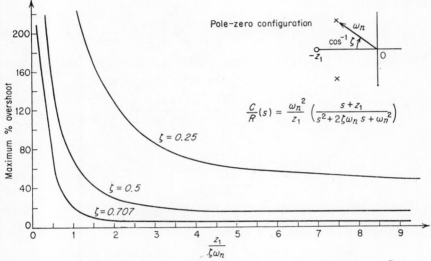

FIG. 10-22. Variation of maximum per cent overshoot with a zero of $\dfrac{C}{R}(s)$.

described by Fig. 4-8. Otherwise the results of Fig. 10-22 must be employed.

It should be understood, of course, that, whenever the time-domain solution is found by using a partial-fraction expansion of $\dfrac{C}{R}(s)$ along with a subsequent inverse Laplace transformation, the foregoing effects are automatically accounted for. The primary purpose of this discussion is to point out that a two-pole and one-zero configuration for $\dfrac{C}{R}(s)$ can lead to results which differ markedly from those of the two-pole configuration. Accordingly, care must be exercised in applying the results of Fig. 4-8.

Nonunity Feedback Systems, $H(s) \neq 1$. As an example of such a system, consider the configuration illustrated in Fig. 10-23. The input command is the aircraft elevator deflection originating with the pilot, and the output quantity C denotes the pitch rate which is fed back through a lead network in order to reduce the tendency to oscillate. The system direct transfer function is clearly

$$G(s) = \frac{137(s + 0.56)}{(s + 10)(s^2 + 1.68s + 8.7)} \tag{10-56}$$

and the feedback transfer function is

$$H(s) = \frac{0.3s}{s + 4} \tag{10-57}$$

Combining these two expressions yields the open-loop transfer function of the system. Thus,

$$HG(s) = \frac{41.1s(s + 0.56)}{(s + 4)(s + 10)(s^2 + 1.68s + 8.7)} \tag{10-58}$$

The corresponding root-locus plot is shown in Fig. 10-24. The four roots

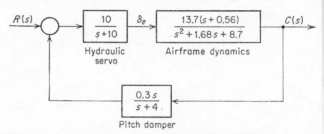

Fig. 10-23. An aircraft control system with a frequency-sensitive feedback element.

corresponding to K' equal to 41 are

$$s_{1,2} = -r_{1,2} = -0.9 \pm j1.85 \qquad \text{for which } \zeta = 0.46$$

and

$$s_{3,4} = -r_{3,4} = -7.0 \pm j6.0 \qquad \text{for which } \zeta = 0.78$$

Also, the quadratic factors associated with each pair of complex conjugate roots are, respectively,

$$(s + 0.9)^2 + (1.85)^2 = s^2 + 1.8s + 4.23$$

and

$$(s + 7)^2 + (6)^2 = s^2 + 14s + 85$$

Whenever the feedback function is other than unity, the closed-loop transfer function is expressed as

$$\frac{C}{R}(s) = \frac{G(s)}{1 + HG(s)} \tag{10-59}$$

Inserting Eqs. (10-56) and (10-57) into Eq. (10-59) and simplifying yields

$$\frac{C}{R}(s) = \frac{137(s + 0.56)(s + 4)}{(s + 4)(s + 10)(s^2 + 1.68s + 8.7) + 41.1s(s + 0.56)}$$

Note the presence of an additional zero in the numerator of the closed-loop transfer function, which arises because of the difference in $G(s)$ and $HG(s)$. As usual, the resulting denominator polynomial is the characteristic equation, and the roots for a gain of K' equal to 41 have already been found. Therefore the denominator may be replaced by the quadratic factors which are computed in the foregoing. Thus,

$$\frac{C}{R}(s) = \frac{137(s + 0.56)(s + 4)}{(s^2 + 1.8s + 4.23)(s^2 + 14s + 85)} \tag{10-60}$$

A partial-fraction expansion can now be introduced and the inverse

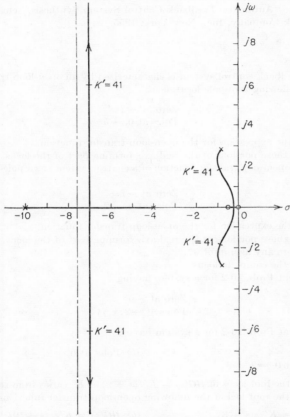

ғıG. 10-24. Root-locus plot of Eq. (10-58) representing the system of Fig. 10-23.

transformation performed to yield the time-domain response. The details are not carried out here since there is nothing new to be learned.

Putting Eq. (10-60) in the form which more readily lends itself to frequency-response analysis leads to

$$\frac{C}{R}(s) = \frac{306}{358} \frac{(1 + 0.25s)(1 + 1.77s)}{\left[\left(\frac{s}{2.06}\right)^2 + \frac{2(0.46)}{2.06}s + 1\right]\left[\left(\frac{s}{9.21}\right)^2 + \frac{2(0.78)}{9.21}s + 1\right]} \tag{10-61}$$

It is interesting to note that now the product of the roots is no longer equal to the constant factor appearing in the numerator, as was the case with the unity feedback system.

SUGGESTED READING

Evans, W. R.: "Control-system Dynamics," chaps. 7, 8, and 11, appendixes B and C, McGraw-Hill Book Company, Inc., New York, 1954.

Truxal, J. G.: "Automatic Feedback Control System Synthesis," chap. 4, McGraw-Hill Book Company, Inc., New York, 1955.

PROBLEMS

10-1. A feedback control system is characterized by an open-loop transfer function having the following zero-pole locations:

Zero at -2
Poles at 0, -5

(a) Write the expression for the open-loop transfer function.

(b) Locate those portions of the real axis forming part of the locus.

10-2. The open-loop transfer function of a control system has a pole-zero configuration given by

Zero at -5
Poles at 0, -2

(a) Write the expression for the open-loop transfer function.

(b) Locate those portions of the real axis forming part of the locus.

(c) Are there any asymptotes?

(d) Sketch the complete locus.

10-3. Repeat Prob. 10-2 for a system having

Zero at -6
Poles at $-2 \pm j4$

10-4. Repeat Prob. 10-2 for a system having

(a) Zero at -4 (b) Poles at 0, -2, -8
      Poles at 0, -2, -8

10-5. Plot the root locus of $HG(s) = K'/(s + 2)$ as K' varies from zero to infinity.

10-6. Plot the root loci of the following open-loop transfer functions:

(a) $HG(s) = K'/s(s + 3)$ (b) $HG(s) = K'/s(s + 2)(s^2 + 2s + 5)$

10-7. A system has an open-loop transfer function given by

$$G(s) = \frac{K(1 + 0.4s)}{(1 + s)(1 + 0.25s)(1 + 0.1s)}$$

(a) Using the spirule, plot the complete root locus.

(b) Find the value of gain which makes the damping ratio of the complex roots equal to 0.5.

(c) Calculate the complete time-domain solution for the output quantity, assuming that the input is subjected to a unit-step command.

10-8. Given the control system shown in Fig. P10-8a. The poles and zeros of $G_1(s)$ and $G_2(s)$ are located as shown in Fig. P10-8b and c.

(a) Draw the root locus for the system, showing all significant information.

(b) At what value of K does the system become unstable?

(c) If $K = 1$, determine r as a function of time when $c(t) = 10 \sin 2t$ in the steady state.

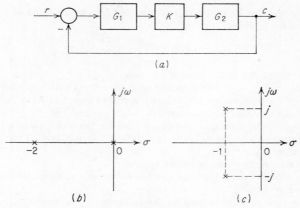

FIG. P10-8

10-9. A feedback control system has an open-loop transfer function with poles and zeros located as illustrated in Fig. P10-9.

(a) Write the equation for the system open-loop transfer function.

(b) Sketch the general shape of the root-locus plot.

(c) Is there any value of gain for which this system will be absolutely stable? Explain.

(d) This system is modified by the introduction of derivative compensation which effectively introduces a double zero at $s = -2$. Sketch the root-locus plot of the modified system.

(e) Is there any value of gain for which the modified system will be absolutely stable? Explain.

(f) Make a list of the type of components which make up the system of part d.

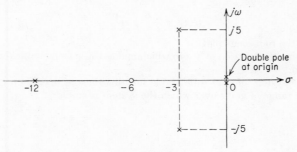

FIG. P10-9

10-10. A system has a direct transfer function of the form

$$HG(s) = \frac{K'}{(s + 16)(s^2 + 2s + 2)}$$

(a) Plot the root locus of this system neatly and to scale.

(b) Compute the value of open-loop gain needed to yield a closed-loop transient response having a damped frequency of oscillation of 2 radians/sec.

(c) For the value of gain found in (b) estimate the per cent maximum overshoot for step inputs to the closed-loop system.

10-11. The system of Example 10-1 is modified by the inclusion of a lag network having the transfer function

$$G_c(s) = 0.20 \frac{s + 0.25}{s + 0.05}$$

(a) Plot the root locus of the modified system.

(b) Determine the value of the damping ratio associated with the complex roots for that value of gain which makes the velocity constant equal to 5 sec^{-1}. Do this for the compensated as well as for the uncompensated system.

10-12. The system of Example 10-1 is modified by the inclusion of a lead network having the transfer function $G_c(s) = (1 + 0.5s)/(1 + 0.035s)$. This includes the required gain adjustment.

(a) Plot the root locus of the modified system.

(b) Find the value of damping ratio corresponding to a velocity constant of 5 sec^{-1} for the modified system.

(c) Compare these results as well as the behavior of the transient modes in this case with those of Prob. 10-11b.

10-13. Repeat Prob. 10-12 by using a compensation network having the transfer function

$$G_c(s) = \frac{s + 1.6}{s + 3.9} \frac{s + 0.45}{s + 0.12}$$

10-14. A controlled system has a transfer function described by

$$G(s) = \frac{K}{s + 5} \frac{1}{s^2 + 4}$$

(a) Sketch the root-locus plot.

(b) Determine the location of a zero which makes the system absolutely stable.

(c) For the modified system of (b) find the maximum value of the damping ratio associated with the complex roots as well as the value of the open-loop gain.

10-15. A unity feedback control system has an open-loop transfer function given by

$$G(s) = \frac{5}{s + 5} \frac{10}{s^2 - 4}$$

(a) Sketch the root-locus plot.

(b) Determine the location of a zero which makes the system stable for the specified open-loop gain.

(c) Will the system of part b be stable for all values of open-loop gain? If not, determine the range of gains over which the system is stable.

11 | Pole-Zero Design Techniques

Basically the principles underlying the design of compensation are the same whether it is performed in the frequency domain or in the s plane. In either case the object is to modify the open-loop system in order to achieve satisfactory closed-loop performance. It is pointed out in Chap. 9 that the success of a compensation transfer function depends quite critically upon the appropriate selection of the breakpoint frequencies of its asymptotic attenuation characteristic. Analogously, in this chapter it is seen that s-plane design of effective compensation likewise depends upon the proper location of the compensation poles and zeros. The selection of these open-loop poles must be such as favorably to influence the shape of the root locus for the compensated system. In this way control over the predominant roots of the system's characteristic equation is obtained.

The s-plane design technique is highly attractive because it offers the designer the advantage of dealing directly with the roots of the characteristic equation. He can now abandon the use of figures of merit to determine the dynamic behavior, which at best could convey only approximate information. However, lest the advantage of the s-plane approach be lost, it is important for the designer to possess a firm understanding of the theory underlying the Laplace transform. For example, he must fully appreciate the effects which the addition of poles and zeros has on the transient response of the closed-loop system. Thus, one must avoid the tendency to identify the dynamic performance solely in terms of the roots of the characteristic equations. If there are zeros present in the closed-loop transfer function, these must be given due consideration because they can greatly deteriorate the dynamic response. In this connection it is recommended that the results appearing on pages 434 to 435 be reviewed at this time. It is worthwhile, too, to review the material of Appendix E. This review offers the opportunity to emphasize that

441

with the s-plane approach the designer exerts simultaneous control over the transient response and the frequency response.

11-1. Effects of Compensation Critical Frequencies on the Root Loci

Often in the composition of a system there is need for compensation because the fixed elements, which are selected on the basis of meeting the steady-state specifications as well as providing the required output power levels, are usually incapable of furnishing a satisfactory dynamic response.   The transient performance is likely to be either too sluggish or too oscillatory.   To correct this situation, the compensation transfer function is made to take on various forms, depending upon the type of system involved and its order.   It is our purpose here to discuss some of these forms in order to emphasize more clearly the importance of properly locating the critical frequencies (poles and zeros) of the compensation transfer function so that a satisfactory dynamic response is achieved. Essentially this is analogous to selecting appropriate breakpoint frequencies for the compensation transfer functions when the design is carried out entirely in the frequency domain.   It will be recalled that the successful design of these corrective networks depends upon a judicious choice of breakpoint frequencies, which frequently are restricted to a limited range of the frequency spectrum.   The careless selection of breakpoint frequencies proves to be ineffectual in achieving suitable transient performance.   This same situation prevails in connection with s-plane design techniques.   It is shown below that, unless the zeros and poles of the compensation transfer function are strategically located, the specified dynamic behavior cannot be realized.

In this section attention is focused solely upon general effects.   Our interest is in the manner in which the root loci are made to change their directions and shapes as a result of the introduction of the poles and zeros of compensation devices.   Specific effects such as the resulting system bandwidth, maximum overshoot, settling time, and so on, corresponding to specific open-loop gains, are treated at length in the subsequent sections.   For the most part this study is confined to a type 1 system of both second and third order.   Moreover, in the interest of providing continuity, the poles and zeros of those types of transfer functions encountered in Chaps. 5, 6, and 9 are treated.

Effect of a Zero on a Second-order Type 1 System.   The root-locus plot of an uncompensated second-order system whose transfer function is

$$HG(s) = \frac{K'}{s(s + p)} \tag{11-1}$$

appears in Fig. 11-1a.   As the plot reveals, there is no finite value of gain which can make this system absolutely unstable.   However, it is possible for the system to be relatively unstable by allowing the damping ratio to become less than some specified minimum value. Although there are several ways of preventing this situation even in the presence of high gains, attention is here directed to the method of error-rate damping,

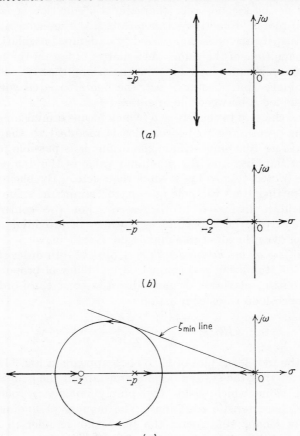

(a)

(b)

(c)

FIG. 11-1. Root-locus plot of (a) $HG(s) = \dfrac{K'}{s(s + p)}$; (b) $HG(s) = \dfrac{K'(s + z)}{s(s + p)}$, where $z < p$; (c) $HG(s) = \dfrac{K'(s + z)}{s(s + p)}$, where $z > p$. (Not drawn to scale.)

which was first introduced in Chap. 4, where the emphasis was on the time-domain analysis. We are now in a position to investigate the effect of this proportional plus derivative control in the complex-frequency domain as well. Recall that the presence of proportional plus derivative control modifies the open-loop transfer function of Eq. (11-1) to

$$HG(s) = \frac{K'(s + z)}{s(s + p)}$$

The particular manner in which the root-locus plot of the original system is affected depends upon the location of the zero of the proportional plus derivative control. Figure 11-1b shows that if $z < p$, that is, the zero is placed between the origin and $-p$, then for any value of open-loop gain the solution of the second-order characteristic equation consists of two negative real roots. Effectively this means that the error-rate damping is so strong that it precludes the possibility of damped oscillations regardless of the magnitude of the gain. As a matter of fact, if the root located to the left of $-p$ is sufficiently far from the origin, the system behaves as if it has a single time constant, viz., the one associated with the root located on the locus between the origin and $-z$.

By locating the zero to the left of p (which means diminishing the error-rate damping term), the root-locus plot is modified to that shown in Fig. 11-1c. Note that under these conditions it is possible for complex roots to exist but that now the minimum value of the damping ratio is definitely restricted to a value greater than zero. By placing the zero closer to or farther from the pole at $-p$, the minimum value of allowed damping ratio is increased or decreased. For the control systems engineer this carries the important significance of providing a means of direct control over the allowable maximum overshoot.

Effect of a Zero on a Third-order Type 1 System. In order to illustrate even better the stabilizing and compensating ability of proportional plus derivative control, attention is next directed to a third-order system having the open-loop transfer function

$$HG(s) = \frac{K'}{s(s + p_1)(s + p_2)} \tag{11-2}$$

A sketch of the root-locus plot of Eq. (11-2) appears in Fig. 11-2a. Here the plot reveals that the system becomes unstable if the gain is increased beyond that value which yields two purely imaginary roots as solutions to the characteristic equation. The manner of finding this gain is outlined in Chap. 10. Again the particular manner in which the root-locus plot of the original system is affected depends upon the location of the zero associated with the proportional plus derivative control. Figure 11-2b shows the new root-locus plot for the modified transfer function $HG(s) = K'(s + z)/[s(s + p_1)(s + p_2)]$ when $z < p_1$, and Fig. 11-2c illustrates the results for $z > p_1$. It is worthwhile to note that in either case the presence of the zero has so modified the system that it is absolutely stable for all values of open-loop gain. This is indeed a significant improvement over the uncompensated system, where the magnitude of open-loop gain was definitely restricted.

Since the magnitude of the zero appearing in Fig. 11-2c is approximately twice that used in the compensated system of Fig. 11-2b, it is to be expected that for the same value of open-loop gain the dynamic response

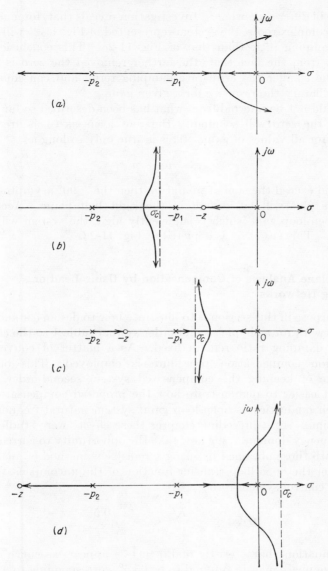

Fig. 11-2. Root-locus plot of (a) $HG(s) = \dfrac{K'}{s(s + p_1)(s + p_2)}$; ($b$) $HG(s) =$ $\dfrac{K'(s + z)}{s(s + p_1)(s + p_2)}$, where $z < p_1$; (c) $HG(s) = \dfrac{K'(s + z)}{s(s + p_1)(s + p_2)}$ where $z > p_1$; (d) $HG(s) = \dfrac{K'(s + z)}{s(s + p_1)(s + p_2)}$, where $z > p_1 + p_2$. (Not drawn to scale.)

of each will differ somewhat.   Investigation reveals that, for a gain which calls for complex roots, the system represented in Fig. 11-2b will exhibit a higher damping ratio than that of Fig. 11-2c.   This conclusion is also apparent from the fact that, the farther removed the zero is from the origin, the smaller the error-rate damping term, and consequently the more oscillatory the response for a given gain.

It should not be inferred from what has been described so far that any value of the zero will so modify the root locus as to assure absolute stability for all values of gain.   This is true only so long as

$$z < p_1 + p_2$$

If z should exceed the sum of p_1 and p_2, then the $\pm 90°$ asymptotes of the root-locus plot will be located in the right half plane.   Accordingly, for an open-loop gain which is sufficiently high, the system will become unstable.   This situation is depicted in Fig. 11-2d.

11-2. s-plane Analysis of Compensation by Using Lead or Lag Networks

Our purpose in this section is to illustrate how to design a standard lead or lag network for a simple second-order system subject to the constraint that the damping ratio remain fixed.   As a matter of convenience a cancellation compensation procedure is employed.   This offers the advantage of keeping the compensated system second-order, thereby making it easier to demonstrate how the proposed compensation influences such quantities as open-loop gain, system natural frequency, and settling time.   In a preceding chapter these effects were studied in the pure-frequency domain.   We now take the opportunity to correlate these results with those obtained by using a root-locus method of analysis.

Consider the open-loop transfer function of the uncompensated unity feedback control system to be

$$G_f(s) = \frac{K'}{s(s + \omega_1)} = \frac{0.5}{s(1 + s)} \tag{11-3}$$

The attenuation characteristic of Eq. (11-3) appears as curve a in Fig. 11-3.   The phase margin is found to be 65.5°, corresponding to which is a damping ratio of 0.707, as obtained from Fig. 7-21.

A root-locus plot of Eq. (11-3) appears in Fig. 11-4 as curve a.   The points along the loci corresponding to the gain $K' = 0.5$ are located by the intersection of the ordinate line passing through -0.5 and the lines drawn at angles of $\pm 135°$ from the origin.   From this root-locus plot it is clear that the damping ratio is 0.707.   Now that the uncompensated system is identified in the sinusoidal-frequency as well as the complex-frequency domains, we may proceed with the compensation design and draw comparisons.

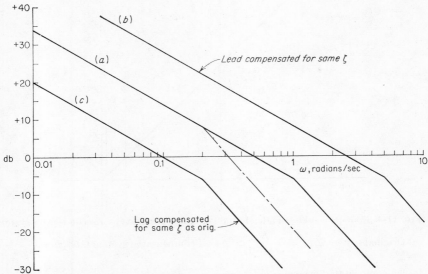

FIG. 11-3. Attenuation characteristics of a lead- and lag-compensated type 1 second-order system. (a) Original system $G_f = \dfrac{K'}{s(s + \omega_1)} = \dfrac{0.5}{s(s + 1)}$; (b) lead-compensated system for same ζ as (a): $G_f G_c(s) = \dfrac{2.5}{s(1 + 0.2s)}$; (c) lag-compensated system for same ζ as (b): $G_f G_g(s) = \dfrac{0.02}{s(s + 0.2)}$.

Series-lead Compensation. The transfer function of the lead network may be expressed as

$$G'_c(s) = \frac{1}{\alpha}\frac{1 + s\alpha\tau}{1 + s\tau} = \frac{s + 1/\alpha\tau}{s + 1/\tau} \tag{11-4}$$

Upon insertion of the preamplifier gain of α, which is needed to offset the attenuation at zero frequency, Eq. (11-4) becomes

$$G_c(s) = \alpha\frac{s + 1/\alpha\tau}{s + 1/\tau} \tag{11-5}$$

Accordingly, the lead-compensated open-loop transfer function becomes

$$G_f G_c(s) = \frac{K'\alpha}{s(s + \omega_1)}\frac{s + 1/\alpha\tau}{s + 1/\tau} \tag{11-6}$$

Design of the lead network requires specifying both τ and α in Eq. (11-6). As explained at the start, the lead-network design is to be such that the value of ζ is to remain the same, viz., 0.707; also, the system is to remain

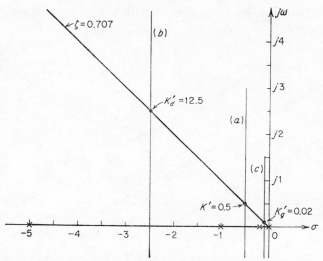

FIG. 11-4. Root-locus plots of a lead- and lag-compensated type 1 second-order system. (a) Original system $G_f(s) = \dfrac{K'}{s(s+1)}$; (b) lead-compensated system $G_c G_f(s) = \dfrac{K'_d}{s(s+5)}$; (c) lag-compensated system $G_g G_f(s) = \dfrac{K'_g}{s(s+0.2)}$.

second-order. The latter condition can be satisfied by selecting the zero of the lead network equal to the pole of the fixed configuration. Thus, select

$$\frac{1}{\alpha\tau} = \omega_1 \tag{11-7}$$

or

$$\frac{1}{\tau} = \alpha\omega_1 \tag{11-8}$$

Inserting the last equation into Eq. (11-6) yields a compensated open-loop transfer function of second order. Thus,

$$G_f G_c(s) = \frac{K'_d}{s(s+\alpha\omega_1)} \tag{11-9}$$

where K'_d refers to the gain needed to make the damping ratio equal to the specified value. If we continue with $\omega_1 = 1$ radian/sec and choose $\alpha = 5$, Eq. (11-9) becomes

$$G_f G_c(s) = \frac{K'_d}{s(s+5)} \tag{11-10}$$

The root-locus plot appears as curve b in Fig. 11-4. The value of K'_d which satisfies the damping-ratio condition may be determined by use of the spirule or else by noting in this simple case that the gain is the product of the distances from the poles at the origin and at -5 to the point of intersection of the ordinate line passing through -2.5 and the line drawn at $+135°$ from the origin. Thus,

$$K'_d = \sqrt{2}\,(2.5)\,[\sqrt{2}\,(2.5)] = 12.5$$

The complete form of the open-loop transfer function which satisfies the specification is

$$G_f G_c(s) = \frac{12.5}{s(s+5)} = \frac{2.5}{s(1+0.2s)} \tag{11-11}$$

A comparison of this equation with Eq. (11-3) indicates that, although both the original and the lead-compensated system have the very same damping ratio, the lead-compensated system enables the gain to take on a value which is 25 times greater. This means smaller steady-state errors where such are called for, as well as a larger system natural frequency, thus providing smaller settling times. The interesting aspect of this comparison is that each of these features is immediately apparent from a glance at the root-locus plot. Thus, the faster settling time is obvious from a comparison of the real parts of the complex roots. For the original system this has a value of -0.5, whereas for the lead-compensated system it is -2.5. Expressed in terms of time constants, the original system has its transients decaying in accordance with a 2-sec time constant, whereas for the lead-compensated system the decay occurs with a 0.4-sec time constant. Moreover, the larger natural frequency is also apparent from the root-locus plot, since it is merely the distance from the origin to the root in question. For the lead-compensated case this has the value

$$\omega_n \Big|_d = \sqrt{2}\,(2.5) = 3.54 \text{ radians/sec}$$

while for the original system the value is

$$\omega_n \Big|_{\text{orig}} = \sqrt{2}\,(0.5) = 0.707 \text{ radian/sec}$$

The ratio is obviously $5:1$.

For the sake of completeness the Bode plot of Eq. (11-11) is shown as curve b in Fig. 11-3. It is worthwhile to note that, if the time constant of the original system had been reduced by a factor of 5 ($=\alpha$) and the gain K' increased by only this same factor, then the damping ratio would have increased. An additional increase in gain K' is required to preserve the original value of damping ratio.

Series-lag Compensation. Attention is now directed to the design of a lag network using the same cancellation compensation procedure outlined in the above text. The standard lag-network transfer function may be described as

$$G_c(s) = \frac{1 + s\tau}{1 + s\alpha\tau} = \frac{1}{\alpha} \frac{s + 1/\tau}{s + 1/\alpha\tau} \tag{11-12}$$

Therefore the lag-compensated open-loop transfer function becomes

$$G_f G_c(s) = \frac{K'/\alpha}{s(s + \omega_1)} \frac{s + 1/\tau}{s + 1/\alpha\tau} \tag{11-13}$$

Applying cancellation compensation for the reasons previously described, it follows that the lag-network time constant is so chosen that

$$\frac{1}{\tau} = \omega_1 \tag{11-14}$$

A comparison of this equation with Eq. (11-8) points out that, for the given value of ω_1, the selected time constant for the lag network is greater than for the lead network. This is a result which is consistent with the conclusions reached in Chap. 9 regarding lag-network design in the sinusoidal-frequency domain.

Inserting Eq. (11-14) into Eq. (11-13) yields the simplified second-order open-loop transfer function

$$G_f G_c(s) = \frac{K'/\alpha}{s(s + \omega_1/\alpha)} \tag{11-15}$$

Putting $K' = 0.5$, $\alpha = 5$, and $\omega_1 = 1$ into this equation leads to

$$G_f G_c(s) = \frac{0.1}{s(s + 0.2)} = \frac{0.5}{s(1 + 5s)} \tag{11-16}$$

Again it is to be noted that, unless the gain is changed after insertion of the lag compensation, the original value of damping ratio cannot be maintained. In fact a Bode plot of Eq. (11-16) reveals that the asymptotic attenuation characteristic crosses the 0-db axis at a slope of -12 db/octave, thereby indicating that the damping ratio is less than the desired 0.707 value. Hence a further reduction in gain is needed. Of course the simplest way to establish the gain needed to yield a damping ratio of 0.707 is to solve for it directly from the root-locus plot. The root-locus plot of Eq. (11-15) appears as curve c in Fig. 11-4. Accordingly, the gain corresponding to a ζ of 0.707 is

$$K'_g = \sqrt{2} \, (0.1) \, [\sqrt{2} \, (0.1)] = 0.02$$

The desired lag-compensated open-loop transfer function then becomes

$$G_f G_c(s) = \frac{0.02}{s(s + 0.2)} = \frac{0.1}{s(1 + 5s)} \tag{11-17}$$

The corresponding attenuation characteristic of this equation appears in

Fig. 11-3 as curve c. A check on the phase margin of this curve yields a value of 65.5°, corresponding to which is a ζ of 0.707.

A glance at the root-locus plot for the lag-compensated system reveals that, although the maximum overshoot to a step command will be the same as for the lead-compensated case, the settling time will be con- considerably longer because the associated time constant is 10 sec. This conclusion is also borne out by the much smaller natural frequency for the lag-compensated system, which the root-locus plot bears out to be

$$\omega_n \Big|_g = \sqrt{2}\ (0.1) = 0.14 \text{ radian/sec}$$

This is considerably less than the value of 3.54 radians/sec found for the lead-compensated case.

On the basis of comparisons made in the foregoing text, it should be clear that the root-locus method of analysis provides significant insight into the manner in which lag and lead compensation influence the dynamic system behavior. In fact it offers the advantage of not only a quicker but also an even more complete description than the frequency-domain approach.

Normally the insertion of a lag network permits an increase in velocity constant while at the same time preventing a highly oscillatory dynamic behavior. This result is not obtained in the foregoing because the stand-ard lag-network design procedure was not employed (see Secs. 9-5 and 11-3). Our purpose here is merely to show the general effects of lag compensation in terms of a reduction in bandwidth, with the consequent increase in settling time.

11-3. s-plane Design of Lag Compensation

Lag compensation is frequently employed in situations where it is desired to improve steady-state performance by increasing the gain while at the same time preserving a satisfactory dynamic response. The manner of designing such a network by using frequency-domain tech-niques is carefully outlined in Chap. 9. Our purpose now is to describe how these same results may be obtained with the use of pole-zero design techniques. As we do so, we shall again correlate the results obtained by each method.

In view of the fact that straight lag compensation finds its greatest application in type 0 and type 1 systems, attention is here centered in the type 1 system. It will be recalled that the ability of a lag network to provide a desired compensation lies in its attenuation characteristic in that portion of the frequency spectrum where the gain curve of the com-pensated system crosses the 0-db axis. To assure that no significant phase lag is introduced in this frequency band, the breakpoint frequencies are chosen small compared with the other nonzero critical frequencies in the system. These very same considerations must be made in designing a lag compensator using the pole-zero approach. In order to illustrate these ideas in terms of the notation used in making root-locus studies, consider a third-order type 1 system whose fixed configuration is described by the open-loop transfer function

$$G_f(s) = \frac{K_v}{s(1 + s\tau_1)(1 + s\tau_2)} = \frac{K'}{(s + 1/\tau_1)(s + 1/\tau_2)s} \tag{11-18}$$

where

$$K' = \frac{K_v}{\tau_1\tau_2} \tag{11-19}$$

Furthermore, imagine that the values of τ_1, τ_2, and K_v are such that a suitable transient response results. However, the difficulty is that the velocity constant is too small, so that an increase is desired. Clearly, we cannot just increase the gain to the value which provides the desired velocity constant, since this adversely affects the dynamic behavior. The use of a lag network is called for to reconcile these two conflicting factors.

Applying the expression for the transfer function of the lag network as given by Eq. (11-12) to Eq. (11-18) makes available the open-loop transfer function of the lag-compensated system. Thus

$$G_fG_c(s) = \frac{K'_c}{s(s + p_1)(s + p_2)} \frac{s + z_c}{s + p_c} \tag{11-20}$$

where

$$K'_c = \frac{K_v}{\tau_1\tau_2} \frac{1}{\alpha} \tag{11-21}$$

and

$$p_1 = \frac{1}{\tau_1} \qquad p_2 = \frac{1}{\tau_2}$$

$$z_c = \frac{1}{\tau} \qquad p_c = \frac{1}{\alpha\tau} \qquad \alpha = \frac{z_c}{p_c}$$

Before proceeding with an explanation of how the increase in gain is accomplished by using the pole-zero approach, let us briefly review how this was achieved in the frequency domain. Refer to Fig. 11-5a. Note that, although the increase in gain raises the log-magnitude curve, yet the attenuation feature of the lag network beyond the frequency $\alpha\omega_b$ restores this portion of the compensated attenuation characteristic to its original position for the portion of the frequency spectrum beyond $\alpha\omega_b$. The significant effect of course is that the position of the very low frequency -6 db/octave slope is raised, and thus the increased velocity constant results. To understand how this same increase is produced by using the s-plane approach, refer to Fig. 11-5b, which shows a sketch of the root-locus plot of the uncompensated system. The squares on the loci indicate the value of K' which yields the desired dynamic response. Examination of Eqs. (11-19) and (11-20) reveals that if the pole and zero of the compensation network are so located that the quantity

$$\frac{s + z_c}{s + p_c} \approx 1\underline{/0°} \qquad (11\text{-}22)$$

when s has the value equal to that drawn from the origin to the square in

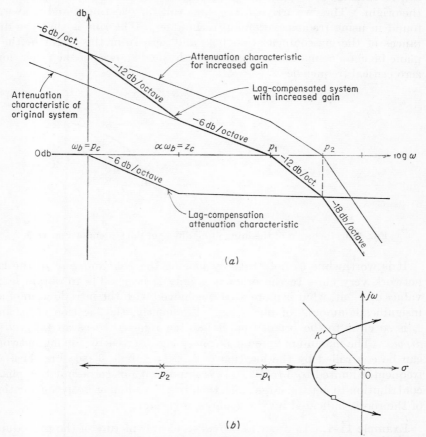

(a)

(b)

FIG. 11-5. (a) Bode representation of a lag-compensated system; (b) sketch of root locus for $G_f = \dfrac{K'}{s(s + p_1)(s + p_2)}$, showing value of K' which yields desired dynamic response.

Fig. 11-5b, then the magnitudes of K' and K'_c are the same. Equation (11-21) then indicates that the value of the velocity constant for the compensated case is increased by the factor α. There remains now the problem of establishing the locations of the pole and zero so that Eq. (11-22) is approximately satisfied. It is important at this point to realize that Eq. (11-22) is not the only condition that needs to be satisfied.

It is also necessary to satisfy the condition that

$$\frac{z_c}{p_c} = \alpha > 1 \tag{11-23}$$

A little thought makes it apparent that the only way both conditions can be satisfied is to place the compensation zero and pole very close to the origin. Thus we arrive at the same rule for selecting z_c and p_c as was found in using frequency-domain techniques. The rule is that the distances of the lag-compensation pole and zero from the origin in the s plane be chosen small in comparison with the distances of the other nonzero critical frequencies.

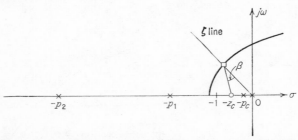

Fig. 11-6. Inclusion of the integrating dipole in the system of Fig. 11-5.

It is worthwhile to note that by placing the pole and zero of the lag network very close to the origin not only is it possible to obtain large values of α but, what is more, this is achieved with the introduction of an insignificant amount of phase lag. Frequently, the location of p_c and z_c is so close to the origin that it is often referred to as an *integrating dipole*. The maximum amount of phase lag inserted by the lag network can be controlled by the location of z_c. The angle β (see Fig. 11-6) is frequently limited to 5 to 10°. It is important not to permit this phase contribution to get too large since then it will no longer keep the location of the roots, indicated by the squares, invariant.

Example 11-1. In order to provide a clearer picture of the procedure, let us apply the foregoing method to an example. Specifically we shall use the example of Sec. 9-5 so that a comparison between the two methods may readily be made. The statement of the problem may be expressed as follows:

Controlled-system open-loop transfer function for meeting the specifications on the output and steady-state performance:

$$G_f(s) = \frac{5}{s(1 + s/2)(1 + s/6)} \tag{11-24}$$

that is,

$$K_v = 5$$

Specifications on the transient performance:

$$\zeta = 0.6$$
Predominant time constant < 2 sec

The root-locus plot of the uncompensated system appears in Fig. 11-7. Before proceeding with the design, it is helpful to investigate just how

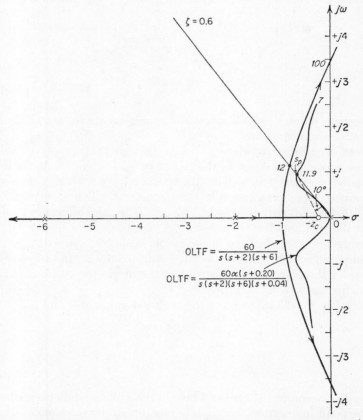

Fig. 11-7. Root-locus plot of type 1 system with and without compensation.

unsatisfactory the original system is under conditions where the gain is adjusted to yield the desired velocity constant. From Eq. (11-24) we have

$$G_f(s) = \frac{60}{s(s + 2)(s + 6)}$$

Corresponding to a value of $K' = 60$ on the root-locus plot, the predominant pair of complex conjugate roots are found to be

$$-r_{1,2} = -0.3 \pm j2.8$$

The associated damping ratio is about 0.1. Hence, although K_v is satisfied, neither the desired value of ζ nor the predominant time constant is met. Therefore lag compensation is required.

Design Procedure. Although concern here is with a specific example, the procedure is presented in generalized form in order to make it more readily applicable to other situations.

1. Obtain the relationship between K_v and K'. For the case at hand,

$$G_fG_c(s) = \frac{12K_v}{\alpha} \frac{s + z_c}{s(s + 2)(s + 6)(s + p_c)}$$

Hence,
$$K' = \frac{12K_v}{\alpha}$$

where
$$\alpha = \frac{z_c}{p_c} = \frac{12K_v}{K'} \tag{11-25}$$

2. Choose a point s_p which meets the requirements on both ζ and the predominant time constant.

3. Select z_c sufficiently close to the origin so that $(s + z_c)/(s + p_c)$ introduces a negligible effect in the region of s_p. A good rule for determining z_c in a manner which meets the specifications without the need for an excessively large time constant is to construct a line at s_p making an angle of $10°$ (or less) with the desired ζ line. Then the intersection of this line with the real axis locates $-z_c$.

Following this procedure for the example leads to $z_c = -0.2$.

4. Compute the value of K' associated with point s_p. In this computation consider the pole p_c to be located at the origin for all practical purposes. This leads to $K' = 11.9$.

5. From Eq. (11-25) determine the required value of α and p_c. Thus,

$$\alpha = \frac{z_c}{p_c} = \frac{12(5)}{11.9} \approx 5$$

and
$$p_c = \frac{z_c}{\alpha} = \frac{0.2}{5} = 0.04$$

6. Locate the computed zero and pole in the s plane, and check whether or not the point in question, viz., s_p is in fact a point on the locus.

If the point does not satisfy the phase criterion, then seek out that point in the vicinity of s_p and on the ζ line which does. For our example s_p satisfies the phase criterion of $180°$.

It is worthwhile to note that the foregoing design procedure does not require drawing the entire root locus of the compensated system. However, for convenience the entire locus is shown in Fig. 11-7.

One final point remains to be discussed, and it involves the introduction of a zero by the compensation network in the expression for $\frac{C}{R}(s)$. An appropriate query to raise at this point concerns the influence this zero has on the amplitude of the transient modes.   (Refer to pages 434, 435 for background in this matter.)   Before this point can be fully explored, the root on that part of the locus lying between -2 and -0.2 must be found, corresponding to that $K' = 12$ which yields the desired velocity constant.   It is usually found located very close to the compensation zero. A few quick trials reveals this root to be located at -0.25.   Accordingly the four roots for $K' = 12$ are

$$s_{1,2} = -r_{1,2} = -0.7 \pm j1$$
$$s_3 = -r_3 = -0.25$$
$$s_4 = -r_4 = -(>6)$$

Thus, the closed-loop transfer function may be expressed as

$$\frac{C}{R}(s) = \frac{\dfrac{K'(s + z_c)}{s(s + 2)(s + 6)(s + p_c)}}{1 + \dfrac{K'(s + z_c)}{s(s + 2)(s + 6)(s + p_c)}} = \frac{K'(s + 0.2)}{(s + r_1)(s + r_2)(s + r_3)(s + r_4)}$$

Inserting the values for the roots yields

$$\frac{C}{R}(s) = \frac{K'(s + 0.2)}{(s^2 + 1.4s + 1.49)(s + 0.25)(s + r_4)} \approx \frac{K'/r_4}{s^2 + 1.4s + 1.49}$$

Examination of this last expression makes it apparent that the effect of the zero is virtually canceled by the root at $-r_3$ so that the dynamic behavior is determined by the newly located complex conjugate roots.

A comparison of the results of the design of the lag compensation by using the s-plane approach with those by using the frequency-domain approach shows them to be identical for the example treated.

11-4. s-plane Design of Lead Compensation

It is pointed out in Chap. 9 that the lead network is capable of furnishing appropriate compensation to a system by virtue of its phase-lead property.   The pole-zero approach to the design of these lead networks is based upon this very same characteristic, as is demonstrated below. As one gains experience with the effects caused by the additions of poles and zeros on the root loci, one comes to appreciate that the design of compensation can be performed quite readily from a cut-and-try procedure.   However, because this text is an introductory one on the subject matter, we shall not take this approach.   Instead, a rather simple and straightforward design theory is developed and subsequently illustrated. A comparison is then made with the corresponding results obtained by using frequency-domain techniques, in order to see better the additional advantages offered by the s-plane approach.   A truly attractive feature of the described method of design is the ability to choose the desired locations of the predominant complex roots of the closed-loop system and then to proceed directly to the pole and zero of the lead compensation which make the selected roots fall on the loci of the compensated system.

Circles of Constant Phase Lead in the s Plane. As a preliminary step in the development of a general design procedure for the standard type of lead network, it is helpful to investigate the nature of the phase-lead

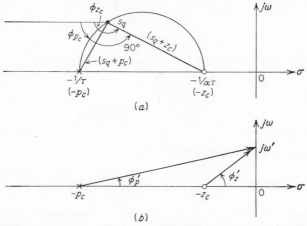

FIG. 11-8. Circle of constant phase lead of 90°. (*a*) *s*-plane representation; (*b*) manner of obtaining the sinusoidal-frequency characteristic of the lead network.

characteristic of the network in terms of its pole-zero configuration in the *s* plane. From Eq. (11-4) we know the transfer function of the lead network to be

$$G_c(s) = \frac{s + 1/\alpha\tau}{s + 1/\tau} = \frac{s + z_c}{s + p_c}$$

An inspection of this equation reveals that the zero is always located closer to the origin than the pole, as is illustrated in Fig. 11-8a. This arrangement is just the reverse of what prevails for the lag network. There is another essential difference. Whereas with the lag network both the pole and the zero are closely located with respect to the origin and with respect to each other, in the case of the lead network they are usually appreciably displaced from the origin as well as from each other. For the lag network the proximity of the pole and zero assures a very small phase-lag contribution to the over-all compensated phase characteristic. For the lead network, however, the farther apart p_c and z_c are, the greater is the phase-lead contribution of the network.

For a given pole-zero configuration the amount of phase-lead contribution of the network corresponding to a selected point s_q in the *s*-plane is readily determined by proceeding as depicted in Fig. 11-8a. The phase-lead contribution of the root factor associated with the zero is ϕ_{z_c}, while the phase-lag component associated with the pole is ϕ_{p_c}. The net phase-lead contribution is described by $\phi_{z_c} - \phi_{p_c}$. In Fig. 11-8a the point s_q is so chosen as to yield a net phase lead of 90°. It is important at this point not to confuse this phase-lead contribution with those discussed in connection with the frequency-domain analysis of lead networks. For example, the net phase-lead angles represented in Fig. 5-28 are determined by *confining the frequency variable to the jω axis*. For any specified values of α and τ the angles represented in Fig. 5-28 as a function of frequency may be determined by proceeding as outlined in Fig. 11-8b.

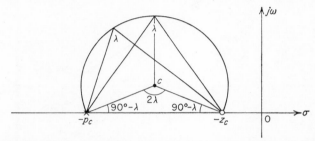

FIG. 11-9. Construction procedure for circles of constant phase in the s plane.

Thus, corresponding to frequency $j\omega'$, the net phase-lead angle is $\phi'_z - \phi'_p$. It is interesting to note that, as long as s is limited to variation along the $j\omega$ axis, the net phase-lead angle cannot exceed 90°, which is a result with which we are already familiar.

Once the pole and zero of a lead network are established (as indicated in Fig. 11-8a), it is possible to seek out those points in the s plane for which the net phase-lead angle is 90°. Clearly, the result is a locus which defines a semicircle whose diameter lies on the negative real axis. In situations where it is desired that the net angular contribution of the pole-zero configuration be other than 90°, it should be apparent that the center of the constant-phase circle must move off the real axis. The procedure for constructing such a circle is simple and straightforward.

Let it be desired to construct that portion of a circular locus on which lie points which yield a constant phase lead of λ corresponding to a specified pole and zero location. Assume that the given pole and zero are located as shown in Fig. 11-9. To establish the location of the center of the desired circle, mark off lines making an angle of $90° - \lambda$ with the real axis originating at $-p_c$ and $-z_c$ in the manner illustrated in Fig. 11-9. The point of intersection of these lines identifies the center of the circle c. Then with c as a center and cp_c as a radius the appropriate portion of the circle is constructed. Thus any point located on the portion of the circle above the real axis provides a net phase-lead contribution due to the pole and zero equal to λ. A little thought should reveal that in those cases where the desired λ is less than $90°$ the center of the circle always appears above the real axis, while for those cases where λ is greater than $90°$ the location occurs below the real axis. The proof of the foregoing construction should be obvious since it merely requires a knowledge of the facts that a central angle is equal to two times its inscribed angle and that inscribed angles which subtend the same arc are equal to each other.

General Design Procedure. Our purpose here is to develop a method which will permit us to choose the locations of the pole and zero of a lead network so that a desired pair of points in the s plane become roots of the

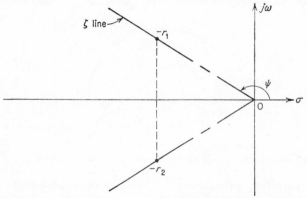

Fig. 11-10. Showing location of roots which yield the desired damping ratio as well as settling time.

characteristic equation of the compensated system. Accordingly, assume that the root locus of an uncompensated system is known and plotted. Assume further that it is desirable to have the s-plane points located at $-r_{1,2}$ (as shown in Fig. 11-10) as the roots of the closed-loop system, which essentially describes the dynamic performance. These locations are selected on the basis of furnishing a desired damping ratio as well as settling time. The latter is determined by the magnitude of the real part of the roots $-r_{1,2}$. Of course, it is understood that the points $-r_{1,2}$ do not fall on the root locus of the original system, for then there is hardly any need for compensation. Knowing the desired locations of $-r_{1,2}$ and the pole-zero configuration of the original system, we can readily determine the total phase lag ϕ existing at the point $-r_1$. It follows then that a phase-lead compensator needs to be designed which satisfies the following equation:

$$\phi + \lambda = -180° \qquad (11\text{-}26)$$

Here ϕ is a negative quantity representing the phase lag at point $-r_1$ owing to the pole-zero configuration of the original system and λ is a positive quantity representing the phase-lead contribution of the lead network. The required amount of lead compensation is therefore

$$\lambda = -\phi - 180° \qquad (11\text{-}27)$$

Equation (11-27) furnishes one of two pieces of information needed to determine the locations of the compensation pole and zero. The second piece of information involves the angle ψ, which identifies the location of the ζ line (see Fig. 11-10).

In order to develop the theory which outlines how p_c and z_c are found by using this information, refer to Fig. 11-11. The constant-phase circle is constructed tangent to the ζ line at the desired root location $-r_1$.

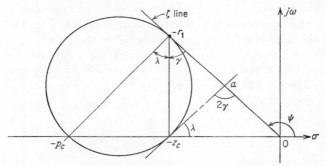

FIG. 11-11. Construction procedure for locating a compensation pole and zero.

The circle intersects the real axis at $-p_c$ and $-z_c$, which together combine to add a net phase-lead angle of λ to the $s = -r_1$ point, thereby assuring that this point is now on the root locus of the compensated system. The angle λ of course is assumed to be found from Eq. (11-27) in the prescribed manner. Since in any given situation the known quantities are λ and ψ, a study of Fig. 11-11 points out that this does not lead directly to the location of p_c and z_c. Rather, what must be established first is the angle γ, since this can be used to locate z_c. Then λ can be used to obtain p_c. Thus, what we need is an equation which relates γ to λ and ψ.

The desired expression is obtained with the aid of plane geometry. At $-z_c$ construct a tangent to the λ circle intersecting the ζ line at point a. It then follows that

$$\psi = \lambda + 2\gamma$$

Hence
$$\gamma = \tfrac{1}{2}(\psi - \lambda) \qquad (11\text{-}28)$$

The design procedure for locating the pole and zero of a lead compensator which makes a pair of selected points in the s-plane roots of the characteristic equation of the compensated system can now be summarized as follows:

1. Measure ψ corresponding to the desired locations of the predominant pair of complex roots (the locations are selected on the basis of a desired

damping ratio, and/or damping factor, and/or bandwidth, and/or damped frequency of oscillation, etc.).

2. At the desired root location find the actual phase lag of the uncompensated system.

3. Compute the required phase-lead angle from $\lambda = -\phi - 180°$.

4. Determine the location of the compensation zero by finding

$$\gamma = \tfrac{1}{2}(\psi - \lambda)$$

and marking off a line γ displaced below the ζ line originating at $-r_1$. The intersection of this line with the negative real axis establishes the value of $z_c (= 1/\alpha\tau)$. For realizability in terms of minimum phase-shift networks γ must be positive in the direction defined in Fig. 11-11. That is, γ must be marked off by a line drawn below the ζ line.

5. To locate the compensation pole, mark off a line displaced by an angle $\lambda + \gamma$ below the ζ line. The intersection of this line with the negative real axis yields $p_c (= 1/\tau)$.

6. *Final design:*

$$\tau = \frac{1}{p_c}$$

$$\alpha = \frac{p_c}{z_c}$$

Example 11-2. Design a lead compensator such that a system with the fixed configuration

$$G_f(s) = \frac{K_f}{s(1 + s/2)(1 + s/10)}$$

meets the following specifications:

Damping ratio $\zeta = 0.6$
Predominant time constant $= \tfrac{1}{3}$ sec

Also, determine the value of the velocity constant for these conditions.

Choose the desired location of the root at ρ_1 in Fig. 11-12. This location satisfies the $\zeta = 0.6$ condition as well as that on the predominant time constant. Measure $\psi = 127°$.

Using the pole-zero configuration of $G_f(s)$, find the phase lag at point ρ_1 with the help of the spirule. Thus

$$\phi = 117° = -243°$$

Hence $\lambda = 243° - 180° = 63°$

Compute $\gamma = \tfrac{1}{2}(\psi - \lambda) = 32°$

This leads to $z_c = 2$.

Mark off a line $95°$ displaced from the ζ line. This yields $p_c = 8$.

Final design:

$$\tau = \frac{1}{p_c} = \tfrac{1}{8} \ \text{sec}$$

$$\alpha = \frac{p_c}{z_c} = 4$$

The value of gain corresponding to point ρ_1 is $K' = 200$. To determine the velocity constant from this requires writing the complete expression

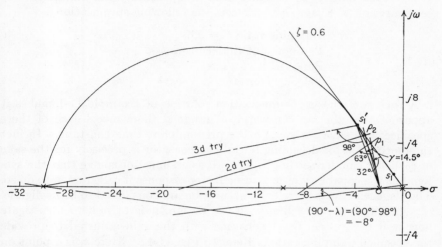

Fig. 11-12. Graphical illustration of the design of lead compensators for Examples 11-2 and 11-3.

for the compensated open-loop transfer function. Thus

$$G_cG_f(s) = \frac{K_f}{s(1 + s/2)(1 + s/10)} \frac{1}{\alpha} \frac{1 + s\alpha\tau}{1 + s\tau}$$

$$= 20 \, K_f \frac{1}{s(s + 2)(s + 10)} \frac{s + z_c}{s + p_c}$$

Therefore from the second equation it follows that

$$K' = 20K_f$$

or

$$K_f = 10$$

From the first form of the equation for $G_cG_f(s)$, the velocity constant is seen to be

$$K_v = \frac{K_f}{\alpha} = \frac{10}{4} = 2.5 \ \text{sec}^{-1}$$

Example 11-3. We consider next a situation which calls for meeting a specification, not only on the nature of the dynamic response as is done in Example 11-2, but also on the magnitude of the velocity constant.

With the introduction of this additional constraint the foregoing procedure must be somewhat modified, especially if attention is to be confined to the design of the usual type of lead network. The method of design must now take on the aspects of a cut-and-try procedure, because with the root-locus approach the gain can be determined only after the point on the compensated locus has been established. In spite of this, however, the method is rapid, as is demonstrated below.

Let it be desired to design a lead compensator such that the fixed configuration of Example 11-2 meets the following specifications:

Damping ratio $\zeta = 0.6$
Predominant time constant $< \frac{1}{3}$ sec
Bandwidth < 2 cps
Velocity constant $= 5$ sec^{-1}

A review of the lag-compensation solution of Example 11-1 makes it apparent that the lag compensator designed there meets each of these specifications save the one on the predominant time constant. In fact the motivation for designing a lead compensator is precisely for the sake of realizing smaller settling times. It is assumed of course that the system has the capability of providing faster response if called upon to do so. That is, such effects as velocity saturation are considered to be negligible.

Again, before proceeding with the design, it is helpful to investigate how well the system $G_f(s)$ performs with the gain adjusted to provide the specified damping ratio. Refer to Fig. 11-12. Here s_1 is a point on the desired ζ line as well as on the root locus of the uncompensated system $G_f(s)$. The value of K' for this point is found to be $K' = 12$, so that the corresponding value of the velocity constant is $K_v = K'/20 = \frac{12}{20} = 0.6$. Accordingly, we see that operation corresponding to s_1 meets only two of the four specifications. It does not meet the requirement on the velocity constant or on the predominant time constant.

Clearly, the lead-network design of Example 11-2 is not a suitable solution because it does not provide the desired velocity constant. Therefore, as a second try consider point ρ_2, which meets the first three specifications. However, a check on the velocity constant is needed. To do this requires first designing the appropriate compensation network. Measure

$$\psi = 127°$$

Find

$$\phi = 92 = -268°$$
$$\lambda = 268 - 180 = 88°$$
$$\gamma = 19.5°$$

Therefore

$$z_c = 2$$
$$p_c = 18$$

Final design:

$$\tau = \tfrac{1}{18}$$
$$\alpha = 9$$

For the pole-zero configuration using this compensation the gain at ρ_2 of the root-locus plot is found to be

$$K' = 664$$

for which

$$K_v = 3.68 \text{ sec}^{-1}$$

Another try is needed. Thus choose point s_1'. Then

$$\psi = 127°$$
$$\phi = 82 = -278°$$
$$\lambda = 98°$$
$$\gamma = 14.5°$$

Therefore

$$z_c = 2.0$$
$$p_c = 30$$

Final design:

$$\tau = \tfrac{1}{30}$$
$$\alpha = 15$$

For this compensated pole-zero configuration the gain is

$$K' = 1{,}440$$

corresponding to which is a velocity constant

$$K_v = \frac{1{,}440}{20(15)} = 4.8 \approx 5$$

Thus by operating at point s_1' each of the specifications is satisfied. As a result of the need to raise the gain to meet the requirement on the velocity constant, it is noted that the predominant time constant is $\tfrac{1}{4}$ sec, which is somewhat less than what was called for.

In summary, then, the compensation transfer function may be written as $G_c(s) = (1 + s/2)/(1 + s/30)$. Applying this to the expression of the fixed configuration makes the open-loop transfer function of the compensated system become

$$G_cG_f(s) = \frac{1 + s/2}{1 + s/30} \frac{5}{s(1 + s/2)(1 + s/10)} = \frac{5}{s(1 + s/10)(1 + s/30)}$$

An examination of this last expression indicates that effectively the designed lead network has removed the troublesome $\tfrac{1}{2}$-sec time constant and replaced it with a considerably smaller one of value $\tfrac{1}{30}$ sec. It is important to understand, however, that this procedure is admissible only as long as saturation effects are negligible. Figure 11-13 demonstrates more clearly the manner in which the root locus is modified by the lead compensation to allow the system to meet all the specifications.

It is instructive at this point to design a lead compensator by using the frequency-domain techniques outlined in Chap. 9 (see Prob. 11-4). If this is attempted, it will be seen that meeting the proposed specifications will be considerably more difficult. The difference lies essentially in the fact that the frequency-domain approach employs figures of merit to describe the time response approximately, whereas with the s-plane

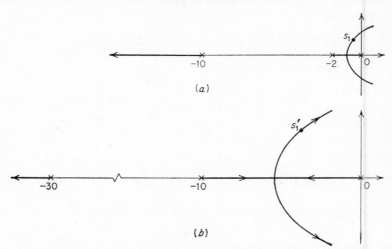

FIG. 11-13. Illustrating how the lead compensator of Example 11-3 modifies the root locus of the original system. (a) Original system; (b) compensated system.

approach this is wholly unnecessary because we are dealing directly with the roots of the characteristic equation.

11-5. s-plane Design of Lag-Lead Compensation

There are several approaches to the design of lag-lead compensation. Here attention is primarily focused on the cancellation compensation method, not only because it is the simplest to handle, but also because it proceeds in a manner very similar to the design method employed in the frequency domain. Sometimes the objection is raised that exact cancellation is difficult to realize in practical systems. However, where minimum-phase[1] transfer functions are involved, the presence of inexact cancellation which is not overexaggerated produces a relatively insignificant effect on the system's dynamic behavior. The theory underlying the s-plane design of lag-lead compensation is merely a combination of what is described in Secs. 11-3 and 11-4. First, it requires the selection of the pole and zero of a lead network to assure that the chosen root locations of the closed-loop system satisfy the Evans phase criterion. Then, it necessitates the design of an appropriate integrating dipole to allow the specification on the open-loop gain to be met. The combination of the

[1] These are transfer functions for which the poles and zeros are located inside the left-half s plane.

two networks then furnishes the required lag-lead compensation. This procedure is best illustrated by means of an example.

Example 11-4. Design a lag-lead compensation such that a fixed configuration described by

$$G_f(s) = \frac{K_f}{s(1 + s/2)(1 + s/6)}$$

meets the following specifications:

> Damping ratio $\zeta = 0.6$
> Predominant time constant $< \frac{3}{4}$ sec
> Bandwidth < 3 radians/sec
> Velocity constant $= 5$ sec^{-1}

Choose a point in the s plane which meets the first three conditions. Such a point is identified in Fig. 11-14 as s_1. The method of designing the

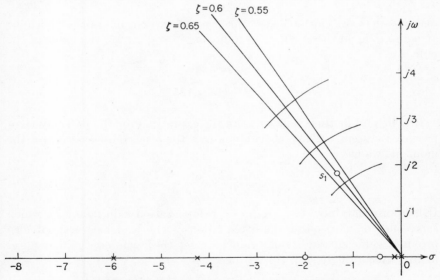

FIG. 11-14. Pole-zero configuration for the solution of Example 11-4.

lead portion of the compensation is to replace the pole of $G_f(s)$ located at -2 by one which enables the point at s_1 to meet the $-180°$ phase condition. Thus, the lead network requires a zero located at -2, that is,

$$z_d = 2$$

(Since we are dealing here with a lag and lead network, the poles and zeros of each of these networks are distinguished by using the subscript d for the lead network and the subscript g for the lag network.) Then the pole which replaces the original one is found by proceeding as follows: Place the pivot of the spirule at s_1, and obtain the phase-lag contributions of the poles of $G_f(s)$ located at 0 and -6. Next rotate the arm and the disk of the spirule until the 180° mark points horizontally toward the left, as depicted in Fig. 11-15. The intersection of the arm with the negative

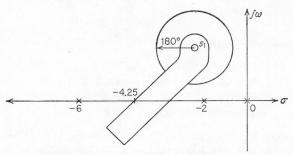

FIG. 11-15. Manner of finding the lead-network pole for cancellation compensation.

real axis determines the location of the pole which makes the phase lag at point s_1 equal to $-180°$. As indicated in Fig. 11-15, the value of the pole is

$$p_d = 4.25$$

Also,

$$\alpha_d = \frac{p_d}{z_d} = 2.125$$

It is helpful at this point to write the expression for the partially compensated system. Thus, considering just the lead compensation for the moment, we have

$$G_f G_d(s) = \frac{K_f}{s(1 + s/2)(1 + s/6)} \frac{1}{\alpha_d} \frac{1 + s/z_d}{1 + s/p_d} \tag{11-29}$$

It is appropriate now to introduce a compensation gain factor K_c which serves not only to offset the attenuation of the lead network but also provides sufficient additional gain to meet the open-loop gain requirement. Accordingly, Eq. (11-29) becomes

$$G_f G_d(s) = \frac{K_f}{s(1 + s/2)(1 + s/6)} \frac{K_c}{\alpha_d} \frac{1 + s/z_d}{1 + s/p_d} \tag{11-30}$$

from which it follows that the expression for the velocity constant for the system is

$$K_v = \frac{K_f K_c}{\alpha_d} \tag{11-31}$$

Putting Eq. (11-30) into the form for root-locus analysis, we get

$$G_f G_d(s) = \frac{12 K_v}{s(s + 2)(s + 6)} \frac{p_d}{z_d} \frac{s + z_d}{s + p_d} \tag{11-32}$$

Inserting the values for z_d and p_d yields

$$G_f G_d(s) = \frac{25.5K_v}{s(s + 4.25)(s + 6)} \qquad (11\text{-}33)$$

This expression represents the lead-compensated system. Of course, if the gain at point s_1 were such that the desired K_v results, then there would be no need to proceed further. However, a check on this gain reveals that the requirement on the velocity constant is not met. Thus, it is found that

$$K' = 37.5$$

so that

$$K_v = \frac{37.5}{25.5} = 1.47$$

which falls far short of the desired value of 5.

As pointed out in Sec. 11-3, the insertion of lag compensation can permit an increase in open-loop gain without upsetting to any significant extent the phase condition at point s_1. Therefore, lag compensation is next introduced to permit the necessary increase in velocity constant. Recall that the lag-network transfer function is given by

$$G_g(s) = \frac{p_g}{z_g} \frac{s + z_g}{s + p_g}$$

Accordingly, the expression for the totally compensated open-loop transfer function becomes

$$G_f G_d G_g(s) = \frac{25.5K_v}{s(s + 4.25)(s + 6)} \frac{p_g}{z_g} \frac{s + z_g}{s + p_g} \qquad (11\text{-}34)$$

A glance at Eq. (11-34) indicates that the expression for the gain K' at point s_1 for the lag-lead compensated system is

$$K' = 25.5K_v \frac{p_g}{z_g} = 25.5 \frac{K_v}{\alpha_g} \qquad (11\text{-}35)$$

where $\alpha_g = z_g/p_g > 1$. Solving for the velocity constant gives

$$K_v = \frac{K'}{25.5} \alpha_g \qquad (11\text{-}36)$$

Equation (11-36) makes it clear just how the velocity constant is increased by the lag dipole. After the selection of z_g, p_g is subsequently determined by assigning it that value which makes α_g take on the value needed to yield the desired K_v.

To determine z_g, draw a line at s_1 in Fig. 11-14 at an angle of about 10° from the ζ line. The intersection with the real axis establishes the value of the lag-network zero as $z_g = 0.45$. It should be kept in mind that, by locating z_g in accordance with a 10° line rather than, say, some other line drawn at a smaller angle, the magnitudes of the corresponding time constants can be kept within reasonable limits. Of course, for greater accuracy in describing the dynamic behavior, it is desirable to relocate point s_1 slightly to offset the lag contribution of the integrating dipole.

The lag-network pole p_g is found from the gain condition as expressed by Eq. (11-36). But first we need to know K', which can be found by assuming that p_g is located practically at the origin. This leads to $K' = 41$. Inserting this quantity as well as $K_v = 5$ into Eq. (11-36) gives

$$\alpha_g = \frac{25.5(5)}{41} = 3.2$$

Thus, $$p_g = \frac{z_g}{\alpha_g} = \frac{0.45}{3.2} = 0.14$$

Substituting the designed values for p_g and z_g into Eq. (11-34) makes the expression for the lag-lead-compensated open-loop transfer function become

$$G_f G_d G_g(s) = \frac{41}{s(s + 4.25)(s + 6)} \frac{s + 0.45}{s + 0.14} \tag{11-37}$$

Rearranging so as to bring the value of the velocity constant into evidence yields

$$G_f G_d G_g(s) = \frac{5.16(1 + 2.22s)}{s(1 + s/4.25)(1 + s/6)(1 + 7.14s)} \tag{11-38}$$

Also, the required lag-lead-compensation transfer function takes the form†

$$G_d G_g(s) = \frac{1}{2.125} \frac{1 + s/2}{1 + s/4.25} \frac{1 + s/0.45}{1 + s/0.14} \tag{11-39}$$

Finally, the value of gain adjustment K_c required in the system to provide this desired velocity constant as well as to make up for the attenuation of the lead portion of the compensation is determined from Eq. (11-31) as

$$K_c = \frac{\alpha_d K_v}{K_f} = \frac{10.375}{K_f}$$

where K_f represents the assumed constant gain factor of the fixed configuration. It is interesting to note that α_g of the lag network does not enter into this computation because the lag network causes no attenuation at steady state.

A check on the phase lag prevailing at s_1 by using the complete pole-zero configuration of Eq. (11-38) shows that it is no longer $-180°$, as already explained. The point that now meets the phase criterion is

† For synthesis procedures to mechanize such transfer functions consult Sec. 12-5 and Prob. 12-18.

located slightly to the right of s_1. This means that the damping ratio as well as the predominant time constant will be a little off the required values. We shall not concern ourselves here with making this adjustment. However, the lesson to be learned from this is that when s_1 is initially selected it should be done in a way which foresees the need for adjustment. Thus, in our example a more appropriate selection for s_1 would have been to place it somewhat to the right of the position shown in Fig. 11-14. This was not done at the beginning of the example in order to illustrate the consequences more emphatically.

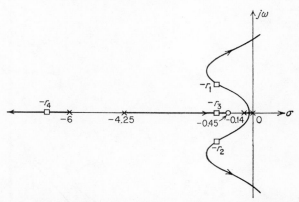

FIG. 11-16. Location of the roots of Eq. (11-40) corresponding to $K' = 41$.

From the form of Eq. (11-38) it should be clear that the expression for the closed-loop transfer function contains a zero. In view of the adverse influence which a poorly placed zero has on the dynamic behavior (cf. pages 434, 435), a check is in order. For a unity feedback system the expression for the closed-loop transfer function is

$$\frac{C}{R}(s) = \frac{41(s + 0.45)}{(s + r_1)(s + r_2)(s + r_3)(s + r_4)} \tag{11-40}$$

where r_1, r_2, r_3, r_4 represent the locations of the roots of the characteristic equation corresponding to $K' = 41$, as depicted in Fig. 11-16. The root r_1 of course corresponds to the selected s-plane point s_1. That is, $s_1 = -r_1$. The root r_2 merely represents the complex conjugate of r_1. The third root r_3 is found to be equal to 0.57. The value of the fourth root r_4 is not determined since it is too far out in the s plane to affect adversely the transient performance. Accordingly, Eq. (11-40) may be written as

$$\frac{C}{R}(s) = \frac{41(s + 0.45)}{(s + r_1)(s + r_2)(s + 0.57)(s + r_4)}$$

A little thought should reveal that, because of the relatively close proximity of the r_3 root to the zero, the coefficient in the partial-fraction expansion for this term is almost negligible. Therefore, the closed-loop transfer function can be represented for all practical purposes by

$$\frac{C}{R}(s) \approx \frac{41/r_4}{(s + r_1)(s + r_2)}$$

so that the dynamic behavior is essentially determined by the roots located at $s_{1,2} = -r_{1,2}$.

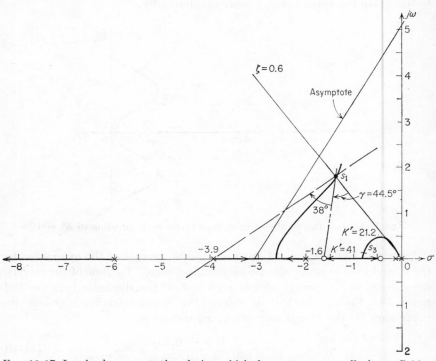

FIG. 11-17. Lag-lead compensation design which does not use cancellation. $G_f(s) =$
$$\frac{K_f}{s(1 + s/2)(1 + s/6)}; \; G_d G_g(s) = \frac{1.6 \, (1 + s/1.6)(1 + s/0.45)}{3.9 \, (1 + s/3.9)(1 + s/0.14)}.$$

When a method of design other than the cancellation procedure outlined in the foregoing is employed, care must be exercised to avoid a situation which makes the selected locations of the complex conjugate roots of the characteristic equation take on a secondary role. For example, if a lag-lead compensation were designed by a direct application of the methods of Secs. 11-3 and 11-4 without making use of cancellation compensation, a solution such as depicted in Fig. 11-17 is very likely to result. In this case the zero and pole of the lead portion of the compensation are located, respectively, at -1.6 and -3.9, whereas the integrating dipole has the same location as in Example 11-4. The resulting root-locus plot reveals that additional root paths are introduced off the axis and in the vicinity of the origin. Now, although the point s_1 is a point on the locus for the desired velocity constant, investigation shows that these roots no longer predominate exclusively in such a design. This is because another pair of complex conjugate roots arise in the vicinity of s_3 in Fig. 11-17, corresponding to the same open-loop gain.

11-6. s-plane Design of Double-lead Compensation

The design of a double-lead network proceeds in a manner very similar to that of the single-lead network. The place where a modification is necessary is dependent upon the magnitude of the computed phase-lead angle λ. If this quantity is found to be very large, then it is best to continue the design in terms of a double-lead network. Then each section of the double-lead network contributes an amount of phase lead which can be expressed as

$$\lambda^* = \tfrac{1}{2}\lambda \tag{11-41}$$

Clearly, in a situation where a triple-lead network may be called for, the appropriate factor to use is $\tfrac{1}{3}$.

Because the design of a lead network involves the insertion of a double zero in the over-all pole-zero configuration of the compensated system, care must be exercised in order to avoid the condition which makes the selected roots exert a secondary rather than a predominant role in determining the system's dynamic behavior. Once again the use of an example serves fittingly to illustrate the ideas as well as the procedures involved.

Example 11-5. Design the appropriate compensation which is needed to make the system

$$G_f(s) = \frac{K_f}{s(1 + s/2)(1 + s/6)}$$

meet the following specifications:

> Damping ratio $\zeta = 0.6$
> Predominant time constant $< \tfrac{1}{3}$ sec
> Bandwidth < 8 radians/sec
> Velocity constant $= 4.5$ sec^{-1}

Refer to Fig. 11-18. Select s_p as the point in the s plane which meets the first three requirements. Measure $\psi = 127°$. Using the pole-zero configuration of $G_f(s)$, find the phase lag at s_p. Thus

$$\phi = 48° = -312°$$

Thus
$$\lambda = 312 - 180 = 132°$$

The large magnitude involved here is an indication that a double-lead network is appropriate. Moreover, the use of this quantity together with the value of ψ in Eq. (11-28) results in a negative value for γ, which of course is meaningless. This can be taken as a clear indication that simple lead compensation should not be attempted.

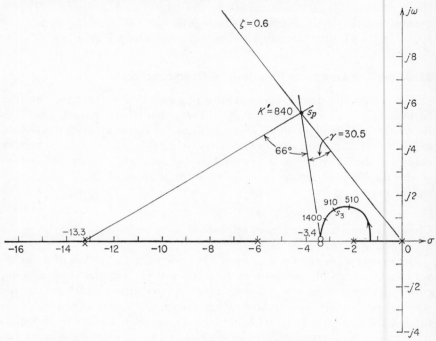

FIG. 11-18. Root-locus plot of a double-lead compensated system.

$$G_f(s) = \frac{K_f}{s(1 + s/2)(1 + s/6)}; \quad G_c(s) = \left(\frac{1}{3.91}\right)^2 \frac{(1 + s/3.4)^2}{(1 + s/13.3)^2}$$

Each section of the double-lead compensator must then provide a phase-lead angle of

$$\lambda^* = \tfrac{1}{2}\lambda = 66°$$

in order that s_p be a point on the compensated root locus. Hence,

$$\gamma = \tfrac{1}{2}(\psi - \lambda^*) = \tfrac{1}{2}(127 - 66) = 30.5°$$

This leads to

$$z_c = 3.4$$

Marking off a line displaced $(66 + 30.5)°$ from the ζ line leads to

$$p_c = 13.3$$

Final design:

$$\tau = \frac{1}{p_c} = \frac{1}{13.3} \text{ sec}$$

$$\alpha = \frac{13.3}{3.4} = 3.91$$

Two such networks are needed.

A check on the value of velocity constant is now needed to determine whether or not s_p needs to be moved farther up on the ζ line but still within the bandwidth specification. The expression for the compensated transfer function is

$$G_f G_c(s) = \frac{K_f}{s(1 + s/2)(1 + s/6)} \frac{1}{\alpha^2} \left(\frac{1 + s\alpha\tau}{1 + s\tau}\right)^2$$
$$= \frac{12 K_v \alpha^2}{s(s + 2)(s + 6)} \left(\frac{s + z_c}{s + p_c}\right)^2 \quad (11\text{-}42)$$

It follows from this that

$$K' = 12 K_v \alpha^2 \quad \text{and} \quad K_v = \frac{K_f}{\alpha^2}$$

The spirule-measured value of gain at point s_p is

$$K' = 840$$

Therefore the velocity constant is

$$K_v = \frac{K'}{12\alpha^2} = \frac{840}{12(3.91)^2} = 4.6$$

which is satisfactory.

The partially completed root-locus plot of the compensated system appears in Fig. 11-18. The point s_p and its complex conjugate are of course on the loci originating from the pole at -6 and one of the two poles at -13.3. It is noticed that the presence of the double zero at -3.4 has created auxiliary root paths in the vicinity of the origin. The point s_3 on this locus corresponds to the gain $K_v = 4.5$. Consequently, it is necessary under these circumstances to investigate whether s_3 or s_p exerts the predominant effect. Such an examination reveals that the root at s_p does predominate. An appreciation of this result can be had by referring to Eq. (11-42) and noting that the evaluation of the residue at s_3 is proportional to $(s_3 + 3.4)^2$. Since this quantity is less than unity and squared, the resulting magnitude is quite small. Note that the smaller the arc of this auxiliary locus, the less important is the role played by the root s_3.

In the interest of correlating s-plane design of the double-lead network with the frequency-domain design, a double-lead compensator was designed by using the procedures of Chap. 9. A 45° phase margin was used as one of the design criteria. At first an attempt was made to use a single-lead network. It required several trials before it became apparent that a double-lead compensation was needed. As already pointed out, the s-plane approach makes this immediately evident. Finally, it was found that the compensation transfer function which allowed the system to meet the specifications was

$$G_c(s) = \left(\frac{1 + s/2.8}{1 + s/11.2}\right)^2$$

In view of the fact that a 45° phase margin was used in this design, the point s_p which meets the $-180°$ phase criterion for this design was found on the $\zeta = 0.4$ line. Refer to Fig. 11-19. A check on the velocity

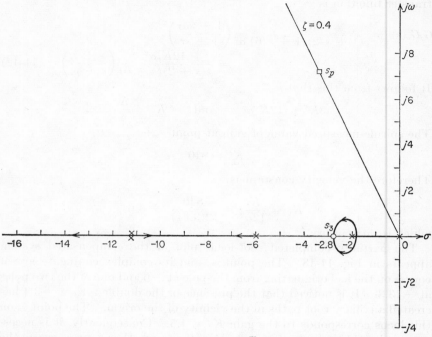

Fig. 11-19. Root locus for $G_cG_f(s) = \dfrac{12K_v\alpha^2}{s(s + 2)(s + 6)}\left(\dfrac{s + 2.8}{s + 11.2}\right)^2$ ($\alpha = 4$).

constant for this point yields

$$K' = 960$$

Therefore

$$K_v = \frac{K'}{12\alpha^2} = \frac{960}{12(4)^2} = 5$$

The auxiliary root path in this case yields a residue at s_3 which is practically negligible, thus leaving the root at s_p (and its complex conjugate) to establish completely the character of the transient performance.

11-7. s-plane Design of Compensation for Configurations Having Complex Poles

The compensation of a system which has a pair of complex roots with poor damping is a difficult task. Our intention here is to discuss several methods of attacking the problem in order to point out some of the limitations involved. An example is again used for the purpose of illustration.

Example 11-6. The fixed configuration of a feedback control system is given by

$$G_f(s) = \frac{K_f}{s[(s/1.68)^2 + 0.7s + 1]} = \frac{2.82K_f}{s(s^2 + 2s + 2.82)} \quad (11\text{-}43)$$

That is, the uncompensated system has open-loop poles located at $-1 \pm j1.35$, for which the damping ratio is 0.6. Essentially the problem is to design compensation such that the damping ratio of the closed-loop system will be made to exceed that of the open-loop poles. Moreover, a specification on the velocity constant is also to be met. (No further detailing of the specifications is given, because the goal here is merely to discuss the methods of solution.)

The Cancellation Compensation Method. The procedure with this method involves replacing the troublesome open-loop poles by means of more suitably placed real poles. It follows therefore that the compensation transfer function should be of the form

$$G_c(s) = \frac{s^2 + 2s + 2.82}{(s + p_1)(s + p_2)} \quad (11\text{-}44)$$

where p_1 and p_2 represent the real poles, which are to be selected in such a manner as to allow the desired performance to be achieved.

Combining Eqs. (11-43) and (11-44) yields the compensated open-loop transfer function

$$G_f G_c(s) = \frac{2.82K_f}{s(s^2 + 2s + 2.82)} \frac{s^2 + 2s + 2.82}{(s + p_1)(s + p_2)}$$

Rearranging gives

$$G_f G_c(s) = \frac{K_f}{s[(s/1.68)^2 + 0.7s + 1]} \frac{2.82}{p_1 p_2} \frac{(s/1.68)^2 + 0.7s + 1}{(1 + s/p_1)(1 + s/p_2)}$$

$$= \frac{K_v}{s(1 + s/p_1)(1 + s/p_2)} \quad (11\text{-}45)$$

where

$$K_v = \frac{2.82K_f K_c}{p_1 p_2} \quad (11\text{-}46)$$

The compensation gain K_c is included in order to provide whatever adjustments are needed to meet the requirement on the velocity constant. Putting Eq. (11-45) in the form for root-locus analysis gives

$$G_f G_c(s) = \frac{p_1 p_2 K_v}{s(s + p_1)(s + p_2)} = \frac{K'}{s(s + p_1)(s + p_2)} \quad (11\text{-}47)$$

where

$$K' = p_1 p_2 K_v \quad (11\text{-}48)$$

From the relationship $1 + G_f G_c(s) = 0$, it follows that specifically the characteristic equation for the closed-loop compensated system is

$$s^3 + (p_1 + p_2)s^2 + p_1 p_2 s + p_1 p_2 K_v = 0 \quad (11\text{-}49)$$

Accordingly, once the desired locations of the roots are selected on the basis of obtaining the desired dynamic as well as static performance, the particular values for p_1 and p_2 can be readily determined.   This is because the characteristic equation may be expressed also in terms of the selected root factors.   Thus,

$$(s + r_1)(s + r_2)(s + r_3) = 0 \tag{11-50}$$

where r_1, r_2, and r_3 represent the chosen locations of the closed-loop system.   Expansion of Eq. (11-50) leads to

$$s^3 + (r_1 + r_2 + r_3)s^2 + (r_1r_2 + r_2r_3 + r_3r_1)s + r_1r_2r_3 = 0 \tag{11-51}$$

Since Eq. (11-49) involves only two unknowns, viz., p_1 and p_2, and since r_1 and r_2 in Eq. (11-51) are known by selection, the determination of the new open-loop poles follows by equating the like coefficients of Eqs. (11-49) and (11-51).   Thus,

$$r_1r_2r_3 = p_1p_2K_v \tag{11-52a}$$
$$r_1 + r_2 + r_3 = p_1 + p_2 \tag{11-52b}$$
$$r_1r_2 + r_2r_3 + r_3r_1 = p_1p_2 \tag{11-52c}$$

Usually r_1 and r_2 are selected to furnish the desired dynamic performance, and a suitable solution for r_3 is one that locates it far to the left of r_1 in the complex plane.

This cancellation compensation procedure is pursued no further, primarily because the synthesis of the compensation network which involves a quadratic term cannot be achieved with simple ladder RC networks to which we are restricting our designs.

Standard Lead-network Design Approach.   The procedure outlined in Sec. 11-4 is attempted next.   For the sake of illustration assume that the damping ratio of the compensated system is to be 0.8 and K_v is to be not less than 10 sec^{-1}.

As a first try choose s_1 located on the $\zeta = 0.8$ line as depicted in Fig. 11-20.   Measure

$$\psi = 143°$$
Measure $\quad\quad\quad\quad \phi = -422°$
Hence $\quad\quad\quad\quad\quad \lambda = 242°$

This large value of λ indicates the need for a triple-lead network.   Thus

$$\lambda^* = 81°$$
$$\gamma = 31°$$
$$\left. \begin{array}{l} z_c = 1.9 \\ p_c = 6.0 \end{array} \right\} \quad \alpha = 3.16$$

A check on the value of K' for point s_1 yields

$$K' = 160$$
which gives $\quad\quad\quad K_v = \dfrac{K'}{2.82(3.16)^3} = 1.35$

Since the velocity constant is too low, select a point s_2 higher up along the $\zeta = 0.8$ line. For this case

$$\phi = -424°$$
$$\lambda^* = 81°$$
$$\gamma = 31°$$
$$\left.\begin{array}{c} z_c = 3.3 \\ p_c = 10.5 \end{array}\right\} \quad \alpha = 3.18$$

Also, at s_2 $\qquad\qquad K' = 850$

so that $\qquad\qquad\qquad K_v = 9.4$

which can be considered satisfactory. However, further investigation

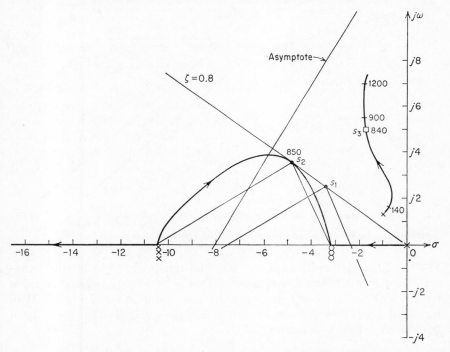

FIG. 11-20. Triple-lead compensation of a fixed configuration having complex poles.

shows that, although the point s_2 does meet the specifications, it is no longer a predominant root. As a matter of fact, as more of the root-locus diagram for this compensated system is drawn, it becomes increasingly evident that the point s_3 on the locus originating from the pole at $-1 \pm j1.35$ (which has almost the same gain as point s_2) is certainly no less important in determining the dynamic behavior than is point s_2. The conclusion that one must draw, therefore, is that here this method of design does not yield a pole-zero configuration for the compensation which works to best advantage.

Use of Bode Plot to Suggest an s-plane Solution. The chief purpose of resorting to a Bode plot of the uncompensated system is to get a quick indication of the most advantageous locations of the zeros and poles of the appropriate lead compensator. A sketch of the uncompensated attenuation characteristic corresponding to a $K_v = 10$ appears in Fig.

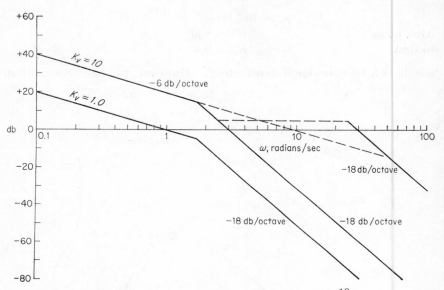

Fig. 11-21. Attenuation characteristic for $G_f(s) = \dfrac{10}{s[(s/1.68)^2 + 0.7s + 1]}$. The horizontal dashed curve shows the effect of the triple-lead network.

11-21. Note that, although $\zeta = 0.6$, the quadratic term is still represented by straight-line asymptotes. This is done only because a guide for the s-plane design is being sought. An examination of Fig. 11-21 in terms of frequency-domain design techniques reveals the need for a triple-lead network characterized by

$$\left. \begin{array}{l} z_c = 2.5 \\ p_c = 25 \end{array} \right\} \qquad \alpha = 10$$

The use of this pole-zero configuration for the compensation results in the root-locus plot shown in Fig. 11-22. It is worthwhile noting that, as a result of spreading the pole and zero of the triple-lead network, a very significant change is brought about in the shape of the root locus. The loci originating from the complex open-loop poles are now forced to move toward the left, as well as down into the negative real axis, as the gain increases. The conclusion is that suitable values of closed-loop damping ratios are now possible. In fact, for a $\zeta = 0.8$, it is found that the value of the velocity constant is slightly in excess of the required value of 10.

The insertion of a triple-lead network of course raises the order of the system. Accordingly, there are other modes present in addition to the desired one. For example, there will be another pair of complex roots

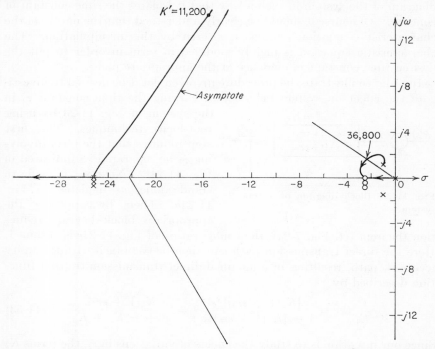

FIG. 11-22. Alternate triple-lead compensation of a system having complex open-loop poles.

which are poorly damped, of high damped frequency of oscillation, and of very small magnitude. Not so small in magnitude, however, is that root which lies on the locus between 0 and −2.5 in Fig. 11-22. This has the effect of increasing the settling time.

11-8. Effect of Time-constant Variation. *s*-plane Analysis

In the root-locus plots the variable parameter is often the constant term of the characteristic equation of the closed-loop system. Frequently this constant term involves the open-loop gain directly, so that the root-locus diagram presents a description of the manner in which changes in open-loop gain influence the dynamic performance. However, in some situations it may be desirable to study the manner in which an increase in a system time constant affects the roots of the characteristic equation. We are already familiar with the way in which such an investigation can be made in the frequency domain. It merely requires changing the position of the breakpoint frequency involved and determining how this in turn changes the gain and phase margins. To perform a similar investigation in the s plane, one needs to manipulate the block diagram of the system in such a way that it isolates the time constant of concern. Of course it should be clearly understood that the nature of the characteristic equation remains unaltered by this manipulation. The characteristic equation is merely modified in form in order to put the desired time constant in evidence at the appropriate place.

In order to illustrate the procedure involved, let it be desired to investigate the effect on system behavior of varying the time constant τ_1 in the system of Fig. 11-23 by using root-locus techniques. The first step requires that the term involving τ_1 be separated as indicated in Fig. 11-24a. Next $s\tau_1$ is made to stand alone, as depicted in Fig. 11-24b. Then by applying the appropriate block-diagram reduction theorem (cf. Fig. 7-2g), the configuration of Fig. 11-24c is obtained.

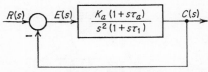

FIG. 11-23. Block diagram of a type 2 system.

Here the direct transmission path can then be combined with the unity feedback path, resulting in a modified direct-transmission transfer function described by

$$\frac{C}{E_1}(s) = \frac{[K_a(1 + s\tau_a)]/s^2}{1 + [K_a(1 + s\tau_a)/s^2]} = \frac{K_a(1 + s\tau_a)}{s^2 + s\tau_a K_a + K_a} \quad (11\text{-}53)$$

Since our intention is to study the effects of variations in τ_1, the terms K_a and τ_a in Eq. (11-53) are considered fixed. Accordingly, the roots of the denominator quadratic may be found. For convenience call these roots $s_{1,2} = -r_{1,2}$. Equation (11-53) may then be written as

$$\frac{C}{E_1}(s) = \frac{K_a(1 + s\tau_a)}{(s + r_1)(s + r_2)} \quad (11\text{-}54)$$

The block diagram of Fig. 11-24c then assumes the form shown in Fig. 11-24d.

An inspection of Fig. 11-24d reveals that the goal we set out to achieve is accomplished. The time constant τ_1 is isolated and appears as the gain factor of an *equivalent* open-loop transfer function of the closed-loop system. Its expression is

$$[HG(s)]_{eq} = \frac{\tau_1 s^3}{(s + r_1)(s + r_2)} \quad (11\text{-}55)$$

A word of comment is in order at this point regarding the rather unconventional form of Eq. (11-55). It must be clearly understood that this is an equivalent open-loop transfer function only in so far as it is capable of describing the closed-loop behavior. One must not lose sight of the fact that Eq. (11-55) resulted from a block-diagram reduction subject to

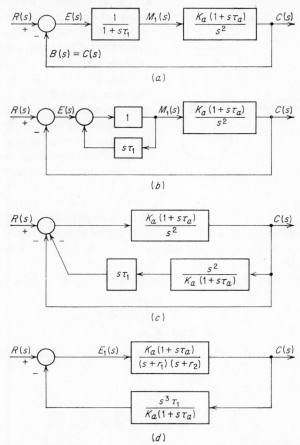

FIG. 11-24. Illustrating the steps in isolating the time constant τ_1 for the purpose of making a root-locus study. (a) Isolating the transfer function involving τ_1; (b) separation of $s\tau_1$ from $1/(1 + s\tau_1)$; (c) further block-diagram reduction; (d) final, desired diagram reduction.

the boundary condition that the ratio $C(s)/R(s)$ with the loop *closed* be in no way altered. Accordingly, Eq. (11-55) is merely an alternate expression of an open-loop transfer function which yields the very same closed-loop transfer function as obtained from Fig. 11-24a. It is incorrect to use Eq. (11-55) for any other purpose than to gain information about the characteristic equation of the closed-loop system. Thus, it is meaningless to use Eq. (11-55) to classify the system or even to identify a phase margin. This is because Eq. (11-55) is not an equivalent open-loop transfer function of the open-loop system of Fig. 11-24a. To determine the latter, the block-diagram manipulation must be subject to the boundary condition whereby an equivalence is provided between $E(s)$ and $B(s)$ with the loop open at the point where $E(s)$ is applied.

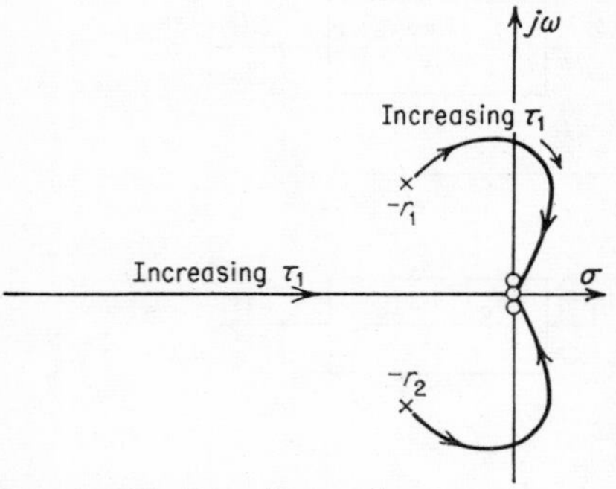

A root-locus plot of Eq. (11-55) furnishes information about the roots of the characteristic equation of the system of Fig. 11-24a. Of course the equation is in such a form that it conveys this information specifically as a function of the time constant τ_1. In order to illustrate the general shape of the resulting root loci, it is assumed that the constants K_a and τ_a in Eq. (11-53) are such that the roots $-r_{1,2}$ are complex conjugate. A typical root-locus plot would then look as shown in Fig. 11-25. The root paths clearly show that as τ_1 is made larger a point is reached which causes the system to become absolutely unstable.

Fig. 11-25. Root-locus plot for

$$\frac{s^3\tau_1}{(s + r_1)(s + r_2)}$$

The characteristic equation of the system of Fig. 11-23 is

$$1 + \frac{K_a(1 + s\tau_a)}{s^2(1 + s\tau_1)} = 0 \tag{11-56}$$

which leads to

$$s^3\tau_1 + s^2 + K_a\tau_a s + K_a = 0 \tag{11-57}$$

The characteristic equation associated with the system of Fig. 11-24d is

$$1 + \frac{s^3\tau_1}{(s + r_1)(s + r_2)} = 0 \tag{11-58}$$

or

$$(s + r_1)(s + r_2) + s^3\tau_1 = 0 \tag{11-59}$$

But

$$(s + r_1)(s + r_2) = s^2 + K_a\tau_a s + K_a \tag{11-60}$$

Hence Eq. (11-59) becomes

$$s^3\tau_1 + s^2 + K_a\tau_a s + K_a = 0 \tag{11-61}$$

which clearly is the same as Eq. (11-57). Of course a similar procedure reveals that the closed-loop transfer functions are also identical for the two systems.

11-9. Effect of Tachometric Feedback. s-plane Analysis

In preceding chapters the manner in which tachometric feedback (or output-rate damping) provides a system with greater stability is studied in the time domain as well as in the frequency domain.   For the sake of completeness we now make a similar study, using s-plane techniques. As is to be expected, the s-plane analysis shows very clearly and thoroughly the way in which the roots of the characteristic equation are affected by the inclusion of output-rate damping.

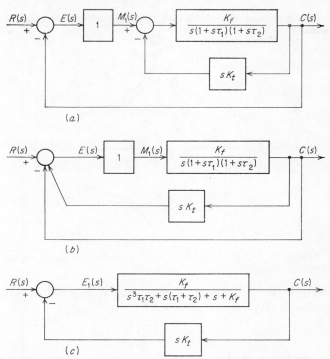

FIG. 11-26. Block-diagram reduction of a system employing output-rate damping. (a) Third-order system with tachometric feedback damping; (b) modified form of Fig. 11-26a; (c) single-loop version of (a).

Figure 11-26a depicts a typical situation in which tachometric feedback may be used to advantage.   By block-diagram reduction Fig. 11-26a is modified to Fig. 11-26b.   Then by combining the direct transmission path with the unity feedback path there results the expression

$$\frac{C}{E_1}(s) = \frac{K_f}{s^3\tau_1\tau_2 + s^2(\tau_1 + \tau_2) + s + K_f} \tag{11-62}$$

which permits Fig. 11-26b to be redrawn as Fig. 11-26c.   Now the stabilizing effect of output-rate damping is best illustrated by assuming the gain in Eq. (11-62) to be adjusted to that value which puts the system just on the verge of absolute instability.   That is, K_f is assigned that value which makes two of the roots of the denominator of Eq. (11-62)

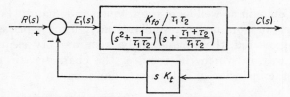

FIG. 11-27. Modification of Fig. 11-26c such that the direct transfer function has poles on the $j\omega$ axis.

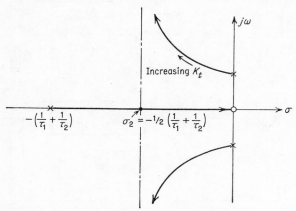

FIG. 11-28. Root-locus plot of an unstable third-order system using tachometric feedback (not drawn to scale).

fall on the $j\omega$-axis. Calling this gain K_{fO}, it can be shown that the required value is given by

$$K_{fO} = \frac{\tau_1 + \tau_2}{\tau_1\tau_2} \tag{11-63}$$

Moreover, the two roots located on the $j\omega$ axis are determined by

$$s_{1,2} = \pm\, j\,\frac{1}{\sqrt{\tau_1\tau_2}} \tag{11-64}$$

The third root is located at

$$s_3 = -\frac{\tau_1 + \tau_2}{\tau_1\tau_2} \tag{11-65}$$

Accordingly, if K_f is made equal to K_{fO}, then Eq. (11-62) may be expressed as

$$\frac{C}{E_1}(s) = \frac{K_{fO}/\tau_1\tau_2}{(s^2 + 1/\tau_1\tau_2)[s + (\tau_1 + \tau_2)/\tau_1\tau_2]} \tag{11-66}$$

The corresponding modification of Fig. 11-26c appears as Fig. 11-27.

The open-loop transfer function of the system of Fig. 11-27 is therefore

$$HG(s) = \frac{sK_tK_{fO}/\tau_1\tau_2}{(s^2 + 1/\tau_1\tau_2)[s + (\tau_1 + \tau_2)/\tau_1\tau_2]} \tag{11-67}$$

The associated root-locus plot appears in Fig. 11-28. An examination of the root paths points out very clearly the manner in which tachometric feedback allows the closed-loop system to achieve a desired dynamic performance. For the case where no output-rate damping is used (that is, $K_t = 0$), the system has two roots on the $j\omega$ axis. This means that the response to a command or a disturbance always results in a sustained oscillation. As tachometric feedback is inserted, the roots of the characteristic equation move farther into the left-hand plane, thereby allowing the system to manifest a well-damped dynamic behavior. In fact the value of K_t needed to yield a specified damping ratio is readily established from a scaled diagram of the root-locus plot.

SUGGESTED READING

Evans, W. R.: "Control-system Dynamics," McGraw-Hill Book Company, Inc., New York, 1954.

Truxal, J. G.: "Automatic Feedback Control System Synthesis," McGraw-Hill Book Company, Inc., New York, 1955.

PROBLEMS

11-1. A feedback control system has a fixed configuration which is described by

$$G_f(s) = \frac{K^1}{s^2(s + p_1)}$$

(a) Sketch the root-locus plot for the fixed configuration.

(b) Show the affect upon this plot of a zero so selected that $z < p_1$. Make appropriate comments upon the nature of the resulting dynamic performance for increasing gains.

(c) Repeat (b) for the case where $z > p_1$.

(d) Repeat (b), using a double zero.

(e) Repeat (c), using a double zero.

11-2. The system of Prob. 11-1 is to be compensated by means of a double-lead network. Sketch the resulting root-locus plots for the following conditions:

(a) The magnitude of the pole of the double-lead network is less than p_1.

(b) The magnitude of the pole of the double-lead network is greater than p_1, and the magnitude of the zero is less than p_1.

(c) The magnitude of the zero of the double-lead network is greater than p_1.

(d) The magnitude of the zero of the double-lead network is equal to p_1.

In each case make appropriate comments regarding the nature of the resulting dynamic performance for increasing gains.

11-3. By using the appropriate theorems of plane geometry as they apply to Fig. 11-11, prove the validity of Eq. (11-28).

11-4. Design a lead compensator of the standard type to meet the specifications of Example 11-3, using the frequency-domain techniques of Chap. 9. Compare and discuss this result with that found in Example 11-3.

11-5. The fixed configuration of a unity feedback control system has the transfer function

$$G_f(s) = \frac{K_v}{s(1 + s/2)(1 + s/6)}$$

Using root-locus techniques, design a compensation network such that the compensated system meets the following specifications:

$$\zeta = 0.4$$
$$K_v = 20$$

Bandwidth not to exceed $\frac{1}{2}$ cps

Time constant of lag network not to exceed 20 sec

Estimate the settling time of the compensated system.

11-6. Using the pole-zero s-plane techniques design a lag-lead compensator so that the system described by

$$G_f(s) = \frac{180}{s(1 + s/2)(1 + s/6)}$$

meets the following specifications:

$$\zeta = 0.4$$

Predominant time constant < 1 sec

Bandwidth < 4 radians/sec

Velocity constant $= 180$

11-7. For the compensated system of Example 11-4 examine and comment upon the effects of inexact cancellation. Consider two cases: (a) the cancellation zero lies slightly to the right of the pole at -2; (b) the cancellation zero lies slightly to the left of the pole at -2.

11-8. A system has a fixed configuration given by $G_f(s) = K_f/[s^2(1 + s/5)]$. Design the compensation for this system such that it meets the following specifications:

Damping ratio $\zeta = 0.4$

Predominant time constant $< \frac{1}{2}$ sec

Acceleration constant $= 10$

11-9. A unity feedback control system has an uncompensated open-loop transfer function given by

$$G_f(s) = \frac{K_f}{s(1 + s/2)(1 + s/6)}$$

Using the cancellation compensation techniques described in Sec. 11-7 design appropriate compensation to enable the corrected system to meet the following specifications:

$$\zeta > 0.5$$

Bandwidth < 10 radians/sec

Predominant time constant $< \frac{1}{3}$ sec

$$K_v = 4.0 \text{ sec}^{-1}$$

11-10. Attempt a solution of Example 11-4, using the cancellation compensation techniques of Sec. 11-7. Give a critical discussion of the results.

11-11. Using sketches of the root-locus diagram, show the effect which variation of the time constant τ_2 has on the system shown in Fig. P11-11.

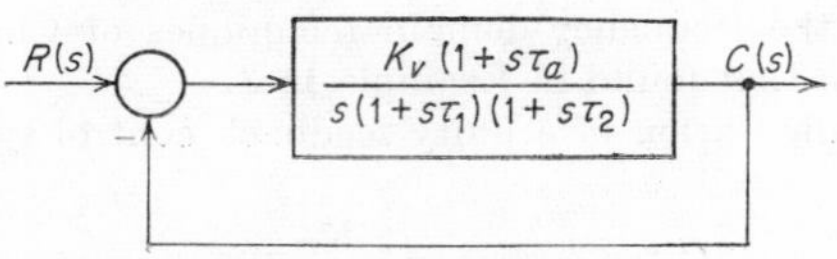

FIG. P11-11

11-12. Using sketches of the root-locus diagram, show the effect which variation of the time constant τ_a has on the system of Prob. 11-11.

11-13. Using sketches of the root-locus diagram, show the effect which variation of the time constant τ_1 has on the system shown in Fig. P11-13.

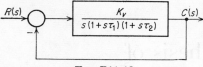

$$\frac{K_V}{s(1+s\tau_1)(1+s\tau_2)}$$

FIG. P11-13

11-14. Prove the validity of Eqs. (11-63) to (11-65).

12 | Synthesis of Compensation Transfer Functions with RC Networks

In this chapter we are concerned with techniques for the synthesis of RC networks. The need for synthesis procedures follows directly from the root-locus method. In the previous chapter it was shown how zeros and poles are placed in the s plane to reshape the root-locus plot and thereby control the closed-loop behavior of a system. When we have decided upon the zeros and poles necessary to achieve the desired system compensation, the question arises as to how to implement this zero-pole pattern, particularly in terms of electrical networks placed in the direct transmission path. Up to now we have concentrated on three basic types of compensation schemes, namely, lag, lead, and lag-lead networks. In the case of these simple networks there is no problem in choosing component values after the transfer function is specified. If two such compensation networks are required (as, for example, a double-lead network), an isolation amplifier may be used between them, as is illustrated in the example of Fig. 9-14, so that the over-all transfer function is given by the product of the individual transfer functions. As a matter of fact, if we consider a generalized transfer function of the following form:

$$T(s) = \frac{E_2}{E_1}(s) = K \frac{(1 + s\tau_1)(1 + s\tau_2)(1 + s\tau_3) \cdots}{(1 + s\tau_a)(1 + s\tau_b)(1 + s\tau_c) \cdots} \quad (12\text{-}1)$$

it is always possible to implement this function by grouping numerator and denominator factors into terms of the form $(1 + s\tau_1)/(1 + s\tau_a)$, where each term corresponds to a basic lag or lead network. Representative networks for each of the terms can then be connected in tandem through isolation amplifiers, as illustrated in Fig. 12-1, to obtain the desired over-all transfer function with a constant numerical gain factor. This isolation-amplifier approach to synthesis is unnecessarily restrictive for two fundamental reasons. (1) The transfer function of Eq. (12-1) is limited to one whose zeros and poles lie on the negative real axis. (2) The use of isolation amplifiers to prevent loading between cascaded network sections is undesirable.   In some situations, such as mechanical or pneumatic systems, isolation amplifiers cannot be used to generate the desired compensation transfer function.   By the use of network-synthesis theory we can remove these restrictions on our design procedure and in the process enhance our knowledge in several important ways.   First, we can examine any zero-pole configuration as derived from the root-locus approach to determine whether or not the transfer

FIG. 12-1. Synthesis by means of basic lag and lead networks and isolation amplifiers.

function represented by this configuration can be implemented with a linear passive network.   Second, we can ascertain the conditions imposed on the location of the zeros and poles of this network to assure the fact that it can be composed of resistors and capacitors only.   Finally, for a known zero-pole configuration, it is possible to follow straightforward procedures to arrive at a specific network which has the required transfer function.

Prior to discussing the details of network synthesis, there are several other pertinent factors to be considered.   First we should recognize that the subject of network synthesis is a broad field with a vast and ever-expanding literature.   Accordingly, all that we can hope to do in this text is to present some of the basic concepts of the subject, with particular emphasis on those topics which pertain to control systems engineering. In particular the discussion is restricted primarily to the synthesis of *RC* networks.   This choice of topic was made for very practical reasons. As pointed out in previous chapters control systems are basically low-pass filters with cutoff frequencies as low as 0.01 cps for process control systems and as high as 100 cps for broader-band systems.   Thus, if a practical electrical compensation network is to operate in this frequency range, it should be composed of resistors and capacitors only.   Any inductance would be too large and costly for practical consideration.

Another point to realize is that in network synthesis there never is a single correct answer.   The techniques outlined are procedures which, if followed step by step, are guaranteed to lead to a specific network configuration which has the prescribed transfer function.   There is no assurance that this is the best network from the point of view of the number of components or practical wiring considerations.   Alternate procedures which lead to different network configurations are possible. At various points in any synthesis procedure it is possible to change synthesis techniques so that a completely different network configuration is obtained. This versatility may seem disturbing at first but should not be unexpected when it is realized that synthesis is basically the problem of design and that there are often as many different designs as there are designers. In fact it is this very versatility of approach which offers the designer an opportunity to obtain the best possible answer for his particular problem.

Finally it should be pointed out that, although we are primarily interested in *transfer* functions, the first few sections of the chapter are devoted to a discussion of the properties of driving-point *impedance* functions and their synthesis. The reason for this is that the problem of *transfer-function* synthesis is normally approached by reducing it to one of *impedance* synthesis. In this connection it is interesting to note that any driving-point impedance function $Z(s)$ can be converted to a transfer function in the form of the

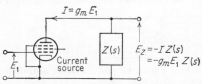

Fig. 12-2. A circuit showing the use of a pentode constant current source to convert an impedance function $Z(s)$ into a transfer function $\dfrac{E_2}{E_1}(s) = -g_m Z(s)$.

ratio of two voltages, $\dfrac{E_2}{E_1}(s) = (\text{constant})[Z(s)]$, by placing the impedance $Z(s)$ in series with a constant current source, such as a pentode, as illustrated in Fig. 12-2. This is not the type of transfer-function synthesis we are discussing in this chapter. It is mentioned merely as a possibility which has been used to advantage in practice.

12-1. Properties of RC Impedance Functions

RC impedance functions are characterized by certain basic properties which enable us always to recognize them and to form the basis for their synthesis. We do not discuss the details of why RC impedance functions exhibit these properties but merely present the results without derivation. It is suggested that the interested reader refer to one of the many excellent texts on the subject of linear-network theory for a complete development of the topic of network realizability conditions.[1]

Before enumerating the properties of RC impedance functions, it is important to emphasize that these characteristics apply to RC *driving-point impedances only*. By the term driving-point impedance we refer specifically to a function $Z(s)$ which gives the ratio between a voltage $E(s)$ applied to the input terminals of a network (called the driving-point terminals) and the resulting current $I(s)$ which flows into and out of these

---

[1] See, for example, E. A. Guillemin, "Synthesis of Passive Networks," John Wiley & Sons, Inc., New York, 1957.

terminals (see Fig. 12-3). By definition, the driving-point admittance is given by $Y(s) = [Z(s)]^{-1}$. In general $Z(s)$ is given by the ratio of two polynomials in s with real coefficients, as follows:

$$Z(s) = \frac{A(s)}{B(s)} = \frac{A_0 + A_1 s + A_2 s^2 + \cdots + A_p s^p}{B_0 + B_1 s + B_2 s^2 + \cdots + B_q s^q} \qquad (12\text{-}2)$$

One of the fundamental properties of any RC impedance function is that the highest and lowest powers of s in the numerator polynomial must be equal to or one degree less than the highest and lowest powers of s in the denominator polynomial. For example, if the highest power of s in the numerator polynomial is s^3, then the highest power in the denominator polynomial must be s^3 or s^4. A similar condition holds at the low-frequency end, i.e., for the lowest powers of s. The reason for this re-striction lies in the fact that any physically realizable RC impedance function must, as $s \to 0$ and $s \to \infty$, vary as either a constant (represent-

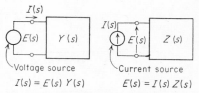

FIG. 12-3. Definition of driving-point impedance and admittance functions. $Z(s) = 1/Y(s)$.

ing a pure resistance) or s^{-1} (representing pure capacitance). Thus we arrive at the first general property of RC impedance functions.

1. The highest and lowest powers of s in the denominator polynomial for $Z(s)$ must be equal to, or at most be one degree higher than, the highest and lowest powers of s in the numerator polynomial.

In addition the following conditions must also be fulfilled:

2. All zeros [roots of the equation $A(s) = 0$] and poles [roots of the equation $B(s) = 0$] of $Z(s)$ must be simple and must lie on the negative real axis.

3. The zeros and poles of $Z(s)$ must alternate along the negative real axis, with the lowest critical frequency (the one closest to the origin) being a pole. The highest critical frequency (the one farthest from the origin) must be a zero.

Figure 12-4a illustrates a typical zero-pole pattern for an RC imped-ance function, namely,

$$Z(s) = K \frac{(s + z_1)(s + z_2)}{(s + p_1)(s + p_2)} = K \frac{s^2 + (z_1 + z_2)s + z_1 z_2}{s^2 + (p_1 + p_2)s + p_1 p_2} \qquad (12\text{-}3)$$

If the variable s is restricted to the real axis, i.e., if $s = \sigma$, it is possible to plot $Z(\sigma)$ vs. σ. Figure 12-4b illustrates this plot for Eq. (12-3). It can be seen that the slope of the resulting curve $\dfrac{\partial Z(\sigma)}{\partial \sigma}$ is always negative, which in fact is equivalent to the statement that the zeros and poles of $Z(s)$ must alternate along the negative real axis.

In the example of Fig. 12-4 both $Z(0)$ and $Z(\infty)$ are finite. It is possible to have an RC impedance function where the lowest frequency, namely, the pole p_1, falls at the origin. For example, consider the function

$$Z(s) = K \frac{(s + z_1)(s + z_2)}{s(s + p_2)}$$

In this case $Z(0) = \infty$, and the equivalent network must necessarily

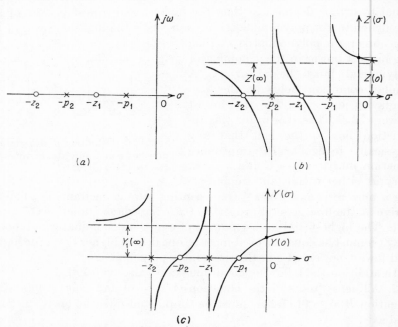

Fig. 12-4. Characteristic behavior of an RC impedance function. (a) s-plane pole-zero pattern for an RC impedance function; (b) plot of $Z(\sigma)$ vs. σ, illustrating that $\partial Z(\sigma)/\partial\sigma$ is always negative; (c) plot of $Y(\sigma)$ vs. σ, illustrating that $\partial Y(\sigma)/\partial\sigma$ is always positive.

have a series capacitance in the input lead. Similarly, it is possible for the highest zero z_2 to occur at infinity so that $Z(\infty) = 0$. For example, consider the function

$$Z(s) = \frac{K(s + z_1)}{(s + p_1)(s + p_2)}$$

The equivalent network in this case must have a capacitance shunting the input leads.

The zero-pole pattern for an RC driving-point admittance,

$$Y(s) = [Z(s)]^{-1}$$

must necessarily have its zero and poles interchanged from those of the impedance function. Thus the zeros and poles of $Y(s)$ again alternate along the negative real axis, but the lowest critical frequency must be a zero and the highest critical frequency a pole. It also follows that the plot of $Y(\sigma)$ vs. σ always has a positive slope (see Fig. 12-4c[1]).

12-2. Synthesis of RC Impedance Functions in Canonic Forms

Owing to the aforementioned properties of RC impedance functions, it is always possible to synthesize them in certain basic, or canonic, forms. The canonic forms contain the minimum number of elements required to realize the impedance function. Two of these forms follow from a partial-fraction expansion of $Z(s)$ or $Y(s)$ and are known as *Foster forms*. Two more follow from a continued-fraction expansion of $Z(s)$ or $Y(s)$ and are called *Cauer forms*.

The First Foster Form. Expansion of $Z(s)$ about Its Poles. This synthesis technique consists in expanding $Z(s)$ as the sum of a series of partial fractions, each one of which corresponds to one of the poles of $Z(s)$. Thus in general $Z(s)$ is expanded as follows:

$$Z(s) = a_\infty + \frac{a_0}{s} + \frac{a_1}{s + p_1} + \cdots + \frac{a_n}{s + p_n} \qquad (12\text{-}4)$$

Each term of Eq. (12-4) can be represented by a simple impedance function. The impedance looking into the series connection of these simple impedances is then the over-all impedance function of Eq. (12-4). Each term of the general form, that is, $a_n/(s + p_n)$, may be synthesized by means of a parallel RC circuit as shown in Fig. 12-5a. Thus the general impedance of Eq. (12-4) may be drawn as shown in Fig. 12-5b. The series capacitor C_0 and resistor R_0 determine the behavior of the network at $s = 0$ and $s = \infty$, respectively, and their presence or absence can be determined readily by examining the behavior of the original impedance

---

[1] For those acquainted with Foster's reactance theorem, the graphs of Fig. 12-4 should look very similar to those obtained for the driving-point impedance of purely reactive (LC only) networks. In the case of purely reactive networks, however, the zeros and poles are simple and alternate along the $j\omega$ axis. In order to complete the picture, it is worthwhile to mention that the zero-pole pattern for the driving-point *impedance* to an RL network also has the zeros and poles alternating along the negative real axis as in the RC case, except that the lowest critical frequency must be a zero and the highest critical frequency must be a pole. For the RL case it follows that $\partial Z(\sigma)/\partial\sigma$ is always positive.

In general, any RLC impedance function must have its zeros and poles restricted to the left side of the complex s plane. However, this is a necessary but insufficient condition for physical realizability; i.e., just because an impedance function has its zeros and poles restricted to the left-half s plane does not necessarily mean that it is realizable as a passive RLC linear network. Conditions 1, 2, and 3, however, are both necessary and sufficient conditions for physical realizability as an RC network.

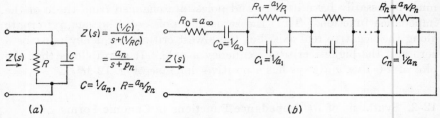

FIG. 12-5. Expansion of $Z(s)$ in the first Foster form. Partial-fraction expansion about the poles of $Z(s)$. (a) Parallel RC combination representing a simple pole of $Z(s)$; (b) network representing the parital-fraction expansion of $Z(s)$ about its poles.

function at these frequencies. The actual technique for determining the network may be demonstrated by some numerical examples.

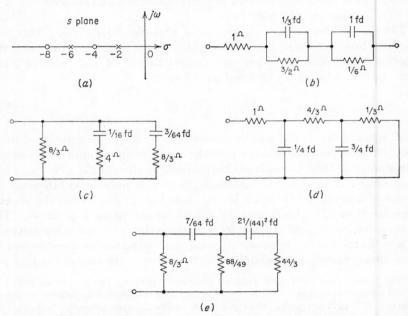

FIG. 12-6. Canonic-form expansions of $Z(s) = [(s + 4)(s + 8)]/[(s + 2)(s + 6)]$. (a) Pole-zero pattern for $Z(s)$; (b) first Foster form; (c) second Foster form; (d) first Cauer form; (e) second Cauer form.

Example 12-1. Determine the first Foster network for the following impedance function:

$$Z(s) = \frac{(s + 4)(s + 8)}{(s + 2)(s + 6)} = \frac{s^2 + 12s + 32}{s^2 + 8s + 12}$$

This impedance function is that of an RC network with poles located at $s = -2$, $s = -6$ and zeros at $s = -4$, $s = -8$ (see Fig. 12-6a). In order to obtain the first Foster form, it is necessary to expand $Z(s)$ into partial fractions about its poles. $Z(s)$

cannot be expanded directly since the numerator polynomial is of the same degree as the denominator polynomial and a preparatory step of long-hand division must be performed first. Thus, after a step of division, we obtain

$$Z(s) = 1 + \frac{4s + 20}{s^2 + 8s + 12} = 1 + \frac{4s + 20}{(s + 2)(s + 6)}$$

If $Z(s)$ had been a proper fraction to start with, this preliminary division would not have been necessary. Expanding the second term of $Z(s)$ into partial fractions, we write

$$Z(s) = 1 + \frac{a_1}{s + 2} + \frac{a_2}{s + 6}$$

The coefficients a_1 and a_2 are evaluated as follows:

$$a_1 = (s + 2)Z(s)\Big|_{s=-2} = \frac{(s + 4)(s + 8)}{s + 6}\Big|_{s=-2} = \frac{(2)(6)}{4} = 3$$

$$a_2 = (s + 6)Z(s)\Big|_{s=-6} = \frac{(s + 4)(s + 8)}{s + 2}\Big|_{s=-6} = \frac{-2(2)}{-4} = 1$$

Hence $Z(s)$ is given by

$$Z(s) = 1 + \frac{3}{s + 2} + \frac{1}{s + 6}$$

The first Foster form for $Z(s)$ is drawn in Fig. 12-6b. It can be noted that at the extreme values of frequency $Z(s)$ can be calculated readily from the network. At $s = 0$, the capacitors can be considered open circuits. At $s = \infty$, the capacitors can be considered short circuits. Thus we may write directly from inspection of Fig. 12-6b

$$Z(0) = 1 + \tfrac{3}{2} + \tfrac{1}{6} = \tfrac{8}{3} \text{ ohms}$$
$$Z(\infty) = 1 \text{ ohm}$$

These values agree with the original algebraic expression for $Z(s)$ evaluated at $s = 0$ and $s = \infty$.

The numerical values of the RC elements appearing in the circuit of this example are impractical in that the resistors are too small and the capacitors are too large. As discussed later in the chapter, it is possible to shift these numerical values so that realistic circuit elements are obtained, with the network maintaining the same frequency and time-domain response as before. The details of this topic are left to Sec. 12-6, and the reader should not be disturbed by the apparent impracticability of present results.

The Second Foster Form. Expansion of $Y(s)$ about Its Poles. To obtain the second Foster form, $Z(s)$ is inverted to obtain the function $Y(s)$, and the latter is expanded as the sum of a series of partial fractions. The partial-fraction expansion for $Y(s)$ takes the form

$$Y(s) = b_\infty s + b_0 + \frac{b_1 s}{s + z_1} + \cdots + \frac{b_n s}{s + z_n} \qquad (12\text{-}5)$$

This expansion is similar to Eq. (12-4) except for the term $b_\infty s$. This term is necessary for a generalized partial-fraction expansion of $Y(s)$

because it is possible for the highest power of s in the numerator of $Y(s)$ to be 1 greater than the highest power of s in the denominator. In other words, $Y(s)$ can have a pole at $s = \infty$, and the first term of the expansion of Eq. (12-5) allows for this possibility.

Each of the terms of Eq. (12-5) can be represented by a simple admittance function, as shown in Fig. 12-7a, and the over-all admittance $Y(s)$

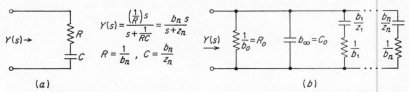

(a)   (b)

FIG. 12-7. Expansion of $Y(s)$ into the second Foster form. Partial-fraction expansion about the poles of $Y(s)$. (a) Series combination representing a simple pole of $Y(s)$ [or zero of $Z(s)$]; (b) network representing the partial fraction of $Y(s)$ about its poles.

is obtained by connecting these simple circuits in parallel, as shown in Fig. 12-7b. The shunt resistor R_0 and the shunt capacitor C_0 determine the behavior of the network at zero and infinite frequency, respectively, and their presence or absence can be checked readily by examining the behavior of the admittance function at these frequencies.

Examination of Eq. (12-5) indicates that for the determination of the unknown coefficients it is easier to expand $Y(s)/s$ rather than $Y(s)$ as indicated. Thus $Y(s)/s$ may be rewritten as

$$\frac{Y(s)}{s} = b_\infty + \frac{b_0}{s} + \frac{b_1}{s + z_1} + \cdots + \frac{b_n}{s + z_n} \tag{12-6}$$

After the coefficients of the expansion of Eq. (12-6) are determined, $Y(s)$ is obtained by multiplication by s. The actual technique involved may be demonstrated best by a numerical example.

Example 12-2. Determine the second Foster form for the impedance function of Example 12-1.

Inverting the expression for $Z(s)$, we obtain

$$Y(s) = \frac{(s + 2)(s + 6)}{(s + 4)(s + 8)}$$

$Y(s)/s$ is given by

$$\frac{Y(s)}{s} = \frac{(s + 2)(s + 6)}{s(s + 4)(s + 8)}$$

$Y(s)/s$ may be expanded into partial fractions directly since it is a proper fraction. Thus we write

$$\frac{Y(s)}{s} = \frac{b_0}{s} + \frac{b_1}{s + 4} + \frac{b_2}{s + 8}$$

The coefficients b_0, b_1, and b_2 are determined as follows:

$$b_0 = s \left. \frac{Y(s)}{s} \right|_{s=0} = Y(s) \bigg|_{s=0} = \frac{2(6)}{4(8)} = \frac{3}{8}$$

$$b_1 = (s+4) \left. \frac{Y(s)}{s} \right|_{s=-4} = \left. \frac{(s+2)(s+6)}{s(s+8)} \right|_{s=-4} = \frac{-2(2)}{-4(4)} = \frac{1}{4}$$

$$b_2 = (s+8) \left. \frac{Y(s)}{s} \right|_{s=-8} = \left. \frac{(s+2)(s+6)}{s(s+4)} \right|_{s=-8} = \frac{-6(-2)}{-8(-4)} = \frac{3}{8}$$

Thus $Y(s)/s$ is given by

$$\frac{Y(s)}{s} = \frac{3}{8s} + \frac{\frac{1}{4}}{s+4} + \frac{\frac{3}{8}}{s+8}$$

Hence $Y(s)$ is given by

$$Y(s) = \frac{3}{8} + \frac{\frac{1}{4}s}{s+4} + \frac{\frac{3}{8}s}{s+8}$$

Identifying the terms of the last expression with the network of Fig. 12-7 yields the second Foster form, as drawn in Fig. 12-6c. The network may again be checked by evaluating $Z(s)$ at extreme values of frequency. Thus

$$Z(0) = \tfrac{8}{3} \text{ ohms}$$

$$Z(\infty) = \frac{1}{\frac{3}{8} + \frac{1}{4} + \frac{3}{8}} = 1 \text{ ohm}$$

These values also agree with the original expression for $Z(s)$ evaluated at $s = 0$ and $s = \infty$.

The First Cauer Form. Removal of Poles at $s = \infty$. In general the Cauer method of synthesis consists in expanding $Z(s)$ into a continued fraction and leads to a ladder-type realization for the network. Mathematically the first Cauer form is obtained by successively removing constants and poles at the point $s = \infty$. The technique can best be explained by considering $Z(s)$ in unfactored form as in Eq. (12-2),

$$Z(s) = \frac{A(s)}{B(s)} = \frac{A_0 + A_1 s + A_2 s^2 + \cdots + A_p s^p}{B_0 + B_1 s + B_2 s^2 + \cdots + B_q s^q} \qquad (12\text{-}7)$$

As explained previously, at $s = \infty$, $Z(s)$ is either zero or finite. In general, let us consider that the exponents are equal, $p = q = n$, so that $Z(\infty) = A_p/B_q = A_n/B_n$. For those cases where $Z(\infty) = 0$ we may consider $A_p = 0$.

If the expression for $Z(s)$ is now rearranged so that the numerator and denominator polynomials appear in descending powers of s, the value $Z(\infty)$ can be obtained by dividing the numerator polynomial by the denominator polynomial. The reason for reordering the polynomials before dividing is that we are interested in the behavior of $Z(s)$ at large values of s, namely, $s = \infty$, and the terms of the highest powers of s are important. After the first step of division, Eq. (12-7) (with $p = q = n$)

can be written as A_n/B_n plus a remainder. Thus

$$Z(s) = \frac{A_n}{B_n} + \frac{C_{n-1}s^{n-1} + C_{n-2}s^{n-2} + \cdots + C_1 s + C_0}{B_n s^n + B_{n-1}s^{n-1} + \cdots + B_1 s + B_0} \quad (12\text{-}8)$$

The constants C represent the coefficients of the remainder after the first step of division. The remainder term of Eq. (12-8) is seen to have the value of zero at $s = \infty$. This follows directly from the division process. If the remainder term is now inverted, it has a pole at the point $s = \infty$. The pole of the inverted remainder term may again be removed by division. Thus the inverted remainder of Eq. (12-8) may be expanded as follows:

$$\frac{B_n s^n + B_{n-1}s^{n-1} + \cdots + B_1 s + B_0}{C_{n-1}s^{n-1} + C_{n-2}s^{n-2} + \cdots + C_1 s + C_0} = \frac{B_n}{C_{n-1}} s$$
$$+ \frac{D_{n-1}s^{n-1} + \cdots + D_1 s + D_0}{C_{n-1}s^{n-1} + \cdots + C_1 s + C_0} \quad (12\text{-}9)$$

The constants D represent the coefficients of a new remainder term. Upon combining Eqs. (12-8) and (12-9), it is possible to write $Z(s)$ as follows:

$$Z(s) = \frac{A_n}{B_n} + \cfrac{1}{\cfrac{B_n s^n + B_{n-1}s^{n-1} + \cdots + B_1 s + B_0}{C_{n-1}s^{n-1} + C_{n-2}s^{n-2} + \cdots + C_1 s + C_0}}$$
$$= \frac{A_n}{B_n} + \cfrac{1}{\cfrac{B_n}{C_{n-1}} s + \cfrac{D_{n-1}s^{n-1} + \cdots + D_1 s + D_0}{C_{n-1}s^{n-1} + \cdots + C_1 s + C_0}} \quad (12\text{-}10)$$

The last term in Eq. (12-10) may be inverted and expanded by division again. Continuing this process until the final remainder term disappears yields a continued fraction expansion for $Z(s)$ in the following form:

$$Z(s) = R_1 + \cfrac{1}{C_2 s + \cfrac{1}{R_3 + \cfrac{1}{C_4 s + }}} \quad (12\text{-}11)$$

$$\cfrac{1}{R_{n-1} + \cfrac{1}{C_n s + \cfrac{1}{R_{n+1}}}}$$

where the R's and C's are numerical constants. Equation (12-11) may be represented by a ladder-type network configuration, as illustrated in Fig. 12-8. After each division the remainder term is inverted to create a pole at infinity. This pole is then removed by division and a new

remainder term generated.   The process is continued until the remainder
is zero.   The actual technique for a continued-fraction expansion by
division, inversion, division, etc., can be carried through quite easily
and is illustrated best by a numerical example.

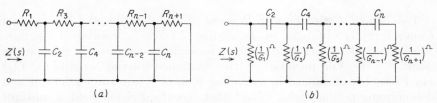

FIG. 12-8. Expansion of $Z(s)$ in a continued fraction yielding the Cauer forms.   (a)
First Cauer form; (b) second Cauer form.

Example 12-3.   Expand the $Z(s)$ of Example 12-1 in the first Cauer form.
$Z(s)$ is first written in unfactored form with the highest powers of s written first.
Thus

$$Z(s) = \frac{s^2 + 12s + 32}{s^2 + 8s + 12}$$

The process of a continued-fraction expansion is carried out as follows:

$$
\begin{array}{r}
1 \quad \text{impedance} \\
s^2 + 8s + 12\overline{)s^2 + 12s + 32} \\
\underline{s^2 + \ 8s + 12} \quad \tfrac{1}{4}s \quad \text{admittance} \\
4s + 20\overline{)s^2 + 8s + 12} \\
\underline{s^2 + 5s} \quad \tfrac{4}{3} \quad \text{impedance} \\
3s + 12\overline{)4s + 20} \\
\underline{4s + 16} \quad \tfrac{3}{4}s \quad \text{admittance} \\
4\overline{)3s + 12} \\
\underline{3s} \quad \tfrac{1}{3} \quad \text{impedance} \\
12\overline{)4} \\
\underline{4} \quad \infty \quad \text{admittance} \\
0\overline{)12}
\end{array}
$$

Since the division process is started with $Z(s)$, it follows that the quotient of the
division is an impedance function.   Thus after the first division we may write

$$Z(s) = \frac{s^2 + 12s + 32}{s^2 + 8s + 12} = 1 + \frac{4s + 20}{s^2 + 8s + 12} = 1 + \frac{1}{(s^2 + 8s + 12)/(4s + 20)}$$

The remainder term $(4s + 20)/(s^2 + 8s + 12)$ corresponds to an impedance function, and the inverted remainder term $(s^2 + 8s + 2)/(4s + 20)$ therefore is an admittance function.   The quotient after the next division is an admittance function, and
the new inverted remainder is an impedance function.   Thus successive inversions
and divisions yield alternate impedance and admittance terms, as indicated above.

Rather than rewriting the results of this process as a continued fraction, the elements of the corresponding ladder network can be determined directly from the
quotient terms above and writing the network as indicated in Fig. 12-6d.   The final

result can be checked by evaluating $Z(s)$ at extreme values of frequency.   Thus

$$Z(0) = 1 + \tfrac{4}{3} + \tfrac{1}{3} = \tfrac{8}{3} \text{ ohms}$$
$$Z(\infty) = 1 \text{ ohm}$$

These results are identical to those obtained with the previous Foster forms.

The Second Cauer Form.   Removal of Poles at $s = 0$.   The second Cauer form is obtained by expanding $Y(s)$ as a continued fraction. Mathematically this is equivalent to removing constants and poles at the point $s = 0$.   For purposes of the continued-fraction expansion, $Y(s)$ must now be rearranged in ascending powers of s in the numerator and denominator polynomials.   The first step of the division yields a constant value [which corresponds to the value of $Y(s)$ at $s = 0$] plus a remainder fraction which has a zero at $s = 0$.   In this expansion the constant value at $s = 0$ is an admittance function.   Inverting the remainder gives us an impedance function which has a pole at $s = 0$.   Dividing again yields a term of the form of a constant times s^{-1} plus another remainder.   Continuing the process of inversion and division enables $Y(s)$ to be expanded into a continued fraction as follows:

$$Y(s) = G_1 + \cfrac{1}{\cfrac{1}{C_2 s} + \cfrac{1}{G_3 + \cfrac{1}{\cfrac{1}{C_4 s} + \cdot}}} \qquad (12\text{-}12)$$

$$\cfrac{1}{G_{n-1} + \cfrac{1}{\cfrac{1}{C_n s} + \cfrac{1}{G_{n+1}}}}$$

The G's and C's are numerical constants generated in the division process.   The continued-fraction expansion of Eq. (12-12) can be represented by a ladder network as drawn in Fig. 12-8b.   The actual technique for obtaining the second-Cauer-form expansion is simple and again is illustrated by an example.

Example 12-4.   Determine the second Cauer form for the $Z(s)$ function of Example 12-1.

$Z(s)$ is inverted and written in ascending powers of s as follows:

$$Y(s) = \frac{1}{Z(s)} = \frac{12 + 8s + s^2}{32 + 12s + s^2}$$

The process of a continued-fraction expansion is carried out as indicated below, where alternate admittance and impedance terms are labeled.

$$\frac{3}{8} \quad \text{admittance}$$

$$s^2 + 12s + s^2 \overline{)\,12 + 8s + s^2}$$

$$12 + \frac{9}{2}s + \frac{3}{8}s^2 \quad \frac{64}{7}\frac{1}{s} \quad \text{impedance}$$

$$\frac{7}{2}s + \frac{5}{8}s^2 \overline{)\,32 + 12s + s^2}$$

$$32 + \frac{40}{7}s \qquad \frac{49}{88} \quad \text{admittance}$$

$$\frac{44}{7}s + s^2 \overline{)\,\frac{7}{2}s + \frac{5}{8}s^2}$$

$$\frac{7}{2}s + \frac{49}{88}s^2 \quad \frac{(44)^2}{21}\frac{1}{s} \quad \text{impedance}$$

$$\frac{3}{44}s^2 \overline{)\,\frac{44}{7}s + s^2}$$

$$\frac{44}{7}s \qquad \frac{3}{44} \quad \text{admittance}$$

$$s^2 \overline{)\,\frac{3}{44}s^2}$$

$$\frac{3}{44}s^2 \quad \infty$$

$$\overline{0\,)s^2} \quad \text{impedance}$$

Rather than rewriting the results of the inversion and division process as a continued fraction, the elements of the ladder network can be determined from the quotient terms as shown in Fig. 12-6e. This result may again be checked by evaluating $Z(s)$ from the network at extreme values of frequency. Thus

$$Z(0) = \tfrac{8}{3} \text{ ohms}$$

$$Z(\infty) = \frac{1}{\frac{3}{8} + \frac{49}{88} + \frac{3}{44}} = 1 \text{ ohm}$$

These values again agree with the previous results.

As a final word on the subject of Cauer-form synthesis it should be noted that in general there are four possible ways of dividing the numerator and denominator polynomials—ascending or descending powers of s, inverted or not inverted. Only two of these lead to networks which have positive real component values. The other two lead to unrealizable forms with negative components. A little thought at the start of a continued-fraction expansion will prevent the designer from embarking on an erroneous division and inversion process.

12-3. The Properties of Two-terminal Pair Networks and Their Use in Obtaining Transfer Functions

In order to discuss the properties of RC transfer functions as distinguished from driving-point impedance we must first discuss the behavior of a two-terminal pair network as illustrated in Fig. 12-9a. In general this network's behavior is characterized by three parameters, which are called z parameters and which are denoted by z_{11}, z_{12}, z_{22}. They are defined as follows (see Fig. 12-9a):

Consider two current sources I_1 and I_2, applied to terminal pairs 1-1 and 2-2. The voltages at these terminal pairs are given by

$$E_1 = z_{11}I_1 + z_{12}I_2 \qquad (12\text{-}13a)$$
$$E_2 = z_{12}I_1 + z_{22}I_2 \qquad (12\text{-}13b)$$

If $I_2 = 0$ (terminal pair 2-2 open), then Eqs. (12-13a) and (12-13b) become

$$z_{11} = \left. \frac{E_1}{I_1} \right|_{I_2=0} \qquad (12\text{-}13c)$$

$$z_{12} = \left. \frac{E_2}{I_1} \right|_{I_2=0} \qquad (12\text{-}13d)$$

Equation (12-13c) states that z_{11} is the impedance looking into terminal pair 1-1 with terminal pair 2-2 open. Equation (12-13d) indicates

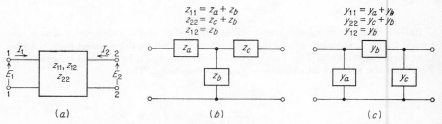

$$z_{11} = z_a + z_b \qquad y_{11} = y_a + y_b$$
$$z_{22} = z_c + z_b \qquad y_{22} = y_c + y_b$$
$$z_{12} = z_b \qquad\qquad y_{12} = y_b$$

FIG. 12-9. Two-terminal pair networks. (a) Two-terminal pair network, general form; (b) T network; (c) π network.

that z_{12} is given by the voltage across terminal pair 2-2 when terminal pair 2-2 is open and a unit current source is applied to terminal pair 1-1($I_1 = 1$). Similarly Eq. (12-13b) can be used to show that z_{22} is the impedance looking into terminal pair 2-2 with terminal pair 1-1 open and that z_{12} is also given by the voltage across the open-circuited terminal pair 1-1 when a unit current is applied to terminal pair 2-2. From the foregoing discussion it is left to the reader to show that the z parameters for the T network of Fig. 12-9b are given as follows:

$$z_{11} = z_a + z_b \qquad (12\text{-}14a)$$
$$z_{22} = z_c + z_b \qquad (12\text{-}14b)$$
$$z_{12} = z_b \qquad\qquad (12\text{-}14c)$$

An alternative way of characterizing the two-terminal pair network of Fig. 12-9a is in terms of a set of y parameters, which give the currents when voltage sources are applied to the terminals. Thus we write

$$I_1 = y_{11}E_1 + y_{12}E_2 \qquad (12\text{-}15a)$$
$$I_2 = y_{12}E_1 + y_{22}E_2 \qquad (12\text{-}15b)$$

Equations (12-15a) and (12-15b) may be derived from Eqs. (12-13a) and (12-13b), indicating the following relationships between the y and z parameters:

$$y_{11} = \frac{z_{22}}{\Delta_z} \tag{12-16a}$$

$$y_{22} = \frac{z_{11}}{\Delta_z} \tag{12-16b}$$

$$y_{12} = - \frac{z_{12}}{\Delta_z} \tag{12-16c}$$

where $$\Delta_z = z_{11}z_{22} - z_{12}{}^2 \tag{12-16d}$$

Conversely the z parameters can be expressed in terms of the y parameters as follows:

$$z_{11} = \frac{y_{22}}{\Delta_y} \tag{12-16e}$$

$$z_{22} = \frac{y_{11}}{\Delta_y} \tag{12-16f}$$

$$z_{12} = - \frac{y_{12}}{\Delta_y} \tag{12-16g}$$

where $$\Delta_y = y_{11}y_{22} - y_{12}{}^2 \tag{12-16h}$$

From Eqs. (12-15a) and (12-15b) it can be seen that y_{11} is the admittance looking into terminal pair 1-1 with terminal pair 2-2 short-circuited ($E_2 = 0$). Similarly y_{22} is the admittance looking into terminal pair 2-2 with terminal pair 1-1 short-circuited ($E_1 = 0$). y_{12} is given by either the short-circuit current through terminal pair 2-2 ($E_2 = 0$) when a unit voltage is applied to terminal pair 1-1 ($E_1 = 1$) or the short-circuit current through terminal pair 1-1 ($E_1 = 0$) when a unit voltage is applied to terminal pair 2-2 ($E_2 = 1$).

In terms of the π network of Fig. 12-9c the y parameters are given as follows:

$$y_{11} = y_a + y_b \tag{12-17a}$$
$$y_{22} = y_c + y_b \tag{12-17b}$$
$$y_{12} = -y_b \tag{12-17c}$$

Two-terminal pair networks can be used to implement a transfer function in several ways. The most general form is shown in Fig. 12-10a, where the network is used to couple a voltage source E_g having an internal impedance Z_g at terminal pairs 1-1 to a load impedance Z_L at terminal pairs 2-2. Rather than consider the general case of Fig. 12-10a, the problem of transfer-function synthesis is greatly facilitated if we define three basic transfer functions as illustrated in Fig. 12-10b to d. Each of these represents another way of obtaining a transfer function, the particular choice depending upon the designer. It should be pointed out that for practical sources the internal generator impedance can often be taken into account by considering it as part of one of the impedances of the network. This point will become more apparent presently.

Let us consider each of the transfer functions of Fig. 12-10 separately.

The Voltage Transfer Function T_{12}. Figure 12-10b illustrates the case where a voltage source is applied to terminal pair 1-1 and the output is taken across terminal pair 2-2, which are open-circuited ($I_2 = 0$). This is a very common arrangement in which the transfer function $T_{12} = E_2/E_1$

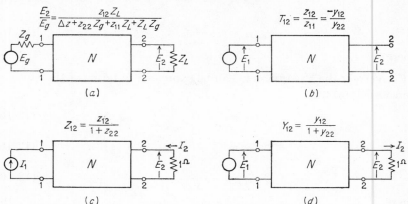

FIG. 12-10. Use of a two-terminal pair network to generate a transfer function. (*a*) General form; (*b*) $E_2 = T_{12}E_1$; (*c*) $E_2 = Z_{12}I_1$; (*d*) $I_2 = Y_{12}E_1$. N is the network.

is dimensionless. From examination of Eqs. (12-13a), (12-13b), and (12-15b) with $I_2 = 0$, it is obvious that

$$T_{12} = \frac{z_{12}}{z_{11}} = \frac{-y_{12}}{y_{22}} \qquad (12\text{-}18)$$

The important conclusion to be drawn from Eq. (12-18) is that in specifying T_{12} we are in effect stipulating z_{11} and z_{12} or y_{12} and y_{22}, that is, two of the three z or y parameters of the network. The third parameter (z_{22} or y_{11}) is unspecified and depends upon the actual synthesis procedure used.

Thus, given a $T_{12}(s)$, the problem is reduced to one of determining a two-terminal pair network which has the prescribed z_{11}, z_{12} (or y_{11}, y_{22}) parameters.

The Current-source to Voltage Transfer Impedance Z_{12}. Figure 12-10c illustrates the case where the driving function is a current source applied to terminals 1-1 and the output is the voltage across a nominal 1-ohm load resistor at terminals 2-2.† The transfer function is usually specified as $Z_{12} = E_2/I_1$, which has the units of ohms. The ratio I_2/I_1 (which is dimensionless) is identical to this expression because of the 1-ohm termination. $E_2 = (1 \text{ ohm})(I_2)$.

An expression for Z_{12} in terms of the z parameters of the network can be derived readily by applying Thévenin's theorem to Fig. 12-10 at

† The discussion of Sec. 12-6 takes care of terminations other than 1 ohm.

terminal pair 2-2. The open-circuit voltage seen at terminals 2-2 is given by $z_{12}I_1$. The impedance looking into terminals 2-2 with terminals 1-1 open is given by z_{22}. Thus, in so far as the load resistor is concerned, the two-terminal pair network can be replaced by a voltage source of $z_{12}I_1$ volts in series with an impedance of z_{22} ohms. By voltage-divider action, the output voltage E_2 is given by the expression

$$E_2 = z_{12}I_1 \frac{1}{1 + z_{22}}$$

Hence it follows that Z_{12} is given by

$$Z_{12} = \frac{z_{12}}{1 + z_{22}} \qquad (12\text{-}19)$$

Equation (12-19) again is useful because it indicates how the transfer function Z_{12} is related to the parameters z_{12} and z_{22} of the two-terminal pair network. The synthesis procedure for a Z_{12} transfer function in the form of Fig. 12-10c is thus again reduced to determining a two-terminal pair network with appropriate z parameters. It is interesting to note that here again Z_{12} is related to only two of the three z parameters of the network.

The Voltage-source to Current Transfer Admittance Y_{12}. Figure 12-10d illustrates the case where the driving function is a voltage source applied to terminals 1-1 and the output is the current through a nominal 1-ohm load resistor at terminals 2-2. The transfer function is usually specified as an admittance $Y_{12} = I_2/E_1$, although its expression is identical to the dimensionless ratio specifying E_2/E_1 since $I_2 = E_2/(1 \text{ ohm})$. As before, Y_{12} can be related to two of the defining parameters of the two-terminal pair network. The result in this case is

$$Y_{12} = \frac{y_{12}}{1 + y_{22}} \qquad (12\text{-}20)$$

This result can also be derived from the application of Thévenin's theorem to Fig. 12-10d and is left as an exercise for the reader. Examination of Eq. (12-20) again illustrates that specifying Y_{12} enables us to stipulate two of the y parameters of the network. Thus the transfer-function synthesis procedure again is reduced to determining a two-terminal pair network with appropriate z or y parameters.

12-4. Properties of Transfer Functions

In general any transfer function associated with a linear passive network has certain restrictions placed on the locations of its zeros and poles in the complex s plane. These are quite different from the restrictions on the zeros and poles of driving-point impedance or admittance functions. The first restriction is quite general and follows from the fact that in a passive network the source-free, or transient, response must decay, or at most remain constant, with time. Consider a general transfer function $T(s)$ as the ratio of two polynomials

$$T(s) = \frac{\text{output}}{\text{input}} = \frac{A(s)}{B(s)} \tag{12-21}$$

If the input function is a unit impulse $\delta(t)$, the transient time-domain response is given by $\mathcal{L}^{-1}[A(s)/B(s)]$, since the Laplace transform of a unit impulse is unity. It follows that if the response is to decay with time all the roots of the equation $B(s) = 0$ must lie in the left half of the complex s plane. This leads to the following conclusion: *For a linear*

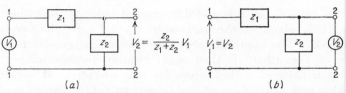

FIG. 12-11. Example illustrating that the reciprocal of a transfer function is not the same as interchanging the input and output. (a) V_1 as the voltage source; (b) V_2 as the voltage source.

passive network all the poles of any transfer function, regardless of its form, must lie within the left half of the complex s plane.

A similar restriction *does not* hold for the zeros of the transfer function, i.e., the roots of the equation $A(s) = 0$. The fact that the zeros of a transfer function need not be restricted to the left half of the s plane is one of the major aspects in which transfer functions are different from driving-point impedance functions. The zeros of a physically realizable driving-point impedance are restricted to the left-half s plane. The reason is basically that the reciprocal of a driving-point impedance function, that is, the input admittance, has physical significance in calculating the response of the network. It gives the current which flows when a unit-impulse voltage is applied ($i(t) = \mathcal{L}^{-1} Y(s)$). Thus the poles of $Y(s)$, which are the zeros of $Z(s)$, must lie in the left-hand s plane for a passive impedance. The same physical interpretation is not possible for the reciprocal of a transfer function. This can be seen by considering the voltage-to-voltage transfer function for the network of Fig. 12-11a. When V_1 is a voltage source, V_2 is given by $V_2 = V_1 z_2/(z_1 + z_2)$ and the transfer function is $V_2/V_1 = z_2/(z_1 + z_2)$. The reciprocal of this transfer function is $V_1/V_2 = (z_1 + z_2)/z_1 = 1 + z_2/z_1$. This expression cannot be used to determine V_1 when V_2 is the voltage source. For the latter case, as can be seen from the network, $V_1 = V_2$, and the transfer function is actually $V_1/V_2 = 1$.

Hence there are no basic restrictions on the location of the zeros of a transfer function. In general these zeros may lie anywhere in the complex s plane. Those networks which have the zeros of a transfer function confined to the left half of the complex s plane are known as *minimum-phase-shift* networks. We are primarily concerned with transfer functions of this type.

Another basic difference between transfer and impedance functions is that the highest and lowest powers of s in the numerator and denominator polynomials of a transfer function can differ by more than unity, with the single restriction that the highest power of s in the numerator polynomial never exceeds the highest power of s in the denominator polynomial. If the highest power of s in the numerator were to exceed the highest power of s in the denominator, the output response to a unit-impulse input would involve derivatives of the impulse, which cannot occur in physical systems.

The foregoing statements apply to network transfer functions in general. In the case of RC networks there are further restrictions imposed upon the location of poles of a transfer function. These follow from the fact that the network does not contain any inductances, so that the impulsive response cannot involve an exchange of energy between electric and magnetic fields. This response must therefore involve simple decaying exponentials only, i.e., terms of the form $\epsilon^{-\sigma t}$, where σ is a real positive number. The following restriction therefore holds for the roots of the equation $B(s) = 0$, that is, the poles of $T(s)$: *In the transfer function of any RC network the poles are restricted to the negative real axis.*

The foregoing restriction is an important guide for design. It is imperative that we restrict the poles of the transfer function of a compensation network to the negative real axis if we hope to implement this network by means of RC's only. It is also important to note that we have not placed any restriction on the zeros, and they, in general, can lie anywhere in the complex s plane. However, for practical reasons it is advisable to restrict the zeros to the left-half s plane, i.e., to make the network minimum-phase-shift. The reason for this is that a nonminimum-phase-shift network must be synthesized in a lattice (or bridge) configuration, as illustrated in Fig. 12-12a. In general the lattice network is undesirable because there is no common connection between one of the input and one of the output terminals so that either the input or the output must float above ground. Nonetheless the lattice is the most general network configuration, and any realizable transfer function can be synthesized in lattice form.

From a practical point of view, however, the most desirable type of network configuration is the ladder form, such as the T or π of Fig. 12-9. We shall confine our discussions mainly to the synthesis of ladder types.

Ladder networks are characterized by being minimum-phase-shift, and RC ladder networks have the additional restriction that the zeros must lie on the negative real axis.

In an RC ladder network any transfer function must have its zeros as well as its poles restricted to the negative real axis. It should be noted that there is nothing in this statement about the locations of the zeros and poles alternating along the negative real axis, as with RC impedance functions. That the foregoing property of RC ladder networks is reasonable may be appreciated by considering a ladder-type network, as shown in Fig. 12-12b. A little thought reveals that there is zero

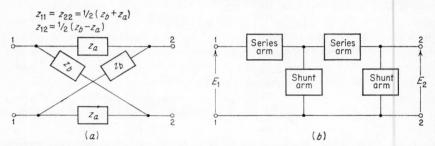

FIG. 12-12. Basic two-terminal-pair network types. (a) A symmetrical lattice or bridge network capable of producing a nonminimum-phase transfer function; (b) ladder-type transfer function.

transmission of voltage between the input and output terminals at those complex frequencies at which the impedance of any one of the series arms by itself is infinite or at which the impedance of any one of the shunt arms by itself is zero. Mathematically this means that the transfer function is zero at those values of s where the impedance of a series arm has a pole (infinite impedance) or at those values of s where the impedance of a shunt arm has a zero (zero impedance). Since each arm of the ladder is to consist of a simple RC network, the zeros and poles of the impedance function for each arm must lie along the negative real axis in the s plane. Thus the transmission zeros of the transfer function are also restricted to the negative real axis of the s plane. The identity of the zeros of the transfer function [i.e., values of s at which $T(s) = 0$] with the zeros of the shunt-arm impedance function and with the poles of series-arms impedance functions is an important consideration in the synthesis of transfer functions.

At this point it is worthwhile to summarize some of the concepts presented in this section. If a transfer function is to be realized by means of an RC ladder-type network the zeros and poles must lie along the negative real axis (the origin is also acceptable). If the zeros are allowed off the negative real axis but are still confined to the left half of the complex s plane, the network is still minimum-phase-shift and realization is possible in nonlattice forms (such as parallel-ladder or split-T configurations, which are discussed in Sec. 12-8).   If zeros are permitted in the right half of the complex s plane a lattice (nonminimum-phase-shift) type of realization is necessary.   In any of the above cases the poles of the transfer function must be restricted to the negative real axis if only RC elements are to be used.

12-5. The Synthesis of Transfer Functions in RC Ladder Forms

The Voltage Transfer Function T_{12}; Synthesis by z Parameters.   Let us consider that a transfer function is specified as the ratio of two polynomials for which the zeros and poles lie along the negative real axis in order to assure that the transfer function can be implemented with an RC ladder network.   Let us also assume that it is desired to obtain this transfer function in the form of a voltage ratio, as illustrated in Fig. 12-10b.   Thus the transfer function is written as

$$T_{12} = K \frac{A(s)}{B(s)} = K \frac{z_{12}(s)}{z_{11}(s)} \tag{12-22}$$

The constant K is a numeric known as the *gain factor* whose exact value depends upon the specific network we arrive at in our synthesis procedure. As is shown later, the value of K is determined after the network has been synthesized.   The larger the value of K, the less the attenuation introduced by the network.   Since many networks are possible in a synthesis procedure, the value of the gain factor is one of the major considerations in choosing one network in preference to others.

Since z_{11} is the impedance looking into terminal pair 1-1 with terminal pair 2-2 open, it follows that z_{11} is an impedance function with the properties of an impedance function (which were discussed earlier in the chapter) and that it is given by the ratio of two polynomials in s.   It is therefore possible to write $z_{11}(s)$ as follows, where $q(s)$ is, for the time being, any arbitrary polynomial in s.

$$z_{11} = \frac{B(s)}{q(s)} \tag{12-23}$$

From Eq. (12-22) it follows that, for the assumed $z_{11}(s)$ of Eq. (12-23), $z_{12}(s)$ is given by

$$z_{12} = K \frac{A(s)}{q(s)} \tag{12-24}$$

It should be noted that finite transmission zeros of T_{12} occur where $A(s) = 0$, so that in general the finite zeros of the transfer function T_{12} are also zeros of z_{12}.   We shall use this fact later on.

Up to this point $q(s)$ can be any polynomial in s.   However, if z_{11} is to be an impedance function looking into an RC network, its zeros and poles must alternate along the negative real axis in the s plane and the lowest critical frequency must be a pole and the highest critical frequency a zero. Thus, if z_{11} is to be an RC impedance function, the polynomial $q(s)$ must be such that its roots are properly interlaced with the roots of the polynomial $B(s)$. Actually there are an unlimited number of polynomials for $q(s)$ which can be chosen to make $z_{11}(s)$ an RC impedance function, and this is a choice left to the network designer.

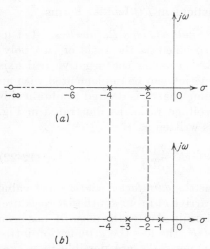

After $q(s)$ is chosen, the synthesis problem reduces to one of finding a network with the proper z_{11} and z_{12} functions. Before proceeding with this part of the problem, let us examine some of the factors which arise in the choice of $q(s)$. Unfortunately, there is no standard way of choosing the best polynomial for $q(s)$ even though the final network complexity, the spread of the element values, and the value of the gain factor K depend upon the choice of $q(s)$. In general, the closer the zeros and poles of z_{11}, the greater the spread of element values. Also, the simplest network often results if z_{11} is chosen with a pole at $s = 0$ or $s = \infty$, indicating a series or shunt capacitor in the resultant network. The arbitrary choice of a polynomial for $q(s)$ is no serious handicap to

Fig. 12-13. Determining the zero-pole pattern for $z_{11}(s)$. (a) Zero-pole pattern for
$$T_{12}(s) = K \frac{s + 6}{(s + 2)(s + 4)} = K \frac{A(s)}{B(s)}; (b)$$
zero-pole pattern for
$$z_{11}(s) = \frac{(s + 2)(s + 4)}{(s + 1)(s + 3)} = \frac{B(s)}{q(s)}$$

the designer since the synthesis procedure which follows is quite simple and many different polynomials for $q(s)$ can be tried to see which leads to the best result.

To illustrate the manner of choosing $q(s)$, let us assume that it is desired to synthesize an RC transfer function of the following form:

$$T_{12}(s) = K \frac{s + 6}{(s + 2)(s + 4)} = K \frac{A(s)}{B(s)} \qquad (12\text{-}25)$$

The zero-pole pattern of T_{12} is illustrated in Fig. 12-13a. The roots of the equation $B(s) = 0$ are located at $s = -2$ and $s = -4$. In choosing a polynomial for $q(s)$, it is apparent that $q(s)$ must have a root in the range $0 \geq s > -2$ and in the range $-2 > s > -4$ if z_{11} is to be an RC impedance function. Let us arbitrarily choose the roots $s = -1, s = -3$

for $q(s)$. Thus z_{11} may be written as follows:

$$z_{11} = \frac{(s+2)(s+4)}{(s+1)(s+3)} \tag{12-26}$$

The zero-pole pattern for this z_{11} is sketched in Fig. 12-13b. From Eq. (12-24) it follows that z_{12} is given by the following ratio of polynomials:

$$z_{12} = K \frac{A(s)}{q(s)} = K \frac{s+6}{(s+1)(s+3)} \tag{12-27}$$

It should be noted that z_{12} has zeros at $s = -6$ and $s = \infty$, which are the same frequencies at which $T_{12}(s)$ has zeros.

After the polynomial for $q(s)$ is chosen, the problem of network synthesis is reduced to one of finding a network having the required $z_{11}(s)$ *provided* that it also has the required zeros for $z_{12}(s)$ which correspond to the transmission zeros of T_{12}. As pointed out in the preceding section, transmission zeros in a ladder structure are obtained by either a series-arm impedance pole or a shunt-arm impedance zero. The simplest RC network which has an impedance pole at a negative real value of s is the parallel RC combination as shown in Fig. 12-5a. Similarly the simplest RC network which has an impedance zero at a negative real value of s is the series RC network as shown in Fig. 12-7a. Thus transmission zeros in the ladder structure may be obtained by means of parallel RC combinations in series arms or by series RC combinations in the shunt arms of the latter. The actual synthesis procedure consists in manipulating the synthesis of the impedance function z_{11} so as to create either series-arm poles or shunt-arm zeros at those frequencies where z_{12} has zeros. These poles or zeros are then removed from z_{11} as either parallel RC combinations in series arms or series RC combinations in shunt arms, respectively. The details of the procedure can be illustrated best by example since so many variations are possible. Let us continue with the preceding example, where z_{11} and z_{12} are given by Eqs. (12-26) and (12-27).

As the first step, sketch $z_{11}(\sigma)$ vs. σ, as shown in Fig. 12-14a. It is noted that at extreme values of frequency $z_{11}(\sigma)$ has the following values:

$$z_{11}(0) = \frac{2(4)}{1(3)} = \frac{8}{3} = 2.67$$
$$z_{11}(\infty) = 1$$

Since z_{12} (and T_{12}) is to have a zero at $s = -6$, it is desirable to manipulate $z_{11}(s)$ so as to create a zero at $s = -6$. This zero can then be removed from z_{11} as a series RC circuit in a shunt arm of the ladder,

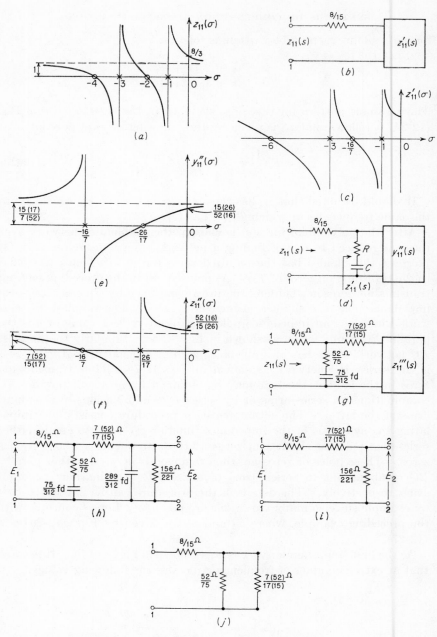

Fig. 12-14. Steps in the synthesis of $T_{12}(s) = K \dfrac{s + 6}{(s + 2)(s + 4)}$. (a) Plot of $z_{11}(\sigma)$ vs. σ; (b) creating a zero in $z_{11}(s)$ by removing a series resistor; (c) $z'_{11}(\sigma)$ vs. σ; (d) removal of zero in $z_{11}(s)$ at $s = -6$; (e) $y''_{11}(\sigma)$ vs. σ; (f) $z''_{11}(\sigma)$ vs. σ; (g) creating a zero in $z_{11}(s)$ at $s = \infty$; (h) the final network; (i) evaluating the constant K_1 from the circuit at $s = 0$; (j) network configuration at $s = \infty$.

514

thereby providing one of the required transmission zeros. At $s = -6$, $z_{11}(s)$ has the following value:

$$z_{11}(-6) = \frac{(-6 + 2)(-6 + 4)}{(-6 + 1)(-6 + 3)} = \frac{-4(-2)}{-5(-3)} = \frac{8}{15}$$

It is obvious from Fig. 12-14a that if $\frac{8}{15}$ ohm were subtracted from $z_{11}(\sigma)$ the remaining function would have a zero at $s = -6$ and still behave as an RC impedance function. Thus write $z_{11}(s)$ as

$$z_{11}(s) = \frac{(s + 2)(s + 4)}{(s + 1)(s + 3)} = \frac{8}{15} + z'_{11}(s) \tag{12-28}$$

where $z'_{11}(s)$ is given by

$$z'_{11}(s) = \frac{(s + 2)(s + 4)}{(s + 1)(s + 3)} - \frac{8}{15} = \frac{(7s + 16)(s + 6)}{15(s + 1)(s + 3)} \tag{12-29}$$

Obviously $z'_{11}(s)$ now has a zero at $s = -6$. In view of Eq. (12-28) $z_{11}(s)$ may be represented as illustrated in Fig. 12-14b. The plot of $z'_{11}(\sigma)$ vs. σ is sketched in Fig. 12-14c.

It should be noted from Fig. 12-14a that if a series resistor greater than 1 ohm were subtracted from $z_{11}(s)$ the resulting expression for $z'_{11}(s)$ would not represent a realizable RC network since the curve of $z'_{11}(\sigma)$ would be negative at $\sigma = \infty$, which is physically impossible since it represents negative resistance at high frequency.

Note that, since $z'_{11}(s)$ has a zero at $s = -6$, the required transmission zero at this frequency can be obtained by removing a series RC combination as a shunt arm of the ladder, as illustrated in Fig. 12-14d. Thus, if $z'_{11}(s)$ is inverted, we may write it as follows:

$$\frac{1}{z'_{11}(s)} = y'_{11}(s) = \frac{15(s + 1)(s + 3)}{(7s + 16)(s + 6)} = \frac{ks}{s + 6} + y''_{11}(s) \tag{12-30}$$

The constant k is evaluated as follows:

$$k = \frac{15(s + 1)(s + 3)}{s(7s + 16)}\bigg|_{s = -6} = \frac{15(-5)(-3)}{-6(-26)} = \frac{15(5)}{52} = \frac{75}{52}$$

Thus the R and C of the series RC combination are given by

$$R = \frac{1}{k} = \frac{52}{75} \text{ ohm} \qquad C = \frac{k}{6} = \frac{75}{6(52)} = \frac{75}{312} \text{ farad}$$

It now remains to determine and synthesize the remaining function $y''_{11}(s)$. The admittance $y''_{11}(s)$ is determined by subtraction. Hence from Eq. (12-30)

$$y''_{11}(s) = \frac{15(s + 1)(s + 3)}{(7s + 16)(s + 6)} - \frac{75}{52}\frac{s}{s + 6} = \frac{15(17s + 26)}{52(7s + 16)} \tag{12-31}$$

It is interesting to note that $y_{11}''(s)$ no longer has a pole at $s = -6$. Figure 12-14e illustrates $y_{11}''(\sigma)$ sketched vs. σ.   Figure 12-14f illustrates $z_{11}''(\sigma)$ sketched vs. σ.

Thus far we have taken care of the transmission zero at $s = -6$. From Eq. (12-27) it is seen that $z_{12}(s)$ and T_{12} also have a zero at $s = \infty$. This transmission zero must be obtained by means of a shunt capacitor in the ladder development for $z_{11}(s)$. Since $z_{11}''(s)$ is finite at $s = \infty$, the necessary zero can be created in $z_{11}''(s)$ by subtracting the value of $z_{11}''(\infty)$ from $z_{11}''(s)$.   Since $z_{11}''(\infty) = [52(7)]/[15(17)]$, we can write $z_{11}''(s)$ as

$$z_{11}''(s) = \frac{52(7s + 16)}{15(17s + 26)} = \frac{52(7)}{15(17)} + z_{11}'''(s) \qquad (12\text{-}32)$$

where $z_{11}'''(s)$ is given by

$$z_{11}'''(s) = \frac{52(7s + 16)}{15(17s + 26)} - \frac{7(52)}{15(17)} = \frac{52(6)}{17(17s + 26)} \qquad (12\text{-}33)$$

In view of Eq. (12-32), $z_{11}(s)$ can be represented as shown in Fig. 12-14g. Equation (12-33) indicates that $z_{11}'''(s)$ now has a zero at $s = \infty$, as required.   This zero can be removed as a shunt capacitance by inverting $z_{11}'''(s)$ to form $y_{11}'''(s)$ and dividing through.   Thus

$$y_{11}'''(s) = \frac{17(17s + 26)}{52(6)} = \frac{289}{312} s + \frac{221}{156} \qquad (12\text{-}34)$$

Equation (12-34) completes the synthesis process in that $y_{11}'''(s)$ is equivalent to a capacitor of $\frac{289}{312}$ farad in parallel with a conductance of $\frac{221}{156}$ mhos. The completed network is drawn in Fig. 12-14h.

It now remains to evaluate the constant K of Eq. (12-25).   From Eq. (12-25) it follows that $T_{12}(0) = \frac{6}{8}K = \frac{3}{4}K$.   At direct current ($s = 0$) the network of Fig. 12-14h reduces to the configuration in Fig. 12-14i. Thus we may write directly from the network

$$T_{12}(0) = \frac{E_2}{E_1}(0) = \frac{\frac{156}{221}}{\frac{8}{15} + 7(52)/17(15) + \frac{156}{221}} = 0.265 = \tfrac{3}{4}K$$

It follows from this equation that $K = 0.353$ for the network found. The network of Fig. 12-14h can be checked by considering the value of $z_{11}(s)$ at $s = 0$ and $s = \infty$.   Figure 12-14j illustrates the network configuration at $s = \infty$, when all the capacitors become short circuits.   Thus we obtain the following from Fig. 12-14i and j directly:

$$z_{11}(\infty) = \frac{8}{15} + \frac{\frac{52}{75}[7(52)/17(15)]}{\frac{52}{75} + [7(52)/17(15)]} = \frac{8}{15} + \frac{7}{15} = 1$$

$$z_{11}(0) = \frac{8}{15} + \frac{7(52)}{17(15)} + \frac{156}{221} = \frac{8}{15} + \frac{32}{15} = \frac{8}{3}$$

These values agree with those obtained from Eq. (12-26).

In the foregoing example the polynomial $q(s)$ was chosen to illustrate the synthesis technique rather than to simplify the resulting network. In order to illustrate what can be done to simplify the result, let us consider the synthesis of the same transfer function but with a more judicious choice of $q(s)$. This time let us choose $q(s)$ so that it has a

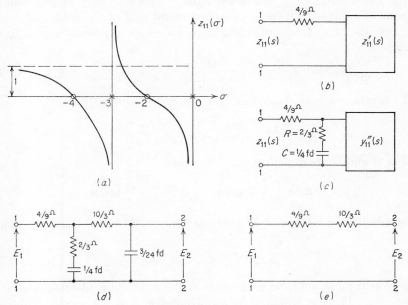

FIG. 12-15. Steps in the synthesis of $T_{12}(s) = K \dfrac{s+6}{(s+2)(s+4)}$. (a) $z_{11}(\sigma)$ vs. σ; (b) creating a zero at $s = -6$; (c) removing a transmission zero at $s = -6$; (d) final network; (e) network at $s = 0$.

pole at $s = 0$. Thus a possible polynomial for $q(s)$ is $q(s) = s(s+3)$, and z_{11} and z_{12} are therefore given by the equations

$$z_{11}(s) = \frac{(s+2)(s+4)}{s(s+3)} \tag{12-35}$$

$$z_{12}(s) = \frac{K(s+6)}{s(s+3)} \tag{12-36}$$

A plot of $z_{11}(\sigma)$ is sketched in Fig. 12-15a. $z_{11}(s)$ has a zero at $s = -4$, whereas $z_{12}(s)$ has a zero at $s = -6$. Since $z_{11}(-6) < z_{11}(\infty)$, it is possible to subtract the value of z_{11} at $s = -6$ from $z_{11}(s)$ to create a zero in $z'_{11}(s)$ at $s = -6$, with the remaining function still being realizable as an RC impedance function. Accordingly,

$$z_{11}(-6) = \frac{-4(-2)}{-6(-3)} = \frac{4}{9}$$

A $\frac{4}{9}$-ohm resistor is now taken out in a series arm as shown in Fig. 12-15b, and $z'_{11}(s)$ is given as follows:

$$z'_{11}(s) = \frac{(s + 2)(s + 4)}{s(s + 3)} - \frac{4}{9} = \frac{(5s + 12)(s + 6)}{9s(s + 3)} \tag{12-37}$$

$z'_{11}(s)$ has a zero at $s = -6$ as expected. This zero may be removed by means of a series RC combination in a shunt arm of the ladder as shown in Fig. 12-15c. Thus, inverting $z'_{11}(s)$ to create a pole at $s = -6$, we obtain

$$y'_{11}(s) = \frac{1}{z'_{11}(s)} = \frac{9s(s + 3)}{(5s + 12)(s + 6)} = \frac{ks}{s + 6} + y''_{11} \tag{12-38}$$

The constant k is evaluated as

$$k = \frac{9s(s + 3)}{s(5s + 12)} \bigg|_{s = -6} = \frac{3}{2}$$

Thus R and C are given by the following:

$$R = \frac{1}{k} = \frac{2}{3} \text{ ohm} \qquad C = \frac{k}{6} = \frac{1}{4} \text{ farad}$$

The admittance $y''_{11}(s)$ is obtained from Eq. (12-38) by subtraction. Thus

$$y''_{11}(s) = \frac{9s(s + 3)}{(5s + 12)(s + 6)} - \frac{3s}{2(s + 6)} = \frac{3s}{2(5s + 12)} \tag{12-39}$$

Up to this point we have taken care of the required transmission zero at $s = -6$. There is still need for a transmission zero at $s = \infty$. This zero is provided readily by inverting $y''_{11}(s)$ to form $z''_{11}(s)$. Thus

$$z''_{11}(s) = \frac{2(5s + 12)}{3s} = \frac{10}{3} + \frac{24}{3s} \tag{12-40}$$

Equation (12-40) indicates that $z''_{11}(s)$ consists of a series connection of a resistor and capacitor. Thus, if the resistor is taken as the series arm of the ladder and the capacitor as a shunt arm, then $z''_{11}(s)$ is arranged to provide the required transmission zero at $s = \infty$. Figure 12-15d illustrates the final network. This network is seen to involve one fewer component than the previous case of Fig. 12-14h, although they both represent the same transfer function. The value of gain constant K for the present network can be found by considering T_{12} at $s = 0$. The network reduces to that of Fig. 12-15e at $s = 0$ so that $E_2/E_1 = 1$, and K is therefore given as follows:

$$T_{12}(0) = \tfrac{3}{4}K = 1$$
$$K = \tfrac{4}{3} = 1.333$$

This is obviously a higher gain constant than obtained previously.

The Voltage Transfer Function T_{12}. Synthesis by y Parameters. As an alternate procedure for the synthesis of $T_{12}(s)$ one can use the y-parameter representation for $T_{12}(s)$ as given by Eq. (12-18). Thus we may write $T_{12}(s)$ as follows:

$$T_{12}(s) = \frac{K(s+6)}{(s+2)(s+4)} = -\frac{y_{12}}{y_{22}} = \frac{A(s)}{B(s)} \qquad (12\text{-}41)$$

The synthesis procedure in this case is very similar to that in the previous examples except that $y_{12}(s)$ and $y_{22}(s)$ are now identified. Thus, if a polynomial $q(s)$ is chosen so as to make $y_{22}(s)$ the input admittance to an RC network, we may write

$$y_{22}(s) = \frac{B(s)}{q(s)} \qquad (12\text{-}42)$$

$$-y_{12}(s) = K \frac{A(s)}{q(s)} \qquad (12\text{-}43)$$

The zeros of $T_{12}(s)$ are again the zeros of $y_{12}(s)$. The synthesis procedure consists in manipulating $y_{22}(s)$ in such a way as to provide the required transmission zeros where $y_{12}(s)$ has zeros. Since we are dealing with $y_{22}(s)$, the synthesis proceeds from the output terminals 2-2 to the input terminals 1-1 short-circuited. This short circuit is required by the definition of y_{22} and is removed after the network is determined. In order to demonstrate the technique, let us again follow through with the example of Eq. (12-41). The simplest choice for $q(s)$ is now a polynomial of the form $q(s) = s + 3$, so that $y_{22}(s)$ and $y_{12}(s)$ may be written as

$$y_{22}(s) = \frac{(s+2)(s+4)}{s+3} \qquad (12\text{-}44)$$

$$-y_{12}(s) = \frac{K(s+6)}{s+3} \qquad (12\text{-}45)$$

Figure 12-16a illustrates $y_{22}(\sigma)$ sketched vs. σ and is seen to correspond to the case of a realizable RC admittance function. $y_{22}(s)$ has a pole at $s = \infty$. If this pole is removed as a shunt capacitance, this will also provide the required transmission zero at $s = \infty$. Thus, if the numerator of Eq. (12-44) is divided by the denominator in descending powers of s, we obtain the following,

$$y_{22}(s) = \frac{s^2 + 6s + 8}{s+3} = s + \frac{3s+8}{s+3} = s + y'_{22}(s) \qquad (12\text{-}46)$$

where $y'_{22}(s)$ is given as follows:

$$y'_{22}(s) = \frac{3s+8}{s+3} \qquad (12\text{-}47)$$

The synthesis thus far is represented in Fig. 12-16b. Figure 12-16c

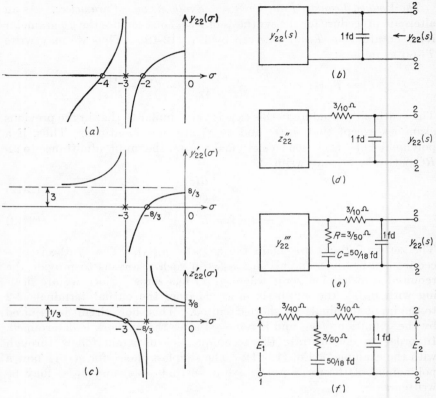

FIG. 12-16. Steps in the synthesis of $T_{12}(s) = K \dfrac{s+6}{(s+2)(s+4)}$ by y parameters. (a) $y_{22}(\sigma)$ vs. σ; (b) removal of pole in $y_{22}(s)$ at $s = \infty$; (c) $y'_{22}(\sigma)$ and $z'_{22}(\sigma)$ vs. σ; (d) creating a zero at $s = -6$; (e) removing a transmission zero at $s = -6$; (f) final network.

represents sketches of $y'_{22}(\sigma)$ and $z'_{22}(\sigma)$ vs. σ. Since we still need to provide a transmission zero at $s = -6$, it is obvious from these sketches that the zero can be created by subtracting from $z'_{22}(s)$ the value of $z'_{22}(s)$ at $s = -6$. Thus $z'_{22}(-6)$ is calculated as

$$z'_{22}(-6) = \frac{-6+3}{3(-6)+8} = \frac{3}{10}$$

The network can now be drawn as illustrated in Fig. 12-16d, where $z''_{22}(s)$ is obtained by subtraction.

$$z''_{22}(s) = z'_{22}(s) - z'_{22}(-6) = \frac{s+3}{3s+8} - \frac{3}{10} = \frac{s+6}{10(3s+8)} \qquad (12\text{-}48)$$

$z''_{22}(s)$ now has a zero at $s = -6$ as required. This transmission zero can be implemented directly by inverting Eq. (12-48) and expanding as follows:

$$y_{22}''(s) = \frac{10(3s + 8)}{s + 6} = \frac{ks}{s + 6} + y_{22}''' \tag{12-49}$$

The first term is seen to correspond to a series RC shunt arm of the ladder and provides the required transmission zero at $s = -6$. The value of k is obtained as usual. Thus

$$k = \frac{10(3s + 8)}{s}\bigg|_{s = -6} = \frac{50}{3}$$

R and C are given as

$$R = \frac{3}{50} \text{ ohm} \qquad C = \frac{k}{6} = \frac{50}{3(6)} = \frac{50}{18} \text{ farads}$$

The network thus far looks as shown in Fig. 12-16e. $y_{22}'''(s)$ is obtained from Eq. (12-49) by subtraction. Thus

$$y_{22}''' = \frac{10(3s + 8)}{s + 6} - \frac{50s}{3(s + 6)} = \frac{40}{3}$$

y_2''' is obviously an admittance of $\frac{40}{3}$ mhos. In this particular procedure we are synthesizing $y_{22}(s)$, and the process proceeds from the output end (terminals 2-2) to the input end (terminals 1-1), short-circuited. The final network, with terminals 1-1 open, therefore appears as illustrated in Fig. 12-16f. This network is seen to be identical in configuration to that of the previous example except that the numerical values are different. In this case the value of K also turns out to be $\frac{4}{3}$.

As another example of the synthesis of a transfer function as a voltage ratio, let us consider the case of a lag-lead transfer function for which the zero-pole configuration is different from the example considered thus far.

Example 12-5. Consider that it is desired to synthesize a lag-lead type of transfer function with zeros at $s = -4, -6$ and poles at $s = -2, -8$. The zero-pole pattern is shown in Fig. 12-17a. The transfer function is

$$T_{12} = K \frac{(s + 4)(s + 6)}{(s + 2)(s + 8)} = \frac{K[(s + 4)(s + 6)/q(s)]}{(s + 2)(s + 8)/q(s)} = \frac{z_{12}(s)}{z_{11}(s)} \tag{12-50}$$

Thus $z_{11}(s)$ is given by

$$z_{11}(s) = \frac{(s + 2)(s + 8)}{q(s)} \tag{12-51}$$

We must choose a polynomial for $q(s)$. Obviously $q(s)$ must have one root in the range $-2 < s < 0$ and another in the range $-8 < s < -2$ if z_{11} is to be an RC impedance function. A simple network is obtained if $q(s)$ is chosen to have a root at $s = 0$ and another at $s = -4$, the latter root occurring exactly at a frequency where $z_{12}(s)$ is to have a zero. By this judicious choice we are assured that $z_{11}(s)$ initially has a pole at $s = -4$, which can be removed as a series-arm parallel RC network, thereby auto-

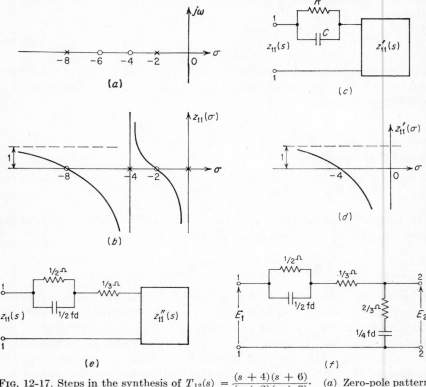

FIG. 12-17. Steps in the synthesis of $T_{12}(s) = \dfrac{(s+4)(s+6)}{(s+2)(s+8)}$. (a) Zero-pole pattern of $T_{12} = K \dfrac{(s+4)(s+6)}{(s+2)(s+8)}$; (b) plot of $z_{11}(\sigma)$ vs. σ; (c) removing a pole at $s = -4$; (d) $z'_{11}(\sigma)$ vs. σ; (e) creating a zero at $s = -6$; (f) final network.

matically providing one of the required zeros of $z_{12}(s)$ and $T_{12}(s)$. Thus let us write $z_{11}(s)$ as

$$z_{11}(s) = \frac{(s+2)(s+8)}{s(s+4)} \tag{12-52}$$

A sketch of $z_{11}(\sigma)$ vs σ appears in Fig. 12-17b. From the choice of $q(s)$, $z_{12}(s)$ is given by

$$z_{12} = \frac{K(s+6)(s+4)}{s(s+4)} = \frac{K(s+6)}{s} \tag{12-53}$$

Notice that the factor $s+4$ occurs in both the numerator and the denominator of $z_{12}(s)$. In order that this required transmission zero is not overlooked, we can remove this pole in $z_{11}(s)$ as a parallel RC network immediately. Thus $z_{11}(s)$ can be expressed in partial-fraction form and represented as illustrated in Fig. 12-17c.

$$z_{11}(s) = \frac{(s+2)(s+8)}{s(s+4)} = \frac{k}{s+4} + z'_{11}(s) \tag{12-54}$$

The factor k is determined as follows:

$$k = \frac{(s+2)(s+8)}{s}\bigg|_{s=-4} = \frac{-2(4)}{-4} = 2$$

Hence C and R of the parallel RC combination are given by $C = \frac{1}{2}$ farad, $R = \frac{1}{2}$ ohm. $z'_{11}(s)$ is determined by subtraction. Thus

$$z'_{11}(s) = \frac{(s+2)(s+8)}{s(s+4)} - \frac{2}{s+4} = \frac{s+4}{s} \tag{12-55}$$

Figure 12-17d illustrates $z'_{11}(\sigma)$ sketched vs. σ. Thus far we have taken care of the required transmission zero at $s = -4$. It still remains to take care of the required transmission zero at $s = -6$. This can be done by shifting the zero in $z'_{11}(s)$ from $s = -4$ to $s = -6$ by subtracting the value of $z'_{11}(-6)$ from $z'_{11}(s)$. From Fig. 12-17d it is seen that this can be done without destroying the realizable RC character of the remaining function. Thus $z'_{11}(-6) = (-6+4)/-6 = \frac{1}{3}$. Hence we write $z'_{11}(s)$ as follows:

$$z'_{11}(s) = \frac{s+4}{s} = \frac{1}{3} + z''_{11}(s) \tag{12-56}$$

From Eq. (12-56) we can draw the next diagram in the synthesis of z_{11}, as illustrated in Fig. 12-17e. $z''_{11}(s)$ is determined by subtraction. Thus

$$z''_{11}(s) = \frac{s+4}{s} - \frac{1}{3} = \frac{2s+12}{3s} \tag{12-57}$$

As expected, $z''_{11}(s)$ has a zero at $s = -6$. In order that this zero become a transmission zero of $z_{12}(s)$, it must be removed as a series RC combination in a shunt arm of the ladder. Inverting $z''_{11}(s)$ to obtain the admittance form yields

$$y''_{11}(s) = \frac{3s}{2s+12} = \frac{\frac{3}{2}s}{s+6} \tag{12-58}$$

This is exactly the expression for the admittance of a series RC combination, and the final network now appears as drawn in Fig. 12-17f, where all element values have been calculated. The value of the gain constant K can be obtained by considering T_{12} at $s = 0$, as determined from the network and from the expression of Eq. (12-50). Thus we can write

$$T_{12}(\infty) = K = \frac{\frac{2}{3}}{\frac{2}{3}+\frac{1}{3}} = \frac{2}{3} = 0.667$$

The Transfer-admittance Form Y_{12}. Let us assume that it is desired to synthesize a transfer function in the form of a transfer admittance, as illustrated in Fig. 12-10d. In this case we write $Y_{12}(s)$ as follows:

$$Y_{12} = K\frac{A(s)}{B(s)} = \frac{y_{12}}{1+y_{22}} \tag{12-59}$$

Here it is necessary to identify polynomials for the parameters y_{12} and y_{22} of a two-terminal pair network. After these are identified, the synthesis process is identical to that in the previous examples. In order to determine polynomials for y_{12} and y_{22}, it is necessary to express $B(s)$

as the sum of two polynomials, $B(s) = B_1(s) + B_2(s)$. Substituting these into Eq. (12-59) and dividing through by $B_2(s)$, we obtain

$$Y_{12} = K \frac{A(s)}{B(s)} = K \frac{A(s)/B_2(s)}{1 + B_1(s)/B_2(s)} \tag{12-60}$$

It is now possible to identify y_{22} and y_{12} as follows:

$$y_{22} = \frac{B_1(s)}{B_2(s)} \qquad y_{12} = K \frac{A(s)}{B_2(s)} \tag{12-61}$$

If $y_{22}(s)$ is to be an RC admittance function, it is necessary that $B_1(s)$ and $B_2(s)$ be chosen so that their zeros and poles alternate along the negative real axis with a zero being closest to the origin. It is always possible to split $B(s)$ into the sum of two polynomials as required, and there are, in fact, many possibilities. In order to avoid the necessity for trial and error in this process, the following procedure can be followed:

1. Express $B(s)$ in factored form, where B_n is a constant.

$$B(s) = B_n(s + p_1)(s + p_2) \cdots (s + p_n) \tag{12-62}$$

2. Form a polynomial $B_2(s)$ as follows:

$$B_2(s) = A(s + p_1')(s + p_2') \cdots (s + p_n') \tag{12-63}$$

where $$p_1 < p_1' < p_2 < p_2' < \cdots < p_n < p_n' \tag{12-64}$$

and the constant A is any nonzero value chosen so that

$$A p_1' p_2' p_3' \cdots p_n' \leq B_n p_1 p_2 p_3 \cdots p_n \tag{12-65}$$

3. Form

$$B_1(s) = B(s) - B_2(s) \tag{12-66}$$

The preceding steps assure that $B_1(s)$ and $B_2(s)$ will be such that $y_{22}(s)$ as given by Eq. (12-61) is the input admittance to an RC network. As an example of this process, consider the following transfer function:

$$Y_{12}(s) = \frac{Ks(s + 2)}{(s + 4)(s + 6)} = \frac{Ks(s + 2)}{s^2 + 10s + 24} = \frac{y_{12}}{1 + y_{22}} \tag{12-67}$$

Following the steps outlined, polynomials for $B_1(s)$ and $B_2(s)$ can be identified as follows:

1. $B(s) = (s + 4)(s + 6)$. Hence $B_n = 1$, and $p_1 = 4$, $p_2 = 6$.

2. Since $B(s)$ is a quadratic, either $B_1(s)$ or $B_2(s)$ must be a quadratic, while the other must be linear. Let us choose $p_1' = \frac{24}{5} = 4.8$. This value satisfies Eq. (12-64) and makes $B_2(s)$ linear. (The reason for this particular choice will become apparent in a moment.) Thus $B_2(s) = A(s + \frac{24}{5})$. The value for A is chosen by numerical substitution into Eq. (12-65). Thus $A(\frac{24}{5}) \leq 4(6)$ so that A can be chosen equal to 5, and $B_2(s)$ is given by $B_2(s) = 5s + 24$.

3. Subtracting $B_2(s)$ from $B(s)$ yields $B_1(s) = s^2 + 5s = s(s + 5)$.

Thus Y_{12} may be written as

$$Y_{12} = \frac{Ks(s + 2)}{(s + 4)(s + 6)} = \frac{Ks(s + 2)}{(5s + 24) + s(s + 5)}$$
$$= \frac{Ks(s + 2)/(5s + 24)}{1 + s(s + 5)/(5s + 24)} \quad (12\text{-}68)$$

y_{12} and y_{22} are now defined as follows:

$$y_{12} = K \frac{s(s + 2)}{5s + 24} \qquad y_{22} = \frac{s(s + 5)}{5s + 24} \quad (12\text{-}69)$$

The synthesis of y_{22} to provide the required zeros of y_{12} is carried out as before. In order to give yet another example of the synthesis process, the steps are outlined briefly. In this example a series-arm parallel RC combination is obtained to provide the required transmission zeros.

A sketch of $y_{22}(\sigma)$ is drawn in Fig. 12-18a and is seen to have zeros at $s = 0$ and $s = -5$ and a finite pole at $s = -\frac{24}{5} = -4.8$. From y_{12} it is seen that there are transmission zeros at $s = 0$ and $s = -2$. The zero in y_{22} at $s = 0$ may be removed as a series capacitor, which also provides the required transmission zero at $s = 0$. Thus, inverting y_{22}, we may write, after division,

$$z_{22} = \frac{1}{y_{22}} = \frac{24}{5}\frac{1}{s} + \frac{\frac{1}{5}s}{s(s + 5)} = \frac{24}{5}\frac{1}{s} + z'_{22}(s)$$

where $z'_{22}(s) = 0.2/(s + 5)$.

The network thus far appears as shown in Fig. 12-18b. A sketch of $z'_{22}(\sigma)$ is drawn in Fig. 12-18c. We have already taken care of the transmission zero at $s = 0$, so that all that remains is to take care of the transmission zero at $s = -2$. This can be done by creating a pole in $z'_{22}(s)$ at $s = -2$. We must therefore examine $y'_{22}(s)$. Thus

$$y'_{22}(s) = \frac{s + 5}{0.2}$$

The function $y'_{22}(\sigma)$ is sketched in Fig. 12-18d. At $s = -2$, $y'_{22}(s)$ has the value

$$y'_{22}(-2) = \frac{-2 + 5}{0.2} = \frac{3}{0.2} = \frac{30}{2} = 15$$

Thus, if we subtract a constant admittance of $3/0.2$ mhos from $y'_{22}(s)$, the remaining admittance function will have a zero at $s = 2$. The circuit will then appear as shown in Fig. 12-18e, where $y''_{22}(s)$ is given by the following:

$$y''_{22}(s) = y'_{22}(s) - \frac{3}{0.2} = \frac{s + 5}{0.2} - \frac{3}{0.2} = \frac{s + 2}{0.2}$$

$y_{22}''(s)$ has a zero at $s = -2$ so that $z_{22}''(s)$ has a pole at $s = -2$. Inverting $y_{22}''(s)$, we obtain $z_{22}''(s)$. Thus

$$z_{22}''(s) = \frac{0.2}{s + 2}$$

$z_{22}''(s)$ has the required pole at $s = -2$ and can be recognized directly

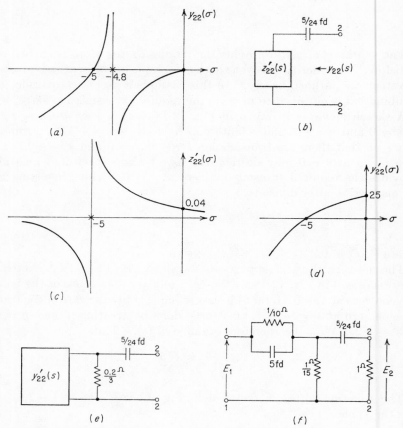

FIG. 12-18. Synthesis of $Y_{12} = K \dfrac{s(s + 2)}{(s + 4)(s + 6)} = \dfrac{K y_{12}}{1 + y_{22}}$. (a) Plot of $y_{22}(\sigma)$ vs. σ; (b) providing a transmission zero at $s = 0$; (c) plot of $z_{22}'(\sigma)$ vs. σ; (d) plot of $y_{22}'(\sigma)$ vs. σ; (e) creating a transmission zero at $s = -2$; (f) final network.

as a parallel RC circuit, as shown in Fig. 12-18f. The 1-ohm terminating resistor as required by Fig. 12-10d is also added to this figure. The value of K is determined from the network's behavior at $s = \infty$ and is seen to be $K = 1$.

12-6. Impedance-level and Frequency Shifting

In the previous sections the reader may have been concerned by the simple values chosen for the locations of the zeros and poles of the transfer function. Obviously these permitted us to simplify the arithmetic involved but led to some impractical component values. In order to change these values into practical ones, there are two transformations which can be applied to the network after a synthesis is completed. The first of these is impedance-level shifting, which enables us to raise or

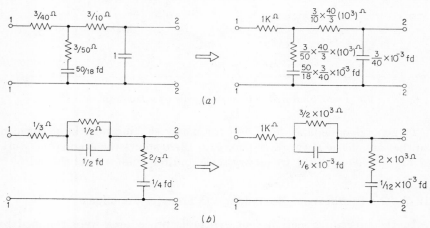

FIG. 12-19. Shifting the impedance level. (a) Network of Fig. 12-16f; (b) lag-lead network of Fig. 12-17f.

lower the impedance level of a network while leaving its transfer function essentially intact. The second is a frequency shift, which enables us to expand or contract the zero-pole pattern in the s plane so as to shift the zeros and poles to more practical values. Let us consider these transformations one at a time.

Impedance-level Shift. In this transformation the impedance level is shifted by a constant factor k, by multiplying all resistance values by the factor k and dividing all capacitance values by the factor k. It can be seen that all time constants, and hence the location of all zeros and poles, remain the same. All impedance functions, however, are multiplied by the constant k, and all admittance functions are divided by k. A dimensionless transfer function, such as T_{12}, remains unchanged, whereas the transfer functions Z_{12} and Y_{12} are multiplied and divided by k, respectively.

Figure 12-19 illustrates some of the networks of the previous sections with the generator impedance (the series-arm resistance) in each case raised to 1,000 ohms.

Frequency Shift. In this transformation the resistance values are unchanged, but all capacitances are divided by a factor k. This has the effect of multiplying all time constants by the constant k so that the location of the zeros and poles is shifted. For example, if the capacitors of Fig. 12-19b are divided by 10^3, the resultant network has the same transfer function as Eq. (12-50) except that the zeros and poles are now located at $s = 4 \times 10^{+3}$, $s = -6 \times 10^{+3}$, $s = -2 \times 10^{+3}$, $s = -8 \times 10^{+3}$.

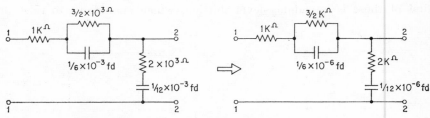

FIG. 12-20. Shifting the frequency scale by a factor of 10^3.

In general impedance-level and frequency shifting may be performed on the same basic network. Thus Fig. 12-20 shows the original network of Fig. 12-19b with the frequency scale and impedance level shifted.

12-7. The Synthesis of Nonladder RC Transfer Functions

In the preceding sections our synthesis procedures were confined to the case of RC ladder-type networks where the zeros and poles of the transfer function were confined to the negative real axis. It is also possible to synthesize minimum-phase-shift (i.e., nonlattice) RC networks if the zeros of the transfer function are allowed to leave the negative real axis, provided that they come in complex conjugate pairs and are restricted to the left-half s plane. In this case simple ladder-type network forms will not be possible, and more complicated networks result.

One simple technique is Guillemin's procedure, which results in a final configuration consisting of the connection of two-terminal pair *ladder networks in parallel.*[1] The parallel connection of two-terminal pair networks is sketched in Fig. 12-21. It can be shown that for this connection the over-all y parameter is given by the sum of the y parameters of the individual networks. Thus

$$y_{11} = y_{11}^{(1)} + y_{11}^{(2)} + \cdots + y_{11}^{(n)} \qquad (12\text{-}70a)$$

$$y_{22} = y_{22}^{(1)} + y_{22}^{(2)} + \cdots + y_{22}^{(n)} \qquad (12\text{-}70b)$$

$$y_{12} = y_{12}^{(1)} + y_{12}^{(2)} + \cdots + y_{12}^{(n)} \qquad (12\text{-}70c)$$

where y_{11}, y_{12}, and y_{22} are the y parameters of the parallel combination

[1] Guillemin, *op. cit.*

and the superscripts in parentheses are used to denote the individual network parameters, respectively.

In order to understand Guillemin's procedure, let us consider that we are given the transfer function $Y_{12}(s)$ as follows:

$$Y_{12}(s) = K \frac{A(s)}{B(s)} = \frac{y_{12}}{1 + y_{22}} \tag{12-71}$$

$A(s)$ and $B(s)$ are again polynomials except that $B(s)$ has its roots

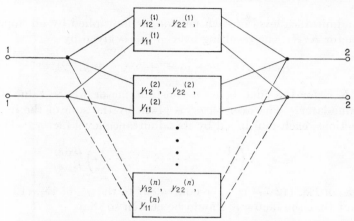

FIG. 12-21. Parallel connection of two-terminal pair networks.

restricted to the negative real axis, whereas $A(s)$ has its roots restricted to the left half plane, including the imaginary axis. Separating $B(s)$ in polynomials $B_1(s)$ and $B_2(s)$ as in the preceding section, we write

$$Y_{12}(s) = \frac{A(s)/B_2(s)}{1 + B_1(s)/B_2(s)} \tag{12-72}$$

$A(s)$ has its roots located throughout the left-half s plane, and it can be written as the sum of individual terms. Thus let us write $A(s)$ in polynomial form,

$$A(s) = a_0 + a_1 s + a_2 s^2 + \cdot\cdot\cdot + a_n s^n \tag{12-73}$$

In terms of Eq. (12-73), Eq. (12-71) can be rewritten as

$$
\begin{aligned}
Y_{12}(s) &= \frac{K[a_0/B_2(s) + a_1 s/B_2(s) + \cdot\cdot\cdot + a_n s^n/B_2(s)]}{1 + B_1(s)/B_2(s)} \\
&= \frac{K(y_{12}{}^{(1)} + y_{12}{}^{(2)} + \cdot\cdot\cdot + y_{12}{}^{(n)})}{1 + y_{22}} \qquad \text{where } y_{12}{}^{(n)} = a_n s^n/B_2(s)
\end{aligned}
\tag{12-74}
$$

From an inspection of Eq. (12-74) it should be obvious that, if we neglect constant multipliers for a moment, Y_{12} can be considered as being made up of the parallel connection of two-terminal pair networks, each having the same $y_{22}(s) = B_1(s)/B_2(s)$ but with respective values of $y_{12}{}^{(1)}, y_{12}{}^{(2)}, \ldots, y_{12}{}^{(n)}$. When synthesized, each one of these two-terminal pair networks is a ladder structure and has its own constant-multiplier gain factor. If we denote these factors by $K_1, K_2, \ldots, K_n$, respectively, then the y_{12} of the parallel combination of these networks is given by

$$y_{12} = K_1 y_{12}{}^{(1)} + K_2 y_{12}{}^{(2)} + \cdots + K_n y_{12}{}^{(n)} \qquad (12\text{-}75)$$

If the admittance level of each network is multiplied by an impedance-level factor K/K_n, the resulting over-all y_{12} is given by

$$y_{12} = K(y_{12}{}^{(1)} + y_{12}{}^{(2)} + \cdots + y_{12}{}^{(n)}) \qquad (12\text{-}76)$$

where K is for the time being a constant factor whose value we shall determine later. The over-all y_{22} is given by the sum of the individual y_{22} functions, each multiplied by its admittance-level factor. Thus

$$y_{22} = K\left(\frac{1}{K_1} + \frac{1}{K_2} + \cdots + \frac{1}{K_n}\right)\frac{B_1(s)}{B_2(s)} \qquad (12\text{-}77)$$

Since y_{22} of Eq. (12-77) is to be equivalent to the y_{22} of Eq. (12-74), it is apparent that the factor K should be chosen so that

$$K\left(\frac{1}{K_1} + \frac{1}{K_2} + \cdots + \frac{1}{K_n}\right) = 1$$

or

$$\frac{1}{K} = \frac{1}{K_1} + \frac{1}{K_2} + \cdots + \frac{1}{K_n} \qquad (12\text{-}78)$$

In order to illustrate the details of Guillemin's synthesis procedure, let us consider a simple example. Let it be required to synthesize the following transfer function:

$$Y_{12} = \frac{K(s^2 + 1)}{2s^2 + 20s + 44} = \frac{KA(s)}{B(s)} \qquad (12\text{-}79)$$

The zeros are located at $s = \pm j$ and the poles at $s = -3.27, -6.73$. As in the previous section, $B(s)$ can be conveniently separated into the sum of two polynomials as follows:

$$B(s) = B_1(s) + B_2(s) = (s + 2)(s + 6) + (s + 4)(s + 8)$$

With $B_1(s)$ and $B_2(s)$ identified it is possible to rewrite Y_{12} as shown, where $B_1(s) = (s + 2)(s + 6)$ and $B_2(s) = (s + 4)(s + 8)$.

$$Y_{12} = \frac{K(s^2 + 1)/[(s + 4)(s + 8)]}{1 + [(s + 2)(s + 6)]/[(s + 4)(s + 8)]} \qquad (12\text{-}80)$$

From Eq. (12-80) it appears that Y_{12} can be synthesized as the parallel combination of two ladder networks with the following y parameters:

$$\text{Network 1:} \quad y_{12}^{(1)} = \frac{K_1 s^2}{(s+4)(s+8)} \qquad y_{22}^{(1)} = \frac{(s+2)(s+6)}{(s+4)(s+8)} \quad (12\text{-}81)$$

$$\text{Network 2:} \quad y_{12}^{(2)} = \frac{K_2}{(s+4)(s+8)} \qquad y_{22}^{(2)} = \frac{(s+2)(s+6)}{(s+4)(s+8)} \quad (12\text{-}82)$$

Starting with network 1, we note that there are two transmission zeros at $s = 0$. In the synthesis of $y_{22}^{(1)}$ these zeros can be provided by a

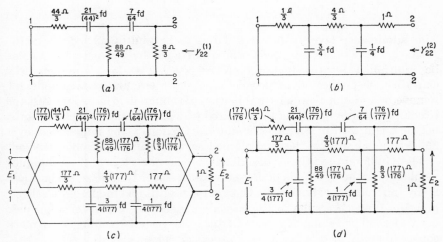

Fig. 12-22. Synthesis of $Y_{12} = \dfrac{K(s^2 + 1)}{s^2 + 20s + 44}$. (a) Network 1; (b) network 2; (c) final network, parallel connection; (d) rearrangement of c.

continued-fraction expansion of $y_{22}^{(1)}$ in terms of a ladder structure with shunt R's and series C's. This particular expansion was carried out in Sec. 12-2, and the resulting network of Fig. 12-6e is redrawn in Fig. 12-22a. It should be noted that the expansion of $y_{22}^{(1)}$ yields the network with terminals 1-1 short-circuited.

Network 2 has the same y_{22} function as network 1 except that there are two transmission zeros called for in $y_{12}^{(2)}$ at $s = \infty$. This means that $y_{22}^{(2)}$ should be expanded in a ladder form with shunt-arm capacitors and series-arm resistors. This expansion was also performed in Sec. 12-2, Fig. 12-6d, and the resultant network with terminals 1-1 short-circuited is redrawn in Fig. 12-22b.

Prior to connecting these networks in parallel, it is necessary to adjust their admittance levels. The gain constant for network 1 can be obtained by checking y_{12} at $s = \infty$. K_1 is given by the short-circuit current through 1-1 when a unit voltage is applied to terminals 2-2 with all capacitors short-circuited. Thus $K_1 = \frac{3}{44}$. Similarly K_2 is determined by evaluating $y_{12}^{(2)}$ at $s = 0$. Using Eq. (12-82) and the network of Fig. 12-22b, we obtain the following:

$$\frac{K_2}{32} = \frac{1}{1 + \frac{4}{3} + \frac{1}{3}}$$

Hence
$$K_2 = 12$$

Using Eq. (12-78), we calculate K,

$$\frac{1}{K} = \frac{1}{12} + \frac{44}{3} = \frac{177}{12}$$

The admittance level of network 1 has to be multiplied by the factor $K/K_1 = \frac{12}{177}\left(\frac{44}{3}\right) = \frac{176}{177}$. Also, the admittance level of network 2 must be multiplied by the factor $K/K_2 = \frac{12}{177}\left(\frac{1}{12}\right) = \frac{1}{177}$. The networks can then be connected in parallel, the short circuits at terminals 1-1 removed, and the parallel combination terminated in a 1-ohm resistor to complete the synthesis of the required transfer function. The resultant network is drawn in Fig. 12-22c and d. Obviously the impedance level and frequency scale of the final parallel network can be shifted as desired.

The Guillemin synthesis described here is one of several techniques available for the synthesis of RC-network transfer functions. The topic is by no means exhausted. One very useful technique is Dasher's procedure, which results in the cascade connection of two-terminal pair networks. The reader is referred to the Suggested Reading for a more complete study of this fascinating aspect of network synthesis.

SUGGESTED READING

Guillemin, E. A.: "Synthesis of Passive Networks," chaps. 4 and 13, John Wiley & Sons, Inc., New York, 1957.
Savant, C. J., Jr.: "Basic Feedback Control System Design," chap. 7, McGraw-Hill Book Company, Inc., New York, 1958.
Storer, J. E.: "Passive Network Synthesis," chaps. 23 and 24, McGraw-Hill Book Company, Inc., New York, 1957.
Truxal, J. G.: "Automatic Feedback Control System Synthesis," chap. 3, McGraw-Hill Book Company, Inc., New York, 1955.

PROBLEMS

12-1. Show that for an RC impedance function $Z(\infty) < Z(0)$.

12-2. Find four canonic forms for the following impedance functions:

(a) $Z(s) = \dfrac{(s + 2)(s + 4)}{(s + 1)(s + 3)}$ (b) $Z(s) = \dfrac{(s + 1)(s + 3)}{s(s + 2)}$ (c) $Z(s) = \dfrac{s + 1}{s(s + 2)}$

12-3. For RC impedance functions show that Re $[Z(j\omega)]$ is a continuously decreasing function of ω and that Re $[Y(j\omega)]$ is a continuously increasing function of ω.

12-4. Find four canonic networks equivalent to the diagram shown in Fig. P12-4.

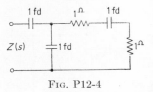

FIG. P12-4

12-5. Determine the z and y parameters for the networks shown in Fig. P12-5a and b.

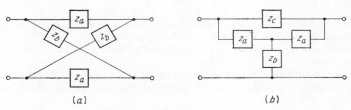

(a) (b)

FIG. P12-5

12-6. Show that the z parameters of a T network are as given by Eq. (12-14). Determine the y parameters of a T network.

12-7. Show that the y parameters of a π network are as given by Eq. (12-17). Determine the z parameters of a π network.

12-8. Prove the general relationships between the z and y parameters as given by Eq. (12-16).

12-9. Prove Eq. (12-20) by applying Thévenin's theorem to the circuit of Fig. 12-10d.

12-10. Prove the generalized form of the transfer function given in the diagram of Fig. 12-10a.

12-11. Synthesize the following transfer functions with RC elements as a voltage-to-voltage transfer function of the form given in Fig. 12-10b:

(a) $T_{12} = K \dfrac{(s + 1)(s + 4)}{(s + 2)(s + 6)}$ $\qquad$ (b) $T_{12} = K \dfrac{s^2}{(s + 2)(s + 6)}$

(c) $T_{12} = K \dfrac{(s + 3)(s + 5)}{(s + 1)(s + 7)}$

Evaluate the gain constant K for each of the networks you have obtained. Check your results by recalculating the transfer function from the network.

12-12. Synthesize the transfer functions of Prob. 12-11 in the form of Z_{12} and Y_{12} as given in Fig. 12-10c and d, respectively.

12-13. Synthesize the following transfer function, using Guillemin's procedure:

$$Y_{12} = \frac{s^2 + 1}{2(s + 1)(s + 2)}$$

12-14. Shift the impedance level of the network found in the foregoing problem so that the terminating resistor is 1,000 ohms instead of 1 ohm.

12-15. Given the network shown in Fig. P12-15.

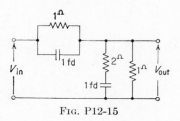

Fig. P12-15

(a) What is the transfer function $\dfrac{V_o}{V_i}(s)$?

(b) Shift the impedance level so that the d-c input impedance is 1 megohm.

(c) Determine V_o when $V_i = u(t)$, a unit-step function.

(d) Shift the frequency scale so that the predominant time constant of the step response is 1 sec.

(e) Draw the log-modulus plot of the transfer function before and after the transformations of parts b and d. How do they differ from the log-modulus plots of the original network?

12-16. The transfer function of a minimum-phase-shift RC network has the log-modulus plot as shown in Fig. P12-16. Find the network. Determine the value of H in decibels for the network you have found.

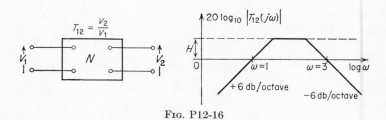

Fig. P12-16

12-17. Given the network shown in Fig. P12-17.

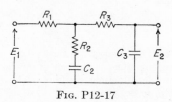

Fig. P12-17

(a) Calculate the transfer function $\dfrac{E_2}{E_1}(s)$.

(b) Show that the networks of Figs. 12-15d and 12-16f have the identical transfer function $\dfrac{E_2}{E_1}(s)$.

12-18. Given the generalized transfer function for a lag-lead characteristic

$$T_{12} = K \frac{(s + z_1)(s + z_2)}{(s + p_1)(s + p_2)}$$

where $p_2 > z_2 > z_1 > p_1$. Show that this transfer function can be synthesized as a voltage ratio as illustrated in Fig. P12-18.   What is the value of K for the network shown?

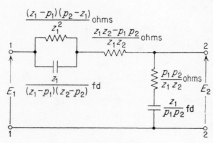

Fig. P12-18

V | Computer Approach

13 | Electronic Analog-computer Techniques

The material of the foregoing chapters is confined entirely to linear systems because it provides the foundation for all subsequent efforts. Now that this objective is accomplished, attention is turned to the analysis and design of systems containing inherent nonlinearities such as saturation, coulomb friction, backlash, and so forth. Basically there are two methods of approaching this problem. One requires that the control engineer learn about the techniques available for treating nonlinear systems such as the describing-function method or the phase-plane method.[1] The second approach makes use of the analog computer as an engineering tool of analysis and design. Effectively the linear as well as the nonlinear elements of the system are simulated, and the solutions are subsequently found by machine methods. The latter approach is more attractive for several reasons. One is that it usually enables the engineer to make a far more comprehensive analysis with considerably less time and effort. Thus, after the problem has been simulated on the analog computer, the solution for the controlled quantity, corresponding to various types of command inputs as well as various combinations of control and system parameters, is obtained with great ease and speed. Moreover, the results are easily interpreted because of the graphical form in which the computer output equipment presents the solutions. This makes it possible then to optimize the values of a nonlinear system's control parameters easily. The corresponding amount of analytical work needed to accomplish the same results is enormous by comparison. A second reason is this: The evaluation of many feedback control systems depends upon the behavior of such systems in the presence of random noise, which exists either as an unwanted quantity or as a system input of a statistical nature. The

[1] J. G. Truxal, "Automatic Feedback Control System Synthesis," chaps. 10 and 11, McGraw-Hill Book Company, Inc., New York, 1955.

electronic analog computer equipped with a suitable random-noise generator can be used to study problems of this kind. Such a procedure is especially valuable if the system is nonlinear, because there is no known general analytical method for treating such cases. For these reasons (as well as others described below) this chapter is devoted to an explanation and description of electronic analog-computer techniques and their application to control systems engineering. However, it should not be construed that this choice in any way belittles the importance of acquiring a solid background in nonlinear analytical techniques. The latter is always useful, especially in applying the analog computer more intelligently. Accordingly the interested reader is encouraged to consult the previously cited reference.

13-1. Classification of Analog Computers

An analog (or a model) of a problem can always be determined if the same equations or set of equations can be used to describe the behavior in the problem as well as in the model. Thus, if the differential equation describing the behavior of a mechanical system containing mass M, spring constant K, and viscous-friction coefficient F is

$$M \frac{d^2x}{dt^2} + F \frac{dx}{dt} + Kx = f \text{ (force)} \tag{13-1}$$

and if the differential equation describing the flow of charge in an RLC electric circuit is

$$L \frac{d^2q}{dt^2} + R \frac{dq}{dt} + \frac{1}{C} q = E \text{ (voltage)} \tag{13-2}$$

then, since the two equations are of the same form, it is possible to build an electrical analog (or model) of the mechanical system. For the analog to be a correct one, it is required that the electrical parameters and variables play precisely the roles called for in the original problem. To accomplish this, it is necessary that self-inductance L be made to take on the role of mass M, R be analogous to F, and $1/C$ be analogous to K. Moreover, the dependent variable x in the original problem is represented by charge q in the analog. Also, the applied force in the mechanical system is represented by a voltage in the electrical model. These results are apparent from a comparison of Eqs. (13-1) and (13-2). Analog computers which are constructed on this principle are called *general-purpose analog computers* of the *direct type.*

A second approach can be employed in solving for the displacement variable of the mechanical system of Eq. (13-1). A study of this equation reveals that the solution can be obtained by interconnecting appropriate equipment capable of performing the mathematical operations called for in Eq. (13-1).   Thus, by making available two computing devices capable of performing integration with respect to time as well as a unit capable of summing, the solution to Eq. (13-1) can be found.   An analog computer built on this principle is called an *indirect-type general-purpose computer*.   It is this type of computer with which this chapter is concerned.   Here all variables are represented as voltages.

Appearing in Fig. 13-1 is a classification of all types of analog computers.   The special-purpose analog computers employ the same basic

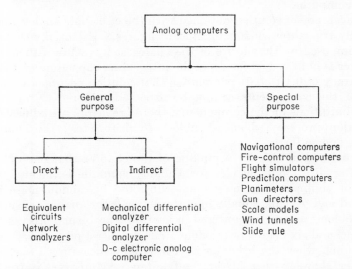

FIG. 13-1. Classification of analog computers.   (*Reprinted by permission from "Analog Computer Techniques" by C. L. Johnson, Copyright 1956, McGraw-Hill Book Co., Inc.*)

principles as those used in the general-purpose units.   The difference is that they are designed to solve a specific set of equations corresponding to specific types of inputs.   In essence, then, they lack flexibility.   They are designed for a special purpose and no other.   The mechanical differential analyzer was the first of the indirect types of general-purpose analog computers built.   It was constructed at MIT by Dr. V. Bush, employing mechanical ball-and-disk integrators.   Although this computer is capable of a fair degree of accuracy, such units are not being built any more because on the one hand they are not as accurate as digital computers and on the other hand they cannot match the ease and speed of operation offered by the d-c electronic analog computer.   With regard to the direct-type general-purpose analog computer it is interesting to note that in 1958 the world's largest computer of this kind was delivered to the Convair Division of General Dynamics Corporation at Fort Worth, Tex.   It measures 29 by 46 by 91 ft and is used to solve complex design problems of high-speed high-altitude aircraft.

Since our attention from this point on is exclusively on the d-c electronic analog computer, it is worthwhile to mention a few additional characteristic features. Because of the method used to obtain integration, time is usually the independent variable. Therefore in this respect the electronic analog computer is different from the digital computer as well as the mechanical differential analyzer because they do not share this restriction. For this reason it should be apparent that the solution of partial differential equations is difficult to achieve on the electronic analog computer.

The accuracy of solution obtained with the electronic analog computer is usually two, three, or four significant figures. Essentially this restriction is imposed by the nature of the analog components with which the computer is built. For example, the integrating capacitors at best have an accuracy of 0.1 to 0.01 per cent so that solution accuracies exceeding those of the components cannot be expected. Moreover, in addition to the limitations of the components, there are errors introduced by the integration process (which is subject to drift, etc.), the summation process, and so forth.

It is pointed out at the beginning of the chapter that one of the big areas of application of the electronic analog computer is the analysis and design of nonlinear control systems subjected to random-noise inputs. A second and perhaps equally important area is the analysis of such complex problems as are encountered in heat-flow problems, process control problems, and six-degree-of-freedom aircraft control problems. In areas of this kind, when the behavior is of a dynamical nature, the electronic computer shows to considerable advantage. Moreover, it frequently offers economy. For example, in the case of the design of an autopilot for a high-performance aircraft it is possible to simulate the flight equations for various altitudes and Mach numbers on the electronic analog computer and then feed the appropriate aircraft output variables to a cockpit installed alongside the computer in the laboratory. In this way, with the pilot in the cockpit, the design can be optimized without incurring the high cost per hour associated with actual flight testing.

The aircraft industry is one of the biggest users of electronic analog computers. One reason for this preference over digital computers, for example, is that frequently the accuracy of the aerodynamic parameters used in the equations of motions is not known to better than 5 or 10 per cent. Accordingly, the limited accuracy of the analog computer is not a drawback, and in fact the analog computer has much to offer in terms of simplicity and ease of operation. Of course in situations where a high degree of precision is needed, as, for example, in computing the trajectory of a long-range guided missile, the digital computer must be preferred.

Another worthwhile feature of the electronic analog computer is illustrated by the following case reported by the Rand Corporation. Several reports were written on the theoretical aspects of applying the calculus of variation to optimizing aircraft flight paths.   However, no conclusions were reached because of the complexity of the equations.   At this point an electronic analog computer was used, and not only were practical answers obtained, but by means of the computer suggested revisions of the theory were verified.

13-2. Basic Computations in D-C Electronic Analog Computers

The electronic analog computer is made up of building blocks capable of performing specific mathematical operations.   In this section attention is directed to the manner in which multiplication, addition, integration, and differentiation are accomplished.

Multiplication by Constant Coefficients.   Very often in analog simulation it is necessary to multiply a machine variable by a constant coefficient.   In those instances where the constant is a number less than unity the multiplication is accomplished by means of a potentiometer, as illustrated in Fig. 13-2.   If it is assumed that there is no loading on the output arm of the potentiometer (that is, $R_L \to \infty$), the output quantity is related to the input by

$$e_o = ae_i \qquad (13\text{-}3)$$

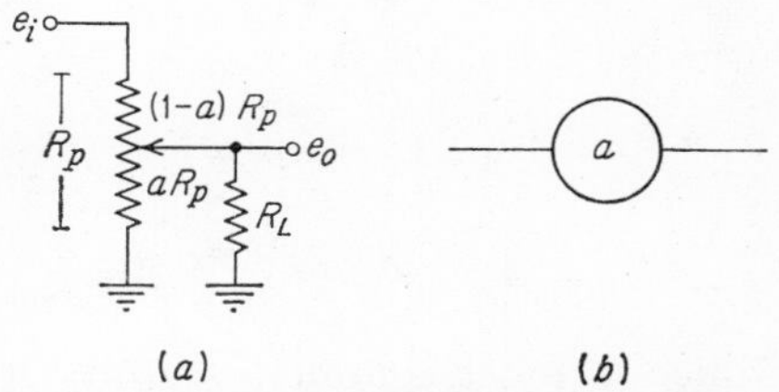

FIG. 13-2. Coefficient setting potentiometer. (*a*) Schematic diagram; (*b*) symbolic diagram.

where a is the slider-arm setting of the potentiometer.   In most of the commercially available computers these potentiometers are designed to make 10 full revolutions and can be set to three places in the range $0.000 \leq a \leq 1.000$.   The total resistance R_p of the potentiometer varies from 10,000 to 100,000 ohms, depending upon the manufacturer. A common value is 30,000 ohms.   In the normal application of these potentiometers the resistor R_L is usually in the range from 0.1 to 1.0 megohm so that the loading effect is not always negligible.   A more exact analysis of the ratio of output to input shows the actual ratio to be

$$\frac{e_0}{e_i} = \frac{a}{1 + a(1 - a)(R_p/R_L)} \qquad (13\text{-}4)$$

where a is the ideal ratio value.   Clearly the ratio error can be kept small by making the value of R_p/R_L small.   The potentiometer resistance R_p cannot be made too small; otherwise it will draw a current in excess of the capacity of the amplifier which supplies it with the input-voltage variable.

In order to multiply a machine variable by a number greater than unity, use is made of the operational amplifier. The operational amplifier is a direct-coupled feedback amplifier having an open-loop gain often in excess of 10^8. It is the basic building block used in most of the computing components of the d-c electronic analog computer. To understand how multiplication by a constant coefficient greater than

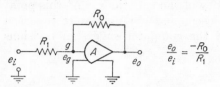

$$\frac{e_o}{e_i} = \frac{-R_0}{R_1}$$

Fig. 13-3. Illustrating multiplication by a constant greater than unity. $R_0 > R_1$.

unity is accomplished, refer to Fig. 13-3. The operational amplifier having a gain A is represented by the symbol ⊳. Applying Kirchhoff's current law to the grid point g and assuming zero grid current permits writing

$$\frac{e_i - e_g}{R_1} + \frac{e_o - e_g}{R_0} = 0 \tag{13-5}$$

But

$$e_o = A e_g \tag{13-6}$$

Inserting Eq. (13-6) into Eq. (13-5) yields

$$\frac{e_o}{e_i} = \frac{A R_0}{R_1[(R_0/R_1) + (1 - A)]} \tag{13-7}$$

Since in most commercial units $A = -10^8$ or more, it follows that Eq. (13-7) may be written as

$$\frac{e_o}{e_1} = -\frac{R_0}{R_1} \tag{13-8}$$

Thus by selecting $R_0 > R_1$ the desired result is accomplished. For $R_0 = 1$ megohm and $R_1 = 0.1$ megohm the output voltage is ten times greater than the input. Furthermore, this multiplication is performed with a precision that is determined by the input and feedback resistors alone. Hence, if 0.1 per cent resistors are used in the arrangement of Fig. 13-3, then multiplication is accomplished with the same degree of precision. A glance at Eq. (13-5) reveals that the result of Eq. (13-8) could be obtained directly by considering the grid to be virtually at ground potential. The use of a feedback circuit round the very high open-loop gain assures this. This same result is obtained by considering that the output voltage is usually limited to 100 volts for linear operation. Therefore for a gain of $A = -10^8$ it follows that e_g must be merely 1 μv above ground to generate the 100-volt output. The grid is accordingly at virtual ground and shall be so considered in all subsequent analysis.

When a machine variable is to be multiplied by a noninteger constant coefficient, as, for example, obtaining $e_o = 3.69e_1$, the arrangement appear-

ing in Fig. 13-4a is used.   By setting the potentiometer for a reading of
0.369 and then multiplying by 10, the desired result is obtained (assuming no potentiometer loading).   Figure 13-4b shows the symbolic diagram
for this mathematical operation.   Note that the high-gain d-c amplifier,
together with the input and feedback resistors, is represented by a triangle
and by the multiplying factor being specifically indicated.

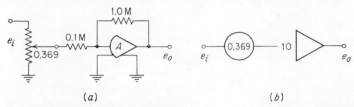

FIG. 13-4. Illustrating multiplication by a noninteger coefficient.   (a) Schematic
diagram; (b) symbolic representation.

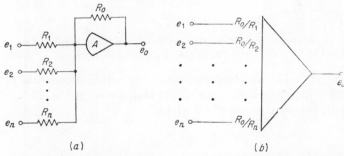

FIG. 13-5. Illustrating the addition of n variables.   (a) Schematic diagram;   (b)
symbolic diagram.

Addition of Several Variables.   The addition of n variables may be performed by the arrangement shown in Fig. 13-5a and b.   Applying Kirchhoff's current law in nodal form at the amplifier grid point and assuming
zero grid voltage gives

$$\frac{e_1}{R_1} + \frac{e_2}{R_2} + \cdots + \frac{e_n}{R_n} = -\frac{e_o}{R_o} \tag{13-9}$$

Therefore, $$e_o = -\left(\frac{R_0}{R_1}e_1 + \frac{R_0}{R_2}e_2 + \cdots + \frac{R_0}{R_n}e_n\right) \tag{13-10}$$

This expression demonstrates that not only is the output the sum of
several variables but each variable may be multiplied by an appropriate
scale factor if desirable.   In the standard electronic analog-computing
equipment manufactured by the Reeves Instrument Company the configuration used for the summing amplifiers is as illustrated in Fig. 13-6.
Note that there are seven input terminals, two of which provide multiplication by 10, two by 4, and three by unity.   With this arrangement,

and by the use of parallel connections of the input variable, the latter can be multiplied by any integer from 1 to 31. Other manufacturers use other arrangements.

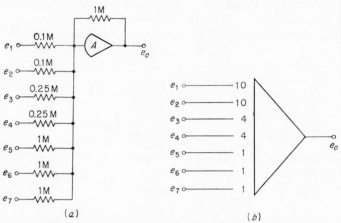

FIG. 13-6. Configuration used in the standard summing amplifier of the REAC (Reeves electronic analog computer). (a) Schematic diagram; (b) symbolic diagram.

Integration. The method for obtaining integration with respect to time in the electronic analog computer is depicted in Fig. 13-7. Writing Kirchhoff's law at the grid point yields

$$\frac{e_1}{R_1} + \frac{e_o}{1/sC} = 0$$

Therefore,

$$\frac{e_o}{e_i} = -\frac{1}{sRC} \tag{13-11}$$

A glance at this result indicates that the transfer function is that of a pure integrator. Accordingly, when Eq. (13-11) is interpreted in the time domain, it states that the output of the circuitry shown in Fig. 13-7

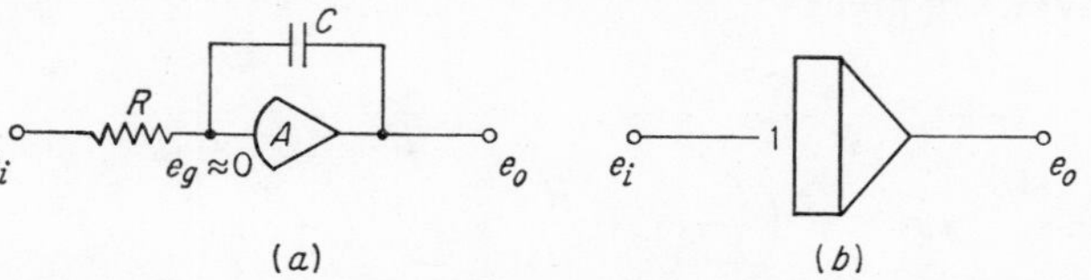

FIG. 13-7. Circuit arrangement for integration. (a) Schematic diagram; (b) symbolic diagram.

is the integral of the input. Moreover, the output may also be modified by the scale factor $1/RC$. It is customary in commercial computers for the feedback capacitor to be fixed at the value of 1 μf and the scaling accomplished by the appropriate selection of R. The standard electronic integrator manufactured by Electronic Associates, Inc., has the configuration shown in Fig. 13-8. Thus multiplication by 1 or 10 may be accomplished if no input potentiometers are used.

Whenever an analog simulation requires integrators, this means that the corresponding physical problem contains energy-storing elements. Consequently, in order for the simulation to be correct, it is necessary at the start of the computer solution of the problem to establish at the output of each integrator that value of voltage which properly represents the initial condition in the original problem. To accomplish this, circuitry similar to that shown in Fig. 13-9 is used. When the master control knob of the analog computer is placed at the so-called *reset* position, switches $S1$, $S2$, and $S3$ are placed at position a. Switch $S1$

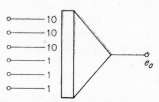

Fig. 13-8. Standard electronic integrator configuration as manufactured by Electronic Associates, Inc.

puts the input terminals to ground, thereby making the simulation inoperative. The switches $S2$ and $S3$ establish a circuit permitting the proper initial-condition voltage to appear across the capacitor. This

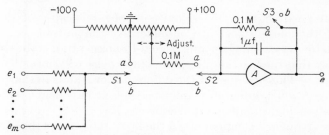

Fig. 13-9. Illustrating how initial conditions are applied to integrators.

voltage is applied to the capacitor in accordance with a time constant of 0.1 sec. When the master control knob is placed at the *compute* position, switches $S1$, $S2$, and $S3$ go to position b in Fig. 13-9. The original simulation is reestablished, and the 0.1-megohm resistor is removed from the capacitor so that it cannot upset the initial-condition voltage.

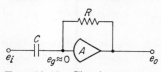

Fig. 13-10. Circuit arrangement for differentiation.

Differentiation. The method for obtaining differentiation in the electronic analog computer is illustrated in Fig. 13-10. Writing Kirchhoff's law at the grid point leads to

$$\frac{e_1}{1/sC} + \frac{e_o}{R} = 0$$

Hence

$$\frac{e_o}{e_i} = -sRC \qquad (13\text{-}12)$$

Inspection of this equation reveals that this transfer function corresponds to that of a pure differentiator in the time domain with a multiplying factor of RC. Thus, if the input signal e_1 is a ramp, then ideally the output signal e_o, as required by Eq. (13-12), should be a step (see Fig. 13-11). The height of the output step clearly depends upon the slope of the input ramp. It is significant to note that, when the input signal to a differentiator contains high-frequency noise (i.e., is not a pure ramp in the example considered), the noise components are amplified

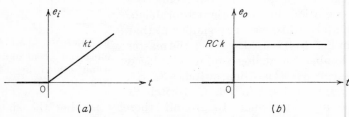

FIG. 13-11. Input and output signals of the differentiator of Fig. 13-10. (a) Input signal; (b) output signal.

to a greater extent than the signal component because of the greater slopes of the noise signals. Consequently, the output signal of the differentiator has a much poorer signal-to-noise ratio. Moreover, it is quite likely that the high amplification of the noise will cause the amplifier to overload. This behavior of the differentiator stands in sharp contrast to the way in which integrators influence noise components. Since noise is generally a high-frequency phenomena, Eq. (13-11) reveals that the higher the frequency components in the noise the greater the attenuation caused by the integrator. This is the frequency-domain viewpoint. In terms of the time domain it is apparent that since integration is an averaging process, the integrator exerts a smoothing effect on the input signal, thus furnishing an output signal with an improved signal-to-noise ratio. Chiefly for these reasons, then, the electronic analog computer provides solutions to problems by performing successive operations of integration rather than of differentiation.

"Impure" Integration and "Impure" Differentiation. Often in the computer study of physical problems, especially in control systems engineering, it is necessary to simulate such important items as proportional plus integral operations, proportional plus derivative operations, simple time lags, quadratic transfer functions, and so forth. The manner of accomplishing this is straightforward. It requires merely a recognition of the fact that in general the output is related to the input in the configuration of Fig. 13-12 by

$$\frac{e_o}{e_i} = -\frac{Z_0}{Z_1} \tag{13-13}$$

where Z_0 and Z_1 are, respectively, the feedback and input impedance functions, which need not be restricted to resistors or capacitors but may be varied combinations of these. Consider, for example, the situation where Z_0 is a parallel combination of a resistor and a capacitor. Then the impedance of the parallel combination is

$$Z_0 = \frac{R_0}{1 + sR_0C_0} \qquad (13\text{-}14)$$

If the input impedance is also made a parallel combination of R_1 and C_1, it follows that

$$Z_1 = \frac{R_1}{1 + sR_1C_1} \qquad (13\text{-}15)$$

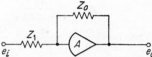

Fig. 13-12. Operational amplifier with general input and feedback impedances.

Inserting the last two equations into Eq. (13-13) yields

$$\frac{e_o}{e_i}(s) = -\frac{R_0}{R_1}\frac{1 + sR_1C_1}{1 + sR_0C_0} \qquad (13\text{-}16)$$

Examination of this result makes it apparent that the standard lead and lag networks discussed in Chaps. 5 and 9 can readily be simulated by such a configuration. Table 13-1 shows some of the more commonly used forms. Note that for case 1 the simulation of a proportional plus derivative operation can be had by removing the feedback capacitor C_0. On the other hand the removal of the input capacitor C_1 instead furnishes a means of simulating a simple time lag.

13-3. Simulation Procedures. Differential-equation Approach. Magnitude Scale Factors

How are the basic mathematical building blocks which are described in the preceding section combined to solve problems? The answer to this question is illustrated by applying the required techniques to the solution of a linear second-order differential equation. In the process of developing the simulation diagram, it becomes necessary to discuss the very important topics of magnitude scaling and time scaling. Although the treatment of these topics is in connection with a linear system, the techniques are applicable in general.

Assume that the behavior of a control system is described by the differential equation

$$\ddot{y} + 5\dot{y} + 100y = f \qquad (13\text{-}17)$$

where f is the forcing function and y the controlled variable. Let it be desired that the dynamic behavior is to be studied on an electronic analog computer. The simulation is to be such that it allows a study to be made of the complete time history of the controlled variable as

TABLE 13-1. SIMULATION OF COMPLEX FUNCTIONS

Case 1:

$$Z_0 = \frac{R_0}{1 + sR_0C_0}$$

$$Z_1 = \frac{R_1}{1 + sR_1C_1}$$

Therefore $\dfrac{e_o}{e_i} = -\dfrac{Z_0}{Z_1} = -\dfrac{R_0}{R_1}\dfrac{1 + sR_1C_1}{1 + sR_0C_0}$

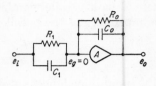

Subcase 1a—C_0 removed:

Therefore $\dfrac{e_o}{e_i} = -\dfrac{R_0}{R_1}(1 + sR_1C_1)$

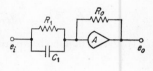

Subcase 1b—C_1 removed:

Therefore $\dfrac{e_o}{e_i} = -\dfrac{R_0}{R_1}\dfrac{1}{1 + sR_0C_0}$

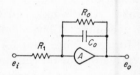

Case 2:

$$Z_0 = R_0 + \frac{1}{sC_0} = \frac{1 + sR_0C_0}{sC_0}$$

$$Z_1 = \frac{R_1}{1 + sR_1C_1}$$

Therefore

$$\frac{e_o}{e_i} = -\frac{Z_0}{Z_1} = -\frac{(1 + sR_1C_1)(1 + sR_0C_0)}{sR_1C_0}$$

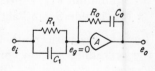

Subcase 2a—R_0 removed:

$$\frac{e_o}{e_i} = -\frac{1 + sR_1C_1}{sR_1C_0}$$

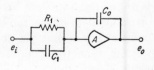

Subcase 2b—C_1 removed:

$$\frac{e_o}{e_i} = -\frac{1 + sR_0C_0}{sR_1C_0}$$

TABLE 13-1. SIMULATION OF COMPLEX FUNCTIONS (*Continued*)

Case 3:

$$Z_0 = R_0 + \frac{1}{sC_0} = \frac{1 + sR_0C_0}{sC_0}$$

$$Z_1 = R_1 + \frac{1}{sC_1} = \frac{1 + sR_1C_1}{sC_1}$$

Therefore $\dfrac{e_o}{e_i} = -\dfrac{Z_0}{Z_1} = -\dfrac{C_1}{C_0}\dfrac{1 + sR_0C_0}{1 + sR_1C_1}$

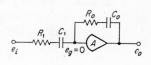

Subcase 3a—R_0 removed:

Therefore $\dfrac{e_o}{e_i} = -\dfrac{C_1}{C_0}\dfrac{1}{1 + sR_1C_1}$

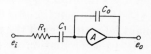

Subcase 3b—R_1 removed:

$$\frac{e_o}{e_i} = -\frac{C_1}{C_0}(1 + sR_0C_0)$$

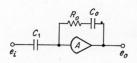

Case 4:

$$Z_0 = \frac{R_0}{1 + sR_0C_0}$$

$$Z_1 = \frac{1 + sR_1C_1}{sC_1}$$

Therefore

$$\frac{e_o}{e_i} = -\frac{Z_0}{Z_1} = -\frac{sR_0C_1}{(1 + sR_0C_0)(1 + sR_1C_1)}$$

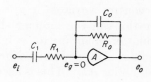

Subcase 4a—C_0 removed:

$$\frac{e_o}{e_i} = -\frac{sR_0C_1}{1 + sR_1C_1}$$

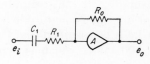

Subcase 4b—R_1 removed:

$$\frac{e_o}{e_i} = -\frac{sR_0C_1}{1 + sR_0C_0}$$

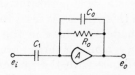

well as its velocity and acceleration as it responds to various types and magnitudes of the forcing function. Also, assume for the purpose of illustration that the maximum value of f is 200 units of forcing function and that all initial conditions are zero.

The first step in simulating Eq. (13-17) is to isolate the highest derivative term on one side of the equation. Thus,

$$\ddot{y} = f - 5\dot{y} - 100y \tag{13-18}$$

This is required in view of the fact that it is desirable to use only integrators to obtain the solution because of the reasons previously cited. Hence by summing and then performing two successive integrations of Eq. (13-18) the solution for the dependent variable is obtained. For the moment let us disregard the need for magnitude-scale factors and proceed directly to a simulation of the last equation. If attention is confined solely to the operations called for in Eq. (13-18), it should be clear that to obtain the second derivative quantity $\ddot{y}$ requires summing f, $-5\dot{y}$, and $-100y$. This can be done by means of a summing amplifier, provided that $\dot{y}$ and y are available. Actually, the latter quantities are made available through feedback connections as they are generated in the analog simulation. Of course the forcing function f is available, since it is the known input quantity. The result of the summation of these quantities yields $-\ddot{y}$, as depicted in Fig. 13-13a. The negative sign is due to the phase reversal of the operational amplifier. Integration of $-\ddot{y}$ yields $\dot{y}$, as illustrated in Fig. 13-13b. A second integration yields the control variable $-y$, as shown in Fig. 13-13c. Combining these operations in the manner shown in Fig. 13-13d furnishes the complete simulation diagram for solving Eq. (13-17). Note that the output of amplifier $A2$ needs to be reversed before it can be applied as an input at amplifier $A1$. This is accomplished by means of the inverter amplifier $A4$.

Although Fig. 13-13d is a correct mathematical simulation of Eq. (13-17), it does not necessarily follow that the correct solution can be measured with this simulation. An incorrect solution comes about when improper magnitude scaling is used in the problem. To illustrate this, let it be assumed that the useful operating range of the d-c amplifiers is ± 100 volts, which is typical of most commercial electronic analog-computing equipment. Clearly, then, if f has a maximum value of 200 units, this quantity at best can be represented by 100 volts. Thus, there is a scale factor for this simulation of $\frac{1}{2}$ volt/unit forcing function. Once this scheme is used to represent f as a voltage and no modifications are made anywhere in the circuitry of Fig. 13-13d, it follows that each of the remaining three variables, viz., $\ddot{y}$, $\dot{y}$, and y, are to be interpreted in accordance with the same scale factor. Thus, in looking at the output of amplifier $A3$ in units of volts, the corresponding value of the physical variable is found by dividing the measured output voltage of $A3$ by $\frac{1}{2}$ volt/unit y. Here then lies the difficulty with Fig. 13-13d. When f has its maximum value of 200 units (assume f to be a step input), Eq. (13-17) shows that the steady-state value of the controlled variable is

$$y_{\max} = \frac{f_{\max}}{100} = \frac{200}{100} = 2$$

Now, because the scale factor for the simulation diagram was chosen to be

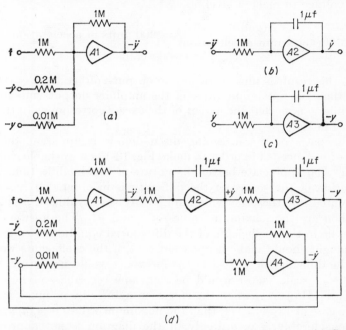

FIG. 13-13. Simulation procedure for a linear second-order system. (a) Summation to obtain acceleration quantity; (b) integration of acceleration to obtain velocity; (c) integration of velocity to obtain the controlled variable; (d) complete simulation diagram.

$\frac{1}{2}$ volt per variable, it follows that the maximum steady-state voltage level appearing at amplifier $A3$ is 1 volt. Yet the full dynamic voltage range of the amplifier is 100 volts. This is indeed a case of poor magnitude scaling, which is very likely to lead to serious errors in the measurement of the quantity y. In fact, when f is not at its maximum value, the output of $A3$ will be less than 1 volt, which practically puts the reading of $A3$ in the amplifier noise region, thereby affording very poor accuracy.

This line of reasoning is likely to prompt one to suggest using as the scale factor for the circuit a value which will allow $A3$ to operate at a maximum level of 100 volts. Proceeding in this manner leads to another serious difficulty. Although the conditions at the output of $A3$ are apparently improved, this is not the case at the remaining amplifiers in the simulation. Operating with a scale factor of 50 volts/variable, which is selected to make full use of the output voltage range of $A3$, calls for a highly excessive voltage at $A1$ if the maximum acceleration of 200 units is to be realized. Equation (13-17) reveals that, if f is given a maximum value of 200 units, the maximum acceleration is also 200 units. However, for the output of $A1$ to represent correctly this physical quantity in terms of a scale factor of 50 volts/variable, it is necessary for the output voltage to reach a level of

$$\frac{e_{A1}(\text{volts})}{50(\text{volts/unit acceleration})} = 200 \text{ units of acceleration}$$

or $$e_{A1} = 10{,}000 \text{ volts}$$

Clearly, this result is unrealistic. The output-voltage level is 100 times greater than the maximum value of the amplifier output voltage. It is worthwhile to note that the extent of the excess corresponds to the coefficient of y in Eq. (13-17).

On the basis of the foregoing discussion it is apparent that some modification is needed in order to make Fig. 13-13d a workable simulation diagram. To appreciate better the nature of this modification, a closer examination of the source of the difficulty is in order. It has already been pointed out that the maximum steady-state value of y is 2 units. What then are the maximum values of $\dot{y}$ and $\ddot{y}$? The answers to this question lie in the coefficients of the differential equation of concern. A little thought should make it apparent that, if the coefficients were each unity, the difficulty described in the foregoing would not occur, because the value of scale factor would be the same regardless of how it was arrived at. However, when the coefficients differ by as much as 100:1, as in the case of Eq. (13-17), then the maximum values of y, $\dot{y}$, and $\ddot{y}$ can differ considerably. Accordingly, if the diagram is not appropriately modified to reflect this situation, the simulation is not a very useful one. An estimate of the maximum value of $\dot{y}$ can be obtained by reasoning in terms of the differences in values of y, $\dot{y}$, and $\ddot{y}$ when the system of Eq. (13-17) responds to a command. Clearly this information is available from the solution to the characteristic equation. Upon using the s notation for derivatives, it follows that for Eq. (13-17) the characteristic equation is

$$s^2 + 5s + 100 = 0 \tag{13-19}$$

Since the general form of the characteristic equation of second-order linear systems is

$$s^2 + 2\zeta\omega_n s + \omega_n{}^2 = 0 \tag{13-20}$$

it is apparent that for the case at hand

$$\omega_n = 10 \text{ radians/sec}$$

Furthermore, the complementary solution is given by

$$y_c = k\epsilon^{-\zeta\omega_n t} \sin(\omega_d t + \phi) \tag{13-21}$$

Inspection of Eq. (13-21) reveals that, in the worst case (that is, $\zeta = 0$), the first derivative quantity $\dot{y}_c$ can have a maximum value which is ω_n times as large as that of y_c. Similarly, the second derivative $\ddot{y}_c$ can have a maximum value $\omega_n{}^2$ times as large as that of y_c. Of course, when $\omega_n = 1$ radian/sec, the maximum values of all three quantities are the same and so no scaling difficulty arises. However, when ω_n is 10 radians/sec, then a definite problem exists because the second derivative quantity has a maximum value 100 times greater than that of the controlled variable. If the same reference voltage is to represent the maximum value of each variable, then the magnitude-scale factors cannot be chosen equal. Rather the scale factors should be chosen to reflect this difference.

One convenient way to accomplish this is to introduce modified machine variables which bear out the difference in scale factors. Thus, if it is known (or estimated) that the maximum steady-state value of y is 2 units, the modified machine variable for y becomes

$$\frac{y}{y_{\max}} 50 \text{ (volts)} = y\left(\frac{50 \text{ volts}}{2 \text{ units of } y}\right) = 25y \qquad \text{volts} \tag{13-22}$$

Note that 50 volts rather than the maximum available 100 volts is used. The reason is to allow enough margin so that even if y undergoes a 100 per cent overshoot during the transient state the operational amplifiers will not exceed the 100-volt limit. Note, too, that the modified machine variable $25y$ carries a number which is in reality the scale factor for the physical variable y. Proceeding in like manner, the modified machine variables for velocity and acceleration become

$$\dot{y} \text{ (units of velocity)} \frac{50}{\dot{y}_{\max}}\left(\frac{\text{volts}}{\text{units of velocity}}\right) = \dot{y}\frac{50}{10(2)} = 2.5\dot{y} \qquad \text{volts} \tag{13-23a}$$

$$\ddot{y} \text{ (units of acceleration)} \frac{50}{\ddot{y}_{\max}}\left(\frac{\text{volts}}{\text{units of acceleration}}\right) = \ddot{y}\frac{50}{100(2)}$$
$$= \tfrac{1}{4}\ddot{y} \qquad \text{volts} \tag{13-23b}$$

In order to simulate the physical problem [described by Eq. (13-17)] in a manner consistent with the modified variables, the procedure is as follows: First, manipulate Eq. (13-17) in such a way that it brings into evidence the modified machine variable $\tfrac{1}{4}\ddot{y}$. Clearly this requires multiplying each term by $\tfrac{1}{4}$. Thus,

$$\tfrac{1}{4}\ddot{y} + \tfrac{5}{4}\dot{y} + 25y = \frac{f}{4} \tag{13-24}$$

It is desirable, too, at this point to manipulate the coefficients of the other variables so that the modified form of the variable appears. Hence Eq. (13-24) becomes

$$\tfrac{1}{4}\ddot{y} + \frac{1}{2}(2.5\dot{y}) + 25y = \frac{f}{4} \qquad (13\text{-}25)$$

The simulation of the summation indicated in this equation to yield acceleration is depicted in Fig. 13-14a. Note that the modified machine

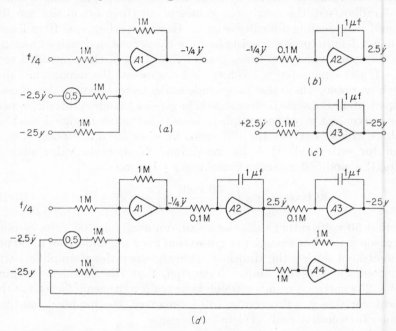

FIG. 13-14. Simulation procedure for a linear second-order system using proper scale factors. (a) Summation to obtain acceleration; (b) integration of acceleration voltage with scale-factor adjustment to obtain velocity; (c) integration of velocity voltage with scale-factor adjustment to obtain controlled variable; (d) complete simulation diagram.

variable representing velocity is multiplied by $\tfrac{1}{2}$, as called for by Eq. (13-25). When f has its maximum value of 200 units, this is represented in the simulation by a voltage of 50 volts.

The integration of the modified form of the machine variable (output of $A1$) representing acceleration must be done in such a way that the modified form of the velocity appears. Clearly, this requires that the integrator also introduce a scale factor change of 10:1-as illustrated in Fig. 13-14b. Of course the significance of such a procedure is that both amplifiers $A1$ and $A2$ are capable of employing the full dynamic range from -100 to $+100$ volts in providing the solution of the variable involved. A similar procedure is followed to get y. This is depicted in

Fig. 13-14c.   The complete simulation diagram appears in Fig. 13-14d. By the selection of appropriate scale factors a simulation diagram can be developed which not only simulates the given physical equation but does so in a fashion which allows each amplifier to operate over its full dynamic range.   Figure 13-14d is a useful simulation diagram because the computing amplifiers are not subjected to overloads or to low voltage levels. Figure 13-15 is the symbolic representation of Fig. 13-14d.

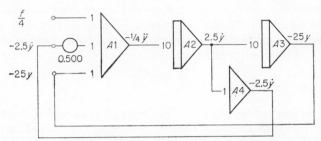

FIG. 13-15. Symbolic representation of Fig. 13-14d.

The presence of the scale factors in the simulating diagram also serves as a convenience in interpreting the meaning of the output voltages of the individual amplifiers.   Thus, if at a particular time the output of $A2$ is found to be 37.5 volts, the corresponding value of the physical quantity is readily obtained by noting that

$$2.5\dot{y} = 37.5 \text{ volts}$$

from which it follows that the physical quantity, namely, velocity, has the value $\dot{y} = 37.5/2.5 = 15$ units of velocity.

13-4. Time Scaling

The dynamic behavior of a system containing energy-storing elements is determined by the roots of the characteristic equation.   Whether or not velocity or acceleration terms will have excessive values depends upon the magnitude of the complex conjugate roots.   Thus, if the natural frequency of these roots is large, there is need for magnitude scaling. On the other hand, if the natural frequency of the predominant complex conjugate roots of a system has a natural frequency of 1 radian/sec (or thereabouts), magnitude scaling is unnecessary because the scale factor for the controlled variable as well as its first- and higher-order derivatives are the same.   In situations where large natural frequencies are known to exist, therefore, it is reasonable to ask whether or not it is possible to introduce an appropriate time-scale change so that the system behaves as if the natural frequency were 1 radian/sec.   To pursue this thought, let us return to Eq. (13-17), which is repeated here for convenience as

$$\frac{d^2y}{dt^2} + 5\frac{dy}{dt} + 100y = f \qquad (13\text{-}26)$$

The rate of change symbol d/dt refers to the rate at which changes take place in the physical problem with respect to time. However, in the simulation of this problem there is no reason why the time required for the controlled variable to respond to commands and disturbances cannot be slowed down or speeded up as long as the functional relationship called for in Eq. (13-26) is satisfied. Thus, it should be possible to take 10 sec of machine time to accomplish what takes 1 sec in the physical problem. Mathematically expressed, we have

$$\frac{d}{dt} = \alpha_t \frac{d}{d\tau} \qquad (13\text{-}27)$$

where α_t represents the desired time-scale change and $d/d\tau$ denotes the rate of change with respect to machine time as contrasted to the rate of change with respect to problem time d/dt. By choosing $\alpha_t = 10$ the rates of change in the analog-computer machine must be one-tenth the rates which occur in the physical problem; i.e., it computes on a sloweddown basis. Inserting the equality expressed in the last equation into Eq. (13-26) yields

$$\alpha_t{}^2 \frac{d^2y}{d\tau^2} + 5\alpha_t \frac{dy}{d\tau} + 100y = f = 200$$

or

$$\frac{d^2y}{d\tau^2} + \frac{5}{\alpha_t}\frac{dy}{d\tau} + \frac{100}{\alpha_t{}^2}y = \frac{200}{\alpha_t{}^2} \qquad (13\text{-}28)$$

A glance at Eq. (13-28) makes it apparent that the selection of α_t equal to 10 makes the computer solution behave in terms of a natural frequency of 1 radian/sec. Hence the magnitude-scale factors for the controlled variable and its first and second derivatives may be the same. By using the dot notation for derivatives as well as the capital letter for the controlled variable and for derivatives with respect to machine time τ in order to emphasize the associated time-scale change, Eq. (13-28) may be written as

$$\ddot{Y} + \tfrac{1}{2}\dot{Y} + Y = 2 \qquad (13\text{-}29)$$

Since the maximum value of Y is not influenced by the time-scale change, the scale factor for the simulation of Eq. (13-29) is chosen to be that of the controlled variable. As given by Eq. (13-22), this has the value of 25 volts/variable. Before proceeding with a simulation of Eq. (13-29), it is desirable to convert it to a computer equation (expressed in volts) by multiplying each term by the common-scale factor 25 volts/variable. Thus Eq. (13-29) becomes

$$25\ddot{Y} + \tfrac{1}{2}(25\dot{Y}) + 25Y = 50 \text{ volts} \qquad (13\text{-}30)$$

The simulation of this equation in symbolic notation appears in Fig. 13-16.

A comparison of Figs. 13-13d, 13-14d, and 13-16 reveals an interesting result.   In Fig. 13-13d note that the loop-gain factor in the y loop is 100 and that in the $\dot{y}$ loop is 5.   These results are consistent with the values of the coefficients of y and $\dot{y}$, as called for in Eq. (13-17).   An examination of Fig. 13-14d indicates that the use of proper magnitude-scale factors in no way alters the total value of these loop gains.   What has happened is that the total gain no longer is put at a single amplifier but rather is distributed throughout the loop in a fashion to assure full

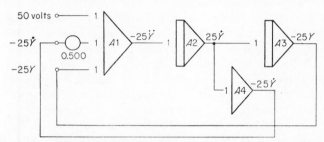

Fig. 13-16. Simulation diagram for the solution of Eq. (13-26).   The machine solution is ten times slower than solution in the physical problem.

use of the amplifiers' dynamic voltage range.   However, the situation is decidedly different in the case of Fig. 13-16.   Here the loop gain for the controlled variable is now 1 as compared with 100 for Figs. 13-13d and 13-14d.   Also, the loop gain for the first derivative quantity is 0.5 compared with 5.   Thus it is apparent that the introduction of *time scaling changes the loop gains*.   This is clearly borne out by Eq. (13-29), which reveals that the coefficient of the Y and $\dot{Y}$ terms are, respectively, 1 and $\frac{1}{2}$.   It is important to keep in mind, too, that Eq. (13-29) is still a physical equation whose proportional gain (or spring constant) has been reduced by a factor of 100.   The application of the appropriate scale factor to this equation then yields the computer version of the equation expressed in volts.   The solutions which are obtained from the electronic analog computer are of course solutions to Eq. (13-29).   To make these solutions applicable to the original problem, one merely needs to introduce the appropriate modification in the time axis.   Thus in the case where the solution is slowed down by a factor of 10, a recorded computer solution which yields $\dot{Y}$ equal to 1 in./sec machine time actually corresponds to $\dot{y} = \alpha_t \dot{Y} = 10(1)$ in./sec of problem time.

Another interesting conclusion which comes from a comparison of Figs. 13-14d and 13-16 is that the time-scale change appearing in Fig. 13-16 is effectively accomplished by increasing the time constant of both integrators of Fig. 13-14d by the time-scale factor α_t.   In fact this is a rule which can be applied in general: *To change the time scale of a given simulation merely requires that all integrator time constants be changed by the same factor.* If α_t is chosen greater than unity, the computer solution is slower than in the physical problem. Conversely, if α_t is chosen less than unity, the computer takes less time to generate the solution than is required in the physical problem.

Although one of the most important factors responsible for introducing a time-scale change is the need to avoid high loop gains, there are other good reasons for doing this. One concerns the limited bandwidth of the galvanometer-type oscillographic recorders which are used to measure the magnitudes of the problem variables. The majority of these units have a bandwidth of 100 cps; some have a bandwidth of 300 cps. Accordingly, if a situation arises which calls for frequencies in excess of 300 cps, time scaling is a necessity if accuracy is to be preserved. Servo-driven vari-plotters and the use of servomultipliers in the total simulation impose similar restrictions. Another factor which influences the need for time scaling is the limit on the available maximum recorder speed. If the problem solution occurs at a speed far in excess of the maximum recorder speed, the time scale will be so compressed as to make it impossible to read the galvanometer oscillographic recordings with any degree of suitable accuracy.

13-5. Simulation Procedures. Transfer-function Approach

Often the mathematical description of a physical problem is given in terms of the transfer functions of the components rather than a set of differential equations. This occurs frequently in the area of control systems engineering. In fact sometimes the output-input relationship cannot be expressed by an appropriate differential equation of a component. Instead, on the basis of measured attenuation and phase vs. frequency characteristics, it becomes necessary for an equivalent transfer function to be written for the component. Now, although it is true that once the transfer function is available the corresponding differential equation can be written, it is usually unnecessary to do this because the simulation diagram can be arrived at directly. For the sake of illustration, assume that the open-loop transfer function of a feedback control system is given by

$$\frac{C}{E}(s) = G(s) = \frac{K}{s(1 + s)(1 + s\tau_1)} \tag{13-31}$$

and that it is desirable to investigate[1] with the computer the effect on the

---

[1] Again it is pointed out that a computer is really not needed for this purpose, because the available analytical techniques are adequate. However, if there were a nonlinearity such as backlash in the feedback path, then indeed the computer would show to advantage.

dynamic performance of varying the loop gain K and the time constant τ_1. Since the transfer function is given in factored form, the simulation is readily determined by making use of the configurations discussed in Sec. 13-1 for performing the operations called for in Eq. (13-31). Note that building blocks are needed which can provide a pure integration and two simple lags. The simulation diagram of Eq. (13-31) appears in Fig. 13-17a. Amplifier $A1$ furnishes the required 1-sec time constant. The circuitry associated with $A2$ makes available the variation in the

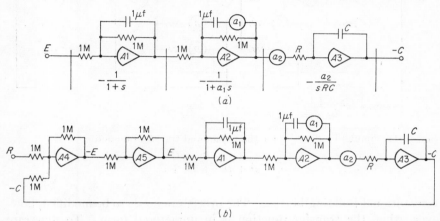

FIG. 13-17. Simulation of a closed-loop system starting from the open-loop transfer function. (a) Simulation of the open-loop transfer function of Eq. (13-31); (b) simulation of the closed-loop system of (a).

time constant τ_1. The arrangement shown allows τ_1 to be varied between zero and 1 sec. If greater values of τ_1 are needed, the feedback resistor must be changed to a larger value. The circuitry associated with $A3$ furnishes integration as well as the variable gain feature called for.

Since the purpose of this computer study is to establish information concerning the dynamic behavior of the closed-loop system, it is necessary to provide the configuration of Fig. 13-17a with a feedback connection. The result is shown in Fig. 13-17b. Note that the output of $A3$, which is $-C$, is summed with the command signal at $A4$ to yield the negative of the actuating signal. However, since $A1$ calls for $+E$, it follows that an additional inverter amplifier is needed. This is shown as $A5$ in Fig. 13-17b.

When the simulation diagram of a transfer function is developed in the foregoing manner, it is important to understand that all initial conditions are assumed equal to zero and that the magnitude-scale factors for the controlled variable and its derivatives are assumed equal. Of course, depending upon the natural frequency of the predominant complex roots of the characteristic equation, this procedure could lead to amplifier overloading. If this should happen, one remedy is to change all time con-

stants by an appropriate time-scale factor. The matter of initial conditions is not important here if the investigation is concerned chiefly
with a study of dynamic behavior.

The simulation of a transfer function when it is expressed in factored
form is easily accomplished because it usually requires a cascading of

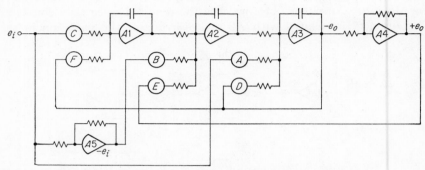

Fig. 13-18. Simulation diagram for the unfactored transfer function

$$\frac{e_o}{e_i} = \frac{As^2 + Bs + C}{s^3 + Ds^2 + Es + F}$$

conventional building blocks. The procedure needs to be modified, however, when the transfer function is in unfactored form. To illustrate
this, consider the simulation of the transfer function given by

$$\frac{e_o}{e_i} = \frac{As^2 + Bs + C}{s^3 + Ds^2 + Es + F} \tag{13-32}$$

In situations of this sort one should not solve for the highest-order
derivative and then proceed to simulate in the usual manner. To
appreciate better why this procedure should be avoided, let us solve
for the highest-order derivative. Thus,

$$s^3e_o = As^2e_i + Bse_i + Ce_i - Ds^2e_o - Ese_o - Fe_o \tag{13-33}$$

A glance at this result makes the reason apparent: it requires that the
input quantity be differentiated twice.

The need for this differentiation can be eliminated by dividing both
sides of Eq. (13-33) by s^2. Hence

$$se_o = (Ae_i - De_o) + \frac{1}{s}(Be_i - Ee_o) + \frac{1}{s^2}(Ce_i - Fe_o) \tag{13-34}$$

The rearrangement of the terms into the form shown is done in order to
avoid the overloading which would otherwise occur at those amplifiers
where the first and second integrals of the input signal are generated.
The final simulation diagram of Eq. (13-34) appears in Fig. 13-18.

13-6. Multiplication and Division of Variables

The electronic analog computer shows to considerable advantage in solving nonlinear problems as well as linear problems having time-varying coefficients. It possesses this capability by virtue of equipment which enables the multiplication and the division of variables to be performed conveniently and accurately. It also possesses this capability because it contains components which allow it to generate many types of non-linearities. The latter is the subject matter of the next section. This

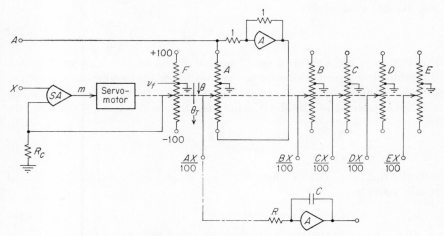

Fig. 13-19. Schematic diagram of a servomultiplier.

section is confined to a brief treatment of how multiplication and division of variables is accomplished.

One of the most commonly used methods for obtaining the product of two variables is the servomultiplier. The circuit arrangement is shown in Fig. 13-19. Usually it is equipped with six potentiometers. Five of these, viz., A through E, are used for multiplication; the sixth one is used as a feedback potentiometer. To understand the operation of this circuit, consider that two variables A and X are applied to the servomultiplier as shown in Fig. 13-19. Corresponding to a specific magnitude of X, there are fed back and summed at the servoamplifier (SA) both X and V_f, where the latter quantity denotes the voltage picked off the feedback potentiometer F. The servoamplifier output can be expressed as

$$(X - V_f)\mu = m \tag{13-35}$$

Here μ is the servoamplifier gain, and the negative sign denotes negative feedback. Since μ is very large, it follows that

$$X = V_f \tag{13-36}$$

Moreover, for a linear feedback potentiometer the magnitude of V_f may be expressed as

$$V_f = \frac{\theta}{\theta_T}(100) \tag{13-37}$$

where θ is the displacement of the slider arm of the potentiometer on which appears the feedback voltage and θ_T is the total travel from the center tap to either end of the potentiometer. The reference voltage applied to the feedback potentiometer is -100 volts at one end and $+100$ volts at the other end. Rearranging Eq. (13-37) and inserting Eq. (13-36) then yields

$$\frac{\theta}{\theta_T} = \frac{V_f}{100} = \frac{X}{100} \tag{13-38}$$

Furthermore, for a given displacement θ of the feedback potentiometer, the multiplying potentiometer undergoes the same displacement because each is ganged to the common servomotor shaft. Accordingly, the voltage appearing on the slider arm of the first multiplying potentiometer is

$$e_{OA} = \frac{\theta}{\theta_T}A \tag{13-39}$$

Substituting Eq. (13-38) into the last equation furnishes the desired result, namely,

$$e_{OA} = \frac{AX}{100} \tag{13-40}$$

The form of Eq. (13-40) is such as to avoid any amplifier-overloading difficulty. Thus, if the variables A and X are supplied to the servo-multiplier with proper magnitude scaling, that is, $A_{max} = 100$ volts and $X_{max} = 100$ volts, then clearly the output voltage will not exceed 100 volts even though both variables may be at their maximum values at the same time. The equation for the output of each of the remaining multiplying potentiometers is, of course, the same as Eq. (13-40) with the one modification that the variable A is replaced by B, or C, or D, or E. It is apparent, then, that with the arrangement of Fig. 13-19 it is possible to obtain computer voltage signals which provide the product of one variable (X) by each of five other variables (A,B,C,D,E).

Before leaving Fig. 13-19, two additional items are worth noting. The first concerns the use of an operational amplifier placed between the ends of the first multiplying potentiometer A. It is included in order to allow four-quadrant multiplication. Thus, Eq. (13-40) gives a correct description of the output quantity irrespective of the combination of signs used for A and X. The second item refers to the presence of a resistor R_c placed between ground and the slider arm of the feedback potentiometer. This is done in order to preserve the equivalence of the potential distributions existing along the feedback and the multiplying potentiometers under conditions where the slider arm of the multiplying potentiometer is fed to a succeeding stage through an input resistor R as depicted in Fig. 13-19. Error in the computation can be avoided by selecting $R_c = R$.

The servomultiplier is used extensively because of its simplicity, its relative economy, and its capability of providing four-quadrant multiplication with a good degree of accuracy. However, in certain applications it does have one serious disadvantage. Because it is essentially an

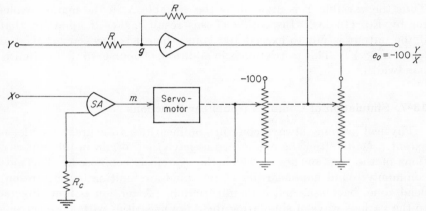

Fig. 13-20. Circuit arrangement for the division of two variables.

electromechanical device containing appreciable inertia, it has a limited frequency response which varies from 5 to 50 cps. Accordingly, if the machine solution to a physical problem requires the use of a multiplier and it is known that oscillatory responses having frequencies in excess of 50 cps will occur, then clearly the servomultiplier cannot be used. However, it can be used if the machine solution is time-scaled. As a matter of fact this is a good reason for introducing time scaling in the simulation of the problem. In those instances where time scaling is not permitted because of other considerations, then it is necessary to employ an all-electronic scheme to provide the product of variables. One method is to use the time-division multiplier; a second method is to use the quarter-squares multiplier. Both are capable of furnishing fast and accurate multiplication of variables. For information about these methods consult the Suggested Reading at the end of the chapter.

The division of two variables can be effected by the use of the servomultiplier and a summing amplifier arranged as illustrated in Fig. 13-20. The division feature of this configuration may be demonstrated as follows: Writing Kirchhoff's current law at the grid of the operational amplifier yields

$$\frac{Y}{R} + \frac{ae_o}{R} = 0 \tag{13-41}$$

where a is the slider-arm setting corresponding to the particular value of X. Solving for e_o gives

$$e_o = -\frac{Y}{a} \tag{13-42}$$

But the quantity a is given by $a = X/100$, so that Eq. (13-42) becomes

$$e_o = -\frac{Y}{X}(100) \tag{13-43}$$

Thus the variable Y is divided by the variable X in the manner called for by Eq. (13-43). Inspection of this result makes it apparent that, if the output is not to exceed 100 volts, then it is necessary that at all times $X \geq Y$. This restriction is in addition, of course, to that of limited bandwidth.

13-7. Simulation of Common Nonlinear Functions

Physical systems always contain nonlinearities to a greater or lesser extent. Quite often the nonlinearities have their origin in the imperfections of the components of which the system is composed. The most commonly found nonlinearities of this kind are limiting (or saturation), dead zone, backlash, and coulomb friction. Attention is now directed to the various ways of simulating these nonlinearities with the electronic analog computer.

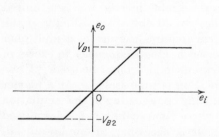

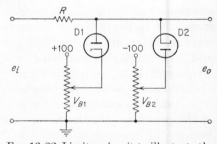

FIG. 13-21. Illustrating the nonlinear character of limiting.

FIG. 13-22. Limiter circuit to illustrate the principle involved.

Limiting. The character of this nonlinearity is depicted in Fig. 13-21. It can occur in many ways, as, for example, saturation in electronic and magnetic amplifiers, hitting the stop of a control surface, or reaching velocity and acceleration limits of output actuators. The principle utilized by the electronic analog computer to generate such a characteristic is illustrated by the circuitry appearing in Fig. 13-22. As the input signal increases from zero in the positive direction, the output voltage increases in direct proportion until it reaches the value V_{B1}. The voltage V_{B1} is the positive potential at which the cathode of diode $D1$ is held.

As e_i attempts to increase beyond this point, diode $D1$ conducts, thereby holding the potential of the output lead at V_{B1}. Of course, as a result of the finite resistance of the potentiometer as well as the diode resistance, the cutoff will not be abrupt. A practical version of this limiter circuit which is used in the REAC computer is depicted in Fig. 13-23. A study of the circuitry reveals that the potential of point 1 prior to the conduction of either diode is $e_1 = [0.25/(0.75 + 0.25)]e_i = e_i/4$. Thus, before conduction takes place there is a one-to-one relationship between

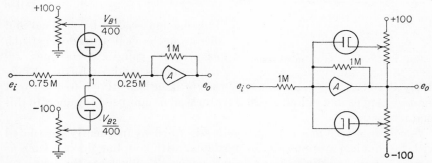

FIG. 13-23. Practical version of Fig. 13-22 as used in the REAC computer.   FIG. 13-24. Generation of limiter characteristic by using output shunt limiting.

input and output. After conduction occurs, the voltage $V_B/400$ appears as the input signal, which in turn is multiplied by 4 by the operational amplifier. If the output of the operational amplifier is to be kept at a maximum of ± 100 volts, it should be clear that the maximum potentiometer setting must correspond to a maximum slider-arm voltage of ± 25 volts. When limiting is performed in this manner, it is referred to as *input shunt limiting*.

Output shunt limiting can also be used to generate a limiter characteristic. This is illustrated in Fig. 13-24. The output voltage of the amplifier is applied to one end of the potentiometer while the reference voltage of 100 volts is applied to the other end. As long as the amplifier output voltage is positive, the upper diode cannot conduct. However, when this output voltage becomes negative, corresponding to a positive input signal e_i, a point will be reached for increasing values of e_i which will cause this diode to conduct. The exact value of amplifier output voltage for which conduction occurs depends upon the potentiometer setting. The relationship between this potentiometer setting a, the 100-volt reference, and the saturation (or limiting) voltage V_B is

$$a = \frac{V_B/100}{1 + V_B/100}$$

When e_i exceeds V_B in magnitude, the amplifier output voltage remains clamped at the bias value V_B so that no further change in amplifier output voltage occurs for increasing input voltages. Output shunt limiting offers the advantage over input shunt limiting of sharper cutoff.

Dead Zone. This term is used to denote the nonlinear variation shown in Fig. 13-25. It may be expressed mathematically as

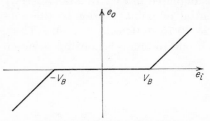

$$e_o = 0 \qquad\qquad -V_B < e_i < V_B$$
$$e_o = e_i - V_B \qquad\qquad e_i > V_B$$
$$e_o = e_i + V_B \qquad\qquad e_i < -V_B$$

It is encountered in mechanical and electromechanical transducers such as pressure gauges, gyroscopes, accelerometers, and so forth. Effectively it refers to a region in which there is no sensitivity to the input signal. Appearing in Fig. 13-26 is a practical circuit used to generate this characteristic.

FIG. 13-25. Illustrating dead zone.

Backlash. This is a type of hysteresis which is frequently associated with mechanical systems and in particular with coupling devices such as spur gears, rack and pinion gears, and so on. To illustrate the character of the output-input relationship, refer to Fig. 13-27a, which shows a rod A which is being used to transmit motion to a body B (as in the case

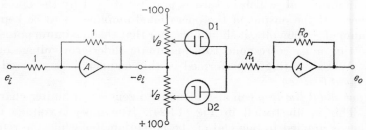

FIG. 13-26. Practical circuit used to generate dead zone.

of gears). When the rod is centered, there is a space of b units on either side, as depicted in the figure. Now, as the rod is displaced, no displacement of the body occurs until a displacement of b units is reached. Beyond this point there is a one-to-one correspondence between the rod displacement and that of the body. If, after a total positive displacement of d units, the direction of the rod is reversed, then clearly the body will not move until the rod has gone through a displacement of $2b$ units. At this point body motion is again restored. It should be apparent that, if the rod is displaced between the limits $\pm d$ in a cyclic fashion, the output-input displacement curve appears as illustrated in Fig. 13-27b.

In the electronic analog computer the input and output displacements are conveniently represented by voltages. A practical circuit for simulating backlash is shown in Fig. 13-28. Each diode is set at a value equal to one-half the total backlash.

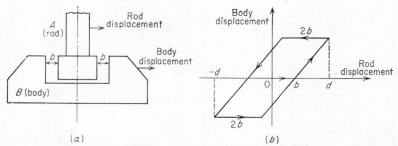

FIG. 13-27. Illustrating backlash. (a) Torque-transmitting device; (b) backlash.

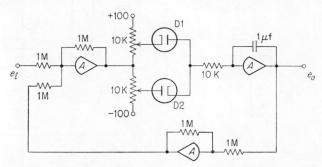

FIG. 13-28. Backlash simulator of the closed-loop type.

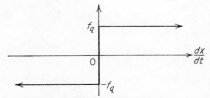

FIG. 13-29. Coulomb friction.

Coulomb Friction. The term coulomb friction is used in reference to the frictional force which exists between two bodies when one moves with respect to the other. The magnitude of the force is equal to the product of the coefficient of friction and the normal force. It is independent of the velocity, and it always opposes motion. A graphical description of this relationship appears in Fig. 13-29. Coulomb friction is frequently found in output actuators such as hydraulic motors, electric

TABLE 13-2. NONLINEAR CIRCUITS FOR SPECIAL APPLICATIONS†

No.	Application	Transfer characteristic, or function generated	Circuit or block diagram	Remarks
1a	Representation of **dead space** (inert zone) in springs, control characteristics, etc. With large values of R_0, these circuits are used for the representation of a pair of **stops**			$m_1 = \dfrac{R_0}{R_1}$ $m_2 = \dfrac{R_0}{R_2}$
1b				$m_1 = m_2 = \dfrac{R_0}{R_1 + R_2}$ Use in older computers with permanently installed shunt limiters. Requires accurate resistance matching
1c				$m_1 = m_2 = \dfrac{R_0}{R_1}$ ($E_{C2} = -E_{C1}$) Easy to adjust

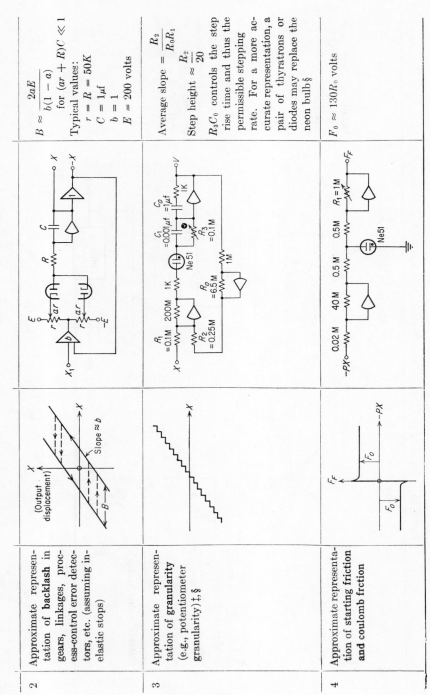

	Graph	Circuit	Formulas
2	Approximate representation of **backlash** in gears, linkages, process-control error detectors, etc. (assuming inelastic stops)		$B \approx \dfrac{2aE}{b(1-a)}$ for $(ar + R)C \ll 1$ Typical values: $r = R = 50K$ $C = 1\mu f$ $b = 1$ $E = 200$ volts
3	Approximate representation of **granularity** (e.g., potentiometer granularity)‡,§		Average slope $= \dfrac{R_2}{R_0 R_1}$ Step height $\approx \dfrac{R_2}{20}$ $R_3 C_0$ controls the step rise time and thus the permissible stepping rate. For a more accurate representation, a pair of thyratrons or diodes may replace the neon bulb§
4	Approximate representation of **starting friction and coulomb frction**		$F_0 \approx 130 R_0$ volts

571

TABLE 13-2. NONLINEAR CIRCUITS FOR SPECIAL APPLICATIONS† (Continued)

No.	Application	Transfer characteristic, or function generated	Circuit or block diagram	Remarks
5	Precision absolute-value device (linear full-wave rectifier)¶	$x_0 = |x_1|$		Obtain $-|x_1|$ by reversing diodes and bias voltage
6	Comparative circuit¶ (also used to represent coulomb friction)			Useful in many switching applications Drives relays A small feedback capacitor may be required for stability
7	Bistable multivibrator¶			

572

TABLE 13-2. NONLINEAR CIRCUITS FOR SPECIAL APPLICATIONS† (Continued)

No.	Application	Transfer characteristic, or function generated	Circuit or block diagram	Remarks
8	Free-running multivibrator¶			$T_1 = \dfrac{1}{ab}\left(1 + \dfrac{E_{C1}}{E_{C2}}\right)$ $T_2 = \dfrac{1}{ab}\left(1 + \dfrac{E_{C2}}{E_{C1}}\right)$

† From G. A. Korn and T. M. Korn, "Electronic Analog Computers," McGraw-Hill Book Company, Inc., New York, 1956; with permission. All formulas are derived for negligible source impedance and infinite amplifier gain.

‡ GEDA Simulation Study of a Carrier-type Instrument Servomechanism, *Rept. GER*-5779, Goodyear Aircraft Corporation, Akron, Ohio, Apr. 21, 1954.

§ C. A. Meneley and C. D. Morrill, Applications of Electronic Differential Analyzers to Engineering Problems, *Proc. IRE*, vol. 41, p. 1487, 1953.

¶ C. D. Morrill and R. V. Baum, Diode Limiters Simulate Mechanical Phenomena, *Electronics*, vol. 25, p. 122, November, 1952.

motors, etc., and in transducers such as potentiometers. Figure 13-30 shows an analog-computer simulation of this characteristic. When the velocity of the controlled variable dx/dt is the slightest bit positive, the output of the high-gain amplifier (without feedback) becomes greatly negative, which causes diode $D2$ to conduct almost instantly, thus applying the coulomb-friction force to the second amplifier. If dx/dt becomes

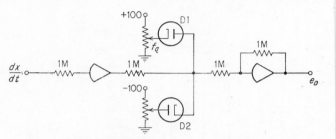

FIG. 13-30. Coulomb-friction simulator.

the slightest bit negative, diode $D1$ immediately conducts, thus changing the sign of the output quantity.

Table 13-2 itemizes additional nonlinear circuits for special applications.

13-8. Example and Concluding Remarks

In the interest of illustrating the procedure involved in simulating a nonlinear differential equation, which requires a servomultiplier as well as unequal magnitude-scale factors, consider a physical system which is described by the equation

$$\ddot{y} + 5\dot{y}y + 100y = f = 200u(t) \tag{13-44}$$

This is a nonlinear equation, and accordingly it is desirable to study the solution on the electronic analog computer. As is usual, before proceeding with the simulation, an estimate is needed of the maximum values of $y, \dot{y}, \ddot{y}$. It is sufficient here to use the same maximum values employed in the simulation of the linear version of this equation. The corresponding scale factors are given by Eqs. (13-22), (13-23a), and (13-23b).

The first step in the procedure requires multiplying Eq. (13-44) by $\frac{1}{4}$ and then solving for the highest derivative term. Thus

$$\tfrac{1}{4}\ddot{y} = 50 - \tfrac{1}{2}(2.5\dot{y})y - 25y \qquad \text{volts} \tag{13-45}$$

A question immediately arises at this point concerning the manner of handling the product $y\dot{y}$. Since a servomultiplier is to be used to obtain this product and because the input voltages to the multiplier will be the properly scaled versions of the physical quantities y and $\dot{y}$, it follows that the multiplier output voltage under these circumstances is necessarily

$$\frac{2.5\dot{y}(25y)}{100} = 0.625\dot{y}y \qquad \text{volts} \qquad (13\text{-}46)$$

A comparison with the corresponding term of Eq. (13-45) reveals that for correctness the output signal of the servomultiplier must be multiplied by a factor of 2 before it is summed with the other terms on the right side of Eq. (13-45) to yield the properly scaled acceleration. The remainder of the simulation procedure is then identical to that of the linear case. The final simulation diagram appears in Fig. 13-31.

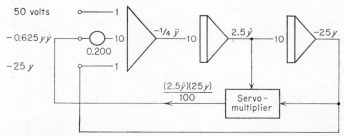

FIG. 13-31. Simulation diagram for the nonlinear equation $\ddot{y} + 5y\dot{y} + 100y = 200$.

It is significant to realize that this simulation diagram is not much more complicated than it is for the linear case. However, the simulation of the nonlinear system enables the engineer to study the effects upon the controlled variable and its derivatives of using various types of forcing functions, even to the extent where noise is included. The attractive part, too, is that very little time is needed to obtain the results. The solution is simple, direct, and complete.

Essentially it has been the purpose of this chapter to provide an introduction to electronic analog computers. Accordingly a description has been given of the most commonly used methods of computation employed in the analysis of linear as well as nonlinear systems. Also, a careful treatment of magnitude and time scaling has been offered and illustrated because useful computer results would be difficult to obtain without such an understanding. There is, of course, a good deal more to the subject matter than appears here. For additional information, therefore, the suggested reading should be consulted. However, before concluding it is worthwhile to mention that, even with the limited background provided in this chapter, it is possible for the control system engineer to see the vast possibilities which the electronic analog computer offers as a tool of analysis and design. Thus, when confronted with a complex system design, the engineer can begin with a simple paper analysis to guide his thinking, then resort to the computer for accuracy and flexibility, then return to the analysis to derive the full benefit from the computer results, and finally modify the computer results consistent with the latest analytical study. Doubtlessly the best way to appreciate the merits of such an approach is for the engineer to try it in the solution of his problems.

SUGGESTED READING

Johnson, C. L.: "Analog Computer Techniques," McGraw-Hill Book Company, Inc., New York, 1956.

Karplus, W. J., and W. W. Soroka: "Analog Methods," 2d ed., McGraw-Hill Book Company, Inc., New York, 1959.

Korn, G. A., and T. M. Korn: "Electronic Analog Computers," 2d ed., McGraw-Hill Book Company, Inc., New York, 1956.

PROBLEMS

13-1. Derive Eq. (13-4).

13-2. Obtain the potentiometer calibration curves by plotting Eq. (13-4) vs. Eq. (13-3) for $R_p/R_L = 0.3$, 0.15, and 0.03.

13-3. For the given input waveshapes and circuitry shown in Fig. P13-3 sketch the output waveshapes.

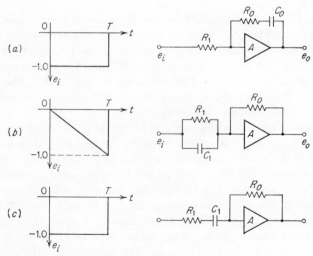

Fig. P13-3

13-4. Derive an expression for the per cent error caused by the leakage resistance of the capacitor (R_l) for a step input. Put the result in terms of the computing time t, the per cent error ϵ, and the time constant represented by the leakage resistance $T_l = R_lC$. Assume $e_o = 0$. (See Fig. P13-4.)

For a value of $R_l = 10^{14}$ ohms compute the permissible computing time within which the error due to this source is 0.1 per cent or less. $C = 1 \mu f$.

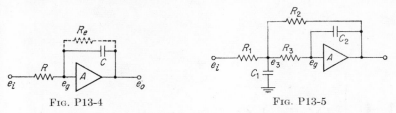

FIG. P13-4   FIG. P13-5

13-5. Derive the transfer function $\dfrac{e_o}{e_i}$ for the computer circuitry illustrated in Fig. P13-5. Assume infinite d-c gain, that is, $e_g = 0$.

13-6. Determine the transfer function which can be simulated with the circuitry of Fig. P13-6. Point out the basic difference in the computational functions performed by the circuits of Figs. P13-5 and P13-6.

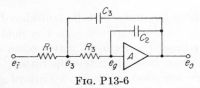

FIG. P13-6

13-7. Develop the simulation diagram to solve Eq. (13-17) subject to the restriction that only three operational amplifiers are to be used. The assumption is that acceleration is not to be recorded. Use appropriate scale factors.

13-8. Develop the simulation diagram to solve the equation $4\ddot{x} + \dot{x} + 4x = f$.

13-9. Develop the simulation diagram to solve the equation $\dddot{y} + 29\ddot{y} + 520\dot{y} + 2{,}000y = f$.

13-10. Repeat Prob. 13-9, introducing a time-scale charge which allows the scale factors for each of the variables to be the same.

13-11. The differential equation which describes the behavior of a servomechanism is

$$\frac{d^2c}{dt^2} + 2\zeta\omega_n \frac{dc}{dt} + \omega_n{}^2 c = \omega_n{}^2 r$$

Simulate this equation for a time-scale change of $\omega_n/1$. The solution must be such that the value of ζ may be set between 0.000 and 1.000 by means of a single potentiometer adjustment.

13-12. Describe the operation of the circuitry of Fig. 13-26 in generating the deadzone nonlinearity.

13-13. Describe the operation of the circuitry of Fig. 13-28 in generating the backlash nonlinearity.

14 | Digital Computers

The electronic digital computer can be considered as one of the most useful tools available to the engineer. In the field of control systems engineering, digital computers are used in two basic ways: as an analytic tool for the numerical analysis of system operation, and as a component used in the direct transmission or feedback path of a closed-loop control system. In this chapter we are concerned with the basic operating principles of the digital computer and its use as an analytic tool.

Prior to discussing the detailed operation and the use of digital computers it is useful to compare them with analog computers in general terms. It will be recalled from the previous chapter that analog computers are basically devices in which the variables of a problem are represented by analogous quantities in either an electrical or a mechanical model. The operation of this model is mathematically identical to the operation called for in the problem, so that there is a direct correspondence between the physical quantities in the computer and the constants and variables of the problem. For this reason the results obtained from an analog computer are easy to interpret in terms of the problem parameters. Thus it is a relatively simple task to investigate the effects of component variations when a control system is studied on an analog computer. Also, in the analog computer there is an exact correspondence (within a numerical time-scale factor) between time as the independent variable of a problem and time as measured during the actual solution of the problem on the computer. For this reason analog computers are said to operate in *real* time in so far as the problem solution is concerned.

Digital computers on the other hand operate on a completely different premise. The function of the digital computer is strictly restricted to numerical calculations with numbers as such. Physical quantities within the computer represent numerical digits. For example, a geared wheel with 10 discrete positions can be used to represent any of the decimal digits from 0 to 9, depending upon the position of the wheel. This technique is used in the office-type adding machine, which is a good example of a digital-computing device. The abacus is another example of a digital-computing machine since the position of the counters (beads) on the rods is used to represent numbers. Since the digital computer is merely a device for numerical calculation, the only relationship it has to the problem being studied is in the way in which the machine operates upon the numbers to arrive at the problem answers. The results obtained from a digital computer are numerical. The numbers, as represented by a physical configuration within the computer or as typed out on a sheet of paper by an output mechanism, represent the numerical magnitudes of the problem variables. Fundamentally digital computers have no limitation (except for those of physical size) on the accuracy of their calculations since greater precision can be had by adding more decimal places to the numerical representations within the computer. For example, more code wheels can be added to an adding machine to provide more significant figures, or more beads and rods can be added to an abacus. When a digital computer is used to solve a problem in which time is the independent variable, the time increment of the solution is just another number to be represented within the computer. There is no *direct* correspondence between the time it takes the computer to calculate a numerical answer and the time scale of the problem. However, when a digital computer is used as an integral part of a dynamic control system, the calculation time of the computer must be considered. In these applications it is important that the computer make the answers available fast enough for them to be used for the dynamic control of the system itself. For example, if a digital computer is used for controlling a chemical process plant, where the input data to the computer arrive periodically from remote sampling points, then the computer outputs (after calculation) must be made available at a fast enough rate for them to be of value in controlling the plant operation. Fortunately the time constants in most process plants are quite long, so that a computer has no difficulty in preparing the answers in time. In fact in these applications, as well as in others, such as operating upon control signals from a space vehicle, the arrival rate of the input data is so slow compared with the computer's calculation time that the same computer can often be used to do other jobs in the interval between data input samples. Thus the operation of the computer is often time-shared to accomplish a variety of tasks. In general, however, time scaling does not exist in the digital computer in the same sense that it exists in the analog computer. If we wish to calculate the solution of a differential equation for 0.1-sec increments of the independent variable rather than 1-sec increments, the result must simply be recalculated for the new time increment. The actual time taken for computation may very well be the same in both cases.

One of the major advantages of digital computation is that nonlinearities can be handled with the same relative ease and precision as linearities. Thus the digital computer is particularly useful for the solution of nonlinear-system problems.

In general, digital computers fall into two basic types: general-purpose and special-purpose computers. The general-purpose computer is a versatile machine which can be programmed to solve many different problems. The special-purpose computer is specifically designed to perform a particular calculation or solve a particular problem type and cannot, in general, be used for other calculations. Obviously the special-purpose computer is smaller and more economical than the larger, general-purpose machine. In this chapter we are concerned with the operation of general-purpose computers; the special-purpose machine is considered as a special case of the latter.

With these basic ideas in mind let us now look further into the detailed operation of general-purpose digital computers. It should be recognized that the discussion which follows is necessarily limited to basic concepts, with the emphasis on the use of digital computers rather than on their internal operation. The reader should consult some of the references listed in the Suggested Reading at the end of the chapter for further detailed study.

14-1. Digital Codes

In a simple decimal adding machine each decimal digit is represented by a discrete position of a 10-position wheel. Addition or subtraction is performed by rotating the wheels, which are linked together so that a complete rotation of the unit's wheel causes the tens wheel to rotate $\frac{1}{10}$ revolution, and so on for higher-order decimal digits. In this connection it is useful to think of a mechanical counter or the mileage indicator of an automobile as an example of a digital adding device. Each wheel in the counter serves as a basic storage cell in which a particular decimal digit is recorded. The electronic digital computer stores numbers in a similar fashion except that the basic storage device is usually a bistable mechanism, i.e., one with only two discrete stable states. For example, the basic storage cell may consist of a switch which is either opened or closed, a relay which is energized or deenergized, the presence or absence of a hole in a punched card or tape, an electronic flip-flop circuit which is in either one state or the other, a magnetic core which is saturated with magnetic flux in either a positive or a negative direction, and many other possibilities. Each one of these devices is capable of equilibrium in either one of two distinguishable states, which are usually designated by the symbols 0 and 1. If numbers are written in the binary number system rather than the decimal number system, then such binary numbers can be represented by a row of bistable storage cells each one of which is in an appropriate 0 or 1 state to correspond to each one of the binary digits.

In the binary (base or radix 2) number system, numerical quantities are represented using only two number symbols, 0 and 1. Each successive digit of a number representation, starting at the right, indicates the presence or absence of higher powers of the number base, 2. Binary numbers can best be understood by first reviewing the exact meaning of the decimal number system with which we are all familiar. In the decimal system each decimal

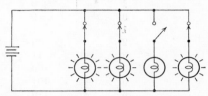

FIG. 14-1. Representation of binary number 1101.

digit, starting at the right, represents the value of successively higher powers of the base 10. Thus when we write the number $N = 12{,}345.6$ we really mean

$$N = 1 \times 10^4 + 2 \times 10^3 + 3 \times 10^2 + 4 \times 10^1 + 5 \times 10^0 + 6 \times 10^{-1}$$

In general a number written to any base or radix r is represented by the sequence $N = A_n \cdots A_2 A_1 A_0 . A_{-1}$, where it is understood that

$$N = A_n r^n + \cdots + A_2 r^2 + A_1 r^1 + A_0 r^0 + A_{-1} r^{-1} + \cdots$$

The terms $\ldots, A_{-1}, A_0, A_1, A_2, \ldots, A_n$ represent the value of the coefficients of successively higher powers of the number base. Each coefficient can have any numerical value from zero up to and including $r - 1$.

In the binary number system the base $r = 2$ and each coefficient must be either 0 or 1. Thus the binary number 10111 means

$$N = 1(2)^4 + 0(2)^3 + 1(2)^2 + 1(2)^1 + 1(2)^0$$
$$= 16 + 0 + 4 + 2 + 1 = 23$$

It is interesting to note the significance of the binary point, which plays the same basic role as the decimal point does in the decimal system. Thus, when we write the binary number 11.01, we mean

$$N = 1(2)^1 + 1(2)^0 + 0(2)^{-1} + 1(2)^{-2} = 3.25$$

Table 14-1 presents the binary numbers corresponding to the decimal numbers from $\frac{1}{4}$ through 17. Figure 14-1 illustrates how the binary number 1101 (decimal number 13) can be represented in a set of bistable storage cells, namely, a series of switches and lights in which a 1 is assumed to be represented by a closed switch and a 0 by an open switch.

TABLE 14-1. BINARY EQUIVALENTS OF DECIMAL NUMBERS

Decimal number	Binary number	Decimal number	Binary number
$\frac{1}{4}$	0.01	8	1000
$\frac{1}{2}$	0.1	9	1001
0	0	10	1010
1	1	11	1011
2	10	12	1100
3	11	13	1101
4	100	14	1110
5	101	15	1111
6	110	16	10000
7	111	17	10001

Bistable storage cells can be used to represent decimal numbers directly without conversion to the binary number system as such. These techniques fall into the general classification of binary-coded decimal-number systems. One such system, known as the excess-three code, is illustrated in Table 14-2. It can be seen that each decimal digit is

TABLE 14-2. A BINARY-CODED DECIMAL SYSTEM—THE EXCESS-THREE CODE

Decimal number	Equivalent binary code
0	0011
1	0100
2	0101
3	0110
4	0111
5	1000
6	1001
7	1010
8	1011
9	1100

represented by the one-zero pattern of four bistable storage cells. Thus the decimal number 1,280 is represented in the excess-three code as follows:

Excess-three code:	0100	0101	1011	0011
Equivalent decimal number:	1	2	8	0

In the excess-three code each of the decimal digits, 0 through 9, is represented by its binary equivalent plus the binary number 11 (which is decimal number 3). Thus the excess-three code for the decimal digit 9 is given by

$$1001 + 11 = 1100$$
$$\text{(binary 9)} + \text{(binary 3)} = \text{(excess-3 code for 9)}$$

In order to help the reader with the process of binary number addition, the following binary addition rules are presented:

$$0 + 0 = 0$$
$$1 + 0 = 1$$
$$0 + 1 = 1$$
$$1 + 1 = 0 \qquad \text{and carry 1}$$

Addition is carried out in exactly the same way as decimal addition. It is interesting to note that in the excess-three code, 9 minus any number (known as the *nine's complement*) is found by merely replacing all the zeros by ones and the ones by zeros in its coded representation. Consider the number 2, which in excess-three is coded as 0101. The nine's complement of 2 is $9 - 2 = 7$, which is coded as 1010. Thus the nine's complement may be found very easily with the excess-three code in a computer by simply reversing the zero-one condition of each one of the storage cells. Nine's complementing is often used in computers to perform subtraction because it allows the process of subtraction to be replaced by addition. For example, suppose that we would like to find the difference, 8 minus 5. We may write as follows:

$$8 - 5 = 8 - 5 + 9 - 9$$
$$= 8 + (9 - 5) - 9$$
$$= 8 + (9 - 5) - 10 + 1$$

In terms of computer operation the last line is relatively easy to perform. To subtract 5 from 8, the number 8 is added to the nine's complement of 5, unity is added to the result, and 10 subtracted from the answer. Subtracting 10 means dropping the unity in the tens place of the answer of the previous step. Thus in the computer subtraction is reduced to the process of determining a nine's complement and adding. Of course many other computer techniques for subtraction exist; the example presented only indicates one of the advantages of the excess-three code.

It is apparent that in general any binary-coded decimal-number representation, such as the excess-three, has the advantage of being easy to translate into its equivalent decimal value. On the other hand the binary-coded decimal representation generally requires more bistable storage cells than the representation of the same number in the pure binary number system. A variety of binary-coded number systems are used in different digital computers. Regardless of the type of binary representation used the transfer or shifting of a number from one set of bistable storage cells in the computer to another set is usually accomplished by sending electrical pulses along wires. For example, the presence of a pulse may represent a 1, and the absence of a pulse (or perhaps a negative pulse) may represent a 0. In this way the computer is capable of storing numbers and, by means of pulses, of shifting them from one storage location in the computer to another.

14-2. Method of Operation of the Computer

Although the detailed design of digital computers varies greatly from machine to machine, they basically contain the same operational units. The functional block diagram of a typical digital computer is drawn in

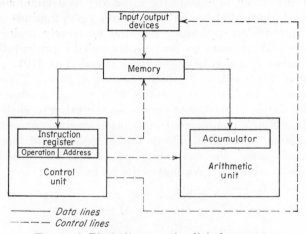

FIG. 14-2. Block diagram of a digital computer.

Fig. 14-2. Its operation can be understood from the function of each of the major blocks. The solid interconnecting lines represent possible paths of data (number) flow, and the dashed lines represent control lines, i.e., lines which control the source and destination of numbers as they are shifted about in the computer. It should be noted that the computer operation to be described is that of a stored-program machine, although the exact meaning of this phrase will not become clear until later on in the discussion.

The *input-output* block is used to indicate those devices by which the operator communicates with the machine. A typical input device is a punched-card reader, which converts the presence or absence of holes appearing on a punched card into the presence or absence of electrical pulses on wires which feed into the storage, or memory, unit of the machine. A typical output device is an electrically operated typewriter which accepts coded electrical pulses from the computer and converts them into readable symbols on a sheet of paper.

The *memory* unit consists of a collection of bistable storage cells in which it is possible to store many numbers in binary form. A typical memory unit is a magnetic drum, as depicted in Fig. 14-3. Numbers are stored on the magnetic surface of the drum in binary form by the presence or absence of magnetic-flux pulses. As the drum rotates, the pulse data stored on the drum surface are "read out" by means of magnetic pickup heads which sense the presence or absence of magnetic flux. These same heads are also used in reverse to "read in," or store, data on the drum surface. The memory drum is organized so that the digits of any multidigit number occur in a line parallel to the axis of the drum.

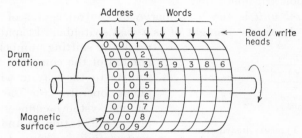

FIG. 14-3. Magnetic-drum storage unit.

Each of these lines is identified by a number called the *address*. The stored numbers at any particular drum address are called a *word*. Electronic circuitry associated with the drum is designed so that the word at any particular drum address may be read out of the drum or, conversely, numbers can be read in at any particular drum address. In most memories "read-out" is nondestructive, i.e., the stored data are kept intact by the reading process, whereas "read-in" automatically replaces the numbers in the storage location by the new data. The address never changes. In a sense the memory unit can be thought of as a series of pigeonholes. Each of the pigeonholes corresponds to a storage location and is identified by its address. Thus it is possible to store any number in any address by simply writing the number on a slip of paper and placing the paper in the proper pigeonhole. In Fig. 14-3 the decimal number 59,386 is stored in address location 003. Each of the decimal digits of the stored number, as well as the numbers designating the address, is stored on the drum surface in binary form as, for example, binary-coded decimals. Thus the number 59,386 would be stored through the use of 20 magnetic recording heads, 4 heads being required to store each decimal digit. Accordingly, the decimal number 59,386 appearing in address 003 in Fig. 14-3 would be recorded in terms of an excess-three code as

$$\underbrace{1000}_{5} \quad \underbrace{1100}_{9} \quad \underbrace{0110}_{3} \quad \underbrace{1011}_{8} \quad \underbrace{1001}_{6}$$

The size of the memory unit determines the capacity of the computer, and usually several thousand "words" can be stored in the memory.

The *arithmetic unit* is basically a group of electronic circuits which are capable of performing certain simple arithmetic operations with numbers as they appear in coded binary form as electrical impulses on the input lines. The detailed operation of the arithmetic unit is of no real concern to the computer operator. He accepts the operations that the arithmetic unit can perform. In the block diagram the arithmetic unit is shown to contain a set of bistable storage cells, known as the *accumulator*, into which numbers are shifted prior to the time when they are to be operated upon arithmetically.

The *control unit* is the basic nerve or control center of the digital computer. It can be thought of as a vast switchboard capable of auto-matically shifting numbers from one portion of the computer to another, similar to the way in which a telephone operator (or the automatic dialing system) connects one telephone toll station to another. The control unit is shown to contain a block known as the *instruction register*.

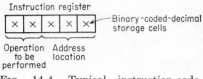

FIG. 14-4. Typical instruction-code format.

The function of the instruction register is to dictate the type of control action to be performed by the control unit. The action to be performed is determined by a number, known as the *program instruction*, which is stored in the instruction register at the time when the control operation is to take place. A typical program single-address instruction number consists of two parts, as illustrated in Fig. 14-4. The first part is known as the *operation code* and designates the type of operation to be performed by the control unit. The second part is known as the *address* and designates the location in the memory where the number to be operated upon is to be found. It is important to remember that the address part of a program instruction is not operated upon by the computer but merely indicates the memory location where the number to be controlled is to be found. In order to illustrate computer operation several control functions for a fictitious computer, and their corresponding operation code numbers, are listed in Table 14-3. This table should be read carefully to acquaint the reader with the type of internal operations a computer can perform. Instruction codes 07 and 08 are rather special, and their function is discussed further in the next section.

Let us now assume that the computer whose instruction codes are given in Table 14-3 has 1,000 memory-address locations and that these are identified by the address numbers 000 through 999. Thus, if we would like to place the number in memory address 653 into the accumulator of the arithmetic unit the program instruction number 01653 should appear in the instruction register of the control unit. The 01 portion of the program instruction indicates the operation to be performed, and the next three digits (653) indicate the memory address of the number to be operated upon. From the foregoing it should be

TABLE 14-3. INSTRUCTION CODES FOR A DIGITAL COMPUTER

Instruction	Code	Control operation
Stop	00	The computer stops, regardless of the digits in the address part of the instruction
Reset and add	01	The accumulator is reset to zero, and the number at the indicated memory address is then placed in the accumulator
Add	02	The number at the indicated memory address is added to the number in the accumulator, and the sum is left in the accumulator
Subtract	03	The number at the indicated memory address is subtracted from the number in the accumulator, and the difference is left in the accumulator
Multiply	04	The number at the indicated memory address is multiplied by the number in the accumulator, and the product is left in the accumulator
Divide	05	The number in the accumulator is divided by the number at the indicated memory address, and the quotient is left in the accumulator
Store	06	The number in the accumulator is placed in the memory storage location indicated by the address part of the instruction. The previous contents of this storage location are lost; the number in the accumulator is unchanged
Jump	07	The next instruction is taken from the address indicated by the address part of this instruction instead of the next sequentially numbered address position
Jump if minus	08	Same as "jump" if the number in the accumulator at the time is negative (zero is assumed to be positive); otherwise, the next instruction is taken from the next sequentially numbered address position
Read	09	The numbers on the punched cards at the input mechanism are placed in memory storage at the address indicated on each card. The previous number at this memory address is lost. After all cards are read, the number in memory address 000 is taken into the instruction register
Print	10	The number at the memory storage location indicated by the address is recorded by the output mechanism. The number in storage remains unchanged

apparent that in order to perform a sequence of arithmetic operations it is necessary only to have the pertinent program instructions appear in sequence in the instruction register of the control unit, sufficient time being allowed between the appearance of each program instruction for the control unit to perform the required operation.

The question now arises as to how the proper sequence of program instructions required for the solution of a numerical problem is made to appear in the instruction register. The answer is that the numbers of the program instructions are stored beforehand within the memory unit itself, thereby giving rise to the term "stored-program" digital computer which was referred to previously. The steps of the program are usually stored in sequence in successive address locations of the memory unit. In the case of our fictitious computer it is assumed that the program is always stored in the memory in sequence starting at memory address 000. When the computer is placed in operation, the number in memory address 000 is automatically shifted into the instruction register of the control unit. This number represents the first program instruction, and the computer performs the corresponding operation. When this first operation is completed, the control unit automatically shifts the number from memory address 001 into the instruction register. The computer now performs the second program instruction. When this operation is complete, the next program instruction is taken from memory address 002. The computer continues to cycle through all the instructions in the memory in this way until the entire sequence of operations required in the program is performed. In synchronous computers the timing of the machine operations is controlled by a clock-pulse generator of fixed frequency. All machine operation takes place in synchronism with this basic pulse rate. However, it should be mentioned that there are some asynchronous computers which do not have a clock pulse.

Before a problem is solved on a digital machine, it is necessary that the memory be cleared (all zeros stored) and that the operator "load" the memory with the numbers of the program as well as any other numerical values that may be required for the solution. Exactly how this is done is discussed in the next section.

14-3. A Simple Computer Program

Let us now consider how the digital computer described previously can be used to perform a simple numerical task such as calculating the function $(a + b)/c$, where a, b, and c are any real numbers. Let us assume that the calculation is to be performed for the case where $a = 325$, $b = 625$, and $c = 526$. The sequence of program instruction required to perform the calculation is given in Table 14-4. In this table it is assumed that the number 325 has been placed beforehand in memory location 500, the number 625 in memory location 501, and the number 526 in memory location 502.

The first step in preparing the machine to perform this calculation is to "load" the program into the machine, starting at memory address 000, and then to store the numerical values for a, b, and c in memory addresses 500, 501, and 502, respectively. This is done by preparing a set of punched cards containing the information of Table 14-5 in binary form.

After the punched cards are prepared, they are placed in the input device and the operator manually sets the instruction register of the

TABLE 14-4

Step no.	Program instruction code	Operation performed
1	01500	The number 325 (at address 500) is shifted into the accumulator
2	02501	The number 625 (at address 501) is added to 325 in the accumulator, thereby forming $a + b$
3	05502	The sum $a + b$ is divided by 526, (at address 502), thereby forming $(a + b)/c$ in the accumulator
4	06503	The answer $(a + b)/c$ is shifted to memory location 503. This location is chosen arbitrarily
5	10503	The number in memory location 503 is printed out by the output mechanism
6	00000	The machine stops

control unit at operation code 09. When the "start" button is depressed, automatic machine operation takes place and the machine follows operating instruction 09. The first thing that happens is that all the punched-card data at the input unit are read into the memory, thereby properly storing the program information and the values of a, b, and c.

TABLE 14-5

Memory address	Number to be stored	
000		01500
001		02501
002	Program, instructions	05502
003		06503
004		10503
005		00000
500		00325
501	Constants a, b, c	00625
502		00526

In accordance with instruction code 09, when all the data at the input unit are read into the machine's memory, the control unit automatically shifts the number at memory address 000 into the instruction register, replacing the 09 which the operator placed there. The number at 000 is the first step of the program sequence so that the machine now automatically starts the calculation, proceeding through the entire list of program instructions, printing out the answer, and stopping at the end.

14-4. Numerical Integration of Differential Equations

Let us now consider how the digital computer of the previous section can be used to determine the solution of a simple second-order differential equation. The technique outlined is one of numerical integration using straight-line approximation and is known as *Euler's method*. Other techniques are available, but attention is directed to this one because it is quite simple and straightforward. Although we are confining ourselves to a second-order differential equation, the method can be extended readily to higher-order equations as well.

Consider the second-order differential equation

$$\frac{d^2c}{dt^2} + 2\zeta\omega_n \frac{dc}{dt} + \omega_n{}^2 c = \omega_n{}^2 r(t) \tag{14-1}$$

where $r(t)$ is a given driving function and $\omega_n{}^2$ and $2\zeta\omega_n$ are known coefficients. Equation (14-1) can be rewritten as follows with the standard dot notation to denote derivatives:

$$\ddot{c}(t) = \omega_n{}^2 r(t) - \omega_n{}^2 c(t) - 2\zeta\omega_n \dot{c}(t) \tag{14-2}$$

We note that if $c(t)$, $\dot{c}(t)$, and $r(t)$ are known at any instant of time t_0, then $\ddot{c}(t)$ can be evaluated at $t = t_0$. From the values of $c(t)$, $\dot{c}(t)$, $\ddot{c}(t)$, and $r(t)$ at $t = t_0$, it is possible to calculate c and $\dot{c}$ at the time $t_0 + \Delta t$, where Δt represents a small increment of time. This calculation is based upon the definition of the derivative given by

$$\dot{c} = \dot{c}_{-1} + \Delta t\, \ddot{c}_{-1} \tag{14-3a}$$
$$c = c_{-1} + \Delta t\, \dot{c}_{-1} \tag{14-3b}$$

The subscript -1 is used to denote the value of the variable at the beginning of the interval Δt, and the variable without a subscript denotes its value at the end of the interval. Thus Eqs. (14-3a) and (14-3b) may be used to determine c and $\dot{c}$ at time t_0 and Δt. Substituting these calculated values and the value of $r(t_0 + \Delta t)$ into the original differential equation then enables us to calculate $\ddot{c}$ at $t_0 + \Delta t$. Similarly by using in Eqs. (14-3a) and (14-3b) the computed values of c, $\dot{c}$, and $\ddot{c}$ prevailing at $t = t_0 + \Delta t$, the values of c and $\dot{c}$ existing at $t_0 + 2\,\Delta t$ can be determined. The process of numerical substitution is continued as long as desired, and a table of the values of c, $\dot{c}$, and $\ddot{c}$ at successive intervals Δt of time is generated.

In order to prepare Euler's numerical integration procedure for programming on a digital computer, it is helpful to outline the procedure in a flow diagram, as drawn in Fig. 14-5. Such diagrams are a great help in programming. At the start of the solution at $t = 0$, it is assumed that $c(0^+)$, $\dot{c}(0^+)$, and $r(0^+)$ are known from the initial conditions. With the aid of the diagram it is apparent that the numerical calculations to be performed must follow the steps of Table 14-6. It is noted that the numerical calculations required for step 7 are identical to those required

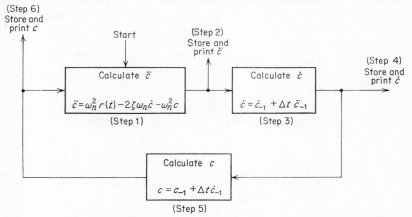

Fig. 14-5. Flow diagram for the numerical solution of a second-order differential equation.

for step 1. In other words, the same calculations are repeated over and over again, and only the numerical values of the variables change.

Let us now see how the procedure outlined can be programmed on the digital computer with the program instruction code of Table 14-3. Assume that the initial values for c and $\dot{c}$ are placed in memory addresses

TABLE 14-6

Step no.	Operation
1	Calculate $\ddot{c}$ at $t = 0$, using $c(0^+)$, $\dot{c}(0^+)$, and $r(0^+)$
2	Store and print $\ddot{c}$ at $t = 0$
3	Calculate $\dot{c}$ at $t = \Delta t$
4	Store and print $\dot{c}$ at $t = \Delta t$
5	Calculate c at $t = \Delta t$
6	Store and print c at $t = \Delta t$
7	Calculate $\ddot{c}$ at $t = \Delta t$

500 and 501, respectively. Also assume the following: The time increment Δt is located at memory address 502. The value of $\omega_n{}^2$ is located at address 503. The value of $2\zeta\omega_n$ is located at address 504. The driving function $r(t)$ is a step of height 15, so that the number 15 is placed at memory address 505. As mentioned previously, the computer's memory must be supplied with this information as well as the program instructions

prior to starting computations. Table 14-7 summarizes the information that must be stored in the memory beforehand. Obviously the number of steps in the program sequence itself should not exceed 500. It should also be noted that assuming $r(t)$ to be a step function simplifies the program greatly. If $r(t)$ were not a constant, its successive values at increments of time Δt would have to be stored in the memory also. With the aid of the flow diagram (Fig. 14-5) it is now possible to write out the

TABLE 14-7

Memory location	Numbers to be stored
000	Reserved for program instructions
001	Reserved for program instructions
002	Reserved for program instructions
.	.
.	.
.	.
500	The value of c at $t = 0$
501	The value of $\dot{c}$ at $t = 0$
502	The value of Δt
503	The value of ω_n^2
504	The value of $2\zeta\omega_n$
505	The number 0015, that is, the value of $r(t)$

individual steps of the program. This is done in Table 14-8. It should be apparent that this programming sequence is not unique. Other possibilities exist.

In Table 14-8 the subscript $+1$ is used to denote the value of a variable at the end of a time increment. In following this program some important points should be noted. Storage locations 600 through 603 are used as temporary storage locations throughout the calculations. Instruction steps 21, 22, 23 shift the newly calculated values of c and $\dot{c}$ to memory-address locations 500 and 501, where the previous values of c and $\dot{c}$ were stored. After step 23 the computer is ready to recycle through the program to calculate the variables at the end of the next increment of time. This recycling is made to occur by means of the jump instruction of step 24, which returns the control unit to the first program instruction at memory address 000. The "jump" instruction is essential for recycling or loop operation of the computer. It should also be noted that, if the solution is desired for a different time increment Δt, all that is necessary is to change the number stored in memory address 502.

The program presented thus far has no provision for stopping the computer calculation. This feature can be added to the program and involves making use of the "jump if minus" instruction, which has operation code 08 in Table 14-3. This type of instruction is also known

TABLE 14-8

Step no.	Memory location	Instruction		Operation performed
		Operation	Address	
1	000	10	500	Print out c
2	001	10	501	Print out $\dot{c}$
3	002	01	503	ω_n^2 shifted to the accumulator
4	003	04	500	The product $\omega_n^2 c$ is formed
5	004	06	600	The product $\omega_n^2 c$ is shifted to memory location 600
6	005	01	504	$2\zeta\omega_n$ shifted to the accumulator
7	006	04	501	The product $2\zeta\omega_n\dot{c}$ is formed
8	007	06	601	The product $2\zeta\omega_n\dot{c}$ is shifted to memory location 601
9	008	01	503	ω_n^2 shifted to the accumulator
10	009	04	505	The product $\omega_n^2 r(t)$ is formed in the accumulator
11	010	03	600	$\omega_n^2 c$ is subtracted from $\omega_n^2 r(t)$ in the accumulator
12	011	03	601	$2\zeta\omega_n\dot{c}$ is now subtracted, yielding $\ddot{c}$
13	012	06	602	$\ddot{c}$ is shifted to memory location 602
14	013	10	602	Print out $\ddot{c}$
15	014	04	502	The product $\Delta t\,\ddot{c}$ is formed ($\ddot{c}$ is still in the accumulator)
16	015	02	501	$\dot{c}_{+1}$ is formed from $\dot{c} + \Delta t\,\ddot{c}$
17	016	06	603	$\dot{c}_{+1}$ is stored in memory location 603
18	017	01	501	$\dot{c}$ is shifted to the accumulator
19	018	04	502	The product $\Delta t\,\dot{c}$ is formed
20	019	02	500	c_{+1} is formed from $c + \Delta t\,\dot{c}$
21	020	06	500	c_{+1} is stored in memory location 500
22	021	01	603	$\dot{c}_{+1}$ is shifted to the accumulator
23	022	06	501	$\dot{c}_{+1}$ is shifted to memory location 501
24	023	07	000	Jump back to the instruction at address 000

as a "conditional transfer." Let us assume that it is desired to stop the computer after 150 increments of time have been computed. The following additional data must then be stored in the computer memory together with the program:

Memory location	Number to be stored
506	The number 1
507	The number 150

Step 24 of Table 14-8, above, is removed, and the program steps of Table 14-9 are added. The function of the "jump if minus" instruction should be apparent from reading the program.

TABLE 14-9

Step no.	Memory location	Instruction Operation	Instruction Address	Operation performed
24	023	01	604	The number in 604 is shifted to the accumulator. This number is initially zero
25	024	02	506	1 is added to the number in the accumulator
26	025	06	604	The number in the accumulator is stored in address 604. This number represents the number of computation cycles which have taken place
27	026	03	507	150 is subtracted from the number in the accumulator
28	027	08	000	Jump to the instruction at address 000 if the accumulator is negative, i.e., less than 150. If the number in the accumulator is positive, go to the next sequentially numbered address position for the next instruction
29	028	00		Stop

In order to enable the reader to check the application of Euler's integration to a second-order differential equation, the method was applied to the following equation, where $r(t)$ was taken as a unit-step function and $\Delta t = 0.0001$ sec:

$$\ddot{c} + 15\dot{c} + 900c = 900r(t)$$

The numerical results for the first few increments of time are tabulated in Table 14-10. It is apparent the accuracy of the numerical solution depends upon the size of the time increment used. In fact a completely

TABLE 14-10

t	$\ddot{c}$	$\dot{c}$	c
0	900.0000	0.0000	0.0000
0.0001	898.6500	0.0900	0.0000
0.0002	897.2900	0.1798	0.0000
0.0004	895.9300	0.2695	0.0000
0.0005	894.5600	0.3591	0.0000
0.0006	893.1900	0.4486	0.0000
0.0007	891.8100	0.5379	0.0001
0.0008	890.4200	0.6271	0.0001
0.0009	889.0300	0.7161	0.0002
0.0010	887.6300	0.8050	0.0003
0.0011	886.2300	0.8938	0.0004
0.0012	884.8200	0.9824	0.0004
0.0013	883.4000	1.0710	0.0005
0.0014	881.9800	1.1593	0.0006

erroneous solution (such as indicating instability) may be obtained by using too large an increment. For this reason it is recommended that with Euler's method the time increment be such that there are at least 50 points for the highest frequency present in the solution. If the highest frequency is denoted by ω_c, then Δt should be chosen so that

$$\Delta t \leq \frac{2\pi}{50\omega_c} \approx \frac{1}{8\omega_c}$$

With the foregoing program sequence in mind it is not difficult to see how the computer can be used to calculate the solution of a nonlinear problem. Let us suppose that one of the coefficients of the original differential equation is a function of the magnitude of the dependent variable. As the dependent variable is calculated at each increment the program can be adapted so that the number stored for this coefficient is changed at each step of the calculation. In this way a good solution to the problem can be achieved. The ability to take the effects of nonlinear behavior into account is one of the major advantages of the digital computer in control system analysis. Another important characteristic is that higher-order systems can be analyzed on a digital computer by simply extending the computer program.

14-5. Weighted-average Method of Numerical Integration of Differential Equations

There are many other methods which can be used for the numerical integration of differential equations. Their chief advantage over the method outlined in the previous section is that larger time increments can be used for the same accuracy of solution. One such method is the weighted-average technique, which uses average values to replace $\dot{c}_{-1}$ and $\ddot{c}_{-1}$ in Eqs. (14-3a) and (14-3b). Thus c is calculated from the equation

$$c = c_{-1} + \frac{\dot{c}_{-1} + \dot{c}}{2} \Delta t \tag{14-4a}$$

where the average value of the derivative during the interval Δt is used rather than its value at the beginning of the interval as in Eq. (14-3b). Similarly Eq. (14-3a) is replaced by the expression

$$\dot{c} = c_{-1} + \frac{\ddot{c}_{-1} + \ddot{c}}{2} \Delta t \tag{14-4b}$$

As it stands, Eq. (14-4b) is useless for numerical calculations since the value at $\ddot{c}$ at the end of the interval, as required by the equation, is not known. This difficulty is overcome by assuming that the *highest* derivative does not change very much between two successive intervals, so that we may write

$$\ddot{c} - \ddot{c}_{-1} \approx \ddot{c}_{-1} - \ddot{c}_{-2} \tag{14-5}$$

From Eq. (14-5) we get the result $\ddot{c} = 2\ddot{c}_{-1} - \ddot{c}_{-2}$, which when substituted in Eq. (14-4b) yields

$$\dot{c} = \dot{c}_{-1} + \frac{3\ddot{c}_{-1} - \ddot{c}_{-2}}{2} \Delta t \tag{14-6}$$

Equation (14-6) is now in a form such that $\dot{c}$ is expressed in terms of the derivatives of c at previous intervals of time. Thus a differential equation can now be integrated by using the equation itself and Eqs. (14-4a) and (14-6).

There are available many other techniques for the numerical integration of differential equations. It is recommended that the interested reader consult the references given in the Suggested Reading at the end of the chapter for further study of this topic.

14-6. Typical Computer Characteristics

Tables 14-11 and 14-12 list the characteristics of some common computers. In the arithmetic-number-system column the number system used by the machine is listed. The expression "alphanumeric" is used to refer to machines in which the letters of the alphabet as well as the decimal digits are represented by a digital (binary) code. The instruction column lists the basic format of a machine instruction. A single-address machine is similar to the type of computer outlined in this chapter. A two-address machine contains two addresses as well as the operation code in its instruction code. In these machines the operation called for by the instruction is performed on the numbers at the designated addresses. For example, in performing an addition it is unnecessary to shift one of the numbers to the accumulator beforehand as with a single-address machine. Thus programming steps are saved. In a three-address machine the third address designates the address where the result of an operation is to be stored. The basic operating speeds of the large-scale calculators are also listed in the tables. The problem of decimal- (or binary-) point location is a major factor in the use of computers. Fixed-point machines operate with numbers, so that the decimal point is always at a fixed location in a word. In these machines the programmer must watch the scaling of the numbers to ensure that the decimal point is always in the correct position for the machine calculation. This problem is avoided in *floating-point* calculators, which automatically take care of the decimal-point location during all arithmetic operations. In these machines numbers are stored together with an appropriate exponent or power of ten to indicate the decimal-point location. Exponents are added when multiplication takes place and are subtracted for division. When performing addition or subtraction, the

TABLE 14-11. CHARACTERISTICS OF SOME LARGE-SCALE DIGITAL CALCULATORS†

Calculator	Arithmetic number system	High-speed storage capacity and type	Word size	Instructions	Operating speeds
IBM—type 701	Binary	2,048 words, electrostatic	36 bits‡	Single-address	Add: 60 μsec Multiply: 450 μsec
ERA—1103A	Binary	Up to 4,096 words, magnetic cores	36 bits	Two-address	Add: 48 μsec Multiply: 266 μsec
IBM—type 704	Binary	4,096–32,768 words, magnetic cores	36 bits	Single-address	Floating add: 84 μsec Floating multiply: 200 μsec
Illiac	Binary	1,024 words, electrostatic	39 bits	Single-address	Add: 75 μsec Multiply: 650 μsec
Whirlwind	Binary	2,048 words, magnetic cores	16 bits	Single-address	Add: 24 μsec Multiply: 40 μsec
NORC	Decimal	2,000 words, electrostatic	16 decimal digits	Three-address	Floating add: 15 μsec Floating multiply: 30 μsec
UNIVAC I (UNIVAC II)	Decimal, alphanumeric	1,000 words, acoustic delay lines (up to 10,000 for UNIVAC II)	12 decimal digits	Single-address	Add: 400 μsec average Multiply: 2,100 μsec average
IBM—type 702	Decimal, alphanumeric	10,000 characters, electrostatic	Variable word length	Single-address	Add: 370 μsec Multiply: 3,360 μsec (on 10 decimal numbers)
IBM—type 705	Decimal, alphanumeric	20,000 characters, magnetic cores	Variable word length	Single-address	Add: 200 μsec Multiply: 2,480 μsec (on 10 decimal numbers)

† Data taken from J. G. Truxal, "Control Engineers' Handbook," McGraw-Hill Book Company, Inc, New York, 1958. Originally compiled by J. W. Carr III and A. J. Perlis for *Control Eng.*, March, 1956.

‡ The term *bits* is an abbreviation for "binary digits."

TABLE 14-12. CHARACTERISTICS OF SOME SMALL DIGITAL COMPUTERS†

Calculator	Arithmetic number system	High-speed storage (words)	Word size
Type 650	Decimal	1,000 or 2,000	10 decimal digits
Datatron	Decimal	4,000	10 decimal digits
UNIVAC File Computer	Decimal	1,000	12 decimal digits
Miniac	Decimal, binary	4,096	10 decimal digits
Elecom 125 Computer	Decimal	2,000–10,000	10 decimal digits
Alwac	Binary	4,096 or 8,192	32 bits
Circle	Binary	1,024	40 bits
Bendix G15A	Binary	2,176	29 bits
Readix	Decimal	4,000	10 decimal digits
Librascope LGP-30	Binary	4,096	32 bits
Monrobot VI	Decimal	100 nos., 200 orders	20 decimal digits
E-101	Decimal	128 orders (pinboard), 100–200 nos.	12 decimal digits
Elecom 50	Decimal	2,400 orders (Mylar tape), 100 nos.	10 decimal digits

† Data taken from J. G. Truxal, "Control Engineers' Handbook," McGraw-Hill Book Company, Inc., New York, 1958. Originally compiled by J. W. Carr III and A. J. Perlis for *Control Eng.*, March, 1956.

machine automatically shifts the numbers so that they have the same exponent when the operation takes place. Obviously machines capable of floating-point arithmetic are more elaborate than fixed-point machines.

SUGGESTED READING

Jeenel, J.: "Programming for Digital Computers," McGraw-Hill Book Company, Inc., New York, 1959.

Kopal, Z.: "Numerical Analysis," chap. 4, Chapman & Hall, Ltd., London, 1955.

McCracken, D. D.: "Digital Computer Programming," John Wiley & Sons, Inc., New York, 1957.

Nixon, F. E.: "Principles of Automatic Control," chaps. 12 and 13, and appendix, Prentice-Hall, Inc., Englewood Cliffs, N.J., 1956.

Proceedings of the IRE: October, 1953. The entire issue is devoted to digital computers.

Scarborough, J. B.: "Numerical Mathematical Analysis," chap. 11, Johns Hopkins Press, Baltimore, 1950.

Staff of Engineering Research Associates, Inc.: "High-speed Computing Devices," chaps. 1–7, McGraw-Hill Book Company, Inc., New York, 1950.

PROBLEMS

14-1. (*a*) Write the following decimal numbers in the binary number system: 19; 22; 324; 3,240.

(*b*) Write the following decimal numbers in the excess-three code: 19; 22; 324.

(*c*) Given the binary-coded decimal number system of Table 14-13, write the following numbers in this code: 19; 22; 236; 3,240.

TABLE 14-13. BIQUINARY SYSTEM

Decimal	Code	Decimal	Code
0	0100001	5	1000001
1	0100010	6	1000010
2	0100100	7	1000100
3	0101000	8	1001000
4	0110000	9	1010000

14-2. Check the following binary addition: $1101 + 1111 + 101 = 100001$.

14-3. The following numbers are written in excess-three code. What are their decimal number equivalents?

(a) 011001011000   (b) 110010110011   (c) 001100110011

14-4. Program the following arithmetic operations on the computer whose instruction is given in Table 14-3.

(a) $(a + b)c$ (b) $\dfrac{a + b + c}{3}$ (c) $\dfrac{ab}{c}$

14-5. The square root of any number can be determined by the following iterative formula developed by Newton:

$$X = \frac{1}{2}\left(X_{-1} + \frac{N}{X_{-1}} \right)$$

where N = number of which square root is desired

X_{-1} = first numerical approximation for square root

X = second approximation for square root

The square root is determined by assuming a first approximation to the answer. This first approximation is substituted into the formula to yield a second approximation. The second approximation is then substituted into the formula to yield the third approximation, and so on. The process converges very rapidly.

(a) Test the Newton formula by finding the square root of 67.2.

(b) Write a program to determine the square root of any number, using the instruction codes of Table 14-3. Use the "jump" instruction so that the computer automatically evaluates higher-order approximations of the answer.

14-6. Program the digital computer whose instruction code is given in Table 14-3 to solve a second-order differential equation, using the weighted-average method of numerical integration. Assume that the driving function is a unit step and that the initial conditions are known.

14-7. Solve the following differential equation, using numerical integration:

$$\ddot{c} + 5.0\dot{c} + 50.0c = 50.0$$

(a) Use Euler's method, letting $\Delta t = 0.01$ sec. Assume zero initial conditions, and carry the calculations up to $t = 0.03$ sec.

(b) Use the weighted-average method, again using $\Delta t = 0.01$ sec and zero initial conditions. Calculate up to $t = 0.03$ sec.

(c) Use the weighted-average method, using $\Delta t = 0.015$ and zero initial conditions Calculate up to $t = 0.03$ sec.

Compare the numerical answers obtained for parts a, b, and c.

14-8. Solve the following equation by numerical integration. All initial conditions are zero

$$\dddot{c} + 3\ddot{c} + 3\dot{c} + 1 = u(t)$$

VI | Special Topics

15 | Self-adaptive Control Systems

A self-adaptive control system is one which is inherently capable of maintaining a desired performance in the presence of a changing environment. It is to be recalled that, in the case of conventional linear design, gain adjustments and compensation designs are usually associated with a controlled system transfer function which is essentially invariant. Although some variations in the parameters are likely to exist, these are usually sufficiently small so that the desired performance is realized. However, in situations where the controlled system parameters vary widely over the operating range a constant loop gain or fixed compensation network can easily lead to a serious deterioration in performance and even to a condition of instability. The flight of hypersonic and supersonic aircraft throughout their entire flight regimes represents precisely such a situation. As the aircraft flies from the heavy atmosphere prevailing at low altitudes to the rare atmosphere at very high altitudes, extreme changes occur in the aerodynamic parameters. A single set of gains and compensation time constants is incapable of providing satisfactory performance throughout the flight regime. Instead, a gain scheduling procedure is required; i.e., changes must be made in the control elements as the surrounding conditions change. The changes are made in a predetermined fashion based upon air-data measurements. Such a procedure is not particularly attractive, for several reasons. First, it requires rather accurate information about the controlled system in its environment (i.e., the aircraft characteristics over the complete flight regime). Second, there is the need to measure air data for all flight conditions. Unfortunately, this is not always easily done. In fact in cases where high altitudes, high Mach numbers, and large angles of attack are involved, the on-board measurements of air-stream quantities is almost impossible. Third, the establishment of the required gain scheduling is a long process which often must be confirmed by flight testing. Finally, any changes in aircraft configuration often require additional testing and adjustment. It was chiefly these reasons that led to the development of self-adaptive control systems. The big advantage offered by the latter type of control system is that it eliminates the need for accurate information about the controlled system and it adjusts the control parameters on the basis of the amount of deviation existing between the actual and the desired output response rather than on some intermediate quantity such as air data, which may be difficult to measure.

The use of self-adaptive control systems in the process industry represents another important area where they can be used to advantage. For example, the case is reported by a leading manufacturer of control equipment of laboring all day in a chemical plant, adjusting gains and limits until the control system was functioning in the desired fashion. A subsequent load shift which caused a few pressures and temperatures to change resulted in a divergent control system. With a self-adaptive control system much greater tolerances to the surrounding operating conditions would have been permitted, and the unstable condition could have been avoided.

As the ideas of the self-adaptive control systems are developed, one begins to appreciate that the same familiar feedback principle is involved, but in a more sophisticated form. Certainly any feedback system which is designed to furnish an output which follows an input command with a minimum of steady-state error can be considered adaptive. The very presence of the negative feedback assures this condition. Such adaptability is best referred to as *static adaptability*. The use of this terminology then permits a distinction to be made between static adaptability and dynamic adaptability. A feedback control system which exhibits essentially the same dynamic response under the influence of changing system parameters possesses *dynamic adaptability* and is called a *self-adaptive control system*. In other words the description of a feedback control system as self-adaptive is determined by whether or not it has dynamic adaptability.

Another distinction worth making at this point is that existing between adaptive and self-adaptive systems. A feedback control system which changes its control parameters in accordance with a predetermined schedule allows the system to adapt to its changing environment, but not in an independent fashion. There is presupposed a fairly good knowledge of the general characteristics of the controlled system as well as the manner in which these characteristics vary in the changing environment. On the other hand a self-adaptive control system avoids the need for this kind of information because it has incorporated within its design a scheme for determining the characteristics of the controlled system along with a means for evaluating the need for control parameter adjustments in the presence of changing parameters of the controlled system.

No attempt is made here to classify the various types of self-adaptive control systems which have been developed in recent years. Rather, attention is confined to presenting a description of some of the concepts involved in several of the more prominent systems. It is felt that any attempt at classification at such an early stage in the development of self-adaptive control systems is likely to become obsolete soon. Moreover, there is the valid argument that perhaps no separate classification is really necessary because such systems offer nothing basically new save the feature of dynamic adaptability.

15-1. Self-adaptive Control by Using a Model-reference System[1]

The block diagram of a model-reference self-adaptive control system appears in Fig. 15-1. The conventional portion of the control system is

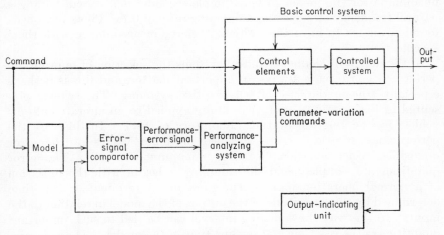

FIG. 15-1. Model-reference self-adaptive control system.

singled out by means of the dashed box. The remaining components in the diagram represent the additional equipment needed to provide the system with self-adaptive features. The figure shows that the command input is applied simultaneously to an appropriately designed model as well as to the main control loop. The system output is then compared with the model output. If a difference exists, an error signal is generated which is then operated upon in some predetermined fashion in order to apply optimum control-parameter variations. These in

[1] H. P. Whitaker, J. Yamron, and A. Kezer, "Design of Model-reference Adaptive Control Systems for Aircraft," *MIT Instrumentation Lab.*, *Rept.* R-164, September, 1958.

turn serve to modify the input to the controlled system in such a way as to bring the system output into correspondence with the output of the model. Examination of the block diagram should make it clear that, as changes in the parameters of the *controlled* system occur, the magnitude of the performance error signal is correspondingly affected because the model parameters remain fixed. This then reflects directly in the extent to which adjustments are made in the *control* parameters to yield the desired performance. Thus, the system is made self-adaptive.

The dynamic-performance specifications are embodied in the model in analog form. The model furnishes the system with the optimum criteria, which are used as a reference standard for the self-adaptive control loop. Of course the model design must be a realistic one and should require a performance of the control system which is entirely within its capabilities. In situations where a different set of specifications are required because of certain peculiar circumstances, the model can be readily modified to reflect such requirements. In aircraft application it is not uncommon for the model to be a simple second-order system having a natural frequency of $\frac{1}{2}$ cps and a damping ratio of 0.7. Pilots have been found to prefer to have their aircraft behave in accordance with these specifications.

In the design of feedback control systems the selection of appropriate performance criteria is always an important matter, and this is perhaps especially true in the case of self-adaptive systems. The scheme presented in Fig. 15-1 has been successfully applied to an aircraft military vehicle by the Instrumentation Laboratory of MIT. In this case the performance criteria involve specified optimum values of the error quantities, which are taken to be a minimum or a null. The error quantities are sampled, and the sampling is begun with the initiation of a normal operating input. The sampling is terminated at a time determined by the magnitude of the output of the model in relation to the input. In this way the sampling interval can be tied to such important quantities as the rise time and settling time of the model. Three parameters are used to control the dynamic response. The first parameter is known to affect the torque applied to the airplane in response to an input command and so is effective in controlling the initial portion of the response (i.e., the rise time). For this reason the error criterion chosen to vary this control parameter is that the integral of the error sampled over the rise time of the model be a minimum. The second control parameter is known to exert the greatest influence on the stability of the system. Accordingly, the error criterion used to adjust this control parameter is that the integral of the error sampled over the settling time of the model be a null (zero). Here the use of a nulling quantity rather than a minimizing quantity is preferred in order to reduce settling time. The third control parameter is adjusted in accordance with the error criterion calling for the integral of the absolute value of the error to be a minimum.   The absolute-value criterion is needed because even when the first two error criteria are satisfied oscillations could result because of low damping.   The chief contribution of the first two error criteria is to provide a reduction in settling time.

Some of the advantages which the system of Fig. 15-1 has to offer, besides that of self-adaptability, are worth noting.   To begin with, the adaptive loop functions independently of the main control loop.   Hence, if the adaptive loop should fail, operation is still possible.   Also, the

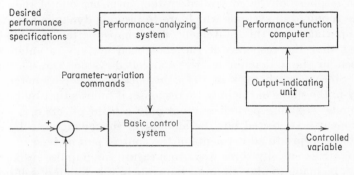

FIG. 15-2. A self-adaptive system using a performance-function computer.

design of the system is such that an error signal is immediately and continuously available.   There is no need for introducing computing lags (as is the case with computer-controlled self-adaptive systems[1]) or disturbing test signals.   Moreover, it is interesting to observe that the self-adaptive loop can be readily added to existing systems without appreciably altering the main control loop.   Furthermore, in instances where several loops are involved (as with aircraft controls) it is possible to use several models.   Thus, for example, an inner-loop model could be used to furnish the desired damping, while an outer-loop model could be used to provide the desired command response.   Finally, since the presence of noise in the input command is treated essentially in the same way in the model as in the system, there should be little if any deterioration in the optimizing process of the self-adaptive control system.

Figure 15-2 illustrates an alternative procedure which can be used to provide self-adaptive features to the basic control system of Fig. 15-1. A comparison shows that the model is replaced by a performance-function computer.   Here the task of the performance-function computer is to detect when changes occur in the performance function of the system components, to determine what the new performance functions are, and to use this information to vary the control parameters so that the output

[1] See Sec. 15-3.

performance is in correspondence with the desired performance-function specifications. The controlled system's performance functions can be measured either continuously or at discrete sampling intervals. A little thought should make it apparent that the use of an analog model offers the very significant advantage of simplicity.

15-2. Impulse-response Self-adaptive System

A design which has the capability of deriving information about the impulse response of the controlled system furnishes one of the essential features required in systems which are to provide dynamic adaptability. The importance of this statement is perhaps better appreciated by recalling that the response of the controlled system to an impulse is described in the s domain by the controlled-system transfer function itself. Since any changes in the controlled-system parameters reflect directly in the shape of the impulse response, it follows that by measuring this impulse response periodically not only can the effects of a changing environment be detected but the amount of this change can be used to generate appropriate adjustments of the control parameters.

There are essentially three ways to measure the impulse response, and each can be made to play an important role in the design of self-adaptive control systems. (This role is described in this section as well as in the next one.) Before proceeding with a description of these methods, it is helpful to keep in mind that the measurement of the impulse response must not be separated from the manner in which the information is to be used. Thus, if a rather complete description of the impulse response is needed, then the designer must be resigned to the need for an excessive amount of equipment. However, if the purpose of measuring the impulse response is merely to convey information about the oscillatory tendency of the system, the equipment requirement can be appreciably reduced.

The first way to find the impulse response is to excite the system by means of an impulse and measure the output as indicated in Fig. 15-3. Of course the specific form of $g(t)$, the impulse response, depends upon the composition of the controlled system $G(s)$. It follows that

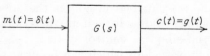

Fig. 15-3. An impulse-excited controlled system.

$$g(t) = \mathcal{L}^{-1}G(s) \qquad (15\text{-}1)$$

If the controlled system is assumed to be second-order, having the transfer function

$$G(s) = \frac{C(s)}{M(s)} = \frac{\omega_n^2}{s^2 + 2\zeta\omega_n s + \omega_n^2} \qquad (15\text{-}2)$$

the corresponding time-domain solution for the impulse response is given by

$$g(t) = \frac{\omega_n}{\sqrt{1 - \zeta^2}} \, \epsilon^{-\zeta\omega_n t} \sin \left(\omega_n t \sqrt{1 - \zeta^2} \right) \qquad (15\text{-}3)$$

for the underdamped case. A plot of this equation for various values of damping ratio appears in Fig. 15-4. These curves are applicable not only for the purely second-order system but quite often for higher-order systems, too, where the behavior is essentially established by a single pair

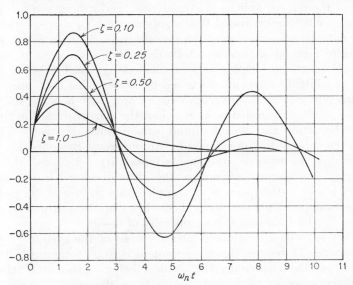

FIG. 15-4. Impulse response for the linear second-order system of Eq. (15-2).

of predominant complex conjugate roots. There are various ways in which these characteristic curves may be utilized. For example, the adaptive control system designed by one company uses the ratio of the positive areas to the negative areas of the impulse response as an indication of the damping ratio and in this way evaluates the system performance. Another procedure is to measure the magnitudes of the successive peaks of the impulse response. A third method samples the impulse response and shapes the response into a series of fixed-amplitude pulses. Then the number of these pulses is used as an indication of the number of reversals occurring in $g(t)$, which in turn can be used as a measure of the damping ratio.

The second method of finding the impulse response of a controlled system involves use of the convolution integral. Thus, if the controlled system is excited by an arbitrary but known function $m(t)$ and the output

$c(t)$ is measured, then the impulse response may be found from the relation

$$c(t) = \int_{-\infty}^{t} g(\tau)m(t - \tau) \, d\tau \qquad (15\text{-}4)$$

In those instances where the initial stored energy of the system is zero, Eq. (15-4) simplifies to

$$c(t) = \int_{0}^{t} g(\tau)m(t - \tau) \, d\tau \qquad (15\text{-}5)$$

One procedure for solving this equation for $g(t)$ involves using a series expansion for $c(t)$ as well as $m(t)$ and then performing the integration over the specified interval and finally solving for $g(t)$, also in series form. A more complete description of the process is available in Sec. 15-3.

The third method of experimentally determining the impulse response makes use of the principles of statistical design theory.[1] Thus, if a process or controlled system is excited by white noise (i.e., noise which has a flat power-density spectrum over a bandwidth considerably wider than that of the controlled system), then the cross-correlation function between the output and the noise input is the impulse response. The self-adaptive control system developed by Aeronutronic Systems, Inc.,[2] uses this principle to provide dynamic adaptability. Because the Aeronutronic system employs several of the ideas discussed in this section, attention is now turned to a more complete description of the system.

The self-adaptive philosophy embodied in the Aeronutronic system is described by the following three principles of design:

1. There is to be a continuous measurement of the system's dynamic performance. Moreover, this measurement is to be accomplished with a minimum of disturbance to the system being optimized. Also, the measurements are to be entirely immune to the effects of corrupting noise signals. This means avoiding such standard procedures as the use of step, impulse, and sinusoidal forcing functions, in order to establish information about the characteristics of the controlled system.

2. The evaluation of performance is to be based on an appropriate figure of merit. Furthermore, the figure of merit must be sign-sensitive so that it exhibits positive or negative values, depending upon the direction of the deviation from the nominal value.

3. There is to be a continuous readjustment of the control parameters based upon the performance evaluation.

The block diagram of the self-adaptive system designed in accordance with these principles appears in Fig. 15-5. Note that the command

[1] Consult J. G. Truxal "Automatic Feedback Control System Synthesis," chap. 7, McGraw-Hill Book Company, Inc., New York, 1955 for background in this subject.

[2] G. W. Anderson, R. N. Buland, and G. R. Cooper, The Aeronutronic Self-optimizing Automatic Control System, Aeronutronic Systems, Inc., Glendale, Calif., published in Wright Air Development Center, *Proceedings of the Self-adaptive Flight Control Systems Symposium*, March, 1959.

and the test signals are applied simultaneously to the basic control system. The basic control system responds to the command in a manner consistent with the dynamics of its loop. However, at the same time, the basic control system is responding to the wide-band noise test signal but in such a fashion as to cause a minimum of disturbance to the system. This result is accomplished because the excitation energy is spread over a wide frequency band with a consequent low noise amplitude. The

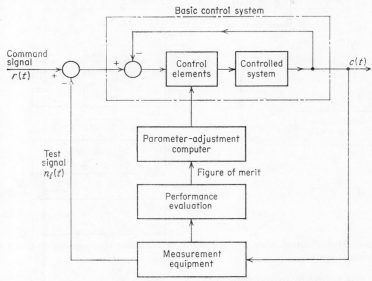

FIG. 15-5. An impulse-response self-adaptive control system.

block in Fig. 15-5 identified as "measurement equipment" contains the cross-correlator mechanization, which serves the very important function of measuring the impulse response continuously and accurately. Figure 15-6 presents a more detailed picture of the cross correlator. Since it is not our purpose here to develop the theory of correlation functions, we shall merely outline briefly how the impulse response is derived, starting with the cross-correlation function.

The cross-correlation function between the input noise and the output is defined as

$$\phi_{io}(\tau) = \lim_{T \to \infty} \frac{1}{2T} \int_{-T}^{T} n_i(t - \tau)[c(\tau) + n_o(\tau)] \, d\tau \tag{15-6}$$

or

$$\phi_{io}(\tau) = \lim_{T \to \infty} \frac{1}{2T} \left[\int_{-T}^{T} n_i(t - \tau)n_o(\tau) \, d\tau + \int_{-T}^{T} n_i(t - \tau)c(\tau) \, d\tau \right] \tag{15-7}$$

where n_i is the noise input and $n_o(t)$ the noise output of the basic control system. The second term of Eq. (15-7) is zero because the input noise and the output $c(t)$ due to the command, arising from separate sources, are uncorrelated. Therefore,

$$\phi_{io}(\tau) = \lim_{T \to \infty} \frac{1}{2T} \int_{-T}^{T} n_o(\tau) n_i(t - \tau) \, d\tau \qquad (15\text{-}8)$$

Furthermore, the output noise is related to the input noise by means

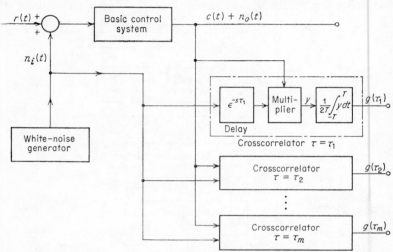

FIG. 15-6. Multichannel cross correlator for determining the impulse response of the basic control system.

of the convolution integral as follows:

$$n_o(t) = \int_{-\infty}^{\infty} g(t') n_i(t - t') \, dt' \qquad (15\text{-}9)$$

Inserting this equation into Eq. (15-8) and interchanging the integration yields

$$\phi_{io}(\tau) = \int_{-\infty}^{\infty} g(t') \left[\lim_{T \to \infty} \frac{1}{2T} \int_{-T}^{T} n_i(t - \tau) n_i(t - t') \, dt \right] dt' \qquad (15\text{-}10a)$$

The quantity in brackets is the autocorrelation function $\phi_{ii}(\tau - t')$ of the input noise. Accordingly, Eq. (15-10a) simplifies to

$$\phi_{io}(\tau) = \int_{-\infty}^{\infty} g(t') \phi_{ii}(\tau - t') \, dt' \qquad (15\text{-}10b)$$

The significant point here concerns the character of the autocorrelation function. It can be shown that if the input autocorrelation is narrow (and this results whenever the noise is wideband), then the autocorrelation function becomes essentially the impulse function $\delta(\tau - t')$. For this condition then, the cross-correlation function becomes

$$\phi_{io}(\tau) = \int_{-\infty}^{\infty} g(t') \, \delta(\tau - t') \, dt' = g(\tau) \qquad (15\text{-}11)$$

Equation (15-11) thus makes it clear that the output of the cross correlator makes available a point on the impulse response. Of course as many points on the impulse response as is desirable may be obtained by introducing additional cross-correlator channels equipped with the appropriate delay. It is interesting to note that the cross correlator of Fig. 15-6 is nothing more than a mechanization of Eq. (15-6).

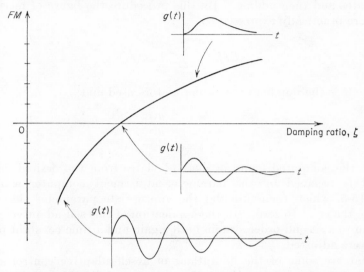

FIG. 15-7. Variation of the figure of merit as a function of the damping ratio associated with the system impulse response.

The evaluation of the performance is determined on the basis of an appropriately selected figure of merit, which in this case is the damping ratio. As already pointed out, information about the damping ratio can be deduced from the ratio of the positive area to the negative area of the time history of the impulse response. It can be shown that for the second-order system this area ratio is given by

$$k = \left| \frac{A_+}{A_-} \right| = \epsilon^{\zeta\pi/\sqrt{1-\zeta^2}} \tag{15-12}$$

where A_+ represents the total positive area of the impulse response and A_- represents the total negative area. Accordingly, the figure of merit may be expressed as

$$FM = A_+ - kA_- = \frac{1 - k\epsilon^{-\zeta\pi/\sqrt{1-\zeta^2}}}{1 - \epsilon^{-\pi\zeta/\sqrt{1-\zeta^2}}} \tag{15-13}$$

A sketch of Eq. (15-13) as a function of the damping ratio is depicted in Fig. 15-7. The function can be made to change sign at the desired damping ratio by a suitable choice of k. The attendant sign sensitivity of *FM* of course makes it suitable as an error signal for the optimizing system.

Since the entire impulse response is not available continuously but rather as a discrete set of finite values, it is necessary to approximate the appropriate areas needed to evaluate Eq. (15-13) by multiplying the computed ordinates $g(\tau_1)$, $g(\tau_2)$, etc., by the spacing between successive ordinates and then adding. By this procedure the figure of merit may be more practically expressed by

$$FM = \sum_{m=1}^{M} A_m\, g(\tau_m) \tag{15-14}$$

where M is the number of cross correlators used and

$$\begin{aligned} A_m &= a_m & g(\tau_m) > 0 \\ &= ka_m & g(\tau_m) < 0 \end{aligned} \tag{15-15}$$

and
$$a_m = \tfrac{1}{2}(\tau_{m+1} - \tau_{m-1}) \tag{15-16}$$

When the computed figure of merit deviates from the desired value, a signal is received by the parameter-adjustment computer shown in Fig. 15-5, which then provides the appropriate parameter changes to reduce the error to zero. In the application of this self-adaptive control system to a second-order system both a gain and a time-constant parameter were adjusted.

What are some of the limitations of a self-adaptive control system based on the foregoing principles? One area of difficulty can arise in a situation where the variation of the controlled parameters occurs in a time which is not excessive compared with the time required to perform the cross-correlation computations. Another objection is that the system does require the use of artificial excitation, and although the use of wide-band noise reduces the effect at the output, still it does cause some disturbance, thereby contributing to the wear of components. Finally, the application to higher-order systems does necessitate a modification in the manner of performance evaluation as well as a change in the parameter-adjustment computer.

15-3. Digital-computer-controlled Self-adaptive System[1]

The inclusion of a digital computer in a feedback control system offers some truly attractive features. It is possible, for example, for it to perform a dual function. It can be made to compute the forcing function needed to bring the output into correspondence with the input (or desired response), as well as to compute up-to-date information about the

[1] L. Braun, Jr., On Adaptive Control Systems, doctoral dissertation, Brooklyn Polytechnic Institute, New York, 1959.

dynamic response of the system. The latter feature, which makes the system self-adaptive, is derived from the manner by which the forcing function applied to the controlled system is generated. This becomes apparent as the theory underlying this type of control system unfolds.

A simplified block diagram of a digital-computer-controlled system appears in Fig. 15-8. The model is included for the purpose of converting the command signal to a desired response signal. The model may be

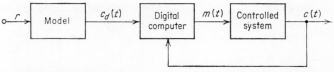

FIG. 15-8. Simplified block diagram of a digital-computer-controlled system.

omitted, if desired. Let it be assumed that this system is subjected to a command input $r(t)$ and that at a particular point in its dynamic time history the actual value of the controlled variable is $c_1(t)$, corresponding to which is a forcing function $m_1(t)$ applied to the controlled system. Then in accordance with the convolution integral these two quantities are related as follows:

$$c_1(t) = \int_{-\infty}^{t_1} m_1(\tau) \, g(t - \tau) \, d\tau \tag{15-17}$$

where $g(t)$ is the controlled-system impulse response. Now, if the controlled variable is to take on the desired value $c_d(t)$, then the manipulated variable should assume the value $m_d(t)$ as described by

$$c_d(t) = \int_{-\infty}^{t} m_d(\tau) \, g(t - \tau) \, d\tau \tag{15-18}$$

In general the desired manipulated variable can be represented as

$$m_d(t) = m_1(t) + \Delta m(t) \tag{15-19}$$

where $\Delta m(t)$ represents the increment in the manipulated variable required to make $c(t) = c_d(t)$. It is the function of the digital computer to calculate these required increments, and it is called upon to do so every T sec. Effectively, then, the digital computer is charged with the responsibility of keeping track of the present state of affairs in the system, comparing the actual response with the desired response, and then generating and applying to the controlled system the increment in forcing function needed to make $c(t) = c_d(t)$. If the computer is designed to make a computation for $\Delta m(t)$ every T sec, and if t is made to represent time variation within the control interval, then clearly in Eq. (15-19)

$$\begin{aligned} \Delta m(t) &= 0 & t &< 0 \\ \Delta m(t) &\neq 0 & t &> 0 \end{aligned} \tag{15-20}$$

Figure 15-9 depicts the notation convention used. The t_1 here is the same as that appearing as the upper limit in Eq. (15-17), whereas t is the time variation starting from zero at the beginning of a control

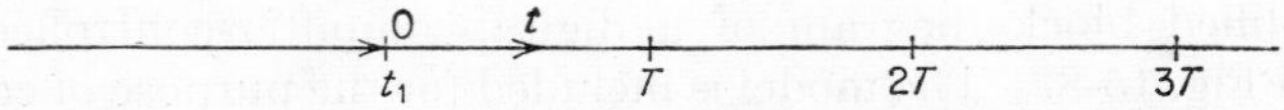

FIG. 15-9. Notation for time variation within a control (computation) interval.

interval. Inserting Eq. (15-19) into the convolution integral yields

$$c(t) = \int_{-\infty}^{t_1+t} m_1(\tau)\, g(t-\tau)\, d\tau + \int_0^t \Delta m(\tau)\, g(t-\tau)\, d\tau = c_1(t) + c_2(t)$$

(15-21)

The first part of Eq. (15-21) is identical to Eq. (15-17). The second term, which we now call

$$c_2(t) = \int_0^t \Delta m(\tau)\, g(t-\tau)\, d\tau$$

(15-22)

represents the increase in output generated by the incremental forcing function $\Delta m(t)$. Equation (15-22) is one of two key equations upon which the digital-computer-controlled system is based.

The error existing in the system immediately before the start of a control interval is

$$e(t) = c_d(t) - c_1(t)$$

(15-23)

Substituting Eqs. (15-17) and (15-18) into the last equation gives

$$e(t) = \int_0^t \Delta m(\tau)\, g(t-\tau)\, d\tau$$

(15-24)

Equation (15-24) is the second of the two key equations. The importance of this equation lies in the following: It states that if information about the error is known at the start of a control interval, as well as up-to-date information about the impulse response, then the value of the required $\Delta m(t)$ can be computed.

One procedure for computing $\Delta m(t)$ from Eq. (15-24) is to use Maclaurin-series expansions of the quantities $e(t)$ and $g(t)$ in the interval $0 < t < T$ as proposed by L. Braun.[1] Thus, the impulse response can be written as

$$g(t) = G_0 + G_1 t + G_2 \frac{t^2}{2!} + \cdots$$

(15-25)

The corresponding Laplace transform expression is

$$G(s) = G_0 s^{-1} + G_1 s^{-2} + G_2 s^{-3} + \cdots$$

(15-26)

[1] *Ibid.*

Similarly the error function may be written as

$$e(t) = \int_0^t \Delta m(\tau)\, g(t - \tau)\, d\tau = E_0 + E_1 t + E_2 \frac{t^2}{2!} + \cdots \quad (15\text{-}27)$$

where

$$E_n = \frac{d^n e(t)}{dt^n}\bigg|_{t=0} \qquad \text{and} \qquad n = 0, 1, 2, \ldots \quad (15\text{-}28)$$

A little thought reveals that these error coefficients are determined from the differences existing between the actual and desired responses and their derivatives at the beginning of a control interval. Thus,

$$
\begin{aligned}
E_0 &= c_d(0^-) - c(0^-) \\
E_1 &= \dot{c}_d(0^-) - \dot{c}(0^-) \\
E_2 &= \ddot{c}_d(0^-) - \ddot{c}(0^-) \\
&\quad \cdot \qquad\qquad \cdot \\
&\quad \cdot \qquad\qquad \cdot \\
&\quad \cdot \qquad\qquad \cdot \\
E_p &= c_d{}^p(0^-) - c^p(0^-)
\end{aligned}
\qquad (15\text{-}29)
$$

where the single dot refers to the first derivatives, the double dot to the second derivatives, and so forth. The Laplace transform of Eq. (15-27) is

$$E(s) = \Delta M(s)\, G(s) = E_0 s^{-1} + E_1 s^{-2} + E_2 s^{-3} + \cdots \quad (15\text{-}30)$$

A glance at Eq. (15-30) reveals that the expression in the s domain for the required incremental forcing function is

$$\Delta M(s) = \frac{E(s)}{G(s)} = \frac{E_0 s^{-1} + E_1 s^{-2} + E_2 s^{-3} + \cdots}{G_0 s^{-1} + G_1 s^{-2} + G_2 s^{-3} + \cdots} \quad (15\text{-}31)$$

Performing the longhand division of this equation yields an expression for $\Delta M(s)$ which is in the form of a series expansion. Thus,

$$\Delta M(s) = \Delta M_{-1} + \Delta M_0 s^{-1} + \Delta M_1 s^{-2} + \cdots \quad (15\text{-}32)$$

where

$$\Delta M_{-1} = \frac{E_0}{G_0} \quad (15\text{-}33)$$

$$\Delta M_0 = \frac{E_1 - \Delta M_{-1} G_1}{G_0} \quad (15\text{-}34)$$

$$\Delta M_1 = \frac{E_2 - (\Delta M_{-1} G_2 + \Delta M_0 G_1)}{G_0} \quad (15\text{-}35)$$

The corresponding time-domain expression of Eq. (15-32) is

$$\Delta m(t) = \Delta M_{-1}\, \delta(t) + \Delta M_0 + \Delta M_1 t + \cdots \quad (15\text{-}36)$$

Equation (15-36) reveals some interesting facts. It states that in a situation where the impulse response is correctly represented by Eq. (15-26), that is, $G_0 \neq 0$, the change in the forcing function which is needed to bring the output response into correspondence with the desired response contains several of the standard types of driving functions. One component is the impulse function having the magnitude given by Eq. (15-33). A little thought shows that the purpose of this impulse is to bring the magnitude of the controlled variable into exact correspondence with the desired value of the variable. The second component it contains is a step function having the magnitude given by Eq. (15-34). As a study of this equation reveals, the purpose of this term of $\Delta m(t)$ is to make the first derivative of the controlled variable equal to the first derivative of the desired output response. Similarly, the purpose of the ramp component of $\Delta m(t)$ is to provide correspondence between the second derivatives of the actual response and the desired response. It should be clearly understood that the basic character of $\Delta m(t)$ is dependent upon the form of $G(s)$, as an inspection of Eq. (15-31) indicates. Herein lies one of the serious limitations of this type of control system. More is said about this presently.

The self-adaptive characteristic of the digital-computer-controlled system revolves about Eq. (15-22). To possess adaptability, the digital controller must be capable of modifying the manipulated variable, not only in accordance with the magnitudes of the error coefficients (as described in the foregoing), but also in a manner which reflects the effects of changing system dynamics in the computation of the coefficients of the incremental forcing function. In other words, the system must be capable of computing the new values of G_0, G_1, G_2, etc., and using these in the computations called for in Eqs. (15-33) to (15-35). Equation (15-22) indicates that, if information about $c_2(t)$ is known at the start of a control interval as well as information about $\Delta m(t)$, then current information about the impulse response $g(t)$ can be determined. However, it should be apparent that the $\Delta m(t)$ in this expression cannot possibly be the incremental forcing function to be used in the present control interval because to compute this quantity requires information about the coefficients of $g(t)$. This difficulty is resolved by using the value of $\Delta m(t)$ which is computed and utilized in the preceding control interval. Clearly some error is thereby introduced, because somewhat "stale" information is being used to compute the coefficients in the series expansion of the impulse response. However, the extent of this error can be kept within bounds by making the control interval sufficiently small. Moreover, there is also the asset that the control interval is quite small in comparison with the time needed for the changes in the parameters of the controlled system to take place.

By proceeding on this basis then and using a series expansion to represent the change in controlled variable caused by the application of $\Delta m(t)$, Eq. (15-22) may be written as

$$c_2(t) = \int_0^t \Delta m^*(\tau)\, g(t - \tau)\, d\tau = C_{20} + C_{21}t + C_{22}\frac{t^2}{2!} + \cdots \quad (15\text{-}37)$$

where $\qquad C_{2n} = \dfrac{d^n c(t)}{dt^n}\bigg|_{t=0^+} \qquad n = 0, 1, 2, \ldots \qquad (15\text{-}38)$

and where t is time starting from zero at the beginning of a control interval. Also, $\Delta m^*(t)$ represents the incremental forcing function of the preceding control interval. The Laplace-transform version of Eq. (15-37) is

$$C_2(s) = \Delta M^*(s)\, G(s) = C_{20}s^{-1} + C_{21}s^{-2} + C_{22}s^{-3} + \cdots \quad (15\text{-}39)$$

from which it follows that information about the system dynamics is deducible from

$$G(s) = \frac{C_2(s)}{\Delta M^*(s)} = \frac{C_{20}s^{-1} + C_{21}s^{-2} + C_{22}s^{-3} + \cdots}{\Delta M_{-1}^* + \Delta M_0^*\, s^{-1} + \Delta M_1^*\, s^{-2} + \cdots} \quad (15\text{-}40)$$

Longhand division of this expression leads to

$$G(s) = G_0 s^{-1} + G_1 s^{-2} + G_2 s^{-3} + \cdots \quad (15\text{-}41)$$

where $\qquad G_0 = \dfrac{C_{20}}{\Delta M_{-1}^*} \qquad\qquad\qquad\qquad (15\text{-}42)$

$$G_1 = \frac{C_{21} - \Delta M_0^*\, G_0}{\Delta M_{-1}^*} \qquad\qquad (15\text{-}43)$$

$$G_2 = \frac{C_{22} - (\Delta M_0^*\, G_1 + \Delta M_1^*\, G_0)}{\Delta M_{-1}^*} \qquad (15\text{-}44)$$

$$\cdot \qquad\qquad \cdot$$
$$\cdot \qquad\qquad \cdot$$
$$\cdot \qquad\qquad \cdot$$

By means of expressions such as those represented by the last three equations, the system can be made to exhibit self-adaptive features. As these equations reveal, evaluation of an up-to-date series expansion of the impulse response $g(t)$ requires measurement of the controlled variable and its derivatives immediately before and immediately after the application of the incremental forcing function $\Delta m(t)$. To make this clearer, recall from Eq. (15-21) that

$$c_2(t) = c(t) - c_1(t)$$

Then in Eq. (15-38) for $n = 0$ and $t = 0^+$ we have

$$C_{20} = c_2(0^+) = c(0^+) - c_1(0^+)$$

But since $c_1(t)$ is the controlled variable without the effect of the incremental forcing function, it follows that $c_1(0^+) = c(0^-)$. Inserting this into the last equation yields

$$C_{20} = c_2(0^+) = c(0^+) - c(0^-) \tag{15-45}$$

Hence information about C_{20} is obtained by measuring the output quantity just before and just after initiation of a control interval. In a similar fashion it can be shown that

$$C_{21} = \dot{c}_2(0^+) = \dot{c}(0^+) - \dot{c}(0^-) \tag{15-46}$$
$$C_{22} = \ddot{c}_2(0^+) = \ddot{c}(0^+) - \ddot{c}(0^-) \tag{15-47}$$

It is worthwhile to note that in this self-adaptive system information about the controlled-system dynamics is deduced from a previously applied corrective signal $\Delta m^*(t)$ and not from an intentionally inserted noise source, as is the case with the system in the preceding section.

In the interest of presenting a clearer picture of the computation sequence as it is to be performed by the digital computer, the following simplified procedure is offered. Refer to Table 15-1. It will be noticed that the computation procedure starts by applying a small impulse for the sake of computing and storing information about the impulse response in order to use it soon after the application of a command. Of course, if even approximate information about the impulse response is known initially, this can be entered directly into memory, thereby eliminating the need for an initial impulse excitation.

Immediately upon application of the command input r, the digital controller computes the error coefficients and then determines the coefficients of the incremental forcing function. Next a summation is made to obtain $\Delta m_1(t)$. Immediately before applying $\Delta m_1(t)$ the values of the controlled variable and as many of its derivatives as are needed are computed. These same quantities are computed immediately after the introduction of $\Delta m_1(t)$. In this way information is available for the computation of the coefficients appearing in Eq. (15-41), which can be combined subsequently with the previously determined values of the coefficients of $\Delta m_1(t)$ to yield more current information about the system dynamics. Then, at some appropriately predetermined elapsed time T_1, the computer compares the actual state of the output with the desired output. If the error coefficients are found to be zero (or within a suitably small tolerance band), there is no further need for correction and so no additional increment in forcing function is generated. On the other hand, if any one error coefficient is not zero, then a proper increment in the forcing function is developed and it acts to reduce these errors to a minimum. The time elapsed between successive applications of the

TABLE 15-1. SIMPLIFIED OUTLINE OF COMPUTATION PROCEDURE

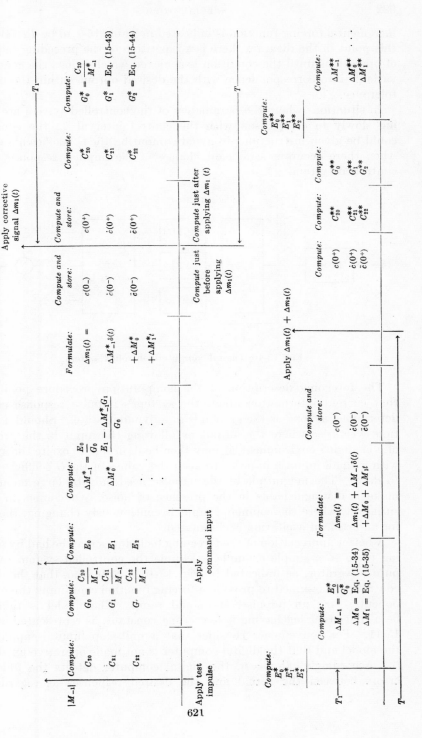

incremental forcing function is indicated in Table 15-1 to be T.   Beyond
this point in the diagram there is a repetition of the preceding sequence
of operations until the condition is achieved which brings the controlled
variable into correspondence with the desired output within the desired
tolerance.

In situations where the parameters of the controlled system are varying slowly in comparison with the control interval T, the computer
could be given instructions to avoid computing the G coefficients except
when there occurs a significant change in the impulse response of the
controlled system.

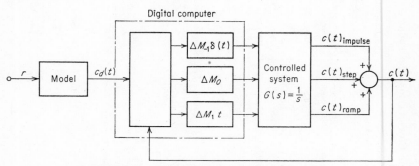

Fig. 15-10. Digital-computer-controlled system.

The foregoing description of the computation procedure points out
that current information about the system's impulse response can be
determined as long as the system is in a dynamic state.   Should a situation ever arise where the output is following the input in the presence
of a changing environment, it may then be desirable to excite the system
with a small impulse in order to keep the values of the G coefficients up
to date.   The magnitude of the impulse need only be large enough to
make it distinguishable in the presence of noise.   Of course, in those
situations where the command input is continuously changing, the need
for an artificial excitation is eliminated.

A better appreciation of the foregoing techniques may be had by applying them to a simple example.   Assume the controlled system to be a
pure integrator, as indicated in Fig. 15-10.   Note, too, that the digital
controller is assumed to provide a forcing function containing three components, viz., an impulse, step, and ramp.   The model is taken to
be a first-order lag having a 1-sec time constant, as represented in Fig.
15-11.   For convenience consider that a unit-step input is applied to
the model and that the digital computer is not made operative until time
t_1.   Accordingly, at $t = t_1$, the digital computer detects the following
errors between the actual and the desired responses as regards the

magnitude of the variable as well as its first and second derivatives:

$$E_0 = c_d(t_1^-) - c(t_1^-) = c_{d1} = 1 - \epsilon^{-t_1}$$
$$E_1 = \dot{c}_d(t_1^-) - \dot{c}(t_1^-) = \epsilon^{-t_1} \tag{15-48}$$
$$E_2 = \ddot{c}_d(t_1^-) - \ddot{c}(t_1^-) = -\epsilon^{-t_1}$$

Thus, through measurement and computation the digital computer

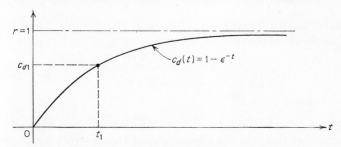

FIG. 15-11. Description of model output for a step command.

determines the error coefficients.   Also, for this simple case

$$g(t) = 1$$
$$G(s) = \frac{1}{s}$$

so that $$G_0 = 1 \qquad G_1 = G_2 = G_3 = \cdots = 0 \tag{15-49}$$

From Eqs. (15-48) and (15-49) the forcing function needed to reduce the error coefficients to zero is determined.   To establish the output corresponding to this forcing function requires merely finding the contribution of each component of the forcing function and then summing.   Thus, the contribution at the output during the first control interval due to the impulse component is as follows:

$$\Delta M_{-1} = \frac{E_0}{G_0} = E_0 = c_{d1} = \text{magnitude of impulse}$$

$$C(s)_{\text{impulse}} = G(s)(\Delta M_{-1}) = \frac{E_0}{s} = \frac{c_{d1}}{s}$$

Therefore
$$c(t)_{\text{impulse}} = \mathcal{L}^{-1}\, C(s)_{\text{impulse}} = c_{d1} \tag{15-50}$$

The contribution of the step component is

$$\Delta M_0 = \frac{E_1}{G_0} = E_1 = \epsilon^{-t_1} = \text{magnitude of step}$$

$$C(s)_{\text{step}} = \frac{1}{s}\frac{\Delta M_0}{s} = \frac{\Delta M_0}{s^2}$$

Therefore $$c(t)_{\text{step}} = \mathcal{L}^{-1}\, C(s)_{\text{step}} = E_1 t \tag{15-51}$$

The contribution of the ramp component is:

$$\Delta M_1 = \frac{E_2}{G_0} = E_2 = -\epsilon^{-t_1} = \text{ramp magnitude}$$

$$C(s)_{\text{ramp}} = \frac{1}{s}\frac{\Delta M_1}{s^2} = \frac{E_2}{s^3}$$

Therefore $c(t)_{\text{ramp}} = \mathcal{L}^{-1}\, C(s)_{\text{ramp}} = \frac{1}{2}E_2 t^2$ (15-52)

Accordingly, the total expressions for the output quantity and its derivatives in the interval $0 < t < T$ are $c(t) = c(t)_{\text{impulse}} + c(t)_{\text{step}} + c(t)_{\text{ramp}}$.

$$c(t) = c_{d1} + E_1 t + \tfrac{1}{2}E_2 t^2 \qquad (15\text{-}53)$$
$$\dot{c}(t) = E_1 + E_2 t \qquad (15\text{-}54)$$
$$\ddot{c}(t) = E_2 \qquad (15\text{-}55)$$

Superposition is valid because the assumption is made throughout that the changes that occur in the parameters of the controlled system always do so at a rate which is very small compared with the time constants of the control system.

At the start of the control interval, i.e., at $t = 0^+$, the controlled variable and its first two derivatives have the values

$$c(0^+) = c_{d1} = E_0$$
$$\dot{c}(0^+) = E_1 \qquad (15\text{-}56)$$
$$\ddot{c}(0^+) = E_2$$

Of course this is as it should be since the magnitude of the forcing function was computed to assure this condition. In other words, with this type of control system correspondence between the desired and the actual response is established at the start of the interval. However, as Eqs. (15-53) and (15-54) reveal, this correspondence no longer prevails as time progresses within the control interval. Thus, from time t_1 to $t_1 + T$ the desired response is described by $c_d = 1 - \epsilon^{-t}$, whereas the output variable is described by Eq. (15-53). Similarly the first derivative of $c_d(t)$ is ϵ^{-t}, whereas for the controlled variable it is given by Eq. (15-54). It should be apparent, then, that the smaller the control interval is made, the more exact the correspondence between the actual and the desired responses.

In order to investigate the effect of changing system dynamics on the computation of the forcing function, consider that in the succeeding control interval the error coefficients are found to be E_0^*, E_1^*, and E_2^*. Consider, too, that the system dynamics change in such a way that the controlled-system transfer function changes from $G(s) = K/s$ to

$$G^*(s) = \frac{K + \Delta K}{s}$$

In such a situation the magnitude of the impulse is found by using the new value of the G coefficient, viz., G_0^*. Thus $\Delta M_{-1}^* = E_0^*/G_0^* = E_0^*/(K + \Delta K)$ and

$$C(s)_{\text{impulse}} = \frac{K + \Delta K}{s} \frac{E_0^*}{K + \Delta K}$$

Therefore $\qquad c(t)_{\text{impulse}} = E_0^*$

which shows that the impulse contribution is still of such a magnitude as to make the magnitude of the output variable equal to the desired value in spite of the changing dynamics. A similar argument holds for the other components of the forcing function.

What are some of the limitations of the foregoing type of self-adaptive control system? There are several serious restrictions, but perhaps one stands out above the others. This system behaves in the manner described provided that the controlled-system transfer function has an excess of poles over zeros of 1 and not more if there is to exist a component of the forcing function no more sophisticated than the impulse. Thus, if the excess of poles over zeros is equal to 2, a doublet would be needed to provide correspondence between the magnitude of the output variable and the desired value. In such a case the impulse component is effective only in furnishing correspondence between the first-derivative terms, the step in the second-derivative terms, and so on. Of course the argument can be offered that the inclusion of a zero in the controlled system remedies the situation. Perhaps a better solution might be to design the controller to furnish correspondence at the end of the control interval rather than at the start.

Another significant factor affecting the success of this type of control system concerns the need to obtain reliable measurements of the controlled variable and its derivatives just before and just after the application of a corrective forcing-function signal. Moreover, the greater the number of terms used in the series expansion of $e(t)$, the more difficult the design becomes, not only in terms of the problems dealing with the measurement of higher derivatives of the output quantity, but also because more time is needed to process this information in the digital computer. The consequent increase in control interval then means increased error.

15-4. Extension of the Concepts of Digital-computer-controlled Systems

On the basis of the limitations described for the system of Sec. 15-3, it may be desirable to seek out a control scheme which avoids the use of an impulse component in the forcing function as well as one which relaxes the requirement of imposing correspondence between the desired and the actual response at the start of the control interval. Elimination of the need of an impulse is generally desired because as a practical matter it is not easily generated. One procedure for avoiding the impulse has been suggested by Haddad and Mishkin[1]—confining the variation of the manipulated variable to step changes, as depicted in Fig. 15-12. This is referred to as a staircase function for obvious reasons. The second restriction is removed by generating the magnitude of the forcing function in such a way that the desired output is obtained at the end of the control interval rather than at the start.

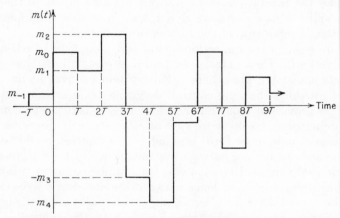

FIG. 15-12. Staircase variation of the manipulated variable.

The underlying theory of this approach is essentially the same; however, some modifications are needed. As a result of the staircase nature to which the forcing function is restricted, it is reasonable to characterize the dynamics of the controlled system in terms of its step response rather than its impulse response. In this connection, then, the controlled output and the manipulated variable may still be related by the convolution integral but in the modified form given by

$$c(t) = \int_{-\infty}^{t} m'(\tau)u(t - \tau)\, d\tau \tag{15-57}$$

where $m'(t)$ is the derivative of the manipulated variable and $u(t)$ is the step response of the controlled system. To remove the effect of the initially stored energy in Eq. (15-57) just prior to the application of a corrective signal at the start of a new control interval, the last equation may be written as

$$c(t) = \int_{-\infty}^{0} m'(\tau)u(t - \tau)\, d\tau + \int_{0}^{t} m'(\tau)u(t - \tau)\, d\tau \tag{15-58}$$

[1] R. A. Haddad and E. Mishkin, On the Identification and Command Problems in Computer-controlled Adaptive Systems, *Proc. Wescon*, 1959.

In fact it can be shown that the effect of the stored energy up to the point in time when a new corrective signal is to be applied to the controlled system is given by the first term of Eq. (15-58), which in turn can be represented by a Maclaurin-series expansion as follows:

$$c_1(t) \equiv \int_{-\infty}^{0-} m'(\tau)u(t - \tau) \, d\tau = c(0^-) + \dot{c}(0^-)t + \ddot{c}(0^-)\frac{t^2}{2!} + \cdots \quad (15\text{-}59)$$

The second part of Eq. (15-58) represents the change in $c(t)$ due to the

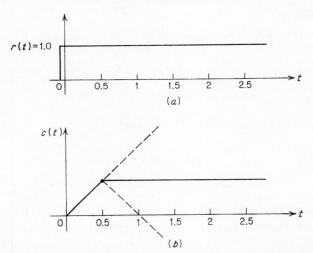

Fig. 15-13. Illustration of desired and actual responses, using the control technique described by Eq. (15-69). (a) Command input signal; (b) description of controlled variable for a control interval $T = 0.5$ sec.

change in forcing function applied at the beginning of the control interval. Thus

$$c_2(t) = \int_{0-}^{t} m'(\tau)u(t - \tau) \, d\tau \quad (15\text{-}60)$$

Since the forcing function is restricted to the variation shown in Fig. 15-12, a general expression may be written to represent it which is of the form

$$m(t) = m_0(t)u + (m_1 - m_0)u(t - T) + (m_2 - m_1)u(t - 2T) + \cdots$$

Upon inserting this equation into Eq. (15-60) and evaluating the result at $t = T^-$, that is, at the end of the control interval, there results

$$c_2(T^-) = (m_0 - m_{-1})u(T^-)_1 \quad (15\text{-}61)$$

Here $m_0 - m_{-1}$ represents the change in the manipulated variable when going into the "first" control interval from the preceding one (see Fig. 15-12). The reason for using a lower limit of 0^- in Eq. (15-60) should now be apparent. The quantity $u(T^-)_1$ represents the unit-step response of the controlled system at the end of the first control interval.

Evaluating Eq. (15-59) also at $t = T^-$ and inserting this result together with Eq. (15-61) into Eq. (15-58) yields

$$c(T^-) = \left[c(0^-) + T\dot{c}(0^-) + \frac{T^2}{2}\ddot{c}(0^-) + \cdots \right] + (m_0 - m_{-1})u(T^-)_1$$

$$c(T^-) = \sum_{n=0}^{m} \frac{T^n c^n(0^-)}{n!} + (m_0 - m_{-1})u(T^-)_1 \tag{15-62}$$

Therefore the unit-step response may be expressed as

$$u(T^-)_1 = \frac{c(T^-) - \sum_{n=0}^{m} \dfrac{T^n c^n(0^-)}{n!}}{m_0 - m_{-1}} \tag{15-63}$$

In general, at the end of the kth control interval,

$$u(T^-)_k = \frac{c(kT^-) - \sum_{n=0}^{m} \dfrac{T^n c^n[(k-1)T^-]}{n!}}{m_{k-1} - m_{k-2}} \tag{15-64}$$

It is through the use of this equation that the self-adaptive feature can be designed into the system. Equation (15-64) states that, by measuring the actual value of the control variable just before the end of the kth control interval, subtracting the value of the controlled variable and its derivatives due to the stored energy at the end of the preceding control interval, and finally dividing by the magnitude of the change in the forcing function existing at the start of the control interval, the unit-step response of the controlled system can be computed. The computations may be accomplished by using either digital or analog procedures. The significant point, however, is that if this computed step response differs from some desired one an error signal can be generated to adjust those system parameters which brings the two into correspondence. Thus dynamic adaptability is realized.

In the analysis so far the step magnitudes of the forcing function were assumed to be known. Actually, of course, these must be generated. Attention is therefore now directed to the manner by which this is accomplished. As previously mentioned, the control strategy to be employed is that the controlled output is to be made equal to the desired value at the end of the control interval. Equation (15-65) expresses this statement mathematically:

$$c(kT^-) = c_d[(k-1)T^-] \tag{15-65}$$

To satisfy this condition, the staircase command signal depicted in Fig.

15-12 suffices. Let us consider the situation where it is desirable to compute the value to be assigned to m_1 in this figure. It is assumed that m_0 is already known. In order to involve the quantity m_1, it is necessary to write the expression for the output at the end of the second control interval, i.e., at $t = 2T^-$. Using $k = 2$ in Eq. (15-64), we get

$$c(2T^-) = \sum_{n=0}^{m} \frac{T^n c^n(T^-)}{n!} + (m_1 - m_0)u(T^-)_2 \qquad (15\text{-}66)$$

In accordance with Eq. (15-65) we have $c(2T^-) = c_d(T^-)$. Thus Eq. (15-66) becomes

$$c_d(T^-) = \sum_{n=0}^{m} \frac{T^n c^n(T^-)}{n!} + (m_1 - m_0)u(T^-)_2 \qquad (15\text{-}67)$$

Examination of this equation reveals that there are two unknowns, viz., m_1 and $u(T^-)_2$. However, for all practical purposes there is really only one unknown, which is m_1. Although $u(T^-)_2$ cannot be known at $t = T^-$, it is quite reasonable to assume that

$$u(T^-)_2 = u(T^-)_1 \qquad (15\text{-}68)$$

The validity of this assumption lies in the fact that the control period T is very small compared with the time needed for changes to occur in the parameters of the controlled system. Therefore the magnitude of the corrective forcing function to be applied at $t = 2T$ is

$$m_1 = \frac{c_d(T^-) - \sum_{n=0}^{m} \dfrac{T^n c^n(T^-)}{n!}}{u(T^-)_1} + m_0 \qquad (15\text{-}69)$$

A generalized version of Eq. (15-69) takes the following form:

$$m_k = \frac{c_d(kT^-) - \sum_{n=0}^{m} \dfrac{T^n c^n(kT^-)}{n!}}{c(kT^-) - \sum_{n=0}^{m} \dfrac{T^n c^n[(k-1)T^-]}{n!}}(m_{k-1} - m_{k-2}) + m_{k-1} \qquad (15\text{-}70)$$

It should be clear, then, that through the use of Eqs. (15-64) and (15-70) the controlled output can be made equal to the desired output at the ends of the control intervals in a way which reflects the influence of changing system parameters.

In order to illustrate the concepts described in the foregoing, let us apply them to a simple example. Assume the controlled system to be a pure integrator so that $G(s) = 1/s$. Also, assume that the desired response is identical to the command, which is a unit step, as depicted in Fig. 15-13a. The command signal is assumed applied at $t = 0^-$ in order that Eq. (15-70) will yield a value different from zero and thereby generate the corrective action needed to provide the desired result. Furthermore, for convenience, consider the system parameter to be invariant. On the basis of this assumption it then follows that the system's unit-step response also remains invariant and may be simply described as

$$u(t) = \mathcal{L}^{-1} \frac{1}{s} \frac{1}{s} = t \tag{15-71}$$

Accordingly, at the end of the first control interval the unit-step response is for $T = \frac{1}{2}$ sec

$$u(T^-) = \tfrac{1}{2}$$

As long as no changes take place in the parameters of the controlled system, Eq. (15-70) may be simplified to

$$m_k = \frac{c_d(kT^-) - \sum_{n=0}^{m} \frac{T^n c^n(kT^-)}{n!}}{u(T^-)} + m_{k-1} \tag{15-72}$$

The magnitude of the step forcing function to be applied to the controlled system $G(s) = 1/s$ at the start of the first control interval is found from Eq. (15-72) for $k = 0$. Thus

$$m_0 = \frac{1 - 0}{\frac{1}{2}} + 0 = 2 \tag{15-73}$$

Applying this step to the controlled system generates a ramp output given by

$$c(t) = 2tu(t) \tag{15-74}$$

Note that at the end of the control interval, i.e., at $t = \frac{1}{2}$ sec $= T$, the output is exactly equal to the desired value. The time behavior of $c(t)$ during the first control interval is depicted in Fig. 15-13b. To investigate the behavior during the second control interval, it is necessary to compute a new value of the forcing function consistent with the initial conditions prevailing at the end of the first control interval. Thus, at $t = T^-$,

$$c_d(T^-) = 1.0$$
$$c(T^-) = 1.0$$
$$\dot{c}(T^-) = 2.0$$

Hence
$$m_1 = \frac{c_d(T^-) - [c(T^-) + T\dot{c}(T^-)]}{u(T^-)}$$
$$= \frac{1 - [1 + \frac{1}{2}(2)]}{\frac{1}{2}} + 2 = -2 + 2 = 0 \tag{15-75}$$

The variation of $m(t)$ over the first two control intervals is shown in Fig. 15-14. It should be apparent that at the start of the second control interval a negative step of amplitude 2 is needed to yield the necessary value for m_1. Clearly, then, the output generated by this negative step is

$$-2(t - T)u(t - T)$$

so that the complete expression for the controlled variable over the first two control intervals becomes

$$c(t) = 2tu(t) - 2(t - T)u(t - T) \qquad (15\text{-}76)$$

Further investigation reveals that this expression is valid for all succeeding control intervals as well.

What are some of the restrictions of this type of control system? The application of the foregoing techniques to more complicated systems [such as, for example, $G(s) = 1/s^2$] shows that although correspondence with the desired output is assured at the ends of the control intervals, i.e., at $t = T, 2T, 3T$, etc., it is possible for the response to be divergent

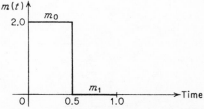

FIG. 15-14. Variation of the forcing function needed to generate the output shown in Fig. 15-13b.

during the control intervals. In such situations an improvement can usually be effected by employing a modified control strategy. For example, an additional restriction can be imposed so that a forcing function is generated to match the slope of the controlled output with the desired slope as well as matching the magnitudes of the actual and desired outputs. Expressing this mathematically, we have

$$c(kT^-) = c_d[(k - 1)T^-]$$
$$\dot{c}(kT^-) = \dot{c}_d[(k - 1)T^-] \qquad (15\text{-}77)$$

It is found that to satisfy both conditions requires that the forcing function contain ramp components as well as steps. Of course this means increased equipment requirements for the controller. Moreover, it may well be that in some situations a considerable extension of the conditions of Eq. (15-77) is needed to assure stability for the system.

The need for reliable measurements as called for in Eqs. (15-64) and (15-70) is as important in the system designed on the basis of these equations as it is for the system of Fig. 15-10. This statement is true also as regards the selection of the period of the control interval T. Now, although it is possible to point to cases where instability results with the use of a simplified control strategy, the chief purpose of treating the subject matter here is to describe the concepts involved, because per se they contain considerable merit.

15-5. Adaptive Control by Using Nonlinear Techniques[1]

One approach to making a controlled system insensitive to changes in its parameters is to measure the characteristics of $G(s)$, and whenever a deviation occurs from a desired standard the measured change is used to adjust appropriate control parameters to maintain the desired performance. This is the subject matter of the preceding sections. In this

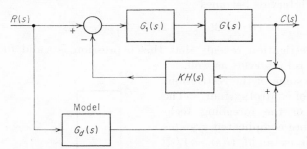

FIG. 15-15. High-gain feedback control system.

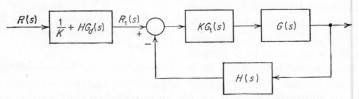

FIG. 15-16. Block-diagram equivalent of Fig. 15-16.

section attention is turned to a second basic approach to the problem. The use of high loop gains as well as intentional nonlinearities is necessary. However, the principles involved are simple ones. Consider, for example, a control system designed in accordance with the configuration depicted in Fig. 15-15. The equivalent block diagram appears in Fig. 15-16. The closed-loop transfer function is

$$\frac{C}{R}(s) = \left[\frac{1}{K} + HG_d(s)\right]\frac{KG_1G(s)}{1 + KHG_1G(s)} \tag{15-78}$$

For a very high loop gain, that is, $K \ggg 1$, Eq. (15-78) becomes

$$\frac{C}{R}(s) = G_d(s) \tag{15-79}$$

[1] Wright Air Development Center, Proceedings of the Self-adaptive Flight Control Systems Symposium, March, 1959. The articles of interest are J. D. McLean and S. F. Schmidt, On an Adaptive Autopilot Using a Non Linear Feedback Control System, NASA, Ames Research Center, Moffett Field, Calif.; O. Hugo Schuck, Honeywell's History and Philosophy in the Adaptive Control Field.

so that the controlled-variable response becomes that of the model. It is interesting to note that this result prevails in spite of changes that may occur in the controlled system $G(s)$ provided that $KHG_1G(s) \gg 1$. In this manner the controlled variable is made insensitive to parameter changes of the controlled system. Of course this is a familiar consequence of feedback. When a control system provides this kind of insensitivity to system parameter changes, it seems more appropriate to call it adaptive rather than self-adaptive. The self-adaptive design normally implies a measurement, evaluation, and adjustment procedure.

The need for very high loop gains rules out the use of a linear system because of the resulting instability that is almost certain to occur. A

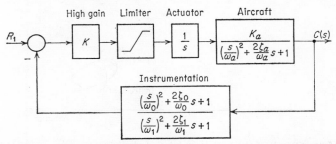

FIG. 15-17. Block diagram of a high-gain nonlinear control system.

nonlinear device is needed such as an "on-off" controller or a limiter which has constant finite gain up to a specified value beyond which saturation occurs. The inclusion of the nonlinear component within the control loop furnishes the system with a variable gain, which is so necessary if stability as well as high loop gains are to be realized. However, it is also responsible for the existence of a high-frequency oscillation (limit cycle), the amplitude of which is determined by the frequency response of the linear elements following the nonlinear device. With proper precaution this amplitude can be kept to acceptably small values.

Appearing in Fig. 15-17 is the block diagram of an aircraft control system. The nonlinear element in this case is a limiter having the characteristic shown. Practically it can be considered as representing the rate limit of the actuator, which here is considered to be an ideal integrator. That is, the actuator dynamics are neglected. The feedback transfer function is selected to provide the desired response as illustrated in the root-locus plot of the system, the nonlinearity being neglected. In Fig. 15-18 it is assumed that the aircraft poles are subject to motion anywhere within the shaded area, depending upon the flight condition. An adaptive control system is accordingly desired in order to make the response insensitive to this variation. Clearly the use of a high gain puts the root of the characteristic equation practically at the instrument zero so that the position of the corresponding aircraft pole becomes almost irrelevant. However, a glance at the locus originating from the instrument pole reveals that this high gain is likely to involve a root located in the right half plane and so to result in instability. The presence of the nonlinear element prevents the system from becoming unstable by limiting the effect of the high gain to a high-frequency low-amplitude sustained oscillation.[1] This conclusion can be predicted by

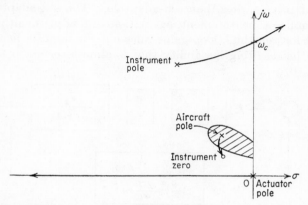

FIG. 15-18. Sketch of the root-locus plot of the linear portion of Fig. 15-17.

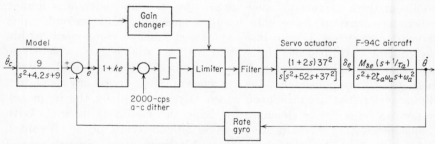

FIG. 15-19. Minneapolis-Honeywell adaptive control system using nonlinear techniques.

considering the limiter as a variable-gain device which is dependent upon the input signal. Thus, for small errors the effective loop gain is large, and for large errors the gain is small. By careful design it is possible to operate at such a gain that the predominant roots of the closed-loop system are located close to the instrument zero, while the oscillation associated with the locus from the instrument pole is of suitably small magnitude.

[1] Cf. Truxal, *op. cit.*, chap. 10.

Illustrated in Fig. 15-19 is the block diagram of the adaptive control system built for the F-94C by Minneapolis-Honeywell and successfully flight-tested. This final design pattern was arrived at only after considerable computer simulation studies were made. For example, these studies revealed that the control system could be made adaptive over a greater flight regime by introducing a gain change on the limiter when the actuating signal exceeds a specified level. The use of the 2,000-cps a-c "dither" frequency on the relay is for the purpose of linearizing the output for small inputs. The relay, of course, is of the electronic type because of the high dither frequency used.

Adaptive control systems designed on the principle of high linear gain combined with a nonlinear element offer three attractive features. They are (1) a fairly high degree of performance, (2) simplicity in terms of equipment, and (3) reliability, which is perhaps most important. On the other hand there are the disadvantages associated with the need to tolerate a sustained oscillation during operation. The attendant limit cycle causes increased wear on some of the equipment in addition to a small amplitude disturbance at the output.

SUGGESTED READING

Aseltine, J. A., A. R. Mancini, and C. W. Sarture: A Survey of Adaptive Control Systems, *Trans. IRE*, PGAC-6, December, 1958. This paper also includes a rather extensive bibliography of the papers written on this subject.

Braun, L., Jr.: On Adaptive Control Systems, doctoral dissertation, Polytechnic Institute of Brooklyn, New York, 1959.

Haddad, R. A., and E. Mishkin: On the Identification and Command Problems in Computer-controlled Adaptive Systems, *Proc. Wescon*, 1959.

Whitaker, H. P., J. Yamron, and A. Kezer: Design of a Model-reference Adaptive Control System for Aircraft, *MIT Instrumentation Lab. Rept.* R-164, September, 1958.

Wright Air Development Center: Proceedings of the Self-adaptive Flight Control Systems Symposium, Lt. P. C. Gregory (ed.), *WADC Tech. Rept.* 59-49, March, 1959.

PROBLEMS

15-1. A feedback control system is designed in accordance with the configuration shown in Fig. P15-1a. When the command input signal is negative, switch S_1 is put to position a; otherwise it remains at position b.

(a) Describe the behavior of this system when the command signal varies as shown in Fig. P15-1b. Assume that all system parameters remain invariant.

(b) Devise a suitable performance criterion to be used for this system.

(c) Assume that the system is following a command input in the steady state. The controlled system then undergoes a change in the velocity constant K_v. Describe the ensuing system behavior. Is this system self-adaptive? Explain.

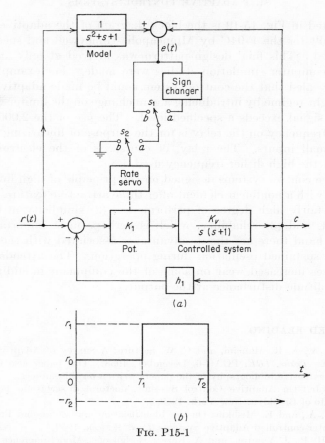

Fig. P15-1

15-2. Demonstrate that Eq. (15-12) is valid.

15-3. Prove the validity of Eq. (15-59).

15-4. Apply the self-adaptive control principles of Sec. 15-3 to a controlled system whose tranfer function is $G(s) = 1/s^2$. Assume that at the start of the first control interval the measured errors of the controlled variable and its first two derivatives are, respectively, equal to E_0, E_1, and E_2. Determine the equation which describes the forcing function needed to reduce these errors to zero immediately after the start of the control interval. Also, find the complete expression for the output quantity as well as its first and second derivatives.

What serious practical disadvantage is there to the design of the controller needed for this system? What recommendation can you make to somewhat simplify the controller design?

15-5. Repeat Prob. 15-4 for a controlled system described by $G(s) = (s + 1)/s^2$.

15-6. Demonstrate the validity of Eq. (15-70).

15-7. Apply the self-adaptive principles described in Sec. 15-4 to a controlled system given by $G(s) = 1/s^2$. Use Eq. (15-65) as the criterion by which the forcing function is derived. Assume that the command signal is a unit step, and sketch the variation of the output as a function of time. Assume $T = \frac{1}{2}$ sec.

Does the system respond in a stable fashion to the step command?

15-8. Repeat Prob. 15-7 for a ramp input command.

15-9. Repeat Prob. 15-7, using Eqs. (15-77) as the criterion for computing the forcing function to be applied to the controlled system.

15-10. By means of block-diagram algebra show how Fig. 15-16 derives from Fig. 15-15.

15-11. An aircraft control system consists of a servoactuator, the aircraft, and an autopilot. The transfer functions of the aircraft and autopilot, respectively, are given by

$$G_a = \frac{(1 + s/\omega_1)(1 + s/\omega_2)}{[(s/\omega_a)^2 + (2\zeta_a/\omega_a)s + 1][s^2/\omega_b^2 + (2\zeta_b/\omega_b)s + 1]}$$

and $\qquad G_1 = $ autopilot transfer function $= K(1 + s\tau_r)$

When the dynamics of the servoactuator are neglected, there is no basic stability problem as a root-locus sketch of the open transfer function reveals. However, when realistic servo dynamics are introduced, a stability problem arises. Assuming the servoactuator transfer function to be

$$G_s = \frac{1}{s^2/\omega_s^2 + (2\zeta_s/\omega_s)s + 1}$$

the corresponding root-locus plot becomes that shown in Fig. P15-11a. The plot

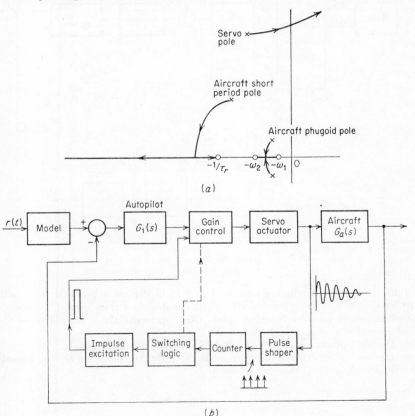

(a)

(b)

FIG. P15-11

shows that for large gains instability can result. To avoid this difficulty, the control system of Fig. P15-11b is proposed.

(a) Deduce the principle upon which this control system functions. Be specific, and clearly point out the function of each component.

(b) Can this control scheme be used in situations where little or no information is known about the controlled system (the aircraft in this case)? Explain.

15-12. A feedback control system has the block-diagram configuration as shown in Fig. P15-12. Also,

$$e = c_d(t) - c(t)$$
$$\dot{e} = \dot{c}_d(t) - \dot{c}(t)$$
$$e^* = \left(k_1 e + k_2 \dot{e} + k_3 \frac{e}{\dot{e}^2} + k_4 \frac{\dot{e}}{e^2} \right)$$

The variable-gain parameter is adjusted in accordance with the values of e and $\dot{e}$ and has fixed lower and upper limits.

(a) Describe the operation of this system.

(b) Comment upon the expression for e^*, which is often referred to as the "all-purpose" performance criterion.

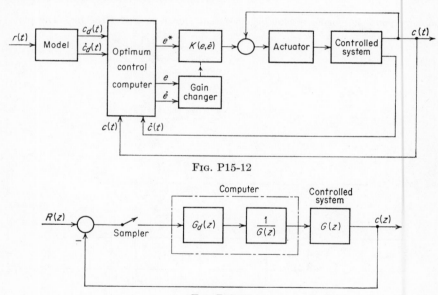

FIG. P15-12

FIG. P15-13

15-13. The block diagram shown in Fig. P15-13 depicts a proposal for a self-adaptive control system. The quantity $G_d(z)$ denotes the z transform of the desired controlled-system transfer function, while $G(z)$ represents the z transform of the actual controlled-system transfer function.

(a) Discuss the relative merits and demerits of such a control system.

(b) Discuss the effects of a root located in the right half plane for $G(z)$ as regards the computer design and the system stability.

Appendixes

A | Conversion Factors for Servo Calculations

To obtain	Multiply number of	By
Length:		
cm	in.	2.540
cm	ft	30.48
in.	cm	0.3937
in.	ft	12.0
ft	cm	3.281×10^{-2}
ft	in.	8.333×10^{-2}
Mass:		
g	oz	28.35
g	lb	453.6
g	slugs	1.459×10^4
oz	g	3.527×10^{-2}
oz	lb	16.0
oz	slugs	514.7
lb	g	2.205×10^{-3}
lb	oz	6.250×10^{-2}
lb	slugs	32.17
slugs†	g	6.853×10^{-5}
slugs	oz	1.943×10^{-3}
slugs	lb	3.108×10^{-2}
Force:		
dynes	g‡	980.7
dynes	oz	2.780×10^4
dynes	lb	4.448×10^5
g‡	dynes	1.020×10^{-3}
oz	dynes	3.597×10^{-5}
lb	dynes	2.248×10^{-6}
Torque:		
dyne-cm	g-cm	980.7
dyne-cm	oz-in.	7.062×10^4

To obtain	Multiply number of	By
dyne-cm	lb-ft	1.356×10^7
g-cm	dyne-cm	1.020×10^{-3}
g-cm	oz-in.	72.01
g-cm	lb-ft	1.383×10^4
oz-in.	dyne-cm	1.416×10^{-5}
oz-in.	g-cm	1.389×10^{-2}
oz-in.	lb-ft	192.0
lb-ft	dyne-cm	7.376×10^{-8}
lb-ft	g-cm	7.233×10^{-5}
lb-ft	oz-in.	5.208×10^{-3}
Rotation:		
deg/sec	rpm	6.0
deg/sec	radians/sec	57.30
rpm	deg/sec	0.1667
rpm	radians/sec	9.549
radians/sec	deg/sec	1.745×10^{-2}
radians/sec	rpm	0.1047
Moment of inertia:		
g-cm^2	oz-in.^{2}	182.9
g-cm^2	lb-ft^2	4.214×10^5
g-cm^2	slug-ft^2	1.356×10^7
oz-in.^{2}	g-cm^2	5.467×10^{-3}
oz-in.^{2}	lb-ft^2	2.304×10^3
oz-in.^{2}	slug-ft^2	7.412×10^4
lb-ft^2	g-cm^2	2.373×10^{-6}
lb-ft^2	oz-in.^{2}	4.340×10^{-4}
lb-ft^2	slug-ft^2	32.17
slug-ft^2	g-cm^2	7.376×10^{-8}
slug-ft^2	oz-in.^{2}	1.349×10^{-5}
slug-ft^2	lb-ft^2	3.108×10^{-2}
Power:		
hp	(oz-in.)(deg/sec)	1.653×10^{-7}
hp	(oz-in.)(rpm)	9.917×10^{-7}
hp	(lb-ft)(deg/sec)	3.173×10^{-5}
hp	(lb-ft)(rpm)	1.904×10^{-4}
hp	watts	1.341×10^{-3}
watts	(oz-in.)(deg/sec)	1.232×10^{-4}
watts	(oz-in.)(rpm)	7.395×10^{-4}
watts	(lb-ft)(deg/sec)	2.366×10^{-2}
watts	(lb-ft)(rpm)	0.1420
watts	hp	745.7

Torque/inertia ratio, or acceleration at stall (stall torque divided by rotor inertia):

radians/sec^2	oz-in./g-cm^2	7.062×10^4
radians/sec^2	oz-in./oz-in.^{2}	386.1

To obtain	Multiply number of	By
Damping coefficient of 2-phase motor (stall torque divided by top motor speed):		
lb-ft/radian/sec	oz-in./rpm	4.974×10^{-2}
dyne-cm/rad/sec	oz-in./rpm	6.743×10^{5}
Time constant of 2-phase motor (rotor inertia divided by motor damping coefficient):		
sec	$\dfrac{(\text{g-cm}^2)(\text{rpm})}{\text{oz-in.}}$	1.483×10^{-6}
sec	$\dfrac{(\text{oz-in.}^2)(\text{rpm})}{\text{oz-in.}}$	2.712×10^{-4}
Loop gain (also called stiffness, sensitivity, torque gradient):		
lb-ft/radian	oz-in./deg	0.2984
dyne-cm/radian	oz-in./degree	4.046×10^{6}

† 1 slug mass accelerates at 1 ft/sec^2 when acted upon by 1 lb force.
‡ Used as force units.

B | Methods for Determining the Roots of Algebraic Equations

In the analysis and design of control systems it is often necessary to determine the roots of an algebraic equation. In this appendix three numerical methods for doing so are presented. The first is known as Lin's method and is particularly suited to a paper and pencil computation. The second method is known as Graeffe's root-squaring method and is easily adapted for programming on a digital computer. The third method is a graphical technique based upon the root-locus approach.

Lin's Method.[1] Lin's method is basically a division technique by which the original equation is factored into quadratic and/or linear terms. It is simple and accurate, and the roots are obtained quickly, particularly when there are pairs of complex roots located far apart. Consider the original algebraic equation

$$s^n + B_{n-1}s^{n-1} + B_{n-2}s^{n-2} + \cdots + B_2s^2 + B_1s + B_0 = 0$$

As the first step a trial division is formed from the last three terms as follows:

$$s^2 + \frac{B_1}{B_2}s + \frac{B_0}{B_2}$$

The trial divisor is divided into the original equation as follows:

$$
s^2 + \frac{B_1}{B_2}s + \frac{B_0}{B_2} \overline{\Big)\begin{array}{l} s^{n-2} + \cdots \\ s^n + B_{n-1}s^{n-1} + B_{n-2}s^{n-2} + \cdots + B_2s^2 + B_1s + B_0 \end{array}}
$$

$$C_2s^2 + C_1s + C_0$$
$$D_2s^2 + D_1s + D_0$$
Remainder

---

[1] Shih-Nge Lin, Methods of Successive Approximations of Evaluating the Real and Complex Roots of Cubic and Higher Order Equations, *J. Math. Phys.*, vol. 20, no. 3, August, 1941.

If the remainder is negligible, then the original divisor is a quadratic factor of the original equation.   If the remainder is not negligible, then a second trial divisor is formed as follows:

$$s^2 + \frac{C_1}{C_2}s + \frac{C_0}{C_2}$$

The second trial divisor is divided into the original equation in a way similar to that in which the first divisor was applied.   If the remainder of this division is negligible, then the second trial divisor is a quadratic factor of the original equation.   If the remainder is not negligible, a third trial divisor is formed from the results of the second division, in a manner identical to that in which the second divisor was formed from the results of the first division.   The process is continued until a negligible remainder is obtained.   The last trial divisor is then a quadratic factor of the original equation, and the quotient polynomial, which must necessarily be of order $n - 2$, is the other factor of the original equation. Lin's method may now be applied to this other factor to yield another quadratic factor of the original equation.

When the highest power of the original equation is odd, a linear factor can be found, whenever terms of order greater than the first are negligible, by using a trial divisor of the form

$$s + \frac{B_0}{B_1}$$

This trial divisor is divided into the original equation, and, as before, the process of finding trial divisors and performing the division is continued, until a negligible remainder results.

Lin's method is best demonstrated by numerical examples.

Example B-1.   Solve for the roots of the equation

$$s^3 + 13s^2 + 30s + 3 = 0$$

The first trial divisor is

$$s + \tfrac{3}{30} = s + 0.1$$

Division yields the following result:

$$
\begin{array}{r}
s^2 + 12.9s + 28.7 \\
s + 0.1)\overline{s^3 + 13s^2 + 30s + 3} \\
\underline{s^3 + 0.1s^2} \\
12.9s^2 + 30s \\
\underline{12.9s^2 + 1.3s} \\
28.7s + 3.00 \\
\underline{28.7s + 2.87} \\
0.13
\end{array}
$$

The second trial divisor is given by

$$s + \frac{3.00}{28.7} = s + 0.104$$

Division yields the following result:

$$
\begin{array}{r}
s^2 + 12.9s + 28.65 \\
s + 0.104 \overline{\smash{)}\ s^3 + 13s^2 + 30s + 3} \\
\underline{s^3 + 0.1s^2} \\
12.9s^2 + 30s \\
\underline{12.9s^2 + 1.35s} \\
28.65s + 3 \\
\underline{28.65s + 3} \\
0
\end{array}
$$

A remainder of zero indicates that $s + 0.104$ is an exact factor of the original equation. Thus the original can be factored as follows

$$(s + 0.104)(s^2 + 12.9s + 28.65) = 0$$

Solving for the roots of the quadratic factor by formula yields the following roots for the original equation:

$$s = -0.104, \ -10.04, \text{ and } -2.86$$

Example B-2. Solve for the roots of the following equation:

$$s^4 + 25.5s^3 + 685s^2 + 8{,}150s + 47{,}400 = 0$$

The first trial divisor is

$$s^2 + \frac{8{,}150}{685}\,s + \frac{47{,}400}{685} = s^2 + 11.9s + 69.2$$

Division yields the following result:

$$
\begin{array}{r}
s^2 + 13.6s + 453.8 \\
s^2 + 11.9s + 69.2 \overline{\smash{)}\ s^4 + 25.5s^3 + 685s^2 \ \ + 8{,}150s + 47{,}400} \\
\underline{s^4 + 11.9s^3 + 69.2s^2} \\
13.6s^3 + 615.8s^2 + 8{,}150s \\
\underline{13.6s^3 + 162s^2 \ \ + 952s} \\
453.8s^2 + 7{,}198s + 47{,}400 \\
\underline{453.8s^2 + 5{,}400s + 31{,}400} \\
1{,}798s + 16{,}000
\end{array}
$$

Comparing the coefficients of the remainder with the coefficients of the term used to form the second trial divisor indicates that the remainder is not negligible. Thus the second trial divisor is formed as follows:

$$s^2 + \frac{7{,}198}{453.8}\,s^2 + \frac{47{,}400}{453.8}\,s = s^2 + 15.85s + 104.5$$

Division yields the following result:

$$
\begin{array}{r}
s^2 + 9.6s + 429 \\
s^2 + 15.85s + 104.3 \overline{\smash{)}\ s^4 + 25.5s^3 \ \ + 685s^2 + 8{,}150s + 47{,}400} \\
\underline{s^4 + 15.85s^3 + 104s^2} \\
9.6s^3 \ \ + 581s^2 + 8{,}150s \\
\underline{9.6s^3 \ \ + 152s^2 + 1{,}000s} \\
429s^2 + 7{,}150s + 47{,}400 \\
\underline{429s^2 + 6{,}800s + 44{,}800} \\
350s + \ \ 2{,}600
\end{array}
$$

The remainder is still not negligible so that a third trial divisor is formed, namely,

$$s^2 + \frac{7{,}150}{429}\,s + \frac{47{,}400}{429} = s^2 + 16.7s + 110$$

Division yields the following result:

$$
\begin{array}{r}
s^2 + 8.8s + 428 \\
s^2 + 16.7s + 110 \overline{)\,s^4 + 25.5s^3 + 685s^2 + 8{,}150s + 47{,}400} \\
s^4 + 16.7s^3 + 110s^2 \\
\hline
8.8s^3 + 575s^2 + 8{,}150s \\
8.8s^3 + 147s^2 + 970s \\
\hline
428s^2 + 7{,}180s + 47{,}400 \\
428s^2 + 7{,}150s + 47{,}200 \\
\hline
30s + 200
\end{array}
$$

The remainder term is seen to be quite small so that the process can be stopped at this point. Greater accuracy can be had by continuing further. On the basis of the results of the last division the original equation can be factored in the following two quadratic factors:

$$(s^2 + 16.7s + 110)(s^2 + 8.8s + 428) = 0$$

Solving for the roots of the quadratic factors yields the following results for the roots of the original equation:

$$s = -8.35 \pm j6.3, \; -4.4 \pm j20.25$$

The Graeffe Root-squaring Method. Graeffe root squaring is a numerical root-finding technique which can be readily adapted for programming on a digital computer. The reason for this is that the numerical calculations required follow a fixed, regular pattern.

Consider an nth-degree algebraic equation of the form

$$f(s) = B_n s^n + B_{n-1} s^{n-1} + \cdots + B_2 s^2 + B_1 s + B_0 = 0 \quad \text{(B-1)}$$

The basis of Graeffe's method lies in transforming the equation into one whose roots are higher powers of those of the original. The roots of the transformed equation are then widely separated from each other and can therefore be found easily. For example, if the roots of the original equation are 2 and 4, the roots of the transformed equation are 2^m and 4^m, where m is the power to which the roots have been raised. When $m = 20$, the ratio of the two roots is $2^{20} = 1{,}048{,}576$ and the smaller root of the transformed equation is certainly negligible compared with the larger root. The process of transforming the original equation consists in successive root squarings; i.e., each step generates an equation whose roots are the squares of the preceding one. Squaring is repeated until the roots of the final equation are far enough apart to be found easily with the accuracy required. The roots of the original equation are then determined from the roots of the final transformed equation.

The process involved in root squaring may be demonstrated as follows. Consider Eq. (B-1) rewritten in factored form,

$$f(s) = B_n(s - s_1)(s - s_2) \cdots (s - s_n) = 0 \quad \text{(B-2)}$$

Now formulate the function $(-1)^n f(-s)$. Thus

$$(-1)^n f(-s) = (-1)^n B_n(-s - s_1)(-s - s_2) \cdots (-s - s_n)$$
$$= B_n(s + s_1)(s + s_2) \cdots (s + s_n) \qquad \text{(B-3)}$$

The product of Eqs. (B-2) and (B-3) yields the result

$$(-1)^n f(s) f(-s) = B_n^2(s^2 - s_1^2)(s^2 - s_2^2) \cdots (s^2 - s_n^2) = 0 \qquad \text{(B-4)}$$

If we now let $s^2 = s'$, a new variable, Eq. (B-4) becomes

$$f(s') = B_n' s'^n + B_{n-1}' s'^{n-1} + \cdots + B_1' s' + B_0'$$
$$= B_n^2(s' - s_1^2)(s' - s_2^2) \cdots (s' - s_n^2) = 0 \qquad \text{(B-5)}$$

Equation (B-5) is recognized as a new algebraic equation whose roots are the squares of the roots of the original Eq. (B-2).

The letters B_n', B_{n-1}', . . . , B_0' are used to designate the coefficients of this transformed equation. The conclusion to be drawn from the foregoing discussion is that to find an equation whose roots are the squares of the roots of a given equation $[f(s) = 0]$ one must formulate the equation

$$(-1)^n f(s) f(-s) = 0 \qquad \text{(B-6)}$$

Obviously the formulation called for by Eq. (B-6) must be performed with the unfactored form of the original. At first this may seem to be a very difficult task, but actually it can be carried out in a routine manner, as demonstrated in Table B-1, which outlines a systematic procedure for performing the operation of Eq. (B-6) by means of calculations with the coefficients of the original equation. The veracity of this table may be checked by multiplying out the expression $(-1)^n f(s) f(-s)$, the unfactored form for $f(s)$ being used as in Eq. (B-1).

The root-squaring process may be repeated as many times as required. If it is repeated twice, the resulting equation has roots which are the fourth power of the roots of the original. If root squaring is repeated m times, the roots of the resultant equation are equal to the roots of the original raised to the 2^mth power. In practice, root squaring should be continued until all the double-product terms are negligible (within the accuracy desired) compared with the squared coefficient in the same column. The number of steps required to reach this point depends upon the separation of the roots in the original equation.

After the final transformed equation is formed, its roots may be found readily because they are widely separated. This can be demonstrated by considering the relationship between the coefficients of an algebraic equation and its roots.

Consider an equation in the form

$$B_n' s^n + B_{n-1}' s'^{n-1} + \cdots + B_2' s'^2 + B_1' s'^2 + B_0' = 0 \qquad \text{(B-7)}$$

TABLE B-1. DETERMINING THE COEFFICIENTS OF THE ROOT-SQUARED EQUATION

	B_n	B_{n-1}	B_{n-2}	B_{n-3}	B_{n-4}	$\cdots$
Original coefficients:	B_n	B_{n-1}	B_{n-2}	B_{n-3}	B_{n-4}	$\cdots$
Squares of original coefficient with alternating signs (starting with $+$)	$+B_n^2$	$-B_{n-1}^2$	$+B_{n-2}^2$	$-B_{n-3}^2$	$+B_{n-4}^2$	$\cdots$
All double products of symmetrically located neighbors with alternating signs (starting with $+$)		$+2B_nB_{n-2}$	$-2B_{n-1}B_{n-3}$ $+2B_nB_{n-4}$	$+2B_{n-2}B_{n-4}$ $-2B_{n-1}B_{n-5}$ $+2B_nB_{n-6}$	$-2B_{n-3}B_{n-5}$ $+2B_{n-2}V_{n-6}$ $-2B_{n-1}B_{n-7}$ $+2B_nB_{n-8}$	$\cdots$ $\cdots$ $\cdots$ $\cdots$ $\cdots$
Coefficients of the root-squared (the transformed) equation. Sums of the squares and double products	B_n'	B_{n-1}'	B_{n-2}'	B_{n-3}'	B_{n-4}'	$\cdots$

649

Assume that the roots are located at $s = s_1', s_2', \ldots, s_n'$.

The roots and the coefficients of Eq. (B-7) are related by the following formulas:

$$\frac{B_{n-1}'}{B_n'} = -(s_1' + s_2' + \cdots + s_n') = -(\text{sum of the roots}) \qquad \text{(B-8}a)$$

$$\frac{B_{n-2}'}{B_n'} = (s_1's_2' + s_1's_3' + \cdots) = \text{sum of the roots taken two at a time}$$
$$\text{(B-8}b)$$

$$\frac{B_{n-3}'}{B_n'} = -(s_1's_2's_3' + s_1's_2's_4' + \cdots)$$
$$= -(\text{sum of the roots taken three at a time}) \quad \text{(B-8}c)$$
$$\cdots\cdots\cdots\cdots\cdots\cdots\cdots\cdots\cdots\cdots\cdots\cdots\cdots\cdots\cdots\cdots\cdots$$

$$\frac{B_0'}{B_n'} = (-1)^n s_1' s_2' \cdots s_n' = (-1)^n(\text{product of all the roots}) \qquad \text{(B-8}d)$$

If the roots are widely separated, i.e., if

$$|s_1'| > |s_2'| > |s_3'| \cdots > |s_n'|$$

these equations reduce to the following:

$$B_n' s_1' + B_{n-1}' = 0 \qquad \text{so that } s_1' = \frac{-B_{n-1}'}{B_n'} \qquad \text{(B-9}a)$$

$$B_{n-1}' s_2' + B_{n-2}' = 0 \qquad \text{so that } s_2' = \frac{1}{s_1'} \frac{B_{n-2}'}{B_n'} \qquad \text{(B-9}b)$$

$$B_{n-2}' s_3' + B_{n-3}' = 0 \qquad \text{so that } s_3' = -\frac{1}{s_1' s_2'} \frac{B_{n-3}'}{B_n'} \qquad \text{(B-9}c)$$

Equations (B-9) are used to determine the roots of the transformed equation directly from its coefficients. When the roots of the original equation are real numbers, it is obvious that the roots of the transformed equation will be real numbers. The roots of the original equation may then be determined by taking the 2^mth root of each one of the transformed equation's roots, where m designates the number of times root squaring was repeated and 2^m represents the power to which the original roots are raised in the transformed equation. It is also apparent that the sign of a real root in the original equation is lost in the root-squaring process and must be checked separately once its magnitude is found. This can be done by substituting positive and negative approximate root values into the original equation and checking which one makes $f(s)$ come closer to zero.

When the original equation has complex conjugate roots, the foregoing analysis still applies. However, before proceeding to a discussion of this case, it is worthwhile to present an example illustrating the solution of an equation having real roots only.

Example B-3.   Determine the roots of the following equation:

$$s^3 + 13s^2 + 30s + 3 = 0$$

The steps of the root-squaring process are given in Table B-2.   It can be seen that all the double-product terms would become negligible (to three decimal places) if a fourth root squaring were to be performed. Therefore only three root squarings are necessary.

TABLE B-2

Original coefficients:	1	13	30	3
Coefficients squared (alternate signs)	1	-169	$+900$	-9
Double products (alternate signs)		$+60$	-78	$+0$
Transformed equation (squared roots)	1	-109	$+822$	-9
Coefficients squared (alternate signs)	1	-1.188×10^4	$+6.757 \times 10^5$	-81
Double products (alternate signs)		0.164×10^4	-0.020×10^5	0
Transformed equation (fourth-power roots)	1	-1.024×10^4	$+6.737 \times 10^5$	-81
Coefficients squared (alternate signs)	1	-1.048×10^8	$+4.539 \times 10^{11}$	$-6,561$
Double products (alternate signs)		0.013×10^8	0.000×10^{11}	
Transformed equation (eighth-power roots)	1	-1.035×10^8	$+4.539 \times 10^{11}$	$-6,561$

The coefficients of the final transformed equation are

$$B'_n = 1 \qquad\qquad B'_{n-2} = 4.539 \times 10^{11}$$
$$B'_{n-1} = -1.035 \times 10^8 \qquad B'_{n-3} = -6,561$$

By using Eqs. (B-9) the roots of the transformed equation are

$$s'_1 = -\frac{B'_{n-1}}{B_n} = 1.035 \times 10^8$$

$$s'_2 = \frac{B'_{n-2}}{B'_{n-1}} = \frac{4.539 \times 10^{11}}{1.035 \times 10^8}$$

$$s'_3 = -\frac{B'_{n-3}}{B'_{n-2}} = \frac{6,561}{4.539 \times 10^{11}}$$

Since three root squarings were performed, the magnitude of the roots of the original equation are found by taking the eighth root of the above values.   Thus

$$|s_1| = \sqrt[8]{1.035 \times 10^8} = 10.04$$

$$|s_2| = \sqrt[8]{\frac{4.539 \times 10^{11}}{1.035 \times 10^8}} = 2.85$$

$$|s_3| = \sqrt[8]{\frac{6,561}{4.539 \times 10^{11}}} = 0.105$$

The signs of the above results may be checked readily and shown to be all negative so that the roots of the original equation are

$$s = -10.04, \, -2.85, \, -0.105$$

When an equation has a pair of complex conjugate roots, the presence of this pair is detected by the behavior of the numbers in Table B-1. The rules for detection are:

1. In one of the columns the double-product terms do not become negligible compared with the squared coefficient regardless of how many root squarings are performed. The double-product terms in the other columns will become negligible so that there is no question as to when to stop root squaring.

2. The coefficients of the transformed equations in the same column fluctuate in sign as root squaring proceeds.

The reason why a complex conjugate root pair causes this peculiar behavior may be seen by considering a simple quadratic equation of the form

$$f(s) = (s - |r|\epsilon^{i\theta})(s - |r|\epsilon^{-i\theta}) = s^2 - (2|r| \cos \theta)s + |r|^2 = 0 \quad \text{(B-10)}$$

The roots of this equation are complex conjugates, $s = |r|\epsilon^{\pm i\theta}$. The root-square transformation of Eq. (B-10) gives the result

$$f(s') = (s' - |r|^2\epsilon^{i2\theta})(s' - |r|^2\epsilon^{-i2\theta}) = (s')^2 - (2|r|^2 \cos 2\theta)s' + |r|^4 = 0 \quad \text{(B-11)}$$

If root squaring is continued for m times, the result is

$$f(s'') = (s'' - |r|^{2^m}\epsilon^{i2^m\theta})(s'' - |r|^{2^m}\epsilon^{-i2^m\theta})$$
$$= (s'')^2 - (2|r|^{2^m} \cos 2^m\theta)s'' + |r|^{2^{m+1}} \quad \text{(B-12)}$$

where $s'' = s^{2^m}$.

It can be seen that the coefficients of the middle term of the transformed equation can be expected to fluctuate in sign as $\cos 2^m\theta$ changes sign for different values of m. Also, if the $m + 1$ root squaring is performed, the double-product term $(2|r|^{2^{m+1}})$ is not necessarily negligible compared with the squared-coefficient term

$$[(2|r|^{2^m} \cos 2^m\theta)^2 = (2)^2|r|^{2^{m+1}} \cos^2 2^m\theta]$$

for all values of m. Hence the foregoing rules can be used to detect the presence of a quadratic factor in the original equation.

The coefficient of the transformed equation in the column where the variations in sign are occurring can be identified as the middle term of a quadratic factor and the terms on either side as the other coefficients. The quadratic factor may now be removed and equated to zero to determine its roots. Since we shall eventually want to take the 2^mth root of these roots, it is worthwhile to put the quadratic factor in the form of Eq. (B-10) and determine its roots in polar form, i.e., to find $|r|$ and θ.

Also, it should be noted that, for the case of complex conjugate roots in the original equation, root squaring gives the same transformed equation for the root pair $s = +|r|\epsilon^{\pm i\theta}$ as for $s = -|r|\epsilon^{\pm i\theta}$. Thus after taking the 2^mth root we must determine the sign ($+$ or $-$) of the result by inspection. The process involved for complex conjugate roots is now demonstrated in a simple example.

Example B-4. Determine the roots of the equation

$$f(s) = s^3 + 94s^2 - 575s + 2,500 = 0$$

The steps of the root-squaring process are presented in Table B-3. The second

TABLE B-3

Original coefficients:	$+1$	$+94$	-575	$+2,500$
Coefficients squared (alternate signs)	$+1$	-8.835×10^3	$+3.306 \times 10^5$	-6.25×10^6
Double products (alternate signs)		-1.105×10^3	-4.700×10^5	0
Transformed equation (squared roots)	1	-9.986×10^3	-1.394×10^4	-6.25×10^6
Coefficients squared (alternate signs)	1	-9.972×10^7	$+1.943 \times 10^{10}$	-3.906×10^{13}
Double products (alternate signs)		-0.028×10^7	-12.483×10^{10}	0
Transformed equation (fourth-power roots)	1	-10.000×10^7	-10.540×10^{10}	-3.906×10^{13}

column of the root-squaring process is seen to be perfectly regular in that the double-product term becomes negligible. Thus a real root of the transformed equation may be found from the first column. Thus

$$s_1' = \frac{-B'_{n-1}}{B'_n} = 10.000 \times 10^7 = 10^8$$

On the other hand the double-product term in the third column does not become negligibly small. This indicates that there must be a pair of complex conjugate roots in the original equation, and hence the final transformed equation has a quadratic factor of the form

$$f(s') = -10 \times 10^7 s'^2 - 10.540 \times 10^{10} s' - 3.906 \times 10^{13} = 0$$

Putting this equation into the form of Eq. (B-10) gives the result

$$s'^2 + 1,054s' + 3.906 \times 10^5 = 0$$

The magnitude of the roots of this equation is given by $|r| = \sqrt{3.906 \times 10^5} = 625$, and the phase angle by $2(625) \cos \theta = -1,054$. Hence $\theta = \pm 147.6°$.

The roots of the original equation can now be found by taking the fourth root of the roots of the transformed equation.

$$|s_1| = \sqrt[4]{10^8} = 100$$
$$s_2 = \sqrt[4]{625\epsilon^{\pm i147.6}} = \pm 5\epsilon^{\pm i36.8} = \pm(3 \pm j4).$$

Checking the results in the original differential equation indicates that the positive sign should be used with all roots. The roots of the original equation are therefore

$$s = -100, +3 + j4, +3 - j4.$$

In cases where the roots of an equation are close together so that Lin's method does not converge rapidly, Graeffe root squaring can be used to form an equation whose roots are higher powers of the roots of the original equation. Lin's method can then be easily applied to this transformed equation.

Root-locus Method. By a successive application of the root-locus techniques it is possible to determine the roots of an nth-degree equation. However, $n-2$ separate root-locus plots are needed. Furthermore, the roots are obtained with an accuracy which can be as poor as 10 per cent. The higher the order of the equation, the poorer will be the over-all accuracy.

The essential idea can be best illustrated by applying the techniques involved to the solution of a quartic equation expressed generally as

$$s^4 + as^3 + bs^2 + cs + d = 0 \qquad (B\text{-}13)$$

The first step in the procedure requires that the original equation be written in such a form that it permits a linear, a quadratic, a cubic, and finally the quartic equation itself to be identified individually. Thus Eq. (B-13) can be rewritten as

$$\{[(s + a)s + b]s + c\}s + d = 0 \qquad (B\text{-}14)$$

Note that within the square brackets there appears a quadratic equation, while within the braces there can be identified a cubic equation. Once the equation is put in this form, a systematic reduction can be effected. To begin with, the quadratic term is replaced by the product of two root factors. Thus,

$$(s + a)s + b = (s + r_1)(s + r_2) \qquad (B\text{-}15)$$

In the case of the quadratic there is no need to resort to a root-locus plot, because those roots can be readily found. Inserting Eq. (B-15) into Eq. (B-14) yields

$$[(s + r_1)(s + r_2)s + c]s + d = 0 \qquad (B\text{-}16)$$

An examination of the cubic equation enclosed within the brackets reveals that the roots may be found by making a root-locus plot of the transfer function

$$G_1(s) = \frac{c}{s(s + r_1)(s + r_2)} \qquad (B\text{-}17)$$

and then selecting those points on the three loci which have the gain c. Calling these roots r_1', r_2', and r_3' permits writing Eq. (B-16) as

$$(s + r_1')(s + r_2')(s + r_3')s + d = 0 \qquad (B\text{-}18)$$

Applying the same technique to this last equation then allows the roots of the original quartic equation to be found. This requires that another root-locus plot be made. This time the transfer function involved is

$$G_2(s) = \frac{d}{s(s + r_1')(s + r_2')(s + r_3')} \tag{B-19}$$

Of course the locations of the poles are known from the previous computations. Once the root-locus plot of Eq. (B-19) is established, the roots of the original equation are found by locating those points on the four root loci for which the open-loop gain is equal to d.

In the interest of furnishing a clearer picture of the details involved, let us apply this method to finding the roots of the cubic equation

$$s^3 + 25.5s^2 + 685s + 8{,}150 = 0 \tag{B-20}$$

The procedure is as follows:

1. Rearrange the original equation in order to bring into evidence the linear, quadratic, and cubic terms. Thus,

$$[(s + 25.5)s + 685]s + 8{,}150 = 0 \tag{B-21}$$

2. Find the roots of the quadratic term,

$$s^2 + 25.5s + 685 = 0 \tag{B-22}$$

Hence, $\qquad\qquad s_{1,2} = -r_{1,2} = -12.75 \pm j22.85 \tag{B-23}$

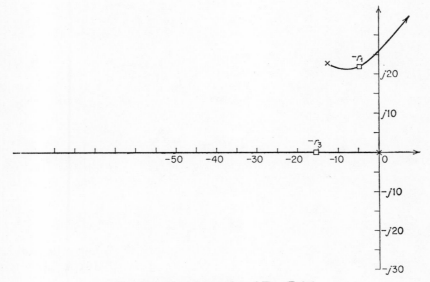

Fig. B-1. Root-locus plot of Eq. (B-25).

3. Rewrite Eq. (B-21) as

$$(s + 12.75 - j22.85)(s + 12.75 - j22.85)s + 8{,}150 = 0 \quad \text{(B-24)}$$

Rearranging leads to

$$\frac{8{,}150}{s(s + 12.75 - j22.85)(s + 12.75 + j22.85)} = -1 \quad \text{(B-25)}$$

4. Plot the root locus of Eq. (B-25). This is shown in Fig. B-1. Then, by locating those points on the plot which have a gain of 8,150, Eq. (B-25) is satisfied. Since the solution of Eq. (B-25) is also a solution of Eq. (B-24), it follows that the roots of the original cubic equation are

$$s_{1,2} = -r_{1,2} = -5 \pm j22.4$$
$$s_3 = -r_3 = -15.5$$

These results are obtained from the plot appearing in Fig. B-1.

C | Table of RC Transfer Functions

Table C-1 lists the transfer function, defined as the ratio of output voltage to input voltage, for some two-port RC networks. The transfer function $T(s)$ is defined in accordance with Fig. C-1.

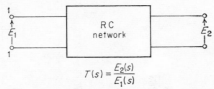

$$T(s) = \frac{E_2(s)}{E_1(s)}$$

FIG. C-1. Definition of voltage transfer function.

It is assumed that a voltage source $E_1(s)$ is applied to terminal pair 1-1 and that the output voltage $E_2(s)$ is taken across terminal pair 2-2. The external load impedance across terminal pair 2-2 is assumed to be infinite.

TABLE C-1

Network	Transfer function
(a)	$\dfrac{1}{1 + RCs}$
(b)	$\dfrac{RCs}{1 + RCs}$
(c)	$\dfrac{1}{1 + (R_1C_1 + R_2C_2 + R_1C_2)s + R_1C_1R_2C_2s^2}$
(d)	$\dfrac{R_1C_1R_2C_2s^2}{1 + (R_1C_1 + R_2C_2 + R_1C_2)s + R_1C_1R_2C_2s^2}$
(e)	$\dfrac{R_1C_1s}{1 + (R_1C_1 + R_2C_2 + R_1C_2)s + R_1C_1R_2C_2s^2}$

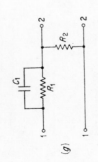

(f)

$$\frac{1 + R_2 C_2 s}{1 + (R_1 + R_2)C_2 s}$$

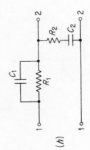

(g)

$$\frac{R_2}{R_1 + R_2} \frac{1 + R_1 C_1 s}{1 + [R_1 R_2/(R_1 + R_2)]C_1 s}$$

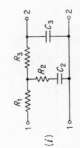

(h)

$$\frac{(1 + R_1 C_1 s)(1 + R_2 C_2 s)}{1 + (R_1 C_1 + R_2 C_2 + R_1 C_2)s + R_1 C_1 R_2 C_2 s^2}$$

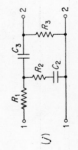

(i)

$$\frac{1 + R_2 C_2 s}{1 + [(R_1 + R_3)C_3 + (R_1 + R_2)C_2]s + (R_1 R_3 + R_2 R_3 + R_1 R_2)C_2 C_3 s^2}$$

(j)

$$\frac{s R_3 C_3(1 + R_2 C_2 s)}{1 + [(R_1 + R_3)C_3 + (R_1 + R_2)C_2]s + (R_1 R_3 + R_2 R_3 + R_1 R_2)s^2}$$

TABLE C-1 (Continued)

Network	Transfer function
(h)	$$\dfrac{R_2C_1s}{1 + (R_1C_1 + R_2C_2 + R_2C_1)s + R_1C_1R_2C_2s^2}$$
(l)	$$\dfrac{R_2}{R_1+R_2}\,\dfrac{1 + R_1C_1s}{1 + [R_1R_2/(R_1+R_2)](C_1+C_2)s}$$
(m)	$$\dfrac{C_1}{C_1+C_2}\,\dfrac{1+R_2C_2s}{1 + [C_1C_2/(C_1+C_2)](R_1+R_2)s}$$
(n)	$$\dfrac{R_2}{R_1+R_2}\,\dfrac{1 + R_1C_1s}{1 + \left(\dfrac{R_1R_2}{R_1+R_2}C_1 + \dfrac{R_1R_2 + R_1R_3 + R_2R_3}{R_1+R_2}C_3\right)s + \dfrac{R_1R_2}{R_1+R_2}C_1R_3C_3s^2}$$

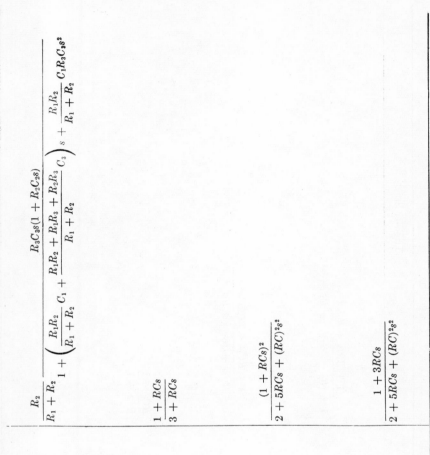

$$\frac{R_2}{R_1+R_2}\cdot\frac{R_3C_3s(1+R_2C_2s)}{1+\left(\dfrac{R_1R_2}{R_1+R_2}C_1 + \dfrac{R_1R_2+R_1R_3+R_2R_3}{R_1+R_2}C_3\right)s + \dfrac{R_1R_2}{R_1+R_2}C_1R_3C_3s^2}$$

$$\frac{1+RCs}{3+RCs}$$

$$\frac{(1+RCs)^2}{2+5RCs+(RC)^2s^2}$$

$$\frac{1+3RCs}{2+5RCs+(RC)^2s^2}$$

(o)

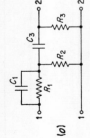

(p)

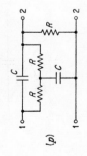

(q)

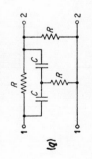

(r)

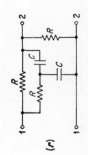

661

TABLE C-1 (Continued)

Network	Transfer function
(s)	$\dfrac{1 + R_2Cs + R_1R_2C'^2s^2}{1 + (R_2 + 2R_1)Cs + R_1R_2C'^2s^2}$
(t)	$\dfrac{1 + RC_1s + R^2C_1C_2s^2}{1 + R(C_1 + 2C_2)s + R^2C_1C_2s^2}$
(u)	$\dfrac{RCs - 1}{RCs + 1}$
(v)	$\dfrac{1 - RCs}{1 + RCs}$

D | Logarithmic Spiral

It is stated in Chap. 10 that phasor multiplication can be accomplished by the addition of angles. Conversely, phasor division can be performed by the subtraction of angles. The validity of these statements is readily established upon an investigation of the equation of the logarithmic spiral.

In general the equation of the logarithmic spiral may be expressed as

$$r = a^{\phi/\Phi} \tag{D-1}$$

where Φ and a are parameters which can be used to set the angular and linear scales. Assume that the product of two phasors expressed as

$$r_1 = a^{\phi_1/\Phi} \qquad \text{and} \qquad r_2 = a^{\phi_2/\Phi} \tag{D-2}$$

is desired. Forming the product yields

$$r = r_1 r_2 = a^{(\phi_1 + \phi_2)/\Phi} \tag{D-3}$$

Taking the logarithm to the base 10 of both sides of Eq. (D-3) leads to

$$\log r = \log r_1 + \log r_2 = (\phi_1 + \phi_2) \frac{\log a}{\Phi} \tag{D-4}$$

This equation makes it apparent that, for fixed values of a and Φ, the logarithm of the *product* quantity is proportional to the *sum* of the individual phase angles. Thus, by the use of an appropriate logarithmic scale and a means of summing angles in conjunction with the logarithmic scale, the product of two or more phasors can be computed.

In performing multiplication in this manner, it is customary to choose a and Φ in such a way that multiplication by 10 corresponds to a rotation of 90°. A study of Eq. (D-4) reveals that one way to accomplish this is to select

$$a = 10$$

$$\Phi = \frac{\pi}{2}$$

Accordingly, Eq. (D-4) becomes

$$\log r = \frac{1}{\pi/2} (\phi_1 + \phi_2) \qquad (D-5)$$

Thus, if two phasors are such that the angles ϕ_1 and ϕ_2 add up to 90°, Eq. (D-5) gives

$$\log r = 1$$

Hence

$$r = 10$$

which indicates multiplication by 10.   Figure D-1 illustrates the result graphically.   It is important to note that the angles ϕ_1 and ϕ_2 associated

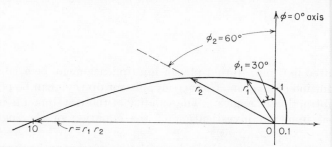

FIG. D-1. Illustrating multiplication by the summation of angles using the logarithmic spiral (curve not drawn to scale).

with the individual phasors must be determined in conjunction with the logarithmic-spiral curve.

In the case of the spirule, which is described in Chap. 10, the parameter a is selected to be 0.1 because of the greater convenience it affords in analyzing the particular type of algebraic polynomial involved in root-locus studies.

E | Bandwidth of Second-order Systems

In terms of conventional notation the bandwidth of a feedback control system is always defined in connection with the frequency characteristic of the *closed-loop system*. Thus the bandwidth is that frequency at which the magnitude ratio of output to input is equal to $1/\sqrt{2}$. It will be recalled that, in analyzing systems in the frequency domain in the body of the book, the exact value of the bandwidth is not determined.

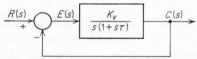

FIG. E-1. Block diagram of two-pole configuration.

Rather we satisfied ourselves with an approximation of this quantity by using instead the crossover frequency of the attenuation characteristic of the open-loop system. Very frequently this approach is satisfactory, because it provides a good "working" figure. It is the purpose here to demonstrate the extent of this approximation for the second-order system having a two-pole configuration as well as the second-order system having a two-pole and one-zero configuration. The latter investigation reveals the manner in which the presence of a zero affects both the bandwidth and the velocity constant.

Two-pole Configuration. The block diagram of the system appears in Fig. E-1. It is assumed that the system characteristic equation has the roots

$$s_{1,2} = -\zeta\omega_n \pm j\omega_n \sqrt{1 - \zeta^2} = -r_{1,2} \tag{E-1}$$

so that the closed-loop transfer function may be written as

$$\frac{C}{R}(s) = \frac{\omega_n{}^2}{s^2 + 2\zeta\omega_n s + \omega_n{}^2} \tag{E-2}$$

Since bandwidth is always concerned with the sinusoidal-frequency domain, it is more convenient to write Eq. (E-2) as

$$\frac{C}{R}(j\omega) = \frac{\omega_n{}^2}{(\omega_n{}^2 - \omega^2) + j2\zeta\omega_n\omega} \tag{E-3}$$

Then in accordance with the conventional definition of bandwidth we have

$$\left|\frac{C}{R}(j\omega)\right| = \frac{\omega_n{}^2}{\sqrt{(\omega_n{}^2 - \omega_{b\omega}{}^2)^2 + 4\zeta^2\omega_n{}^2\omega_{b\omega}{}^2}} = \frac{1}{\sqrt{2}} \tag{E-4}$$

where $\omega_{b\omega}$ is the bandwidth frequency. Rearranging Eq. (E-4) and letting

$$x \equiv \omega_{b\omega}{}^2 \tag{E-5}$$

yields

$$x^2 + (4\zeta^2\omega_n{}^2 - 2\omega_n{}^2)x - \omega_n{}^4 = 0 \tag{E-6}$$

Thus

$$x = -2\zeta^2\omega_n{}^2 + \omega_n{}^2 + \omega_n{}^2\sqrt{4\zeta^4 - 4\zeta^2 + 2} \tag{E-7}$$

The negative radical term is discarded because the bandwidth must be a physically real quantity.

Combining Eqs. (E-5) and (E-7) provides the desired result. Thus the bandwidth is

$$\omega_{b\omega} = \omega_n[1 - 2\zeta^2 + \sqrt{2 - 4\zeta^2 + 4\zeta^4}]^{\frac{1}{2}} \tag{E-8}$$

for

$$\zeta = 0.7 \qquad \omega_{b\omega} = \omega_n$$
$$\zeta = 0.5 \qquad \omega_{b\omega} = 1.27\omega_n$$

Clearly the bandwidth is influenced by the value of the damping ratio.

Next for the sake of comparison let us correlate these results with those obtained from the attenuation characteristic of the open-loop transfer function for the system of Fig. E-1. First, however, it is desirable to put the expression for the open-loop transfer function in a more convenient form in order that it correspond with the formulation of Eq. (E-2). Since the general form of Eq. (E-2) is

$$\frac{C}{R}(s) = \frac{G(s)}{1 + G(s)} \tag{E-9}$$

for unity feedback systems, it follows that

$$\frac{1}{G(s)} = \frac{R}{C}(s) - 1 \tag{E-10}$$

Inserting Eq. (E-2) into the last equation gives

$$G(s) = \frac{\omega_n{}^2}{s(s + 2\zeta\omega_n)} = \frac{\omega_n}{2\zeta}\frac{1}{s(1 + s/2\zeta\omega_n)} \tag{E-11}$$

Clearly, then, the expression for the velocity constant is

$$K_v = \frac{\omega_n}{2\zeta} \tag{E-12}$$

An alternate procedure for finding the velocity constant for type 1 unity feedback systems is to recognize that the inverse velocity constant is equal to the sum of the inverse poles minus the sum of the inverse zeros of the closed-loop transfer function.[1] Hence

$$\frac{1}{K_v} = \frac{1}{r_1} + \frac{1}{r_2} = \frac{1}{\zeta\omega_n - j\omega_d} + \frac{1}{\zeta\omega_n + j\omega_d} = \frac{2\zeta}{\omega_n} \qquad \text{(E-13)}$$

A sketch of the attenuation curve of Eq. (E-11) is depicted in Fig. E-2. This particular orientation of the magnitude characteristic of $G(s)$ is valid

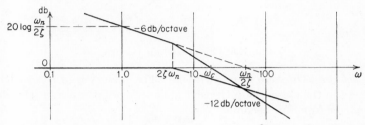

FIG. E-2. Plot of the attenuation characteristic of $G(s) = \dfrac{2\zeta}{\omega_n}\dfrac{1}{s(1 + s/2\zeta\omega_n)}$ for $\zeta < 0.5$.

provided that $\zeta < 0.5$. The crossover frequency is shown to be ω_c. Solving for ω_c analytically yields

$$\omega_c = \sqrt{2\zeta\omega_n\frac{\omega_n}{2}} = \omega_n \qquad \text{(E-14)}$$

Accordingly, it follows that, if the attenuation characteristic is approximated by the straight-line asymptotes, then for $\zeta < 0.5$ the crossover frequency is equal to the natural frequency. A comparison with the results of Eq. (E-8) reveals that for $\zeta = 0.5$ the actual system bandwidth is approximately 27 per cent greater than the crossover frequency of the open-loop transfer function.

For the case where $\zeta > 0.5$ the positions of the frequencies $2\zeta\omega_n$ and $\omega_n/2\zeta$ are interchanged so that the attenuation characteristic assumes the orientation depicted in Fig. E-3. Now the crossover frequency is given by

$$\omega_c = \frac{\omega_n}{2\zeta} \qquad \text{for } \zeta > 0.5 \qquad \text{(E-15)}$$

Hence, for $\zeta = 1/\sqrt{2}$, $\omega_c = \omega_n/\sqrt{2}$. A comparison with the result obtained from Eq. (E-8) puts the actual bandwidth at the value ω_n. Although the difference in values is about 30 per cent, this is not disturb-

[1] Cf. J. G. Truxal, "Automatic Feedback Control System Synthesis," p. 282, McGraw-Hill Book Company, Inc., New York, 1955.

ing, because often all that is needed is an approximation of this order. It is interesting to note, however, that, if the bandwidth is identified in Fig. E-3 by extending the -12 db/octave line until it intersects the frequency axis, the result is the same as Eq. (E-14).

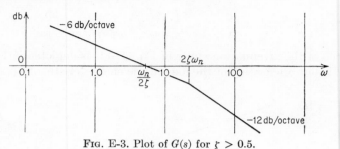

FIG. E-3. Plot of $G(s)$ for $\zeta > 0.5$.

Two-pole and One-zero Configuration. The inclusion of a zero located at $s = -z$ in the closed-loop transfer makes the expression for the closed-loop transfer function become

$$\frac{C}{R}(s) = \frac{1 + s/z}{(s/\omega_n)^2 + (2\zeta/\omega_n)s + 1} = \frac{\omega_n^2}{s^2 + 2\zeta\omega_n s + \omega_n^2} \frac{s + z}{z} \quad \text{(E-16)}$$

The corresponding equation for the open-loop transfer function becomes

$$G(s) = \frac{\omega_n^2 z}{2\zeta\omega_n z - \omega_n^2} \frac{1 + s/z}{s[1 + s/(2\zeta\omega_n - \omega_n^2/z)]} \quad \text{(E-17)}$$

It therefore follows that the velocity constant is

$$K_{vz} = \frac{\omega_n^2 z}{2\zeta\omega_n z - \omega_n^2} = \frac{\omega_n/2\zeta}{1 - (\omega_n/2\zeta)/z} = \frac{K_v}{1 - (\omega_n/2\zeta)/z} \quad \text{(E-18)}$$

where K_v refers to the velocity constant in the absence of a zero as given by Eq. (E-12). An examination of Eqs. (E-17) and (E-18) reveals a limit on the value which the zero can assume if the type of the system is to remain the same. Thus, if the breakpoint frequency in the denominator of Eq. (E-17) is to remain a real number, then the zero must satisfy the condition

$$z > \frac{\omega_n}{2\zeta} \quad \text{(E-19)}$$

The same conclusion follows from Eq. (E-18). Setting $z = \omega_n/2\zeta$ in this equation leads to an infinite velocity constant. Effectively this means that the type of the system has been changed from type 1 to type 2.

The bandwidth for the system of Eq. (E-16) is readily determined from

$$\frac{\omega_n^2 \sqrt{z^2 + \omega_{b\omega}^2}}{z^2 \sqrt{(\omega_n^2 - \omega_{b\omega}^2)^2 + 4\zeta^2\omega_n^2\omega_{b\omega}^2}} = \frac{1}{\sqrt{2}} \quad \text{(E-20)}$$

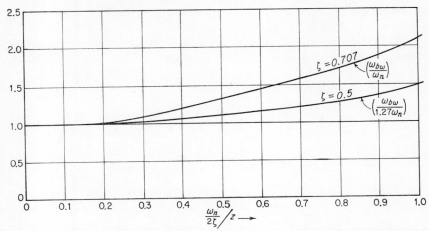

F IG. E-4. Variation of bandwidth for a two-pole and one-zero closed-loop transfer function of a type 1 system.

Solving for $\omega_{b\omega}$ and plotting the results for various values of z as well as ζ leads to the curves shown in Fig. E-4. Clearly, as the zero is made larger, the bandwidth increases in the manner shown. A little thought reveals that similar results prevail for the crossover frequency of the open-loop attenuation characteristic upon the insertion of a lead term (zero), subject of course to the restriction of Eq. (E-19).

Answers to Selected Problems

1-9. (a) 105 volts; (b) -0.952 volt; (c) 0.4 volt

1-10. (c) $\frac{1}{9}$ volt; (d) no

1-11. (a) 9.5 ma; (b) -2.34 amp

2-1. (b) $c(t) = [K_1 + K_2 t + K_3 \sin (t + K_4)]e^{-t}$

2-2. (a) $c(t) = \frac{1}{2}$; (d) $c(t) = \frac{1}{2}(-11 + 9t - 3t^2 + t^3)$
(h) $c(t) = 1.14e^{-2t} \cos (t - 127.9°)$

2-3. (c) $c(t) = \dfrac{\sqrt{5}}{5} e^{-t} \cos (t + 26.6°)$

2-4. (a) $c(0^+) = 0$, $\dot{c}(0^+) = 1$, $\ddot{c}(0^+) = -2$

2-5. $c(t) = \frac{1}{2} + e^{-t}\left[-1 + \dfrac{\sqrt{2}}{2} \cos (t - 45°)\right]$

2-6. (b) $c(t) = t + \dfrac{a - \beta}{\beta} \sqrt{\dfrac{\beta}{g}} \sin \sqrt{\dfrac{g}{\beta}} t$

2-7. (a) $s^2 + 2s + 1 = 0$; (b) $\dfrac{d^2 c}{dt^2} + 2 \dfrac{dc}{dt} + c = r(t) + \dfrac{dr(t)}{dt}$
(c) $c(t) = 1 + (t - 1)e^{-t}$

3-1. (a) $s^2 C(s) + 2\zeta\omega_n s C(s) + \omega_n{}^2 C(s) = \omega_n{}^2 R(s)$; (b) $M_2(s) = \left(\dfrac{1 + sT}{sT}\right) M_1(s)$

(c) $s^2 M(s) + s M(s) = A \dfrac{2\omega}{s^2 + 4\omega^2}$

(d) $M(s)\left[s^3 + a_2 s^2 + a_1 s + a_0 + \dfrac{a_{-1}}{s}\right] = \dfrac{1}{(s + \alpha)^2}$

(e) $(s^2 + 3s + 2)C(s) = \dfrac{1}{s^2} - s - 1$

3-2. (a) $\mathcal{L} \sin (\omega t + \theta) = \dfrac{\omega \cos \theta}{s^2 + \omega^2} + \dfrac{s \sin \theta}{s^2 + \omega^2}$

(b) $\mathcal{L}e^{-\alpha t} \sin (\omega t + \theta) = \dfrac{\omega \cos \theta}{(s + \alpha)^2 + \omega^2} + \dfrac{(s + \alpha) \sin \theta}{(s + \alpha)^2 + \omega^2}$

(c) $\mathcal{L} \dfrac{\epsilon^{-\alpha t} + \alpha t - 1}{\alpha^2} = \dfrac{1}{s^2(s + \alpha)}$; (d) $\mathcal{L} \dfrac{1 - (1 + \alpha t)\epsilon^{-\alpha t}}{\alpha^2} = \dfrac{1}{s(s + \alpha)^2}$

(e) $\mathcal{L} \left(\dfrac{1}{2\beta} + \epsilon^{-\alpha t} \sin \beta t \right) = \dfrac{1}{2\beta s} + \dfrac{\beta}{(s + \alpha)^2 + \beta^2}$

(f) $\mathcal{L}$ sawtooth $= \dfrac{1}{s^2 T_1} (1 - \epsilon^{-sT_1}) - \dfrac{\epsilon^{-sT_1}}{s}$

(g) $\mathcal{L}$ triangular pulse $= \left(\dfrac{1 - \epsilon^{-s}}{s} \right)^2$

(h) $F(s) = \dfrac{A}{s} \left[\epsilon^{-sT_1} \left(1 + \dfrac{1}{sT_1} \right) - \epsilon^{-sT_2} \left(\dfrac{T_2}{T_1} + \dfrac{1}{sT_1} \right) \right]$

3-6. $i(t) = 200t - 300 + 200t\epsilon^{-t} + 300\epsilon^{-t}$

3-7. $f(0^+) = 2$

3-10. (a) $V_i(s) = \dfrac{V}{s^2 T} (1 - \epsilon^{-sT})$; (b) $I(s) = \dfrac{V}{TL} \dfrac{1}{s^2(s + R/L)} (1 - \epsilon^{-sT})$

(c) $i(t) = \dfrac{V}{RT} tu(t) - \dfrac{VL}{R^2 T} (1 - \epsilon^{(R/-L)t})u(t) - \dfrac{V}{RT} (t - T)u(t - T) + \dfrac{VL}{R^2 T}$
$$(1 - \epsilon^{(R/-L)(t-T)})u(t - T)$$

3-11. $f(t) = \frac{1}{2}t^2\epsilon^{-2t}$

3-12. $i(t) = -\frac{1}{2}\epsilon^{-(t/2)} \left(\cos \dfrac{t}{2} + \sin \dfrac{t}{2} \right)$

3-13. $c(t) = 0.852 + 3.33\epsilon^{-0.9t} \cos (1.85t - 92.7°) + 1.99\epsilon^{-7t} \cos (6t + 110.6°)$

3-15. $f(t) = 2\epsilon^{-t} - t\epsilon^{-2t} - 2\epsilon^{-2t}$

4-2. (a) $\omega_n = 10$ radians/sec, $\zeta = 0.8$, $\omega_d = 6$ radians/sec; (b) 1; (c) 4

4-3. (b) $\omega_e(t) = \omega_i \left(\dfrac{1}{1 + K} + \dfrac{K}{1 + K} \epsilon^{-\frac{1+K}{J/F}t} \right) u(t)$, where $K = hK_A K_G K_M/F$

(c) no (theoretically)

4-5. (a) $\zeta = 0.6$; (b) 0.179 radian; (c) no; (d) $1,880 \times 10^{-4}$

4-6. (a) 0.14 radian; (b) $\zeta = 0.7$; (c) $1.4 \times 10^{-5} \dfrac{\text{lb-ft}}{\text{radian/sec}}$; (d) 42×10^{-6}

(e) for error-rate damping, $t_s = 0.286$ sec; for output-rate damping, $t_s = 0.143$ sec

(f) provided by error-rate damping only

4-7 0.77 sec

4-8. (a) $s^2 + \dfrac{F + Q_\varepsilon + Q_t}{J} s + \dfrac{K}{J} = 0$, where $Q_\varepsilon = hAK_s K_M$, $Q_t = G_t K_t K_A K_M$,

and $K = hK_A K_s K_M$; (b) 0.694; (c) 0.52 radian

(d) modify Q_t by changing p or K_t or G_t

4-13. (a) and (b) $\omega_n = 13.32\pi$ for $\zeta = 0.8$, $\omega_n = 10\pi$ for $\zeta = 0.6$

(c) $F = 0.377 \dfrac{\text{lb-ft}}{\text{radian/sec}}$; (d) 0.00562 and 0.01 slug-ft^2

4-14. (a) $a^2 J \dfrac{d^2 c_M}{dt^2} + (a^2 F + D + aK_p AB) \dfrac{dc_M}{dt} + aK_p K_A B c_M = K_p K_A Br + K_p AB \dfrac{dr}{dt}$

(b) $K = 1610$, $A = 1.39$

4-15. (a) 87.2 volts/volt; (b) $\omega_n = 100$ radians/sec, $\omega_d = 96.7$ radians/sec

(c) 0.01 radian; (d) zero, assuming ideal components

4-19. (a) 0.13 radian/sec; (b) $\zeta = 0.6$; (c) 265×10^{-6}; (d) 30.4 radians/sec

4-20. (a) 645×10^{-4}; (b) 964×10^{-6}
   (c) use of tachometric damping yields smaller settling time because of the larger natural frequency

4-22. (a) 612 rpm; (b) -2.36 rpm; (c) 0.024 volt

4-23. 10 radians/sec

5-1. The asymptotes of the log-modulus plots consist of the following:
   (a) initial slope of -12 db/octave followed by a slope of -6 db/octave, breakpoint at $u = 1$ and 20 db
   (b) initial slope of 0 db/octave followed by a slope of -6 db/octave, breakpoint at $u = \frac{3}{2}$ and -9.54 db

5-5. $\bar{T}_4 = \dfrac{18.1}{(ju)(1 + j0.125u)}$

6-3. $\dfrac{E_o}{E_i} = \dfrac{\tau_1 \tau_2 s^2}{1 + (\tau_1 + \tau_2 + \tau_{12})s + \tau_1 \tau_2 s^2}$; $\tau_1 = R_1 C_1$, $\tau_2 = R_2 C_2$, $\tau_{12} = R_1 C_2$

6-4. (c) $\dfrac{E_o}{E_i} = \dfrac{1}{\alpha} \dfrac{1 + \alpha \tau s}{1 + \tau s}$, $\alpha = \dfrac{C_1 + C_2}{C_1}$, $\tau = \dfrac{R C_1 C_2}{C_1 + C_2}$

6-5. (a) $\dfrac{X_o}{X_i} = \dfrac{1}{\alpha} \dfrac{1 + \alpha \tau s}{1 + \tau s}$, $\tau = f/k_1 + k_2$, $\alpha = 1 + k_2/k_1$

6-7. $100 \dfrac{d^2\theta_o}{dt^2} + 504.6 \dfrac{d\theta_o}{dt} = e_i$

6-8. $\tau_m = J/F = 31.2$ msec; the time constant of the control winding $= L/R$ $= 0.26$ msec, which is negligible compared with τ_m

6-9. $\tau_m = 50$ msec; no-load speed $= 14,300$ rpm

6-14. $\dfrac{K_2}{R_a} K_1 R_f v_f + \dfrac{K_2}{R_a} K_1 L_f \dfrac{dv_f}{dt} = \dfrac{K_2 K_3}{R_a} K_1^2 v_f^2 \dfrac{d\theta_M}{dt} + JR_f \dfrac{d^2\theta_M}{dt^2} + JL_f \dfrac{d^3\theta_M}{dt^3}$

6-15. $R_1 = 10$ kilohms, $R_2 = 90$ kilohms, $C_2 = 20 \mu f$

6-19. $\theta_i = (K/F_p)\theta_c$

6-21. $\omega_n = \sqrt{\dfrac{C_2 a}{Mb}}$, $\zeta = \dfrac{1}{2}\left(\dfrac{1}{C_1} + \dfrac{F}{C_2}\right)\sqrt{\dfrac{C_2 b}{Ma}}$

6-23. $\dfrac{X}{e}(s) = \dfrac{K(a/b)}{FLs^2 + [FR + Lk + K^2(a^2/b^2)]s + kR}$

6-25. $\dfrac{E_2}{E_1}(j\omega) = \dfrac{2}{(1 + j\omega)^2}$

6-26. $\dfrac{X}{P}(s) = \dfrac{A}{M(a/b)s^2 + (b/a)Fs + (a/b)K_b + (b/a)K_s}$

7-2. (a) The reduced block diagram for isolation of H_1 consists of a direct transfer function given by $\dfrac{G_1 G_2 G_3}{1 + H_2 G_2 + H_3 G_2 G_3}$ and a feedback transfer function of $\dfrac{H_1}{G_3}$; for isolation of H_2 the direct transfer function is $\dfrac{G_1 G_2 G_3}{1 + H_1 G_1 G_2 + H_3 G_2 G_3}$ and the feedback transfer function is $\dfrac{H_2}{G_1 G_3}$

   (b) The reduced block diagram for isolation of H_2 consists of a direct transfer function of $\dfrac{G_1 G_2}{1 + H_3 G_1 G_2}$ and a feedback transfer function of $H_2\left(\dfrac{1}{G_1} + H_1\right)$

7-3. (b) $C(s) = \dfrac{G_1 G_2 R_1 + G_2 R_2 - G_1 G_2 H_1 R_3 - G_2 R_4}{1 + G_2 H_2 + G_1 G_2 H_1}$

7-4. (a) From the actual curves $\phi_{pm} = 45.6°$, gain margin $= 4.76$
  (b) for the ramp input
$$c(t) = t - 0.1 + 0.00259e^{-33.4t} + 0.108e^{-4.6t}\cos\,(10.1t + 24.6°)$$

7-7. $\dfrac{\omega_o}{\omega_e} = \dfrac{\beta K_A K_G K_T}{R_f(FR + K_1 K_T)}\dfrac{1}{1 + s\tau_f}\dfrac{1}{1 + s\tau_m}$, where $\tau_f = \dfrac{L_f}{R_f}$ and $\tau_m = \dfrac{JR}{FR + K_1 K_T}$

7-8 Servo 1: (b) $\zeta = 0.5$, $\omega_d = 6.94$; (c) $e(t) = 1.154e^{-4t}\cos\,(6.94t - 30°)$
  Servo 2: (b) $\zeta = 0.5$, $\omega_d = 9.8$; (c) $e(t) = 1.02e^{-5.65t}\cos\,(9.8t - 13.5°)$

7-9. (b) $\dfrac{de_o}{dt} + \dfrac{250\sqrt{2}}{\pi}e_o = \dfrac{de_i}{dt} + \dfrac{25{,}000\sqrt{2}}{\pi}$; (c) $e_o = 100$ volts;
  (d) $\tau = \pi/250\sqrt{2}$

7-10. (a) $\omega_n = 12$ radians/sec, $\zeta = 0.333$; (b) $K_v = 18$, $\varepsilon_{ss} = 0.556$ radian

7-13. (a) From the actual curve $\phi_{pm} = 16.6°$, $\zeta = 0.16$ (from Fig. 7-21)
  (b) from the polar plot $M_P = 3.6$, $\zeta = 0.16$ (from Fig. 5-6)
  (c) from the 0-db crossover frequency of the actual open-loop transfer function we get $\omega'_c = 5.55$ radians/sec

8-1. (a) Unstable; (b) unstable

8-4. (a) Unstable; (b) yes at $\omega = 0.35$ radian/sec

8-5. (b) Always unstable; (c) $s^3 + s^2 + 1 = 0$
  (d) always unstable, $s^3 + s^2 + 10 = 0$
  (e) stable, $s^3 + s^2 + 4s + 1 = 0$

8-6. (a) $HG = \dfrac{K}{(1 + \tau_1 s)(1 + \tau_2 s)}$; (b) $HG = \dfrac{K(1 + s\tau_1)}{s^2(1 + s\tau_a)}$, provided $\tau_1 > \tau_a$

9-1. Lead network only

9-4. One possibility is $G_c(j\omega) = \dfrac{1 + j(\omega/0.22)}{1 + j(\omega/0.035)}$

9-5. (a) $-0.1°$; (b) lead network having $G_c(j\omega) = 0.2\left(\dfrac{1 + 0.05s}{1 + 0.01s}\right)$

9-6. Double lead network having $\alpha = 20$ and the first breakpoint frequency occurring at about 3.5 radians/sec

9-7. (b) $-12°$ (corresponding to crossover frequency using asymptotic attenuation characteristic)
  (c) one possibility is $G(j\omega) = \dfrac{[1 + j(\omega/0.88)]^2}{[1 + j(\omega/0.05)][1 + j(\omega/15.5)]}$

9-8. (b) $G_c(s) = \dfrac{1 + j(\omega/1.53)}{1 + j(\omega/0.12)}$; (c) approximately 1.25 sec

9-10. (a) 2d, 3d; (b) 2d; (c) 3d; (d) 3d; (e) 20%, 0.24 sec

10-1. (a) $HG = \dfrac{K(s + 2)}{s(s + 5)}$

10-2. (a) $HG(s) = \dfrac{s + 5}{s(s + 2)}$

10-7. (b) $K = 8.25$; (c) $c(t) = 0.88 - 0.04e^{-2.4t} + 0.97e^{-6.3t}\cos\,(10.8t - 210°)$

10-8. (b) $K = 1.25$; (c) $r(t) = 60\sin\,(2t + 260.5°)$

10-9. (a) $HG = \dfrac{K'(s + 6)}{s^2(s + 12)(s^2 + 6s + 34)}$; (c) no, unstable for all $K' > 0$
  (d) $HG = \dfrac{K'(s + 6)(s + 2)^2}{s^2(s + 12)(s^2 + 6s + 34)}$; (e) stable for all $K' > 0$

10-10. (b) $K' = 46$; (c) percentage overshoot $= 24\%$

10-11. (b) $\zeta = 0.6$ for the compensated system.

10-14. $-5 < z < 0$

11-5. $G_c(s) = \dfrac{(s + 2)(s + 0.4)}{(s + 4)(s + 0.05)}$

11-8. One possibility is $G_c(s) = \left(\dfrac{1 + 0.357s}{1 + 0.074s}\right)^2$

11-9. One solution is $G_c(s) = \dfrac{(s + 2)(s + 6)}{(s + 13.4)(s + 22.6)}$

12-2. Series combination of $R = 1$ ohm, $R = \frac{3}{2}$ ohms in parallel with $C = \frac{2}{3}$ farad, $R = \frac{1}{6}$ ohm in parallel with $C = 2$ farads; parallel combination of $R = \frac{8}{3}$ ohms, $R = 4$ ohms in series with $C = \frac{1}{8}$ farad, $R = \frac{8}{3}$ ohms in series with $C = \frac{3}{32}$ farad; a ladder as follows: series $R = 1$ ohm, shunt $C = \frac{1}{2}$ farad, series $R = \frac{4}{3}$ ohms, shunt $C = \frac{3}{2}$ farad, series $R = \frac{1}{3}$ ohm, shunt short circuit; a ladder as follows: shunt $R = \frac{8}{3}$ ohms, series $C = \frac{7}{32}$ farad, shunt $R = \frac{88}{49}$ ohms, series $C = 42/(22)(88)$ farad, shunt $R = \frac{88}{6}$ ohms

12-5. (b) $z_{11} = z_{22} = z_b + \dfrac{z_a(z_a + z_c)}{z_c + 2z_a}$, $z_{12} = z_b + \dfrac{z_a{}^2}{z_c + 2z_a}$

12-11. (b) Start at terminals 1-1; the network consists of series $C = \frac{1}{3}$ farad, shunt $R = \frac{5}{4}$ ohms, series $C = \frac{1}{25}$ farad, shunt $R = 5$ ohms; the output is taken across the 5-ohm resistor; $K = 1$

     (c) Starting at terminals 1-1 the circuit consists of a series arm of $\frac{8}{15}$ ohm in series with $\frac{3}{8}$ ohm in parallel with $\frac{8}{9}$ farad; the output is taken across a shunt arm consisting of $\frac{7}{15}$ ohm in series with $\frac{9}{21}$ farad; $K = \frac{7}{18}$

12-15. (a) $\dfrac{V_o}{V_i} = \dfrac{s^2 + \frac{3}{2}s + \frac{1}{2}}{s^2 + 3s + 1}$; (c) $V_o = \frac{1}{2} - 0.0585e^{-0.38t} + 0.585e^{-2.62t}$

12-17. $\dfrac{E_2}{E_1} = \dfrac{1 + \tau_2 s}{s^2[\tau_{12}\tau_3 + \tau_{13}\tau_2 + \tau_2\tau_3] + s[\tau_{12} + \tau_{13} + \tau_2 + \tau_3] + 1}$

     $\tau_2 = R_2C_2,\ \tau_{12} = R_1C_2,\ \tau_3 = R_3C_3,\ \tau_{13} = R_1C_3$

13-4. $\epsilon = 50\dfrac{t}{T_l},\ t = \dfrac{10^7}{50}$ sec

13-5. $\dfrac{e_o}{e_i} = -\dfrac{R_3}{R_1}\left[\dfrac{1}{s^2R_2R_3C_1C_2 + sC_2(R_2R_3/R_1 + R_2 + R_3) + 1}\right]$

13-6. $\dfrac{e_o}{e_i} = -\dfrac{1}{s(sR_1R_3C_2C_3 + R_3C_2 + R_1C_2 + R_1C_3)}$

14-1. (a) $(324)_{10} = (10100010)_2$; (b) $(324)_{10} = 011001010111$

     (c) $(324)_{10} = 010100001001000110000$

14-3. (a) 325

14-5. In the program below it is assumed that the first approximation is always chosen to be too small:

Memory location	Data stored
000	Store N
001	Store first approximation
002	Store the minimum allowable error ϵ
003	Store the number 2
004	02000 (shift N to accumulation)
005	05001 (form N/X_{-1})
006	02001 (form $X_{-1} + N/X_{-1}$)
007	05003 (form X_{-2})
008	06001 (shift X_{-2} to 001)
009	04001 (form $X_{-2}{}^2$)
010	03000 (form $X_{-2}{}^2 - N$)
011	03002 (compare $X_{-2}{}^2 - N$ with ϵ)
012	08004 (jump if minus)
013	10001 print
014	00000 stop

14-7.

	ΔT	c	$\dot{c}$	$\ddot{c}$
(a)	0	0	0	50
	0.01	0	0.5	47.50
	0.02	0.005	0.975	44.875
	0.03	0.015	1.424	42.144
(b)	0	0	0	50
	0.01	0.0025	0.5	47.375
	0.02	0.0098	0.961	44.707
	0.03	0.0168	1.394	42.188
(c)	0	0	0	50
	0.015	0.0056	0.75	45.970
	0.030	0.0218	1.409	41.864

15-1. (b) Use $\int e(t)\, dt$ to position the rate-servo output shaft

15-4. Forcing function expressed in the s domain is

$$\Delta M(s) = \frac{E_0}{G_1} s + \frac{E_1}{G_1} + \frac{E_2}{G_1} s^{-1} + \cdots;$$ the corresponding expression in the

time domain is $\Delta m(t) = \dfrac{E_0}{G_1} \dot{\delta}(t) + \dfrac{E_1}{G_1} \delta(t) + \dfrac{E_2}{G_1};$ the output quantities are

$c(t) = E_0 + E_1 t + \frac{1}{2}E_2 t^2,\ \dot{c}(t) = E_1 + E_2 t,$ and $\ddot{c}(t) = E_2$

15-5. $c(t) = c(t)_{\text{impulse}} + c(t)_{\text{step}} + c(t)_{\text{ramp}}$

$$= (E_0 + E_0 t) + [(E_1 - E_0)t + \tfrac{1}{2}(E_1 - E_0)t^2] + [\tfrac{1}{2}(E_2 - E_1 + E_0)t^2$$
$$+ \frac{1}{3!}(E_2 - E_1 + E_0)t^3]$$

$\dot{c}(t) = E_1 + (E_1 - E_0)t + (E_2 - E_1 + E_0)t + \frac{1}{2}(E_2 - E_1 + E_0)t^2$

$\ddot{c}(t) = E_2 + (E_2 - E_1 + E_0)t$

15-7. During the first control interval, namely, $0 < t < T: c(t) = 4t^2,$ for $T = 0.5$ sec; during the second control interval, namely, $T < t < 2T: c(t) = 4t^2 u(t) - 12(t - T)^2 u(t - T);$ during the third control interval, namely, $2T < t < 3T:$ $c(t) = 4t^2 u(t) - 12(t - T)^2 u(t - T) + 16(t - 2T)^2 u(t - 2T)$

Index